Peter Bornedal
The Surface and the Abyss

Monographien und Texte zur Nietzsche-Forschung

Begründet von

Mazzino Montinari · Wolfgang Müller-Lauter
Heinz Wenzel

Herausgegeben von

Günter Abel (Berlin)
Josef Simon (Bonn) · Werner Stegmaier (Greifswald)

Band 57

De Gruyter

The Surface and the Abyss

Nietzsche as Philosopher of Mind and Knowledge

by

Peter Bornedal

De Gruyter

Anschriften der Herausgeber:
Prof. Dr. Günter Abel
Institut für Philosophie
TU Berlin, Sekr. TEL 12/1
Ernst-Reuter-Platz 7, D-10587 Berlin

Prof. Dr. Josef Simon
Philosophisches Seminar A der Universität Bonn
Am Hof 1, D-53113 Bonn

Prof. Dr. Werner Stegmaier
Ernst-Moritz-Arndt-Universität
Institut für Philosophie
Baderstr. 6–7, D-17487 Greifswald

ISBN 978-3-11-048160-0
e-ISBN 978-3-11-022342-2
ISSN 1862-1260

Library of Congress Cataloging-in-Publication Data

Bornedal, Peter.
  The surface and the abyss : Nietzsche as philosopher of mind and knowledge / by Peter Bornedal.
     p. cm. – (Monographien und Texte zur Nietzsche-Forschung, ISSN 1862-1260 ; Bd. 57)
  Includes bibliographical references and index.
  ISBN 978-3-11-022341-5 (hardcover : alk. paper)
  1. Nietzsche, Friedrich Wilhelm, 1844–1900.   I. Title.
  B3317.B6554   2010
  193–dc22
                                                    2009036202

Bibliografische Information der Deutschen Nationalbibliothek

Die Deutsche Nationalbibliothek verzeichnet diese Publikation in der Deutschen Nationalbibliografie; detaillierte bibliografische Daten sind im Internet über http://dnb.d-nb.de abrufbar.

© 2010 Walter de Gruyter GmbH & Co. KG, Berlin/New York
Einbandentwurf: Christopher Schneider, Laufen
Druck und buchbinderische Verarbeitung: Hubert & Co. GmbH & Co. KG, Göttingen
∞ Gedruckt auf säurefreiem Papier
Printed in Germany
www.degruyter.com

Table of Contents

Introduction

1. The Polemical Context 1
2. Nietzsche's Theoretical Consistency 4
3. On the Difference between Deconstructive
   and Reconstructive Thinking 6
4. Nietzsche and the Intentional Object 9
5. Chapter-Descriptions 11
   5.1. Chapter 1: The Concepts of Truth and Metaphor 11
   5.2. Chapter 2: The Ontology and Epistemology 15
   5.3. Chapter 3: The Concept of the Split Subject 17
   5.4. Chapter 4: The Concept of the Fragmented Subject 20
   5.5. Chapter 5: A Theory of the Ideological Subject and the Ideologue 23
   5.6. Chapter 6: Affirmation of the Hyper-Surface of the Present as an
        Intrinsic Psychological Possibility 25

Chapter 1
The Narcissism of Human Knowledge. Truth – Metaphor – Concept: An Interpretation of Nietzsche's "Über Wahrheit und Lüge" in the Context of 19th Century Kantianism 29

0. Introduction 30
1. A Human Being with no Natural Disposition for
   Producing Knowledge 36
2. A Polysemous Notion of 'Truth' 39
   2.1. The Fundamental Opposition: Things-in-themselves versus
        Appearances 39
   2.2. From Truthfulness to Truth: On the Evolution of a 'Truth-Drive' 50
3. The Production of Metaphor: Nerve-Stimulus – Image –
   Word 55
   3.1. Contemporary Context and Background 55
   3.2. The Logic of Metaphor as 'Replacement' and 'Arbitrariness' 58
   3.3. A Distinction between 'Living Metaphor' and 'Dead Metaphor' 63
   3.4. Metonymy and Surface-World 71
4. The Theory of the Concept 73
   4.1. Concept-Formation Distinguishing Human from Animal 73
   4.2. The Surface-World and the Tautological Structure of the Concept 78

4.3. Failed Attempts to Uphold a Rigorous Distinction between
       'Word' and 'Concept' 79
  4.4. The Logic of the Concept and Interpretability 84
  4.5. An Interlude on Stanley Fish's Notion of Interpretability 88
5. Contingency and Narcissism of Human Knowledge 92
  5.1. Recapitulating Nietzsche's Polysemous Notion of Truth 92
  5.2. Connecting 'Truth as Illusion' and the 'Logic of the Concept' 94
  5.3. A Clever, All-Too-Clever Animal 95

Chapter 2
A Silent World: Nietzsche's Radical Realism: World, Sensation, Language 97

1. Introductions to and Descriptions of the Position 98
   1.1. Nietzsche's Rejection of Idealism and Abstract Truth-Claims 98
   1.2. Juxtaposition to an Analytic Philosophical Approach 104
   1.3. An Outline of the Position 110
2. Substantiation and Elaboration of the Position 117
   2.1. Ur-Ground and Sensation 117
   2.1. Human Ground and Sensation 128
   2.3. Sensation and Word 134
3. Two Brief Control-Readings to Put the Position to Test 145
   3.1. Explaining Nietzsche's 'Negative Ontologie des Dinges' 145
   3.2. How Come that 'Lightning Flashes' only in Language? 148

Chapter 3
Splitting the Subject: Nietzsche's Rethinking of the Cartesian and Kantian 'I Think' 153

0. Introduction 154
1. A Preliminary Determination of the Problem of the
   'I Think' in Nietzsche 158
   1.1. The Problem of 'thinking' in 'I think' 158
   1.2. The Problem of 'I' in 'I think' 160

Part I: Thinking the 'I' in Descartes, Kant, and Benveniste

  2. Descartes and Nietzsche; Nietzsche's Criticism of the
     Cartesian 'I Think' 164
     2.1. The Desire for Immediate Certainty 164
     2.2. The Reality of Immediate Uncertainty 166
     2.3. Descartes' Confusion of Linguistic and Cognitive 'I' 171
  3. Kant and Nietzsche: Deconstructing the Cartesian Cogito 174
     3.1. Preliminary; the Multiple-Self Subject in David Hume 174
     3.2. The Paragoristic Confusion of Logical and Empirical
          Subject in Kant 176
     3.3. A Glassy 'Rational Subject' 184
  4. The Linguistically Constituted 'I' in Benveniste 187

Part II: Nietzsche's Theories of the Split Subject

  5. Nietzsche's "General Theory" of the Split Subject 193
     5.1. Spir and Nietzsche's Interpretations of the
          Kantian Double-Determination of the Subject 193
     5.2. The Fictions of 'I' and 'Will' versus the Reality of
          'Thinking' and 'Wills' 200
        5.2.1. Chaos and Becoming in the Empirical Subject 200
        5.2.2. On Willing: A Reading of JGB 19 204
  6. Nietzsche's "Special Theory" of the Split Subject 213
     6.1. Nietzsche's 'Dividuum' as Foundation for the Moral Subject .. 213
     6.2. The Unique Formula for the Commanding Voice 217
     6.3. The 'Perverse' Soliloquy of the Moral Judgment 219
     6.4. Formal Consciousness and Spatialization of Self 220
     6.5. The Metaphor of the Ear:
          To Hear the Differences in the Same 224
  7. From a Theory of the Split Subject to a Theory of Ideology 226
     7.1. Why Re-Introducing Nietzsche's Notion of a Split Subject? 226
     7.2. A Theory of Ideology 228

Chapter 4
Theory of Knowledge as 'Neuro-Epistemology': Toward a
Biological-Linguistic Subject in Nietzsche and Contemporaries 231

  0. Introduction 232

Part I: Nietzsche's Contemporaries on Sensation, Cognition, and Language

1. Schopenhauer, Helmholtz, and Lange on the Retinal Image 241
2. Gustav Fechner's Analysis of Sensations 246
   2.1. On the Threshold for Subjective Sensations 246
   2.2. The Psychophysical Energy-Subject 249
3. Freud's Analysis of Sensation, Memory, & Consciousness 253
   3.1. A Neurological Distinction between
        Stimulus & Sensation, phi & psi 253
   3.2. A Neurological Explanation of the Sense of Reality 259
   3.3. Ego-Clusters and Will-to-Power-Formations 264
   3.4. The Psychological Origin of Entity and Identity 271
   3.5. Toward a Theory of Language:
        Three Variations over a Theme 274
        3.5.1. Word- and Thing-Presentation 274
        3.5.2. The Replacement of Thing with Word 277
        3.5.3. From Ego-Cluster to Semantic Ego-Cluster 280

Part II: Toward a 'Biological-Linguistic' Nietzschean subject

4. Fundamentals in the Constitution of a Biological-Linguistic
   Subject 282
   4.1. On the Constitution of the Experience of Identity 282
   4.2. On the Constitution of the Sense and the
        Evaluation of Reality 288
   4.3. On the Constitution of the Experience of Causality 292
        4.3.1. Causality as Humanization 292
        4.3.2. Causality and Time-Reversal 300
   4.4. On Nature & Constitution of Language:
        Proposition, Word, Meaning 303
        4.4.1. The Judgment and the Categories 303
        4.4.2. The Emotional Word 314
        4.4.3. The Fluidity of Meaning 321

Part III: Reconciling Positions and Drawing up Implications

5. The 'Confused-Aggressive' Subject as the Condition of
   Possibility for Ideology 325
   5.0. Introduction 325
   5.1. Ego-Clusters as Competing Power-Configurations 325
   5.2. The Master-Analogy:

Inner-Mental Life as a Game of Chess 328
5.3. On Intrinsic Irrationality 330
5.4. On 'Irrationality' as Frenetic Defense of 'Truth' 332
5.5. On Ideology as Imaginary Repair of the Subjective
     Sense of Loss 336
5.6. Two Brief Applications 339
6. In Defense of a Cognitively Modified Nietzschean Realism 342
   6.1. On the Reception of Nietzsche's Philosophy of Mind as
        Idealism 342
   6.2. The Mind Creates Perception, not Matter 345
   6.3. Nietzsche's Master-Axiom: the World as
        Language-Independent 348
   6.4. Reconciling Realism and Cognitive Theory 351
   6.5 The Dubious Evolutionary Value of 'Explanations' 353

Chapter 5
The Meaning of Master, Slave, and Priest: From
Mental Configurations to Social Typologies 358

0. Introduction: Servile and Assertive Configuration 358

Part I: The Incredible Profundity of the Truly Superficial

1. Superficial and Profound Subjectivity 361
   1.1. Defending Superficiality 361
   1.2. The Magnificent Shallowness of Woman 365
2. Two Economies: Hyper-Cathected and De-Cathected Self 371
3. The Dialectics Between Forgetfulness and Memory 380
   3.1. Necessary Forgetfulness; Impeding Memory 380
   3.2. Nietzsche's Chiasma: Reversed Valuations of Forgetfulness
        and Memory 383
   3.3. Justice and the Institution of Law 385

Part II: On the Ideological Formatting of the Servile Configuration

4. The Institution of Guilt 389
   4.1. 'Schuldig' as Being Indebted and as Being Guilty 389
   4.2. Internalization of Guilt 393
      4.2.1. From Proto-Sadism to Proto-Masochism 393
      4.2.2. Identical Positions on Conscience & Guilt in

>   Nietzsche & Freud 396
>   4.3. The Unstable Opposition Between 'Good' and 'Evil' 400
>   4.4. Nietzsche's Affirmation of Cruelty as 'Primary Aggression' 403
> 5. Exploiting "Suffering": On the Meaning of the Ascetic Ideal
>   and the Ascetic Priest 407
>   5.1. The Ascetic Ideal as a Will-to-Nothing 407
>   5.2. The 'Ascetic Priest' as Exploiting "Suffering" 413
>   5.3. Soft-Core and Hard-Core Strategies for the
>   "Toleration of Life" 417
>   5.4. Strategies for Fanaticization of the Depressed Individual 424
> 6. Insight and Blindness in Nietzsche; On Defensive Retaliation 430

Chapter 6
Eternal Recurrence in Inner-Mental Life: Eternal Recurrence as Describing the Conditions for Knowledge and Pleasure 435

> 1. Introducing Three Different Kinds of Return 435
>   1.1. A Brief Preliminary about Repetition and Joy 435
>   1.2. Return as Simple and Mechanical Rebirth 438
>   1.3. A Preliminary Introduction to Two Alternative
>   Interpretations of Recurrence 442
> 2. Recurrence as Circle or Loop 446
> 3. Return as a Repetitive Interpretation-Process; Two Cases 450
>   3.1. First Case: Sensation and Perception 450
>   3.1.1. Knowledge as Familiarizing the Strange 450
>   3.1.2. Time-Reversal and 'Delayed Perception' 452
>   3.1.3. Living in the Mirror of Consciousness 456
>   3.2. Second Case: How One Becomes What One Is 463
>   3.2.1. The Polemical Environment 463
>   3.2.2. The Principle of Self-Development 465
>   3.2.3. Amor Fati as Anti-Narcissistic Love of the Inner
>   Interpretation-Machine 468
>   3.2.4. To 'Become What One Is' in a
>   'Vertical Dimension' of Time 472
> 4. Return as Self-Repetition of Self-Presence; Four Encounters 478
>   4.1. Introducing the 'smallest possible loop' 478
>   4.2. First Encounter: The Environment Facilitating the
>   Thought of Eternal Recurrence 479
>   4.3. Second Encounter: An Early Example of Self-Unconsciousness,
>   the Forgetful Animal 484

    4.4. Third Encounter: Empty Perception of Hyper-Reality and the
          Celebration of the Super-Superficial 488
    4.5. Fourth Encounter: The Erotic Unification of the Eternal
          Recurrence-Subject and the Eternal-Recurrence-Universe 492
5. Temporal Construction and Deconstruction of the
   Interpreted World 496
    5.1. The Temporally Constructed World of Being 496
    5.2. Deconstructing the Temporally Constructed World of Being 500

Appendixes 507

Appendix 1
Nietzsche and Ernst Mach on the Analysis of Sensations 508

1. Ernst Mach's Analysis of Sensations 508
   1.1. Deconstructing the Cogito in Mach 508
   1.2. The Dissolution of the World into Sensation-Elements, and the
        Introduction of Perspectivism as Scientific Ideal 510
   1.3. The Suspension of the Cause-Effect Relation 513

Appendix 2
A Theory of "Happiness": Nietzsche's Theory of
Pain and Pleasure 517

1. Nietzsche's Pleasure Principle Reversing the Tradition 517
2. A Relativistic Theory of Pleasure 522
3. The Rhythm 527
4. Beyond the Logic of Desire. What if Desire is Nothing but
   Representation? 528
5. Pain-Sensation as Fantasy and Hallucination 534

Appendix 3
The Fragmented Nietzschean Subject and Literary Criticism: Conflicting Images of Woman in Jacobsen's "Arabesque to a Drawing by Michelangelo" 540

1. On Severe Confusion and Fundamental Ignorance 540
2. Me, on the Contrary 543
3. Reading the Poem 547
   3.1. First Stanza: Repetition and Rebellion 547
   3.2. Second Stanza: Implosion and Castration 550

  3.3. Third Stanza: The Blind Eye of Desire 554
  3.4. Fourth Stanza: Poetry and Death 557
  3.5. Fifth Stanza: A Pen through the Heart of Night 560
 4. Fundamental Ignorance 461
 5. Jacobsen's Poem 564

List of Literature & Index 567

List of Literature 568

Index   593

Preface

It is difficult, if not impossible, to pinpoint date and origin for the conception of a work. Partly because the decision about writing a work on this or that topic rarely comes in a flash, but rather surfaces slowly and gradually. One does not remember all these minute degrees of gradual maturation; one is hardly aware of them. Only after they have accumulated, one experiences perhaps something like a 'flash,' which now emerges as nothing more that the articulation in a sentence of a plan that has been germinating for a long time.

Such plans start to germinate, mature, and sprout ultimately thanks to nourishment. One is offered certain opportunities, encouragements, and rewards, and responds to these rewards in the hope of more of the same. Homo sapiens sapiens is so sufficiently close to other primates on the evolutionary ladder that it still needs its nuts and raisins for motivation. There is always something rudimentarily biological about the decision-processes preceding an activity.

About eight years ago, it was for example my intention to write a work on methodology, on interpretation, and 'reading-strategy.' I had finished a work practicing readings of some key-philosophical texts, and wanted to supply a theoretical statement. I regarded Phenomenology, Hermeneutics, and Grammatology as the three most promising disciplines for working out such a unified theory of interpretation and methodology, but – besides the prohibiting ambition of the project, which might in any case have stalled it in its early stages – nobody were interested. Methodologists are an exclusive group on today's academic scene; they live exclusive lives somewhat like the theoretical mathematician trying to figure out what a six-dimensional universe might look like. Especially in language and literature departments, dealing in 'interpretations,' one would expect that theory and methodology had to be foundational disciplines, but no; mutadis mutandis, there was, still is, no interest.

At that point in time, reading Nietzsche was mostly relaxation; although it had been an activity enjoyed, on and off, for about thirty years. Nietzsche is generally pleasant philosophical reading, because his aphorisms are brief and still brimming with insight. He tends to turn abruptly from subject to subject, which is pleasing to the mind, because he engages the mind in short bursts of energy, whereupon the mind is allowed to relax again, ready to start something new – unlike reading, for example, Kant, where one is forced to follow long tracts of argument in constant fear of losing one's understanding.

Thus, whereas there was obviously no interest in methodology, there seemed to be an interest in the pleasures of Nietzsche. This brings us back to the above-mentioned nuts and raisins of 'rewards' and 'opportunities.' In this narrativized statement of acknowledgment, it was for example a 'reward' to be invited to participate in a Nietzsche-conference under the auspices of SPEP in 2002; it gave me a much needed opportunity to meet notable colleagues, such as Babette Babich, Tracey Strong, David B. Allison, and Lawrence Hatab. It was encouraging to have an early article on Nietzsche and literary interpretation (which in revised version is included as *Appendix III* in the present work*)*, first invited and since accepted for *The Comparatist* under the editor MaryAnn Freese Witt. As my Nietzsche-project started developing, and I began to see his thinking as a version of a neurological model of the subject one could find in outlines in Freud's early writings too, I allowed myself to send a section on Freud's *Project for a Scientific Psychology* for review to Mark Solms (renown psychoanalyst and neuroscientist, and the preeminent international authority on Freud's early work). Again, it was encouragement that Solms took the time to read the long section, and returned a positive response. Finally, as the project started to mature, I had in rapid succession three long essays (included here as *Chapters 2, 5 (part 1), & 6*) accepted for the prominent German *Nietzsche-Studien*, which was so much the more pleasing because the three editors, Josef Simon, Günter Abel, and Werner Stegmaier, not only stood out as distinguished Nietzsche-scholars, but even better, were also renowned philosophers in their own right. As such, what started as pleasure-reading and -writing, gradually to took the form of a serious book-project. As the manuscript developed, and the separate chapters approached final draft form, I called upon Dr. Kasper Nefer Olsen as critical reader and copy-editor of the work. As an accomplished translator of the German, he also checked my translations of Nietzsche into English.

Given this history of conception, the present work was never *planned* as a book; such a plan was conceived quite late into the writing-process. Most of the chapters originated as independent essays of single aspects of Nietzsche's thinking, with the essay's relative independence and self-sufficiency. Redundancies throughout the work are therefore not completely avoided; sometimes a passage, sometimes a quotation, is repeated in different chapters, but when in the relatively few instances it happens, these passages or quotations are then interpreted from the different perspective of the chapter's theoretical context.

The surface-structure of the work is, as one will notice, classical. This work, as so many previous works on Nietzsche, conventionally starts with what seems the most general and abstract of Nietzsche's philosophical concerns, that is, his theories of truth, ontology, and epistemology, and ends with what seems more specific and unique to his thinking, his theories of master/slave and eternal recurrence.

Since the work is not planned as a whole, the reader is also free to begin his or her reading from any point of departure. A strategy, which seems to me to make good sense, might be to first read the subsequent 'Introduction,' and then, according to the brief chapter-descriptions offered here (a kind of elaborate menu for the work), continue reading whatever chapter appeals to the reader's own philosophical interest, engagement, or taste.

Introduction

1. The Polemical Context

When one, some years ago, read commentators of Nietzsche from the post-modernist and deconstructionist tradition, one got the impression that there was nothing more to say of Nietzsche's philosophy as philosophy; it was as if the reception of Nietzsche's philosophy as philosophy was closed. Only because Nietzsche was a fascinating poetical-rhetorical writer, the commentator was preoccupied with him, especially with exploring a rich material of poeticisms, images, allegories, or metaphors left in his texts. There was little or no description of Nietzsche's thinking as a conceptual system, or as a response to problems in the prevailing contemporary, evolutionary-cognitive-psychological, paradigm. Instead, one focused on a single image, an allegory, or a metaphor, which was supposed to 'generate' Nietzsche's discourse, but so far had gone undetected. To understand Nietzsche's discourse as a conceptual system was not seen to be important, but to understand its 'origin' as ambiguous non-origin – as generating, from a root that was in-decidable and oscillating, a discourse that was purely rhetorical – became important.

The assumption behind the approach was that a word, an image, or a metaphor would linger in the text as an un-thematized, but over-determining density, and from that position influence subsequent theoretical decisions taken in the text. This word or image – as 'original non-origin,' as 'decisive in-decidability' – was symptomatically repeated in the entire discourse. Nietzsche (in effect suffering from a kind of theoretical repetition-compulsion regarding these mantras) was unbeknownst by himself ultimately writing on a word. This magical word, the commentator would see reflected in different aspects of the theory, and it could be put into play in numerous possible permutations; permutations one could multiply by consulting dictionaries and encyclopedias to trace its history and etymology to reveal new, hidden, and surprising meanings. The effect of this approach was that after one had had a first encounter with some significant Nietzschean text (which might be represented by a single or a few passages), one could suspend the reading of Nietzsche in his totality. The strategy allowed the post-modern deconstructionist to playfully exercise his or her associations over a word, feeding these associations with carefully selected textual material, in the assumption that these selections would epitomize

Nietzsche's thinking. As such, one was in own self-understanding exploring the deepest depth of Nietzsche's thinking.

Partly because the strategy became heavily dependent on the technique of association, the language exercised was seen as 'playful.' Thinking was exercised in the horizontal, so to speak. The theorist reclined on the couch, and started associating, committed only to the golden rule of free association, 'everything that comes to my mind has importance.'

As such, one was confirming and re-confirming the 'eternal truth' of post-modernism, the playful character of language. One believed in the truth of a constative that one was performing as one's thinking and writing activity. According to the paradigm, Nietzsche was himself seen as confirming this eternal post-modernist truth, and the post-modern deconstructionist meant to pay Nietzsche an exquisite complement when appointing him master of the playful discourse. Had Nietzsche not promoted a 'cheerful' or 'gay' science? And had not Jacques Derrida (authority on Nietzsche, and unchallenged master-thinker of deconstruction) more than once suggested that there was something utterly suspect about classical philosophy's recourse to *seriousness*? It is therefore not surprising that in these readings of Nietzsche, one did not address theoretical-conceptual problems; nor did one solve any; one hardly seemed to be even aware of any. Emphasis on logical and conceptual problems had become a suspect reiteration of this *metaphysics of seriousness*, deriving from that *phallo-logo-phono-centric* malady characterizing all Western Thinking ('*phallo-logo-phono-centrism*': the ethnocentric belief in a masculine-rational-self-conscious subjectivity).

The present work has several aspects, and undersigned may hope that its polemic aspect is the least interesting. But now introduced, the work can be seen as an argument against the above theoretical approach, which may perhaps belong more to the past than to the present, but still lingers as a part of Nietzsche's recent reception-history. The present work argues that important issues in Nietzsche's thinking has rarely been addressed, is largely under-explored, and has never been attempted reconstructed (except in isolated cases; a lonely book or an article, which in due time, we will of course acknowledge). We shall argue that exposing Nietzsche to 'deconstruction' (in skilled hands, sometimes a strong reading-strategy) becomes an empty and idle exercise, if one does not have a clear understanding of the conceptual and argumentative machinery, to which one applies the deconstructive reading.

We see a problem in relying on the technique of free association, namely that the nodal point, which is chosen as the first link in the chain of associations, is often selected randomly ('random,' relative to the text as system, but hardly 'random' relative to the interpretive desire of the commentator), and the following associations become equally random, or emerge from highly selective readings. There is nothing to keep this double randomness in check, if the recourse to the conceptual problem that Nietzsche has been struggling to represent is prohibited from the outset. If or when one promotes Nietzsche first and foremost as a stylist and a poet-philosopher, ironically, the interpretations of Nietzsche have gone full circle. After one century, one is back to the beginning of Nietzsche-reception. The newest is also the oldest.

We see another problem in the strong emphasis on style, vocabulary, image, and metaphor in some of these approaches. When commentators express themselves exclusively in 'style' and 'vocabulary,' but rarely or never in concepts, arguments, structures, or diagrams, then, when we read them, we do not and cannot 'see' their thinking. We cannot 'see' this vague form of a *structure*, a *diagram*, or a *picture* that always comes to mind when one reads a conceptual thinker (let it be Aristotle, Locke, Kant, Husserl, Freud, or even Nietzsche). We are for example able to discuss Kant, and endlessly so, because he produces these vague structures or diagrams in our minds (these 'pure and abstract intuitions'), which are rarely reproduced exactly as the same in every reader, but are nevertheless sufficiently obvious to prompt discussion. When discussing Kant with a colleague, we therefore discuss whether this thing is so or so in relation to this other thing, whether it is 'before' or 'after,' 'above' or 'below,' 'primary' or 'secondary,' 'inclusive' or 'exclusive,' etc. In contrast, in their interpretation of language, the post-modern deconstructionists have decided that language is style and 'rhetoric'; and since they are performatively consistent, they express themselves in a language that is stylistic and rhetorical. Consequently, we find it impossible to truly discuss them, insofar as we 'see' nothing. If in their discourse there is nothing, which we can get our hands on, there is also nothing for us to think about. Their theoretical choice of 'style' over 'content,' 'vocabulary' over 'concept,' is intentional in their discourse, which is often deliberately escaping argument and discussion. This escape from reason is seen as a virtue and a higher purpose of the discourse.

Perhaps one can sum up the conceptually deepest disagreement between post-modernistic deconstructionism and the re-constructive thinking we shall pursue below (and which is not without affinity to the early Derridian project, cf. below). In a neo-rational re-constructive thinking, one intuitively feels that thinking is *spatial*, while in post-modernist deconstructionism one feels it is *temporal*. In the first view, thinking is conceptual structure, and structure can only be thought in space; in the second view, thinking is speech, and speech advances along a temporal line. In the post-modern paradigm, the *architecture* of genuine thinking, its many dimensions and many compartments, has been collapsed into a one-dimensional plane of indifferent linearity. Undersigned, representing a loosely defined neo-rationalist position with affinities to technical disciplines like structuralism, linguistics, and phenomenology, is happy to appropriate William James' observation as his own:

> In reasoning, I find that I am apt to have a kind of vaguely localized diagram in my mind, with the various fractional objects of the thought disposed at particular points thereof; and the oscillations of my attention from one of them to another are most distinctly felt as alternation of direction in movement occurring inside my head.[1]

2. Nietzsche's Theoretical Consistency

When introducing Nietzsche's philosophy in several of its most general philosophical aspects, it is of course impossible to pretend originality. Much of what has been said about Nietzsche throughout the reception of the last three-quarters of a century is necessarily said again. Our understanding of Nietzsche's concept of truth is for example shared by earlier commentators from the Hermeneutic and Pragmatic traditions (e.g. M. Heidegger, E. Fink, H. Rudiger-Grimm, R. Rorty).[2] The presentation of the so-called 'split' and/or 'fragmented' subject was introduced into Nietzsche-reception already in the sixties, and regularly onwards (e.g., G. Deleuze, J. Derrida, M. Foucault, A. Nehamas, H. Staten).

---

[1] James, William: The Principles of Psychology, vol. I. New York (Dover Publications), 1890/1950; p. 300.

[2] The present introduction, I understand as an outline and summation of positions more detailed described, and further elaborated, in the main text. For that reason, I abstain at this point from detailing my references to the work of Nietzsche-scholars I am using, since they are copiously cited in what follows. For the same reason, I also abstain from quoting Nietzsche himself in order to substantiate my claims, since this too is scrupulously done in the main text. The introduction is a recapitulation of the entire work; it is written as the last phase in a long journey as an outline and summation of research already performed; it seems redundant to repeat this research process yet again, and expand the text beyond what is strictly necessary. Therefore, in the present introduction, I limit my acknowledgment of commentators of importance for the interpretations of Nietzsche to a brief string of names.

Still, however unavoidable this repetition of the well-known and well-consolidated may be, it is in the present work differently contextualized and theorized.

Moreover, in the present work, Nietzsche's philosophy has been attempted reconstructed and rebuilt into a coherent philosophical system, spanning the traditionally distinct disciplines, epistemology, mind, subject, psychology, and ideology. In this reconstruction effort, we have addressed both the published and the unpublished work, although the disciplines mentioned above in particular are being developed in the unpublished work, Nietzsche's so-called *Nachgelassende Fragmente*. In this *Nachlaß* material Nietzsche has left us with a seeming confusion of notes, which, for the latter parts, we assume that he intended to edit into the a relatively more solid form in the magnum opus he was planning, but never completed – the work, which in his notes often appears by the tentative working-title, *Der Wille zur Macht: Versuch einer Umwerthung aller Werthe*.

We will thus rely heavily of Nietzsche's *Nachgelassende Fragmente*, as we shall argue and demonstrate that this seeming confusion of notes is only a mess on appearances. Behind the surface, the fragments are usually always informed by the same (at most, a few) guiding philosophical idea(s). Even though Nietzsche quite frequently exposes himself to 'brainstorming' sessions in his notes – 'experimental' sessions that are meant to drive his thinking to the edge of the logically possible, and to reveal to himself the ultimate logical consequences of a thought – it is always the same fundamental assumptions we find underlying these sessions, for example, the chaos of the human mind, its tendency to 'simplify,' etc. In these sessions, he leaves behind the nitty-gritty; he bypasses dozens of possible intermediate propositions, and allows himself to ask fundamental questions addressing directly the core of a problem; for example, if the human is a chaos, how then to think the human?

In the present work, we aspire at least *ideally* to reconstruct these fundamental assumptions guiding, as logics, diagrams, or figures, Nietzsche's thinking. If or when we succeed in reconstructing semi-consistent theoretical statements from this apparent confusion of notes, we become evidently better able to appreciate the consistency of the thinking underlying them. In this, our perception of Nietzsche as philosopher changes: no longer is he regarded as a philosophical wild-card, as some exuberant poetizing mind, good at expressing provocative but beautiful ideas, but rather is he a precocious proto-scientific experimenter in the theories of mind and knowledge, struggling to establish the most radical consequences of an emerging 19th century scientific understanding of the subject.

If therefore we introduce the five theoretical subjects listed above – the five subjects of Nietzsche's thinking we have adopted as the principal subject-matter of this particular work – we believe there is *consistency* between Nietzsche's epistemology, his theory of the subject, his analyses of religious/ideological psychology, and even his exotic proposals of a so-called *Übermensch* and an *Ewigen Wiederkunft*. We believe that Nietzsche has a 'general plan' behind whatever new aspect he introduces into his philosophy; a 'plan' not necessarily followed consciously, but rather emerging from a deeply internalized core, an internalized 'theorem' or 'diagram,' manifesting itself symptomatically in different materials (something like a 'strange attractor' in Chaos Theory – a peculiar figure all values in a 'map' seek to satisfy; an ordering principle hidden in the chaos).

3) On the Difference between Deconstructive and Reconstructive Thinking

Like much of the newest Nietzsche research, the present work too understands itself as 'post' post-Modernism. Like several recent Nietzsche-scholars, we too believe that this post-Modernist Nietzsche has had his day. If or when post-modernism is advertised as cutting-edge theory, half a century after these interpretations were first proposed, we believe that the commentator reveals a rather conservative bend of mind.

We read with interest Nietzsche's recent receptions by more historically and philologically interested commentators (including for example, C. Emden, G. Moore, T. Brobjer, R. Small, C. Cowan, & A. Urs Summer). We see in this new reception an intention to understand Nietzsche in his historical, cultural, and intellectual contexts; implying that the scholar takes upon him or herself reading a large material of texts that would have constituted the intellectual background and inspiration for Nietzsche. Placed into this historical-intellectual context, it becomes also far more evident to see the Nietzschean project as a reaction to the contemporary evolutionary-cognitive-psychological debates of his day; a dimension almost entirely lost in the post-modern paradigm.

While thus we find this historical research highly valuable, and we generally see it as indispensable to be acquainted with some of the textual material that inspired Nietzsche (in the present work, we put a strong emphasis of the trinity, Kant, Schopenhauer, and Lange, but include also discussions of a number of philosophical and scientific texts that may today have only historical interest, but had significance to Nietzsche), still, the present work is *not* and does *not* pretend to be a historicist investigation. Its higher purpose is not a reconstruction of Nietzsche's sources, his readings, or his library.

It rather pretends to be 'reconstruction' of Nietzschean concepts of world, mind, knowledge, and language, combined with an over-determining interest in the theories of mind and cognitive theory (which incidentally was one of Nietzsche's own over-determining interests). *Theoretically*, theories of perception, cognition, mind, and language occupy the center-stage in the present work. *Methodologically*, the work continues in the vein of the work of the early Derrida – Derrida, we emphasize, *the philosopher of Grammatology*.

This needs some explanation. We allow ourselves to distinguish between Derrida, the grammatological phenomenologist, and Derrida, the masterthinker of post-modernist deconstruction. We distinguish between *Grammatology*, as a phenomenologically inspired reading-strategy, and *Deconstruction*, as a post-Modern reading-strategy challenging New Criticism, mostly adopted in North America. We believe that there was a brief opportunity for a Phenomenology-inspired *Grammatology* to develop, a window of opportunity that was lost again, when *Grammatology* was transformed into *Deconstruction*.

In its American appropriation, Derrida's 'Deconstruction' became a discipline mostly exercised in Language and Literature Departments, and often denounced in the Philosophy Departments. Scholars appropriating Deconstruction came typically from the Language Departments (so, for example, Paul de Man and Jonathan Culler; later the 'Yale School' was established, etc.), and seemed to be continuing the strictly formal approach to texts that had been internalized, but exhausted in important aspects, in New Criticism. The strategy, which could now replace the basic New-Criticism project, focused on textual *lack of consistency*, rather than on *consistency*. This branch of Deconstruction would emphasize inconsistency on the rhetorical surface, it would emphasize the playful interchangeability of positions in an opposition (so-called 'in-decidability'), or the rhetorical nature of all language, implying that philosophy and science were also kinds of rhetoric.

In the original Grammatological project (literally a 'logic of writing'), Derrida had been introducing new readings of the philosophical concept *vis a vis* re-readings of Husserl's phenomenology, Saussure's Linguistics, and Levi-Strauss' Structuralism – like Jacques Lacan had been offering new readings of psychoanalysis, and Michel Foucault new readings of history. Philosophy had been exposed to *re-thinking* by a so-called 'Grammatology,' which was organically related to, although superseding in important aspects, these three highly *technical* disciplines: Phenomenology, Structuralism, and Linguistics. When this context for Grammatology disappeared, one no longer saw Derrida's thinking as practicing the Phenomenological *epochè* applied to conceptual structure, as such opening up a new kind of deep-analysis of the philosophical text, which was neither Analytic nor Psychoanalytic, and the *theoretical analysis* of this new application of phenomenology was never well developed (although bright minds would be *practicing* the strategy).

If, in its earliest project, Grammatology is essentially applying the Phenomenological *epochè* to conceptual structure, we need no longer think that Grammatology necessarily merely 'deconstructs.' It may also, and perhaps more often so, 'reconstruct.' In adopting a possible and legitimate 'theoretical attitude' to conceptual structure, one erases the 'world' to which the concept refers, and has now an unhindered access to understanding the formal structure in itself (this 'theoretical attitude' we see as a purely methodological posture, which in no way commits us to Idealism). The guiding question becomes, what is the concept *inside* the 'logic of writing,' temporarily ignoring ('suspending') that to which the concept refers *outside* the 'logic of writing.' If temporarily we accept that there is "nothing outside the text," the text lays open to another kind of elucidating reading. By *reconstructing* the in the text appearing concept-structure, one necessarily also becomes aware of the weak or absent 'joints' in the structure; that is, the problematic points of connection that might bring about a collapse of the entire system, if or when they are illuminated. The reconstructive work must therefore always *precede* the deconstructive work. A Deconstruction that emphasizes only the 'play' or the 'poetry' of theory we see as nonsensical, and is often merely an ideological position from where to challenge two designate 'enemy' disciplines, professional philosophy and the sciences.

When we reconstruct concept-structures in Nietzsche's thinking, we necessarily become of aware of 'elements' in the structure that have been allowed to pass through Nietzsche's thinking unidentified and anonymously; or elements that may be entirely lacking in the structure. We know, that the human mind has a capacity for, not just perceiving what *is there*, but also for perceiving what *is not there*, *if and when* a pattern points to the missing element. In reconstructive thinking, one therefore also names the unnamed; one points to and identifies an absence; one locates differences in a material that on appearances seems undifferentiated. This is the hardest challenge in reconstructive thinking, namely to 'see' something that is not originally there. In meeting this challenge, the dictum 'read the text' ('back to the text,' as one might paraphrase this phenomenologically inspired strategy) has to be properly understood. One necessarily is committed to the text, but not exactly as the philologist is committed. We read conceptual structure; philology reads history and development of word-meaning. We are committed to the 'text' as a system, and nothing but the system revealed in the text can give us the necessary indications of absences. But this also implies that in some instances, word-meaning is not particularly important, or more precisely, words are only important as naming a position in a structure. In order to understand 'words' we therefore do not believe it is as important to understand their history and etymology, as it is to understand their positions in a structure. Historical development of word-meaning becomes the important business of scholars; systems are the business of philosophers. In the first case, one must rely on the library; in the second, one must rely on spatial and abstract thinking.

To provide an example! We surely believe that Nietzsche's word 'priest' is a word for something. We also believe that the word has a connotation to what in everyday-language we call a 'priest.' Still, we do not believe that we have in any way exhausted Nietzsche's meaning of the word by knowing this connotation. We even assume that this connotation is relatively unimportant in determining the rich and expanded meaning the word 'priest' gets in Nietzsche's texts. Consequently, we have to 'reconstruct' this expanse of meaning. We have to investigate the system and context in which 'priest' repeatedly occurs. In this reconstruction, we move far beyond its conventional word-meaning (the 'priest' as 'clergyman,' 'preacher,' etc., in a Christian church), and far more importantly construct in what kind of relation Nietzsche's 'priest' stands to the 'slave' or to the 'master'; in what his so-called 'remedies' for 'suffering' consist; how they are disseminated; why Nietzsche's intemperate tone when introducing this particular 'priest,' etc. The 'priest' becomes a nodal-point, an intensified semantic cluster, from where antennas reach out to other and different semantic clusters, which may or may not have something to do with 'priest' as conventionally defined. We mention *en passant* that this strategy is in perfect harmony with Nietzsche's general understanding of language, as we shall see in especially *Chapter 4* (see especially the discussion of 'the emotional word').

4. Nietzsche and the Intentional Object

We believe that Nietzsche is always thinking positively *about* something, positively *explaining* something. He is certainly keenly aware of his language and his style, but his object is not 'the text,' and he is not producing a self-reflexive philosophy about 'the text.' His philosophy might take as its object the individual's perceptive and cognitive abilities; or the genealogy and disciplinary techniques of morality; or the degeneration of Nietzsche's contemporary Germany and the Germans. But in any case, his thinking has positively defined objects.

The truistic fact that we represent an object in a text, does not imply that the object *is a text*, as little as events represented on the television-screen are 'in' the television. Writing surely is our most typical means of representation, but that does not mean that what we represent by means of writing is also writing. The misunderstanding comes about thanks to a confusion of *means of representation* and *represented*. The text is always in Nietzsche only a *means* of *representing* something *outside* the text. It is not his idea that the text's *outside* represents the text's own *inside*. The internalization of a moral imperative is supposed to have happened; the human being subjected to the moral imperative is supposed to feel actual guilt; the suggestion of a 'super-human' that might transgress the current situation is supposed to address a possible real future, etc. That we are able to suspend references to 'outside' objects by applying the phenomenological *epochè* in order to study formal conceptual structure, is a purely 'theoretical attitude' – a methodological pose, as we say – that does not contradict the general proposition that Nietzsche must always be seen as thinking *about something*.

So, what is Nietzsche thinking about; what is Nietzsche's thinking about? In the aspects of his philosophy that we are here pursuing, Nietzsche is most fundamentally thinking about *cognition and mind*. This aspect was suppressed in much late 20th century commentary (however, rediscovered by the above-mentioned cultural and intellectual historians, and also frequently addressed by a newer generation of German commentators; e.g., W. Müller-Lauter, J. Simon, G. Abel, W. Stegmaier, R. Gasser, & E. Schlimgen) for the understandable reason that if Nietzsche's philosophy is frequently about the mind, then he can be seen, not only as thinking *about something*, which is supposed to have an empirical manifestation, therefore a 'self-presence.' Moreover, it becomes doubtful if Nietzsche is really such a good ally to the post-modernists in the current "science wars" fought between the humanities and the sciences in especially North America. If Nietzsche is solidly imbedded in the scientific paradigms of his day, it casts doubts on the cultivated image of Nietzsche as the poeticizing philosopher engaged in playful transgressions; the thinker who is never *serious*, who knows all the traps of metaphysics, and dances his way out of their reach.

In Nietzsche's epistemology and subject-philosophy, we are always returning to the mind, cognition, and knowledge. It is the mind that perceives (what has consequences for his theory of perception); it is the mind that 'simplifies' (what has consequences for his cognitive theory); it is the mind that 'interprets' (what has consequences for his theory of meaning). It is because we have a mind that we cannot have a notion of truth in the classical sense. What is per definition located beyond the reach of our mind – as either the Platonic *forms* or the Kantian *in-itself* – cannot be of any consequence to the human being, because our mind, controlling our perception and our thinking, prevents us from perceiving or thinking the absolutely independent and self-sufficient. It is also thanks to our malleable minds that it is possible to *format* different human 'types,' like so-called 'master' and so-called 'slave.' It is even because of a certain repetition-automatism characterizing our cognitive processes that we may experience something like 'eternal recurrence of the same' (at least in what we shall defend as the strongest and most pertinent interpretation of this enigmatic concept).

If Nietzsche's evolutionary-cognitive-psychological understanding of mind and cognition is his main project, he suddenly becomes a highly 'timely' philosopher. This interpretation of Nietzsche is eminently relevant for contemporary theories of mind, cognition, and neurology. An evolutionary-cognitive-psychological epistemology has several advocates in modern thinking, some of who nicely continue the Nietzschean project and focus on both evolutionary and cognitive descriptions of the mind (e.g., R. Penrose, P. Churchland, D. Hofstadter, M. Solms, H. Tetens, & D. C. Dennett). Still, it is not our explicit purpose in this work to juxtapose Nietzsche and modern neuro- and cognitive sciences. That would require another treatise. In this work, we shall confine ourselves to the contemporary, or near-contemporary, discourses and paradigms of which Nietzsche was a part.

5. Chapter-Descriptions

5.1. Chapter 1: The Concepts of Truth and Metaphor

In our first chapter, we start with what best represents Nietzsche's philosophical beginning; we start with a reading of the brief essay *Über Wahrheit und Lüge im aussermoralischen sinne* (WL). The essay is probably the most frequently commented about of Nietzsche's texts, attracting commentators from a wide range of different traditions (cf., S. Kofman, P. de Man, W. Klein, C. Crawford, M. Clark, R. Schacht, C. Emden, & G. Moore). The essay has ignited a debate especially on Nietzsche's concept of truth and his concept of metaphor; less about his concept of concept, which we find equally important and shall include below.

For some traditions, Nietzsche's discussions of truth are full of contradictions, because he is apparently discussing truth in more than one sense.

These, especially Anglo-Saxon, traditions take truth to be a uniform concept best determined as correspondence between a proposition and a fact or a state of affairs. Nietzsche seems to have such a concept of truth, since in the context of his essay, it is possible to make false statements. However, he also frequently asserts that 'truth is an illusion,' and equally frequently that the Kantian in-itself is 'truth.' The Anglo-Saxon philosophers find this bewildering, since they have a strongly internalized concept of truth as correspondence between proposition and fact. If now someone questions this correspondence, they by default also question the existence of facts, or at least our access to facts; they even question the existence of the world, or our access to the world (this being seen as wild, indefensible, and nonsensical Idealism). In this interpretation, the Anglo-Saxon philosophers seem committed to Francis Bacon's conception of reality; the fact is *there* in its own self-evident self-presence, and our sentences can refer, or fail to refer, to this self-evident self-presence.

To Nietzsche, this direct access to reality is not an option, because we per human constitution necessarily receive reality as *perceived* reality (according to our so-called "human optics"), which thereupon, we transform into *conceptualized* reality (according to our language). The truths we as such produce about reality are *per force* mediated by these two layers, perception and cognition. Therefore Nietzsche's modest proposal, 'truth is an illusion'; implying that if or when our reflective point of departure is the classical correspondence theory of truth presupposing accessibility to the fact itself, 'truth' – pragmatically speaking – could only be 'illusion' because it has to traverse these two mediating layers. In Nietzsche's early essay, our epistemological nether limit is always *perceived reality*, never reality as such, never the Kantian in-itself. We have no way of transgressing perceived reality in order to get a peek at what reality in-itself might look like as a kind of *perception-free hyper-surface*. We are stuck with our perceived reality; a reality that appears as "images in our eyes."

Therefore, measured against a hypothetical universal 'truth-in-itself,' truth, as our species-specific production, is 'an illusion.' However, this does not imply that we suspend the possibility for uttering sentences that may correspond to, or fail to correspond to, what is *perceived reality*. It is still possible to lie or to tell the truth in Nietzsche. One the one hand, 'truth is an illusion,' because it has undergone a perceptive-linguistic formatting; on the other hand, it is possible to lie or tell the truth about the 'illusion' that our perceptive-linguistic apparatus has so concocted. The two notions of truth are type- and category-different, and they do as such not collide, nor do they produce a self-contradiction. They are proposed within two different contexts or 'compartments' of the theory, and have as such two different comparison-backgrounds on which to be understood and evaluated. As we might say with Nietzsche, they are proposed from two different perspectives.

We therefore generally propose that Nietzsche has a polysemeous theory of truth, where his different notions of truths are proposed from different perspectives, and therefore engender no contradiction in-between themselves, even when the same signifier is assigned a variety of different significations. Similarly, I am not guilty of self-contradiction because I organize my cabinet, and allocate one drawer for shorts, another for T-shirts, and a third for socks. I am in this example only guilty of self-contradiction, if T-shirts and shorts are found in the same drawer. Philosophy is like such a cabinet; it has several different compartments or 'drawers.' Discovering different articles in different 'drawers' does not reveal a 'contradiction.' In order to read philosophy properly, one has to take upon oneself the work of locating its theorems within their proper compartments. Not before this work is done can one meaningfully start passing verdicts about the logical consistency of a theory.

In our interpretation, Nietzsche essentially introduces three type-different notions of truth. First, he calls the thing-in-itself 'truth'; secondly, he proposes that 'truth' is an 'illusion'; thirdly, he introduces a notion of truth as 'truthfulness' or accountability. His primary interest is to determine 'truth as illusion.' This concept of truth he can only express if he asserts a background that would hypothetically be free of 'illusion.' Language therefore forces him, temporarily and as a heuristic device, to suggest that the Kantian in-itself is Truth. This 'Truth' becomes a linguistically and structurally necessary concept that nobody believes actually exist; it is a concept without which we cannot express that 'truth is an illusion'; it is a concept rejected in the very instant it is proposed; it is a concept under erasure. Therefore, the thing-in-itself is ~~Truth~~, and compared to ~~Truth~~, truth is an illusion.

In Nietzsche, 'truth' is also determined as a 'metaphor.' This claim has ignited at least as much debate as his claim that 'truth' is an illusion. The two claims are in fact complementary and codependent. In Nietzsche's essay, the images we receive of perceived reality, as well as our conceptualization of images qua words, are so-called 'metaphors.' The radical determination of both our perceptions and our language as 'metaphorical' – thus rhetorical, thus figurative, thus creative and poeticizing – has received two greatly different responses in respectively the post-modernist and the analytic tradition. The post-modernist commentators have been confirmed in their basic dogma, everything is language, and language is always play and poetry. The Anglo-Saxon commentators have on the contrary been offended in their basic dogma, the strongly internalized belief in the correspondence theory of truth, and the accessibility to the world as fact. The latter also do not see any reason for erasing the difference between literal and metaphorical language, because then one is merely left with an inflated notion of metaphoricity, unable to distinguish different language-uses, which does not seem to be a theoretical gain (e.g., A. Danto, A. Nehamas, M. Clark).

In our work, we have articulated the problem differently. Only in a highly qualified sense, we see Nietzsche's notion of metaphoricity as 'inflated.' Preferably, we see it as a completely new concept, with only *system-specific meaning*. Like in our example of Nietzsche's *priest*, Nietzsche's *metaphor* has only superficially connotations to 'metaphor' as used in classical rhetorical theory from Aristotle to Perelman. Its conceptual range has been expanded; in the expansion, it has perhaps retained a few elements from classical theory, but largely, Nietzsche has given the concept a new conceptual sphere. 'Metaphor' has in Nietzsche lost its commonsensical value, and been re-invested with new values. Now it lingers in his theory as an incomprehensible 'x,' whose meaning-structure it is the commentator's task to reconstruct and better describe. In the classical sense, a metaphor replaces a literal expression with a figurative expression; one word or phrase in a sentence-construction is replaced with another word or phrase. We immediately see that Nietzsche's 'metaphor' *replaces nothing*. (1) Images supposedly replace nerve-stimuli, but nerve-stimuli have no representation to begin with, why the 'image' as a 'metaphor' 'replacing' it can be nothing but pure and spontaneous creation. (2) Words supposedly replace images, but images belong to visual perception, not to our linguistic capabilities. Images do not make up a language replaced with a more poetic and figurative language in the form of words. Nerve-stimuli, images, and words are distinct spheres, and when something is 'transferred' from one sphere to another, the transfer is uniquely original. Therefore, Nietzsche's 'metaphor' replaces a void, *implying* that it replaces nothing, *implying* that Nietzsche's 'metaphor' is pure and spontaneous creation, *implying* that it gives representation to something, which originally have no representation. Nietzsche's 'metaphor' is thus another word for 'sign.' By means of signs, we orient ourselves in the world. Images are such signs, as are words. Nietzsche's notion of 'metaphor' can therefore be said to be 'inflated,' but only because its *system-specific meaning* equals 'sign,' and because we can think of no science that does not employ signs.

This reading makes Nietzsche's theory of 'metaphor' entirely harmless (perhaps even trivial, but we fear not the trivial – especially not when it provides the best explanation!), and we furthermore understand that in this sense of 'metaphor,' Nietzsche does not see language as playful in the postmodernist sense, since signs are employed, not only in creative and imaginative writing, but also in rigorously formalized languages, such as logic and mathematics. Nietzsche's 'metaphor' has meaning only within a highly abstract epistemology that generally asserts that our access to so-called 'reality' is necessarily sign-mediated. It is in the best sense a foundational theory, reaching several levels deeper into the enigma of knowledge-formation, than the superficial distinction between 'literal' and 'figurative' in classical rhetoric.

5.2. Chapter 2: The Ontology and Epistemology

In our second chapter, we continue to elaborate our theory on Nietzsche's ontology and epistemology. Our access to reality is necessarily sign-mediated (the 'sign' being both a perceptive image and a linguistic word). This however, does not imply to Nietzsche that reality has evaporated. Contrary to what is often suggested, we find in Nietzsche a strong emphasis of so-called 'language-independent' reality as the paradoxical 'ground' that grounds nothing. The reason for our inadequate ability of producing knowledge is exactly the existence of this language-independent reality. 'Reality' is in Nietzsche always something *absolutely other*; something existing without intention, design, and purpose; something that was never preformatted in language or according to rules or structures that we can understand. 'Reality' is the *absolutely other*, the *chaos*, the *becoming*, the *ground that grounds nothing*, that we cannot understand; only from this abyss of incomprehension do we describe it in our (sign-dependent) scientific languages. If by any chance reality were already 'language' or 'structured as language' (which in Nietzsche's context would be a nonsensical assumption), it would be superfluous to start describing it once more in yet another language. If reality was already lingering as 'language,' we only needed to press the 'record' bottom.

Since reality is always the *absolutely other*, we are not able to understand the *nature* of reality; still, we are able to describe the *appearances* of reality. This limited ability to describe 'reality' is secured thanks to three human capabilities, (i) we are able to perceive a surface, (ii) we are able to form languages about what we perceive, and (iii) we are able to conceptualize, that is, group together into distinct classes, the linguisticized perceived surface. We have for example the ability to perceive objects as either big or small, as either near or far, as either bright or dim, etc. Thanks to this perceptive capability, we can now classify stars according to their mass, their distance, and their luminosity. This again enables us to set up tables that determine a near-constant value for the proportionality between for example mass and luminosity. This table may give us the illusion of a law-governed universe, thanks to which we may quickly identify a newly observed star according to our preconceived parameters; but – however impressive the scientific achievement is – we have exclusively addressed a *surface*, not a *nature*, of things. We have classified only an appearance, that is, an *appearance for-us*, *appearing* according to our exclusive human optics, our perceptive designs, as we shall explain in better detail in the chapter below.

Beneath the surface, Nietzsche suggests his so-called chaos or world of becoming. To live in a world of chaos remains our fundamental condition. It is upon this chaotic foundation, we build our fragile conceptual systems. Chaos is the nether limit in Nietzsche's ontology. If being is ultimately *chaos*, it implies that there *is* no *nature* of things, no thing-in-itself, no hidden laws or principles or designs for us to discover, or which by happy accident we might tumble into. This implies again that our conceptualizations and classifications are exclusively *our* work, that science necessarily has this inescapable anthropomorphic (or 'narcissistic') dimension. Nietzsche's ontological foundation is the chaos that we cannot access as such, but can approach only through simplifying processes. Our perceptive image-making as well as our linguistic language-making are such simplifying processes.

We as such simplify in two stages; and we even seem to be simplifying two qualitatively different grounds. First we simplify thank to our 'human optics.' This fundamentally means that we see the world as we are capable of seeing it. That is, the world as it appears to us through our perceptive designs, strongly favoring *visual* perception, but a visual perceptive system exclusively designed for humans. (For example, humans see the world in color (some mammals do not); humans see a limited band of wavelengths (birds see the world in a far broader band of colors); humans see the world in three-dimensional perspective (insects do not, and may not even have visual perception), etc.) As such we see a *surface*, and habitually believe that the world *is* a *surface*; a *surface* that may retreat into the horizon, or draw near just under our noses. Since there is no law guaranteeing that the world in-itself 'looks' exactly as we see it (nor, indeed, that it *is* a surface), we must have 'falsified' something originally *there*, but which may look different from, as Nietzsche says, another "point." That which is originally there, that which is open to all possible perception – visual, auditory, tactile, olfactory – we will now call the *Ur-ground*. We have no choice but to simplify, thus falsify, this Ur-ground. Per human constitution, we have perceptive designs, and are not equipped with extraordinary means by which to bypass these human designs. We therefore necessarily falsify the Ur-ground, and cannot help doing so.

However, in Nietzsche we also falsify a ground constituted for-us; the ground that is constituted already in human perception; the ground that as such announces itself as surface, as having dimension, being colorful, near and far, bright and dim, up and down, right and left, etc. We shall call this ground the *Human ground*. We falsify also this ground in Nietzsche, but for different reasons, since it is qualitatively different from the Ur-ground. If we falsify the Ur-round out of physiological necessity, we falsify the Human ground out of psychological necessity. The Human ground, constituted thanks to our perceptive designs, still encounters us as too chaotic, too abundant, and too complex. The problem with this human ground, this reality for-us, is that it is always too abundant. There is always too much reality, too much information, impinging on our sensory apparatus. We as such need to filter and abbreviate this multitude of impressions into something manageable. Our mind provides this service; our mind is a filtration-, abbreviation-, simplification-apparatus. The problem is never in Nietzsche that there is *no reality*, the problem is always that there is *too much reality*. To protect ourselves against too much reality, we develop a cognitive 'reality-defense'; we automatically screen impressions before we let them pass as conscious sensations.

5.3. Chapter 3: The Concept of the Split Subject.

In this work, we distinguish between a 'split' and a 'fragmented' subject in Nietzsche. The issue in *Chapter 3* is the split subject, the issue in *Chapter 4*, the fragmented. We have not attempted to work out a *unified theory* for both 'split' and 'fragmented' subject. It is to undersigned not clear how to think this unification with sufficient accuracy. It is also not a unification attempted by Nietzsche himself. Nonetheless, we believe that the distinction is justified and does frequently appear in especially the *Nachlaß* material. Nietzsche speaks sometimes as if the subject is split, and sometimes as if it is fragmented. In the first case, we assume that a whole is split into two pieces, which are still determinable and definable as two parts of the whole (this assumption pulls the rug from under the subject understood as self-conscious and self-present self-identity, but it does not necessarily see the subject's inner life as an inaccessible chaotic in-itself). In the second case, we assume that the subject has broken into several pieces so multifarious that it is no longer possible to put the pieces back together into either identifiable unity or identifiable parts. According to this assumption, there is no 'personality' (nor, for that matter, any 'personality-split'), but rather an indefinite number of 'ego-positions' or 'ego-clusters' competing against each other for 'power' in the chaotic self.

In the theory of the split subject, we notice that there is in Nietzsche two ways in which a subject may split; consequently, two levels for discussion of the condition. When Nietzsche addresses the 'split subject' in its most general sense, he inherits a discussion introduced by Descartes and continued by Kant as its two major representatives. This discussion concerns the nature of the *I* and the 'thinking' in 'I think.' We see Nietzsche continuing and radicalizing the critique of the Cartesian 'I think' first introduced by Kant in his famous chapter on the "Paralogisms of Pure Reason" (from KrV). Already here Kant recognized that there was an unbridgeable gap between a formal 'I' and empirical 'thinking.' The *I* was in Kant no longer understood as a substance, but as a formality. That to which the *I* might be 'referring' had at best the status of an unknowable and inaccessible thing-in-itself, explicitly labeled 'x'. We see Nietzsche continuing this conception, since he too conceives of the *I* as a purely fictional construction, with no reference to a substantive nature of the self. However, Nietzsche explains the temptation in the Rationalist tradition to misinterpret *I* as substance differently from Kant. At the core of this misinterpretation, Nietzsche too locates a 'paralogism,' but if in Kant, the rationalist tradition misunderstood the notion *subject*, and applied to it two different meanings in respectively the major and minor of a syllogism, in Nietzsche analysis, the rationalist tradition imitates the *subject-predicate* logic from conventional grammar, and applies it as a *substance-accidence* scheme to subjectivity. In Kant, one had been seduced by *reason* itself. In Nietzsche, one had been seduced by *language*. To Nietzsche, the tradition had appropriated the *grammatical subject* and made it a matrix for the *existential subject*.

As we shall see, the *I* as a formality (in Kant) and as a grammatical subject (in Nietzsche) has a strong family-resemblance to Emile Benveniste's recent determination of the *subject of enunciation* (subject of discourse). In Benveniste too, the subject is without essence, determined merely by the performance of "the one who says I in the instance of enunciation." This *I* is instrumental for communication, because *in use*, it necessarily constitutes itself as *self* opposed to the *other* addressed, the *you*. It thus constitutes an elementary *self-other* opposition in the dialogical situation. In Benveniste, this *I* designates, in all instances, the one who *says I*, as such designating nobody in particular, therefore cannot provide us as speakers with any substantive knowledge of ourselves. Still, it is necessary in the communicative or dialogical situation, since without this ability to refer a discourse to an *I* speaking, there would be no communication. In Saussure's vocabulary, there would be no *parole*, but only *langage*. The language-system would at best exist as some abstract, isolated, and divine potentiality; some kind of 'dark matter,' we could not access and not comprehend.

With Benveniste, we understand that the emergence of the simple dialogical structure, *I-you*, has several consequences. For one thing, it sets us apart from most animals, which do not refer to themselves as *I* when communicating (i.e., signaling). We therefore believe that language-acquisition and development of an ego-consciousness are simultaneous processes (what happens to be also Nietzsche's position). For another thing, the structure introduces into our mental life the possibility of a split between self and other, insofar as the dialogical situation is internalized and transferred to inner life. We therefore suggest that as well as an *I* can address a *you*, the *I* – thanks to internalization and transference – can also address *itself* as *you*. However, with the substantial difference that now the *you* is another part of the *I*; a part we label *me*.

If the simple structure *I-you* is imitated in inner dialogue (soliloquy), the subject imitates a speech-situation with which it is already familiar in the outside world. (We assume in general in this treatise that experience of inner life can be nothing substantially different from experience of outer life. If for example fantasies are spatially-temporally organized, it is because the subject experiences in a spatial-temporal world; if they are played out in three dimensions, it is because the subject perceives its world in three dimensions, etc. Similarly, if the subject speaks to itself as another in inner-life, it is because it is familiar with speaking to another in outer life. Therefore, nothing uniquely 'inner' develops out of itself as object of experience – something uniquely 'inner,' like digestion, we are hardly able to experience.) We believe that the soliloquizing subject internalizes the dialogical situation, implying that, (i) a dialogical *I-you* distinction becomes a soliloquizing *I-me* distinction; (ii) a self-other opposition becomes a self-self opposition; (iii) a subject constituting itself as individuality, constitutes itself as dividuality; (iv) pragmatic discourse becomes self-reflective discourse.

The two positions *I* and *me* become empty forms that can now be filled with contents; with or without Nietzsche, we know that all kinds of dialogues are carried out in inner life. Out of the constitution of an *I-me* grows eventually the possibility of a subject communicating with itself. We argue that a *special case* of this self-communication is the moral discourse. Here an *I* as one part of the self sets itself up as a commander over another, subservient, part of the self.

Therefore, *first*, we see the abstract constitution of the two positions as the most general possibility for dialogue in inner life. This happens thanks to the subject taking over the *I-you* distinction from communication, and depends of language-use in general. *Second,* in a special case of this possibility of dialogue in inner life, the *I* and *me* set themselves up over and against each other, with an *I* demanding the *me* to subject itself to various morals imperatives.

Subjected to the moral discourse, the subject turns into Nietzsche's 'herd' or 'slave.' The *me* is subjected to imperatives issued by the *I*. Internalization of *outer* to *inner* is accomplished in three steps: first, the *I* is subjected to a discourse of an authoritarian other (a parent, a teacher, a priest, etc.); second, it appropriates this discourse as his or her own; lastly, it exercises the immediate demands of the discourse on that other part of itself we call *me*. Since one can internalize several authoritarian voices, the moral subject is typically constructed as several *clusters of signification*, each of which is defending different cases. The self does not constitute a single uniformly commanding 'super-ego,' but, as we shall see, a number of competing *ego-clusters*; the self does not internalize a single set of logical coherent ideas, but rather, it internalizes a number of discourses, depending on their appeal and intensity in the moment. As such, the subject is not simply divided between one voice set over and against another voice; it is fragmented into several of such *groups, clusters*, or *configurations*. There are potentially an infinite number of *I-me* dialogues carried out in the heterogeneous subject.

5.4. Chapter 4: The Concept of the Fragmented Subject

The heterogeneous, or fragmented, subject is the issue in the fourth chapter. This is also the chapter where we most elaborately describe Nietzsche's biological-linguistic (i.e., proto-neurological) model of the subject. In a certain way, the chapter can be seen as a *translation* of well-known concepts into the new context of a neurological-evolutionary, a biological-linguistic, model of the subject. The chapter discusses notions like stimulus, sensation, cognition, memory, language in this new context; it gives an account of how sense of 'reality' and belief in 'truth' are biologically-evolutionarily constituted; it explains what more precisely we understand by 'ego-cluster'; it argues that Nietzsche, in his notion of 'will-to-power,' is envisioning a constitutionally aggressive subject, almost constitutionally configured to be subjected to, and subject itself to, ideological deception. The last aspect gives our exposition a new politically relevant dimension, which has so far been absent. Nietzsche's thinking, in at least one of its important aspects, can be seen as a 'critique of ideology.' In the third chapter, we were already building up to that conclusion; in the fourth, we develop it; finally, in the fifth, we consolidate.

We will address here only a few selected issues. First, what does it mean that *sense* of reality (but *not* reality) and *belief* in truth are biologically constituted? It most elementarily means that the individual internalizes the surface of the outside as representing what is real and what is true. The individual 'chooses' the surface of the outside over and above a possible alternative candidate – from an evolutionary perspective, a very poor candidate – namely the surface of the inside in the form of hallucinations. Since our engagement of the inside cannot provide gratification of simple needs, and the engagement of the outside can, the outside surface comes to represent what is true and what is real. Hence, the human subject biologically acquires an ability to distinguish between *outside* and *inside*, between *perceptive* representations and *hallucinatory* representations, between *true* and *false*. In this evolutionary-neurological context, the 'true' is now determined as what is *not* my hallucination, while the 'false' *is* my hallucination. The subject needed to learn to fight off its inner chaos, and evolve a psyche under the auspices of *will-to-power*. Still, in the fragile inner-mental life of the subject, 'the true' is in perpetual *competition* with the 'un-true,' the hallucination, when particularly well-cathected and intensified memory-traces or 'clusters' (for example if intensified by *desire* or *hatred*), without any corresponding 'reality,' take over the control of existence, and sometimes perception (the human subject frequently believes, and sometimes even perceives, what it *desires*).

Another master-distinction like good and bad, we also regard as biologically constituted. In a biological context, the 'good' and the 'bad' derive from the evolutionary earlier distinction between 'friendly' and 'hostile.' It was necessary for survival to quickly establish something as threatening, thus hostile or 'bad,' in order for our prehistoric ancestor to escape the danger.

These two master-distinctions, *true and false* & *good and bad*, were originally merely distinctions necessary for survival. They come down to self-preservation: 'true' is what aids my perception of the real, and 'good' is what assures me that there is no danger. These simplifying and schematic perceptions of the surface were constituted thanks to evolutionary necessity. It was never necessary for humans to build up memory-systems retaining all possible data; it was necessary to evolve much simpler systems that could for example crudely distinguish between trees that yielded edible fruits and trees that did not. We shall argue that these elementary simplifying processes are pre-linguistic, that our mental system therefore starts to *interpret* the world in simple distinctions *before* language properly speaking is introduced into the system. In Nietzsche, the *interpretive processes* are always primary, and the *linguistic processes* secondary. Both processes, however, 'simplify.'

With the formation of an 'ego,' the subject is capable of judging and gaining control over reality (external as well as internal). This 'ego' Nietzsche now sees as collection of several egos, or so-called 'cells,' competing in and between themselves for control. 'Will-to-Power,' applied to inner-mental life, becomes more correctly 'wills-to-power,' where several conflicting 'wills' collide in their battle for power (an aspect of Nietzsche strongly emphasized in the newer German tradition; e.g., W. Müller-Lauter, G. Abel, W. Stegmaier, & E. Schlimgel). Given this situation, we encounter in Nietzsche an *inner perspectivism* in every subject, insofar as the subject, as a multiplicity of subjects, is populated with several wills. In this conception, there is no rational supervision of the psyche, because there is no overarching *logical super-self.*

Our inner experiences exist primordially as unstructured chaos. However, upon this chaos we impose a certain order. This implies that we, by means of language, impose our interpretations on a certain material, as such, shape, organize, and fashion that material to fit a new linguistic medium. This implies again that the translation from *inner experience* into *language* involves an inevitable distortion, falsification, and simplification of the inner experience. Still, Nietzsche emphasizes that language introduces us to the *only* inner world, which we can know. We can know only this simplified and falsified inner world. Our simplifying language transforms the strange and the other into the familiar; reduces the other into a *for-us*.

Will-to-power-complexes manifest themselves as local (ideological or quasi-ideological) formations and configurations in a subject. If now the psyche explicitly operates according to will-to-power-processes, then the psyche is a *battleground* for defending its most cherished beliefs, and attacking anything threatening these beliefs. Consequently, the psyche is most essentially *aggressive*. In such an aggressive psyche, there is no commitment to logic and reason. This psyche does not bother itself about solving contradictions, incompatibilities, irrationalities, or other subtle logical tensions in inner-life. If a tension ever surfaces, the psyche does something much easier and faster. It creates a new 'perspective' from where to 'see'; a new inner-mental compartment, where something unacceptable can suddenly be seen as acceptable. This *perspectival 'method'* by which to solve contradictions overrides the methods of formal logic. Thanks to this 'method,' it is now possible to mean both A and non-A. With this, we notice that the human being possesses an almost infinite flexibility and plasticity. It has in its *intrinsic constitution* the ability to adopt and to mean everything, if not at once and simultaneously, then under *rapidly shifting* perspectives, whose coherence and consistency is a small matter.

The subject remains a fragile construction because its self-interpretations are fragile; or, to put it more strongly, the subject is fragile because interpretations are *always* fragile. We now suggest that because the subject, unconsciously, knows this – but knows it as repressed knowledge that cannot be admitted into consciousness – it also puts up a tenacious fight to keep its interpretations, its 'truths,' intact. It is because interpretations are the *always fragile* foundational network of the self that there is in Nietzsche a "will to truth." Will-to-power becomes a will-to-truth, where 'truth' here designates the individual's strongest beliefs, the individual's master-signifiers, according to which he or she projects meaning into his universe. We therefore see the lonely and soliloquizing subject as engaged in a perpetual war within itself to hold on to its 'truths,' its 'master-signifiers.'

Irrationality we now see as the *frenetic defense* of hyper-cathected truth-positions (and the complementary offenses against anti-cathected truth-threatening positions). It is when language comes into 'touch' with these intensities (desire or hatred), this hot inner core of the subject, that logic breaks down. Formal knowledge of the rules of logic is no guarantee for coherent thinking or dialogue. The pull downward toward randomly hyper-cathected positions is too strong, and overrides immediately the agent's whatever superficial awareness of existent rules for argument. As soon as the mind is no longer under extreme discipline, no longer occupied with the formal organization of x, y, and z, the surface cracks, and the mind slips immediately back from these acknowledged rules; rules it only kept extended for a brief moment and with too great an effort. The logical mind is like extended in free air with no support, why therefore it only sustains itself with an enormous effort, and only for brief moments of time. The logical mind is without strength, and it is only too happy to slip back to its initial and much more comfortable positions, the old well-known hate and love objects.

5.5. Chapter 5: A Theory of the Ideological Subject and the Ideologue

We believe that one of the most promising prospects of the theory of the subject we have extracted from Nietzsche is its superior ability to explain *ideology*. We start out with a confused-aggressive subject, which is constitutionally empty, and which, exactly because it is empty, craves to be filled with contents. That which we call 'ideology,' whether religious or political, satisfies this need. It provides meaning in a meaning-less universe, and purpose in a purpose-less existence. Thanks to ideology, positions in the subject become hyper-cathected as semantic clusters; they become intensified or 'super-charged,' and are thereupon tenaciously defended by the subject as its so-called 'truths.' The commander 'shouting' his commands to the receptive subject is essentially a description of the *ideologue* disseminating his *ideology*. The subject is receptive to this 'shouting' because of its cravings for meaning. Ideology as such always repairs *a loss*; it also tends to appeal to the *original aggression* of the subject; it is like a catalyst accelerating the reactions of these two original subjective deficiencies, confusion and aggression. Generally, ideology creates hyper-cathected love-objects as well as anti-cathected hate-objects with the aim to create a group of self-righteous individuals, who, in their protection of some idea, can legitimately unload their hatred on other groups, who are seen as either opposed or indifferent to the cherished idea.

It is in this light that we interpret Nietzsche's criticism of the moral subject and moral discourse in GM. We consequently read Nietzsche's 'priest' as a label for the consummate *ideologue*; we read Nietzsche's 'slave' as the ideologically *infected subject*; and his 'master' as the promise of an ideologically *emancipated subject*. This is to some extent interpretation on our part, since Nietzsche's object of criticism is the distinct Judeo-Christian socialization of European man. Through this socialization history, the slave has come to dominate Europe, and has developed as the universal type at the cost of the rarer masters. Christianity becomes an attempt to make equal what is intrinsically unequal. It is for example a basic motive in Christianity to declare every man equal 'in the eyes of God.' However, from Christianity, as the European master-ideology *par excellence*, slave-morality has proliferated into other contemporary ideologies where equality has also being promoted, even when these ideologies were ostensibly opposed to Christianity; for example socialism, anarchism, and feminism.

Christianity has as such provided the general matrix for the dogmatic form of other ideologies. To interpret Nietzsche's criticism of the Judeo-Christian religious-moral discourse in general terms as Critique of Ideology is for that reason alone justified by Nietzsche. Furthermore, since we abstractly concentrate our analysis on the conditions of the possibility of the religious-moral discourse, as well as the general structure and dynamics between priest and slave, ideologue and ideological subject, we are investigating an essence that must be identical for both religion and ideology (*religion* would indeed seem to be merely a sub-class of *ideology*). Like religion, ideology too is disseminated by a 'priest' and received by a 'slave'; like religion, ideology too provides relief, and issues promises; like religion, ideology too helps the individual forgetting an unsatisfying actual world; like religion, ideology too socializes a self-righteous individual disposed to divide the world in self and other.

A theory of ideology extracted from Nietzsche's discussions of morality and the moral subject must be generally applicable. It cannot be allowed to set up another ideology; and can for that reason alone not be identical to Marx's theory, which, for political reasons, defines ideology narrowly as an instrument of the ruling classes. An ontological theory makes ideology a universal condition ameliorating subjective emptiness (– unless we are as hopeful as Nietzsche and believe that a 'noble' or a 'master' will eventually evolve and invalidate the need for ideology). In the context of a general theory of ideology, Marx's theory, by contrast, is itself ideology created on behalf of the socially aspiring classes: first and foremost, *the intellectuals*. Allegedly, it is advanced in the name of the proletariat, but historically, it has always best served the intellectuals.[3] This discrepancy, we might add, is one of the cheap tricks in the considerable arsenal of the ideologue – one always speaks in the name of somebody else (some minority, suppressed, disenfranchised, etc.) in order to disguise the brutal fact that one really speaks for oneself.

5.6. Chapter 6: Affirmation of the Hyper-Surface of the Present as an Intrinsic Psychological Possibility

How does one escape from this subjective condition, the emptiness of the subject, and the false (ideological) remedies that are being offered as cure? Nietzsche cannot allow himself to suggest an alternative ideology; all alternative religious and political utopias must be ruled out, since they are exactly priest-generated false promises. Nietzsche cannot allow himself to become another 'priest.'

In our final *Chapter 6*, we suggest that Nietzsche, in his enigmatic concept of *Eternal Recurrence of the Same*, attempts to think himself *out* of a condition that he has thought himself into. However, the notion of Eternal Recurrence in Nietzsche is notoriously vague, not least because it has sev-

---

[3] For a critical analysis of Marxism, see Alvin Gouldner's two first volumes of his trilogy, *The Dark Side of Dialectic*: Gouldner, Alvin: Dialectic of Ideology and technology. New York, 1979; and Gouldner, Alvin: The Future of Intellectuals and the Rise of the New Class. New York, 1979

eral different applications, which, seemingly, are related neither explicitly nor immanently.

In its two traditionally best-known applications, the notion has a cosmological interpretation (critical expositions in G. Simmel, I. Soll, and G. Abel), and an ethical interpretation (e.g., W. Müller-Lauter, B. Magnus, G. Deleuze, and L. Hatab). According to the former interpretation, the universe allegedly 'recurs as the same.' The interpretation has always been regarded as outlandish, but is perhaps less so today, since contemporary physics has reiterated Nietzsche's original suggestion, and proposed that our universe is only one among an infinity of universes, where somewhere in this ocean of universes, we would likely find a universe, a galaxy, a solar system, a planet, etc., identical to our own (i.e., with the exact same composition of particles). With or without the mathematical support of modern physics, the idea remains highly speculative, and without practical consequences (it cannot be verified; we cannot see, even less travel, outside our universe to check the hypothesis; we can hardly see into our own universe, and, on a cosmological scale, our 'traveling about' is just pitiful). According to the latter interpretation, 'eternal return of the same' is proposed as an ethical command asserted in the hypothetical conditional entreating the individual to live his or her life eternally as the same life. The interpretation is strongly supported by the famous aphorism from FW, where a 'daemon' challenges our protagonist to affirm his willingness to re-live his life eternally as the same, as such, confirm his current existence and renounce the promises of Heaven. The interpretation is often understood as an 'existential imperative' providing an emancipative alternative to Kant's 'categorical imperative.'

It can no longer come as a surprise to the reader that we in this work prefer to see 'recurrence' as an 'inner-mental' possibility; that we prefer to understand 'recurrence' as a possibility that emerges thanks to the organization of our *mind*. In this sense, we see 'recurrence' as something that immanently structures two existential human concerns: our 'knowledge-formation,' on the one hand, and our 'pleasure-constitution,' on the other.

There is recurrence in 'knowledge-formation' because knowledge is not produced in unique acts of insights, but is in Nietzsche rather produced in layers of interpretation-processes, where one rudimentary interpretation is *transferred* to, but essentially *repeated* in, the language of another interpretation, which yet again may be *transferred* to, and thus *repeated* in, another language. Something, which we already tacitly know, returns as something we explicitly know. In this sense, there is always recurrence of the same in the production of knowledge (M. Heidegger and G. Abel foreshadow this interpretation). To know thanks to some spontaneous act of insight in the absolutely new is not an option in Nietzsche; one always knows according to schemes and taxonomies that are absolutely old, and are therefore just variations and repetitions of the same. We are not conscious of all the interpretation-processes our bodies are responsible for and capable of; we only become conscious of knowledge when the interpretation-process becomes a sign-process. In other words, it is only on the linguistic surface we become conscious about what we know; still, beneath the linguistic surface – "under the table," as Nietzsche puts it – we already 'know' (immanently, passively, and pre-consciously) what subsequently we come to know consciously, that is, as expressible in language. (E.g., on the Triple-A meeting, the member stepping up to the lectern and declaring his 'I am an alcoholic!' is not supposed to state something he did not already know; he is stating something he has known for thirty years. But now, what was before a blur of fleeting and transitory suspicions (emerging momentarily in-between drinks just to drift away again) has found a precise expression, and it is easier to engage and fight the 'alcohol-devil' if he has a voice.)

We believe that we discern 'recurrence' in 'pleasure-constitution' as well (foreshadowing this interpretation are P. Klossowsky and J. Stambough). In this context, we understand 'pleasure' as 'aesthetic pleasure' – thus related to *perception*. Thus, we see knowledge-constitution and pleasure-constitution as representing respectively an epistemological and an aesthetic attitude. As aesthetic pleasure, pleasure concerns perception, and especially visual perception, of the environing world. It is a pleasure that in Nietzsche manifests itself as a pleasure of immersing oneself in the presence of the self-present. It always involves a halt to time in our otherwise time-constituting consciousness, insofar as it emerges as a pleasure that dreams of turning off and shutting down our conscious operations. Our thinking, memories, and desires are being suspended, and we re-enter as clean tablets the surface-world we call the hyper-surface; we re-enter the hyper-surface only as *gaze*. If, when experiencing this surface, time is forced to a halt, experiences must necessarily arrive to the subject as absolutely new and context-independent in each instant, since we have shut down our memory-systems and therefore our ability to contextualize. Nietzsche expresses on various occasions a yearning for *living* this surface-existence where all troubles have evaporated, and we live happily in the moment like the "cattle" "fettered to the pale of the moment" that Nietzsche introduced already in UB2 (the cattle that cannot speak, because it always forgets what it is just about to say). Thanks to the suspension of our conscious operations, every now returns eternally as the same, with the same 'value,' 'weight,' and 'intensity' as the previous now. The universe is eternally new; worries about death have evaporated as well as worries about life. Heidegger's so-called 'Being toward Death' cannot be experienced.

The attitude is in-itself grandiose affirmation, an extreme 'Yes' to world and existence, since the negation cannot be experienced. Only the *gaze* is activated; one can only *see*, one cannot see that something is *not* what it ought to be.

Although the idea is never explicitly worked out in Nietzsche's thinking, we regard it as his *last* thought – 'last' chronologically as well as structurally. It becomes Nietzsche final resolution to the subjective conundrum, apparently reached by some kind of method of elimination. In a philosophy, where we are not allowed to introduce new ideologies, religions, or political utopias, *eternal recurrence* as an *inner-mental suspension of time* seems to offer the only viable path out our rotten subjectivity. Although radical in the extreme, it is the only way left for defeating the aggressive, the envious, the confused, and the easily seduced individual, the 'slave,' which has been cultivated as the standard model of the human being in Nietzsche's 19th Century Europe.

It may be speculative, but undersigned find it difficult not to relate this Nietzsche's last and most radical thought to Nietzsche's own last years. When, in beginning of 1889, Nietzsche was found in a state of ecstatic joy, dancing about in his bed and on his table, he had found and accepted eternal recurrence of the now; he was simply entering the hyper-presence of eternal recurrence. And when, in the last ten years of his life, he lived as a speechless autistic and catatonic, he only lived the cherished idea he had intimated, but never made completely explicit. He had fallen into the abyss, and had come out on the surface. *We* call such life 'demented'; but *he*, he lived the desired time-stop, where finally thoughts, memories, and desires had disappeared, and he had become no more than that desired *gaze* that unifies the eternal-recurrence-subject with the eternal-recurrence-world. As well as the world repeats and renews itself in every moment, the eternal-recurrence-subject, joined to the world thanks to the gaze, repeats and renews itself in every moment.

CHAPTER 1

The Narcissism of Human Knowledge

An Interpretation of Nietzsche's *Über Wahrheit und Lüge* in the Context of 19th Century Kantianism.

> In endless space countless glowing spheres, around each of which a dozen smaller illuminated ones revolve; hot at the inside and covered with a hard cold crust, on which a musty film has produced a living and knowing being – this is the empirical truth, the real, the world. Yet for a being who thinks, it is a troublesome position to stand on one of those numberless spheres freely floating in boundless space, without knowing wherefrom and whereto, and to be only *one* of innumerable similar beings that press, and push, and suffer, restlessly and rapidly arising and passing away in beginningless and endless time.
>
> — Schopenhauer: *Die Welt als Wille und Vorstellung.*[4]

> We: bits of dust on the surface of our planet, itself hardly worth calling a grain of sand in the universe's infinite space; we: the most recent race among the living on earth, according to geological chronology barely out of the cradle, still in the learning stage, barely half-educated, declared of age only out of mutual respect, and yet already, through the more powerful force of the causal law, grown beyond all our fellow creatures and vanquishing them in the struggle for existence.
>
> — Helmholtz: Popular Lectures.[5]

> In a remote corner of the universe, dispersed throughout an indefinite number of flickering solar systems, there was once upon a time a star, upon which a clever animal discovered knowledge. This was the most arrogant and dishonest minute in "world history": but it was after all only a minute. After nature had taken a few breaths, the star stiffened, and the clever animal had to die.
>
> – Nietzsche: Wahrheit und Lüge.[6]

---

[4] Schopenhauer, Arthur: W2, SW 2, p. 11.
[5] Helmholtz, Hermann von: Science and Culture: Popular and Philosophical Lectures. Edited by D. Cahan. Chicago (The University of Chicago Press), 1995, p. 366.

0. Introduction

Nietzsche's brief essay "Über Wahrheit und Lüge im aussermoralischen Sinne" (hereafter WL) is best understood against the epistemological background of 19th century Kantianism and neo-Kantianism.[7] Against this background, Nietzsche's essay gains both a 'value' and a 'meaning' quite different from the value and meaning it was oftentimes given in some of the more recent receptions from the latter part of the 20th Century. Inserted into this precise epistemological context, we will for example notice that it is *not* Nietzsche's intention to reduce all knowledge to "rhetoric" and "metaphor" understood in the *classical sense*. Knowledge is 'metaphorical' in a *specific sense*. 'Metaphor' becomes a metaphor for a particular Kantian model of thinking.

---

[6] Nietzsche: WL, KSA 1, p. 875.

[7] We shall in the present chapter give a first presentation of Nietzsche's well-known influences from Kant, Schopenhauer, Fr. A. Lange, Hermann von Helmholtz, and Gustav Gerber; in the following *Chapters 3* and *4*, we continue this contextualization of Nietzsche in more detail. For our purposes, the most crucial readings have been Kant, Immanuel: Kritik der reinen Vernunft & Prolegomena, Werkausgabe Band III, IV, and V. Frankfurt am Main (Suhrkamp), 1977; Schopenhauer, Arthur: Über die vierfache Wurzel des Satzes vom zureichenden Grunde & Die Welt als Wille und Vorstellung bd. 1 & 2. (Sämtliche Werke Band I, II, and III. Frankfurt am Main (Suhrkamp), 1986). Lange, Friedrich Albert: Geschichte des Materialismus und Kritik seiner Bedeutung in der Gegenwart, bd. 1 & 2. Iserlohn (Verlag von J. Baedeker), 1873. Hartmann, Eduard von: Philosophie des Unbewussten bd. 1-3. (Berlin (Carl Dunker's Verlag), 1870,); Helmholtz, Hermann von: Science and Culture: Popular and Philosophical Lectures. (Edited by D. Cahan. Chicago (The University of Chicago Press), 1995); Zöllner, Johann: Transcendental Physics. (Kessinger reprint edition 1881); Gustav, Gerber: Die Sprache als Kunst bd. 1 & 2 (Berlin (R. Gaertner's Buchverhandlung), 1885). (In recent Nietzsche-commentary, Nietzsche's inspiration from Lange has been pointed out by Salaquarda, Jörg: "Nietzsche und Lange." Nietzsche Studien 7. Berlin, New York (Walter de Gruyter), 1978; by Stack, George: Lange and Nietzsche. Berlin, New York (Walter de Gruyter), 1983; and by Crawford, Claudia: The Beginnings of Nietzsche's Theory of Language. Berlin, New York (Walter de Gruyter), 1988. His inspiration from Gerber is addressed in Meijers, Anthonie: "Gustav Gerber und Friedrich Nietzsche" (Nietzsche Studien 17. Berlin, New York (Walter de Gruyter), 1988; &, in the same volume, Meijers, A. & Stingelin, M.: "'Konkordanz' between Gerber's *Die Sprache als Kunst* and Nietzsche's WL.")

0. Introduction

In earlier receptions (like S. Kofman's, P. de Man's, H. Miller's, & W. Klein's) one interprets Nietzsche's 'metaphor' hyperbolically as an inherent criticism of the objectivity of the sciences. If the language the scientists are using for formation of knowledge is 'metaphorical' through and through, then, according to the conventional definition of 'metaphor,' they can at best be producing narratives; i.e., other kinds of creative writing; other kinds of poetry (– although they are in denial about this aspect their activity, refusing to acknowledge the intrinsic figurative and rhetorical nature of their field.)[8] These receptions see Nietzsche as being engaged in a "science war," ideologically similar to the contemporary 'science war' that was or is fought out between the humanities and the science departments.[9]

---

[8] We find this view represented by de Man, Paul: "Anthropomorphism and the Trope in the Lyric" in The Rhetoric of Romanticism. New York (Columbia University Press) 1984; & de Man, Paul: Allegories of Reading: Figural Language in Rousseau, Nietzsche, Rilke and Proust (New Haven (Yale University Press), 1979; Miller, Hillis J.: Topographies (Stanford (Stanford University Press) 1995.); Kofman, Sarah: Nietzsche and Metaphor. Translated by Duncan Large. Stanford (Stanford University Press), 1993; and Klein, Wayne: Nietzsche and the Promise of Philosophy. New York (State University of New York Press), 1997. We may regard Jacques Derrida's essay "White Mythology" (from *Margins of Philosophy*. (Chicago (The University of Chicago Press), 1982), as breaking the ground for this hyperbolic interpretation of the notion 'metaphor.' In *Nietzsche on Language, Consciousness, and the Body*. (Urbana and Chicago (Illinois University Press) 2005), Christian Emden pursues Nietzsche interest in rhetoric and introduces the hyperbolic interpretation of 'metaphor' as well, but with more hesitation and skepticism than any of the above (and laudably with much scholarship and awareness of Nietzsche's influence from the scientific and physiological literature of his day).

[9] Nietzsche's description of how the sciences are incapable of discovering essences and must resign themselves to explain only surface-structures, according to the neo-Kantianism of his day (see later), is for example by Sarah Kofman translated into what she thinks is a diatribe directed against the sciences (I allow myself to comment on a few of her most poignant passages): "The scientific edifice, full of splendour, is compared to that of a miserable insect, with such small cells, in order to ridicule science's claim to cut the world down to its size, a presumption which takes metaphors for essences." [It would be as foreign to Schopenhauer and Nietzsche to regard the bee as "miserable," as it would be for them to "ridicule" science. PB] "Science's need to conceal its metaphorical character is symptomatic of its weakness, since it cannot admit that its perspective is a perspective lest it should perish as a consequence." [Scientists usually do not "need to conceal," and are typically painfully aware of the metaphoricity of many of their descriptions; they are also rather ruthless in letting a perspective "perish" if or when they discover

However, it is not Nietzsche's intention to challenge the sciences; it is rather his intention to describe their condition of possibility. His project is epistemological. He intends to investigate the dynamics and interactions between perception, cognition, and language in the formation of knowledge. These dynamics can be outlined as a trinity of three important relations: a) stimulus and sensation, b) sensation and cognition, and c) cognition and language. As we move from a to b to c, something becomes manifestly known. The questions are: When does something become a sensation, and when does it become a cognition, and by what means? What role does language play for something to transform into cognition? At what point do we say that something is 'true,' and what do we mean by that, when it is plain that what we call 'true' can have nothing to do with the original stimulus? Is 'truth' now a 'metaphor' in a particular sense? And if so, does not our 'metaphorical' conceptualizations imply a necessary distortion of original material? – As such, Nietzsche's essay introduces a hard-core epistemological program, endeavoring to account for the conditions for the formation of scientific knowledge.

'Truth' is a well-known stumbling-block for commentators of Nietzsche's early essay. Many commentators see Nietzsche as contradicting himself, because he introduces several different and incompatible concepts of truth. We agree that Nietzsche *does indeed* introduce different notions of 'truth,' and we seem to be able to count in the essay exactly three such notions (or four, depending on how we count): *Truth as truthfulness*, *Truth as illusion* (which branches out in two forms, because truth can be illusion thanks to *perception*, or illusion thanks to *concepts*), and *Truth as the thing-in-itself*. However, in introducing these three or four concepts of truth, we

---

that a perspective it was. PB]. "Just as the bee makes honey from the flowers whose nectar it gathers ceaselessly, so science diverts the individual form himself and his own metaphorical power." [This "diversion" from some supposed 'creative human nature' (hypothetically accepting the idea) would not be unique to science; it starts already in perception, it continues in language, and is sustained in all production of knowledge. PB]. "Thus the 'greatness' of science is merely an impoverished greatness, a poor man's greatness; purely fictional, it is a mask designed to scare and deceive." [No! That "greatness" is truly great; that it is "purely fictional" does not diminish the endeavor (. . . but why are the sciences suddenly accused for being 'purely fictional,' when two seconds ago, they were blamed for not embracing the metaphor?); it only means that science must obey the general predicament: not being able to understand the thing-in-itself. Science is most definitely not meant to "scare and deceive" us; this is paranoid projection. PB]. See Sarah Kofman: Nietzsche and Metaphor, loc. cit., pp. 62-65.

do not see Nietzsche contradicting himself, since the notions have different *definition*, *application*, and *context* (see table, page 96). If truth is defined differently according to context, it is not surprising that truth is celebrated as 'truthfulness' in one context, while in another, truth is held to be 'illusion.' We see this as a fully rational application of the idea that words can have different uses or jobs in our language. It is indeed rare that a word has only one job in a language; for that reason alone, it is not a very deep insight to conclude that Nietzsche has a *polysemous notion* of truth – how could we not, in general, have 'polysemous notions' of just about any word we put into play in different circumstances and contexts?

Nietzsche's concept of 'metaphor' has been another contentious issue in commentary – sometimes embraced with enthusiasm, in the commentators mentioned above, and sometimes denounced as nonsensical in explaining knowledge-formation, in commentators from the Analytic tradition. Both of these schools adopt the conventional meaning of 'metaphor'; that is, its classical definition as a stylistic device, which is now seen as being amplified and magnified into a fundamental principle for all knowledge-production. Some of the problems in such a radical conception vaporize, when 'metaphor' is seen as a notion with (again) various jobs; it has one job in Aristotle, and another in Nietzsche, where it is uniquely applied within a specific context. In Nietzsche, 'metaphor' has a specific and discrete signification, distinguishing it from the notion of 'metaphor' we know from Aristotle over Port Royal to Perelman. We claim that Nietzsche's 'metaphor' has *system-specific meaning*, that is, a unique meaning within the system of the text. We argue that Nietzsche's notion is always meant to help *explicating* and *re-articulating* a general theory of perception and cognition (*not* a theory of *rhetoric*), as this general theory is steeped in Kantian and Schopenhaurian thinking. Therefore, we shall explain why it is quite reasonable to see this *re-defined notion* of 'metaphor' as indispensible in the production of knowledge. The explanation, however, relying as it does on a new definition of the notion, becomes so harmless, straightforward, and self-evident, that it will hardly offend even the most hard-core scientist. On the contrary, the explanation appreciates the difficulties that confront every scientist, when for example he or she desires to communicate a scientific observation (that may be counter-intuitive) in a way that can be understood by the general public. It becomes immediately obvious why 'metaphor' in this general sense must be instrumental in meaning- and knowledge-production. There are things in modern physics we cannot observe, others that we cannot explain in terms of classical physics, and again others for which we have only mathematical language. In order to give a representation of such things, we resort to linguistic approximations, or 'metaphors.'

Part of the job of a contemporary scientist is to render in language something, which *is* not language, and which may never before have been represented in language, but which needs to be linguistically represented, granted that he or she wants to define, and make accessible to an audience, his field of research.

That Nietzsche's 'metaphor' has system-specific meaning is easy to substantiate, because both perceptive images and conceptional words are in Nietzsche's thinking 'metaphors,' and since it is obvious that a perceptive image cannot be a metaphor in the classical sense, the classical rhetorical definition breaks down almost immediately. We are forced to begin looking in other directions.

Images and concepts both 'translate' something into something else – in this translation-process transferring something from one sphere into another sphere. Regarding perceptive images, nerve-stimuli impinging themselves on our sensible system are translated into to the simpler 'perceptive images' – "images in our eyes" as Nietzsche precisely describes them. Regarding the concept, a multifarious world of images is translated into still-easier-to-handle word-forms. In the last translation, the world becomes 'linguisticized,' and 'metaphors' as words and concepts become primarily responsible for meaning- and knowledge-production. As we shall notice later, Nietzsche does not make a clear distinction between 'word' and 'concept,' and uses often the terms interchangeably – partly because he sees them essentially doing the same thing (more below).

In Nietzsche's vocabulary, both perceptive images and linguistic signs (words) are 'interpretations,' because they 'transfer,' 'simplify,' and 'distort' a material. However, we notice that whereas images and words are *conventionally locked interpretations* (implying that one is not free to choose what one sees as anything different from what one sees, nor to call things by a name different from the name convention applies), regarding the concept, meaning is *unlocked* and starts 'floating.' As we shall argue, it is with the introduction of *the concept* that the semiotic world loses its firmament; it is now the pandemonium of Babel enters the stage.

The *concept* (in contrast to the nominally used *word*) has a unique 'logic' or 'essence' that makes this 'floating' virtually unavoidable.[10] We shall introduce this logic in better detail in the last part of the chapter, and argue that we here find the true culprit for the situation that in whatever discipline

---

10   The notion of 'floating meaning' I have first seen in Stegmaier, Werner: Nietzsches 'Genealogie der Moral'. Darmstadt (Wissenschaftliche Buchgesellschaft), 1994. I shall have more to say about 'floating meaning,' and Stegmaier's definition, in especially *Chapter 4*.

one comes across, one is always presented with worlds of (competing, opposing, incompatible, contradictory, etc.) *interpretation*. In this, we suggest a *logic or theory of interpretability*, and give ourselves an opportunity to juxtapose ourselves and respond to American neo-Pragmatist, Stanley Fish, who too, in the eighties and nineties, made *interpretability* a key-term in his radical and revisionary critical theory – as he here offered a theory of interpretability significantly different from what we shall here suggest.

The outlined interpretive strategy for the present essay is meant to resolve some of the paradoxes and difficulties many commentators have seen in Nietzsche's early essay. We hope that the problem of the 'many *truths*' is resolved. We hope to suggest a sensible understanding of Nietzsche's *metaphor*; and finally, we hope – by proposing a theory of the concept – to propose a correct foundation for the phenomenon of *interpretability*.[11] The strategy is also meant to restore to Nietzsche a sensibility and rationality that we have often seen him being deprived of.[12]

---

[11] Many of the problems, and some of the resolutions, I here suggest, one will have seen introduced previously in a number of other commentators of Nietzsche's essay. I see especially three strong commentators often orbiting the same problems – however different their agendas may be from my own: Clark, Maudemarie: Nietzsche on Truth and Philosophy. Cambridge (Cambridge University Press), 1990. Crawford, Claudia: The Beginnings of Nietzsche's Theory of Language. Berlin, New York (Walter de Gruyter), 1988; and Emden, Christian: Nietzsche on Language, Consciousness, and the Body. Urbana and Chicago (Illinois University Press) 2005.

[12] The present work is methodologically neither philological nor historicist, although I would agree with the philologists and the historicists that careful/precise reading and knowledge of historical/intellectual context, are necessary requirements for a proper understanding of Nietzsche. It for example improves one's understanding of Nietzsche's '*Nervenreize*' to know the contemporary context suggesting the term; it improves one's understanding to know that Nietzsche's '*Bild*' corresponds to what some of his contemporaries would discuss as '*Vorstellung*.' Still, the present work is in own self-understanding *philosophical*; it is a thinking-through of concepts, and a systematic effort to *solve problems*, whether these problems appear to be immanent in Nietzsche's text, and/or seem consistently to excite puzzlement in different generations and schools of Nietzsche's commentators.

1. A Human Being with no Natural Disposition for Producing Knowledge

Early in his philosophical development, Nietzsche shows an interest for the problem of knowledge, an interest that he will sustain into his very latest writings.

As he necessarily must, he addresses this problem as it is being thought and articulated within the context of the late 19th Century; this means, as it has been advanced by a number of contemporaries or near-contemporaries like, Immanuel Kant, Arthur Schopenhauer, Friedrich A. Lange, Hermann von Helmholtz, Eduard von Hartmann, Johann Zöllner, and Gustav Gerber; to mention just a few of the philosophers and scientists that had cultivated a paradigm that he will further develop.

WL is Nietzsche's first consistent attempt to address the problem. As has been documented in newer Nietzsche-scholarship, his readings are extensive, and span everything from the canonical classics to scientific treatises on physics, physiology, and psychology.[13] Nietzsche seems determined to solve the problem of knowledge. His focal point is the intricate and elusive problem of the interaction between mind and matter; especially as this problem had been articulated within the Kantian and neo-Kantian traditions.

Depending on whom we read from these traditions, there are different attitudes to the solution of this problem. We encounter a situation where the essential same paradigmatic framework gives rise to two basically different attitudes: either to an arching 'scientific pessimism' or to a vigorous 'scientific optimism' (– as we shall here simplify the problem). Within the Kantian paradigm, a deep-structural inner tension makes it possible for writers within the same tradition to put their emphases differently on either our constitutional inability to understand the thing-in-itself, or our newly-won ability to understand phenomena with an amazing and exceptional clarity. These 'attitudes' are not necessarily followed consistently in single authors, but Schopenhauer and Hartman tend to come across as a 'scientistic pessimists' (– since in the last analysis scientific discovery 'objectifies' on- ly an irrational and unconscious *will*), whereas Helmholtz and Lange tend to come across as 'scientistic optimists.' If we look at Nietzsche's ear-

---

[13] See G. Moore & T. Brobjer (eds.): Nietzsche and Science. London (Ashgate), 2004. See especially the articles: Moore, Gregory: "Introduction"; Brobjer, Thomas: "Nietzsche's Reading and Knowledge of Natural Science: An Overview," and – of particular interest for WL – Emden, Christian: "Metaphor, Perception and Consciousness: Nietzsche on Rhetoric and Neurophysiology."

ly essay in the light of this preliminary distinction, Nietzsche, like Schopenhauer and Hartman, will appear to be in his essay a 'scientistic pessimist.'[14]

This pessimism is apparent from the beginning of Nietzsche's essay.[15]

> In a remote corner of the universe, dispersed throughout an indefinite number of flickering solar systems, there was once upon a time a star, upon which a clever animal discovered knowledge. This was the most arrogant and dishonest minute in "world history": but it was after all only a minute. After nature had taken a few breaths, the star stiffened, and the clever animal had to die. – As such one could invent a fable and would still not have sufficiently illustrated how lamentable, how shadowy and evanescent, how aimless and random, the human intellect is treated in nature. (WL, KSA 1, p. 875).[16]

The human being is in the passage reduced to a 'clever animal,' implying that we are first and foremost 'animals,' but nonetheless distinguish ourselves by being 'clever.' The idea behind this notion was most prominently developed by Schopenhauer. In Schopenhauer, we share with the animals

---

[14] Claudia Crawford reports that in the 1870ies Nietzsche is still strongly influenced, not only by the pessimistic philosophy of Schopenhauer, but also by Eduard von Hartman's even more pessimistic philosophy: "[In] a letter written in December of 1870 [. . .] we find Nietzsche championing Hartmann and aligning himself with him in the common cause of promoting fundamentally Schopenhauerian principles." Crawford, Claudia: The Beginnings of Nietzsche's Theory of Language. Loc. cit., p. 142.

[15] The passage appears to be a favorite of Nietzsche's, since he is using it also in the essay "Über das Pathos der Wahrheit." (cf. KSA 1, p. 759). We also notice that the passage has a certain resemblance to both the Schopenhauer- and the Helmholtz-passages that we used as epigraphs above; the three authors use the same imagery, and manifest a fascination with this evolving animal, the human being, with its random position in the universe, and for who 'truth' is no longer a credible destiny.

[16] Translations from the German, whether Nietzsche, Schopenhauer, or Kant, are usually my own. In the translation of WL, I cross-check my own with two good previous translations of Nietzsche's essay: Daniel Breazeale's in *Philosophy and Truth: Selections from Nietzsche's Notebooks of the Early 1870's*. Amherst: (Humanities Books), 1999; and Maudemarie Clark's in *The Birth of Tragedy, And other Writings*. Cambridge (Cambridge University Press), 1999. The Schopenhauer-translations are revised translations from E. F. J. Payne's earlier translations; and the Kant-translations are guided by respectively Norman Kemp Smith's translation of *Critique of Pure Reason* (Houndsmill (Palgrave Macmillian), rev. 2nd ed. 2003); and Werner S. Pluhar's translation of same (Indianapolis (Hackett), 1996).

both *Vorstellung* and *Wille*. On one hand, man and animal perceive the world according to the same essential parameters, the three fundamental categories, time, space, and causality that Schopenhauer had extracted from Kant's more elaborate scheme; on the other hand, we share with animals the primitive drives and impulses for survival and reproduction that Schopenhauer labels *will*. In other words, in our cognitive and volitional make-up, we are like the animals; and yet, we distinguish ourselves from the animals by means of a single ability that animals do not possess. Compared to our fundamental cognitive and volitional make-up, this one ability is superficial and artificial. It nonetheless accounts for the momentous and, to Schopenhauer's mind, calamitous, difference between animal and human. Schopenhauer labels it *Vernunft*: reason or intellect.

However, there is nothing divine about Schopenhauer's 'reason'; it has emerged from the primordial human being as something exterior added to our natural animal constitution. It is underpinned by something as mundane as our ability to form *concepts*. It is this superficial-artificial *addition*, this *technicality*, which transforms us into Schopenhauer and Nietzsche's 'clever animal.' Compared to our cognitive and volitional make-up, our 'cleverness' must consequently be understood as a relatively accidental feature. As it is exterior to our nature, it is impossible to maintain our confidence in our treasured 'reason,' since it is now seen as up against forces that are so much older, inevitably dragging it down into the anonymity and dimness of animal nature. Still, Nietzsche must admit with Schopenhauer that this 'clever animal' has been indefatigable in its attempts to secure for itself an understanding of its world.

Hence, Nietzsche starts his essay by rehearsing this theory about human insignificance. Situated in an otherwise meaningless universe, and with all odds stacked against it, the human being attempts to build significance into its universe. Nietzsche wonders at this human creature, this irrelevant speck of dust, which in happy ignorance belies its fundamental condition, and heroically labors to create meaning in its little nook of an incomprehensible world.

> [The intellect] is nothing but an aid [*Hülfsmittel*] supplied to the most unfortunate, delicate and transient of beings so as to arrest them for a minute within existence; otherwise, without this supplement [*Beigabe*], they would have every reason to flee existence as quickly as did Lessing's son. The arrogance inherent in cognition and feeling casts a blinding fog over the eyes and senses of human beings." (WL, KSA 1, p. 876).

We notice that reason is explicitly described as "an aid" [*Hülfsmittel*] and "a supplement" [*Beigabe*]; thus, as we elucidate, as a superficial-artificial *ad-*

dition, a mere *technicality*. Granted this point of departure, the purpose of Nietzsche's essay is to explain in better detail how we, who obviously have no inherent designs for producing knowledge, nevertheless manage to do so, and what now the status is of the knowledge we produce. Nietzsche therefore addresses an issue often pursued in Schopenhauer's philosophy (and which in Schopenhauer-commentary is often under-described, if not entirely ignored[17]), Schopenhauer's theory of the concept, and generally speaking, his theory of knowledge.

2. A Polysemous Notion of 'Truth'

2.1. The Fundamental Opposition: Things-in-themselves versus Appearances.

Since in WL, Nietzsche is informed by the neo-Kantianism of his day, he takes for granted – like most of his contemporaries – the dichotomy between a world of *appearances* and a world for the *thing-it-itself*, even if this dichotomy increasingly has become a purely heuristic device. Nietzsche readily admits, like 'educator' Schopenhauer and contemporaries like Helmholtz and Lange, that we as humans have no access to the things-in-themselves. We are therefore consigned to a surface-world of appearances, and must resign a 'transcendent' world beyond appearances to the realm of the inaccessible.

Thus, Kant's great anti-dogmatic insight, we can only know what we can see (in Kant's idiolect, we can know only *phenomena*), is taken for granted. Sense-perception is our primary guidance in the production of knowledge,

---

[17] Schopenhauer scholarship typically pursues, as the main issues in Schopenhauer's thinking, his Idealism, his Aesthetics, or his Pessimism, while the young Nietzsche in his essay is engaged in Schopenhauer's theory of knowledge, as this theory is paradoxically proposed within a general Idealist paradigm, but is simultaneously reiterating compelling materialist and scientific themes of his day. See the following introductions to Schopenhauer: Janaway, Christopher: Schopenhauer. Oxford (Oxford University Press), 1994; & Janaway, Christopher: Self and World in Schopenhauer's Philosophy. Oxford (Clarendon Press), 1989; Magee, Brian: The Philosophy of Schopenhauer. Oxford (Clarendon Press), 1983; Spierling, Volker (ed.): Materialien zu Schopenhauers 'Die Welt als Wille und Vorstellung'. Frankfurt am Main (Suhrkamp), 1984; Spierling, Volker: Arthur Schopenhauer. Zur Einführung. Hamburg (Junius), 2002 & Spierling, Volker: Schopenhauer ABC. Leipzig (Reclam), 2003.

and only thanks to sense-perception do we gain information about the 'world' – the neo-Kantians always, however, adding the qualification, information not about the world *itself*, only as it appears for us and arrives to us mediated through our sensory and cognitive apparatus.

We necessarily perceive and situate a world of objects in *space* and *time*. As a unity, these two parameters provide the single *form* for perception. We could not in the concrete perceive according *only* to time, and neither according *only* to space. If time were the only form, we would not know co-existence, and could not experience *permanence*; if space were the only form we could only know co-existence, but could not experience *change*; therefore, as Schopenhauer says, the "*intimate union* of the two is the condition of reality."[18] It is to Schopenhauer and the neo-Kantians impossible to imagine a world beyond this *unity*. We might with a little effort imagine a world from where we had subtracted *time* – a world of things in absolute rest (something like a picture). We might also imagine a world where we had subtracted *space* – a world of things in complete flux (something like a film sped up). But it is impossible to imagine a world from where we have subtracted both space and time. Beyond the *space-time unity*, we would supposedly find the enigmatic 'thing-in-itself,' but the 'thing' is now mere hypothesis, because according to the theory itself we are prevented from further investigations into it.[19] It is thanks to space-time and the law of causality that the world now comes into being as *experience* or *representation* – as expressed in Schopenhauer's arch-doctrine: "The world is my representation."[20]

---

[18] Schopenhauer: SzG, SW 3, p. 43

[19] Cf. Lange: "But that there exist 'things-in-themselves,' which have a spaceless and timeless existence, Kant could never prove to us out of his principles, for that would be a transcendental, even though negative, knowledge of the properties of the 'thing-in-itself,' and such a knowledge is, on Kant's own theory, entirely impossible." Lange: The History of Materialism, 2nd book, 1st section, p. 201.

[20] "The world is my representation [*Die Welt is meine vorstellung*] [. . .] It becomes clear and certain to [man] that he does not know a sun and an earth, but always only an eye, that sees a sun, and a hand, that feels an earth; that the world around of him, is only representation [*Vorstellung*] thanks to the one who represents, which is himself. [. . .] No truth is therefore more certain, more independent of all others, and less in need of proof than this, that what exists as knowable, hence the whole world, is only an object in relation to a subject, only perception of a perceiver, in a single word, representation [*Vorstellung*]." (Schopenhauer: W1, SW 1, p. 31). This doctrine crucially *does not* contradict Schopenhauer's firm conviction that experiences are real. The

2. A Polysemous Notion of Truth

However, in the emerging neo-Kantian paradigm, Kant's world *for-us* is re-interpreted within a scientific theory of stimuli, transport of stimuli, and the brain's interpretation of stimuli. As Lange puts it in a chapter titled, *The Physiology of the Sense-Organs and the World as Representation*, "The physiology of the sense-organs is developed or corrected Kantianism, and Kant's system may, as it were, be regarded as a programme for modern discoveries in this field."[21] In this scientific paradigm, appearances 'for-us' have now become identical to our brain's interpretation of nerve-stimuli. In this scientistic-epistemological reformulation of Kant's thinking, the *thing-in-itself* is more than simply Kant's enigmatic "X"; it is certainly still enigmatic, but now it is understood as sense-impressions impressing themselves upon us "beneath the skin," as Schopenhauer says. The 'thing' is as unknown and inaccessible as ever, but now its incomprehensibility has a scientific-physiological explanation.[22]

---

world that presents itself *is* 'empirical reality' and *is* 'objective'; however with the implied understanding that it is real only as "object for a subject"; i.e., as *phenomenon*. In this, Schopenhauer repeats Kant's own conviction that phenomena are real, and knowledge of them true: "Even if the phenomena are essentially only copies [*Abbilder*] and not original images [*Urbilder*] of the things, and even if they do not express inner and unconditional properties about things [*Gegenstände*], then the knowledge of them is nonetheless completely true." Kant: De Mundi Sensibilis, § 11, WA VI, p. 43.

[21] Lange: *History of Materialism*, loc. cit., 2nd Book, 2nd Section, p. 202. In his article "Nietzsche und Lange" Jörg Salaquarda reports that Lange's work is familiar to Nietzsche after year 1866: "In the years after 1866 [Lange's] *Geschichte des Materialismus* belonged to the books that Nietzsche used to re-read, when he wanted to orient himself in certain philosophical questions and problems." Salaquarda: "Nietzsche und Lange" in Nietzsche Studien 7. Berlin, New York (Walter de Gruyter), 1978, p. 237.

[22] Kant's distinction between the thing-in-itself and the thing-for-us has in Schopenhauer been moved 'into the head' insofar as both subject and object are internalized as two positions within the phenomenological subject: a position for the perceived and a position for the perceiver. Without being able at this point to go into detail with a difficult epistemological discussion, it seems on a first reflection that Kant's distinction can only make sense as a distinction between the *outside* and the *inside*, between *other* and *self*, between 'it' and 'us.' When in Schopenhauer, this distinction is moved entirely *inside* as part of the self, as *Vorstellung*, effectively, we encompass *in the head* both of the two extremities. The implication must be that they only *verbally* correspond to Kant's thing-in-itself and thing-for-us, but in fact have a significantly different epistemological status. By moving Kant's original distinction 'inside the head,' his thing-in-itself is re-interpreted into a *quantity-in-us* ('matter') to

Unknown sense-impressions are now transformed into known perception thanks to what Schopenhauer calls understanding (*Verstand*), a capacity we as humans share with other higher animals. Thanks to *Verstand*, sense-impressions are interpreted as objective reality, but not yet according to reason (*Vernunft*), which requires the ability to conceptualize (an ability animals do not possess). So, human beings experience the world in much the same way as animals do, but in addition, humans are endowed with reason.[23]

Up through the nineteenth century, the scientists and physiologists began to understand the functioning of the eye. Johannes Müller makes pioneering work in the field, and Hermann von Helmholtz continues with meticulous empirical investigations of vision and the mechanics of the eye. This research also testifies to the new "corrected Kantianism." Pointing out facts like 'blind spots' within the eye, stereoscopic vision, color perception, and the inverted retinal image of the outer world, Helmholtz sufficiently documented how erroneously the eye receives data from the external world, implying that these data undergo a necessary interpretation before they are restored as proper perceptive images. That is, one had *scientific evidence*

---

be transformed into a *quality-by-us* ('form'). The 'thing-in-itself' is no longer *in-itself*, existing independently, and it is no longer a *thing*, but a stimulus. In Schopenhauer's reinterpretation, the 'thing-in-itself' is always-already a primitive 'thing-for-us' existing on the periphery of our "sensuous bodies." Or better, it becomes a hybrid that we might as well label accordingly, *thing-in-itself-for-us*. It is thereupon – thanks to Schopenhauer's three categories – finally appropriated as a genuine *thing-for-us*. In an attempt to give Schopenhauer's new distinction a formulaic expression, we might describe it as follows: *thing-in-itself-for-us* versus *thing-for-us*. In other words, everything is *for-us*; everything is inexplicable auto-production, auto-creation. Everything emerges *ex nihilo* "under our skin" in order to manifest itself as images "in our eyes."

[23] Simply put, Schopenhauer as well as Schopenhauer's famous poodle experiences a world extended in space, and progressing in time, like Schopenhauer as well as Schopenhauer's poodle understands cause-effect relationships. However, Schopenhauer's poodle cannot form the concept of a world extended in space. Schopenhauer does not shy away from using his beloved pet as example in his scientific treatises: "At my bedroom window large curtains were recently installed reaching down to the floor the kind that are drawn apart from the center when a cord is pulled. One morning I got up and pulled the cord for the first time and, to my astonishment, noticed that my very intelligent poodle stood there in amazement, looking up and to the side for the cause of the phenomenon. He was looking for the change which he knew a priori must have previously taken place." (SzG, SW 3, p. 98).

for one of the major Kantian axioms: the *mind* was apparently assisting the *eye* in understanding the stimuli received as perceptive images.

Kantianism had become biology. That the external world was 'in-itself' was no longer a mere metaphysical postulate; now, one could *prove* that the external world *was indeed* 'in-itself'; it was inaccessible *as a matter of fact*. We would receive impressions of this external world as mere stimuli, but the stimuli had to be transmitted to the brain and interpreted before we could become conscious of them. As Helmholtz explained:

> All that we apprehend of the external world is brought to our consciousness by means of certain changes which are produced in our organs of sense by external impressions, and transmitted to the brain by the nerves. It is in the brain that these impressions first become conscious sensations, and are combined so as to produce our conceptions of surrounding objects. If the nerves which convey these impressions to the brain are cut through, the sensation, and the perception of the impression, immediately cease.[24]

Direct access to the external world was therefore ruled out, and Helmholtz could confidently conclude: "We have already seen enough to answer the question whether it is possible to maintain the natural and innate conviction that the quality of our sensations, and especially our sensations of sight, give us a true impression of corresponding qualities in the outer world. It is clear that they do not."[25]

---

[24] Helmholtz: "The Recent Progress of the Theory of Vision," in Science and Culture, loc. cit., p. 148.

[25] Helmholtz: "The Recent Progress of the Theory of Vision," in Science and Culture, loc. cit., p. 165. Another scientist of the day, physicist Johann Zöllner, would subscribe to the same neo-Kantian paradigm, when he states: "In accordance with Kant, Schopenhauer, and Helmholtz, the author regards the application of the law of causality as function of the human intellect given to man a priori, i.e., before all experience. The totality of all empirical experience is communicated to the intellect by the senses, i.e., by organs with communicate to the mind all the sensual impression which are received at the surface of our bodies." Johann Zöllner: Transcendental Physics (Kessinger reprint edition, 1881, p. 32). Nietzsche writes a letter to Erwin Rohde in 1872 in which he gives a positive assessment of Zöllner: "Did you hear about the Zöllner-scandal in Leibniz? Take a look at his Nature of the Comets; there is amazingly much for us in it. This honest man is, after this deed, in the most contemptible manner excommunicated in the entire learned society [*Gelehrtenrepublik*]; his best friends renounce him and he is in the entire world decried as 'mad' ["*verrückt*"]! Quite seriously as 'mentally ill' ["*Geisteskrank*"]." (Nietzsche to Erwin Rohde, November 1872, KSB 4, No. 272). [After reading

Nietzsche is writing from within this generally accepted paradigm; our eyes – not even particularly accurate instruments as Helmholtz had shown – can at best only glide over the surface of things, about which they only "receive stimuli": "They [human beings] are deeply immersed in illusions and dream-images; their eyes glide only over the surface of things and see "forms"; their sensations never lead to the truth, but are satisfied about receiving stimuli, and to play a fumbling game on the back of things [*ein tastendes Spiel auf dem rücke der Dinge zu spielen*]." (WL, KSA 1, p. 876).

But, as we already indicated, whereas Lange and Helmholtz remain 'scientistic optimists,' Nietzsche strikes a romantic note, and turns the insight into 'pessimism.' All hope of achieving 'truth' is now gone, since there is only *us* receiving stimuli and attempting to make sense out of the received stimuli. So, Nietzsche writes within the familiar neo-Kantian paradigm, and represents a variety of Kantianism that he has encountered in some of the scientists of the day – perhaps most prominently, as Jörg Salaquarda has pointed out, in Fr. Albert Lange, with his strong emphasis on the biological preconditions of knowledge[26] – however, he remains faithful to Schopenhauer's conviction of the ultimate vanity of the total scientific project.

Nietzsche as such subscribes to the general cognitive paradigm, but gives it a 'pessimistic' interpretation. The world that we consciously see (or 'experience') is generated thanks to our perceptive capabilities, but capabilities are interpreted as *limitations*. We create forms, but always *false* forms, in something, which is, supposedly, in-itself formless. Any access to the 'thing' – which Nietzsche now calls *truth* – beyond the surface is self-evidently impossible, because that would imply that we could suspend our perceptive apparatus, and engage ourselves in paradoxical and absurd operations like 'seeing without eyes.' In order to experience the 'thing' –

Zöllner's *Transcendental Physics*, I must side with the German "Gelehrtenrepublik," and against Nietzsche, in its uncompromising assessment of Zöllner; filled as his book is with the description of exotic "experiments" in the occult: magnetism, invocations of spirits, inexplicable actions of ghosts or creatures of a "fourth dimension." A thin veneer of Kantianism apparently justifies to Zöllner's mind the belief in this 'fourth dimension' and its invisible creatures. Fortunately, we do not detect any serious trace in Nietzsche's philosophy of these aspects of Zöllner's "Transcendental Physics."]

26 "Nietzsche in fact represents a variety of [Kantian] criticism [*Kritizismus*], which emphasizes even stronger the biological a priori conditions [*Biologisierung der apriorischen Bedingungen*] of knowledge than Lange had already suggested." Salaquarda, loc. cit., p. 239. This 'Biologisierung' of *a priori* conditions is in fact already present in Schopenhauer.

granted we could wander off into the strange *thereness* of this world of 'things' – we would necessarily need our perceptive apparatus, and thus we would again be caught up in experiences. In a later formulation, Nietzsche repeats the view succinctly: "We sit within our nets, we spiders [. . .] and we can catch nothing at all except that which allows itself to be caught in precisely our nets." (M 117, KSA 3, p 110). Lange gives another succinct characterization of the thinking: "The objects of experience altogether are only *our* objects; the whole objective world is, in a word, not absolute objectivity, but only objectivity for man and any similarly organized beings, while behind the phenomenal world, the absolute nature of things, the 'thing-in-itself,' is veiled in impenetrable darkness."[27]

Adopting this position, one might expect that contemporary thinkers would have suspended the thing-in-itself as a superfluous construction – as Nietzsche in fact does in later writings.[28] However, in Schopenhauer, Lange, and the young Nietzsche, the 'thing' continues to provide a framework for their reasoning. They understand perfectly well, and keep reiterating, that the 'thing' is inaccessible; nonetheless, it is still conceived as the "innermost kernel of being" (Schopenhauer),[29] as "the absolute nature of things" (Lange, cf. above), or as "truth" (Nietzsche); and it does as such set up a *standard* by which to measure everything else as *un-truth*. It is, on one hand, a world forever hidden on the backside of appearances, a "*something = x,*"[30] which hides itself behind the tain of the mirror. On the other hand, if by any chance we were able to know this backside, if by any chance we were able to look through this tin-foil without first seeing our-

---

[27] Friedrich A. Lange: The History of Materialism, 2nd Book, 1st Section, loc. cit., p. 156.

[28] This for example also becomes Ernst Mach's solution in his *The Analysis of Sensations*: "The book [*Prolegomena to any Future Metaphysics*] made at the time a powerful and ineffaceable impression upon me, the like of which I never afterwards experienced in any of my philosophical reading. Some two or three years later the superfluity of the role played by "the thing in itself" abruptly dawned upon me. On a bright summer day in the open air, the world with my ego suddenly appeared to me as *one* coherent mass of sensation, only more strongly coherent in the ego." Mach, Ernst: The Analysis of Sensations. New York (Dover Publications), 1959; p. 30n.

[29] "[The] objective world, the world as representation, is not the only side of the world, but merely its external side, so to speak [. . .] the world has an entirely different side which is its innermost being, its kernel [*ihr innerstes Wesen, ihr Kern*], the thing-in-itself." (Schopenhauer: W1, SW I, p. 67).

[30] The notation is originally Kant's own. Cf. KrV, A 250.

selves, then we would encounter the *revealed truth* about this *something = x*.

When now Nietzsche labels this 'backside' "truth,"[31] the label seems at least odd, because on this 'backside,' we do not find 'truth' in any pragmatic or humanly relevant sense. The notion is dogmatic and speculative, and has nothing to do with the perspectival-pragmatic notion of truth that Nietzsche will be developing from this early essay onwards, into his latest writings.[32] It emerges possibly as so-called 'truth' in Nietzsche, because he pre-reflectively understands Kant's 'thing' as something absolutely hidden 'under' or 'beneath' our accessible 'cover' of appearances. He thus – erroneously, to this author's mind – understands Kant's 'thing' as a self-present and self-identical 'essence' or 'substance' of sorts; an *essence/substance* traditionally understood as unconditioned, permanent, original (*causa prima*), and as such *true*. We notice in passing that as absolutely hidden, Kant's thing as 'truth' – even in Nietzsche's understanding – can have no 'correspondence' to the intellect (there is no *adaquatio intellectus et rei* in this conception), and Nietzsche therefore does not confirm the celebrated 'correspondence-theory of truth' in regard to this notion of truth (contrary to Heidegger's claim, namely that Nietzsche, in a round-about way, happens here to confirm the correspondence-theory of truth; see fn. 38). Rather, if the inaccessible 'thing' is an inaccessible 'truth,' this insight is meant to provide a contrast to Nietzsche's shocking revelation of what 'truth' *really* is: certainly nothing deep, now that Truth in the strong sense has disappeared.

In labeling the 'thing' 'truth,' and in the professed regret (one hears the elegiac and plaintive tone!) that we have no access to this 'truth,' we also seem to witness the last vestiges of a metaphysical hope. *If* we could somehow get around the appearances and enter the mysterious backside, *if* we could suddenly see with new and divine eyes, then finally, the world would open up itself no longer disguised. However, the hope is irrational and the

---

[31] Later in the essay, Nietzsche talks about the thing-in-itself as "pure truth without consequences" [*reine folgenlose Wahrheit*]." (KSA 1, WL p. 879). Neither Kant himself nor later neo-Kantians seem to adopt this label for, or this understanding of, the thing-in-itself.

[32] For a general account of Nietzsche's notion of truth, see Josef Simon: "Grammatik und Wahrheit"; in Nietzsche Studien 1. Berlin, New York (Walter de Gruyter), 1972; and Simon: "Die Krise des Wahrheitsbegriffs als Krise der Metaphysik"; in Nietzsche Studien 18. Berlin, New York (Walter de Gruyter), 1989. and also Werner Stegmaier: "Nietzsches Neubestimmung der Wahrheit" in Nietzsche Studien 14. Berlin, New York (Walter de Gruyter), 1985.

desire is residual, and it is immediately rejected from within the paradigm itself. In this context, 'Truth' is Nietzsche's misnomer for something that hides itself entirely as essence, that which keeps itself disguised and *a priori* never reveals itself, but *if* perchance it did, would open up its own secrets and inform us of a supposed nature of the world. It becomes synonymous with constructions like 'the ideal,' the 'true world,' the 'really real,' as that which is lost to Nietzsche; and while he laments this lack of depth, he adopts, heroically but reluctantly, a cynical acceptance of the world's shallowness. – Is the world deep? Oh, no, my friends, curb your enthusiasm, it is utterly shallow! The tension is better resolved in later writings in the acceptance of 'untruth': "Suppose we want truth: W h y n o t r a t h e r untruth? [*Unwahrheit?*]" (JGB 1, KSA 5, p. 15).

Nietzsche and Schopenhauer criticize the Kantian thing-in-itself in their favored conception. However, as we indicated above, they both replace the re-interpreted Kantian 'thing' with a new 'some-thing,' which, at the very least, has some strong family-resemblances with the old Kantian thing. This replacement starts already in Schopenhauer's two early essays *Über die vierfache Wurzel des Satzes vom zureichenden Grunde* (hereafter SzG) and *Über das Sehn und die Farben*.[33] Here the 'thing' is – within the new epistemological-cognitive framework – refashioned into the above-mentioned 'nerve-stimulus.'[34] The 'thing' would therefore retain a strange limbo-existence in Schopenhauer (and in Nietzsche repeating Schopenhauer). They are both sure that it cannot exist in the concrete sense that *allegedly* Kant had imagined,[35] but they keep returning to this other 'some-thing,' this

---

[33] See Schopenhauer: SW III.

[34] In his later *Die Welt als Wille und Vorstellung*, Schopenhauer refashions the 'thing' into his famous *will*. In the context of the present chapter, we shall allow ourselves to ignore this well-known metaphysical aspect of Schopenhauer, and concentrate on the Schopenhauer, who has a more obvious relevance for our present cognitive perspective.

[35] This Kant-criticism of Schopenhauer and Nietzsche appears to this author as a sleight of hand. Kant himself had emphasized that he doesn't regard a 'thing' as anything concrete, factual, or 'thingly,' but as a *limitative* concept [*Grenzbegriff*], which we could 'know' only as a negation to what positively we do know. "Ultimately, we can have no insight at all into the possibility of such noumena, and the range outside the sphere of appearances is (for us) empty. [. . .] The concept of a noumenon is therefore only a b o u n d a r y c o n c e p t [*G r e n z b e g r i f f*] serving to limit the pretension of sensibility, and therefore only of negative use. Nonetheless, it is not arbitrarily invented; rather, it relates to the limitation of sensibility, yet without being able to posit anything positive outside its range." (Kant: KrV B 311, WA III, p. 282). The 'thing,'

construction of a biological nether limit for receptivity that has the approximately the same structural position and locus as the Kantian 'thing' – and, like the Kantian 'thing,' has the structural effect that 'appearances' are necessarily seen as *derived*. It is as if the ghost of the dead continues to haunt the living.

Thus, the complicated situation is that Schopenhauer and Nietzsche are criticizing the inaccessible Kantian 'thing,' yet remain committed to a 'thing' redefined, but inaccessible like Kant's. Simplifying a complex logic, Schopenhauer and Nietzsche assert in their discourse an 'old thing' and a 'new thing.' The 'old thing' is Kant's thing understood as hidden essence; it has in Schopenhauer and Nietzsche's re-interpretation become a *thing-in-and-for-itself* – an impossibility and a paradox that Nietzsche will be returning to as such throughout his writings (we shall later explain why the current paradigm cannot allow a 'thing-in-and-for-itself'). The 'new thing' is their re-articulated thing as stimulus. A stimulus is also inarticulate, and it is also always in need of the mind's interpretation before becoming conscious, but it must crucially and perforce relate to a subject, since it becomes stimulus only conditional upon being received. It must imprint itself on our bodies and sense-organs, or in Schopenhauer's phrase, "beneath the skin," and can as such not be 'for-itself.' As such, it has become (adopting homologous terminology) a *thing-in-itself-for-us*, and may be seen as a precursor to Nietzsche's later 'forces.' We encounter in the discourse these two 'things': the old Kantian thing, re-interpreted as an (absurd and impossible) *Thing-in-and-for-itself*; and the new 'thing,' not conceptualized as 'thing,' because it is conceived as a *Thing-in-itself-for-us*.

In Nietzsche's early discourse the re-interpreted old Kantian 'thing' is as concept not entirely rejected; it is in-and-for-itself, and as such inaccessible, but it is still understood as an essence that would reveal itself as such if it could; while the 'new thing,' which Nietzsche now – after Schopenhauer, Lange and other neo-Kantians – sees as a nerve-stimulus, is not understood as 'thing' at all. Since the Kantian 'thing' still exerts its old magic on Nietzsche's discourse, Nietzsche 'pessimistically' realizes that he is left

---

Kant says, is nothing more than "a something = x" (Kant: KrV A 250, WA III, p. 280); it is "a something [. . .] of which, as it is in itself, we have no concept whatsoever" (Kant: KrV B 726, WA IV). See also Lange: "In Kant's own view; the 'thing-in-itself' is a mere idea of limit." Lange: *The History of Materialism*, 2nd book, 1st section, p. 216. Stephen Houlgate too, in a fine article about Nietzsche's ambivalence regarding Kant's thing-in-itself, regards his Kant-criticism as precipitate. See Houlgate: "Kant, Nietzsche, and the Thing-in-itself" in Nietzsche Studien 22; Berlin, New York (Walter de Gruyter), 1993.

with derived appearances, which he can now only see as 'metaphors' and 'illusions' for that inaccessible old 'truth-thing.'[36]

At this early point in his development, Nietzsche does not seem to appreciate a certain dynamics played out between the opposition of 'thing' and 'phenomenon,' which is adopted in much neo-Kantian writing: the more the 'thing' withdraws itself and becomes inaccessible (the more "veiled in impenetrable darkness"), the more validity is transferred to the phenomenon. As one had started to internalize the Kantian discourse, his best recipients would eventually admit a so irremediable ignorance regarding the 'thing' that they refused to make any claims as to its actual existence (it became a limit, a hypothesis, or a concept without conceptual content). In 'scientific optimism,' however, this didn't constitute a problem and it threw nobody into despair, because one could be sure that phenomena exist; and since as such we had complete access to reality in the form of presentations (*Vorstellungen*), the objectivity of the sciences were fully restored. Nietzsche has still not adopted the economy, *the more reality 'things' loose, the more reality 'phenomena' gain*, and its immediate consequence: if we end up considering for 'real' only what is 'real' as phenomena, then knowledge can be knowledge of phenomena only; consequently, our 'truths' must be validated in relation to *phenomena*, not in relation to '*things*.'

At this stage, this is obviously not Nietzsche's thinking. He believes that 'truth'— at least in one of its significations – ought to be validated in relation to 'things,' in which case he can only arrive to what is now a foregone conclusion: *truths are illusions*.

---

[36] This interpretation of the status of the 'thing' in Nietzsche's early essay is, from different positions, confirmed by a number of commentators. Alexander Nehamas asserts: "Mainly under the influence of Schopenhauer and of his reading of Kant, Nietzsche seems to have believed that there are some ultimate facts, some non-interpretive truths, concerning the real nature of the world. But he denied that these facts could ever be correctly stated through reason, language, and science." Alexander Nehamas: Nietzsche, Life as Literature. Cambridge (Harvard University Press), 1985. P. 42. Maudemarie Clark has a similar interpretation: "In TL [. . .] Nietzsche accepts the Kantian position that we can conceive of the thing-in-itself and assumes that truth requires correspondence to it. That is, TL accepts metaphysical realism in precisely the sense in which Nietzsche would later reject it." Clark: Nietzsche on Truth and Philosophy. Cambridge (Cambridge University Press), 1990; p. 86.

2.2. From Truthfulness to Truth: On the Evolution of a 'Truth-Drive'

Since now 'Truth' has become irreparably absent, Nietzsche asks himself the next logical question: what is the status of that which we *call* truth? Consequently, there is a *Truth*, which we cannot know, and which exists in the position of Kant's old thing; and then there is that which we *call truth*, which obviously we do know, since we call it into language.

Nietzsche is presupposing these two forms of truth. That the two forms have the same designation in Nietzsche's text, namely *Wahrheit*, must not obscure the fact that they are crucially distinct. There is a Truth, which is absent and remains so, and then, we have the many truth-*candidates* filling the airwaves of the day. Since there is an irreparable gap between these two forms of truths, that which we *call truth* becomes a mere mockery of *Truth in the absolute sense*; in other words, an illusion or a 'metaphor.'[37]

As we continue our reading of Nietzsche's essay, there is indeed a third concept of truth at stake in the text. This is a concept Nietzsche addresses in his attempt to explain why humans have developed this propensity to posit candidates for truth (truth as *illusions*) in the first place.

Humans have evolved something as peculiar as a 'truth-drive,'[38] Nietzsche explains. In order to understand the specific character of this 'drive,' we may start by contrasting it to a better known drive. If a *sexual drive* is a result of biological evolution, a *truth-drive* is a result of social evolution; if a *sexual drive* has a biological origin, a *truth-drive* has a proto-historical origin, and it can be traced in a genealogical analysis. Nietzsche assumes an early pre-history, some early beginnings of a social evolutionary process, where truth was still 'unknown,' or at least, was still not generalized into something abstract, permanent, and in-itself. There would be, in these early pre-historical societies, no truth, and nobody would be positing abstract candidates for truth. So far, 'truth' was only known in an embryonic form, as something one could ascribe to certain individuals as their 'truthfulness.' As such, 'truthfulness' was being adopted by society as something beneficial in interaction, since, in complex political societies, it

---

[37] En passant, we notice the apparent paradox: when it has been often reiterated that in Nietzsche 'there is no truth,' it is only because an *absolute Truth* has withdrawn itself from our inquisitive investigations, and now refuses to inform our *candidates for truth*. Differently put, if in Nietzsche 'there is no truth,' it is only because he presupposes a much more recalcitrant, a metaphysical-speculative, concept of Truth as that which remains inaccessible, but nonetheless wields authority.

[38] Trieb zur Wahrheit or Wahrheitstriebes (cf. WL, KSA 1, p. 877).

became necessary to have truthful, instead of deceptive, individuals. As Nietzsche argues, nobody likes a liar, not because one dislikes the lie itself, but because it may have harmful consequences for society (a lie *without consequences*, for example as performed in the arts, is on the contrary a source of great enjoyment). The liar abuses established social and linguistic conventions, when uttering a lie. He uses language as anyone else, but introduces a discrepancy between his utterance and its content. As such, he does not observe the mandate of society, which dictates that there has to be correspondence between utterance and content. As Nietzsche explains, one cannot be allowed to claim 'I am wealthy,' if one is in fact 'poor.'

> The liar uses valid designations, the words, in order to make the unreal appear as real [*das Unwirkliche als wirklich erscheinen zu machen*]; he says, for example, 'I am wealthy,' although the proper description of his condition would be 'poor.' He abuses the fixed conventions by arbitrarily exchanging or reversing names. When he does so for self-serving and harmful purposes, the society will stop trusting him, and will exclude him. (WL, KSA 1, p. 877-78).

In this early for-form of truth, truth is understood as *accountability*; in complex political societies, accountability is rewarded, while lying is punished. To be *accountable* means to obey the established convention; it means, to obey that which counts as existing in the society. In a note from the *Nachlaß* material from the period, Nietzsche clarifies:

> In a political society, a firm agreement is necessary, which is founded on the habitual use of metaphors. Everything unusual upsets and annoys [*regt sie auf*], yes, destroys. Therefore, it is politically convenient and moral to use every word like the masses use it. To be t r u e means from now on not to deflect from the habitual meaning of things [*Sinn der Dinge*]. The true is that w h i c h i s [*Das wahre ist das Seiende*], in contrast to the non-existing [*Nichtwirklichen*]. The first convention is about what ought to count as 'being' [*seiend*]. (Nachlaß 1872-1873, KSA 7, 19[229]).

It is an issue Nietzsche will address again, and in much better detail, in the later *Zur Genealogie der Moral*, where he will argue that it is important to cultivate a *sovereign* capable of making and of keeping promises (see *Chapter 5*). *Truth as accountability or truthfulness* has so far a practical purpose, the preservation of society, with its political institutions, its commerce, and trading. Man desires the "pleasant, life-preserving consequences of truth." (WL, KSA 1, p. 878).

In the notion of *truthfulness*, Nietzsche has indeed a 'correspondence-theory' of truth. However, it does not produce *correspondence* between more than enunciation and content, sign and reference; and it is therefore trivial and tautological. It is "of limited value," as Nietzsche says, since it does not aspire to access reality 'in-itself.' It is something in the order of *pointing*. For example, I exclaim, "there is a camel!" if I happen to see a camel. Or (only slightly more complicated), 'there is a mammal!' if I happen to see a camel, which I think is a mammal. In both cases there is correspondence between enunciation and reference, but I have not produced any revelatory knowledge about the world. I have essentially only confirmed that I know my dictionary. Nietzsche:

> If I create the definition of a mammal, and then, after observing a camel, declare: look, there is a mammal, then a truth has certainly been brought to light, but it is of limited value; I mean, it is through and through anthropomorphic and contain not a single point, which would be 'true in itself,' real and universal, independently of humans. (WL, KSA 1, p. 883).

This for-form of truth has, however, through generalization and extrapolation, been transformed into the idea of *truth as pure knowledge*. Truth has thus become an abstract ideal, i.e., 'truth' in our second sense above, as *illusion* and *metaphor* for Truth in our third sense above, as metaphysical-speculative idea. In this evolution of the concept of truth, one has concluded that as well as there ought to be correspondence between an utterance and a content (which in communicative action is a simple correspondence to achieve; there is nothing problematic about being honest[39]), there ought to be correspondence also between a judgment and a thing. From 'truth' as necessary social self-preservation, one generalizes, and invents truth as an all-encompassing concept applied to all relationships. 'Truthfulness' is 'transferred' from man to nature, the transference engendering the fallacy: as well as *man* is able to be truthful, it is possible also for *nature* to be 'truthful.' Thanks to this 'transference,' one indeed starts to believe that nature has to (ought to) be inherently truthful, and impresses on nature what is a fundamental *moral* requirement and imperative. "But the drive to be true, transferred to nature, produces the belief that also nature has to confront us

---

[39] There is nothing problematic about being honest, we say, except – we might add – in extreme and exotic cases of communicative action, such as for example in the psychoanalytical situation, where the patient has lost sight of what honesty *means*. When deconstructionists have a problem with 'honesty' and 'sincerity,' they tacitly presuppose these extreme and exotic forms of communicative action. They are romantics drawn to the exorbitant; not to everyday communication, such as if 'honestly' I say 'I just had a cup of coffee,' because I just had a cup of coffee.

as true. The drive for knowledge [*Erkenntnißtrieb*] relies on this transference." (Nachlaß 1872-1873, KSA 7, 19[229]).

In these three meanings of truth, we are moving from the concrete and practical to the ever-more abstract and ideal. If we distinguish the three meanings of truth by adding a number in subscript to the basic form, then we have, first, a *Truth$_1$*, understood as *truthfulness*; characterized by the ability to distinguish a lie from a fact, deception from sincerity, in order to cultivate *accountability* in communicative action. Secondly, we have a *Truth$_2$*, understood as an *illusion* of pure knowledge, an abstract ideal developed from the cultivation of accountability. This transforms into the illusion that the world could be 'abstractly true'; however, it is an illusion, which is unwittingly and unconsciously reliant on 'un-true' interpretations. Finally, we have a *Truth$_3$*, understood as the entirely absent and inaccessible Truth that would have revealed itself behind appearances as the 'old thing,' if it could. It becomes the indispensable metaphysical construction that structurally underpins Truth$_2$, as it sets up a *super-abstract and impossible-to-satisfy standard* by which to measure truth.

When Nietzsche in this essay asks about the status of truth, he is always asking about the status about Truth$_2$; that which we *call truth*; that which we *decide is* and *designate as* truth; that which we *hold-to-be-true* [*Fürwahrhalten*].[40] These truths are being upheld as such thanks to our limited cognitive and linguistics capacities, and since they do not enter the nature of things, they are *untrue* or *illusions*. "Insofar as he [the human being] is no longer satisfied with truth in the form of tautologies, i.e., as empty husks [*leeren Hülsen*], he will always replace illusions with truths." (WL, KSA 1, p. 878).

In the passage, Nietzsche is again referring back to Kant. He is making clear that given that *analytic statements* cannot satisfy us, then the truths we seek are always 'illusions.' Analytic statements are statements, Kant taught, whose negation is self-contradictory and logically impossible. In analytic statements, the predicate is already included in the subject; such statements are per definition always true, but they are also tautological, or *leeren Hülsen*, which do not give us knowledge of the world. Consequently, they

---

[40] The notion of the *Fürwahrhalten* is not Nietzsche's but Kant's. Kant often introduces it in his KrV, and it is being developed in different directions in his *Logic*: "The judgment whereby we r e p r e s e n t / i m a g i n e [*vorgestellt*] something to be true – the relation between reason [*Verstand*] and a certain subject – is taken s u b j e c t i v e l y holding-to-be-true [*Fürwahrhalten*]. [. . .] There are three forms or modi of holding-to-be-true: opinion, belief, and knowledge [*Meinen, Glauben, und Wissen*]. Kant, Logik, WA VI, p. 494.

are dismissed by Nietzsche (or, as he believes, by mankind as such), as he allows himself to concentrate on truths that do interests us, but happens to be 'illusions.' These have necessarily the form of the *synthetic statement* (a statement whose negation is not self-contradictory but logically possible). They are statements from which we learn something about the world, since the predicate adds knowledge to the subject with which it is synthetically associated. In other words, we can ignore all analytic statements, which are trivially true, and of which we might say that Nietzsche has a 'correspondence theory of truth' (however trivial). However, man has an interest only in synthetic statements, and it is as such that man replaces "illusions with truths." When these statements aspire to 'truth' they are rather 'illusions,' because the predicate that adds knowledge to the subject is always only extracted from a surface-world; i.e., the explicative predicate – which is supposed to amplify our knowledge – is merely gliding over the world of appearances; never does it relate or 'correspond' to a reality itself; never does it penetrate into the things-in-themselves.[41]

---

[41] Nietzsche and 'the correspondence theory of truth' has been discussed by numerous commentators. On Heidegger's reading Nietzsche presupposes a notion of 'correspondence' or 'correctness' because "Only if truth in its essence is correctness can it be *in*correctness and illusion according to Nietzsche's interpretation." (Heidegger, Martin: Nietzsche, v. III, "The Will to Power as Knowledge." Edited & translated by D. F. Krell. San Francisco (HarperSanFrancisco) 1987, p. 64.) In other commentators, the verdict is usually that Nietzsche undermines or attacks the correspondence theory; so Danto: "[Nietzsche] means that there is no order in the world for things to correspond to; there is nothing, it terms of the Correspondence Theory of Truth, to which statements can stand in the required relationship in order to be true." Danto, Arthur: Nietzsche as Philosopher. New York (Columbia University Press), 1965; p. 75. If, as we here suggest, Nietzsche has several concepts of truth, then the verdict one pronounces on Nietzsche and the 'correspondence theory' will have to depend on what concept of truth one is discussing. For example, Maudemarie Clark too believes that Nietzsche cannot be defending a 'correspondence theory,' because he proclaims that 'truth are illusions' – but then she notices that Nietzsche, in one of his 'self-contradictions,' defends a kind of 'correspondence theory' when he denounces the liar for lying. When Nietzsche describes the social ideal of *truthfulness*, he must be presupposing a "truthful person . . . using words to make the real appear real": "Nietzsche fails to show that we can understand truth without suggesting the existence of something to which truths correspond. If, as he claims, the liar uses the "valid designations, the words, to make something which is unreal appear real," for example to make himself appear rich when he is actually poor, then the truthful person must use the words to make the real appear real, that is, to convey

As we shall see in more detail below, Nietzsche's second notion of truth, so-called Truth$_2$, splits itself out in two different forms: Truth$_2$ is illusion either thanks to *perceptions*, or thanks to *conceptions*. We shall below designate these two forms respectively *Truth$_{2P}$* and *Truth$_{2C}$*.

3. The Production of Metaphor: Nerve-Stimulus – Image – Word

3.1. Contemporary Context and Background

In a synthetic judgment, the synthesis of subject and predicate necessarily has linguistic form, and Nietzsche continues his interrogations in good logical order by asking: "what is a word"; answering himself that a word is a "representation of a nerve-stimulus in sounds [*abbildung eines Nervenreizes in Lauten*]." (WL, KSA 1, p. 878). This is at best an over-hasty and imprecise answer, which fortunately Nietzsche does not adhere to throughout his essay, because *if* the word represented a nerve-stimulus, the claim would be that we have direct access to unconscious physiological processes. The word would not unite sound and image, but sound and stimulus. We would consequently no longer communicate a world perceived in images, but a world perceived in impulses; i.e., in quanta of energy and forces. As our brains would directly translate stimuli into sounds, language would now become a strange verbalized measuring-device for bodily sensations. When he returns to the problem, Nietzsche has corrected himself, as he will consistently be addressing the trinity indicated by the title of the present section: nerve-stimulus – image – word.

Nietzsche's preliminary answer, however imprecise, still reveals his adherence to the cognitive paradigm of his day, as introduced by Schopenhauer, and elaborated by Lange, Helmholtz, and Hartmann. And as

---

information that corresponds to reality." Clark, Maudemarie: Nietzsche on Truth and Philosophy. Cambridge (Cambridge University Press), 1990; p. 68. If Nietzsche has a notion of *truth as truthfulness*, and a notion of *truth as illusion*, then he has two different notions, which have different attributes, and which have different contexts of application, and the so-called 'self-contradiction' disappears. Accordingly, the appeal to *truthfulness* presupposes a 'correspondence' between statement and content, which does not extent to other notions of truth. There are simply two different notions – like I can have two different drawers for my shirts and for my socks, without being guilty of a 'self-contradiction.'

he continues the quote above, he repeats this strong cognitive motive in neo-Kantian epistemology. A word is a "representation of a nerve-stimulus," whereupon he warns – in complete agreement with Schopenhauer: "But from the nerve-stimuli to refer back to a cause outside us, is only the result of a false and unjustified application of the principle of sufficient reason [*des satzes von Grunde*]." (WL, KSA 1, p. 878).

Nietzsche refers to Materialism's 'naïve' belief in the so-called 'projection-theory,' according to which the outside world is seen as projecting itself onto our sense-apparatus, and 'causing' our sensations, which are therefore comprehended as copies of the material world.[42] Both Schopenhauer and Lange were adamant in their rejection of Materialism; so Schopenhauer: "One must be forsaken by all the gods to imagine that the world of perception [*anschauliche Welt*] outside [. . .] had an entirely objective-real existence without our participation, but then found its way into our heads through mere sensation, where it now had a second existence like the one outside"[43]; or Lange: "The ancient Materialism, with its main belief in the sensible world, is done for."[44] Nietzsche is affirming this essential neo-Kantian position.

In the new 'corrected' Kantianism, the nether epistemological limit had become a sense-impression, or, in Nietzsche's language, a 'nerve-stimulus' [*Nervenreize*]. Sense-impressions or nerve-stimuli we only know as they are presented for-us. Although we naturally infer the existence of an objective world from them (thanks to the principle of sufficient reason, and helped by

---

[42] In his translation of Nietzsche, Daniel Breazeale adds a note to this passage explaining that Nietzsche is here criticizing Schopenhauer: "Note that Nietzsche is here engaged in an implicit critique of Schopenhauer, who had been guilty of precisely this misapplication of the principle of sufficient reason in his first book, *The Fourfold Root of the Principle of Sufficient Reason*." (Breazeale, Daniel (ed.): Philosophy and Truth, loc. cit., p. 81n.) Breazeale reads the "false and unjustified application of the principle of sufficient reason" as *Schopenhauer's* application, thus construing Schopenhauer to be referring a nerve-stimulus to an outside and external world. Quite the contrary, we must believe that Nietzsche is here referring to Schopenhauer's sustained argument from SzG that causes cannot and must not be seen as effecting the subject from without. This is a founding axiom in Schopenhauer's Transcendental Idealism, taken up again in his criticism of Kant (See W1, SW 1, Anhang), and it is unlikely that Nietzsche could have misunderstood Schopenhauer on such a crucial point. The "false and unjustified application of the principle of sufficient reason" is *Materialism's* application.

[43] Schopenhauer: SzG, SW 3, p. 68.

[44] Lange: The History of Materialism, 2nd book, 1st section, p. 204.

3. The Production of Metaphor

our in-built sense of space), it is not possible to go beyond sense-impressions, and investigate the world that we infer from having them, because "sensation of every kind is and remains an event within the organism itself; but as such it is restricted to the region beneath the skin; and so, in itself, it can never contain anything lying outside the skin and thus outside ourselves."[45]

Sense-impressions, stimuli, are in-themselves not yet constituted as sensations or empirical reality; but they are eventually translated as such, thanks to the categories of space, time, and causality. In this, they pass from being mere stimuli into being sensations or presentations ('images' in Nietzsche's language), appearing as such as the only manifestations of the world that we can know. The process has a neurological origin, according to Schopenhauer; explicitly, the transformation of stimuli into sensations happens in the "enigmatic structure of the brain":

> It is only when the *understanding* [*Verstand*] begins to act – a function not of single delicate nerve extremities, but of that complex and enigmatic structure of a brain that weighs three to sometimes five pounds – only when the understanding applies its only possible form, the law of causality [*das Gesetzt der Kausalität*], does a powerful transformation takes place whereby subjective sensation [*Empfindung*] becomes objective intuitive perception [*objective Anschauung*]. [. . .] The understanding has first to create the objective world, for this cannot just walk into our heads from outside, already done and fully finished, through the senses and the openings of their organs. Thus the senses furnish nothing but the raw material [*rohen stoff*], and this the understanding reforms – by the means of the simple forms already mentioned, space, time, and causality – into the objective understanding and apprehension of a corporeal world governed by laws. Accordingly, our daily *empirical intuitive perception is intellectual* [*unsere alltägliche empirische Anschauung ist intellektuel*].[46]

Perception is as such always *intellectual*, implying that sensations are always-already undergoing an *interpretation* before they are perceived *as if* independent reality. The view is repeated by Nietzsche throughout his writings (we shall return to it in *Chapter 2*).

On this neo-Kantian theory, the world has no independent existence as something *out-there-outside-us* – or, what Schopenhauer calls 'objective-real.' It is rudimentarily and originally intertwined with our "sensitive bodies"; accordingly, we cannot assert another 'world' to be *causing* the stimuli, since this other 'world' would falsely imply, what is prohibited in

---

[45] Schopenhauer: SzG, SW 3, p. 69.
[46] Schopenhauer: SzG, SW 3, p. 69-70.

the paradigm, a world *out-there-outside-us*. This false Materialist conclusion is consistently criticized by Schopenhauer, and by Friedrich Lange, and it recurs in Nietzsche's thinking, from the present early essay to the late *Nachlaß* material. For example, Nietzsche's later 'chronological reversal' is easily understood as a variation over the neo-Kantian idea that, first, we receive stimuli, thereupon and only after-the-fact, we make sense of them, insofar as the Kantian categories (albeit a notion that the later Nietzsche will abandon) transform them into possible experience. With or without Kantian categories, so-called 'empirical reality' is in any case an *interpretation* constructed *Nachträglich*; i.e., after reception of a primordial impression (we shall return to this so-called '*Nachträgliche*' constitution of reality in several of the following chapters).

3.2. The Logic of Metaphor as 'Replacement' and 'Arbitrariness'

In *Chapter 4.2*, we return to Schopenhauer and Helmholtz's discussions of sensation, in their examinations of the mechanics of the eye. For now, let us explore how Nietzsche develops the theory of *nerve-stimulus – image – word*. The theory is summarized in the following often-quoted passage (we break it up into two).[47]

> A nerve-stimulus is first transferred [*übertragen*] into an image [*Bild*]! First metaphor [*Metapher*]. The image is again transformed [*nachgeformt*] into a sound! Second metaphor. In each case, there is a complete jump from one sphere into the middle of a quite different and new one.

---

[47] As has been pointed out by Meijers and Crawford (see Anthonie: "Gustav Gerber und Friedrich Nietzsche" in Nietzsche Studien 17. Berlin, New York (Walter de Gruyter), 1988; and Crawford, Claudia: The Beginnings of Nietzsche's Theory of Language. Loc. cit.), this theory imitates Gustav Gerber's almost identical theory of the genesis of language. "Gerber reconstructs the genesis of language. [. . .] First the thing in itself presumably prompts a nerve stimulus (*Nervenreiz*), which produces in the human being a sensation (*Empfindung*). The sensation, quite spontaneously produces a sound (*Laut*). This sound is a purely natural reaction to stimulus, whether a cry, a scream, or any other sound, it is primarily an action which reduces the tension created by the perception of the stimulus. Already in this first phase of its development, the language sound produce by the sensation does not directly represent the original prepetition. The movement between sensation and sound is arbitrary and here the art instinct becomes active." Crawford, Claudia: ibid., p. 203.

First, a nerve-stimulus is transferred, or carried over [*übertragen*], into an *image* [*Bild*]; that is, it is re-fashioned as a *presentation* organized according to the categories space and time. This transference is *pre-linguistic*, since it transforms original sense-impressions into experienced objects. Nietzsche calls the resulting 'image' a 'metaphor'; but why would it be a 'metaphor' when we are explicitly talking about perception? How can a *Vorstellung*, a presentation, a perception, be a 'metaphor'? How could a scenery presenting itself to us possibly be seen as a metaphor? I look out of my window, see the blue immensity of the Mediterranean Sea, and say to myself, "What a beautiful metaphor." – There must be something about language I have misunderstood! – Or Nietzsche must be using the concept 'metaphor' metaphorically.

We recall that according to Aristotle's classical theory, a metaphor is produced when one sets up an analogy between two sets of four terms, as follows: *A is to B* what *C is to D*. In Aristotle's example of the metaphorical expression, 'the evening of life,' one has tacitly related old age to life, and evening to day. When one then relates these two sets of relations again, the two expressions A and D go out, and the formula produces the final expression, 'the evening of life,' which corresponds to and is the *metaphorical expression* for the *literal expression*, 'old age.'[48] We can formalize the logic:

$$\frac{A\ [\text{old age}]}{B\ [\textit{life}]} \ \ X\ \frac{C\ [\textit{evening}]}{D\ [\textit{day}]} \ = \ B + C\ [\textit{evening of life}] \sim A\ [\textit{old age}]$$

In the formula, 'old age' has been cleansed from language, and is replaced with a less blunt expression. This expression, 'evening of life,' does not positively mean 'old age,' and is therefore an arbitrary expression we can only understand from its context. We therefore say it is 'metaphorical,' and not 'literal,' meaning for example that there is no 'objective' or 'ostensive' relation between *evening* and *old*.

So, what does a metaphor essential do? – It *replaces*, and it does so *arbitrarily*, i.e., without any factual correspondence between what is replaced and what is replacing. We therefore suggest that when Nietzsche tells us that the 'image' is a *metaphor*, he does not mean that it is *literally* a metaphor (an image or a presentation cannot be a stylistic device); he means that it has the *structure* and *logic* of a metaphor, because Nietzsche's *image* also (1) *replaces* (2) *arbitrarily*. As such, the 'image' remains an arbitrary sensual 'sign' for an original sense-impression. There is no pictorial

---

[48] Cf. Aristotle, Poetics, XXI, 1457a.

correspondence between *stimulus* and *image*; the image is not a copy of something it is copying. Rather, if the stimulus is a 'force' and the image a 'sign,'[49] the relationship between force and sign is arbitrary. The two orders are *type-different*; something belonging to *one order* is carried over into something of an entirely *different order*. This is the idea behind the formulation that something is 'transferred' from 'one sphere into another sphere.' Hence, Nietzsche calls this transference *metaphor* for two reasons: First, because a neurologically defined reality is formed into a reality for-us, that is, is *replaced* with a sensational sign, an image. Secondly, because the replacement is *arbitrary*, since the original neurological defined reality is not in the slightest way depicted in the image resulting from it (we do not see 'quanta,' 'forces,' or 'electrical impulses' in the image).[50]

If this is the nature of the first transfer, in the second transfer, the image is transformed [*nachgeformt*] into sound [*Laut*].[51] In this second transformation, it is again implied that something of a distinct order is carried over into something of an entirely different order. This time, an image is translated into a word, why this transfer is of *linguistic* nature. These two orders are *type-different* as well; and again, this transfer is therefore 'metaphorical,' meaning that it (1) *replaces* (2) *arbitrarily*, because the resulting word has no necessary and intrinsic connection to the image of which it becomes a

---

[49] This is identical to how Helmholtz understands the process: a perceptive image is a "sign"; it is therefore also an *arbitrary* stand-in for that which is a sign for; see also *Chapter 4.2*.

[50] In Erwin Schlimgen, we find the following account: "Nietzsche's concept of image should here not be thought as a copy in relation to reality; it already replaces something (and has as such sign-character) which has no ontic status, of which it could not be a copy." Schlimgen: Nietzsches Theorie des Bewußtseins. Berlin/New York (Walter de Gruyter), 1998, p. 73. In Christian Emden we read: "The transition from perception to language accordingly proceeds in a 'metaphorical' manner [. . .] and does not start with any kind of external reality or some pseudo-Kantian thing-in-itself." Emden: Nietzsche on Rhetoric and Neurophysiology, loc. cit., p. 101. The two commentators may be right in saying that Nietzsche's interpretation-processes do not start in any 'ontic' or 'external' reality, since these processes are meant to explain the constitution of exactly such an ontic-external reality, but they do start in *something*, namely in the nerve-stimulus, which to this author's mind is a perfect candidate for a 'pseudo-Kantian' thing-in-itself.

[51] An accurate dictionary-translation might translate 'nachgeformt' to 'imitate.' However, whether Nietzsche actually intended to convey the concept 'imitation' or not, it is and would be inaccurate theory, because a 'sound' in no way 'imitates' an 'image.' Nietzsche too cannot truly mean that.

sign. (I will assume that the arbitrariness of the sign is well-known from Structural Linguistics, and in no need of further explanation.)[52]

Hence, in two steps, a *nerve-impulse* is transformed into, first, a *sensible sign*, and second, the *sensible sign* is transformed into a *linguistic sign*, but in both cases according to translation- or interpretation- or replacement-processes that are arbitrary. We will now suggest that it is the *arbitrariness* of the entire process that fascinates – indeed, *mesmerizes* – Nietzsche; it is thanks to the ascribed arbitrariness of *sensible* and *linguistic* signs that they are conceived as 'metaphors' – that is, they are always *random replacements* of '*something* = *x*' (the impossible-to-satisfy 'thing'). This view is substantiated further, when Nietzsche continues the passage:

> One can imagine a human who is totally deaf, and never have had a sensation of tones and music: he would gaze in amazement at the Chladnian sound-figures in the sand [*die Chladnischen Klangfiguren in Sande*], discover their causes in the vibrations of the string, and swear that he now knows what humans call tones; this is how it is with us regarding language. We believe that we know something about the things themselves [*den Dingen selbst*], when we talk about trees, colors, snow, and flowers, and yet, we possess only metaphors of things [*Metaphern der Dinge*], which in no way correspond to the original essences [*den ursprünglichen Wesenheiten*]. Like the tone appears as a sand-figure, so appears also the mysterious X of the thing-in-itself [*das räthselhafte X des Dings an sich*] first as a nerve-stimuli, then as image, and finally as sound. (WL, KSA 1, p. 879).

Nietzsche's illustrates his two transfers by 'Chlandnian sand-figures.' The idea behind this image is that if one lets a violin-string vibrate over a metal

---

[52] Meijers and Stingelin have pointed out that Nietzsche is here repeating a somewhat identical formulation found in Gustav Gerber's *Die Sprache als Kunst*; cf. "Kondordanz"; Nietzsche Studien 17. Berlin, New York (Walter de Gruyter),1988, p. 368. I find it more likely that Nietzsche is simply repeating Schopenhauer's much more stringent formulation: "Reflection is necessarily the copy or the repetition of the originally presented world of perception though a copy of quite a special kind *in a completely heterogeneous material*. Concepts, therefore, can quite appropriately be called representations of representations. [Italics added]." (Schopenhauer: W1, SW I, p. 79). In general, it must be the case that succinct theoretical ideas find numerous different formulations, and are repeated in a variety of different materials, throughout a century. 'Inspiration' or 'influence' as a one-to-one relation between a mentor and an adept could only occur in extremely primitive and ill-informed writers. In writers of Nietzsche's stature, 'inspiration' or 'influence' must be seen rather as an infinitely complicated *net* that will remain unfathomable for even the acutest Nietzschean scholar.

plate covered with sand, the vibrations will produce a pattern in the sand.[53] A deaf, who cannot hear sounds, will now know 'sound' only from looking at the sand figures, which of course will give him no conception of 'sound.' Similarly, we can know truth only by looking at our sensible and linguistic signs. The Nerve-stimuli we know nothing about, and they become now – in Nietzsche's new scientistic-epistemological paradigm – identical to the *räthselhafte X des Dings an sich*.[54]

When in the second transfer, we transfer 'image' to 'sound,' we *name* an image. We have said that this naming is arbitrary, but it is indeed *doubly arbitrary*, because not only are the sounds we attach to various mental images arbitrary, as the existence of multiple different languages testifies, but the unity of image and sound (the sign) is also arbitrary in relation to the quality it signifies. In different languages, we will for example describe the stone as hard, whatever is the *arbitrary word* for 'hard' (e.g., French *'dur'*; German *'hart'*; Danish *'hård'*). However, in whatever language, the stone is *arbitrarily described* as 'hard' (*'dur,' 'hart,'* or *'hård'*), because the hardness of the stone is a specific human perception. It is an antropomorphism that uniquely places the stone in relation to the human being, and adds to its substance an attribute that only makes sense within that relationship. The stone in-itself is neither hard nor soft, but to the human touch, it feels 'hard' (an observation, which was originally John Locke's, mentioned in the beginning of the *Essays Concerning Human Understanding*): "Why should we say: the stone is hard; as if 'hard' was already known to us and not merely a completely subjective stimulus." (WL, KSA 1 p. 878).[55] If now we take it to be *true* that stones are hard, then truth is in this like in other cases, only *antropomorphic*.

---

[53] The well-known example is familiar 19th century scientific repertoire; before Nietzsche, Lange states: "That *our* things are different from things *in themselves* may be made plain to us, therefore, even by the simple opposition between a tone and the vibrations of the string that occasions it." Lange: The History of Materialism, 2nd book, 1st section, p. 188.

[54] In the Nachlaß-material Nietzsche offers a near-identical formulation: "To see the minutest transmissions from nerve-activities [*Ausstrahlungen von Nerventhätigkeit*] on a surface: they behave like the Chlandnian sound-figures to the sound itself: the same with these images to the underlying mobile nerve-activity [*bewegenden nerventhätigkeit*]." (Nachlaß 1872-73, KSA 7, 19[79]).

[55] In their "Kondordanz" between Gustav Gerber's *Die Sprache als Kunst* and Nietzsche's WL, Meijers and Stingelin cite a near-identical statement of Gerber: "We say: the stone is hard, as if the hardness was something different from our judgment." Gerber quoted from Meijers/Stingelin: Kondorkanz. Nietzsche Studien 17. Berlin. Yew York (Walter de Gruyter), 1988, p. 366.

We now begin to see an answer to Nietzsche's initial question, *Was ist ein Wort?* The word becomes the medium for transmitting that which we *call* truth, truth as *untruth* (our so-called Truth$_2$ above). But as such the word skates over its false surface-world, and never does it enter into the thing-in-itself, which is now labeled "pure non-consequential truth": "The thing-in-itself [*Das Ding an sich*] (that is to say, the pure non-consequential truth [*reine folgenlose (lit: without consequences) Wahrheit*]) is to the creator in language [*dem Sprachbildner*] quite incomprehensible and is not worth striving for at all." (WL, KSA 1, p. 879).

"Pure non-consequential truth" we labeled Truth$_3$ above. It was the metaphysical-speculative concept of truth that Nietzsche inherits from Schopenhauer; the truth that is at once inaccessible, and still, despite its inaccessibility, structures the discourse by posing itself as an abstract standard for *truth as untruth. Present false truth* can only be perceived and understood as such within a structural relationship with the *absent true Truth*. One detects in the passage above some disappointment about this *Sprachbildner*, who does not find it worth his while striving for pure truth.

In the paradoxical Schopenhauerian/Nietzschean discourse, pure truth (Truth$_3$) behaves somewhat like a deleted file on a computer: it *is* actively being *deleted*; but it still exists as *retrievable*, and it continues as such to take up as much memory on the hard-drive as it always did. First later, Nietzsche will work hard to *purge* this deleted file from memory.

3.3. A Distinction between "Living Metaphor' and "Dead Metaphor.'

What is now truth, Nietzsche asks, and offers another famous and often-quoted definition:

> What is now truth? [*Was ist also Wahrheit?*] A moveable army [*Ein bewegliches Heer*] of metaphors, metonymies, and anthropomorphisms; in brief, a complex of human relations, which, poetically and rhetorically intensified, have been transferred and beautified. [. . .] The truths are illusions, which one has forgotten that they are so. They are metaphors that are worn out, and have become sensuously powerless [*sinnlich kraftlos geworden sind*]; they are coins, that have lost their stamp, and now are only considered metal, but no longer coins. (WL, KSA 1, p. 880-81)

Let us first be clear about what is asked in this question. The question is only, what is Truth$_2$; truth as illusion; truth as untruth. Nietzsche questions neither Truth$_1$, truth as truthfulness, nor Truth$_3$, pure truth as the thing-in-itself. So, what are now such truths$_2$? They are unsurprisingly 'illusions';

but we have forgotten them to be so, and instead we take them to be real. They are unsurprisingly 'metaphors'; but we take them literally; they are coins having lost their stamp, now worth only their metal; they have in fact become *sinnlich kraftlos*, that is, they have lost the figurative power they presumably once had. So, these so-called 'metaphors' have in themselves undergone a transformation, and as a result they are no longer metaphors at all according to the classical rhetorical definition – they no longer lend figurative power to language, as metaphors supposedly do; they have instead become 'literal' and 'real.'[56]

These transformed 'metaphors' designate a reified, coagulated, and petrified language of sorts. It is as if they have started to live a life of their own, like Marx's commodity on the capitalist market, and, like Marx's commodity, have 'forgotten' their 'origin,' their conditions of production. They act as if they no longer belong to the symbolic order, but to the order of the real. They have become reified words, now reduced to literal and direct representations of things. Apropos Marx, they have become fetishes. The problem is here that language, which is *only symbolic* (which can only be *about something*), has been turned into reality, and the word only *representing* the thing is confused with the thing itself. Such reified language we for example see performed in religious and psychotic pathologies; words or sounds become fetishes, totems, or mantras, and are worshipped as such. When truths are 'coins' having lost their stamp, worth only their metal, when they have become *sinnlich kraftlos*, they are reduced to such empty 'pathological' mantras. Nietzsche continues to call these words 'metaphors' because they are still arbitrary signs for *something* = *x*, but on a classical rhetorical definition they have in fact lost all metaphorical quality. Nietzsche thinking seems to be that *originally* they served as metaphors, i.e., as the most expedient and economic expression for a certain state-of-affairs, but since then they have coagulated, and it is forgotten that they only, once upon a time, provided a convenient model. Now, Nietzsche's 'metaphors' are instead a kind of *dead anti-metaphors*.[57]

---

[56] As an authoritative work on rhetoric, which I often consult and follow in matters rhetorical, I refer to Perelman and Olbrechts-Tyteca's *The New Rhetoric: A Treatise on Argumentation*. Notre-Dame (University of Notre dame Press) 1969.

[57] Christian Emden notices correctly that Nietzsche does not understand 'metaphor' merely as stylistic device: "Language, Nietzsche seems to suggest, is a figurative discourse in itself [. . .], but the metaphoricity of language result from a more fundamental metaphorical process located beyond or perhaps before language. At stake here are the relationships among the materiality of nervous processes, the formation of introspective mental images, and the en-

3. The Production of Metaphor

Truths have now become *signs* that erroneously are understood as *things* existing in the order of the *real*.[58] Scientific explanations will necessarily resort to representing such 'truth-things.' If science is essentially 'creative writing'; composed in a 'metaphorical' 'figurative language'; and engaged in an age-old 'art of persuasion' – as some postmodernists have claimed – this is only in the context of an unavoidable epistemological-linguistic condition. In our re-definition of Nietzsche's 'metaphor,' the modest claim is merely that scientists necessarily *use signs* in order to express an observation, and signs are necessarily arbitrary relative to what they express (signs are of a *type-different* order, as we say). On the standard rhetorical definition, we can be sure that scientists will as always to do their best to *avoid metaphor*, or, as we now can say more precisely, *avoid the living metaphor*. Relative to the standard definition, scientists are as always a kind of hardcore *anti-poets*. In own self-understanding they do not invent, do not create, and do not engage in the rhetorical art of persuasion; they *observe, discover, deduce, test,* and *prove*. If they use ('the living') metaphor, as they sometimes do, and know that they do, they always aspire to understand the 'truth-thing' (the empirical fact) for which the metaphor is a temporary stand-in. The discourse of the scientist always aspires to validate itself exclusively in the order of the real.

Still, even if scientists try hard to avoid the *living metaphor*, they cannot avoid the *dead metaphor*; because the *dead metaphor* is exactly *imagery* turned into *convention*; it is exactly 'coagulated language,' which is simply . . . *language* . . . as such. The *dead metaphor* has become the naming of a

---

[58] suing representations of these images in verbalization. Nietzsche's use of the term *metaphor* here might be confusing, for metaphor can exist only within language. What he seems to mean, however, is metaphor as an explanatory model that can comprise the complexity of nervous processes, mental representation, and language, and this model rest on the most basic understanding of metaphor as a form of transferring or transmitting some kind of information, content, or impulse from one level to another." Emden, Christian: Nietzsche on Language, loc. cit., p. 106. However, despite seeing that Nietzsche's 'metaphor' is "located beyond or perhaps before language," I do not see Emden trying to explain this peculiar location; this unusual notion of metaphoricity.

If truths are seen as things existing in the order of the real, this is one compelling reason why it is so often impossible to discuss truth (what *counts* as truth) with a believer, since it will appear nonsensical to the advocate of his/her truth, to discuss the existence of a *thing*, For example, one cannot tell a religious fanatic that he is only playing a language-game, because he takes for granted that his 'truth' exists in the order of the real.

'thing,' a 'truth-thing,' a 'fact.' This naming of a thing is nothing different from a sign being an indicator of a reference. So again, a *dead metaphor* is *coagulated language*, which is nothing but *language* itself; and a *'truth-thing'* is nothing but a *reference to a fact*. As such, there is no scientist that *cannot* be using language, and in using language *cannot* be referring to a fact.

A few examples on such represented 'truth-things' or 'dead metaphors' may aid the understanding, and provide us with the appropriate perspective on Nietzsche's thinking. (1) For a long time, it was believed that light propagates like a wave; it was then observed that it also sometimes behaves like a particle. Both 'wave' and 'particle' seem in these accounts like 'metaphors' for a complex phenomenon, not fully understood, because on account of the quantum theory emerging in the beginning of the 20th Century, light sometimes would behave like a 'wave' and sometimes like a 'particle,' depending on *the observer*. Here, 'wave' and 'particle' is what we can describe as *dead metaphors* for something in-itself (an inaccessible *nature* of light), which is not clearly understood. (2) About a century ago, one constructed a model of the atom that seemed like a solar-system *en miniature*: one had a positively charged nucleus consisting of protons and neutrons, and a sphere of negatively charged orbiting electrons. Positive and negative charge supposedly kept the electrons in orbit, like gravitation keeps the planets in their orbits. This was for a long time the established 'truth-thing' of atoms, which today we know was only a model, because we know, for example, that electrons do not actually 'orbit' the nucleus, but occupy distinct energy levels around the core, and they furthermore change energy-level in jumps given specific conditions. Furthermore, the so-called 'nucleus,' which one had thought were composed of 'elementary' (indivisible) particles, is a complex of multiple lesser elements: leptons, hadrons, and quarks – where the latter, *apropos metaphorical language*, can have different 'flavors,' which again can have different 'colors.' Again we are using signs to simplify matters. We know full well the solar-system, so it is easy to imagine that something is *like* the solar-system (it may even have been comforting to know that the universe is organized around identical principles on macro- and micro-level). (3) Today, we believe that the universe started in a so-called 'Big Bang explosion'; the wording compels us to see a huge 'explosion.' This appears to be only a new 'truth-thing,' because, in this truly strange and paradoxical so-called 'explosion,' nothing apparently explodes, nothing ignites the explosion, and there is finally nothing (no space) into which to explode. Nonetheless, it is nearly impossible not to think of the Big Bang as an 'explosion.' How otherwise is it possible to imagine something expanding rapidly from a point – we hardly have a cognitive ability for summoning forth other images? In these three examples, we facilitate things by creating so-called *metaphors*, which in none of the cases are in fact – and in the standard 'classical' sense – metaphors. 'Waves,' 'particles,' 'orbits,' and 'explosions' we instead describe as *dead metaphors*; once upon a time they were perhaps 'metaphors' (i.e., *living metaphors*) and understood as such (like 'flavors' and 'colors'), but when they became established knowledge they coagulated into the representations of 'things.' Because they are 'dead,' because they have coagulated, the physicist does not regard himself as speaking metaphorically when he talks about 'particles' or 'explosions.' He would have spoken metaphorically – in the ordinary sense – had he been in the habit of describing a 'particle' as, e.g., 'this the smallest seed of matter.'

We notice that if Nietzsche can be said to 'question' (I prefer to see him 'describing') unconscious metaphorical language-use in the sciences, he is only 'questioning' such language in its coagulated and reified state; i.e., as *dead metaphorical language*. He is 'questioning' the metaphor *after* it has evolved into a non-metaphor; into a represented fact; into *literal language*. He wants to draw to our attention that words, which we are now using innocuously and with a clear fact-oriented consciousness, have had *a history*, a 'beginning,' albeit it is now forgotten, where words were still *living metaphors*, convenient short-hand expressions for something *other* . . . always something *completely other*.

As Nietzsche sees it, this 'otherness' is the general condition and problem in our use of language. Nature as the *other* is itself asleep and withdrawn onto itself. Nature is the Kantian *something* = x that stays indifferent to our attempts to linguistically describing it. It belongs to an entirely different order, another sphere, which manifests neither language nor structure. Our classificatory systems are therefore always poorly equipped to describe this in-itself. When nonetheless, the scientist attempts to represent it, he or she can do so only by means of 'signs': crude approximations to this nature that remains indifferent and withdrawn onto itself.

Saying this, it is not the claim that 'nature' is a 'fiction'; on the contrary, nature as the in-itself *is*. This means that light *does* exists and it *does* propagate, but the question is, can our language represent light's existence? Does light propagate in 'waves' or in 'particles' or in 'packets'? We emphasize instead, nothing is *less fictional* than nature as the in-itself. The *fictional* would be something made-up (by men or gods or evil demons); the *fictional* would have intention, design and purpose; but the stumbling-block for comprehending 'nature' is precisely that it was never 'made-up'; it was never endowed with intention, design or purpose in any which way. Nature we can therefore describe as the abysmal *void of the real*; that void of impenetrable darkness into which man cannot gaze without eventually seeing himself. One the other hand, it is also not the claim that science is a 'fiction,' at least not in the sense that *Lord of the Rings* is a fiction. Whatever the sciences express themselves about *does exist*;[59] but there is always a *human interference* in the *form and manner* by which the scientists express themselves. Human language is necessarily 'scrambling the signals' the scientists receive from the world in the form of 'images,' or today, mathematical formulas, deduced on the basis of observation.

'Metaphor' has in Nietzsche's discourse become a type of concepts I once attempted to describe as *anasemic*; that is, a seme beyond and outside the established (dictionary-defined) universe of semes.[60] This implies that 'metaphor' has become a term 'x' with a novel 'system-specific meaning,' a meaning one cannot 'look up,' because it is generated exclusively within its local textual environment. To read anasemic terms on their conventional nominal definition, instead of purely structurally and contextually, results therefore in serious mis-readings and misunderstandings of such terms. Instead, one must be ready to tease out the particular logic, the exotic economy, which is tacitly presupposed in such concepts, and avoid accepting the terms on their conventional face-value, as ascribed by the dictionary. To take Nietzsche's 'metaphor' on its face-value, concluding that to Nietzsche 'everything' is rhetoric, figure, style, vocabulary, etc., is to reduce him to an over-zealous rhetorician, a whimsical poet-thinker, and a bad philosopher.

A little further reflection will confirm that Nietzsche is not using 'metaphor' in what I have called an 'ordinary classical sense.' In rhetoric, 'metaphor' indicates that one replaces an expression with another expression, where the first expression is understood as 'literal' and the second as 'figurative.' In Aristotle's example, we saw how 'old age' was replaced with 'the evening of life.'[61] So, where in the tradition (from Aristotle to Pe-

---

[59] In the following chapter, I will argue in more detail that it was never Nietzsche's intention to deny 'reality' or so-called 'language-independent reality.' It is never the problem in Nietzsche that there is 'no reality,' the problem is always that there is *too much reality*. I shall say that 'reality' is infinitely 'deep' and it has infinitely many 'combinations.' It is the task of the sciences to give expression to some of these possible combinations.

[60] See especially Bornedal, Peter: Speech and System. Copenhagen (Museum Tusculanum Press), 1997.

[61] As a result of too many rhetorical replacements, a metaphorical language tends to become ornamented and oftentimes stilted and labored, because it is always possible to say the same thing straightforwardly, that is, by using literal terms. To a scientist at least, and to many philosophers, it would be

relman), the 'metaphor' is defined as a specific rhetorical technique in which an expression is replaced with another expression, Nietzsche's so-called 'metaphors' do not replace expressions with expressions, or words with words; they exclusively 'replace' an *unzugänglichen und undefinirbaren X*. Strictly speaking, Nietzsche's 'metaphor' does not 'replace' anything at all. If we insist on saying that it 'replaces' something, then this is in itself a *metaphorical expression*, because, at most, it 'replaces' *a void*.[62]

Applied to Nietzsche, our classical Aristotelian formula for 'metaphor' therefore has to be re-written. In the place of the 'literal' term, the A ('old age' in the example), we must insert a *void*, an *x*, or *the thing-in-itself*. In the metaphorical transformation, *x does something D, like some C to B*; where 'C to B' becomes the *expression* for the unknown.

$$\frac{\cancel{X}}{B} \; X \; \frac{C}{\cancel{D}} \;=\; \text{C to B} \sim X$$

Exactly because there is no communication possible between the world as thing-in-itself and our so-called 'metaphors,' because it is impossible to overstep and transgress the bar between these two realms, Nietzsche's 'metaphor' cannot in the ordinary sense 'replace' something with something else; nor can it in the ordinary sense 'picture' something as something else. It can only be *replacing the void*. Therefore, when truths are so-called 'metaphors,' they substitute themselves for, and give a first description of, something that had *no prior* linguistic existence. When something is "replacing a void," it is *radically arbitrary*, as such 'creating,' 'inventing,' or 'producing' something new. Our *Vernunft* is therefore, as Nietzsche always reiterates, *dichtende*. It does not mean that we are literally all *poets*, it means that, necessarily, we create out of nothing; that which we hold-to-be-true [*Fürwahrhalten*] is the result of such a creation.

Given that 'metaphors' can only inform us on a surface-world, there can be no correct and adequate communication between thing and knowledge, object and subject:

---

[62] convoluted and roundabout to describe a 'particle' as 'the smallest seed of matter.'
See also Meijers: "Words and concepts designate neither individuals nor generalities in the world. The opposition between individual and species is anthropomorphic; it belongs to our abstractions and is not founded in the essence of the things." Anthonie Meijers: "Gustav Gerber und Friedrich Nietzsche" in Nietzsche Studien, loc. cit., p. 385.

> It seems to me that correct perception – in other words, the adequate expression of an object in a subject – is only self-contradictory nothingness/foolishness [*widerspruchsvolles Unding*]: for between two absolutely different spheres, as between subject and object, there is no causality, no expression, but at most only an aesthetic relation; I mean a suggestive transference, a stammering translation into a completely different language [*eine andeutende Uebertragung, eine nachstammelnde Ueberstezung in eine ganz fremde Sprache*]. (WL, KSA 1, p. 884).[63]

In the context of this passage, we notice that we are talking about so-called Truth$_{2P}$. In this context, there is no communication possible between the two spheres, for example, in the form of the celebrated notion of correspondence. If the image, our sensuous sign or perception-metaphor is not the mirror of an outside 'object,' there can at best be an *andeutende Uebertragung, eine nachstammelnde Ueberstezung* of something into something else; since we have no clue about what we in fact translate, the translation can only be "suggestive" or "stammering."

In conclusion: *Nietzsche's 'metaphor' replaces nothing!* Let us illustrate this 'replacement of nothing' and return to one of our examples from physics, and at the same time emphasize that the scientists in their production of knowledge are crucially *dependent* on this sense of 'metaphor.' There is today hardly no better example of the Kantian thing-in-itself than the 'Big Bang'; the 'big bang' is the insurmountable frontier for our knowledge; what happens in the Big Bang is forever hidden from our view; if we knew it, we would – as Stephen Hawking has said – "know the mind of God."[64] The Big Bang in-itself is x. It is unknown; scientists aspiring to describe this inaccessible x can only describe what happens a millionth of a millionth of a millionth of a millionth second after. They cannot describe the point zero when everything starts, so they create, as they must, a 'metaphor' for the unknown. They only know that this x is *doing something*, for example 'expanding' or 'inflating.' So, the task it to find an expression for something 'expanding.' The following formula is not perfect, and it hardly describes the actual thought-processes of a scientist, but let us for illustration suggest:

---

[63] It is possible that Nietzsche is here inspired by another source than Schopenhauer, because in Schopenhauer, the *Object* is precisely understood as the *appropriated* "Thing," that is, the thing as construed by the Subject; therefore, thanks to the subjective categories, completely accessible. An object, Schopenhauer keeps repeating, is only object for a subject; it is never in-itself. However the lax vocabulary, the logic of Nietzsche is clear enough.

[64] Cf. Hawking, Stephen: A Brief History of Time. New York (Bantam), 1988.

3. The Production of Metaphor 71

~~X [in itself]~~
--------------- X
B [zero]

C [explosion]

~~D [expansion]~~

C to B (= zero to cosmic explosion) ~ X (= 'Big Bang')

The in-itself of the X go out; and for the void we have inserted "zero to cosmic explosion," which is abbreviated into the metaphor "Big Bang." For most scientists today, the 'big bang explosion' is a *living metaphor*; they know that it is a metaphorical description, which in no way corresponds to whatever processes it describes. But for a layperson, one could easily imagine that the 'big bang' is a *dead metaphor*; he or she will then believe that the 'big bang' is a precise and exact explanation of the origin of the universe; as dead metaphor it has become a representation of a fact: "this 'explosion' was what really happened!"

Thus, from a certain perspective, the distinction between *living* and *dead* metaphor depends on *memory*. Insofar as a metaphor is *living*, one remembers its metaphoricity; when it is *dead*, its metaphoricity has been forgotten. It only *was*, once upon a time, a *living metaphor*; that is, at one point, one was still aware of its metaphoricity, but eventually that for which it had been a metaphor disappeared from memory, and the metaphorical expression became the conventional *literal* expression. Therefore we say that the *dead metaphor* is in fact *a literal expression*!

In conclusion, Nietzsche's 'metaphor' implies nothing more than whenever a scientist, a philosopher, or a theorist is engaged in the production of knowledge, he or she must find a language or a model by which to express that which does not express itself. This language or this model must necessarily reflect *the human perspective*, since language is human, and we find thus in the scientific expression an *unavoidable interference* of the human perspective. Cf. our example: something 'expands' from zero to everything, and with 'relativistic speed' – how do we comprehend this? . . . Maybe it 'explodes'! . . . Why? . . . Because we know what an explosion is!

3.4. Metonymy and Surface-World

Nietzsche's notion of 'metonymy' must again be understood within the perspective of a general cognitive theory. In classical rhetorical theory, in metonymy one replaces a word for a thing with another word associated with it. In Nietzsche's discourse, 'metonymy' must instead be seen in relation to an epistemological discussion of the nature of synthetic judgments. Discussing 'metonymy,' he addresses another aspect of the production of knowledge out of the indifferent and superficial surface-world. In his so-called 'metonymy,' one accumulates and adds predicates to entities, in the (false) belief that such predicates will explain the essences of entities. We remain, however, firmly consigned to the surface, unable to access the 'thing' (the so-called Truth$_3$); and on this surface we can only count, calculate, and understand relationships between entities, but never their nature, substance, or essence. We understand only quantities, never qualities, as Nietzsche will reiterate throughout his writings. "All laws of nature are only relations from x to y and z. We define laws of nature as the relations between xyz, from where again they are known to us only as relations to other xyz." (Nachlaß 1872-1873, KSA 7, 19[236]).

The discussion goes back to, and is in fact faithful to, Kant and Schopenhauer's contention that substances remain unknown. Kant would contend that reason requires us to seek for a thing its absolute nature, but due to the limitations of our conceptual thinking, we can at best only produce predicates, however deeply we desire to peek into absolute essences. To Schopenhauer, elaborating this Kantian doctrine, this means that there is as such no hope of finding a resting place for our reason in an ultimate cause. This conception of finite human knowledge and limitation of human understanding, Kant for example describes in his *Prolegomena*:

> Pure reason requires us to seek for every predicate of a thing its own subject, and for this subject, which is itself necessarily nothing but a predicate, its subject, and so on indefinitely (or as far as we can reach). But hence it follows that we must not hold any thing at which we arrive to a be an ultimate subject, and that substance itself never can be thought by our understanding, however deep we may penetrate, even if all nature were unveiled to us. For the specific nature of our understanding consists in thinking everything discursively, i.e., by concepts, and so by mere predicates, to which, therefore, the absolute subject must always be wanting.[65]

Nietzsche's theory of 'properties' as mere quantifiable 'relations' synthetically added to a subject, is expanded in a long aphorism, which, given its fragmentary style, seems like Nietzsche is brain-storming himself on the issue:

> On the essence of definition: the pencil is an elongated, etc., body. A is B. That which is elongated is at the same time colored. Properties [*Eigenschaften*] only contain relation. A certain body is exactly made up of so and so many relationships. Relations can never be identical to essence [*Wesen*], they are only consequences of essences. The synthetic judgment describes a thing according

---

[65] Kant: Prolegomena § 46, WA V, p. 205.

to its effects [*Folgen*], that is, essence and effect become identical, that is, a metonymy.
Therefore, at the foundation [*im Wesen*] of a synthetic judgment we have a metonymy,
that is, a **false equalization** [*eine false Gleichung*],
that is, synthetic inferences are illogical [*Synthetischen Schlüsse sind unlogisch*]. When we apply them, we presuppose the popular metaphysics, that is, one that sees effects as causes.
The concept, "pencil," is confused with the "thing" pencil. The "is" [*Das "ist"*] in the synthetic judgment is false, it contains a transference, where two different spheres are posited next to each other, between them equalization never happens. (Nachlaß 1872-1873, KSA 7, 19[242]).

When 'truth' is an "army" [*Heer*] of metaphors and metonymies, humans are inundated by this amassment of false knowledge, which can only address the surface, but never anything deeper like the thing-in-itself. This ultimately implies that we form knowledge only of that which we see (of the *phenomena*); but since in a synthetic judgment, the subject is as visible as is the predicate, and vice versa, our judgments remain on the visible surface, and touch never anything deeper. This implies again, that our judgments are tautological, because judgments are merely repeating that which is already visible, therefore self-evident. Knowledge is in other words, and in "the strongest sense," "empty": "Knowledge [*Das Erkennen*] has, in the strongest sense, only the form of a tautology, and is **empty**." (Nachlaß 1872-1873, KSA 7, 19[236]).

Addressing the theory of the concept below, we shall explain this logic in more detail.

4. The Theory of the Concept

4.1. Concept-Formation Distinguishing Animal from Human

In conceptualization, we usually say that individual cases are transferred from the sphere of the concrete to a sphere of the abstract. The abstract conceptual representation is now no longer of perceptive, but of linguistic, nature.

To Schopenhauer, it is thanks to this transfer, humans distinguish themselves from animals. Humans are able to transfer images into concepts, although, in their *primordial* constitution, they like animals 'think' in images. To both Schopenhauer and Nietzsche, language is indispensible in concept- and knowledge-formation⁶⁶; still, images are always the root for the (correctly used) concept; so Nietzsche: "The concept corresponds first and foremost to the image; images are proto-thinking [*Urdenken*], i.e., the surfaces of things are condensed in the mirror of the eyes. [. . .] Images in the human eye! This determines all human essence!" (Nachlaß 1872-1873, KSA 7, 19[66]). In our most primitive constitution, we as such think in images, and this proto-thinking [*Urdenken*] we share with animals (it is reactivated in dreams, which also proceed as imaginary proto-thinking). Image-thinking therefore also "determines all human essence," or, to be a notch more precise than Nietzsche himself, it constitutes the *animal essence* of all humans. While proto- or image-thinking already constitutes a first primary condensation (an abbreviation and thus 'interpretation') of the surface of things, the 'concept' represents now a further, secondary, condensation ('interpretation') of the images as they exist "in the mirror of our eyes." In this secondary condensation, the particular is generalized, and the unequal equalized: "Every concept emerges from equalizing the non-equal [*durch gleichsetzen des Nicht-Gleichen*]." (WL, KSA 1, p. 880).⁶⁷

---

[66] This is also what Eduard von Hartman had concluded: "[A]ll conscious human thought is only possible by the help of language, since we see that human thought without language [. . .] in the most favorable case, very little exceeds that of the cleverest domestic animals." Hartman, Eduard von: Philosophy of the Unconscious bd. 2. Reprint. London (Routledge) 2000; p. 298. In several letters, Nietzsche denounces Hartman as a charlatan, as "dishonest," etc.; the judgment is to my mind fully justified. Hartman's writing is full of pretentious and idle 'scholarship'; but in this desert of idle knowledge, we nonetheless find remarks that have obviously inspired Nietzsche, for example the notion of language's grammatical structure as formative for the substance-accidence dichotomy (see Hartman, loc. cit., p. 293, and my following *Chapter 3*); or we find this remarkable passage anticipating Nietzsche's famous aphorism on Eternal Recurrence from FW (*The Greatest Weight*, no. 321): "Let us imagine Death to draw nigh this man and say, 'Thy life-period is run out, and at this hour thou art on the brink of annihilation; but its depends on thy present voluntary decision, once again, precisely in the same way, to go through thy now closed life with complete oblivion to all that has passed. Now chose!'" (Hartman, loc. cit., bd. 2, p. 9).

[67] This distinction between intuitive perceptions and concepts is already present in Kant, for example when in the Logic, he observes: "All knowledge, that is, all representations consciously related to an object, are either i n t u i t i v e   p e r c e p t i o n s   or   c o n c e p t s [*entweder A n s c h a u u n g e n   oder   B e - g r i f f e*]. – The intuitive perception is an i n d i v i d u a l [*einzelne*] representation, the concept a g e n e r a l [*allgemeine*] or r e f l e c t i v e representation. (Kant: Logik, WA VI, p. 521).

4. The Theory of the Concept

Concept-formation is a particular human endeavor. It is taken for granted, in both Schopenhauer and Nietzsche, that animals are unable to form concepts. This inability comes about because animals are living exclusively in the moment. They are inundated with perception. Every instance is being replaced infinitely by ever-new instances, while the past glides back into indistinct darkness. Animals therefore remain bound to the narrow horizon of the present; ever-new instants always cancel out what was the most recent previous instant. They have no retentional horizon, and can consequently not retain strings of material. As a result, they cannot remember neither 'life' nor 'death,' and know only death "when they die," as Schopenhauer observes:

> [Animals] live in the present alone; [man] lives at the same time in the future and the past. They satisfy the need of the moment; he provides by the most ingenious preparations for his future. [. . .] They are given up entirely to the impression of the moment, to the effect of the motive of perception; he is determined by abstract concepts independent of the present moment. [. . .] The animal feels and perceives; man, in addition, *thinks* and *knows*; both *will*. The animal communicates his feeling and moods by gesture and sound; man communicates thought to one another. [. . .] The animal learns to know death only when he dies, but man consciously draws every hour nearer his death.[68]

This Schopenhauer passage finds identical formulations in the beginning of the second *Unzeitgemäße Betrachtungen*, where Nietzsche contemplates the 'happiness' of 'the forgetful cattle' "fettered to the pale of the moment." (UB II, KSA 1, p. 248).[69]

In both Schopenhauer and Nietzsche, humans have lost their original innocence and thoughtless happiness, thanks to their ability to form concepts. This is their Fall. They have been expelled from paradise because they learnt to master language. Thanks to this new mastery, they have removed themselves from a full life lived in the self-presence of the present; they have started instead to communicate, to think, and to remember – with the inevitable consequence to learn also to lie (an option not available to animals). *Logos*, scandalous reason, has entered the stage.

Animals still live in the presence of the present; they only perceive; while concepts remove us from perception. Concepts are in Schopenhauer

---

[68] Schopenhauer: W1, SW 1, p. 74.
[69] We return to this passage in *Chapter 6*: "Eternal Recurrence in Inner-Mental-Life." Günter Figal has a reading closely resembling my own in Figal: Nietzsche: Eine philosophische Einführung. Stuttgart (Reclam), 2001; p. 46-52.

defined as, "non-perceptive representations [*nichtanschauliche Vorstellungen*]," or as, "abstract, non-perceptive, general, not in time and space individual representations."[70] They are also described as "representations of representations" [*Vorstellungen von Vorstellungen*], implying that they are still 'representations,' but of a second order. They are on one remove from representations of the first order, i.e., perceptive images. Concepts still have, and ought to have, first-order perceptive representations as their indispensable root,[71] but they have detached themselves from this root, when – out of a heterogeneous world of matter and forces, stuff and activity, and out of the many individual images we receive in perception – they abstract a *name* condensing and abbreviating this multitude of particular and heterogeneous cases. This *abstract name* is now becoming an average and approximation of all these cases, and consequently, individual cases cease to exist when conceptualized, since they are being adjusted to a single abstract 'representation' symbolizing them all. The theory of the concept is reiterated in Nietzsche, for example in the *Nachlaß* material: "The concept originates from equalizing the non-equal. [. . .] The equal is taken for granted because one presupposes identity; therefore because of false perceptions. One sees a human walking, and names it 'walking.' Then a monkey, a dog: and one says again, 'walking.'" (Nachlaß 1872-1873, KSA 7, 23[11]).

Concept-formation also removes us a step further from the things-in-themselves. According to the Kantian paradigm, perceptions would already have made this removal inescapable; we must perforce organize the world in space and time, and are per human constitution fettered to this surface-world into which we are thrown. However, in conceptualizing our perceived world, we add to it a new layer of artificiality, which in principle could have been avoided (*ex hypothesi*, we might regress into or could perhaps have halted our evolution at some primitive animal state). Our so-called 'truth-drive,' understood as a 'drive' to conceptualize, is therefore (cf. above) not part of human constitution, despite described as 'drive.' In Nietzsche it is

---

[70] Schopenhauer: W1, SW I, p. 78.

[71] The primacy of perception, is an often sounded theme in Schopenhauer: "Although the concepts are fundamentally different from intuitive-perceptive representations [*Anschaulichen Vorstellungen*], they still stand in a necessary relation to these, without which they would be nothing." (W1, SW 1, p. 79). And further: "The whole world of reflection rests on, and is rooted in, the world of perception. All ultimate, i.e., original, *evidence* is one of *intuitive perception* [*ist eine anschauliche*]." (W1, SW 1, p. 113). Nietzsche reiterates the view: "The concepts can only emerge from intuitive perception [*Anschauung*]." (Nachlaß 1872-1873, KSA 7, 23[13]).

often seen, rather, as a piece of human folly and pretension. It indicates a certain human tenacity for creating meaning-structures and classificatory systems that interpret a perceived world, but always in its own light. Our 'truth-drive' therefore gives the world a certain gloss; it is intended to reflect essences, but it is uniquely human, and therefore foreign to nature itself. "By overlooking the individual and real we gain the concept, as well as the form. Whereas nature knows of no forms and concepts, nor of species, but only of a for-us inaccessible and indefinable X [*ein für uns unzugänglichen und undefinirbaren X*]." (WL, KSA 1, p. 880).

However artificial an "addition" the concept is, it is nonetheless thanks to our concept-formation we start to know. As the human forms concepts of the apparent world, he or she brings it under control.

> [The human being] as a r a t i o n a l being [*vernünftiges Wesen*] places now his behavior under the control of the abstractions: he will no longer tolerate, from sudden impressions [*eindrücke*], to be carried away by intuitions [*Anschauungen*]; he universalizes all these impressions into colorless, cooler concepts, in order to adopt them as guidance of his life and actions. Everything that distinguishes a human from an animal depends of the ability to dissolve and transfer a perceptive metaphor into a schema [*die anschaulichen Metaphern zu einem Schema zu verflüchtigen*], therefore to dissolve an image into a concept. [. . .] While every perception-metaphor [*Anschauungsmetapher*] is individual and without equal, and therefore escapes all classification, the impressive edifice of concepts displays the rigid regularity of a Roman columbarium, and lives from the rigor and coolness that characterizes mathematics. Everybody who have felt this coolness, is hardly able to believe that the concept – bony and cubic like a dice – still remains the r e s i d u u m   o f   a   m e t a p h o r   [*Residuum einer Metapher*], and that the illusion resulting from the artistic transference of a nerve-stimulus to an image is – if not the mother – then at least the grandmother of every concept. (WL, KSA 1, p. 881-82).

The percept is a metaphor of the first order, and the concept is a metaphor of the second order. Ultimately, concepts stem from nerve-stimuli, but only indirectly; the perception-metaphor, the 'image,' mediates between nerve-stimulus and concept – this is the reason why the nerve-stimulus is described as, not the 'mother,' but "then at least the grandmother," of the concept.

As one forms the concept, one throws away specificity. "Sudden impressions" are universalized and replaced with "colorless, cooler concepts." Whereas the perception-metaphor is "individual and without equal," the concept transfers and dissolves the individual images into classificatory and schematic systems.

4.2. The Surface-World and the Tautological Structure of the Concept

When the concept universalizes, structures, and classifies, its material is always the heterogeneous universe of images; the concept can never step beyond images (phenomena or presentations). We are as such destined to live in this one and only available surface-world; a surface-existence that is both unsatisfactory, and heroically must be affirmed. Schopenhauer offers in *Die Welt* a simile depicting this human condition: "Man is like somebody walking around a castle, in vain looking for an entrance, and in the meantime sketching the façades."[72] The world is this castle: we only see the outer walls, but like Kafka's K., we will never be able to enter its interior.

The same principle applies when we explain things. We remain outside the castle, and can do no better than describe its surface, give sketchy outlines of the outer walls. Explanations are therefore only surface-observations that are artificially added to phenomena as their presumed causes. They are devoid of real explanatory power, because they only repeat what is already self-evident from observing the surface. In the *Nachlaß* material, Nietzsche explains in more detail how this condition consigns us to only describing the above-mentioned *quantities* in nature, but never *qualities*; only *relationships* are accessible.

> Our understanding [*Verstand*] is a surface-ability [*Flächenkraft*], it is superficial [*Oberflächlich*]. It understands [*Erkennt*] through concepts [*Begriffe*]; that is, our thinking is classification, a name-giving [*Benamsen*]; therefore, it is something that derives from the human condition and never touches on the thing itself [*Ding selbst*]. Only as calculating and qua the spatial forms do humans have absolute knowledge, i.e., the ultimate limit for all things knowable [*alles Erkennbaren*] are quantities; he [*man*] understands no quality, only quantity. (Nachlaß 1872-1873, KSA 7, 19[66]).

This condition gives all explanation a tautological and circuitous structure. The concept we use to explain the surface, is itself drawn from the surface. In WL, Nietzsche's gives us the example, 'honesty.' We observe a man behaving honestly, and then we 'explain' his honest behavior with his honesty. "We call a person honest; why did he behave so honestly today? We ask. Our answer usually is: because of his honesty. Honesty! [*Die Ehrlichkeit!*]." (WL, KSA 1, p. 880).

We notice the paradoxical chronological sequence of the explanation: first, we experience the phenomenon of *honest behavior*; second, in our urge to 'explain' this phenomenon we see it as an effect to which we, third-

---

[72] Schopenhauer: W1, SW 1, p. 156.

ly, attach the cause, *honesty*; finally, we interpret *honesty* as preceding our initial observation of *honest behavior*. The following table illustrates the logic of this tautological and circuitous reasoning:

Step 1: Phenomenon ☐
    Step 2: Phenomenon is interpreted as effect ☐
        Step 3: Cause is attached to effect ☐
Step 4: Cause is interpreted as preceding Step 1

The point is here that the explanatory cause is nothing but a generalization of the initially observed phenomenon. Qua this generalization, a *concept* has been formed; in this case, the concept of *honesty*; that is, the notion of an 'honest' quintessence that uniformly informs a multitude of individual human behaviors.

4.3. Failed Attempts to Uphold a Rigid Distinction between 'Word' and 'Concept'

Before going any further in Nietzsche's theory of the concept, we have to address an imprecision in his exposition. We notice that Nietzsche, throughout his essay, has no rigorous distinctions between *sound*, *word*, and *concept*. Throughout his essay, he essentially posits a tripartite model, and any of these three terms will in various contexts designate the third component in his model: *nerve-stimulus – image – sound/word/concept*. Sometimes the third component is labeled 'sound,' often it is labeled 'word,' and in several passages, it is introduced under the label 'concept.'[73] However, these three terms are not identical; and they were not understood to be identical in the tradition Nietzsche was responding to. It was for example commonly understood, also in Nietzsche's days, that animals use sounds differently from human use of sounds; to animals 'sounds' are at best signals, but not words uttered with subjective self-awareness. Moreo-

---

[73] One notices that other commentators seem to have pondered the same arrangement, and encountered the some difficulty about it. Anthonie Meijers offers this schema for Nietzsche's model (oddly leaving out Nietzsche's 'nerve-stimulus'): "Ding an sich → Bild (oder Anschauungsmetaphor) → Laut (oder Wort) → Begriff" Meijers: "Gustav Gerber und Friedrich Nietzsche" in Nietzsche Studien 17, loc. cit., p. 386. Meijers also takes 'sound' and 'word' to be synonymous, which is of course a correct *reading* of Nietzsche. Then he adds 'concept' after word, which is an *interpretation* of Nietzsche, but which seems logical.

ver, to Schopenhauer and Nietzsche's knowledge, animals also do not form 'concepts.' Nietzsche most probably know from Schopenhauer that 'name' and 'concept' are understood as two different things: "So important an instrument of intelligence as the *concept* obviously cannot be identical to the mere *word*, that mere sound, which as a sense-impression passes away with the present moment."[74] Here Schopenhauer himself confounds 'word' and 'sound,' since a word is described as "that mere sound . . ." However, whatever unit Schopenhauer believes *word* and *sound* to be, naming (thanks to the *word-sound unit*) and conceptualizing are describing two different processes, insofar as in naming one attaches (*mutatis mutandis*) a word/sound to a concrete perceptual image; while in conceptualizing one subsumes an indefinite number of perceptual images under an abstract label. Even if it is likely that Nietzsche knows of these distinctions, in his essay, he does not attempt to clarify them. Nietzsche uses the three distinct terms to describe the one and same idea. In his discourse, *sound* is used interchangeably with the *word* (as also Schopenhauer did), and the *word* is used interchangeably with the *concept* – in what seems to be his general and most urgent intention, namely to describe the *logic of the concept*.[75]

We shall in the following try to explain and clear up some of these confusions. We will ignore the confusion of *sound* and *word*, since to Nietzsche and Schopenhauer – writing before Saussure – the distinction is not obvious; and since sound is, after all, the most typical manifestation of the word (moreover, the confusion does not seem to have serious theoretical repercussions). The confusion of *word* and *concept* is theoretically more interesting.

When Nietzsche uses the two terms interchangeably, we will suggest that it is because there are profound and objective problems related to their definition. According to Nietzsche's epistemological model, *word* and *concept* must seem largely to be doing the same thing; they both seem to subsume multifarious material under a single heading. Doing so, they both seem to 'linguisticise' a universe of diverse images. We will describe these processes in better detail in *Chapter 2*, but let us for now notice that when,

---

[74] Schopenhauer: W2, SW II, p. 86. One or two generations later, the distinction between sound and concept of course finds its best formalized expression in Saussure's model of the sign: his signifier/signified, or sound-image/concept model (see also fn. 76, and *Chapter 4*).

[75] Claudia Crawford is one of the relatively few commentators, who is aware of Nietzsche's profound influence by Schopenhauer's theory of concept and language; and she spends a chapter outlining some of the convergences. See Crawford, Claudia: The Beginnings of Nietzsche's Theory of Language, loc. cit.,. pp. 184.

4. The Theory of the Concept 81

for example, one 'invents' the word 'dog' to describe a well-known four-legged creature, one has circumscribed a segment of the universe, making it possible for us to *see with self-conscious awareness* a distinction between 'dog' and other animals, e.g., 'dog' and 'cat.' In fact, one has made it possible to *see* 'a dog,' i.e., see a *dog as dog*. One has thus brought a multifarious material under a single heading; one has created, as we say, a *class*. In this classification of the universe, the word functions like a concept.

Still, we have the intuition that *word* and *concept* cannot be entirely the same thing. This was at least Schopenhauer's position: "The *concept* is entirely different not only from the word to which it is tied, but also from the perceptions from which it originates."[76] However, not even Schopenhauer is completely clear in his thinking on this distinction, when for example he famously claims (cf. above) that the *concept* is a *representation of a representation*; where is now the word supposed to go in this formula; is the *word* an entirely different logic? We understand that the first representation in the formulaic expression is a *perception-image* with spatio-temporal form; and we understand that the *concept* is seen as a representation of that representation; therefore as a second-order representation. Consequently, the concept is without spatio-temporal form, and since it does not belong to perception, it must be without ostensive definition. From Schopenhauer's formula, we understand perfectly well the distinction between *image* and *concept*; the *concept* being an "abstract representation of reason," whereas *images* are "particular representations of perception"[77] (an idea he underscores in the second volume of *Die Welt*: "The concept does not preserve what is perceived or what is felt; rather it preserves what is essential thereof in *an entirely altered form*, yet as an adequate representative of those results [*italics added*]"[78]). Still, we have no explanation of the *word*; is the *word* also "an abstract representation of reason"; does it also "preserve what is essential" in what is perceived?

It seems that this must be the case; and still Schopenhauer will insist on a radical difference between *word* ("that mere sound" – pure materiality) and *concept*. Schopenhauer is not making matters easier, when thereupon he insists that the concept can be represented *only as a word*. Concepts must always *appear as*, or *disguise* themselves in, words. Although a concept seems like an *abstract intuition*, it can only present itself in *language*, attached to a *word*; without the word to represent it, there is also no concept.

---

[76] Schopenhauer: W2, SW II, p. 86.
[77] Cf. Schopenhauer: W1, SW I, p. 81.
[78] Schopenhauer W2, SW II, p. 87.

It is only as *sign* the concept can be examined and manipulated in the mind – they are not like *ideas* swimming around in the mind, they must have *material clothing*.

We must conclude that it is difficult to uphold a rigorous distinction between word and concept, and we therefore suggest that it is exactly this difficulty that Nietzsche reflects in his interchangeable use of *word* and *concept*. When Nietzsche presents us with his famous 'leaf-example,' we notice that he has in fact only two leaves: one corresponding to the *image*, and another corresponding to the *concept*. He is implicitly following Schopenhauer. There is a 'leaf' designating *this particular leaf*, with all its individual characteristics; and then there is a second 'Leaf' designating *The Leaf as such*, described as "the idea that in nature there exists, apart from leaves, the 'Leaf': like an original form [*Urform*], from which all leaves have been woven." The *word* seems again as if it has disappeared; but we must assume that it has in fact fused with the *concept*.

> As sure as a leaf is never quite the same as another, as sure is the concept 'leaf' formed through the arbitrary disposal of these individual differences, through a forgetfulness of the dissimilarities. This awakes now the idea [*Vorstellung*] that in nature there exists, apart from leaves, the 'Leaf': like an original form [*Urform*], from which all leaves have been woven, drawn, colored, bended, painted, but by incompetent hands, so that no copy [*Exemplar*] turned out as a correct and faithful true image of the original form. (WL, KSA 1, p. 880).

Leaves are uniquely distinctive regarding form, thread-pattern, color, etc., while, as we conceptualize leaves, we overlook this indefinite number of differences and create a so-called *Urform* for leaves: the *Leaf* as such, the concept, *Leaf*. The concept-Leaf in thus invented as something like an original form, which all individual leaves seem to derive from and attempt to imitate. In forming the concept-Leaf we have equalized the unequal, simplified multiplicity, and made abstract the concrete. The concept-Leaf is now a *Vorstellung von Vorstellungen*. In Nietzsche's example, we are presented to concept and image. We see no distinct *word* for leaf in the example; because Nietzsche takes for granted that the word has melted into the concept.[79] Nietzsche's missing distinction is symptomatic on the unsolved

---

[79] A few generations later, Ferdinand de Saussure will clear up the relations between sound, word, and concept, in proposing the structure of the linguistic sign. In this structure, the 'word' is made up from the association between a 'sound,' on one hand, and a 'concept,' on the other. The 'sound' is understood as signifier, and the 'concept' is understood as signified. There is as such in Saussure no *progressive sequence of development*, like in Schopenhauer and

problems related to word and concept. Partly, Nietzsche is following Schopenhauer, who is himself not entirely clear about the distinction; and partly (more importantly) the word seems in *most* cases to function like a concept: it circumscribes a class.

It seems now that only in the cases where a *word* is used nominally, and with an ostensive definition, does it lose its infiltration with the concept, and becomes a 'pure word.' Let us at least try to pursue this possibility. There seems to be a distinction between a word in its pure *nominal* function, a word with a definite *ostensive referent*, and the concept with no *ostensive* referent; thanks to its loss of *specificity*. Instead of having a relation to the empirical world of 'things,' like the word typically has, the concept gains instead a "range" or a "sphere," as Schopenhauer says. Implying: a *word* has a *referent*, a *concept* has a '*range*.'[80] In only being 'defined' by its 'range,' the concept now becomes unclear, ambiguous, and indefinite about referent, because nobody can be completely sure about where this 'range or 'sphere' begins or ends; that is, nobody knows for sure the number and nature of its connotations. When we use a word for its nominal value, we *see* a particular leaf, *point* at it, and *pronounce* the word 'leaf'; thus, we refer to a specific referent, and, moreover, we do not engage ourselves in much interpretive activity. The abstract concept-leaf, by contrast, is often inserted into worlds of interpretation, where it can be

---

Nietzsche, where first 'sound' is constituted as the most material linguistic element, then 'words' (although almost disappearing in the paradigm), and finally, most abstractly, 'concepts.' In Saussure, the sound/concept becomes a unity with two abstract components; and this unity designates the 'word' (or strictly speaking, the 'linguistic sign'). In the Saussurian sign, we as such find a necessary solidarity between *sound*, *word*, and *concept*, because the entire trinity is one single unit, which only in the abstract can be separated. Especially, the *word* and the *concept* is always 'melted together' in this conception, since a word existing in isolation is inconceivable; that would presume that we could have a sign of pure sound, and without ideational content, which would constitute no sign at all, but only noise, a hiss in the background.

[80] The distinction here suggested is similar to a distinction suggested by Quine between words with 'intentional meanings' versus words with 'extensional meanings.' A 'purely nominally used word,' in our terminology, would approximately correspond to Quine's extensional meanings, the word has reference; and a concept, having no reference, but only a 'range,' would approximately correspond to Quine's intentional meanings. (See Quine, W. O.: "Two Dogmas of Empiricism." In *Challenges to Empiricism*. Edited by H. Morick. Indianapolis (Hackett), 1980.) We will not at this point further elaborate on these similarities between Schopenhauer/Nietzsche and Quine's distinctions.

'debated.' We may notice that a concept-leaf can indeed be 'good' or 'bad'; it can be remedial or poisonous; it can indicate a healthy fashionable diet, or a primitive diet fit only for animals, etc. While the nominally used *word* points to specificity, the concept-leaf simplifies and abstracts away specificity; now it is possible to subsume several different objects under its heading. As such, 'pure words' (without conceptual infiltration) would occur only in cases like *pointing*: I see a leaf, *point*, and say 'leaf.' In this case, the 'leaf' I point at, and whose name I then pronounce, seems concrete, and is supposedly not an abstraction: it is this and only this leaf.

This 'solution' is attractive, but not completely satisfying; one asks oneself: is not this purely nominal use of language (besides being an exclusive case) still infiltrating concept-formation? Does not the word in its nominal function still select a segment of the universe?

4.4. The Logic of the Concept and Interpretability

Although it seems impossible to uphold a rigorous distinction between word and concept, we understand the drift of the thinking; we understand what Schopenhauer and Nietzsche see as the great achievement of the concept.

Instead of dealing with the complexity and multiplicity of an entire empirical field, conceptualization gives us the opportunity to reduce a field to a small number of abstract ideas, which we are now able to organize, arrange, and combine in a logical order that seems coherent and satisfying. Let the empirical field be a text. In itself the text is always too detailed and abundant in information, which is why, when starting to so-called 'interpret' a text, we always reduce it to a few abstract ideas supposedly conveying its 'message,' its 'intention,' its 'theme,' or the like. We do, what Schopenhauer is saying we always do in any abstraction: "In our reflection, abstraction is a throwing off of useless luggage for the purpose of handling more easily the knowledge to be compared and maneuvered in all directions. Thus, much that is inessential, and therefore merely confusing, in real things is omitted, and we operate with few but essential determinations conceived in the abstract."[81]

Formally, Schopenhauer illustrates the concept by a circle; this circle has a 'range' or a 'sphere' that may contain a number of sub-concepts (i.e., the concept 'animal' contains the concept 'dog' within its sphere). Or reversely, it may be contained within a larger sphere itself (the concept 'dog' is contained within the larger sphere 'animal'). Or one concept-sphere can

---

[81] Schopenhauer W2, SW II, p. 87.

overlap partly or in total another concept-sphere (i.e., the concept 'flower' may partially overlap the concept 'red,' since some flowers are red).

Schopenhauer, with his rational and rigorous mind, now understandably prefers to believe that when we argue rationally and consistently, we keenly observe the relations and distinguish between the different concept-spheres, and we carefully keep an account of all their possibilities and arrange them in their logical order. Whereas, when we argue irrationally or for the sake of persuasion, we deliberately omit certain concept-spheres or put our emphases on other, perhaps inferior, spheres, resulting in invalid arguments where one can argue, from almost any given point of departure, anything imaginable. Schopenhauer explains this logic in more detail:

> Correct and exact conclusions are reached by our accurately observing the relation of the concept-spheres, and admitting that one sphere is wholly contained in a third only when a sphere is completely contained in another, which other is in turn wholly contained in the third. On the other hand, the art of persuasion depends on our subjecting the relations of the concept spheres to a superficial consideration only, and then determining these only from one point of view, and in accordance with our intentions. Mainly in the following way. If the sphere of a concept under consideration lies only partly in another sphere, and partly also in quite a different sphere, we declare it to be entirely on the first sphere or entirely in the second, according to our intentions. For example, when passion is spoken of we can subsume this under the concept of the greatest force, of the mightiest agency in the world, or under the concept of irrationality, and this under the concept of powerlessness or weakness.[82]

In the passage, Schopenhauer's example is 'passion.' From the concept *passion*, one can in opposite directions argue that *passion* is evil or *passion* is good, because passion has a 'sphere.' We can follow Schopenhauer, and illustrate this 'gliding' of the concept *passion* in two different directions as follows:

Evil ← Bodily ← Passion → Spiritual → Good

---

[82] Schopenhauer: W1, SW I, p. 89-90.

In our illustration, every concept, understood as a 'sphere,' becomes a 'bubble' that partly overlaps different other 'bubbles' regarding content; this condition enables the *floating nature* of the argument. From any given 'bubble,' one will selectively choose a content that serves one argument. We understand now that given their 'spherical' character, meaning of concepts is 'floating' and unstable, rather than stable;[83] and everything reduced to concepts are by implication interpretable. As an elaborate example on this floating meaning, one can peruse a model Schopenhauer offers in paragraph 9 of *Die Welt* (See W1, SW 1, p. 93). His example on a concept is here 'traveling' [*Reisen*]. Let us imagine that someone has told us, "He spent his entire life traveling," and we, being inquisitive, now want to know whether this life was spent well, or it was wasted. As Schopenhauer's model demonstrates, 'traveling' can now *float off* in multiple directions. It can for example be "expensive" to travel, in which case the man ends up as "poor," which is "evil"; or it can be an opportunity to gain experience, increase one's knowledge, which is "useful," and therefore "good."

Although Schopenhauer envisions an ideal argument, where we could keep track on the logical order of all the connotations of the 'spherical concept,' let us here suggest, that it is the 'disorder,' the floating nature of the concept that has pragmatic reality in our social world.[84] *Because* the concept is a 'sphere,' that is, because it is indefinite and ambiguous, it is from any given concept possible to arrive to multiple different interpretations and argue multiple different cases.

We therefore restate Nietzsche's famous "all is interpretation."

'All is interpretation,' because the concept is a sphere.
'All is interpretation,' because the concept never contains only one component, but a multiplicity, indefinite in number, and therefore impossible to account for.
'All is interpretation,' because any concept points in multiple different directions, and 'floats off' into the spheres of other concepts.

---

[83] The same idea has been suggested also by Werner Stegmaier; cf. Nietzsches 'Genealogie der Moral' (Darmstadt, 1994), p. 70ff. More about Stegmaier's notion in *Chapter 4*.

[84] Note that Habermas is a modern exponent of the possibility of this ideal debate. One notices that nearly the entire philosophical tradition, from Plato to Schopenhauer to Habermas, seems to suffer from the same nostalgia; this yearning for a rational discourse transcending all contingency. It is certainly a beautiful ideal, and it cannot leave anybody completely cold. The 'only' problem with this ideal is that it is virtually never *practiced*. In *Chapters 3* and *4*, I shall explain why, *per human constitution*, this ideal is always frustrated.

An example one this unavoidable interpretability, which we always encounter in any field, might be Hamlet's famous 'hesitation.' In the history of the reception of *Hamlet*, 'hesitation' became in the critical tradition a *concept*; and interpretations of *Hamlet* often consisted in how to determine the *meaning* of this apparent 'hesitation.' One would in the critical tradition find religious, existential, psychoanalytic, formalistic, etc., explanations on the notion, the result being a dissemination of multiple competing interpretations of Hamlet's 'hesitation' – eventually so multifarious that only a very dedicated Shakespeare-scholar could keep track on them all.

We encounter the following paradox emerging thanks to the concept. Thanks to the concept, we simplify a world; we make it easy; we reduce a multiplicity to something we can handle; in this, we also discipline our thinking and give it direction and precision; as such, the concept seems to stabilize a universe. – But then again, not really, because the concept itself remains unstable; it floats off in all directions; in order to understand it, we have to subject it to interpretation, which is always dependent on our quasi-random selection of any of its multiple components; or as we say, dependent on our *interpretive perspective.*

We may not be able to set up a rigorous distinction between word and concept, but as we say, we can still understand the drift of the thinking. We have in the notions *image, word,* and *concept* three different types of representation; the three types are the result of three different types of transfer. The *image* emerges thanks to the transfer from nerve-stimulus to 'image'; the image is therefore seen as a 'metaphor,' because it *replaces arbitrarily*, and as such, 'interprets.' However, our so-called 'interpretations' of the never-stimuli in our reception of images must be *conventionally locked*, since we cannot decide to see a thing as anything other than the thing we see. The *word* emerges thanks to a transfer from image to word; the word is also seen as a 'metaphor,' because also the word *replaces arbitrarily*, and as such, 'interprets.' However, the same qualification applies, since our so-called 'interpretations' of images into words must again be *conventionally locked*, because, in using language, we cannot decide to name a thing as anything other than what linguistic convention has decided is its name. In both cases, images and words do not give the user a choice of personal preference in his or her so-called 'interpretations.' If *image* and *word* were not *conventionally locked interpretations*, we would see and speak differently from individual to individual: we would experience different worlds and be unable to communicate in conventional languages. This, obviously, is not happening; so, although Nietzsche labels these two types of representation 'interpretations,' none of them give rise to serious debate between individuals (or between theoretical, ideological, and religious communities).

To recapitulate: *First*, our perceptive apparatus 'interprets' an environing world according to our given "human optic" (more about this notion in the following *Chapter 2*); but this 'optic' is exactly given – part of human organization and constitution – implying that it is not up to the individual to 'interpret' the perceived object in anyway different from its appearance. *Second*, when our language 'interprets' the world by replacing perceptive images with linguistic signs, this replacement is also given, insofar as it is not up to the individual to use language differently from the conventional use it has found through social-historical development. We do not start debating between ourselves the name 'dog,' partly because it is understood that the name is arbitrary, and it makes no sense to start debating the replacement of one arbitrary term with another arbitrary term. In these two forms of representations, we do not detect any *hermeneutical-productive activity*.

The situation changes with the introduction of the *concept*, because it has a peculiar propensity to introduce ambiguities into an issue, which require further interrogation and debate. We say that we cannot meaningfully debate whether a dog should be called 'dog,' because we have grown into, and are now locked up, in our language; we can, by contrast, debate a multitude of issues under the *concept* 'dog' (for example, whether dogs are intelligent; whether they have feelings; whether they are an appropriate food-source; where on the evolutionary tree, the dog started to appear, etc.) When words are turned into concepts, meaning typically gets *unlocked*, and it starts *floating*. It is now the pandemonium of Babel starts. It is now the world loses its firmament.

4.5. An Interlude on Stanley Fish's Notion of Interpretability

We say that *interpretability* is an effect of problems in the *logic* of the concept; not primarily an effect of "competing interpretive communities," suggesting new "authoritative interpretations," as American neo-Pragmatist, Stanley Fish, recently has suggested.[85] In this we obviously do not dispute that 'competing interpretive communities' may develop as an outcome of essential conceptual problems. If 'passion' can be interpreted as 'good' as well as 'evil,' depending on the direction the concept of passion takes in the

---

[85] Introduced best in Fish's two major works; Fish, Stanley: Is there a Text in this Class: The Authority of Interpretive Communities. Cambridge (Harvard University Press), 1980; and Fish: Doing what comes Naturally. Durham/London (Duke University Press), 1989.

interpretive process, then one can easily imagine that different 'interpretive communities' will emerge defending any of the two possible interpretations. However, when Stanley Fish explains interpretability with the existence of 'competing interpretive communities,' he reverses the order of cause and effect. He notices that literary texts have multiple interpretations, and then he explains this state of affairs by the existence of different societies. He explains the obvious with the even more obvious; a strategy that one even assumes has a certain appeal to Stanley Fish. We say instead that literary texts have multiple interpretations, because we always interpret a conceptualized version of the text, where the concept is multifarious, ambiguous, and heterogenous and therefore offers a range of possibilities. As an effect of this freedom to choose, 'interpretive communities' emerge, defending now one, now another of these possibilities.

Fish is tacitly relying on the distinction, subject and object, which is in itself never further contemplated or elaborated. The text, as object, is complete passivity and potentiality; the reader's interpretation, as subject, is complete activity and actuality. If in Aristotle, a block of granite is potentially a statue of Zeus, while the sculptor is the activity (the *efficient cause*) forming the granite into the actuality of a statue, in Fish, the interpretive community is the *efficient cause*, the *complete activity*, forming the text into a meaning-structure. Interpretation and text stand over and against each other as subject to object: text being object, passivity and potentiality; interpretation being subject, activity and actuality.[86]

The text therefore does not exist in isolation; in Fish's words, "no text reads itself." This entails that we cannot hope to understand the meaning of the *text*; we can only hope to understand the text through the *interpretation of the text*; that is, insofar as we belong to an 'interpretive community.' Here we notice a first problem related to this idea, because, how do we understand an interpretation of a text, if we cannot understand a text? An *interpretation* of a text would also be a text; in principle, it would be object

---

[86] Fish is aware of this conundrum; it is for example succinctly articulated in the essay "Change": "What is the source of interpretive authority: the text or the reader? Those who answered 'the text' were embarrassed by the fact of disagreement. Why, if the text contains its own meaning and contains its own interpretation, do so many interpreters disagree about that meaning? Those who answered 'the reader' were embarrassed by the fact of agreement. Why, if meaning is created by the individual reader from the perspective of his own experience and interpretive desires, is there so much that interpreters agree about?" Fish: "Change" in Doing what Comes Naturally, loc. cit., p. 141. Fish's solution to the dilemma is the well-known idea of an interpretive community accounting for both the fact of agreement and disagreement.

of the same exigencies as the text. If I cannot adjust my interpretation to the text, then I also cannot adjust my interpretation to the authority of an 'interpretive community,' which is also presented as *text*. If both interpretation and text is made from the same fabric – let us call this fabric 'writing' – and are to a large extent employing the same rhetorical means, narrative, argument, thematic, example, metaphor, etc. – it ought to be as easy or as difficult *in principle* to understand the text and the authoritative interpretation of the text as a meaning-structure. To put the point differently, if I do not know what to say about James Bond after reading Ian Fleming, why is it that I know what to say about Bond after reading Umberto Eco? – Fish seems to have painted himself into a corner.

Fish relies on a distinction between subject and object, but regarding *interpretability*, there seems to be exactly no clear distinguishing mark between object-text and interpretation-text. They are both opening themselves up for *interpretation*, that is, for simplification and falsification. The object-text, in all its supposed *passivity*, seems to be interpreting its own fictive world no less that the interpretation-text, in all its supposed *activity*. When reading a novel, we experience that texts interpret incessantly. They, for example, interpret human emotions, the remedial value of love, the serenity of solitude, the corrupting influence of power, man's relationship to his gods, etc. Some novels, plays, or poems even seem to interpret much more, and much more *interestingly*, than the critics that subject them to professional interpretation. Texts tend – within their fictive universes – to insert a text-segment, of which they subsequently carry out an interpretation by another text-segment (for example, one character suppresses a sly smile, which in turn gives another character the opportunity to elaborate on the meaning of that smile – in other words, *interpret* that smile). To Fish, texts do not interpret themselves, because "no text reads itself"; but it is closer to the mark to assert that fictional texts, exactly, have always been civilizational exercises in *interpretation*; for example, the interpretation of human behavior.

We may even extrapolate this objection, and venture the diametrically opposite assertion, "all texts read themselves." This assertion is only absurd if too squarely and empirically we understand, as the only possible framework for *interpretation*, the text and its reader as two entities necessarily opposing each other as subject to object. Phenomenologically speaking, all texts are always-already reading themselves. That is, they reach the reader partly interpreted, since they have built into their texture what we might call an *implicit interpreter* engaged in interpreting events happening in the text for the sake of easing the reader's understanding. Concrete examples on *implicit interpreters* could be the classical Greek chorus, the soliloquies in

Shakespeare, the inner monologues in psychological novels, or M's briefings of Bond in James Bond movies. This self-interpretive activity is in other words original and primary. The work of the implicit interpreter is what we might call the *primary interpretation* or the *proto-interpretation* of the text. It is the proto-interpretation that subsequent interpretations will have to take into account if they want to demonstrate an elementary understanding of the text. The existence of a proto-interpretation also puts up limits to a text's 'interpretability.' The primary interpretation becomes a measuring rod against which certain interpretations are ruled to be 'wrong' (in scare quotes – as odd, far-fetched, strange, or silly), or simply wrong (bluntly and without quotes – as misleading, incorrect, or false).

Now, also Fish emphasizes that interpretations can be 'wrong' – so we agree that interpretations can be 'wrong.' But to Fish, they are always 'wrong' in scare quotes, because they are wrong relative to the interpretative community as the stabilizing force.[87] Fish would say that an interpretation is wrong when there is no 'interpretative community' to take it seriously; it is wrong for conventional reasons. However, as the flip-side of this coin, one can always expect him to argue for the *possibility* of a *hypothetical* 'interpretive community' where the interpretation might be 'right.' On Fish's neo-Pragmatism, interpretations may be 'wrong,' but only in scare-quotes; thus, they can never be absolutely wrong, and therefore he has this odd tendency to argue *hypothetical* cases for their weird *possibility*. Therefore this typical double-strategy in much of his writing: *something that is conditionally wrong, is always possibly right*

---

[87] Fish's view has incited several objections; some of them he easily shrugs off; for example, the objection that if Fish were right, all interpretive activity would disintegrate into relativism and chaos. With no text-immanent meaning, the text is fundamentally destabilized, and all critical activity degenerates into a vicious relativism. Fish has responded by referring to the 'interpretative community' as the stabilizing force. All interpretations are exactly not permitted, he contends, because the *interpretative community* regulates interpretation; that is, it rules out some interpretations and rules in some others. The interpretive community becomes the final authority confirming or disconfirming interpretation. Fish's meta-criticism, therefore, cannot result in interpretive chaos and anarchy; it just sees textual stability constituted by another agency than the text itself, namely by the *community*.

5. Contingency and Narcissism of Human Knowledge

5.1. Recapitulating Nietzsche's Polysemous Notion of Truth

When Nietzsche asks himself the question *"Was ist also Wahrheit?"* his answer almost exclusively concerns truth only in one of the senses that we have addressed above: namely what above we called Truth$_2$; and here again especially the case where Truth$_2$ relates to concepts. We gave this notion of truth the formal expression, Truth$_{2C}$. In his interest for Truth$_{2C}$, *truth as illusion thanks to concepts*, Nietzsche has simultaneously lost sight of the other concepts of truth that he has been discussing. Let us recapitulate these different notions of truth, and give a full picture of the several incompatible concepts of truth introduced in Nietzsche's essay. We were able to count exactly three (or four) such notions.

First, the plainest notion, *truth as truthfulness*. It indicates the commonsensical fact that humans are able to be truthful or deceitful, sincere or insincere, tell the truth or tell a lie. Truth in this sense is a well-know phenomenon in communicative action, and it is senseless to debate its possibility, since it is contrived to debate the possibility of that which is and has always been the case. In this sense, we can say without hazard that Nietzsche 'believes in truth.' In this sense, he even believes in the celebrated 'correspondence theory of truth.' If I say 'this is a camel' and I point to a camel, then my statement corresponds to the state of affairs, and I have told the truth (although it is not an insight of great consequence). Nietzsche believes in this common standard like anybody else; and if for no better reason then because it is this concept of truth, which – according to his genealogical analysis – prompts or 'seduces' humans into the belief in an abstract concept of truth, invented thanks to the false inference: what is possible for humans, is possible for nature too.

Therefore, Nietzsche has a second notion of truth: *truth as illusion* (which is branching out in two, because truth can be illusion thanks to *perception*, and illusion thanks to *concepts*).[88] We erroneously believe that we

---

[88] In this sense, truth is and remains a 'human, all too human' construction. It is what we *call* truth, and what we *hold* to be true [*Fürwahrhalten*], but Truth (in the absolute sense) it is not. This does not necessarily have to throw us into despair; it may indicate a Nihilism, but in later writings, we can adopt different attitudes to Nihilism: a 'passive' for the despairing nihilist, and an active for the exuberant nihilist, who now realizes that he suddenly has the freedom to create. In the words of the present essay, man becomes a *künstlerisch schaffendes Subjekt* (WL, KSA 1, p. 883); in later works we read, for example: "One is much more of an artist than one realizes." (JGB 192, KSA 5, p.

are able to re-apply simple cases like the one above – 'this is a camel' where the camel is given in intuitive self-evidence – to other more complex cases like for example 'the Moon gravitates toward Earth' where by analogy, we think that we ought to account for 'the gravitational force' with the same ease as above; where by analogy 'the gravitational force' also ought to reveal itself in intuitive self-evidence. We erroneously believe that as well as *we* are able to be truthful, *nature* is also able to be truthful. But here, we have been seduced by commonsense, which serves us so well in communicative action. The gravitational force remains out of sight, and we are able to only detect its effects – or what we *interpret* to be its effects. That is, in *truth as illusion*, we assert universal truth-*candidates*, and suppress the fact that we remain glued to a world of appearances, which can never fulfill the inherently high aspirations associated to these 'candidates.' We remain thrown into a world of appearances; we walk around Schopenhauer's castle and make 'observations,' but further we cannot penetrate into 'things.'

Therefore, Nietzsche presupposes a third (or fourth) notion of truth: truth as *pure non-consequential truth*. This is a concept of truth we call metaphysical-speculative, as it is supposedly residing in or as the *thing-in-itself*. In the neo-Kantian paradigm of the nineteenth century, it seems unavoidable and virtually compulsory. Like the neurotic compulsively repeats the fictions of his trauma, the nineteenth century thinker cannot resist the magic spell of this notion of truth. It is presupposed in the thinking of Schopenhauer, Lange, and Nietzsche (in this his early essay), where it receives the peculiar double-status of both being inaccessible and practically worthless *and* providing an absolute transcendental standard by which to measure truths that are accessible and have practical value, if only locally. As such, it functions teleologically as a regulative idea for truth, and structurally, as a comparison-background on which to evaluate truth. Against this fictive-authoritative background, nothing survives as more than pale shadows; truth is 'illusion' only because seen in contrast to this background. However, the notion has not emerged out of nothing, and it is supported by powerful arguments, in themselves rigorous and convincing, suggesting for example that insofar as humans have cognitive limitations, consequently, also the knowledge they form of the world must be subjected to these cognitive limitations. In later writings, Nietzsche disengages himself from this metaphysical concept of truth and the intractable problems it generates. It will manifest itself in his repeated criticisms of the Kantian 'thing,' of the opposition 'thing' versus 'appearance,' and his attempts to answer the question that emerges out of these criticisms: If there is no 'thing,' what then?

---

114)

A table summarizes the three (or four) concepts of truth (with their definition, application, and context), as we find them in WL:

FORMS OF TRUTH	DEFINITION	APPLICATION	CONTEXT
TRUTH$_1$	Truth as truthfulness	Communicative action	Society
TRUTH$_{2P}$	Truth as illusion thanks to percepts	Perception	World
TRUTH$_{2C}$	Truth as illusion thanks to concepts	Conceptualization	Knowledge
TRUTH$_3$	Pure Truth	Thing-in-itself	Regulative Idea/Comparison background

5.2. Connecting 'Truth as Illusion' and the 'Logic of the Concept'

We now understand why truth is an illusion thanks to concepts; the concept has no longer any reference; it is a so-called 'sphere,' implying that in its essence it is 'gliding' and 'floating' rather than representing stability.

The self-present spatio-temporal world gave itself primarily as representation [*Vorstellung*] to animal and humans alike; but humans have secondarily evolved an ability to practice also reason [*Vernunft*] – this thanks to their linguistically mediated ability to form concepts. Thanks to this ability, they are able to detach themselves from the world as self-presently given 'now,' and organize the world into abstract schematic and classificatory systems that transcend all 'now'-perception. As Kant, Schopenhauer, and Nietzsche argue, the concept necessarily detaches itself from the perceptive image, because, as an abstract sign for a generic type, it cannot have any perceptive representation. The concept lures us away from the world of the self-presently present, and entices us to enter the abstract kingdom of schemes, tables, and classifications.

This has both painful and beneficial consequences: we have lost the immediacy of the self-presently given world, but we have found a way by which to simplify and abbreviate a world that is in itself too multifarious to be cognized. Thanks to this 'simplification,' we are in general able to 'think,' that is, we are able to move around (in "pure intuition") our abstract concepts in ever-new and surprising constellations. As such, the concept gives, on the one hand, our thinking direction and precision; on the other, however, it remains frustratingly 'open' and 'unstable,' partly because it is detached from perceptive representations, and is as such arbitrary in relation to the 'thing' it supposedly represent; and partly because in itself, it represents an open-ended universe of multiple 'components,' and may as such float off in different directions, depending on which of its multiple components one chooses to pursue in one's argument.

The conclusion must be that the meaning, the *truth*, we, thanks to the *concept*, produce of the world must also be open-ended and inconclusive. The doubly arbitrary concept becomes a logical foundation for interpretability; that is, in its inherent logical foundation, in its *essence*, Truth$_{2C}$ is arbitrary – therefore "an illusion." Interpretability comes about as an effect of the doubly arbitrary concept, that 'floats off' in various directions because it harbors this inherent paradox: as much as it gives our thinking direction and precision, it is essentially unstable and interpretable, and harbors as such the unavoidable potential of being exploited for religious, political, ideological, or just personal, expediencies.

5.3. A Clever, All-Too-Clever Animal

It seems that the human animal, this clever animal with its incomparable reason, has become too clever for its own good. One can at best only admire this enterprising animal, but one can no longer believe that it ever gets beyond the *fundamental language-dependency*, and that means ultimately, the *fundamental narcissism* of its epistemological project. When it looks self-indulgently at the world in front of it, it only sees – like Narcissus gazing into his pond – the world smiling back.

It is the narcissism of this project Nietzsche labels *antropomorphism*. All knowledge, in one way or other, is ultimately 'antropomorphic.' It is not necessarily understood and recognized as such, but researchers and scientists pursuing 'truth' do after all transform an indifferent world into a possible *human* form. In the *Nachlaß* it says:

> The philosopher does not seek truth, but the transformation [*Metamorphose*] of the world into man. He struggles to understand the world with self-consciousness. He struggles to achieve a s s i m i l a t i o n [*Er ringt nach assimilation*]: he is relieved, when he is able to lay out something as anthropomorphic. As well as the astrologer regard the world as serving the single individual, so the philosopher sees the world as serving man. (Nachlaß 1872-1873, KSA 7, 19[237])

This idea is repeated in WL: "In such truths, the researcher seeks essentially only the transformation [*Metamorphose*] of the world in man." The scientist becomes like "the astrologer who regards the stars as serving human beings, relating to their luck and suffering." [. . .] "His proceeding is to hold man as the measure of all things." (WL, KSA 1, p. 883).

Now, 'truth' – in the sense of *Truth$_{2C}$* – is in Nietzsche something one *produces in language*; the *sign* is indispensible for the expression of an experience, and nobody therefore avoid, what we have called, the *human interference* in what is still actual and objective observation. Like the bees build their bee-hives and the spiders spin their nets, also the human being makes constructions meant to serve their survival. They, however, build from a material far more delicate than both the wax of the bee and the silk of the spider, namely from concepts; that is to say, from nothing.

> One must admire man as a great genius of construction [*gewaltige Baugenie*], who succeeds in erecting infinitely complicated domes of concepts [*Begriffsdormes*] on unstable foundations that are like flowing water. In order to find foundational support, his constructions have to be, like a spiders web, so delicate that they can moved along by the waves, and so strong that they do not blow apart by the wind. As such a genius of construction, man raises himself far above the bees, because whereas the bee builds from wax gathered in nature, man builds from the far more delicate material of concepts, which he himself has to manufacture. In this he is truly admirable – but not because of his drive for truth, or of pure knowledge of things. (WL, KSA 1, p. 883).

Given that 'truth' is the result of a production-process, we no longer need to act so reverently and awestricken when it is beheld, because the manufactured item is identical to the blueprints with which one entered the production. "When somebody hides something behind a bush and then looks for it again at the same place and finds it there, there is in such seeking and finding not much to applaud. Yet, this is how we seek and find of 'truth' within our realm of reason [*Vernunft-Bezirkes*]." (WL, KSA 1, p. 883).

As such, we remain locked up in a circle that we cannot break out of. If we suppose that the Things-in-themselves are situated outside the circle, and we remain on the inside, then the progression from asserting a problem to solving it, is merely traversing the circumference of the circle. To ourselves the solution may look revelatory, but tacitly, we have only returned to the point from where we started. Our 'truth' is self-referentially referring back to our own *Vernunft-Bezirkes*, and is now merely an articulation of an image of ourselves projected outside and exteriorized. However, since the image has never before been articulated, it is not immediately recognizable as an image of ourselves. Truth, in the sense of Truth$_{2C}$, is therefore human, antropomorphic, and contains a healthy dose of narcissism.

CHAPTER 2

A Silent World

Nietzsche's Radical Realism:
World, Sensation, Language

> In the great silence [*Im grossen Schweigen*]. [. . .] Now everything is silent! The sea lies there pale and glittering, it cannot speak. The sky play its everlasting silent evening game with red and yellow and green, it cannot speak. The small cliffs and strips of rock that run down into the sea as if to find the place where it is most solitary, none of them can speak. This immense stillness [*ungeheure stummheit*], which suddenly intrudes upon us, is beautiful and terrible; the heart swells at it. [. . .] Ah, it is growing yet more still, my heart swells again: it is startled by a new truth, it too cannot speak, it too mocks when the mouth calls something into this beauty, it too enjoys its sweet silent malice. I begin to hate speech, to hate even thinking; for do I not hear behind every word the laughter of error?
> — Nietzsche: Morgenröte.[89]

> The world lies there complete — a golden shell/skin of everything good [*eine goldne Schale des Guten*]. But the creative spirit wants to create also what is complete: so it invented time — and now the world rolled away from itself, and rolled together again in large rings.
> — Nietzsche: Nachlaß 1882-83.[90]

> The world does not speak. Only we do.
> — Rorty: Contingency, Irony, and Solidarity.[91]

---

[89] Nietzsche: M 423, KSA 3, p. 259.
[90] Nietzsche: Nachlaß 1882-83, KSA 10, 5[1/266].
[91] Richard Rorty: Contingency, Irony, and Solidarity. Cambridge (Cambridge University Press), 1989; p. 6.

1. Introductions to and Descriptions of the Position

1.1. Nietzsche's Rejection of Idealism and Abstract Truth-Claims

Throughout a long epistemological tradition, culminating in Idealism, when we perceive the 'world,' we essentially perceive ourselves – or qualities and attributes of ourselves. Looking at the 'world' becomes like looking in a mirror mirroring ourselves. The human-world, self-other relationship is *really* – according to long treatises of ingenious argument – a human-human and a self-self relationship. The world as *other*, as *resistance*, as *appearance* is either (1) deceptive; *or* (2), it does not exist itself but only insofar as it is constituted by us; *or* (3), if it *does* exists in-itself, it has no bearings on us, because it is inaccessible, why the knowable world is again uniquely constituted *by-us* and *for-us*.

Whichever of these epistemological positions one picks – roughly representing Rationalism, Empiricism, and Kantianism – one notices a certain hostility towards the outside, a hostility that is immediately turned into an attempt to appropriate the outside as a projection of the inside; that is, as a part of *us*. In the newly produced *self-self* relationship between world and human, it becomes a preeminent task for the philosopher to explain how the first self in the relationship is identical to the second, how the flesh of the world is our flesh. The overwhelming perceptive intuition, which impresses upon the philosopher and the layman alike a sense of difference, is discarded as appearance, or perhaps just as strangely insignificant and trivial.

Throughout the epistemological tradition before Nietzsche, 'reality' is invariably the problem, and invariably the problem is solved by neutralizing the outside, alien, in-human, and indifferent world, by replacing it with a world humanized, a world for-us, a world interpreted. When the first terms in the epistemological dichotomies, *world* versus *human*, *other* versus *self*, *it* versus *us*, are canceled and reduced to the human, the self, the 'us,' it is in part justified by means of the truism that the world we perceive, is as perceived *by us* necessarily reduced to fit our perceptive capabilities (– we admittedly don't perceive, for example, electric and magnetic fields, as some animals). From this point it seems warranted to draw the conclusion that the world itself is unknown and inaccessible (Kant), or simply non-existent (Berkeley and Schopenhauer). It is from the entanglement in this *epistemological narcissism* (everything is in the final analysis *us*) that Nietzsche increasingly, and especially in later writings, tries to extricate himself – as we shall here try to demonstrate and argue.

It is clear that in his emerging epistemological program, Nietzsche is primarily reacting to Kant and Schopenhauer. Although he reveals his philosophical erudition by confidently referring to Descartes, Spinoza, Leibniz, Hume, Hegel, Feuerbach, Comte, and a variety of lesser known philosophers of his day, it is the arguments of Kant and Schopenhauer that are repeatedly rehearsed, as Nietzsche often – as least so in the *Nachlaß* material – brainstorms himself as to clarify the fallacies inherent in their major presuppositions. Two such major presuppositions are, first, the Kantian doctrine of the *thing-in-itself*, and secondly, Schopenhauer's interpretation of the thing-in-itself as *will*.[92]

---

[92] When Nietzsche, in numerous places around in the work, reiterates that 'there is no will,' it typically refers to Schopenhauer's notion of 'will.' If therefore Nietzsche's rejection of the 'will' – as the renowned philosopher of the 'will-to-power' – has had some commentators confused, it is because they do not appreciate the fundamental difference between Schopenhauer and Nietzsche's notions of will. This discrepancy is often reiterated in Nietzsche. "Philosophers are given to speaking of the will as if it were the best-known thing in the world; Schopenhauer, indeed, would have us understand that the will alone is truly known to us, known completely, known without deduction or addition. But it seems to me that in this case too Schopenhauer has done only what philosophers in general are given to doing; that he has taken up a p o p u l a r p r e j u d i c e and exaggerated it. Willing seems to me to be above all something c o m p l i c a t e d, something that is a unity only as a word." (JGB 19, KSA 5, p. 31-32). This objection to Schopenhauer is repeated in the late Nachlaß material: "Is 'will-to-power' a kind of 'will,' or is it identical to the notion 'will'? Does it mean as much as desire? Or command? Is it a 'will' as Schopenhauer understood it, i.e., as an in-itself of things [*An sich der Dinge*]? My proposal is that the 'will' of psychology so far is only an unjustified generalization, that this will d o e s n o t e x i s t a t a l l. [. . .] This is in the highest degree the case in Schopenhauer: what he calls 'will,' is merely an empty word." (Nachlaß 1888, KSA 13, 14[121]). *Schopenhauer's will* is merely an empty word. Nietzsche's succinct sentence, "We set up a word at the point where our ignorance begins, where we cannot see any further" (WM 482), is perfectly applicable to Schopenhauer's *will*. Schopenhauer's *will* is a genuinely metaphysical principle: an indivisible singularity, unconditioned by anything but conditioning everything; the reason why it cannot be intelligibly explained. *Nietzsche's will* by contrast – as will-to-power – is a result of a competition between forces engaged in a perpetual struggle against one another. Nietzsche's 'will' is therefore not an unmoved mover of everything, it is not the first link in a causal chain of beings, but emerges as the result of a struggle. As we shall see in more detail in *Chapters 3* and *4*, Nietzsche's 'will' is never a singularity, it always implies several *wills*. As the opportune constellation of forces, Nietzsche's 'will' materializes as just a local and temporary order of rank. Müller-Lauter has aptly pointed out that Nietzsche's 'will' is always conceived as an *organization* of quanta of forces: "*The* will to

To Nietzsche, there are only appearances and surfaces, and still, we are capable of producing knowledge of these appearances. It is now Nietzsche's sustained epistemological project to explain (1) *how* is knowledge being produced, and (2) *what* is knowledge in a world that is entirely superficial – that is, a world that is *not*, as surface, the cover of some deeper located 'truth,' and is *not* designed according to, and does not abide by, any anthropomorphic principles like Schopenhauer's *will*. Nietzsche's project is then an aspiration to explain how we conform an utterly de-humanized world to our own needs, a world that is essentially indifferent to *us*: our evaluations and our measurements. We stand in the midst of the world; we look into a night full of stars; there is in truth nothing but a surface, but at an early point in our civilizational development, we have started to 'see' 'constellations'; we have started to 'recognize' star-patterns *as* something; we have begun to 'know.' With a sense of relief, we have made the night familiar and human. "The humanization [*Vermenschlichung*] of nature – a construal according to us." (Nachlaß 1885, KSA 12, 1[29]).

It is in itself puzzling why humans have a compulsion to familiarize and label. As far as we know, it is a desire shared by no other animal, seemingly living just as well without it. Hence, adding to the two epistemological questions above (*how* and *what*), one might add as essential to Nietzsche's project the *anthropological-psychological* question: *why* do humans want knowledge in the first place; *why* this insistence on 'truth'?

As Heidegger too reminds us, it is not the case that in Nietzsche, 'there is no truth'[93] (although measured against the naked flesh of the world, this

---

      power is a manifold of forces that are mutually engaged in a struggle. Also *the* force, in Nietzsche's sense, can only be understood as unity in the sense of organization. Accordingly, the world is "a fixed, even expanse of power," it forms "a quantum of force." However, this quantum only exists in opposition to other quanta." Müller-Lauter: Über Werden und Wille zur Macht – Nietzsche Interpretationen I. Berlin, London (Walter de Gruyter), 1999; p. 40. Günter Abel talks appropriately about "Wille-zur-Macht-*Komplexe*." (In: Abel: Nietzsche: Die Dynamik des Willen zur Macht und die Ewige Wiederkehr. Berlin, New York (Walter de Gruyter), 1998).

[93] Heidegger has asserted that Nietzsche must necessarily presuppose the concept of truth as correctness, since insofar as truth *does not* conform to the world of becoming, it is because it cannot give a *correct* representation of this becoming world; consequently, presupposed is the notion of truth as correctness. A non-conforming truth, a truth that cannot grasp the flow of becoming, is now necessarily incorrectness, error, and 'illusion.' "Only if truth in its essence is correctness can it be *in*correctness and illusion according to Nietzsche's interpretation." (Heidegger, Martin: Nietzsche, v. III, "The Will to Power as Knowledge." Edited & translated by D. F. Krell. San Francisco

1. Introductions to and Descriptions of the Position 101

is still the case); it is rather the case that humans are basking in truths, with an insatiable appetite lapping up every possible candidate. In one context, and according to one definition, 'there is no truth'; in another context, according to another definition, since the dawn of civilization no notion has been pursued more persistently, no other concept has been so over-produced and over-promoted.[94] Nietzsche's three major questions, *how*, *what*, and *why*, are posed in order to come to an understanding of and to diagnose this situation. With these three questions, he wants to produce a knowledge of the production of knowledge, or, in other words, to produce a knowledge of 'truth.' What inevitably happens in inquiries that take their investigations such a step deeper is that the object they investigate can no longer claim of itself to be the first and primary condition. Inevitably, the object under investigation has been demoted and its significance reduced, also such sanctified and revered objects as 'truth.'

(HarperSanFrancisco) 1987, p. 64.) According to this interpretation of Heidegger's, Nietzsche misunderstands himself; as tacit presupposition, truth, seen as correspondence, is still controlling his writing. However, Heidegger also asserts that Nietzsche elsewhere criticizes exactly this concept. He notices, for example, that the concept of truth as conformity is usually by Nietzsche placed in quotation marks, implying, as he correctly sees, that Nietzsche as such quotes the notion from somebody else – i.e., he is commenting on a notion as it is handed down from the history of Western Thinking. "Nietzsche often expresses this thought pointedly and exaggeratedly in the quite misleading form 'There is no 'truth' (WM, 616). Yet, here too he writes truth in quotation marks. This 'truth,' according to its essence, is an 'illusion,' but, as illusion, a necessary condition of 'life.' So, is there 'truth after all? Certainly, and Nietzsche would be the last to want to deny that." (Heidegger, loc. cit., p. 66.). How Heidegger reconciles these two positions, I cannot speculate about here, but in the last statement, he would seem to be right. Only if we place a too high a premium on the concept of truth is there 'no truth.' I.e., if truth is understood as correspondence between proposition and thing (*adequatio intellectu et rei*), and given that the 'thing' is in constant change, then 'truth' as *being* must be of a categorically different nature than *becoming*, and it must necessarily represent 'falsely' the 'flux' (– like Van Gogh on his two-dimensional canvas represents 'falsely' the cypresses waving in the wind). *Stabilization* of the flux must have the character of production or creation, provisionally *added* to a world in flux, but not *discovered* in an unmovable and permanent world.

94 The position is not as inconsistent as it may sound. If there are *many* truths, there is no single truth as the absolute notion of truth philosophy traditionally has been pursuing. Compare to Günter Abel: "But when there are several truths (not several partial truths [*Teilwahrheiten*]), then there is exactly none." Abel: *Nietzsche*, loc. cit., p. 154.

Therefore, it may be befitting to offer a brief remark on a recurrent criticism of Nietzsche. Ever since the beginning of Nietzsche-reception, his interrogation of knowledge and 'truth' has been regarded, by various commentators, as self-defeating, and throughout the 20th century we have seen the following purportedly devastating objection being leveled at Nietzsche: 'If Nietzsche says there is no truth (and either one of two possible conclusions follows), (1) then this is also not true, or (2) then Nietzsche is contradicting himself since he asserts *as true* that there is no truth.' Today, the objection is usually introduced as 'the problem of self-reference.' (The often repeated objection has even filtered down as layman's knowledge; when the conversation falls upon Nietzsche, one can be sure that at some point somebody eventually delivers the fatal *coup de grâce*: '. . . but if Nietzsche says that there is no truth, then this is also not true!' Checkmate!) However, it is only when 'truth' is regarded as *unconditioned* (and this is exactly the premise in question) that Nietzsche's research-strategy can be seen as absurd, paradoxical, or self-defeating. On that traditional assumption, the truth Nietzsche produces on 'Truth,' is also 'Truth,' and he has done no more than confirming the absolute hegemony of 'Truth' (with a capital T). On that traditional assumption, 'Truth' is like an umbrella that encompasses all philosophical, even all human, discourse; one is preconditioned to think *about* this umbrella *under* the umbrella; thus, the project is in the last analysis futile. On that traditional assumption, 'Truth' is like a protective shield protecting philosophy against all kinds of ills, and it is therefore an assault against this metaphysical sanctuary when Nietzsche has the audacity to, so to speak, climb up on top of the umbrella, and begin describing it.

Nietzsche, the anti-idealist, wants to describe the means of production of 'Truth.' However, he realizes that his project is fraught with difficulties, because something as indispensable for his investigations as *language* has been formed under the projective shield of the umbrella; elementary metaphysics is repeated already in our syntax and grammar. There is only one way out of this dilemma; it is not perfect, but there is (*a priori*) no other: one is compelled to use the language one has inherited, ignoring provisionally – through some act of deliberate forgetfulness – that language in itself is permeated with *truth-claims*. There is no purely descriptive and value-free language in which to describe 'Truth'; there is no language *from nowhere*. Hence, Nietzsche – as he, in his revolutionary project, engages in answering his *how*, *what*, and *why* – is obliged to *assert* and *confirm* and *validate* and *substantiate* and *justify* whatever he says about 'Truth' as a human invention and construct.⁹⁵ If Nietzsche wants to communicate to us that 'there is no truth,' *he necessarily has to say it*. More precisely, in order to make any philosophical claims, he has to engage the illocutionary component of language we call 'assertion.' Since we know of no language without illocutionary components, the only *truly consistent alternative* to talking about non-existent, 'illusory' Truth would be (absurdly) *not to talk* about it. In other words, the purportedly devastating objection to Nietzsche has a single, distinct message (. . . perhaps its underlying and unspoken desire?): "Nietzsche! Shut up!"⁹⁶

---

⁹⁵ In his work on Nietzsche's theory of knowledge, Ruediger Grimm has described precisely this condition. Grimm reconstructs the traditional criticism of Nietzsche's 'there is no truth' in the passage, "Nietzsche tells us again and again that there is no truth. But by claiming that there is no truth, is he not in fact offering us another truth? Is he not claiming, in effect, that the statement 'there is no truth' is a true statement? And, if so, is this not a flagrant self-contradiction?" (Grimm, H. Ruediger: Nietzsche's Theory of Knowledge. Berlin, New York (Walter de Gruyter), 1977, p. 26). Heidegger refers in volume three of his *Nietzsche* to the same so-called 'self-referential problem,' rejecting in a mocking exposition the position: "Herr Nietzsche says that truth is an illusion. And if Nietzsche wants to be 'consistent' – for there is nothing like 'consistency' – his statement about truth is an illusion, too, and so we need not bother with him any longer." Heidegger: loc. cit., p. 25. The answer Grimm provides to his rhetorical question above is similar to the view I am indicating: "Nietzsche wishes to deny that there exists any absolute, unchanging standard for truth, but the language in which he is forced to express such an idea is already based upon the tacit metaphysical assumption that such a standard exists. [. . .] Obviously, using language to deny something which that language one is using already presupposes is a proceeding fraught with difficulties, and Nietzsche is very much aware of this." (Grimm, loc. cit., p. 28-29). Finally, essentially the same insight has been advanced by Jacques Derrida in the essay "Structure, Sign, and Play": "We have no language – no syntax and no lexicon – which is foreign to this history [of metaphysics]; we can pronounce not a single destructive proposition which has not already had to slip into the form, the logic, and the implicit postulations of precisely what it seeks to contest." Derrida, Jacques: Writing and Difference. Chicago (The University of Chicago Press), 1978, p. 280.

⁹⁶ It is bitter irony that Nietzsche eventually did in fact 'shut up.' Thus, granted the premise that one could only consistently criticize truth if also annihilating the truth-claims suffusing language, Nietzsche ended up *performing* a life in greater consistency with the *content* of his thinking than any philosopher before and after.

1.2. Juxtaposition to an Analytic Philosophical Approach.

The criticism of Kant's *thing* (= *X*) and Schopenhauer's *thing* (= *will*) is during the eighties still better articulated by Nietzsche; but before he reaches this point, he adopts in earlier writings – as several commentators have noted – positions similar to those of Kant and Schopenhauer. These positions we find represented in writings from the early seventies, especially in Nietzsche's unpublished so-called *Philosophenbuch* (explicitly in the essay *On the Truth and Lies in a Nonmoral Sense*; cf. previous *Chapter 1*[97]), and in *The Birth of Tragedy*.[98] Several commentators thus see a development in Nietzsche's thinking: from an early acceptance of the Kantian-Schopenhauerian thing-in-itself, to a later rejection of this *thing*; from an early acceptance of the dichotomy *truth versus appearance*, to a later rejection of this dichotomy.[99] Furthermore, some have argued that Nietzsche in this late position also relinquishes the often reiterated conception that *senses or concepts falsify* reality – a conception which has been labeled Nietzsche's 'falsification-thesis' (in Maudemarie Clark[100]), or 'error-theory' (in Martin Steven Green[101]).

In Clark's reconstruction of Nietzsche, 'the problem of self-reference' is once again seen as one of the most damning charges one can level against Nietzsche; however, since Clark is a sympathetic reader, her reading is meant to rescue Nietzsche from the supposed logical inconsistency it implies.[102] The strategy is, in brief, to restore to Nietzsche *a belief in Truth*. In

---

[97] These notes have recently been translated into English by Daniel Breazeale as *Philosophy and Truth*. See, Nietzsche: Philosophy and Truth: Selections from Nietzsche's Notebooks of the Early 1870's. New York (Humanities Books), 1999.

[98] Nietzsche: The Birth of Tragedy and Other Writings. Translated by R. Speirs. Cambridge (Cambridge University Press), 1999.

[99] This so-called *Kehre* in Nietzsche's thinking has been addressed by for example Alexander Nehamas (see, Nietzsche: Life as Literature. Cambridge, Mass. (Harvard University Press), 1985, p. 43); by Maudemarie Clark (see, Nietzsche on Truth and Philosophy. Cambridge: (Cambridge University Press), 1990, p. 95); by Michael Steven Green (see, Nietzsche and the Transcendental Tradition. Urbana, Chicago (University of Illinois Press), 2002, p. 9); or from a De Manian perspective, Wayne Klein in Nietzsche and the Promise of Philosophy. New York (State University of New York Press), 1997.

[100] Clark: Nietzsche on Truth and Philosophy, loc. cit.

[101] Green: Nietzsche and the Transcendental Tradition, loc. cit.

[102] Different stratagems are employed to argue that Nietzsche either cannot make inconsistent claims on 'Truth,' or if he actually does, he cannot mean it, because he then would end in "hopeless self-contradiction." "The problem with

pursuit of this strategy, Clark argues that Nietzsche ends up rejecting his early so-called 'falsification-thesis': he rejects in later works "as contradictory the very idea of a thing-in-itself."[103] and since this rejection to Clark implies that Nietzsche *confirms* 'truth,' she can draw the following conclusion: "He thereby lost all basis for denying truth, or for its equivalent, the thesis that human knowledge falsifies reality."[104] In greater detail, the argument runs as follows: If Nietzsche rejects the 'thing-in-itself,' 'truth' (understood as residing in this inaccessible 'thing') no longer hides itself; therefore, if no longer 'hidden,' it must be out in the open; therefore, if it is out in the open, it must *be there* for us all to see; therefore, senses no longer produce *false knowledge*, they produce *true knowledge*. Consequently: Nietzsche ends up rejecting the 'falsification-thesis,' finally confirming 'truth'!

> Because he [Nietzsche] treats logic and mathematics as formal sciences that make no claims about reality, Nietzsche must surely abandon his earlier claim that they falsify reality. He also rejects as 'miscarriage' doctrines, which can get off the ground only on the assumption that the senses deceive us, that they tell

---

this influential view of truth is that it seems to lead Nietzsche into hopeless self-contradiction. There is, first of all, the problem of self-reference. If it is supposed to be true that there is no truth, then there is apparently a truth after all; and if it is not supposed to be true, it seems that we have no reason to take it seriously, that is, accept it or its alleged implications." Clark, loc. cit., p. 3. The argument is introduced in several variations, for example in the discussion of Nietzsche's Perspectivism. If it is true that interpretations are only deriving from different 'perspectives,' and therefore always relative to beliefs, then Nietzsche again ends up in "hopeless self-contradiction," because he must deny the absolute truth of his own 'perspective.' If all perspectives or beliefs are equally true, then the belief we consider true is as true or false as the belief we consider false. Nietzsche criticism of Christian morality, for example – introduced with such fervor and zeal – is no truer than Christian morality. "But of all perspectives are of equal cognitive value, perspectivism then entails that every perspective falsifies – since each perspective induces us to consider beliefs false when they are actually as true as the ones we consider true. [. . .] However, this interpretation of Nietzsche's perspectivism trivializes his other claims. [. . .] Unless perspectivism implies its impossibility, there is every reason to assume that Nietzsche claims superiority for his own perspective. [. . .] Nietzsche's commitment to the genealogical perspective makes it seem ridiculous to deny that he does consider it cognitively superior to the religio-moral perspective." Clark, loc. cit., p. 139-40.

[103] Clark, loc. cit., p. 95.
[104] Clark, loc. cit., p. 95.

us only about 'appearance,' and not reality. [That is, senses do not deceive; they do not inform us merely on appearances – to Clack, *illusions*, but on reality, i.e., *true* reality. PB]. [. . .] These passages from TI [*Twilight of the Idols*] and A [*Antichrist*] contain no hint of the view that human truths, science, logic, mathematics, or causality falsify reality. Instead, they exhibit a uniform and unambiguous respect for facts, the senses, and science. [. . .] Nietzsche does not claim that knowledge falsifies in his last six works.[105]

Nietzsche's last six books therefore provide no evidence of this commitment to the falsification thesis, no reason to deny his commitment to the possibility of truth in science, nor to the truth of his own theories. Given his earlier works, this seems remarkable and in need of explanation. [. . .] My next section provides evidence that it took Nietzsche some time to realize that his denial of truth depended on the assumption of a thing-in-itself.[106]

Rejecting the 'falsification-thesis,' i.e., asserting as *false* that senses or concepts *falsify*, implies that senses or concepts are veridical accounts of 'reality.' Since, during Nietzsche's development, truth 'moves' from concealment to disclosure, and since 'true knowledge' is to Clark something we acquire qua *perception*, Nietzsche can no longer mean that senses falsify. So, after having rejected Kant's *thing*, Clark's Nietzsche arrives at his final position, according to which senses do not falsify and 'truth' is reconstituted or reestablished as the proper guarantor of philosophy.

Clark's reading is obviously meant to rescue Nietzsche from the reception of many recent 'relativistic' neo-pragmatist and post-modernist commentators, but also to appropriate him for, and re-situate him within the context of, Analytic Philosophy. However, the rescuing reading is fraught with problems, some of them obvious, others less so.

The implicit model for Clark's reading is in-itself questionable; Clark reads Nietzsche's development as a journey towards 'truth.' There are three stadia in this development: *First*, Nietzsche believes in the 'thing-in-itself,' and 'truth' is consequently inaccessible (in *The Brith of Tragedy* and *On the Truth and Lies in an Extra-moral Sense*); *second*, he rejects the notion of the 'thing-in-itself,' but continues *inconsistently* to believe that 'truth' is inaccessible (in work up till and including *Beyond Good and Evil*); *third*, he rejects the notion of the 'thing-in-itself,' and arrives to his final *consistent* position, 'truth' is accessible (from *The Genealogy of Morals* onwards; the "last six works"). In this narrative, 'truth' becomes an entity with a movement: first, it hides itself in the thing-in-itself, then gradually it moves out

---

[105] Clark, loc. cit., p. 105.
[106] Clark, loc. cit., p. 109.

of hiding and manifests itself in the open. Contemplating this narrative, one wonders that insofar as 'truth' is supposed to mean 'true or positive knowledge of the world,' how it could possibly be seen as residing in Kant's thing-in-itself in the first place. Kant's *Ding-an-Sich* was never residence for 'true knowledge,' since to Kant 'true knowledge' could never be generated by consulting something that per definition is inaccessible. 'True knowledge' is rather generated by imposing on the world principles formed by the transcendental subject (cf. Kant's famous statement: "Reason – has insight only into what it itself produces according to its own plan."[107]) However, the understanding of Kant is obviously crucial to Clark, since according to her master-argument, as long as Nietzsche believes in the thing-in-itself, true knowledge is inaccessible; but as soon as Nietzsche rejects the thing-in-itself, true knowledge is accessible again. Everything hinges of Nietzsche's initial acceptance, then non-acceptance, of the Kantian *thing*.

On an explicit level of Clark's reading, the 'final position' that is assigned to Nietzsche is contradicted by so many explicit passages that one is tempted to say that it is refuted by the entire textual corpus of Nietzsche.[108]

---

[107] Kant: Critique of Pure Reason. Translated by W. Pluhan. Indianapolis, Cambridge: (Hackett Publishing Company), 1996, "Preface" Bxiii; p. 19.

[108] In general, although also Analytic commentators come in shades and degrees of hermeneutic sensitivity, often, when Analytic philosophers explain Nietzsche's epistemological views, the resulting representations of Nietzsche's texts appear lacking in detail and precision. We do not discern much commitment to philological exactitude. My suspicion is that the main methodological device of the Analytic commentator, the syllogism, is ill-suited to represent complexity; the complexity, for example, of the context-dependent 'floating meanings' of Nietzschean concepts. Since the syllogism gives us only a *linear* and *diachronic* representation of propositions that remains self-identically the same, complexity within such a linear logic must necessarily read as contradiction or self-contradiction. Now – depending on the commentator's allegiances – it becomes the undertaking to resolve or underscore 'Nietzsche's contradictions.' In sympathetic approaches, the project is to find a syllogistically satisfying 'fit' for Nietzsche within the formal universe of Analytic philosophy. Nietzsche's text is no longer a text, but an assemble of a few well-known philosophical positions and set-problems; reading him becomes a question of navigating him in and between these set-problems as they stand in some conventional logical relationship to one another. This, indeed, is a perilous odyssey for the Analytic philosopher, committed as he or she is to an inventory of concepts (Truth, Fact, Objectivity, Reason, Commonsense, etc.) that usually only draws scorn from Nietzsche. Dangers lurk everywhere, and one asks oneself what possibly motivated the Analytic philosopher to embark on this journey in the first place.

What does it mean that Nietzsche in his last two years of writing, his last six works, purportedly ends up rejecting his 'falsification-thesis' in the sense indicated above? – It can only mean that Nietzsche completely reverses the direction of his essential thinking! Now, since the falsification-thesis is false, senses and concepts no longer falsify, simplify, or interpret; now 'truth' is no longer an 'illusion,' since there is a one-to-one relationship between world and perception, as well as between perception and proposition. Ultimately, according to the 'final position,' *the proposition communicates true knowledge as experienced in non-falsifying perception.*[109] Nietzsche purportedly makes this complete U-turn in his thinking, but without a word of explanation; this is truly, as Clark says, "remarkable and in need of explanation." Not only does Nietzsche not address this radical change of mind, but in his *Nachlaß* (especially), he is even so conceited as to continue his old theory – an 'old theory' that oftentimes reads like a critical comment on Clark's Nietzsche.

> Man seeks 'truth': a world that does not contradict itself, does not deceive, does not change; a t r u e world – a world in which man does not suffer: from contradiction, deception, change – the origins of suffering! Man does not doubt that such a world, as it should be, exists. [Consequently], he has to pursue the path that leads to it. [. . .] The conviction [*Glaube*] that the world, as it should be, *is*, really exists, is the conviction of the unproductive, w h o d o e s n o t w a n t t o c r e a t e t h e w o r l d as it should be. He assumes it is present [*vorhanden*], and searches for the means and manners by which to reach it. – ' T h e W i l l t o T r u t h ' – as the powerlessness [*Ohnmacht*] o f t h e w i l l t o c r e a t i o n. (Nachlaß 1887, KSA 12, 9[60]).[110]

---

[109] This view announces an epistemology, which seems to best conform to Francis Bacon's epistemological optimism from *The New Organon*. Given careful observation of the world as it is, and avoiding certain treacherous 'idols,' i.e., illusions that lead us astray in our investigations (language being one of them), we are potentially all capable of producing true knowledge of the world. Applying this epistemology to Nietzsche has, to my knowledge, never been contemplated before. One has typically compared Nietzsche to modern epistemologists like Feyerabend and Kuhn. Habermas, Rorty, and (for obvious reasons) Foucault have all had an inclination to see Nietzsche as foreshadowing certain aspects of their own epistemological programs. One might also suggest that Nietzsche may be seen as anticipating aspects of Niels Bohr, Henri Poincaré, or Karl Popper's theories of knowledge.

[110] Also from the late *Nachlaß* material we read: "It is of cardinal importance that we abandon t h e t r u e w o r l d. She is the great distruster [*Anzweiflerin*] and value reducer [*Wertverminderung*] o f t h e w o r l d t h a t w e a r e: She is the so far most dangerous a t t e m p t [*Attentat*] on life." (Nachlaß 1888, KSA

1. Introductions to and Descriptions of the Position

So says Clark: in his last six works, Nietzsche ends up confirming 'truth'! But in the notes from Spring, 1888, Nietzsche is preparing a chapter for the work that, in the *Nachlaß*, he entitles sometimes *Der Wille zur Macht*, sometimes *Umwerthung aller Werthe*. According to several outlines, the chapter was to be called *Der Wille zur Wahrheit*. In these sketches, we encounter the repetition of positions that he has been advancing during the eighties. We read for example:

> The claim, that t r u t h e x i s t s, and that there is an end to ignorance and error, is one of the greatest existing seductions.
> [...]
> – it is more comfortable to obey than to prove . . . It is more flattering to think "I have the truth" than to peek around in the dark . . .
> – first and foremost: it appeases, it gives comfort, it alleviates life – it 'improves' the c h a r a c t e r, insofar as it m i n i m i z e s m i s t r u s t . . .
> 'The peace of mind,' 'the calm of consciousness,' mere inventions that are possible only under the presupposition, that t r u t h exists.
> (Nachlaß 1888, KSA 13, 15[46]).

> Chapter: the Will to Truth
> [...]
> the methodology of truth c a n n o t be found in truth as motive, but in p o w e r as motive, in a want-to-become-superior [*Überlegen-sein-wollen*].
> h o w does truth prove itself? Through the feeling of increased power (a "certainty-belief" [*Gewißheit-Glaube*]) – through its usefulness – through its indispensability – in b r i e f, through **advantages**
> namely, presuppositions concerning how a truth s h o u l d b e in order to be recognized by us
> but this is p r e j u d i c e: a sign that shows that it is not at all about t r u t h . . .
> [...]
> why knowledge? why not rather deception? . . .
> what one wanted, was always belief, – and n o t t h e truth . . (Nachlaß 1888, KSA 13, 15[58]).

Here, it cannot help to argue, as Clark tentatively suggests in her introduction (and many commentators, especially from the Anglo-Saxon tradition, have suggested less tentatively[111]), that the *Nachlaß* is inferior source ma-

---

[111] 13, 14[103]).
Brian Leiter – in his *Nietzsche on Morality*. London, New York (Routledge), 2002) – makes a similar claim. Leiter reports that Nietzsche should have expressed a wish to have his notebooks burned; readers of these notebooks are

terial, and that only the published work deserves consideration. It cannot be the case that Nietzsche in his *thinking soliloquies* manifests himself as one philosopher, but as soon as he puts the final touches on a manuscript for publication, transforms himself into an entirely different philosopher. Nothing could account for such a radical transformation of a written corpus other than magic or divine intervention. (A radical transformation of a philosophical position would only require *other* thinking soliloquies, *other* unpublished sketches, which we do not find in Nietzsche's *nachgelassene* work.) And even *if* (hypothetically) a radical distinction existed between published and unpublished material, still, we would have no sure criteria of demarcation by which to decide whether Nietzsche's published work is a more authentic expression of 'Nietzsche' than is his *Nachlaß*.[112]

1.3. An Outline of the Position.

Although we see Clark's commentary as designed to appropriate Nietzsche for (a particular branch of) Analytic Philosophy, still, it raises some pertinent questions regarding Nietzsche's ontology and epistemology. Its thrust to understand the status of reality, sensation, and knowledge in Nietzsche, in a reversionary interpretation that tempers and qualifies some of the recent radical (neo-idealistic) accounts of Nietzsche, is fundamentally interesting. Even if we see problems with this reading, it is fertile enough to give us a polemic point of departure for outlining an alternative reading, which we shall here summarize, and in the remainder of the essay elaborate and substantiate.

There is no doubt that Nietzsche, relatively early, discards the notion of Kant's thing-in-itself. Already in *Menschliches, Allzumenschliches* we read that the thing-in-itself is worthy only of "Homeric laughter" (MA I, 16, KSA 2, p. 38),[113] and in statements from *Morgenröte, Die fröhliche Wissenschaft, Jenseits von Gut und Böse, Götzen-Dämmerung,* and the *Nachlaß*

---

consequently in violation of Nietzsche's personal wishes. I don't know where Nietzsche have expressed such a wish, but I understand that if the unpublished material is invalid, then Nietzsche's reported 'wishes' would be *utterly* invalid.

[112] We shall not at this point go deeper into the Nachlaß-problematics in Nietzsche; for a balanced account, one may refer to Müller-Lauter: Über Werden und Wille zur Macht – Nietzsche Interpretationen I. Berlin, London (Walter de Gruyter), 1999, pp. 28-30.

[113] Nietzsche: Human, All too Human, translation R. J. Hollingdale Cambridge (Cambridge University Press), 1996.

from the Eighties,[114] we encounter time and again the rejection of *thing-in-itself* and *true vs. apparent*. However, this rejection oftentimes comes *alongside* the profession of falsifying and arbitrary sense-perceptions. Up through the eighties till his last years of writing, Nietzsche continues to refer to deceptive senses in a number of contexts, while we also see him dismissing, in other contexts, the notion as philosophical nonsense. In the latter position senses do *not* deceive, but apprehend the world in its self-manifestation – this is by Clark seen as Nietzsche's conclusive position, but as such, it appears to be only half the truth. The task must be to understand, rather, in which sense *senses deceive*, and in which sense *senses do not deceive* (however frustrating such an apparently open contradiction may be).[115] Furthermore, even if senses are redeemed as adequate instruments for apprehending the world, this *still* does not entail that Nietzsche has abandoned his 'falsification-thesis' completely, because *concepts*, in any circumstance, are guilty of falsification.

When senses *do* deceive, they deceive us about – what seems plain – 'reality'; but the simplicity of this statement is deceptive. Clark believes that insofar as senses deceive (in Nietzsche's 'early position'), then 'reality' must be inaccessible, and when they no longer deceive (in Nietzsche's 'final position'), then 'reality' must be immediately accessible for knowledge. This conception may seem straightforward, but in our reading it misunderstands, at the least, Nietzsche's notions of 'deception' and 'reality.'

One may say for a start that senses do not only deceive us about *what we see*; more profoundly, they deceive us in *how we see 'what we see.'* What *we see* is the termination of a process, by which an apparatus distorts im-

---

[114] All references to the German work are from Nietzsche: Sämtliche Werke: Kritische Studienausgabe, edited by G. Colli & M. Montinari. Berlin, New York (Walter de Gruyter), 1980. The English translations consulted are the following: Daybreak, translated by R. J. Hollingdale. Cambridge (Cambridge University Press), 1997. The Gay Science. Translated by W. Kaufmann. New York (Vintage), 1974; and The Gay Science, translated by J Nauckhoff. Cambridge (Cambridge University Press), 2001. Beyond Good and Evil, translated by J. Norman. Cambridge (Cambridge University Press), 2002. The Will to Power, edited by W. Kaufmann; translated by J. R. Hollingdale & W. Kaufmann. New York (Vintage Books) 1968.

[115] To find a deliberate and explicit solution to these problems in Nietzsche's own texts appears to be impossible (although I believe it is possible go reconstruct a solution). Rereading Nietzsche's *Nachlaß* from the eighties (the last five volumes in Colli & Montinari's standard edition), I have at no point come across a definitive and conclusive explanation of these senses that apparently are sometimes 'deceptive,' sometimes not.

pressions arriving from the exterior world. *How we see* has thus always-already falsified *what we see*, because *what we see* has had to pass through a "simplification-apparatus," a "filtration-device," before properly seen (more about these two Nietzschean notions below). What we therefore *see* in Clark's so-called 'non-deceptive' perception is already stamped with the limitations of our perceptive apparatus; or, to put it differently, 'non-deceptive perception' is not an available option. This implies that whenever we see something, this something has been through a structuring process (the so-called 'how' of seeing), which is indispensable, and, moreover, that 'access to reality' is necessarily access to a *falsified reality*. This may sound like high philosophical speculation, but it has been common knowledge in contemporary neuroscience for several years.[116]

We see 'reality' as we best can! But what arrives to us as conscious perception is, according to Nietzsche, simplified, thus falsified, thus interpreted. As such, one must now assume that 'Reality,' strictly speaking, must be different from what announces itself as *perceived reality*. In Nietzsche, as well as in the tradition, this 'Reality' is usually described as 'chaos' or 'becoming.' Heidegger is inclined to talk about chaos; Eugen Fink, Ruediger Grimm, and Müller-Lauter often speak of a 'world of becoming.'[117] In any case, we are addressing a relationship between form-

---

[116] It is relevant to relate Nietzsche to the findings of a new generation of cognitive- and neuro-scientists such as Antonio Damasio, Daniel Dennett, and Mark Solms. If for example Damasio in his recent *Looking for Spinoza* has labeled Spinoza a 'proto-biologist' – since anticipating recent discoveries about mind and body – one may well contend that an even more obvious candidate for that label might be Nietzsche. In this context, it is also worth mentioning that Günter Abel, in a recent essay from Nietzsche Studien, has made comparative analyses between neuroscience and Nietzsche's positions on perception, mind, and consciousness. To my knowledge, it is the first time anybody has highlighted this relationship. It thus comes across as pioneering work that may well inaugurate a new direction for current Nietzsche-reception, offering us the opportunity to appraise, with much more theoretical gravitas, Nietzsche as a precocious early philosopher of brain, mind, and consciousness. (See Abel, Günter: "Bewußtsein – Sprache – Natur. Nietzsches Philosophie des Geistes." In Nietzsche-Studien, Bd. 30. Berlin, New York: (Walter de Gruyter), 2001, pp. 1-43).

[117] Heidegger, Fink, Grimm, and Müller-Lauter usually talk about only one world of chaos or becoming, which is, given various will-to-power processes, stabilized into a world of being, *or rather*, into several *worlds* of being (since the perspectival character of interpretations would seem to grant us several *interpreted* worlds). However, the world of *becoming* is always discussed in *the singular*. Fink, for example, speaks of "*the* fluctuating flow of life [*Le-*

giving sensations and a form-less fleeting world of becoming. ("Masses in movement and nothing else," says Freud less than ten years after Nietzsche, referring to an 'exterior world' impinging itself on our sense-organs, but without yet having penetrated into our memory systems, thus without being recognized as *so and so*.[118]) These 'fleeting masses in movement' is 'Reality' in the strictest sense, but as such, 'reality' does not *by itself* opens itself up for knowledge; it is not like a cornfield just waiting to be harvested. If some unfortunate fool had 'immediate access to reality' in this sense, he would be suffering from the severest psychopathological condition imaginable. These fleeting masses of becoming *are being opened* by the sense-apparatus, for sensation; they do as such nothing by themselves. They are certainly *there*, but they do not perform processes that have *us* as their final purpose. They *give* as such nothing. It is in the very *opening of 'Reality'* that senses 'falsify.'

In the strictest sense, senses are falsifying thanks to our specific perceptive designs. When Nietzsche refers to these specific perceptive designs, he often speaks of an *Optik*, and sometimes of a *menschliche Optik* – a phrase

---

bensflut], [. . .] *the* stream of becoming, *the* ceaseless to-and-fro of its drift; there is nothing enduring, unchanging, permanent – *everything* is in flux." Fink: Nietzsches Philosophie. Stuttgart, Berlin (Verlag Kohlhammer), 1960. p. 163; my italics. At this point I modify the tradition, and suggest that much in Nietzsche's texts is easier to read, and simpler to understand, if *the world* of becoming is (abstractly) seen as *two* (cf. below): an Ur-ground and a Human ground, since these 'grounds' are subject to two *fundamentally different* simplification-processes. – To express the view with complete simplicity: our eyes are engaged in one kind of simplification; our language is engaged in another kind of simplification.

[118] As we shall see also Nietzsche be claiming, Freud believes that originally we receive impressions only as *quantities*, which are subsequently transformed, in his neurological apparatus, into *qualities*. At this point, we shall not go into detail with Freud's neurological conception of the psyche, since we return to that discussion in *Chapter 4*, but it is interesting to note that to Freud the 'external world' *beyond* or *before* conscious perception is explicitly conceived as *a world of becoming*; in Freud's words: "Consciousness gives us what are called quality-sensations, which are different in a great multiplicity of ways and whose difference is distinguished according to the relations with the external world. Within this difference there are series, similarities, and so on, but there are in fact no quantities in it. [. . .] Where do qualities originate? Not in the external world. *For out there . . . there are only masses in motion and nothing else.*" Freud: Project for a Scientific Psychology; Standard Edition, v. I. Translated & edited by J. Strachey. London (The Hogarth Press), 1966, p. 308; my italics.

that seems to have been consistently, but misleadingly, translated into the English, 'human perspective.' Optics and perspective are of course two different things. *Human optics* refers to our faculty of sight, our visual perception; thus, we speak of the mechanics of our eyes, enabling us to perceive things in depth; three-dimensionally; shades of lightness and darkness; colors; movement and rest, etc. To translate *menschliche Optik* by *human perspective* waters down the notion (it might also suggest a science-phobic translation, since the notion now refers to various points of view, various ideological stances, that humans apply to intellectual, existential, cultural, or religious issues). (i) *Optics* designates the mechanical designs of our eyes; *perspective* suggests individual idiosyncrasies underpinning opinions. (ii) *Optics* belongs in Biology and Anatomy; *perspective* belongs in the Humanities. (iii) We are free to choose between *perspectives*, but no one has the freedom to choose between *optics*.

Discussions of whether Nietzsche means that 'everybody are entitled to their own perspective'; or whether 'there are as many of them as there are individuals'; or whether he can mean that 'all perspectives are equally good' (without degrading his own 'perspective,' etc.) are completely superfluous if, or rather *when*, 'perspective' means 'optics.' It is also immediately obvious that there can be no *neutral perspective* in the sense of a *neutral optics* (a notion that does not even begin to make sense – an eye that is not species-specific is an eye that has never evolved; a *neutral eye* is a nonsense and an absurdity).

Therefore, if it is Nietzsche's contention that we falsify 'reality' thanks to our human optics, it is hardly possible to disagree. As such, we see masses in movement and becoming *on our terms*, i.e., our human optics narrow down a ground that we know is perceived differently by other animals – having different perceptions of, for example, space and time, or perhaps none at all. as such, we live as such on what I will call an 'Ur-ground' – as the ground we share with all perceiving creatures, but which we form and shape according to our exclusive designs, our 'human optics.' The Ur-ground *itself* is *being opened* by an indefinite number of creatures, seeing it according to their specific perceptive designs; we, however, *open 'reality'* according to our own perceptive designs. The Ur-ground is therefore an infinite expanse of possibilities, but when we open this expanse according to our human possibilities, we create a human horizon, which becomes the world for us. In contrast to the Ur-ground, I shall label this human horizon, the 'Human ground.'

In order to express the distinction between *Ur-ground* and *Human ground* more succinctly, we might say that the Ur-ground is the ground that is open for *all possible perception*, while the human ground is open only for *possible human perception*. Since it is clear that *all possible perception* includes humans only as a single point (more about 'points' is just a moment) within this ocean of possibilities, humans must inevitably 'falsify' the Ur-ground. Against the Ur-ground, falsification is a condition and an ontological given. The Human ground is now a single horizon, a single 'point,' on the Ur-ground; it designates the world as we see and know it, the world according to, for example, our three-dimensional time and space perception.

Now, if necessarily our senses 'falsify' the Ur-ground, what do our senses do to the Human ground? – Senses 'falsify' also this ground, but for somewhat different reasons. We 'falsify' the Ur-ground because our perceptive design is unique (we have three-dimensional vision, color-perception, etc.), but we falsify the Human ground, because we cannot process the overload of information made available *within* our perceptive horizon.[119] Thus, to Nietzsche, the problem is never that there is *no reality* (but 'only interpretations,' as current academic fashion often stipulates); the problem is that there is always *too much reality*. To deal with this abundance, we have evolved a mental apparatus that reduces and simplifies these overloads. We have evolved something we might call a *reality-defense*, i.e., certain defense-mechanisms that allow us to be selective while scanning the exterior world according to our interests and survival-benefits.[120] What ex-

---

[119] Even if the Ur-ground has been considerably narrowed down by human perception, the human ground is still conceived as a world of becoming, and sensations falsify this ground as well. We notice in Nietzsche the promotion of an idea, which may at first seem counter-intuitive, but which is in fact in good accordance with modern science: complexity never stops. If the Ur-ground is unfathomable as an expanse of possibilities where we are, so to speak, only specks of dust, our speck of dust is no less complex than the expanse itself. Complexity always remains an unspecified *constant*, however much we narrow down a field. If, for example, we simplify our speck of dust according to our mental apparatus, this apparatus is as complex as everything above. Our utterly *superficial* world is *also* infinitely *deep*. – It even occurs to me that the infinite depth of the world is a function of its utter superficiality; but at this point I shall not try to explain why this must be the case!

[120] Compare to Werner Stegmaier: "In the ongoing dialogue between our mind and the surrounding world, it is not primarily about taking possession of as much information as possible, but *on the contrary to limit, as much as possible, the impinging overflow of information*, and only allow action-relevant information access to consciousness. The simplification- and abbreviation-apparatus, as Nietzsche describes thinking, must therefore be organized as an "inhibition-apparatus" ["*Hemmungsapparat*"]." Stegmaier, Werner: Nietzsches 'Genealogie der Moral.' Darmstadt (Wissenschaftliche Buchgesellschaft), 1994, p. 134; my italics. Also of relevance is Stegmaier's

actly these defense-mechanisms are and how they work, Nietzsche tries – with his formidable philosophical intuition – to determine, but since he is well ahead of advances that will later be made in linguistics, and in the theories of mind and consciousness, his thinking on the issue remains a torso. He realizes, however, that our memory-systems – and closely related to memory, language – must be accountable for these necessary defenses. Our sensations are like tentacles shooting out and being withdrawn in order to test snippets of a dangerous world. In this *reality-testing*, sensation constantly consults memory in order to cross-check a current sensation against the memory of an identical sensation (the mechanism for this cross-check or testing we shall describe in detail in *Chapter 4*).

The overflow of impressions that as 'exterior reality' impinges and invades the virgin, still unprepared, sensual system, I will below describe as *hyper-reality*. I suggest this neologism[121] since the simpler 'reality' has become so highly inflated, therefore useless, that it is virtually impossible to guess what people are talking about when they refer to 'reality.' 'Reality' refers sometimes to Kant's, sometimes to Plato's, reality; sometimes to the world of becoming; sometimes to perceived reality, etc.

With this notion in hand, I shall address the interesting issue that Clark in her Analytic account is engaged in promoting as Nietzsche's final position. Does Nietzsche think, by any chance, that 'senses do not deceive'? In my reformulation, is it possible to perceive *hyper-reality*? Is it possible to shut down consciousness, and just *see*? (– Within the vistas of current neo-pragmatic and post-modernist thinking: is access to a 'language-independent reality' an available option?) We can obviously not suspend our perceptive designs, and we have as such no perceptive access to the so-called Ur-ground (to put it forcefully and in paradox: we cannot see without eyes!). The question is therefore: is it possible to suspend the defenses we normally put up when we orient ourselves on our Human ground?

As a first provisional, and somewhat simplified, answer, I suggest, that insofar as the Human ground is 'falsified' and 'interpreted' thanks to language, thereby made conscious and communicable, we are in fact capable of suspending consciousness and short-circuiting certain components of our mental system. When we do, we see – as in a blank or empty stare – a muted reality lying there in the presence of itself. In this mode of seeing, we reduce our humanity, and deliberately approach animal stupidity – which, in

---

article: "Weltabkürzungskunst. Orientierung durch Zeichen" (in Simon, Josef (ed.): Zeichen und Interpretation. Berlin (Surhkamp Verlag), 1994).

[121] The notion I have also seen in Babich, Babette E.: Nietzsche's Philosophy of Science. New York (SUNY Press), 1994; but used somewhat differently.

the first place, was always our ontogenetic residual. Reading Nietzsche with the 'suspended attention' of a psychoanalyst, it escapes nobody that he often displays the temptation and desire to access an 'exterior world' in non-conscious and pure perception, as what would seem to be the fascinating entrance into the self-presence of the present. However, this mode of perception – since it presupposes ideal suspension of consciousness – could offer us no promise of access to positive knowledge of the exterior world (as is Clark's contention). On the contrary, it at best indicates the adoption of a purely *aesthetic attitude* in which the subject indulges in the *pleasures of seeing*: with eyes wide open, absorbing, assimilating, *affirming* everything; with eyes wide open, sounding an emphatic '*Yes*' to the eternity (or more precisely, the *timelessness*) of the self-present. Since everything in this mode returns to itself as self-identity, there is no assertion of difference, and hence no production of knowledge.

2. Substantiation and Development of Position

2.1. Ur-Ground and Sensation.

In the following quote from the *Nachlaß*, included also in *Der Wille zur Macht*, the dichotomy 'true vs. apparent' world is again rejected, and then follows a speculation on what constitutes appearance after the 'true' world is annihilated. The result of the speculation is the proposal of *two worlds*: (1) *one apparent world* that serves our practical needs; a world calculable; a world arranged and simplified, as such "perfectly true for us"; (2) *another world* beyond our practically arranged life-world; a world not reduced to our own being; a world extending itself beyond us, but still not understood as identical to the world 'in-itself'; the world I have been labeling the *Ur-ground*.

> Will to Power as Knowledge
> Critique of the concept 'true and apparent world.'
> of these, the first is a mere fiction, constructed of entirely fictitious entities.
> 'Appearance' in itself belongs to reality; it is a form of its being; i.e.
> in a world where there is no being [*Sein*], a calculable world of i d e n t i c a l cases must first be created from a p p e a r a n c e s : [in] a tempo at which observation and comparison are possible, etc.
> 'Appearance' is an arranged and simplified world, at which our p r a c t i c a l instincts have been at work: it is perfectly true for us; namely insofar as we l i v e, are able to live in it: p r o o f of its truth for us –

> The world, apart from our condition of living in it, the world that we have not reduced to our being, our logic, and psychological prejudices
> does not exist as a world 'in-itself'
> it is essentially a world of relationships [*Relations-Welt*]: it has, under certain conditions, a different look [*Gesicht*] from each and every point [*Punkt*]; its being [*Sein*] is essentially different in every point; it presses upon every point, every point resists it – and the sum of these is in every case quite incongruent.
> The measure of power [*Maß von Macht*] determines the nature [*Wesen*] of the other measure of power; in what form, force, constraint it acts or resists.
> Our particular case is interesting enough: we have produced a conception in order to be able to live in a world, in order to perceive just enough to endure it.
> (Nachlaß 1888, KSA 13, 14[93]).

We are introduced to two cases, two aspects of the world described as respectively 'being' and 'becoming' (we are obviously not introduced to two distinct and separate worlds, but to two aspects under which we live in, or stand out in, one single world). The world of 'being' is the world stabilized by us in order to satisfy our practical needs. It is reminiscent of the world that the late Husserl would describe as 'life-world.' It provides us with our historical, social, cultural memory and identity. It is the world I shall describe – referring to Structural Linguistics below – as our *linguistically mediated life-world*. It is primarily (but *not* exclusively) *language* that makes this world habitable to humans.

The world of 'becoming' is much more difficult to describe, and in this quotation, Nietzsche offers us only a *cosmology*. We learn that it is a world of relationships of "points"; that its "being" is different from one point to another, with a different "look" from every point; that "it presses" upon every point, while every point also resists pressure; that the sum of these pressures are in "every case" incongruent. How are we to understand and make sense of this 'theory'? – We are apparently introduced to an extreme relativism, where each 'point' in cosmos sees the rest from its own perspective, or perhaps rather, *optics*. There is in this cosmos, like later in Einstein, neither absolute space nor absolute time, but only relationships of 'points' warping time and space. Every 'point' exerts a pressure on its environing universe, and is being 'pressurized' by a counter-pressure that is *not congruent* to the pressure the point exerts. If a 'point' can be seen – in the biological universe – as an organism, the organism puts a pressure on the environment, and is countered with a pressure of the environment. The incongruity between the strengths of the forces in the action (of the organism) and the reaction (of the environment) would account for the organism's survival and ability to grow; its so-called 'will-to-power.' If the force of the reaction is stronger than the force of the action, we must assume that the organism becomes extinct. We must assume, moreover, that in Nietzsche's theory of relativity, *space* would be measured from the optics of the organism according to its *means* of perception, and *time* according to its *speed* of perception. Thus, both space and time is relative to the perceptive mechanisms of the organism. Every organism (or 'point') thus sees *being* from its own perspective optics: "being is essentially different in every point." The world as such 'a relationship of points' is thus the primordial Ur-ground for all living entities.

In its relation to this Ur-ground, the human being is now just one 'point,' and it sees *being* from the perspective of its own point. *From within that perspective*, senses are *no longer necessarily* deceptive, although they *necessarily* falsify the Ur-ground. That perforce, we see the world humanly – not by the *means of perception* of a bat (echolocation), nor with the *speed of perception* of a fly (perceiving the world three times faster than the human eye; thus living in a world of slow-motion humans trying to catch it) – does not imply that the world is an inaccessible thing-in-itself. We perceive *from within our perspective* the Ur-ground, and as such, 'simplify,' i.e., 'falsify,' the Ur-ground. However, if our senses by perceiving humanly 'deceive' and 'falsify' the world as this Ur-ground, the deception and falsification would seem to be inconsequential; no more an 'error' than if, during the evolutionary process, we have been 'deceived' into breathing a corrosive gas like oxygen.[122]

---

[122] In the last aphorism included in *Der Wille zur Macht*, we encounter again a description of this in-human Ur-ground, a description of an 'impersonal' cosmos of forces played out against each other; a cosmos essentially being will-to-power: "This world: a monster of energy, without beginning, without end; a firm, iron magnitude of force that does not grow bigger or smaller, that does not expend itself but only transforms itself; as a whole, of unalterable size, a household without expenses or losses, but likewise without increase or income; enclosed by 'nothingness' as by a boundary; not something blurry or wasted, not something endlessly extended, but set in a definite space as a definite force, and not a space that might be 'empty' here or there, but rather as force throughout, as a play of forces and waves of forces [. . .] a sea of forces flowing and rushing together, eternally changing, eternally flooding back. [. . .] [A world] without goal, unless the joy of the circle is itself a goal; without will, unless a ring feels good will toward itself – do you want a name for this world? [. . .] This world is the will to power – and nothing besides! (WM 1067).

If Nietzsche sees the organism as a 'point' in a cosmos of becoming, perceiving cosmos from within its own 'point' (from within its own means and speed of perception), the human being would be such a point. However, as such, the human being inevitably perceives 'qualities,' never quantities, although quantities, minor gradations and differences in degree, are understood as the 'objective' foundations for qualities. By perceiving qualities, we *construct an object*, i.e., *solidify* a flow or a sequence, create it as unity, as such making it appear (*ob-jectum* from *ob-jacere*: 'to throw something before someone'; 'to make appear'; to 'present'). We thereupon assign to the objectified flow a *value*. From prehistoric days, we must assume that *appraisal and evaluation of an object* was a biological necessity. From an evolutionary point of view, it was a requisite for the early hominid to know whether an object was 'good' or 'bad': "In brief, an object is the sum of experienced o p p o s i t i o n s [*Hemmungen*] that have become c o n s c i o u s for us. A quality always expresses something that is useful or harmful." (Nachlaß 1885-86, KSA 12, 2[77]). The early hominid thus had to, first, apprehend something in the unity of an object, and, secondly, judge whether this unity was good or bad. Thus, the early hominid made an in-itself fluid state a *thing*, endowing this thing with its specific valuations. It created a *quality*; and this is, Nietzsche says, our "insurmountable limit."[123]

> Qualities are our insurmountable limit; we cannot keep from feeling that mere differences of quantity [*Quantitäts-differenzen*] are something fundamentally different from qualities, which are no longer reducible to one another. However, everything, for which the word 'knowledge' [*Erkenntnis*] has any meaning is related to a realm that can be counted, weighed, or measured – i.e., according to quantity; while, on the contrary, our sense of value exclusively depends on qualities, that is, on our perspectival 'truths,' exclusively belonging to us – and which cannot be known [*Erkannt*] at all. It is obvious that every creature, different from us, would sense other qualities, and consequently would live in a world different from the one we live in. (Nachlaß 1886, KSA 12, 6[14]).

If we grant that creating and perceiving qualities is what *humans do*, do not other creatures perceive *other qualities*; create *other ob-jects*; assign to them other *values*? And if so, do they not live in 'another world' than the one we live in; not on another *'ground'* (we are all assigned the same

---

[123] Also Freud believes that originally we receive impressions only as *quantities*, which are subsequently transformed, in his neurological apparatus, into *qualities*; and also Freud maintains that in conscious perception, we can only perceive *qualities*; see *Chapter 4* for a detailed analysis of Freud's neuroscience.

ground, the same *Environment*), but in another 'life-world'? – Any creature thus lives on an Ur-ground as an abundance of possibilities that the creature from its own narrow 'perspective' cannot fathom, since perforce it must perceive the ground through its distinctive optics.

Since this construal would apply to humans as well, the Ur-ground *itself* – although it does not hide as the thing-in-itself does – is therefore indifferent to the human perspective; it is the absolutely non-human and in-human, merely providing the ground for a play of forces between an indefinite numbers of 'points.' It is a ground that has nothing to do with us, except for the fact that we happen to be one of its 'points.' It is to this Ur-ground Nietzsche is referring in the aphorism, *Let Us Beware*, from FW.

> Let us beware! [*Hüten wir uns!*]. – Let us beware of thinking that the world is a living being. Where would it stretch? What would it feed on? How could it grow and procreate? [. . .] The total character of the world, however, is in all eternity chaos – in the sense not of a lack of necessity but of a lack of order, arrangement, form, beauty, wisdom, and whatever other names there are for our aesthetic anthropomorphisms [*ästhetischen Menschlichkeiten*]. [. . .] How could we reproach or praise the universe? Let us beware of attributing to it heartlessness and unreason or their opposites: it is neither perfect nor beautiful, nor noble, nor does it wish to become any of these things; it does not by any means strive to imitate man. None of our aesthetic and moral judgments apply to it. Nor does it have any drive for self-preservation or any other drive; and it does not observe any laws either. Let us beware of saying that there are laws in nature. There are only necessities: there are no one who commands, no one who obeys, no one who transgresses. Once you know that there are no purposes, you also know that there is no accident, for only against a world of purposes does a word 'accident' have a meaning. (FW 109, KSA 3, p. 468-69).

Since the Ur-ground has nothing to do with us, it is indifferent to the interpretations we apply to it. Thus, we necessarily 'falsify' the Ur-ground when unto it we apply our interpretations, as such, projecting into this indifferent universe our measurements and ourselves. Nietzsche's prudent proposal is therefore: *let us beware* of our human *narcissism*; our truths are not true *in an absolute sense*; that is, measured against the proposed Ur-ground. They are after all only *ours*.

In Nietzsche, we are condemned to live in this cold and indifferent universe (a universe – one might notice in a symptomatic reading – that characteristically *does not like us*, ignoring for a second the obvious fact that it does not express emotion). Nietzsche's universe has been emptied of all anthropomorphic principles. God has surely disappeared, but so has everything else that could give the universe 'identity,' such as *purpose* (*intention*), *design*, *causes*, or scientific *laws*; "let us beware of saying that there are laws in nature," Nietzsche cautions.

Thanks to humanization, nature becomes like a living organism, having the freedom to abide by laws or not. However, that from which we are deducing laws in the first place, *regularity of events*, does not guarantee Law. In Nietzsche as in Hume, the repeated occurrence of an event does not guarantee *a priori* knowledge of cause-effect relationships. There is no *objective nexus* between cause and effect. Nietzsche, however, adds to Hume's skepticism a 'psychological' analysis of the sciences. If the scientists display a propensity to see causes, it is because, ultimately, they have an inclination to *humanize*, i.e., to discover *intentions* in nature: purposes, designs, causes, or Laws. In Nietzsche as in Hume, cause-effect relations are constituted merely as a result of *experience*, as a result of *custom and habit*; but furthermore, to Nietzsche there is an even *older habit* behind our habit of positing cause-effect relations, namely the habit of impressing upon the world the *belief in ourselves*, i.e., the beliefs in intentions and subjects.

> Therefore, Hume is fundamentally right, habit (but n o t only the habit of the individual) makes us expect that a certain often-observed occurrence follows from another: nothing more. What gives us extraordinary belief in causality is not just the habit of seeing a repetition of events, but our i n a b i l i t y to i n t e r p r e t an event as anything but an event from i n t e n t i o n s. It is belief in the living and thinking as the only effective force – in will, in intention – it is belief that every event is a deed, that every deed presupposes a doer, it is belief in the 'subject.'" (Nachlaß 1885-86, KSA 12, 2[83]).

The Ur-ground we cannot understand; it is beyond our sensational capacities, not because it is *hidden* (on the contrary, it is absolutely present), but because we cannot fathom its super-abundance. Thus, we do not know this self-manifesting Ur-ground, because we have never evolved a need to perceive from more than our own modest perspective.[124] A perspective – or more abstractly, a 'point' – is therefore necessarily a 'narrowing' of the universe. *A fortiori*, *without* this 'narrowing' (i.e., 'simplification,' 'falsification'), there would be no sensation and no knowledge. A 'point' is

---

[124] A hominid starting (*ex hypothesi*) to evolve more than a single perception of the world – if for example its three-dimensional image of the world suddenly had to compete with a two-dimensional image – would just be an aberration and would have had such an evolutionary disadvantage that (in some absurd logic) it would become extinct before the new feature could evolve and become species-typical.

2. Substantiation of Elaboration of the Position

the *absolutely necessary*, and *absolutely beneficial*, 'narrowing' of the universe.

> Our knowledge and sensation is like a point in a system: it is like an eye whose visual strength and visual field [*Sehkraft und Sehfeld*] slowly grows and includes still more. With this the real world d o e s n o t change, but this constant activity of the eyes changes everything to a constantly growing streaming activity. [. . .] We are l i v i n g m i r r o r - i m a g e s. What is consequently knowledge [*Erkenntnis*]? Its starting point is an erroneous narrowing, as if measurement existed for sensations; wherever mirror and taste-organs come about, a sphere is formed. If one thinks away this narrowing, one also thinks away knowledge. (Nachlaß 1880, KSA 9, 6[441]).

The 'real world' Nietzsche refers to in this quote, is his (not too fortunate) term for what I am discussing as *Ur-ground* (. . . but we understand him!). This 'real world' is of course not affected by our perception; it remains what it is with or without us. With the activity of 'our eyes,' says Nietzsche, "the real world does not change." So, it is clear that there are no remnants of idealism in Nietzsche's position. The 'real world' does not 'disappear' if we close our eyes (Berkeley); it is not constituted in subjectivity (Fichte); it is not our 'representation' (Schopenhauer); nor is it constituted in language (20th century post-modernist neo-Idealism). It is finally also, in Nietzsche's interpretation, different from Kant's Thing-in-itself.[125]

It is this chaotic ground that stands in opposition to *our apparent world*: the world as *we* see it. Nietzsche's principal opposition is therefore not between an *apparent world* and a *true world*, but between an *apparent world* and *chaos*. "The opposite of this phenomenal-world is n o t 'the true world,' but rather the world as a formless-inexpressible chaos of sensations [*die formlos-unformulirbare Welt des Sensationen-Chaos*] – consequently another kind of phenomenal-world, 'incomprehensible' ['unknowable': '*unerkennbar*'] to us." (Nachlaß 1887, KSA 12, 9[106]). As such, this sensation-chaos is *also* an apparent world. It is not *our* apparent world, but it is Nietzsche's idea that it can be appropriated, or 'raised' into *our world* depending on the interest we invest in certain of its aspects. "[There is] no 'being-in-itself' [*Sein an sich*], no criteria of 'reality,' but only gradations of

---

[125] That I, following some of Kant's 20th century exponents, was never convinced about Nietzsche's understanding of Kant's thing-in-itself, and should be only too happy (at another point in time) to elaborate on the *resemblance* between Kant's *thing* and Nietzsche's *Ur-ground*, must here be left as an entirely different issue that cannot concern us at this point.

appearances measured according to the strength of the interest that we apply to something appearing." (Nachlaß 1886-87, KSA 12, 7[49]).

Commentators frequently describe Nietzsche's epistemology as 'fictionalism,' 'subjectivism,' and/or 'aestheticism.' Thus, Eugen Fink describes Nietzsche's epistemology as a "fictional theory of knowledge";[126] while Jürgen Habermas have seen Nietzsche as over-emphasizing the playfulness of a purely *aesthetic dimension* over and above his own cognitive, intersubjective, and expressive dimensions of knowledge.[127] Although such interpretations tally with certain of Nietzsche's fragments (e.g., the famous ". . . there are only interpretations."), the labels give the wrong impression that Nietzsche means that scientists are working with the same freedom of spirit as poets: they both 'invent.' Accordingly, a poem by William Blake and the

---

[126] Fink, Eugen: Nietzsches Philosophie. Stuttgart (Verlag W. Kohlhammer), 1960; p. 165.

[127] See Habermas, Jürgen: The Philosophical Discourse of Modernity. Cambridge (MIT Press), 1988. Referring to the will-to-power, Habermas states: "This is at the same time a will to illusion, a will to simplification, to masks, to the superficial; art counts as man's genuine metaphysical activity, because life itself is based on illusion, deception, optics, the necessity of the perspectival and of error. Of course, Nietzsche can shape these ideas into a "metaphysics for artists" only if he reduces everything that is and should be to the aesthetic dimension. [. . .] The famous sketches for a pragmatic theory of knowledge and for a natural history of morality that trace the distinction between "true" and "false," "good" and 'Evil," back to preferences for what serves life and for the noble, are meant to demonstrate this. According to this analysis, behind apparently universal normative claims lie hidden the subjective power claims of value appraisals." Habermas, loc. cit. p. 95. Behind this appraisal of Nietzsche lies Habermas's elaborate diagrams of different types of communicative action. In *On the Theory of Communicative Action*, Habermas outlines four such types; the so-called: (1) Teleological action producing knowledge of technologies; (2) Constative Speech acts producing knowledge of theories; (3) Normatively Regulated Action, producing knowledge of legal and moral representations; and finally (4) Dramaturgical Action producing knowledge as works of art. According to Habermas, there is thus, in the production of knowledge, a division of labor between types of communicative action, which Nietzsche ignores, since he promotes the final "dramaturgical action" as the overarching type of action. That is, Nietzsche superimposes the aesthetic dimension on all of the three preceding types of action: "reduces everything that is" to the "aesthetic dimension" (loc. cit.). For these diagrams, see for example Habermas: On the Theory of Communicative Action v. I, loc. cit., p. 334.

DNA molecule supposedly have the same ontological status; are as such the results of the same poetic-creative-inspirational processes.

However, following Nietzsche in his *Nachlaß*, there are reasons to believe that this was never his intended position. It does not seem to be the claim that a poem and a scientific discovery have the same status, but rather that something like the DNA is *not* an exclusive human 'invention' or 'fiction,' *not* exclusively 'constituted in and by language.' It is surely an 'interpretation,' but then an 'interpretation' of *something*. Following Nietzsche, DNA would be understood, rather, as a *single layer* in an infinitely deep and proliferous nature; a nature which consists of multiple *layers* and *combinations* that we do not care about (do not *yet* care about, etc.), and consequently, do not *see* and do not *know*. We only see and learn that which, under the pressure of our reductive observations, seem to give us a perceived advantage in existence. We *observe* according to *the promise of a reward*. Since our interpretations are *interested*, they are – relative to the world of becoming (the Ur-ground) – 'false.' Since scientific knowledge is a construct resulting from our selective observations, it is in this sense 'false.' "The world t h a t c o n c e r n s u s is false, i.e., it is no matter of fact, but rather an invention [*Ausdichtung*] and something rounded up from a meager sum of observations. It is 'in flow'; as something becoming; as a forever forward thrusting falsity that never reaches truth – there is no 'truth.' (Nachlaß 1885-86, KSA 12, 2[108]). However, our interpretations are still true for us. They are the constructs by which we understand fragments of an abundant world, selected according to what concerns our humanity.

In order to *classify and understand* single layers, or a particular combination, in proliferous nature, in order to *see and to bring it into knowledge*, language is now indispensable. Language as such does not create that which is, but it brings something that *is* (e.g., the DNA) on formula. Thanks to language, we write up a model for this existing something, but we realize (or we ought to realize) that this something (regarding DNA, the famous 'helix') could have been represented in numerous alternative models (or it could have been represented as *another combination*).[128]

---

[128] In his important work on Nietzsche's theory of knowledge, Rudiger Grimm is also addressing this so-called 'fictionalism,' but seems in various passages undecided as to whether knowledge is pure *invention*, or knowledge *of* something. Nietzsche is cited for the following passage, corroborating my position as indicated above, "Schaffen – als Auswählen und Fertig-machen des Gewählten." (Nachlaß 1887, 9[106]), and Grimm comments: "Creation here does not mean creation *ex nihilo*. For Nietzsche, a thing, object, quality, etc., is constituted within the sphere of perspectival activity of a power-center.

The pioneers in the discovery of the DNA were in fact experimenting with a number of different representations of the DNA, before, eventually, they reached a consensus about Watson and Crick's simple and elegant helix that most efficiently solved the problems of representing this 'string.'[129] (Thanks to powerful microscopes, we have today enhanced visibility of the world; thus, we see a 'string' tightly wrapped up in the nucleus of the cell; this is today part of our *appearing* universe.) The model of the helix is currently our 'truth' about the DNA; what 'DNA' is beyond that 'truth,' on the inexplicable Ur-ground, that we cannot imagine. We can of course always imagine other models; and one must expect that some day our present model will be replaced with something else; maybe our old 'string' will still be there, but merely as a remnant, as an insignificant loop within something more complicated, more sophisticated, solving other problems, etc. Maybe one day, advances in mathematics will give us completely different ways of representing inner nature; maybe we will realize that inner nature is much more precisely represented in four, five, or six dimensions. Maybe one day, computers will give us the means to perceive the inner workings of the 'DNA' according to another *speed*, different from the cumbersome human timeframe that we always apply to observations.

But still, if DNA had been a mere 'fiction,' 'a playful creation,' 'a conceptional invention,' 'a construction in language,' how could one explain the repeated success of DNA fingerprinting (a few rape victims have been vindicated thanks to DNA analysis)? Nietzsche's position is sufficiently

---

> What or how anything is, is a function of this activity and, as we have seen, there can be no thing apart from an interpretative act. Thus the interpretative-cognitive act is entirely creative: not only is this act responsible for its contents – it is also identical with them." (Grimm: Nietzsche's Theory, loc. cit., p. 185). Now, if a creative act is responsible for and identical to its content, then it is exactly creation *ex nihilo*. The Nietzsche-quote Grimm comments upon is completely lucid in this matter: "creation is selection." So, *something* is selected, which as such must be independent of the creative act – i.e., it does not spring from the creative act itself. As Grimm continues, he sinks deeper and deeper into the trap of Idealism: "The 'external world' is not something simply and univocally present, apart from any observer. It is a function of that activity of perspectival interpretation and falsification through which each power-center actively structures and creates its own world." (Grimm, loc. cit., p. 185). I would reformulate to the opposite: 'the external world is absolute presence, existing apart from any observer; however, in our perspectival interpretations and falsifications, we structure and create our own world 'on top of' that 'external world."

[129] See Watson, James: The Double Helix: A Personal Account of the Discovery of the Structure of the DNA. Touchstone (New York) 1968/2001.

pragmatic to save him from the embarrassment of having to choke back such simple and straightforward questions.[130]

---

[130] This defense of 'reality' in Nietzsche has been suggested by other commentators. Thus, Günter Abel asserts: "There is no in-itself of things, but only interpreting and interpreted processes of establishing [*Fest-stellung*]. This does not imply that reality does not exist, as if interpretation were identical to fantasizing. But it implies that something, which appears as and is addressed as reality, is not something in an ontological sense *given* [*Gegebenes*] and cannot be fixated as an in-itself-always-lasting permanence [*sich-gleich-Bleibender Bestand*] of that *which is*. Reality is always *constructed* reality. It is all about production, not about re-production [*Wiedergabe*] and mirroring." (Abel: Nietzsche, loc. cit., p. 173). From a pragmatic position, Nehamas repeats the necessity of selectivity in our production of knowledge; we could not "begin with all data": "We must bring something into the foreground and distance others into the background. We must assign a greater relative importance to something than we do to others, and still others we must completely ignore. We do not, and cannot, begin (or end) with 'all the data.' This is an incoherent desire and an impossible goal. 'To grasp everything' would be to do away with all perspective relations, it would mean to grasp nothing, to misapprehend the nature of knowledge. If we are ever to begin a practice or an inquiry we must, and must want to, leave unasked indefinitely many question about the world." Alexander Nehamas: Nietzsche – Life as Literature Cambridge, Mass. (Harvard University Press), 1985, p. 49. From an Analytic position, Peter Poellner as well appears to advocate the notion of a "perception-independent" reality that eventually may or may not be correlated with possible "variables in scientific equations": "The theoretical entities which are eventually observed by suitable procedures are *phenomena* [. . .] whose intrinsic qualities nature remains unknown. Nothing of what Nietzsche says in this connection requires him to deny that there may be real, perception-independent items of some sort corresponding to variables in scientific equations which have as yet not been correlated with observable phenomena, but which may in the future be successfully correlated with observables. What he does deny is rather that such newly discovered correspondences usually enlighten us about the qualitative nature of these entities." Peter Poellner: "Causation and Force in Nietzsche" in Babech (ed.): Nietzsche, Epistemology, and Philosophy of Science, loc. cit., p. 295.

2.2. Human Ground and Sensation

The distinction between 'Ur-ground' and 'Human ground' is not clear in Nietzsche, and he never suggests it explicitly and deliberately. However, it is implied in several of his statements, for example:

> We can only understand intellectual processes; that is, the part of matter that becomes – and can become – visible, audible, and tangible. We understand the changes in our seeing, hearing, and touch that hereby occur. That for which we have no sensation does not exist for us – but this doesn't mean that the world goes no further." (Nachlaß 1881, KSA 9, 11[75], p. 470).

Here, we are again introduced to our suggested 'two' worlds (i.e., as two aspects of one and the same ground): a world we can possibly perceive (so-called 'Human'), and a world we cannot possibly perceive (so-called 'Ur-'). In the latter case, the world "for which we have no sensation does not exist for us," but it does not means that the "world goes no further." In its totality, it is beyond our perception, but it is *not* therefore non-existent, as Nietzsche cautions, against for example Berkeley's radical subjectivism.[131]

We said in the summary above that the Ur-ground could be determined as the expanse that presents itself to *all possible perception*. *All possible perception* was an abstract construction meant to signify the inclusion of not only what humans perceive, and not only what animals (lower and higher) may perceive, but also, somewhat exotically, what any extraterrestrial might perceive, what a Cartesian demon might perceive, what God might perceive, etc. In a world open for *all possible perception*, every 'layer' would be visible, every 'combination' would reveal itself (we would no longer need scientists to make 'discoveries'). If the Ur-ground indicates a ground open for *all possible perception*, the Human ground, more modestly, indicates the ground open for *possible human perception*. It is the expanse that presents itself *to us*; that which is or can be (or *could possibly be*) seen from our perspective or 'point.'

Whether we are talking about Ur-ground or Human ground, the grounds are being falsified. The Ur-ground is absolute chaos, a world of becoming, a maelstrom of entropy and disorder we cannot fathom. However, the Human

---

[131] This critical stance against Idealism is expressed explicitly and frequently in Nietzsche. We are regarded as 'mirrors' bringing a world in flux into the stabilizing parameters of our organizing mental 'mirror.' However, it is never the position that *without us* (as these so-called 'mirrors') the world would also cease to exist: "[That] 'there is no world where there is no mirror,' is nonsense." (Nachlaß 1880, KSA 9, 6[429]).

ground is also chaos, but rather because this reality impresses itself upon us with all its detail and multiplicity – a level of detail we do not and cannot 'take in' and 'process.' In both cases, we simplify, thus 'falsify,' these worlds. In the first case, we 'falsify' out of intrinsic *ontological* necessity; in the second case, we 'falsify' out of intrinsic *psychological* necessity.

The *Human ground* is the ground, on which we live and perceive; it is (*mutatis mutandis*) the world we see. It appears as if 'outside us,' 'next to us,' and 'in front of us'; it appears in three dimensions, organized in up and down, near and far, left and right, etc. (On the Ur-ground it has no meaning to talk about up and down or left and right; for one reason, because it is not the organization of the world according to every creature.[132]) Still, we never see *everything* 'next to' or 'in front' of us. We do not travel through the world hyper-conscious of every minor detail; we rather select, suppress, ignore, and forget. When we pull ourselves together, we are capable of 'focusing,' but mostly, the mode and mindset in which we see the world is distracted, distant, and absent. – And even *when* we 'focus,' how 'focused' are we in fact, how attentively do we see (it takes painters years to learn to see with attention)?

Our sense-organs have evolved in order to respond to certain human needs, as such they 'falsify.' The sense-apparatus reduces, compresses, and abbreviates. When we perceive, we are tirelessly gathering information, our eyes scans the world in rapid saccades for information, but we are becoming conscious of and using only a fraction of the information we gather. As such, we are only *browsing* and *skimming* the world, but (almost) never seriously *reading* or *studying* it. This analogy to 'reading' is suggested by Nietzsche himself:

> Just as little as today's reader takes in all the individual words (or especially syllables) on a page (he catches maybe five out of twenty words and 'guesses' what these five arbitrary words might possibly mean) – just as little do we see a tree precisely and completely, with respect to leaves, branches, colors, and shape. We find it so much easier to imagine an approximate tree instead. (JGB 192, KSA 5, p. 113).

---

[132] One may also note that on the scale of the infinitely large and the infinitesimal small it makes no longer sense to talk about up and down, left and right. We don't admit into our repertoire statements like 'The Andromeda Galaxy is located a bit to the left of, and slightly above, our Milky Way.' 'Near' and 'far,' 'large' and 'small,' 'up' and 'down,' 'left' and 'right' etc., makes no sense in the universe; whether the Andromeda Galaxy is 'near to' or 'far from' the Milky Way is completely relative to the frame of reference we adopt.

When we read, which is also perception of an outside world (a point typically ignored by Derrida and Derridians[133]), we are being exposed to an information-overload that we necessarily reduce and simplify in order to 'understand.' The page is here a world of becoming, a world in flux, but a world by no means beyond our perceptive capacities, as little as the tree in its detailed manifold. However, the text, as well as the tree, overwhelms us with information, and this triggers our natural defense: to 'compress,' 'truncate,' and 'interpret.' We notice here that we, as already mentioned, *defend ourselves* against *too much reality*. As such self-defensive readers, we create 'forms' that are easier to conceive, but are in fact mere approximations to the information that is available on the page, information that our senses make available, only to be reduced by us to what we call the 'message' or 'meaning' of the text.[134]

Nietzsche explains himself in more detail in the Nachlaß:

> We are not sufficiently refined to see the supposedly absolute flow of becoming [*absoluten Fluß des Geschehens*]. Our crude organs only have a capacity for the enduring [*Bleibendes*], and summarize and exhibit a surface that does not exist as such. The tree is in every immediate now

---

[133] One of the more interesting problems in Derrida's famous slogan, "There is nothing outside the text," which during the seventies and eighties became the battle-cry for a new generation of textualists, is that the text itself is exactly 'outside' us; and we, as readers, must consequently be "outside the text." Rephrasing Derrida's slogan accordingly would open a new problematic: "There is nothing outside the text, except the reader." It is precisely because we as "outsiders" have to *perceive* a text that we are must reduce it to *meaning*; indeed, *a* meaning, which is, as Derrida repeatedly demonstrates, often incongruent with the existence of the original information-overload present on the page. See also the following note.

[134] Jacques Derrida internalized this insight, as he tried hard, almost uniformly in his earlier writings, to defeat this human tendency to reduce a text to 'meaning.' He is exercising Nietzsche's ideal philology, to read a text as text; as such, to be aware of all minor details and nuances as they *appear* on the textual surface. But whether Derrida has succeeded in realizing this very Nietzschean program is another matter that is still debated, and a discussion which I cannot engage myself in here. I am inclined to think *not*; adding as extenuating explanation that it may never be humanly possible to be absolutely successful in this ambition (– we *reduce*, thanks to our so-called 'reality-defense,' what apply also to the world of texts). In the final analysis, we can only 'reduce' the text to certain abstract forms, such as (in Derrida's case) a certain 'logic of writing' (existing in a variety of descriptions in his philosophy).

[*Augenblick*] something n e w ; but we postulate a f o r m , because we are incapable of perceiving the minute absolute movements [*die feinste absolute Bewegung*]. We expertly add [*legen . . . hinein*] a m a t h e m a t i c a l a v e r a g e - l i n e [*mathematische Durchschnittslinie*] to the absolute movement. We indeed i n v e n t lines and surfaces, because our intellect takes for granted the e r r o r : the assumption of equality and stability; since we can only s e e the stable and only r e m e m b e r the equal. (Nachlaß 1881, KSA 9, 11[293]).

Again, the *tree* is the favorite example. In a world of absolute becoming, the tree would be something new from one moment to the next, like the clouds on the sky, or the waves of the ocean. In a world of becoming, everything renews itself again and again . . . unendingly. This renewal, however, we cannot grasp. Throughout a long evolutionary history, we have invented simplifying forms, such as the line and the surface, on which to organize the *flow* in stable and equal *things*. When we look at the tree, we no longer see a multitude of branches and leaves waving in the wind, endlessly changing the shape of the crown of the tree, we see a 'gestalt,' a 'shape,' or a 'schema' – literally, we see a *ghost tree.*

We realize now that there is no discrepancy between rejecting the notion of a thing-in-itself and still maintain that senses 'falsify.' On the contrary! In Nietzsche's interpretation of Kant, rejecting the thing-in-itself implies denouncing the notion of an abstract content beneath or beyond our apparent world. If we live in a world of *nothing but appearance*, senses *falsify* because they reduce, simplify, and compress the impressions we receive of these appearances, *not* because they inform us *incorrectly* about a presumed thing-in-itself beyond the cover of the appearances. One might say that senses deceive because they are *lazy*, not because they are *inadequate*. (In that case, they are of course *phylogenetically* 'lazy'; biologically *taught* to be 'lazy'; 'lazy' as a part of *acquired* human constitution. To paint the world with the broadest brush was always a biological advantage; it was never advantageous to immerse oneself in detail and sophistication. But why not? – Because that would delay our response-time when we needed to quickly identify and respond to a situation, e.g., danger!) It therefore comes as no surprise when, in numerous places, we encounter the rejection of the thing-in-itself *alongside* the proposal of falsifying and arbitrary sense-perceptions.

In the published work, we find statements to that effect in *Morgenröte, Die fröhliche Wissenschaft*, and *Jenseits von Gut und Böse*.

> I n p r i s o n . – my eyes, however strong or weak they may be, can see only a certain distance, and it is within the space of this distance that I live and move, the line of this horizon constitutes my immediate fate, in great things and small,

> from which I cannot escape. Around every being there is described a similar concentric circle, which has a mid-point and is peculiar to him. Our ears enclose us within a small room, and so does our sense of touch. Now, it is by these horizons, within which each of us encloses his senses as if behind prison walls, that we m e a s u r e the world, we say that this is near and that far, this is big and that small, this is hard and that soft: this measuring we call sensation – and it is all of it an error! [. . .] The habits of our senses have ensnared us in the lies and deceptions of sensation [*haben uns in Lug und Trug der Empfindung eingesponnen*], these again are the basis of all our judgments and 'knowledge' – there is absolutely no escape, no backway or bypath into the r e a l w o r l d ! [*die wirkliche Welt!*] We sit within our net, we spiders, and whatever we may catch, we can only catch that which allows itself to be caught in precisely o u r net. (M 117, KSA 3, p. 110).

According to this passage, we are 'imprisoned' by our senses, since they can give us only the information that they are *arbitrarily* designed to give. (The following specification may be in order: granted that our sense-organs are the result of evolution, and not of design, they must be *a priori arbitrary*; but they are of course *biologically (a-posteriori) necessary*.) We are in the quotation seen as 'imprisoned,' because we exist as if surrounded by the world, with ourselves as center. Whether we perceive by sight, hearing, or touch, we perceive within a given periphery. The world appears like a giant disk with a boundary that moves as we move, always equidistant to the point we happen to occupy; a boundary, therefore, impossible to transgress. It is from this world that there is 'no escape into a *real world*' (the 'real world' here implied may designate either Plato, Kant, or Christianity's 'real world'; a 'reality' I would label – in order to keep track on all these 'realities' – the *extra-real*). In his description of the world as a 'disk' and a 'horizon,' Nietzsche is describing the *apparent* (the *hyper-real*) world; the world we know, the world that binds us, and the world from which there is no escape into anything more 'real' than what we already know is *real*. Expressing oneself less ambiguously, from the *hyper-real* there is no escape into the *extra-real*. As explained in the concluding section, the world according to Nietzsche is always only *one*, never *two*; there is no possibility of escaping this *one* world.

In *Morgenröte*, both the world as *thing-in-itself* and the distinction *real vs. apparent* are under deconstruction. Still, our senses 'ensnare' us in their deception, they are 'errors.' The nets, in which we sit as spiders, are the nets of our sense-apparatuses. Given our limited sense-apparatus, we are prejudiced in our sensations of the world. Our limited senses are selective, designed to catch only a certain portion of the world; as such, they generate erroneous knowledge of the world.

This conception is repeated in a passage from *Die fröhliche Wissenschaft*. Here, explicitly, the notion of the unknown Kantian 'X' is again rejected, and it is once more confirmed that there are only appearances. However, these appearances are again *deceptive* ("there is appearance and a will-o'-the-wisp").

> What is appearance' to me now! [. . .] Certainly not a dead mask that one could put on an unknown X and probably also take of X! To me, appearance is the active and living itself, which goes so far in its self-mockery that it makes me feel that here there is appearance and a will-o'-the-wisp and a dance of spirits and nothing else [*dass hier Schein und Irrlicht und Geistertanz und nichts Mehr ist*]. (FW 54, KSA 3, p. 417).

Finally, in the following passage from *Jenseits von Gut und Böse*, we produce knowledge of the world by filtering an already existing manifold, thus simplifying a world of becoming and producing distinctions where originally there are only continua. It is not clear which of the grounds is object of simplification in the passage: the *Ur-* or the *Human*. It is also not clear, who is being singled out as the primary culprit of deception, the senses or the concepts. On the one hand, it is to our senses that we have given a "*carte blanche* for everything superficial"; but on the other, it is language that "cannot get over its crassness" as it keeps asserting oppositions and distinctions where there is only a fluidity of gradations.

> O s a n c t o s i m p l i c i t a s ! What a strange simplification and falsification people live in! one never stops wondering, when first one's eyes are opened to such wondering. We have made everything around us so bright and easy and free and simple! We have given our senses a c a r t e b l a n c h e for everything superficial, given our thoughts a divine craving for high-spirited leaps and false inferences! – We have from the beginning understood how to hold on to our ignorance in order to enjoy a barely comprehensible freedom, thoughtlessness, recklessness, bravery, and joy in life; to delight in life itself! And first on this solid and granite foundation of ignorance could science arise – the will to know [*Wille zum wissen*] was arising on the foundation of a much more powerful will, the will to not know [*Wille zum nicht-wissen*]; the will to uncertainty, to untruth! Not as its opposite, but rather – as its refinement! Even when l a n g u a g e, here as elsewhere, cannot get over its crassness and keeps talking about opposites where there are only degrees and multiple, subtle shades of gradation. (JGB 24, KSA 5, p. 41).

We notice that Nietzsche has three agencies responsible for falsification: first senses, then (metonymically associated to 'senses') thoughts, and finally, language. He does not seem to recognize distinctions between these three agencies. Whether senses, thoughts, or concepts deceive, they perform the same simplifying operation, the very operation which makes science possible. Thanks to our perceptive, cognitive, and linguistic simplifications of the world, science raises itself on a "solidified, granite foundation of ignorance" – ignorance, of course, of the original ground, the world in perpetual flux and eternal becoming, i.e., the chaos as Ur-ground and/or the sensation-chaos as Human ground that we do not access and cannot process as such. We therefore simplify out of necessity. As repeated time and again, falsification is "necessary for life." If our perceptive, cognitive, linguistic simplifications are 'errors,' they are surely 'errors' that need not alarm us; 'errors' that most emphatically we should not try to 'correct' – nor could we![135]

2.3. Sensation and Word.

Hyper-reality is what we encounter before we impose any interpretation upon the world (we ignore for now that relative to the so-called Ur-ground, our perceptive designs always – but in a general, almost metaphorical, sense – 'interpret'). Nietzsche suggests in this context that it is possible, or it might be possible, to *see* without thinking. Senses deceive *relative* to the degree of thinking by and through which we apprehend the world. *Hyper-reality* is thus suggested as the realm offering a *possibility* for non-deceiving sense-perception, but typically, we pass up the possibility by perceiving the world through our cognitive and linguistic filters. Insofar as we see the world through this filter, senses 'deceive.'

> The model of the perfect [*vollständiger*] f i c t i o n is logic. [. . .] Something like that does not happen in reality [*Wirklichkeit*]: reality is unutterably more complicated. By imposing this fiction as a s c h e m a, i.e. by filtering the factual event, as we think, through a simplification-apparatus: we arrive at a s i g n -

---

[135] When we therefore read Nietzsche's Analytic commentators excusing, amending, or mitigating Nietzsche's 'falsification' or 'error-theory,' they are committing a mistake so essential, that if by any chance they were right about Nietzsche being wrong, they would have annihilated their own cognitive and linguistic capabilities. Nietzsche's 'error' is the condition of the possibility for the reasoning of Analytic commentators (for example, the many "I shall argue that . . ." are *falsifications* of a text that is both *much more* than, and often *much different* from, the proposed 'argument'). One 'forgets,' that Nietzsche's 'false' is not identical to Tarski's 'false'; his 'Truth' not identical to Tarski's 'true.'

language [*Zeichenschrift*], [at the] c o m m u n i c a b i l i t y and k n o w a b i l i-
t y [*Merkbarkeit*] of the logical procedures. [. . .] That something remains
unknown does not worry me; I a m d e l i g h t e d that still, there exists an art of
knowledge [*Erkenntniß*] and admire the complexity of this possibility. The method is: the introduction of absolute fictions as schemata, by which we may
conceive our intellectual processes [*geistige Geschehen*] as simpler than they
are. Experience [*Erfahrung*] is only possible by means of memory
[*Gedächtniß*]; memory is only possible by truncating [*Abkürzung*] intellectual
processes into s i g n s . (Nachlaß 1885, KSA 11, 34[249]).

The interpreting linguistic expression is not an expression of nothing and
knowledge does not generate itself *ex nihilo*. Instead, as expressly stated,
interpretation is to "*filter* a *factual event* through a *simplification-
apparatus*" – a *factual event*! But in fact, Nietzsche's choice of words in describing the interpretive activity – 'simplification,' 'schematization,'
'filtering,' etc. – already suggests a process where there is a reality to be
'filtered,' 'schematized,' etc. It is because it is *there* – as the *too much* and
the *too chaotic* – that we 'filter' it through our 'nets.' It is our human predicament to be exposed to these information-overloads, and our response is to
simplify – according to the process, I have called *reality-defense*. We thus
truncate a phenomenal complex into simple forms that become the conceivable stand-in for (i.e., 'falsifying') the complex.[136]

Through our interpreting 'filter,' we do not secure any *a priori* knowledge of the world. Given the inherent arbitrariness and contingency of the
filter, we aspire in vain to conceptualize, schematize, and stabilize a perpetually changing world in any *absolute* sense. There is as such no *arche-
interpretation*, but there are surely interpretations. These interpretations are

---

[136] In *Nietzsches 'Genealogie der Moral'*, Werner Stegmaier offers an interpretation of the 'logic' of the simplification-process that corresponds to my own:
"Abbreviation in itself does not follow logic in the traditional sense; it is rather an art, an "*abbreviationsart*" [*Abkürzungskunst*]. It is the art to simplify,
to 'prepare' an infinitely complex world for our ability to orient ourselves in
it; a complex world, which is always something else when we try to think it
with our most subtle concepts; which is, as Nietzsche often says, "unutterably
more complicated." [, , ,] To speak of 'knowledge' of 'things' as if 'things'
existed in the world and thinking is representing them as they are, is now to
cater to a "mythology" that already "has had its time." "Logical thinking," as
Nietzsche has learnt to see it, is "the model of a complete Fiction," and "Logic," as the logical thinking of logical thinking, is consequently the fiction of a
fiction. When thinking of 'things,' we already simplify the reality according
to Schemata; we "*filter*" it "through a simplification apparatus"." Stegmaier:
Nietzsches 'Genealogie der Moral,' loc. cit., p. 81.

applied to a ground, which neither withdraws itself from, nor does it yield itself to, interpretation. It is simply *there*. It is always 'in existence,' but fleetingly as the evanescent flicker of a world in incessant change. Interpretation is the attempt to hold on to snippets of this fleeting world.

In the above passage, the 'simplification-apparatus' is first and foremost a *linguistic* construct. Experience, says Nietzsche, "is only possible by means of memory, memory is only possible by truncating intellectual processes into signs."

Here, Nietzsche is repeating a notion from Leibniz' *New Essays of Human Understanding*[137]; in Leibniz too we simplify our universe thanks to memory that so to speak assists perception in becoming conscious of itself. In his *New Essays*, Leibniz observed that as we go about our average daily lives, consciousness does not seem to be as dominant a feature as we tend to think. Due to either the habitualness or superabundance of impressions, we become conscious of only fractions of our surrounding world. As we grow accustomed to a sight, we tend to stop noticing it. "This is how we become so accustomed to the motion of a mill or a waterfall, after living beside it for a while, that we pay no heed to it."[138] Also when impressions are too minute or too numerous they do not engage our attention. "At every moment there is in us an infinity of perceptions, unaccompanied by awareness or reflection."[139]

If this is granted, according to what principle does our perception eventually 'lighten up' the world surrounding us? – Leibniz says that attentive perception requires *memory*.

> *Memory is needed for attention*: when we are not alerted, so to speak, to pay heed to certain of our own present perceptions, we allow them to slip by unconsidered and even unnoticed. But if someone alerts us to them straight away, [. . .] then *we remember them* and are aware of just having had some sense of them.[140]

From the immediate past, memory informs present perception. This would be the first mental mechanism for stabilizing and fixating a world of becoming: I see, and become aware of, *something as something*. It is by engaging our memory in our perceptive present that we become *conscious*. We are

---

[137] G. W. Leibniz: New Essays on Human Understanding. Translated & edited by J. Bennett and P. Ramnant. Cambridge (Cambridge University Press), 1982.
[138] Leibniz: New Essays, loc. cit., p. 54.
[139] Leibniz: New Essays, loc. cit., p. 54.
[140] Leibniz: New Essays, loc. cit., p. 54; italics added.

thus endowed with a psychological capability that does not seem to be strictly necessary. Both Leibniz and Nietzsche are certain that animals do not possess this capability, and we, in the better part of our waken life, also do fine without it – although eventually, consciousness always seems to interfere with and disturb this original unconscious celebration of the pure perceptive present.

In aphorism 354 from *Die fröhliche Wissenschaft*, Nietzsche elaborates on Leibniz's observation. He explicitly refers to Leibniz's insight,[141] and remarks: "We could think, feel, will, remember, and also 'act' in every sense of the term, and yet none of all this would have to 'enter our consciousness' (as one says figuratively) [*wie man im Bilde sagt*]." (FW 354, KSA 3, p. 590). 'Enter consciousness' is here an image [*Bilde*], a metaphor; it indicates that something can either enter our consciousness or 'stay outside.' If it 'stays outside,' it is in Nietzsche's sense 'unconscious.' It is obviously not 'repressed,' as is Freud's unconscious, *it is merely not noticed*.

Nietzsche ends up taking Leibniz's insight a step further: we perceive thanks to *memory* (so far Leibniz), but we remember thanks to *language* (Nietzsche). This step is taken qua the notion of the 'simplification-apparatus.' More precisely, a 'simplification-apparatus' is an apparatus by which we *condense*, and then *identify*. But then we must ask: why is it that *condensation* and *identification* are interrelated processes? – A simplification-apparatus is a device by which to *identify something as*; it allows us to recognize *something as something*. In identifying or recognizing something *as* something, we cannot rely only on the masses or stuff in eternal becoming; because these masses, such stuff, cannot be compared to itself. Stuff cannot *in and by itself* be *identified as something*; in order to be recognized, it must be compared to something *radically different* from itself – paradoxical as this may sound. That which is radically different from stuff, and by which it is identified, is the *sign*. Now stuff becomes an 'entity,' and furthermore, through its encounter with the sign, an 'id-entity.' In its 'natural

---

[141] In the present aphorism, it may not be clear which of Leibniz's insights Nietzsche alludes to when writing that first now we able to catch up with "Leibniz's precocious suspicion" that there is a "problem of consciousness." In the following aphorism 357, however, he explicitly refers to "Leibniz's incomparable insight [. . .] that consciousness is merely an *accidens* of the power of representation and *not* its necessary and essential attribute; so that what we call consciousness constitutes only one state of our spiritual and psychic world (perhaps a sick state) and *by no means the whole of it*." (GS, 357; KSA 3, p. 598). This would refer to Leibniz's discussions of perception and memory from *New Essays on Human Understanding*.

habitat,' in the world of becoming, it is never an *entity-identity*, but a nameless complex or multiplex. However, Nietzsche's 'simplification-apparatus,' the sign, (1) *condenses* 'stuff' into a single indivisible *entity*, and simultaneously, (2) *identifies* this entity *as* such and such by labeling it via the *sign*.[142]

Before the sign, there is for example no 'dog-entity/dog-identity.' There are these four-legged, growling, barking, friendly creatures roaming around, but there are many of them and they are all different – so far, they are only 'stuff.' The sign, (1) condenses them all into the same abstract entity, and (2) identifies these creatures *as something*. The word 'dog' is doing this job. The word 'dog' is thus a 'simplification-apparatus' that simultaneously *condenses* and *identifies*. This does not mean that we are all of a sudden unable to see different dogs running about. Language is *not* like a gray blanket we throw over the world of appearances; it does not make the world disappear by transforming it to 'signifiers'; it does not make our eyes fall out of

---

[142] In many respects, Heidegger's analysis of how the 'thing' is constituted from a fleeting world of chaos is similar to the analysis above, except for the fact that Heidegger believes that he can account for these complex matters without recourse to linguistics. Heidegger discusses the 'thing' as the blackboard behind him in his lecture hall, and says, correctly, that "to know this thing as a blackboard, we must already have ascertained what we encounter as a 'thing' as such, and not, say, as a fleeting occurrence." Heidegger, loc. cit., p. 78. Right! And what does Heidegger now think a 'fleeting occurrence' (my 'stuff') is before it is constituted as a 'thing': "Kant speaks of the '*mass* of sensations,' meaning by that the chaos, the jumble that crowds us, keeps us occupied, concerns us, washes over and tunnels through us [. . .] not only in the moment of perceiving this blackboard, but constantly and everywhere, [. . .] what appears so harmlessly and quietly and conclusively to us as an object, such as this blackboard or any other familiar thing, we do meet up with the mass of sensation-chaos. It is what is nearest." Heidegger, loc. cit., p. 78-79. Heidegger is talking about Nietzsche's 'sensation-chaos,' Freud's 'masses in movement,' my 'hyper-reality.' In all cases, we are talking about the constant impingement of impressions on our mental apparatus, before this apparatus has had a chance to remember these sensations as *the same*; a memory partly (but not exclusively) constituted by means of the *sign* with which a certain selection of impressions are associated, thus retrieved and 'remembered.' However, since Heidegger never consults linguistics, the constitution of 'things' appears to be abstract and medium-less. In Heidegger, it just happens thanks to a purely cognitive drive to 'schematize.' Undoubtedly, Heidegger would have been able to take his analysis more than a few steps further, had he not been in the grip of a permeating 'science-phobia' and 'technology-fear' that also seems to extend into the field of Linguistics.

their sockets. However, after the introduction of the word, we are paradoxically capable of seeing individual dogs *as if* the self-same thing. And more importantly, we are able to retrieve them from memory as the abstract self-same thing: somebody says 'dog,' and suddenly, but without seeing any particular dog in my imagination, I remember some abstract 'form' corresponding to 'dog.' So, somebody says 'dog,' and the sound interacts with old memory-traces, reaches deep back into unconscious memories (memory is always unconscious, as Freud and Breuer would insist), and now it retrieves, not an exact *picture* of a dog, but merely some kind of rough 'outline,' some vague 'silhouette,' or some 'aggregate' of dog-attributes. The word 'dog' is thus a most economical means by which to remember *dogs*. It is in fact so economical and abstract that the word sometimes makes me remember *dogs*, without I have to take a detour around an actual *representation* of *dogs*, that is, without having to evoke a corresponding *picture*.

As another example, the sign allows me to *identify* a leaf as a leaf – not as an individual entity with its unique and matchless characteristics. By identifying a leaf as *leaf*, I give abstract form to something, create an entity out of something, which – in unspoiled and pure perception – I could only have apprehended in its enigmatic individuality. Hence, following Nietzsche, the 'thing' is an abstraction, and the 'thingness' of a thing does not grow naturally out of the stuff itself, but is formed by superimposing on stuff the label by which it becomes a thing, and to which it will have to answer: its name, its *sign*. Nietzsche is precise in describing this identification-process as depending on *memory* and *language* – both! I must necessarily remember this multitude of glistering, rattling, greenish entities as *some*-thing, more precisely, as some *thing*, before being able to bestow upon it a name. We would be utterly incapable of remembering millions of glistering, rattling, greenish entities in their matchless uniqueness.

Because of this linguistic intermeddling with our perceptions, the universe has been *logicized*, as Nietzsche says in another passage from the late *Nachlaß*.

> Our psychological optics is determined by the following:
> 1. That c o m m u n i c a t i o n is necessary, and that to achieve communication, something has to be made stable, simple, and precise (above all, in the i d e n - t i c a l case). Before something can be communicable, however, it must be experienced as c u s t o m i z e d [*zurechtgemacht*], as 're-cognizable' [*wieder erkennbar*]. The material of the senses customized by the understanding, is reduced to rough outlines, made similar, and subsumed under familiar matters. Thus, the haziness and chaos of the sense-impressions are, as it were, l o g i c i z e d [*logisiert*].

2. The world of 'phenomena' is the customized world, which we feel as real. The 'reality' lies in the continual recurrence of identical, familiar, related things in their logicized character, in the belief that here we are able to reckon and calculate;
3. The opposite of this phenomena-world is not 'the true world,' but rather the world as a formless-inexpressible chaos of sensations [*die formlos-unformulirbare Welt des Sensationen-Chaos*] – consequently, another kind of phenomena-world, 'incomprehensible' ['*unerkennbar*'] to us.
4. Asking what things 'in-themselves' may be like, apart from our sense-receptivity and intellectual activity, must be rebutted with the question: how could we know that things exist? 'Thingness' was first created by us. (Nachlaß 1887, KSA 12, 9[106]).

In this passage, several of the problems introduced above have been solved. It is clear that there is no conflict in, on one hand, discarding the notion of things-in-themselves, and on the other, maintaining that senses 'deceive.' It is also clear that it is not inconsistent to claim, in one context, that senses 'deceive,' and in another that they don't. Senses deceive or not *relative* to how 'logicized' they have become. To the extent that we have customized our surrounding world, made it simple and familiar as life-world, senses interpret, thus 'deceive.' But to the extent that we transgress this customized, logicized life-world, we rediscover "the haziness and chaos of sense-impressions." In the latter case, we stand out in a relation to a world that is given in its self-presence, a world of which we may not be entirely conscious (since consciousness depends on linguistic logicization), and a world therefore described as a "formless inexpressible chaos of sensations," but still a world self-given in its self-presence, and therefore within the range of our perceptive possibilities (therefore also radically different from Kant's so-called 'true' world 'in-itself').

Before the emergence of Structural Linguistics, Nietzsche is articulating insights that later Ferdinand de Saussure, Roman Jakobsen, and Louis Hjelmslev would systematize and clarify. It is in Nietzsche the *sign*, as linguistic unit, that is responsible for so-called 'deception' (in this context: relative to the Human ground). Before the emergence of the form-giving sign, perceptions and thoughts are just chaotic, indistinct, and subconscious. In Saussure's words, they are "vague and nebulous . . . chaotic . . . confused";[143] in Hjelmslev's words, they are an "unanalyzed, amorphous

---

[143] Ferdinand de Saussure: Course in General Linguistics, translation, W. Baskin. New York (McGraw Hill), 1966; p. 112. Baskin's translation is in the following compared to Saussure's French original: Cours de linguistique générale, edited by C. Bally & A. Sechehaye. Paris (Payot), 1972.

continuum."[144] Not until the application of the *sign* are amorphous thoughts and perceptions made distinct by being segmented into distinct parts, which, after segmentation, we conceive as ideas or concepts. The segmentation occurs when the signifier, the sound-image, and the signified, the idea, delimit and circumscribe a certain content. Repeating Saussure's model of the sign, there is a relation between signifier and signified, which is *a priori arbitrary*, but *a posteriori necessary*. That is, it is *a priori arbitrary* that we describe glistering, fluttering, rattling, greenish entities as 'leaves,' but as soon as the description has caught on, it forces our hand, or rather our perception. Now we cannot but see these entities as 'leaves.'

Thanks to the signifier, we have an abstract concept of 'leaf'; thanks to the signified, the sound-image 'leaf' circumscribes and defines an abstract content. In isolation, the two layers are merely two amorphous masses, a mass of thought (or impressions) and a mass of sound. In isolation, they both elude linguistic description. 'Thinking' before the expression might constitute what we call a *mood*, or vague feelings and sensations. Sounds without concepts might constitute *noise* (or perhaps music). Separately, none of the entities constitutes a linguistic unit.

Only through their attachment, the two masses of thought and sound are segmented into distinct units, representing meaningful and comprehensible signs. The actual procedure for this reciprocal attachment is admittedly an enigma to Saussure.

> Without language, thought is a vague, uncharted nebula [*Prise en elle-même, la pensée est comme une nébuleuse où rien n'est nécessairement délimité*]. There are no pre-existing ideas, and nothing is distinct before the appearance of language. [. . .] Phonic substance is neither more fixed nor more rigid than thought; it is not a mold into which thought must of necessity fit but a plastic substance [*a matière plastique*] divided in turn into distinct parts to furnish the signifiers needed by thought. The linguistic fact can therefore be pictured in its totality – i.e. language – as a series on contiguous subdivisions marked off on both the indefinite plane of jumbled ideas [*des idées confuses*] and the equally vague [*indéterminé*] plane of sounds. [. . .] Thought, chaotic by nature, has to become ordered in the process of its decomposition [*est forcée de se préciser en se décomposant*; better: 'is made precise in the process of segmentation']. Neither are thoughts given material form nor are sounds transformed into mental entities [*Il n'y a donc ni matérialisation des pensées, ni spiritualisation des sons*]; the somewhat mysterious fact is rather that 'thought-sound' implies division, and that language works out its units while taking shape between two shapeless masses [*masses amorphes*]. [. . .] Linguistics then works in the bor-

---

[144] Louis Hjelmslev: Prolegomena to a Theory of Language, translation, F. J. Whitfield. Madison (University of Wisconsin Press), 1961; p. 52.

derland where the elements of sound and though combine; *their combination produces a form, not a substance.*[145]

It is in the context of this quotation that Saussure suggests two models representing the interaction of the two layers. The *first model* underscores their 'mysterious' interaction. The signified and the signifier interact as air-pressure acts in the formation of waves in the ocean. Between the two layers of air and water, there is an invisible interaction going on, represented, in a drawing by Saussure, by vertical, fragile-looking, punctuated lines. The linguistic sign would similarly be an entity represented not by any of the layers, but by the invisible strings between them holding them together. Saussure's model below can be seen as a formalized version of the air-pressure/wave analogy; level-a represents the sequence of sounds, and level-b the sequence of concepts.[146]

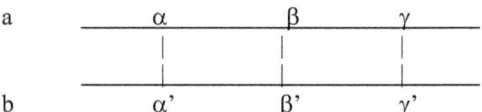

Saussure's *second model* underscores the inseparability of the layers. Signified and signifier are like two sides of the same sheet of paper. Cutting the paper means cutting front and back, signified and signifier, simultaneously; changing one side implies simultaneously changing the other. However, although there would be infinite possibilities of configuring the paper, front and back would always stick together. No pair of scissors could separate the two sides from each other.

In Saussure's model, the vertical separation-lines form concept- and sound-levels into linguistic signs. According to these separation-lines a world is sliced up into abstract entities, simplifying, thus 'distorting,' a world of becoming, a world originally and essentially *language-independent*. This is the 'world' Saussure describes as 'a substance,' and Hjelmslev describes as an 'amorphous continuum.' In Hjelmslev's famous illustration of how this continuum is differently formatted, he notices how the color-spectrum (which is, as far as we know, a 'continuum') is differently described in disparate languages

> In Welsh, 'green' is *gwyrdd* or *glas*, 'blue' is *glas*, 'gray' is *glas* or *llwyd*, brown is *llwyd*. That is to say the part of the spectrum that is covered by our

---

[145] Saussure, Course, loc. cit., p. 112-113; or *Cours de linguistique Generale* (1975), p. 155-157.
[146] Cf. Saussure: Course, loc. cit., p. 103.

word *green* is intersected in Welsh by a line that assigns a part of it to the same area as our word *blue* while the English boundary between *green* and *blue* is not found in Welsh. Moreover, Welsh lacks the English boundary between *blue* and *gray*, and likewise the English boundary between *gray* and *brown*. On the other hand, the area that is covered by English *gray* is intersected in Welsh so that half of it is referred to the same area as our *blue* and half to the same area as our *brown*.[147]

This implies that in Welsh there is, for example, no sharp distinction between our green, blue, and gray, which is all *glas*; neither between gray and brown, which is *llwyd*, etc. If thus we adhere to Saussure's model above, there would exist a c-level below the a-b sign-level. This c-level would represent Saussure's *uncharted nebula*; Hjelmslev's *amorphous continuum*; Nietzsche's *sensation-chaos*; or what above I called *hyper-reality*. If I illustrate this continuum simply by means of a continuous number line (which most appropriately is called *a real line* in mathematics), we can give a formalized illustration on how two languages segment this continuum in two different ways.

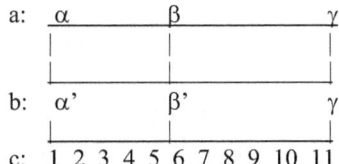
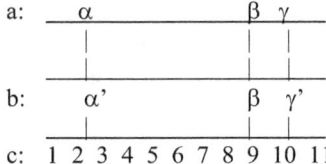

The c-level, the continuum, would now represent the amorphous world, Nietzsche's world of becoming. If the signifier-signified entities, α-α', β-β', and γ-γ' are the signs for *stem, leaf,* and *petal*, then the two different languages in the model would produce different definitions of how much of the continuum constitutes a *stem*, how much a *leaf*, and how much a *petal*. (Without having to go into technical details, we notice that in language I, the sign β/β' (say 'leaf') determines a leaf as the continuum from approximately 5 to 11, while in language II, a 'leaf' is determined as the continuum from approximately 8 to 10. The continuum from 5 to 11, 8 to 10, etc., is here merely a schematic metaphor for a particular segment of what we call *hyper-reality*.) The c-level would now correspond to the continuum of impressions received of the tree; the tree in its amorphous and chaotic totality of detail; the 'original' tree we seem to sacrifice to the linguistic sign as soon as we start naming a few of its properties.

---

[147] Hjelmslev, loc. cit., p. 52-53.

In conclusion, senses *as such* are not inadequate instruments of observing the world, they have not evolved *in order to* deceive (not regarding what I have called 'the Human Ground'). Relative to the Human Ground, they are not in-and-of-themselves deceptive, but they are bound up with a mental apparatus that *does* 'deceive' about (i.e., simplify and interpret) the world. As the mental apparatus during upbringing deepens and expands, a pure and virgin perception of the world also becomes increasingly impossible.

In his *Project for a Scientific Psychology* (to which we return in *Chapter 4*), Freud explains how the psychic apparatus, thanks to the intensity and the repetition of certain impressions, forms certain 'facilitating passages' [*Bahnungen*] that assist and adjust the reception of future impressions. As such, the psychic system creates a 'shell' that during upbringing and adulthood hardens or coagulates, thus setting up the threshold for what in the future may and may not enter the system. Eventually, *memory* (and thus *language*) comes to play an important role in conscious perception. Nietzsche seems to be on a par with Freud. When Nietzsche asserts that senses 'deceive,' they do so relative to the degree of cognitive and linguistic generalization and simplification they have undergone (by mental processes that Nietzsche elsewhere also explains, but a discussion I suspend until *Chapter 4*). In an empty stare into the depth of a lingering, self-manifesting world, there is possibly no 'deception' (at least, it seems to be an option to bypass some, if not all, of the defensive layers developed by a normal mental system). However, there is also in this attitude no self-conscious perception. The world is 'seen' like Leibniz on his daily stroll 'sees' the habitual sights of the windmill and the waterfall; i.e., in a mode of distracted, passive perception. Let us call this mode of perception *subconscious, unmediated*, and *non-falsifying*. However, sensations 'deceive' when in full self-consciousness we see actively; i.e., we see and remember the seen as being such and such. We now recall from memory the gestalt that uniquely corresponds to the seen, as this gestalt has been formed in and by language. I see and know I see a leaf only because a leaf-entity is defined in language (if there were no language for leaf-entities, I would *still* see leaves, but I would hardly notice, and possibly not remember. I would see this unnamed leaf-stuff like a mass of impressions rather than as a thing). We will call the mode of perception where I see and know what I see, *conscious, mediated*, and *falsifying*.

Thus, it is *not* the case that senses shut down themselves as soon as language with its form-giving power defines the seen; it is *not* the case that language makes us 'see' only *signifiers*; it does not *disable* access to 'language independent reality.' If it did, Nietzsche had simply recreated *appearance* as a new *thing-in-itself*, and *language* as a new *appearance*.

The diagram below may now summarize some of the relationships having been discussed. As appears from the diagram, there are two relationships of solidarity between, first, *the human ground and subconscious sensations*, and, second, *conscious sensations and language*. Neither of these two relationships of solidarity is negatively evaluated in Nietzsche. Although the first relationship exerts a special attraction to Nietzsche (and to numerous other 19th century poets and thinkers), since it seems like the fascinating entry-point to a world of becoming, the second relationship – as solidifying the *world of becoming* as a *world of being* – is acknowledged as both necessary and indispensable. That language in this relationship 'falsifies' does not entail a negative evaluation of language, and it should definitely not prompt us to a search for a language that does not 'falsify.' Language falsifying in a negative sense is the language I have equated with metaphysics in the diagram; this metaphysical language has no 'relationship of solidarity'; it exists in-and-for-itself, referring to *nothing*.

	LATE EPISTEMOLOGICAL POSITION
Concepts (= Falsifying) {	Language (= Metaphysics; destruction of life)
	Language (= Simplifying; necessary for life)
	Sensations (= Conscious; mediated; falsifying)
Sensations (= Neutral) {	
	Sensations (= Subconscious; unmediated; non-falsifying)
	Human ground (= pre-linguistic hyper-reality; 'continuum')
Thing-in-itself (= Non-existent). Instead: relativistic 'Ur-ground' of 'forces' and 'points.'	

The Ur-ground lives an isolated existence in my diagram. This is deliberate, since, although we are compelled to think the existence of such a ground, its being is as such inaccessible. As said, the Ur-ground withdraws itself from us; it is cold, indifferent, and inhuman.

3. Two Brief Control-Readings to Put the Position to Test

3.1. Explaining Nietzsche's 'Negative Ontologie des Dinges.'

As soon as we perceive a 'leaf,' named and circumscribed as such in language, we condense a mass of impressions in form of the glister, the flutter, the rattling, or the green of the tree's majestic crown of leaves. We now perceive the original manifold *as* a new abstract entity, called 'leaf.' And still, we must insist with Nietzsche, that the 'real continuum' is there to be perceived; it has not all of a sudden sunk down behind the world of appearances as a thing-in-itself. It is not an inaccessible 'X,' but an expanse of impressions intruding upon our sense-organs. If the majestic crown of the tree is 'hidden' in and by the abstract entity 'leaves,' it is no more 'hidden' than an entire color-spectrum is 'hidden' in an object I for shorthand call 'white' – the shirt is surely 'white,' but truly, it reflects from its immediate environment a variety of color-nuances. I *see* the shirt as white; I *say* the shirt is white; but I am also capable of going beyond my abstraction, my short-hand perception, and re-discover a world of colors 'hidden' in the white. As in Leibniz and as in Freud, also in Nietzsche there is always *too much reality*; our ability to respond to this reality – indeed our 'health' – depends on how effectively we are able to fend off this reality; with this, reduce it.

We now understand how Nietzsche can call our belief in 'things' a fiction; for example, as this belief is described as a fiction necessary for logic in the late *Nachlaß*:

> Let us suppose that there were no self-identical A [*sich-selbst-identische A*], such as every proposition of logic (and mathematics) presupposes, and the A were merely a p p e a r a n c e , then logic would have a merely a p p a r e n t world as its condition. In fact, we believe in this proposition under the influence of an endless empirical world which seems continually to c o n f i r m it. The 'thing' – that is the real substratum of A: o u r b e l i e f i n t h i n g s is the precondition for our belief in logic. The A of logic is, like the atom, a reconstruction of the 'thing' [*eine Nachkonstruktion des 'Dings'*] . . . If we do not understand this, but make logic a criterion for true being, we are already positing as realities all those hypostates: substance, attribute, object, subject, action, etc.; that is, conceiving a metaphysical world, that is, a "real world" (– b u t t h i s i s o n l y t h e a p p a r e n t w o r l d o n c e m o r e . . .). (Nachlaß 1887, KSA 12, 9[97], p. 389-90).

In *Nietzsches Philosophie* (half a century after its publication still a superior introduction to Nietzsche), Eugen Fink labels this lack of belief in enduring things, Nietzsche's *'negative Ontologie des Dinges.'*

> Nietzsche's thesis is: there are [*es gibt*] in truth [*in Wahrheit*] no things, no substances, there is no 'reality' [*'Seiendes'*]; there is only the fluctuating flow of life [*Lebensflut*], only the stream of becoming, the ceaseless to-and-fro of its drift; there is nothing enduring, unchanging, permanent – everything is in flux. However, our knowledge falsifies reality; it misrepresents the flow as the being of enduring things, fluctuation as cessation, and transformation of events as

standstill. The 'thing,' the substance, is a fiction, is a power-image of Will to Power, which as 'Knowledge' [*'Erkenntnis'*] of reality subdues, arrests, misrepresents [*umlügt*], stabilizes becoming, by subordinating it to the concept. Subsequently, it forgets its violation to the extent that it begins to believe that it has comprehended reality in its self-produced concepts like substance, causality, etc. The human being believes in 'things' – but there are none; it believes in 'Reality' [*'Seiende'*], but this 'Reality' is its own creation, the conceptual net [*Begriffsnetz*] that the human repeatedly casts into the tide of becoming. The world is not the sum of different and separate things for Nietzsche, coexisting in relation with one another. It does not consists of things at all. [. . .] At the beginning of Knowledge stands the Original Fall, stands the lie of the conceptual interpretation. [. . .] The Thing is a human thought-object [*Denkegebilde*]. [. . .] There is no Knowledge of the Being of Reality [*Seiendheit des Seienden*], as Metaphysics has it, because there are no Things whatever, nothing final, no in their finality solidified Things. [. . .] Nietzsche's fictional theory of Knowledge is in a decisive sense a negative Ontology of Things: there are no Things [*eine negative Ontologie des Dinges: es gibt keine Dinge*].[148]

Reading Fink, we notice that he, in conformity with the general Nietzsche-reception, does not distinguish between a so-called *Ur-ground* and *Human ground*. As Fink sees it, *Becoming* and *Being* is simply a complementary two-fold relationship: a single ground of becoming, complemented by the conceptual falsifications of this ground. In this 'falsification,' the biggest 'lie' of all is the fabrication of 'things.'[149] Fink can therefore conclude "*es gibt keine Dinge*." Although this statement in itself reiterates statements by Nietzsche to the same effect (for example: "Die 'Dingheit' ist erst von uns geschaffen." (Nachlaß 1887, KSA 12, 9[106]) – Fink's interpretation therefore remaining faithful to Nietzsche), in isolation, it is almost incomprehensible in what sense there can be *no things*, and how Nietzsche could arrive at such a thesis. Things are after all what surround us all the time, whether asleep or awake. Why would not the massive rock protruding

---

[148] Fink, Eugen: Nietzsches Philosophie, loc. cit., p. 163-165).

[149] This view echoes Heidegger, who is also seeing the fundamental opposition as between becoming and being, where being, since erecting its 'truth' on the more fundamental ground of becoming, necessarily becomes an 'illusion': "If the world were constantly changing and perishing, if it had its essence in the most perishable of what perishes and is inconstant, truth in the sense of what is constant and stable would be a mere fiction and coagulation of what in itself is becoming; measured against what is becoming such fixating would be inappropriate and merely a distortion. The true as the correct would precisely not conform to Becoming. Truth would then be incorrectness, error – an 'illusion,' albeit a perhaps necessary one." Heidegger: Nietzsche. loc. cit., p. 64.

from the surface of the ground in its undeniable self-presence be a *thing*? And why would not the rock be exactly an 'enduring,' 'permanent,' 'solid' *thing*, rather than a thing in flux?

It is my argument here that it is impossible to answer and make sense of these elementary questions without rethinking Nietzsche within the framework of Structural Linguistics. Accordingly, it is not the rock as a substance that moves itself about in a world of eternal becoming, it is our *impressions* of the rock – before the arrival of the sign – that moves about in a world of eternal becoming. It is not the rock that needs to be solidified, it is our *impressions* of the rock that need solidification. Nietzsche's negative ontology of things does not apply to things as matter and substance, but to things as constituted for a consciousness.[150]

As such, there are 'in truth' no things. There is (*es gibt*) only Saussure's uncharted nebula, or Hjelmslev's amorphous continuum. Before the sign, 'rocks' would be only large individual masses, hard to the touch, protruding from everywhere in nature – on familiar places or on threatening unfamiliar places. Every 'rock' would be an *individual* – by the early hominid only known (perhaps . . . in truth nobody knows!) by its characteristic individual shape and form. First with the emergence of the sign, these hard individual substances become *one* thing, a universal rock-thing. The rock gains permanence and solidity thanks to something as flimsy and ethereal as the word.

3.2. How Come that 'Lightning Flashes' only in Language?

Sometimes Nietzsche introduces the two relationships, *cause-effect* and *subject-predicate*, as if synonymous. And sometimes the *subject-predicate* relationship is introduced now as an ontological theme (as what one would strictly call a *substance-attribute* relation), and now as a linguistic theme (as what one would strictly call a *noun-verb* relation). One asks oneself, are

---

[150] Commentators lesser than Fink seem oftentimes clueless regarding this question. One encounters long, and longwinded, accounts of Nietzsche's 'becoming world' and 'non-enduring things' by authors that obviously can't get past their own pre-theoretical and commonsensical perception of the world. Accounts that have little or no theoretical approach to Nietzsche, applying to Nietzsche only the impoverished comprehension of the average and ordinary: 'Yes, the world changes, but is it not stable 'in-between' the changes? Things don't change 'all the time,' do they? Only 'sometimes' they do!' And if nothing else, the commentator can always try to give the trivia an appearance of logic: 'If A changes to B, A is still A and B is still B.'

these relationships supposed to express the same thing: *cause-effect, subject-predicate, substance-attribute, noun-verb*?

It is clear that in all cases, the relationships 'falsify' the world. They express something, which in itself is *one*, as *two*. They double the world in first, an *actor*, and then, an *action*. This implies that in these relationships we encounter the unique *method* and *logic* by which humans humanize the world. A world seen as only *one* is fundamentally in-human. To escape this in-humanity, humans invent a world that is always *two*.

The world as *one*, is the world we perceive; the world as surface; the world that opens itself up to us as *hyper-reality*; the *human ground* on which we stand. There is truly nothing but this appearing world; but, on the other hand, this is intolerable – there must be a reason, a purpose, an intention; there must be something that gives meaning and explains; there must be a hidden double. Consequently, the world must be *two*. The above relationships all express the *two*.

> Every judgment presupposes the whole deep belief in subject and predicate or in cause and effect; and the latter belief (that is, the claim that every effect is an activity, and that to an activity one must presuppose an actor) is even only a special case of the former. So the fundamental belief remains: there exist subjects. I observe something, and look for a r e a s o n for it: this means originally, I am looking for an i n t e n t i o n ; first and foremost for someone with an intention, i.e., for a subject, for an actor. (Nachlaß 1885-86, KSA 12, 2[83]).

To look for a subject, an intention, in what we observe, is in the epistemological tradition to look for causes. As mentioned above, Nietzsche is taking Hume a step further. The cause-effect relationship is not to be found as an inherent objectivity in nature – as Hume correctly understood; but Hume's epistemological skepticism is still only a special case of our fundamental beliefs in subjects and intentions; that is, our beliefs *in life in what is dead.* Hume's cause-effect relationships are formed through 'habit,' but to Nietzsche there is a 'habit' for that habit, namely our 'habitual' *belief in life*. The world as *one* is dead; the world as *two* is resurrected and alive. The resurrection is a falsification.

Language stabilizes this misconception. The *subject-predicate*, or strictly speaking *noun-verb*, relationship corroborates the idea that for an action there has to be also an actor. Inherent in our grammatical structure we thus find elementary metaphysics. Since from early on, we internalize this grammatical structure, we are by language seduced into thinking the world according to an actor-action model: I think, I sleep, he expresses, she does, it acts, etc.[151]

In *The Genealogy of Morals*, Nietzsche explains this doubling of the world as resulting from the seductions of language, and illustrates his idea by a favorite example to which he returns several times in the *Nachlaß* material: the lightning flashes [*der Blitz leuchtet*]. He is discussing how the strong cannot be separated from his strength, and he adds the following general explanation.

> A quantum of force is equal to an identical quantum of drive, will, and effect – moreover, it is nothing but exactly this drive, willing, and effect itself; and only because of the seduction of language [. . .] which understands and misunderstands all action as conditioned by an actor, by a 'subject,' does this appear otherwise. Exactly like the people separate the lightning from its flash, and makes the latter a d e e d, an effect of a subject they call lightning, so people-morality also separates strength from the expressions of strength, as if behind the strong there were some indifferent substratum, which h a d t h e f r e e d o m to express itself as strength or not. But there exist no such substratum; there is no 'Being' behind the deed, the effect, the becoming. 'The doer' is simply creatively added [*hinzugedichtet*] to the deed – the deed is everything. People essentially double the deed when they make the lightning flash; it is a deed-deed; it posits the same occurrence first as cause and then again as its effect. The scientists are no better, when they say 'the force moves, the force causes,' etc. (GM I 13, KSA 5, p. 279).

And in the *Nachlaß* material, the same idea is expressed.

> The predicate expresses an effect, which is brought before us, not the effect in itself. The sum of the predicates are condensed [*zusammengefaßt*] into one single word. It is a mistake that the subject is made *causa sui* – mythology of the notion of subject. The lightning 'flashes' – a doubling – the effect turned into a thing [*verdinglicht*]. [. . .] When I say that the lightning flashes, then I have first taken the lightning as an activity, and then as a subject. (Nachlaß 1885-86, KSA 12, 2[78] & 2[84]).

It is clear that the separation of lightning from its flash is seen as a falsification of a reality (here, a *hyper-reality*) where there is no such separation.

---

[151] Since the noun-verb relation is near universal, elementary metaphysics would seem to be promoted in virtually all languages. (We will have to consult the linguists to know exactly how universal this structure is; and perhaps more interestingly, how people with a language where it *does not* apply, perceive the world.)

When people thus express themselves about the flashing lightning they invent the lightning first as cause, and then add the flashing as its effect – or more precisely, language *as such* establishes this cause-effect relation (humans can do no better than using the language they have; they are as such 'seduced').

In *hyper-reality*, when 'lightning flashes,' it only 'does' a single thing (since the world is always only *one*): it makes this characteristic zigzag line on the background of the black sky. This zigzag line is only one. But this is not how we report our perception of the zigzag; language impels us into saying instead that the 'lightning flashes,' introducing thus into the zigzag an actor-action relationship. Tacitly, language has introduced an intention into the flash. We ask, 'who/what is doing the flashing?' – And answer, 'lightning is!' And again, 'what is lightning doing?' – 'It is flashing!' This linguistic seduction has an unconscious effect upon the subject, since the lightning is now understood as an actor that *does* something, namely lighting up the sky. The zigzag has intention. The world has been humanized.[152]

This doubling of the world is, we notice, a formal requirement for the *foundation* of science. Only on the condition of such a doubling, the physicist is capable of asking: "*Why* is lightning doing such a flashing?" – And first now can he attempt an answer: "This is because . . ," and then follows a scientific explanation of what kind of actor lightning is. The *why* can only be asked if there is more to the zigzag than the zigzag. Language postulates

---

[152] Müller-Lauter too refers to this Nietzschean example on subject-predicate logic, and makes the following comment: "As qualities [the predicates, PB] attributed to a fictional entity [the subject, PB] "wherein" they are said to "subsist," they are thereby transformed into something apart from us. We posit this entity as the "casual origin" of these changes, because we are incapable of thinking them otherwise. Whenever we say – to cite one of Nietzsche's favorite examples – "lightning flashes," we have within ourselves the "state" of flashing. Yet we do not stop at this, but rather invent an extra cause (the lightning) (KSA 12, 2[84]). Through this reification of the effect we bring about a linguistic "doubling" (KSA 12, 2 [70])." (Wolfgang Müller-Lauter: "On Judging in a World of Becoming" in B. Babich (ed.): Nietzsche, Theories of Knowledge, and Critical Theory loc. cit., p. 168.) One wonders what precisely is meant by "we have within ourselves the "state" of flashing"? – Müller-Lauter appears to repeat here Nietzsche's "'leuchten' ist ein Zustand an uns" (KSA 12, 2[84]), which, however, does not make the phrase more lucid; lightning obviously does not flash in our selves! The idea must be that we receive the impression of a flash; or, we see a zigzag, this being our "state"! To this we add, "invent," "an extra cause," although the added cause is the same as the effect as "state" that it aspires to explain. See also Stegmaier's "Weltabkürzungskunst" in J. Simon, loc. cit.

this additional layer. We are now in a position to understand why the subject-predicate relationship over-determines the cause-effect relationship, why there is an *older habit* behind Hume's *habit*.

In Nietzsche's cold and indifferent world, there is only the zigzag; and this is confirmed to us, when in pure and unspoiled perception, we gaze into this empty world as it opens itself up to us as *hyper-reality* (as appearance and nothing but appearance). However, we have created a world where this elementary truth is rejected and denied, a false world where lightning flashes, forces move, and I think. But in *hyper-reality*, there are only flashes, movement, and thinking, without something or someone doing the flashing, moving, and thinking.

CHAPTER 3

Splitting the Subject

Nietzsche's Radical Rethinking of the Cartesian and Kantian 'I Think'

> When I enter most intimately into what I call *myself*, I always stumble on some particular perception or other, of heat or cold, light or shade, love or hatred, pain or pleasure. I never can catch *myself* at any time without a perception, and never can observe any thing but the perception.
> – David Hume: *A Treatise of Human Nature.*[153]

> We are a sign, un-interpretable. We are without pain and have almost lost language in the unfamiliar. [*Ein Zeichen sind wir, deutungslos, Schmerzlos sind wir und haben fast die Sprache in die fremde verloren.*]
> – Hölderlin: *Mnemosyne.*[154]

> And when I say I said, etc., all I mean is that I knew confusedly things were so, without knowing exactly what it was all about. [. . .] In reality I said nothing at all, but I heard a murmur, something gone wrong with the silence, and I pricked up my ears, like an animal I imagine, which gives a start and pretends to be dead. And then sometimes there arose within me, confusedly, a kind of consciousness, which I express by saying, I said, etc.
> – Samuel Beckett: *Molloy.*[155]

---

[153] David Hume: A Treatise of Human Nature. London (Penguin Classics), 1984; p. 300.

[154] Hölderlin: Mnemosyne; In, Hölderlin Werke und Briefe. Frankfurt a/M (Insel Verlag), 1969; p. 199.

[155] Samuel Beckett: Molloy; in, Three Novels: Molloy, Malone Dies, The Unnamable. New York (Grove Press), 1958; p. 88.

0. Introduction

It was Kant who remarked that 'I think' was the "sole text" [*alleinige Text*] of rational psychology. In order to make such a small text-fragment an object of interpretation, one must assume that it has certain implications and ramifications, which extend its logical universe beyond its unassuming appearance.

The 'text' derives from Descartes; it becomes the abbreviation for a number of well-known pronounced or tacit presuppositions, such as, 'I think, therefore I am'; or 'Thanks to my thinking, I am a thinking thing'; or 'I can know only that I am a thinking thing.' In Descartes, the 'I think' becomes the beginning for the formation of indubitable knowledge, an anchoring-point from which knowledge can be flawlessly inferred, and simultaneously, an inner-mental principle, a mover or a motor, through which thinking is executed. Accordingly, the mind is conceived to be – in the last analysis – a singularity, or, more precisely, to be controlled by and from the singularity-principle, the 'I' in 'I think.' If we imagine that our thinking is like the action and dialogue happening on a theater stage, the 'I' is like a small homunculus sitting behind the curtain, which is, as a puppet-master, pulling the strings for the events happening on the stage.[156]

As we shall see in more detail below, Kant's objection to this theory is in brief that we can know nothing about the existence of such a small homunculus 'behind the curtain.' We are not able to *see* behind the curtain, although on Kant's stage, we are allowed to imagine the ideal and formal existence of such an 'I' – a formal existence whose nature we cannot know, because it is itself the *ultimate* ground for knowledge.

Nietzsche radicalizes the objection: not only are we *ignorant* about the existence of a homunculus, there *is* no small homunculus, no small puppet-master controlling the mind[157] – or if there 'is,' it is no more than a fictional construction. *A fortiori*, there is indeed no 'curtain,' and consequently no 'behind'; consequently nothing *hidden* and nothing to *find*. There is only a

---

[156] Descartes' famous anatomical equivalent to the 'I' is the 'pineal gland' as a small area in the brain allegedly controlling the various interactions of the brain; see also fn. 12.

[157] One may compare Nietzsche's rejection of the theory of the 'I' with Antonio Damasio's recent neuroscientific rejection of the theory of "a little person inside our brain" controlling all brain-activity: "The self is *not* the infamous homunculus, a little person inside our brain perceiving and thinking about the images the brain forms. It is, rather, a perpetually re-created neurological state." Damasio, Antonio: Descartes's Error: Emotion, Reason, and the Human Brain. New York (Quill-HarperCollins), 2000; p. 99-100.

'performance'; a 'performance' which is not particularly 'rational'; which does not follow a script; where there is no hero and villain, no *deus ex machina*, and no poetic justice. And if on this stage we seem to encounter some protestations of 'good' and 'evil,' they are merely pathetic and rhetorical.

We shall in the following argue that from Descartes over Kant to Nietzsche,[158] there is an increased awareness of the subjective condition that we here label, 'the split subject.'[159] So far, this condition is only a formality

---

[158] The three philosophical masters represent as names only an abbreviation of a historical process infinitely more variegated; they are necessary 'sign-posts' or 'anchoring-points' in a flurry of historical-intellectual events that it would make no sense to try to represent in a single essay; or which would reduce the present essay to a piece of library research.

[159] This is of course not, and it does not pretend to be, a novel recognition. For several years now, nearly throughout the entire last half of the 20th century, philosophers on the continent, and American philosophers with some delay, have been discussing the 'split' or 'decentered' or 'heterogeneous' subject; and some might say – not without some justification – that to take the discussion up again, is a moot, if not trivial, enterprise. If the single purpose were to make yet another postmodernist defense of the 'irrational' (read Emancipated) subject against the 'rational' (read Conformist) subject, they would be right. We believe, however, that (i) we are here working out the thesis differently from what has been seen before, (ii) that we work within an entirely different context, and (iii) with entirely different purposes. Thus, it is the aim of the present essay to place Nietzsche as a forerunner of a discourse that enjoys still greater success and relevance today, the discourse of the cognitive and neurosciences (this purpose will become even more explicit in the following *Chapter 4*, where we shall juxtapose Nietzsche's subject-theory and Freud's early neurological models, and as such prepare an almost direct path to contemporary neuroscience). It is also the aim to understand in which way, what it means, and what implications it has, to conceive the subject as split, multiform, or fragmented; and how, and to which extent, this understanding changes the view of the subject held by philosophical tradition before Nietzsche (especially Descartes, Hume, and Kant); still widespread today. It is even the ambitious aim to try to grasp how such a radical, and sometimes counter-intuitive, model of the subject affects the understanding of ourselves as thinking, speaking, and acting beings – with some, after all, 'rational' capabilities of forming and reforming our surrounding life-world and our societies. In many instances, and to various degrees, the essay has been positively influenced by a number of recent commentators on Nietzsche especially from the recent German tradition. To mention a few of the most influential: first and foremost, and clearly foreshadowing the present work, Schlimgen, Erwin: Nietzsches Theorie des Bewußtseins. Berlin, New York (Walter de Gruyter),

in Descartes. When he infers that if we have thoughts, there must be a cause for them, that is, an 'I,' the two realms he introduces are doing essentially the same thing: the 'I' is doing the thinking, and the thinking is the result of what the 'I' is doing. There is a supposedly complete transparency between the two spheres; we assume a kind of distortion-free communication from one sphere to the other. We shall therefore say that the Cartesian split is purely formal, coming about only thanks to the application of the cause-effect relation to the 'I think.' In this sense, Descartes' subject is still 'homogeneous' (as frequently asserted and generally agreed), although he has introduced the split as a *theme*.

In Kant, by contrast, there is a qualitative difference between 'I' and 'think'; they now occupy two distinct epistemological regions: the 'I' being *logical* and 'thinking' being *empirical*. This distinction is so pronounced that we cannot, from asserting the formal unity of the logical 'I,' conclude anything about the unity of a being doing the empirical thinking. The 'I' is truly alienated from thinking, because whereas thinking undoubtedly *exists*, it becomes a problem to determine what kind of *existence* an 'I' – now merely a logical ideality – may claim.

It is this thought that Nietzsche draws to its conclusion (we therefore believe that Nietzsche not so much opposes Kant as he 'revises' or 'radicalizes' him[160]). The 'I' has indeed no *existence*; it is a "fiction." When nonetheless we use it to signify something, it is because we adopt a grammatical convention. We mistakenly believe that a model we know from grammar, subject-predicate, applies also to the ontological subject, 'I'-

---

1999; and also Abel, Günter: Nietzsche: Die Dynamik des Willen zur Macht und die Ewige Wiederkehr (Berlin/New York: Walter de Gruyter, 1998; & Abel, Günter: "Bewußtsein – Sprache – Natur. Nietzsches Philosophie des Geistes." In Nietzsche-Studien bd. 30. New York/Berlin (Walter de Gruyter), 2001; the authoritative work on Nietzsche and Freud by Reinhard Gasser contains several illuminating chapters (and becomes especially relevant in the next chapter); see Gasser, Reinhard: Nietzsche und Freud. Berlin, New York (Walter de Gruyter), 1997; finally, we find many of our own conclusions in Günter Figal's introduction to Nietzsche: Figal, Günter: Nietzsche: Eine Philosophische Einführung. Stuttgart (Reclam) 1999. From the American tradition, outstanding are especially: Staten, Henry: Nietzsche's Voice. Ithaca, London (Cornell University Press), 1990; Nehamas, Alexander: Nietzsche: Life as Literature. Cambridge, MA (Harvard University Press), 1985; and the recently published, Emden, Christian J.: Nietzsche on Language, Consciousness, and the Body. Urbana, Chicago (University of Illinois Press), 2005.

160 This position is of course at odds with Nietzsche's own self-understanding, who in several notes describes his positions as anti-thetical to Kant's.

thought. In our conception of the subject, we apply and mix up a total of three models, subject-predicate, cause-effect, and 'I'-thought, in a confusion that generates the false promise that we shall eventually understand the 'I' as a unified cause and substance for our thinking (and as such, understand the essence of our subjectivity). We are thanks to a grammatical convention seduced into believing in a substantive 'I'; but we miss the point that we have only access to 'thinking' as it appears in all its fragmentation, and not to the promised unifying nodal point of departure for all these fragments, which we call 'I'.

We will call this particular Nietzschean theory of the 'split subject,' the "General Theory." It describes a split between a *'fictional I'* and *'real thinking,'* introduced thanks to the application of a grammatical subject-predicate logic. However, we find in Nietzsche, in different contexts and on different epistemological levels, another theory of the split subject; a theory introduced in MA under the label of the so-called "dividuum" (contrary to "individuum"), concerning the ability of subjects to split themselves into different, often opposing, 'voices'; for example, one voice 'commanding' something from the subject, which another voice resists.[161] It is this theory of the split subject that becomes the psychological foundation for understanding a phenomenon like the 'moral subject.' Courtesy of Einstein, we shall allow ourselves to label this theory of the split subject, the "Special Theory." The argument is clear: whereas the 'General Theory' applies generally (to anyone using language), the 'Special Theory' would typically apply to Nietzsche's moral subject; whereas the 'I' constituted thanks to grammatical convention is "a fiction," the 'I' "shouting" (see later) its moral commands into the ear of a subservient recipient is anything but fictitious.

Toward the end of the chapter, we shall explain how this so-called 'special theory' of split subjectivity, and Nietzsche's parallel introduction to a moral subject, is eminently well equipped to explain a phenomenon like ideology – so well equipped, indeed, that we tend to see Nietzsche's criticisms of morality and culture as *critique of ideology*. Correspondingly, we see his 'priest' as the *ideologue*, his 'slave' as the *ideological subject*, and his 'master' as the hope and promise of a possible human type *emancipated from ideology*.

We return to Nietzsche's theory of split subjectivity in juxtaposition to Freud's early neurological models of the psyche in the following *Chapter 4*,

---

[161] In the Postmodernist tradition, the theory has been best represented by Henry Staten: Nietzsche's Voice, loc. cit., and Jacques Derrida, in several works, but in relation to Nietzsche, in Otobiographies, loc. cit.

and shall here develop the thesis that the psyche does not consist of something like a single Ego (or a single Superego), but rather of a multiplicity of distinct *Ego-Clusters*, internally competing, and in the last analysis linguistically constituted. Toward the end of that chapter, as well as in the following *Chapter 5*, we will further develop and detail our tentative thesis, and explain how Nietzsche's theory of subjectivity in its practical implications and applications turns into a critique of *ideology*, the *ideologue*, and the *ideological subject*.

1. A Preliminary Determination of the Problem of the 'I Think' in Nietzsche

1.1. The Problem of 'thinking' in 'I think'

We are often recommended by Nietzsche to think beyond the Cartesian and Kantian 'I think'; this recommendation is famously made in aphorism 16 from JGB:

> When I analyze the event expressed in the sentence 'I think,' I acquire a series of rash assertions which are difficult, perhaps impossible, to prove – for example, that it is *I* who think, that it has to be something at all which thinks, that thinking is an activity and operation on the part of an entity thought of as a cause, that an 'I' exists, finally that what is designated by 'thinking' has already been determined – that I k n o w what thinking is. For if I had not already decided that matter within myself, by what standard could I determine that what is happening is not perhaps 'willing' or 'feeling'? Enough: this 'I think' presupposes that I compare my present state with other known states of myself in order to determine what it is. (JGB 16, KSA 5, p. 30).

In commentary, it is usually well understood that Nietzsche in this passage is criticizing the 'I', that is – translated into contemporary language – the homogeneous and centered subject. This understanding is generally accepted, and we shall only clarify it by differentiating the different levels involved in the 'I think' being questioned. *First*, Nietzsche's criticism of the 'I think' is more abstract and radical than much contemporary commentary has it. On its most fundamental level, it involves a questioning of the concept of 'thinking' as such (we emphasize: the *concept* of thinking; not the fact that we do something 'thinking-like'!). *Secondly*, it involves a criticism of the concept of 'I' as a unifying principle, 'doing' or regulating our thinking. *Thirdly*, it involves a deconstruction of the alleged cause-effect relation in inner-mental life between this supposed 'I' and its thinking activity. We

1. A Preliminary Determination of the 'I Think'   159

shall start by discussing the most abstract and fundamental level, then return to some of the consequences of this criticism of 'I', 'thinking', and their interrelation.

In the passage above, Nietzsche admits knowledge of only an absolute minimum; essentially no more than this: we experience 'something in our heads'; an activity of sorts; an operation on part of our minds. However, from this minimum, everything else that we claim to know is up for grabs. The question is, as often in Nietzsche, a question of what, how, and to which degree of certainty we can know anything at all.

We claim to be familiar with an activity called 'thinking'; but already here are we too rash in our judgment, because how can we *start* by determining an activity *as something*, if the point is that we as yet do not know it? We grant that something is 'happening in our heads,' but how do we arrive at the idea that this happening is exactly 'thinking' and not, for example, 'willing' or 'feeling' (cf. "by what standard could I determine that what is happening is not perhaps 'willing' or 'feeling'?")? I can only *know* on basis of a comparison; that is, I must compare a present state to some already known state in order to know the present state. In the case in question, in order to know what is 'happening in my head,' I must compare my present state of ignorance to a known standard. Only given such a comparison, I could perhaps realize that my present state fulfills certain criteria of the known standard, and this would give me the right to call it 'thinking' (cf. "this 'I think' presupposes that I compare my present state with other known states of myself in order to determine what it is.").

However, how do we come to know the known standard – the dilemma would only repeat itself at this one-step deeper level? It seems then that when 'something is happening in my head,' and given that I compare this 'happening' to a standard, then the standard to which I compare my present state can only be asserted as dogma. It must be taken for granted without examination and interrogation. It is asserted as certainty, but the certainty emerges only thanks to the tacit dogmatism of the position. Hence if I ask, 'what is happening in my head right now?' the question cannot be adequately answered, 'it is thinking!'; because then I am comparing my 'activity' to something I pre-reflectively determine as 'thinking'; I am presupposing the knowledge I am looking for; I am begging the question.

We must assume that this argument of Nietzsche's applies to all other 'activities in our heads,' such as, sensations of pleasure and displeasure; emotions like love, hate, anger, fear, and envy; inclinations like cravings and desires; sentiments like elation, curiosity, boredom, indifference, etc. In each case, something 'happens' and precipitately we interpret it as *so and so*. I may find myself in a present state of so-called 'boredom,' but how can

I know that this present state is exactly 'boredom' – it must be nearly impossible to unravel and analyze the actual multiplicity of 'emotions' that amalgamate into something called 'boredom'?

As we will see in more detail below, Nietzsche's criticism of the subject most fundamentally presupposes an assumption of what we shall here call a 'chaotic organism'; an organism beyond our control and cognition, but of which we nonetheless form erroneous and arbitrary knowledge. The mind is also such a 'chaotic organism'; it functions according to secret principles that cannot be understood in language. To label some of the activities of this organism 'thinking' is merely the crudest simplification and abbreviation.

1.2. The Problem of 'I' in 'I think'

Now, furthermore, there is supposedly an agent 'doing' the thinking; we suppose habitually that an 'I' thinks. This is one of the "immediate certainties" that one takes for granted.[162] Explicitly, this 'I' is understood as a substance for thinking as accidence, and simultaneously as a cause for thinking as an effect; as such, it is comprehended as an essential mover or force inherent in the thinking mind, and thanks to which we think. When it comes in the form of an 'I', we comprehend this thinking substance as a consciousness responsible for and in control of its thinking; but more abstractly, it does not matter whether we think of the thinking substance as a conscious 'I' or as something else.

> [...] a thought comes when 'it' wants, and not when 'I' want. It is, therefore, a falsification of the facts to say: the subject 'I' is the condition for the predicate 'think.' It thinks [*Es denkt*]: but to assume that the 'it' is just that famous old 'I' – it is, to put it mildly, just an assumption, an assertion, and by no means an 'immediate certainty.' Already in this 'it thinks' [*'es denkt'*] too much is supposed: already this 'it' [*'es'*] presupposes an interpretation of a process, and does not belong to the process itself. People are following grammatical habits in concluding, 'thinking is an activity, to every activity belongs somebody who is active, therefore – .' (JGB 17; KSA 5, p. 31)

Whether a cause comes in the form of an *Ich* or an *Etwas*, the presupposition of a 'mover' for our thinking is in any case erroneous; in either case, it cannot be proved that "it is I [*ich*] who think, that it has to be something

---

[162] "There are always harmless self-observers [*Selbst-Beobachter*], who believe that 'immediate certainties' exist, for example 'I think.'" (JGB 16, KSA 5, p. 29)

[*Etwas*] at all which thinks" (JGB 16, KSA 5, p. 30). Independently of how the thinking substance is determined, there is in all generality no 'doer' for the 'deed'; no 'agent' for the 'activity'; and no 'mover' for the 'movement.' Therefore Nietzsche can made the statement – seemingly precociously anticipating 20th century psychoanalysis – that even the 'it thinks' [*'es denkt'*][163] makes the same unwarranted assumptions as the 'I think' (cf.: "Already in this 'it thinks' [*'es denkt'*] too much is supposed: already this 'it' [*'es'*] presupposes an interpretation of a process, and does not belong to the process itself.") This is also why Nietzsche starts the aphorism by saying that a thought comes when 'it' wants, not when 'I' want. When a thought comes when 'it' wants, it becomes a self-moving, self-sufficient event without origin; it emerges in an auto-affective circuit, independent of any motivating force inside or outside of the circuit. The 'I' as motivating force is surely absent from this process, but not even the thought itself can truly be identified as an 'it'; i.e., it is not a unified entity *wanting* something (once again, according to subject-predicate logic). The 'it' is therefore placed in distancing quotation-marks, because in the stronger sense the thought ('it') wants nothing. (In the weaker sense, it is of course grammatically necessary to refer to the noun by a pronoun. Like anybody else, Nietzsche cannot help being a slave of language; and since as a stylist, he could not simply allow himself to write something like, 'a thought wants to come when a thought wants to come,' he does the next best, he marks the inadequacy of the grammar he necessarily obeys in his discourse.)

When Nietzsche subtracts the 'I' from the 'I think,' we are introduced to a new logical-psychological determination of the 'subject' – or more correctly, the *mind*. This new logical-psychological determination of the 'subject' (or mind) concerns metaphysics; it does not pretend to alter the way in which we *experience* subjectivity; it only pretends to alter the way in which philosophers have *thought* or *interpreted* subjectivity. First and foremost, when we subtract the 'I' from 'I think,' we end up with a mind without any unifying and centering principles. There is now nothing – no 'Ich' and no 'Es' – accompanying the activities that are seen as just 'hap-

---

[163] This "Es denkt" becomes, as known, an axiom in psychoanalysis, twenty to thirty years after Nietzsche writes. Anecdote has it that Freud does in fact borrow the term 'Es' from Nietzsche, but mediated through George Groddeck. If indeed it is the case that Groddeck first saw the expression in Nietzsche, and since used it as a convenient designation for the anonymous realm of the unconscious, he must obviously have misunderstood Nietzsche, since in Nietzsche it is rejected, not confirmed, that thinking derives from the 'Es.' As we shall see below; Nietzsche thinks explicitly of Descartes' "Es": the *res cogitans*.

pening' in the mind.¹⁶⁴ In the inner-mental activity we call 'thinking,' we find no 'original synthesis' (and we do not need to look for syntheses) that binds together thoughts as derivable from, and as the combined product of, the always present, but tacitly asserted 'I think.' The mind is instead a battleground for thoughts, but without a commander to organize, plan, and carry out the battle.¹⁶⁵

The polemical context for this criticism is most prominently Descartes and Kant. It was Descartes and Kant who before Nietzsche made the 'I' an indispensable foundation for thinking. Rather than questioning 'consciousness' and 'self-consciousness' in a psychoanalytic sense, Nietzsche is

---

¹⁶⁴ We must therefore conclude that Nietzsche is not simply criticizing the 'conscious' or 'self-conscious subject,' present to its intentions, speech, and actions, as psychoanalytic inspired receptions of Nietzsche has it. Again, Nietzsche's criticism is more fundamental and abstract. Most importantly, Nietzsche's 'I' is *not* identical to Freud's 'ego'; and he is, in his questioning of the 'I,' *not* recommending the dissolution of the 'ego,' with the radical consequences this would have within a psychoanalytic framework, namely the defense of an entirely psychotic subject-structure beyond conscious ego-control (something in the order of Deleuze and Guatteri's 'schizo-hero' from *Anti-Oedipus*. Cf., Deleuze, G. & Guattari, F.: Anti-Oedipus. Capitalism and Schizophrenia. Minneapolis (Minnesota University Press), 1993.

¹⁶⁵ This view has recently been repeated in Daniel Dennett: *Consciousness Explained* (New York, London: Little, Brown and Company, 1991). Dennett defends a so-called "Multiple Drafts" model of consciousness, as opposed to what he calls the "Cartesian Theater" model. In the "Cartesian Theater" model we tend to believe in a single location from where all the brain's activities derive, whereas in the "Multiple Drafts" model, 'drafts' are submitted from everywhere in the brain, finally resulting in a comprehensible 'article.' Günter Abel too has noticed the similarity between Nietzsche's model of the mind, and Dennett's, and its implied criticism of Descartes: "Dennett sees in this an alternative model [the 'multiple drafts' model] to the Cartesian conception of consciousness, to what he calls the mythos of the "Cartesian Theater." Descartes made the mistake, as mentioned above, to introduce a centralistic idea regarding where consciousness and conscious experience are seated in the brain. The pineal gland was for him the center of the brain, as if some inner station, where all sense-impressions had to arrive, after thereupon to be transformed or not, in a specific transaction, into the consciousness of the individual. It is important in the context of this idea, that the brain has *a single* center, and that this center is the precise causal point of departure for the occurrences of conspicuous contents as well as conscious experiences." Abel, Günter: "Bewußtsein – Sprache – Natur. Nietzsches Philosophie des Geistes." In Nietzsche-Studien bd. 30. New York/Berlin (Walter de Gruyter), 2001; p. 18.

questioning 'identity' as it has been thought in the modern Western tradition: sometimes in the form of Descartes' *cogito*, and sometimes in the form of Kant's synthesizing transcendental subject.

Part I

Thinking the 'I' in Descartes, Kant, and Benveniste

2. Descartes and Nietzsche: Problems in the Cartesian 'I Think'

2.1. The Desire for Immediate Certainty

Before Descartes can assert his *cogito*, he asserts his *dubito*, the *de omnibus dubitare*. He suggests a number of familiar assumptions about the possible deceptiveness of his senses and cognitions. That senses might be deceptive was no new insight in his day; this idea had been reiterated throughout the history of philosophy; it had also been noted that dream-life is sometimes as vivid as reality itself, and Descartes starts by rehearsing these two familiar assumptions. It might be that perceptions, like dreams, be illusory and deceptive. The whole perceived field of our waking life might then be regarded as seen as in a long dream – as well as Descartes himself, sitting now in front of this fire with this piece of paper in his hand, might be only dreaming of himself sitting in front of the fire, etc. We have after all no objective criteria by which to distinguish waking and sleeping life, as Descartes soliloquizes. Still, even lacking such criteria, something seems certain, and to Descartes, the axioms of mathematics and geometry seem like good candidates for absolute certainty. However, in order to prepare his mind to doubt everything (ultimately, in order to prepare a ground for the absolutely indubitable), Descartes takes his *de omnibus dubitare* to its absolute climax as he imagines that "an evil demon" could have fashioned a world with the singular purpose of deceiving this his precious self, Renatus des Cartes. Now, not only sense perceptions but also intellectual cognitions might be deceptive. The "evil demon" could have inserted Descartes into the matrix for an illusory false world, within which he now perceives and cognizes all these devilries, concocted by the demon, in the naïve belief that they represent certainties.

> I will suppose therefore that not God, who is supremely good and the source of truth, but rather some malicious demon of the utmost power and cunning has employed all his energies in order to deceive me. I shall think that the sky, the air, the earth, colours, shapes, sound and all external things are merely the delusions of dreams which he has devised to ensnare my judgement. I shall consider

myself as not having hand or eyes, or flesh, or blood or senses, but as falsely believing that I have all these things.[166]

After have entertained this exercise in absolute doubt for a while, Descartes eventually arrives to his well-known conclusion: "let him deceive me as much as he can, he will never bring about that I am nothing so long as I think that I am something."[167] Almost defeated, lingering on the brink of the abyss, Descartes turns around, and creates, with much elegance and cleverness, a counter-final conclusion: if everything is false and deceptive, then (surprise!) everything can*not* be false and deceptive. If I am the object of a mighty god's interest, then I must at least conclude that *I am*.[168] Exactly *where I am the object of deceit, I find myself as subject.*

In several Nachlaß fragments, Nietzsche expresses his doubts about the strategy of this Cartesian *de omnibus dubitare*, and its seemingly inevitable consequences. (Nietzsche is far from alone in expressing this skepticism; Descartes' argument already failed to convince several of his esteemed contemporaries; so for example, Thomas Hobbes and Pierre Gassendi[169]):

> Let us assume, that in the essence of things [*Wesen der Dinge*] there were actually something deceptively mad and fraudulent; then even the very best will to de omnibus dubitare, in the style of Descartes, could not protect us from the trap of this essence [*Wesen*]. Indeed, even that very Cartesian device might be the main trick by which to pull our legs and make fools out of us. [. . .] Enough, "I will no longer be deceived" could be the means for a deeper, more refined and more fundamental [*gründlicheren*] will, which wanted exactly the opposite, namely to deceive itself. (Nachlaß 1885, KSA 11, 40[2].

The problem, as Nietzsche sees it, is that when first one has positioned oneself within this circle of generalized doubt, there is no longer any legitimate exit point. Only the repetitious execution of a vicious auto-

---

[166] Descartes: *Meditations* p. 15. in: *The Philosophical Writings of Descartes* vol. II. Translation, J. Cottingham, R. Stoothof, & D. Murduoch. Cambridge (Cambridge University Press) 1984.

[167] Descartes: *Meditations*; *The Philosophical Writings* vol. II., loc. cit., p. 17.

[168] A kind of metaphysical paranoia, one is tempted to add: 'I am maliciously persecuted, therefore *I am*'; we notice in passing the general rule for the paranoid disorder: the more powerful the persecuting agent, the more important (in own self-understanding) the paranoid patient.

[169] We find these objections to Descartes in the debates that followed his *Meditations*, issued under the title, *Objections and Replies*; *The Philosophical Writings*, vol. I, loc. cit.

affective (or solipsistic) circle seems possible: I doubt, that is, I think, ergo I must *exist*; – I exist as thinking and everything else can be doubted; – there is certain existence in doubting and thinking only, and not in anything outside my skull. This auto-affective paralysis cannot tell us anything, and it does not bring Descartes a step closer to understanding either what he is *as* thinking, or the ontological status of that which he is thinking *about*.

This condition Descartes acknowledges insofar as he realizes that he cannot yet determine himself as an 'I' (an *Ich*), but merely as a 'something' (an *Etwas* – or in Descartes' language, as a *res cogitans* (a 'thinking thing')). The 'I' in the 'I think' remains featureless and nondescript, since it is so far no more than a conventional pronoun introducing any first-person indicative. It is merely the 'I' performing the speech-act, the linguistic 'I' uttering the statement while referring back to itself in the instance of enunciation.

What this 'I' *is*, in an ontological sense, and what it *does* while 'thinking' remains a complete mystery. If Descartes perchance thinks that he has gained an insight into his thinking *cogito* by determining it as a 'thinking thing,'[170] then this would be mere make-believe.

Moreover, if one is exposed to this generalized deception, everything could be deceptive, including the apparently rescuing 'I think'; 'I think' could still be instilled by the powerful demon as the subject's illusory belief in own existence; as also Nietzsche contends: "Once I thought that our existence was an artistic dream [*künstlerische Traum*] of a God, and all our thoughts and feelings essentially his inventions in his creation of a Drama – even our belief that 'I think' or 'I act' would be his thought." (Nachlaß 1881, KSA 9, 11[285]).

2.2. The Reality of Immediate Uncertainty

Nietzsche's objection is in fact already symptomatically inscribed and intimated in Descartes text as his growing frustration, throughout the second and third meditation, over not being able to proceed in his investigations.

As said, when first one has positioned oneself within the circle of generalized doubt, no escape route is available – *except* through a logically invalid *protestation*; something in the order of Nietzsche's "Enough, I shall no longer be deceived"; a protestation that has no logical ground, but is only

---

[170] On a close-reading of his text this is debatable, and it may underestimate Descartes' sagacity, as we shall see in a moment

a form of will to power. In a note from 1885, this is precisely Nietzsche's contention.

> Let us assume that there were in fact something deceptive about things, from where we came, how would it help, de omnibus dubitare! It might be the most wonderful means by which to deceive oneself. First and foremost, is it possible?
> "Will to truth" as "I will not be deceived" or "I will not deceive" or "I will convince myself and remain steadfast", as a form of the will to power. (Nachlaß 1885, KSA 11, 39[13]).

At a certain point in his Meditations – we may designate it as Descartes' *true* "Archimedian point" – Descartes asserts his will-to-power, and decides that he can brush aside the extremely powerful demon as old cobweb; the same powerful demon he once needed as a construction to establish his *fake* 'Archimedian point,' the *ego cogito*. In order to break asunder the self-reflexive circle of doubt, it is necessary to apply a measure of force to its perimeters; logical rigor is a small matter for this overriding will-to-truth, will-to-power. Suppression of logical rigor is even necessary for Descartes to sustain the progress of his discourse. The background motive for the celebrated 'rational subject' becomes as such a resolute and tenacious will, a will-to-power-to-truth.

If we take a step back, we notice how this is staged in the text: the deceived subject is, for all that he knows, locked up in an imaginary solipsistic fantasy world. He knows minimally that he is the author of this fantasy world, and can minimally conclude that, "I think, therefore I am." As such, the deceived subject knows minimally that he exists as something; that the evil demon can never cause him "to be nothing, so long as I think I am something." When Descartes from this point onwards starts his investigations into *what* he is as 'something,' these investigations always terminate in the same redundant dead-end conclusion: 'I know I am thinking, so, what am I? – Oh, there is it, thinking!'

The philosophical narrative is well-known: after having suggested to himself that he might be a 'body' and then a 'soul,' and rejected the suggestions again, Descartes wonders again about his true essence, and arrives to his well-known maxim: "Thinking? At last I have discovered it – thought [*Cogitare? hic invenio: cogitatio est*]; this alone is inseparable from me."[171] and once again, he repeats: "I am, I exist – that is certain [*Ego sum, Ego existo, certum est*]. But for how long? For as long as I am thinking. For it

---

[171] Descartes: *Meditations*; *The Philosophical Writings* vol. II., loc. cit., p. 18.

could be that were I totally to cease from thinking, I should totally cease to exist."[172]

This repetitive pronunciation of being, where Descartes as 'I' refers back to himself as utterance-subject, assures him minimal (albeit, strictly *formal*) existence, but he remains trapped in a performative: he is exactly capable of *saying* what his is *doing*, but is capable of no more, and he is consequently unable to determine his identity as anything but this incomprehensible *doing* that he calls 'thinking.'

This does not stop Descartes from trying again, repeating his one and only certainty: "I am, then, in the strict sense only a thing that thinks, that is, I am a mind. [. . .] But what kind of thing? As I have just said – a thinking thing."[173] This assertion of existence continues into the third meditation, where Descartes makes a last effort to break through the self-reflexive circle of doubt. Now he mobilizes all his intellectual resources in a last effort to break out of this language-trap, and *see* what hides behind the 'I think'; he stops his ears and closes his eyes in order to see and hear himself better. He listens to the silence within his own muted self, and gazes into a darkness that stays pitch-black: "I will now shut my eyes, stop my ears, and withdraw all my senses. I will eliminate from my thoughts all images of bodily things [. . .] I will converse with myself and scrutinize myself more deeply, and in this way I will attempt to achieve, little by little, a more intimate knowledge of myself."[174] In this dark and silent world, he fails again to find himself; in vain, he beseeches the same old inscrutable sphinx. The only possible conclusion reads once more, 'I am a thinking thing.' He just has to say it again. For the last time . . .

---

[172] Descartes: *Meditations*; *The Philosophical Writings* vol. II., loc. cit., p. 18. This repeats the first statement of existence: "I am, I exist, is necessarily true each time I pronounce it." The criticism of Descartes' proof of existence is anticipated by Gassendi in his objections to Descartes *Meditations;* Gassendi responds to Descartes: "You add that thought alone cannot be separated from you. Certainly there is no reason not to grant you this, particularly if you are simply a mind, and you are not prepared to allow that your substance is distinct from the substance of the soul except conceptually. Nonetheless I want to stop here and ask whether, in saying that thought cannot be separated from you, you mean that you continue to think indefinitely, so long as you exist. This would accord with the claims of those noted philosophers who, to prove that we are immortal, assume that we are in perpetual motion or, as I interpret it, that we are perpetually thinking." Gassendi, Pierre: *Objections and Replies*; *The Philosophical Writings* vol. I, loc. cit., p. 184.

[173] Descartes, *Meditations*; *The Philosophical Writings* vol. II., loc. cit., p. 18.

[174] Descartes: *Meditations*; *The Philosophical Writings* vol. II., loc. cit., p. 24.

2. Descartes and Nietzsche: Problems in Determining the 'I Think'   169

I am a thing that thinks, that is to say, that doubts, affirms, denies, that knows a few things, that is ignorant of many (that loves, that hates), that wills, that desires, that also imagines and perceives [*Ego sum res cogitans, id est dubitans, affirmans, negans, pauca intelligens, multa ignorans, volens, nolens, imaginans etiam & sentiens*]; for as I remarked before, although the things which I perceive and imagine are perhaps nothing at all apart from me and in themselves, I am nevertheless assured that these modes of thought that I call perceptions and imaginations, inasmuch only as they are modes of thought, certainly reside in me.[175]

A long list of attributes describes the 'thinking thing' (*res cogitans*), the 'something,' the *Etwas*, or the *Es*.[176] We notice from this list that a 'thinking thing' has several properties, and is not accountable only for thinking (in the narrow sense), but for an entire spectrum of intellectual and emotional manifestations. Far from being a so-called rational, homogeneous, self-conscious subject, a thinking thing, also called a "mind" by Descartes, is characterized by a rather bewildering lack of determination.

This paralysis of the Cartesian discourse would and should have been the conclusion of Descartes' *Meditations* if Descartes had stayed as truthful to himself as Nietzsche would have wanted. When they do not stop here, it is because Descartes mobilizes his will to power; or what Nietzsche dubs his "Enough." This is a quite precise characterization, although it comes in a somewhat more elaborate version in the text; Descartes' 'Enough!' reads: "Since I have no cause to think that there is a deceiving God, and I do not yet even know for sure whether there is a God at all, any reason for doubt which depends simply on this supposition is a very slight and, so to speak, metaphysical one."[177]

---

[175] Descartes: *Meditations*; *The Philosophical Writings* vol. II., loc. cit., p. 24.

[176] Again this observation is anticipated by Gassendi, who questions the fecundity of Descartes' conclusion that he is a 'thinking thing': "And so you refer us to your principal result, that you are a thing that thinks – 'thing' is not to give any information. This is a general, imprecise and vague word, which applies no more to you than it does to anything in the entire world that is not simply a nothing. You are a 'thing'; that is, you are not nothing, or what comes to the same think, you are something. But a stone is something and not thinking, and so is a fly, and so is everything else. When you go on to say that you are a *thinking* thing, then we know what you are saying; but we knew it already, and it was not what we were asking you to tell us. Who doubts that you are thinking?" Gassendi, Pierre: *Objections and Replies*; *The Philosophical Writings* vol. I, loc. cit., p. 192.

[177] Descartes: *Meditations*; *The Philosophical Writings* vol. II; loc. cit., p. 25.

Descartes' decision from the beginning, the assumption of the existence of an evil demon is undone; and he is in a sense back to a *before* of the logical beginning of the Cartesian project; back to his pre-philosophical, commonsensical, and pragmatic self. Between these two proclamations – first, one asserts a deceitful god; second, one neutralizes him again – nothing has happened except reflections on how to begin philosophy. With this last sleight of hand, Descartes has now rescued all intellectual certainties that were previously lost in doubt. With his evil demon neutralized, he can again trust the veracity of certain self-evident truths, either because they announce themselves "clearly and distinctly" [*clare et distincta*] or because they are illuminated by the "natural light" [*lumine naturali*].

Following this neutralization of the evil demon, Descartes re-introduces himself to what he has always regarded as the most self-evident truth of all, the law of cause and effect: the related notions that (1) there must be a cause for an effect; (2) that the cause must have at least as much "reality" as the effect; and (3) that the more perfect cannot follow from the less perfect.

> Now it is manifest by the natural light that there must be at least as much reality in the efficient and total cause as in the effect of that cause. For where, I ask, could the effect get its reality from, if not from the cause? And how could the cause give it to the effect unless it possessed it? It follows from this both that something cannot arise from nothing, and also that what is more perfect – that is, contains in itself more reality – cannot arise from what is less perfect.[178]

It is not necessary for us here to go into detail with the intricacies of the different steps in Descartes' argument – all these applications of the cause-effect relation to 'formal' and 'objective' reality, to the more and the less perfect, etc. – we will merely note that in the form of cause-effect, Descartes finds a logical instrument by which to demonstrate the existence of something outside his own thinking; namely, God and world.[179] It is as such

---

[178] Descartes: *Meditations*; *The Philosophical Writings* vol. II; loc. cit., p. 28.

[179] From now on, Descartes can argue that interior ideas, 'phenomena,' which are perceived as evident because of the 'light of nature,' must have a correlative objective reality. They are not just shadows in the mind of the reflective subject. As phenomena, they must have a cause with at least as many 'degrees of reality' as these effects themselves have. This notion of real causes for the images in the mind saves the world as a real world. The idea of a God, which is good and almighty, absolute and perfect, must have infinitely many 'degrees of reality' causing it, inasmuch as the *cause of the idea* of God (namely God himself) is more than the idea itself. God, as the most perfect idea Descartes can imagine, must consequently, have the most perfect creature as its cause,

not the 'ego cogito,' that constitutes the true beginning of 'the rational subject' in the Meditations; it is Descartes' absolute faith in the cause-effect relation's applicability to metaphysical matters.

2.3. Descartes' Confusion of Linguistic and Cognitive 'I'

Descartes of course believes in a 'homogeneous' and transparent subject; for him it is evident that the cause-effect relation between 'I' and 'think' would be direct and straightforward, meaning that a 'will' or 'intention' emerging in the 'I' would manifest itself undistorted in the corresponding 'thinking' – as unproblematically as heat applied to an object warms the object. There is as such no 'unconscious' 'will' or 'intention' in the 'I' that could produce unexpected, unwanted, or contradictory results in its actions, speaking, or thinking. Instead, there is complete transparency between 'thinking' and the supposed intention to think emerging in the 'I.' Nonetheless, Descartes has introduced a split into his homogeneous subject: he postulates that we know only our thinking; but therefore, furthermore, also know that something is *doing* the thinking. He is convinced that the fact that he knows thinking, automatically entails that he knows also that '*something*' is thinking. The split therefore has the form of a cause-effect relation. Thinking must have a 'cause,' "for where," as Descartes asserts, "could the effect get its reality from, if not from the cause? [. . .] Something cannot arise from nothing." In Descartes' optimistic scenario, it is now only a matter of time before we can more precisely describe this 'cause,' this 'something' (and this becomes, according to Kant, the project of 'rational psychology'). Hence, although Descartes never envisioned a disruptive rift or gap between the 'something' and its thinking; although he assumes distortion-free communication between the two regions, he has still introduced a formal distinction between a thinking agent and its activities, since something is cause and something is effect, something is substance and something is accidence, something is subject and something is predicate.[180]

In Nietzsche's view, it is the last matrix (subject-predicate) that overdetermines Descartes' theoretical *modus operandi*. Descartes is "stuck in

---

namely, a real, good God. The logic is, abbreviated: 'I have an idea of God, therefore there is a God, therefore I am.' Or even shorter: 'I have an idea of God, therefore I am.'

[180] See also Günther Abel for a detailed criticism of the Cartesian subject; in Abel: "Bewußtsein – Sprache – Natur"; loc. cit., p. 28-29 & 36-37.

the trap of words"; his 'I think,' entailing that thinking "is an activity for which a subject must be thought," is only "a belief in grammar":

> Let us be more cautious than Descartes, who is stuck in the trap of words. It is true that Cogito is just one word: but it has multiple meanings. [. . .] In that famous cogito hides, 1) I think, 2) and I believe that I am the one who thinks, 3) but assuming that this second point remains undecided, as a matter of belief, the first 'it thinks' [*'es denkt'*] still includes a belief, namely that 'thinking' is an activity, for which a subject, at least an 'it' [*ein 'es'*], must be assumed – the ergo sum means no more that this! But this is only belief in grammar, which already presupposes 'things' and their 'activities'; we are far from immediate certainty. (Nachlaß 1885, KSA 11, 40[23]).

As indicated above, the 'I think' is not rescued by replacing the 'I' with an 'it.' The seemingly precocious *es denkt* (which today we tend to associate to Freud's *Es*) is merely a translation of Descartes' *res cogitans*; the thinking thing as *Es*, following the subject-predicate logic no less than the 'I think'.

In any case, *I* or *Es*, Descartes bases his most fundamental assumptions on grammar. Whether an 'I' or an 'it' precedes thinking, in both cases, Descartes is merely following the linguistic convention that a subject precedes a predicate, and that language as such already presupposes "things and their activities."[181] In some of the latest Nachlaß material, the criticism of Nietzsche's is repeated:

> 'Something is being thought: consequently something thinks' [*Es wird gedacht: folglich giebt es Denkendes*]: this is the outcome of Descartes' argument. But that means that we posit our belief in the concept of substance as 'true a priori'; – that when something is being thought, there must be something 'that thinks,' is simply an expression of our grammatical convention that adds to every deed a doer. In short, a logical-metaphysical postulate is made here – and n o t m e r e l y e s t a b l i s h e d / s t a t e d [*nicht nur konstatiert*] . . . Along the lines of Descartes, one does n o t arrive at something absolutely certain, but only at the fact of a very strong belief. [. . .] If one reduces the proposition to 'something is being thought, therefore there are thoughts,' one has produced a mere tautology, and exactly that which is in question, the 'r e a l i t y of thought' is not addressed. (Nachlaß 1887, KSA 12, 10[158]).

---

[181] Descartes may be deceived by the evil demon, but evidently not regarding his linguistic competencies; the demon has been benevolent enough to let Descartes keep his fundamental sanity; he still speaks and reasons within the rules of language and logic.

Nietzsche's criticism implies that Descartes wants to understand his mind, this 'chaotic organism,' ultimately according to pragmatic surface-rules. He falsely infers that as well as there is a linguistic 'I,' there must be a cognitive 'I'; as well as a predicate is attached to the linguistic 'I,' a thinking activity is attached to the cognitive 'I'; and as well as a subject always precedes a predicate, so the cognitive 'I' must as agent precede its thinking activities.[182]

Most fundamentally, Descartes confounds linguistic 'I' and cognitive 'I.' This is why Descartes is stuck in "the trap of words." He is seduced by language, and does not see that in the 'I think' he is dealing with a pragmatic-linguistic subject-predicate logic. He therefore believes that gazing hard enough into this abyss shall give him knowledge of himself as a thinking substance. He erroneously thinks that the linguistic province of words, sentences, and grammar extends into the domain of the 'thing-in-itself,' and might help him to explain this 'chaotic organism' of the mind.[183]

Especially because Descartes never succeeds in giving a good explanation of this 'something' that he is convinced is the cause of thinking, acute minds after him, such as Kant, begin to question the status and nature of this supposed agent of thinking, as we shall see in more detail below, Nietzsche's objections to Descartes can be seen as further elaborations of Kant's critical analysis of the Cartesian 'I think.

---

[182] See also Erwin Schlimgen: "The Quintessence of Nietzsches Descartes consists in that a subject is not subject as (free) origin for its conscious thinking. We are, according to Nietzsche, "spectators to, rather than creators [*urheber*] of, these processes." Schlimgen, Erwin: Nietzsches Theorie des Bewußtseins. Berlin, New York (Walter de Gruyter), 1999; p. 108.

[183] Cf. Schlimgen: "The Cartesian *ego* is according to Nietzsche an unconscious derivation, which follows from the grammatical subject-predicate-scheme: 'I' is the condition, 'thinking' is the predicate and the conditioned. Descartes succeeds thanks to this schema to think the concept of a thinking substance to which thinking as accidental modus is added; the I is being thought as causal [*ursächliche*] substance, from where thinking becomes an effect. The substance-accidence-schema mirrors then itself *syntactical* in the agent-patient-schema: the I is *cause* for thinking." Schlimgen, Erwin: Nietzsches Theorie; loc. cit., p. 26.

3. Kant and Nietzsche: Deconstructing the Cartesian Cogito

3.1. Preliminary; the Multiple-Self Subject in David Hume

In Descartes, *cogito, ergo sum* is supposed to warrant that only thinking has indubitable certainty. The *de omnibus dubito* declares everything else doubtful.

The assumption is that we have immediate access to our thoughts, but only intermediate access to the objects our thoughts are about. The immediate must have a higher truth-value than the intermediate, to which we seem to arrive only through inferences and conjectures; consequently, nothing can be more certain than our thinking, which therefore, so it must seem, provides us with a true beginning for knowledge. Now, from our new point of departure, we can in good order let our investigations proceed in two different directions: firstly, what we are as 'thinking things'; and secondly, what is constituted outside our thinking.

As we have seen above, these investigations end in paralysis. With a paradoxical formulation, the self-present ground of the *cogito* can be nothing but *beginning*; that is, a self-repetitive 'beginning' from which nothing can follow; a false start frozen in its own momentum. This paralysis is already inscribed in Descartes' text, and is keenly noticed by Nietzsche. However, it had been noticed and discussed well before Nietzsche, notably by Hume and Kant. Hume's introduction to his idea of the so-called "bundle-self" or "multiple self" would radically alter the direction for the discussion of the introspective subject of Descartes,[184] and Kant would, in his analysis of the cogito, relate to this re-directed discussion of the introspective subject.

Hume, like Descartes, had asked himself what kind of impressions could give rise to the idea of a single unified self. His answer, however, had eliminated any Cartesian hope of encountering through introspection a rational substance, corresponding to the *ego cogito*. Instead, as soon as we interrogate ourselves, and try to assert the essence of self-identity, we seem to stumble only upon different perceptions and sensations. In inner perception, we never encounter any perception of a unified self, and may not even be able to produce a notion of such a simple self, because, as we start our introspection, we perceive ourselves only as constantly changing impressions,

---

[184] Nietzsche does not seem to be aware of Hume's discussions of self-identity; he has in any case no references to Hume's concept of identity. This is a peculiar omission, since Hume's reflections on the self are close to Nietzsche's own.

3. Kant and Nietzsche: Deconstructing the Cartesian Cogito 175

and these impressions cannot give rise to any stable principle of identity and unity:

> If any impression gives rise to the idea of self, that impression must continue invariably as the same, through the whole course of our lives; since self is supposed to exist after that manner. But there is no impression constant and invariable. [. . .] [Man is a] bundle or collection of different perceptions, which succeed each other with an inconceivable rapidity, and are in a perpetual flux and movement.[185]

Hume pictures this inner-mental fluctuation of perceptions as a theater-stage where actors make their successive appearances only to disappear again, and without referring to someone or something guiding them; a stage, therefore, without our 'puppet-master' from the beginning, sitting behind the curtain directing the events happening on the stage.[186] There is therefore in Hume no homogeneous, united, or continuous self-identity, but only the perception of distinct impressions.

When nevertheless, we are inclined to ascribe identity to these distinct and successive perceptions, it is because we connect that which in itself is unconnected. We achieve this thanks to a certain confusion, insofar as we ascribe identity to different objects existing in close proximity; and in a similar manner we ascribe a unifying principle (for example in the form of 'soul,' 'self,' or 'substance') to our rapidly changing, but associated, perceptions. As such, the myth of a unified identity is created. The unification of different and distinct perceptions is something we *attribute* to perceptions, but it belongs only to the '*ideal world*' and not to the '*real world*' where as a rule there is disconnection between objects in the mind:

> The identity which we ascribe to the mind of man is only a fictitious one. [. . .] 'Tis evident that the identity which we attribute to the human mind, however perfect we may imagine it to be, is not able to run the several different perceptions into one, and make them lose their characters of distinction and difference, which are essential to them. [. . .] In our understanding we never observe any

---

[185] Hume, David : A Treatise of Human Nature. Oxford (Oxford University Press), 1978; p. 251-52.

[186] "The comparison of the theater must not mislead us. They are the successive perceptions only, that constitute the mind; nor have we the most distant notion of the place where these scenes are represented, or of the materials of which it is composed." (Hume: loc. cit., p. 253.)

real connection among objects [. . .] identity is nothing really belonging to these different perceptions.[187]

3.2. The Paragoristic Confusion of Logical and Empirical Subject in Kant

Kant was aware both of the paralysis in Descartes' determination of the subject, as well as of Hume's intervention, and an important part of *Kritik der reinen Vernunft* is dedicated to the analysis of these two, seemingly, contradictory determinations of self. The self is seemingly both a thinking unity, and a container of a multiplicity of representations; the self seems ambivalently determined as both *one* and *many*. The analysis of this conundrum comes in Kant's section on "The Paralogisms of Pure Reason," where he manages to both deconstruct, acutely and effectively, the Cartesian project of the *ego cogito*, and simultaneously, to qualify and soften some of the most radical consequences of Hume's claims.

Giving a new orientation to Western Thinking, Descartes had focused his philosophical attention on inner-mental life. The totality of this inner life, we label 'consciousness' today, and in Kant's days, 'self' or 'soul' or 'ego.' It seems plain that since the self accompanies inner-mental life in all its many variegated manifestations as the same self, the self must be an unchanging entity or identity in a flood of impressions. The simple assumption is that when a subject 'has' experiences, it simultaneously experiences that it has them; the subject always experiences itself as accompanying its representations as *something*; they always seem to derive from 'something,' and always from this particular 'something' called 'I.' As such, the self is understood as *substance*; and since it is also understood as the *same substance* accompanying multiple representations, it must be a unity; or (so Kant) *simple*. (As an example, in experiencing *a yellow car speeding past us*, we do not have three different experiencing 'selves': one experiencing the out-

---

[187] Hume: loc. cit., p. 259-60. When we reflect upon our perceptions we form ideas about them, and we are able to associate these ideas 'in the imagination.' These associations are primarily due to the principles of resemblance and causation, two principles by which we connect ideas so that we understand the succession of thoughts as a single uninterrupted process in a thinking person. Thanks to these principles, we combine present perceptions with perceptions of the past. Memory becomes thus an original source of identity: "As memory alone acquaints us with the continuance and extent of this succession of perceptions, 'tis to be considered, upon that account chiefly, as the source of personal identity." Hume: loc. cit., p. 261.

line of a car; another experiencing the 'yellow'; and a third experiencing the speed. There is one *simple self* 'accountable' for, and to which we ascribe, the total experience; not three different selves co-operating in representing the experience.) Therefore, the self is *simple substance*. Being a *simple substance* implies furthermore that in all the changes experienced in inner-mental·life, the self remains the *same* simple substance; the states may change in inner life, but the self remains the same throughout all changes (continuing the example given above, now I see the car in front of me; now next to me; and now behind me; in all instances, I remain the same self, while my perceptions of the car change over time.) Therefore, the self is so-called "numerical identical" – it remains the same identical self in all inner-mental changes; it is as such a "self-conscious being," or in Kant's words, *person*. Finally, whereas as all other kinds of objects are situated outside the self, and thus separated from the self, the self is its own object, existing in absolute proximity to itself. Nothing therefore seems to be more certain than the existence of the self, whereas outer objects are less certain. In Kant's words, the self is *ideal*.

These four interrelated qualifications characterize the subject as defined in 'rational psychology': the subject is *substance*, is *simple*, is *person*, and is *ideal*. In Descartes' 'rational psychology,' the 'I think' implies and abbreviates this fourfold definition of the subject.

In Descartes, this self is furthermore understood as a *thinking* substance (a "thinking thing"), and it is assumed that one can produce knowledge of this substance, while in Kant, the 'I think' is merely a *subject of judgment*; that is, it only *receives* representations, which it 'judges' (i.e., distinguishes and compares and synthesizes), but it can never itself be representation. In Kant, the thinking-'judging' subject therefore is the *condition* for all knowledge, and is not itself conditioned by some other extraordinary principle of knowledge (there is no background where we find a subject supporting and representing the first subject).[188] The 'I think' can never become an object

---

[188] See several commentators of Kant. So, Werner Stegmaier: "[Apperception] is thought as "form" or the possibility of condition for knowledge, therefore "transcendental." When the I, the subject and consciousness is merely thought as the "highest" possibility of condition of experience, as the "original-synthetic unity of the transcendental apperception," then one thereby envisions nothing more than "a transcendental subject of thoughts = x, [. . .] whereof, in isolation, we can never form the slightest concept [KrV, A 345f]." Stegmaier, Werner: Interpretationen: Hauptwerke der Philosophie von Kant bis Nietzsche. Stuttgart (Philipp Reclam), 1997; p. 41. Also Friedrich Kaulbach: "The word 'I' is "only" a sign for something that cannot be objectified, [. . .] and therefore remain an indeterminable 'thing'." Kaulbach, Friedrich:

of intuition; it can never become a phenomenon; it can never *appear*; and in Kant we can only form knowledge of phenomena and appearances. If, by any chance, the 'I' in 'I think' was an actual substance, it would have to be situated in space; it would be a permanent object existing over time at a place, but inner-mental phenomena do not exist in space and have no place, they only exist in time; they cannot be intuited as permanent, and can never be cognized as substances. The 'I think' is therefore no more than an empty formal condition, an anonymous 'x,' preceding knowledge.[189]

> We can lay at the basis of this science nothing but the simple, and by itself quite empty, presentation *I*, of which we cannot even say that it is a concept, but only that it is a mere consciousness accompanying all concepts. Now through this *I* or *he* or *it* (the thing) that thinks, nothing more is presented than a transcendental subject of thoughts = *x*. This subject is cognized only through the thoughts that are its predicates, and apart form them we can never have the least concept of it. Hence we revolve around it in a constant circle, since in order to make any

---

[189] Immanuel Kant. Berlin, New York (Walter de Gruyter), 1982; p. 168. Also Kevin Hill: "As Hume pointed out, when we introspect during an act of judgment, we find no substantial self amid the objects of introspection. What we do find, Kant claims, is the peculiarly empty fact that 'all these contents are mine'. This further judgment reflects nothing more than the potential unity a plurality of content must possess if I am to join them together in a judgment. Yet this further judgment [. . .] is utterly empty of all but formal content." Hill, R. Kevin: Nietzsche's Critiques: The Kantian Foundations of this Thought. Oxford (Clarendon Press), 2003. Also Kuno Fischer: "Every object which can be known presupposes the *Ego* as the formal condition of all knowledge, as the logical subject of all judgments. The *Ego* itself, then, can never be the object of a possible cognition, as it its condition; or it must presuppose itself, which is absurd." Fischer, Kuno: A Commentary on Kant's Critick of the Pure Reason. London (Longmans), 1866; p. 178. Finally Kant himself: "The constant logical subject thought is passed off by it as the cognition of the real subject of the inherence of thought. With this real subject we are not, and cannot be, in the least acquainted. For consciousness alone is what turns all presentation into thoughts, and hence solely in it as the transcendental subject must all perceptions be found; and apart from this logical meaning of the I we are not acquainted with the subject in itself that, as substratum, underlies this I as it underlies also all thoughts." (KrV, A 350).

By contrast, in Descartes the 'I' in 'I Think' had an actual manifestation in the brain. Descartes believed that he had found it by locating the pineal gland in the brain. Whereas several areas in the brain have parallel right and left versions, the pineal gland is located in the midline of the top part of the brain, as if a 'center' for the transactions of the brain. See also Daniel Dennett: Consciousness Explained, loc. cit., pp. 104-106.

judgment regarding it we must always already make use of its presentations. (KrV, A 346/B 404).

Whereas in Kant, the 'I' in 'I think' becomes (what we call) 'an empty-formal principle = x' (a so-called 'transcendental,' 'pure,' or 'logical' subject), in rational psychology by contrast, the 'I' is seen as a substance for what is represented in thought. Descartes applies to the 'I think' a substance-accidence schema. The 'I' in 'I think' becomes substance for the accidences p, q, and r (where p, q, and r indicate generic inner representations), and the purpose of 'rational psychology' is now to investigate in more detail the nature of this one unchanging subject/substance. Thus, Descartes takes for granted that *the subject is a substance*, and he assumes that one can gain *a priori* knowledge of this substance.

We have already seen how problematic it was to realize this intention from our close-reading of Descartes' text itself. Now, Kant offers an alternative analysis of how Descartes reaches his conclusion thanks only to a logical mistake. Descartes, says Kant, is guilty of a so-called 'paralogism'; that is, he employs a syllogism which on appearances seems valid, but where one of the terms is being used with two different meanings in respectively the first and the second premise, thus making the conclusion inapplicable.

Since Kant sees the Cartesian 'I think' as having four different characterizations – indicated above as substance, unity, personality, and ideality – he also believes that a paralogism is being tacitly employed in each of the four cases; there is consequently a 'paralogism of substance'; a 'paralogism of simplicity'; a 'paralogism of identity'; and a 'paralogism of ideality.' For the purposes of understanding Kant's argument, we will only need to give a detailed account of the first paralogism, and summarize the conclusions of the second and third, since he here applies identical arguments (the fourth we will permit ourselves to ignore, since it will take us into the complicated discussion of the nature of Kant's Idealism).

When one constructs a syllogism, the first and second premise has to share a predicate, a so-called 'middle' term. The middle term must apply to and be specific for both premises; if it is not, no conclusion can be drawn. Kant contends that the first and second premises of Descartes' syllogism of substance share no middle term, thus turning the syllogism into a paralogism [a "*Trugschluß*"]. Therefore, a syllogism which on appearances has the following valid form . . .

180   Chapter 3: Splitting the Subject

>   p is q
>   r is p
>   Therefore, r is q

... has, under scrutiny, in fact this invalid form ...

>   p is q
>   r is p'
>   Therefore r is q

The latter is the 'paralogism' (where p' indicates a term, which on appearances is identical to p, but disguises a fundamental difference). Kant introduces the paralogism of substance as follows:

> That whose presentation is the *absolute subject* of our judgment and hence cannot be used as determination of another thing is **substance**.
> I, as a thinking being, am the *absolute subject* of all my possible judgments, and this presentation of myself cannot be used as predicate of any other thing.
> Therefore, I, as thinking being (soul), am **substance**. (KrV, A 348)

If we break down and simplify Kant's argument, it has the following form in three (progressively simpler) possible reconstructions:

First Reconstruction:
- That 'something,' which presents itself as absolute subject for all possible judgments, is substance.
- The 'I' in 'I think' is absolute subject for all its possible judgments.
- Therefore, the 'I' in 'I think' is a substance.

Second Reconstruction:
- Given certain conditions, 'something' which is an absolute subject, is a substance.
- The 'I' is an absolute subject.
- Therefore, the 'I' is a substance.

Third Reconstruction:
- An Absolute Subject is a substance. (AS is s)
- The 'I' (in 'I think') is an Absolute Subject. (I is AS)
- Therefore, the 'I' is a substance. (Ergo: I is s)

Several authoritative commentators (for example, Holm Tetens[190]) see the ambiguous term in Kant's syllogism to be 'substance'; I can only construe

---

[190]   Cf. Holm Tetens: Kants "Kritik der reinen Vernunft": Ein systematischer

3. Kant and Nietzsche: Deconstructing the Cartesian Cogito   181

Kant's syllogism to be fallacious thanks to the ambivalent meaning of the middle term, 'absolute subject' (in this I follow other commentators, for example Paul Guyer, and 19th century Kant commentator, Kuno Fisher[191]). In the first premise, the 'subject' is a substance as 'some*thing*,' which is located or localizable in space and time. This subject cannot be predicated from something else; but it can itself have predicates. This subject has existence in space and time, and we can form 'judgments' about it as an entity;

Kommentar. Stuttgart (Reclam), 2006. Among commentators, Holm Tetens (in his altogether succinct introduction to Kant's Critique) is particularly clear about how he reaches this conclusion. "1. The expression 'substance' in the first premise of the logical reasoning [*Vernunftschluss*] of Rational Psychology means: something in intuition given, which only emerges [*vorkommt*] as an in time persistent subject. 2. The expression 'substance' in the second premise of Rational Psychology means however the logical I as the (logical) subject, thinking certain objects. 3. The logical I is not identical to something, which is given in intuition. // 4. Therefore, the expression 'substance' in the logical reasoning of Rational Psychology is being used ambivalently." Tetens, Holm: Kants "Kritik der reinen Vernunft": loc. cit., p. 221. It seems to me that Tetens' conclusion (the fourth statement) is not supported by his three premises. The problem is exactly that 'substance' – understood as a persistent object with permanence, existing in space and time – is being applied to differently understood notions of 'subject'; in the first premise, the subject is a empirically existent entity, which can be a 'substance'; in the second premise, the subject is a transcendental non-existent entity, only 'existent' in flow of time in the mind, and which can never appear as 'substance.'

[191] Paul Guyer has a particularly cogent presentation of Kant's argument: "Kant's charge is that his inference is invalid because the term "absolute subject" is being used in different senses in the major and minor premises. In the major premise, an "absolute subject" is that which can have properties but cannot be the property of anything else, and that is just the traditional definition of "substance" (so the first premise is analytically true). But in Kant's view, the second premise is talking about something entirely different: I am the "absolute subject" of all my judgment in the sense that I attribute them to myself, or can make myself the subject of any of my judgments – instead of just saying "p" I can always say "I think that p" – but this just means that I can include a *representation* of myself in all of my judgments, or represent my self as the subject of all my judgments. It does not tell my anything about what the actual physical or psychological basis of my capacity to think is, so even though the *representation* of myself may be the subject of all my judgments, I have no basis for inferring that the self itself is a substance." Guyer, Paul: Kant. London/New York (Routledge), 2006; p. 136. See also, Fischer, Kuno: A Commentary on Kant's Critick of the Pure Reason. London (Longmans, Green, & Co.) 1866; p. 188.

it can as such become an *object* for our judgments. In the second premise, the 'absolute subject' is the 'I' in the inner-mental 'I think,' which we have already seen can never become an entity or objectivity in Kant; it can have no existence in space; it can only be a *subject* of judgment; it is therefore *transcendental*. If the first subject is a *thing*; the second subject is a mere *sign*. Hence, the fallacy comes about because one infers that a fundamental condition for something actual and 'real' (a thing) also applies to something transcendental and 'unreal' (a sign). Like the substantive 'I' as *thing* have existence, it is believed, thanks to the false inference, that the *sign 'I'* have existence as an actual substance guiding thinking. The inference postulates that if something actual can be a substance, then something transcendental can also be a substance, and this, precisely, is what Kant will insist is impossible. The Absolute Subject in the first premise and the Absolute Subject in the second are two different subjects. In the first premise, the Absolute Subject is a substance (it has 'reality'; or it has 'thing-reality'); in the second premise, the 'I' in thinking is only a subject for thinking (it has no 'reality'; or it has only 'sign-reality'[192]), and since there is no awareness of the two different uses of the term 'subject,' the conclusion seems now to draw itself: the 'I' must be *substance*.[193]

Through the false inference, the 'I' has been objectified. One invents an imaginary version of the 'I' *as if* some inner image of something external, projected backwards as objectified 'I.'[194] Let us call this imaginary inner version of a real self, the *me* (i.e., the *objectified* 'I'). A 'me' is always ambivalently situated both *inside* and *outside* ourselves. The *'me' as*

---

[192] This empty form of a subject is the ultimate condition of possibility of all synthetic judgments, and therefore cannot have some extra-ordinary condition of possibility of its own; it therefore cannot become object of synthetic judgments itself. This is as such the formal reality of the Cartesian 'I think.' The subject of introspection, the empirical subject, is, on the other hand, a fluctuation of thoughts without any identifiable agent responsible for the thoughts.

[193] From a non-critical position, Kant says that this error is unavoidable (an illusion inherent in the mode of functioning of our reason); only by critical thinking can we expose the illusion, and remedy the error.

[194] We grant of course that such an imaginary version of the inner 'I' must be conceived as some sort of abstract miniature-'I' situated somewhere in the brain; and that it will not appear as a cartoon-image of a little man with head, arms, and legs. No abstract thinker imagines that our actual body-selves 'speak' in the brain; rather, the false inference allows that some*thing* (with supposed abstract qualities: body, size, substance, extension, etc.) in the brain functions as nodal-point for all mental transactions – cf. Descartes' pineal gland theory.

objectified 'I' is: (i) as *'I'* supposedly the most inside of all inside, situated as the subject's true essence; (ii) as *'objectified,'* adopted from the outside, taking upon itself spatial form, and first thereupon sent back to the inside.[195] Thanks to this ambivalence, we can perceive and address this *inside* 'me' *as if* something *outside*, and do so habitually: I can always *see* myself (*me*) inserted into this or that scenario (in dreams and fantasies); I can always say to myself (*me*) this or that (in soliloquies).[196] I consequently split myself into an 'I' and a 'me' all the time, and conduct lively discussions between this 'I' and 'me.' Simultaneously, I believe, if asked, that the 'me' constitutes my innermost identity; even though I always address it as a *you* (we shall return in more detail to this fundamental dialogical situation below).

According to this vocabulary, it seems that Descartes' fundamental mistake comes about due to a confusion of the 'me' and the 'I.' Descartes thinks that it is *me* who thinks (i.e., something with an 'outside' spatial form thinks inside the brain). Correlatively, Kant's fundamental correction consists in pointing out that it can only be an 'I' who thinks; and this 'I,' we cannot grasp as an image; it has no objectivity.

Whether it is *me* who thinks, or it is *I*, in both cases, *me* and *I* are endowed with the same qualifying characteristics: substantiality, simplicity, unity, and ideality. But whereas in Kant, the characteristics qualify the 'I' merely formally (they define the 'I' analytically), in Descartes, thanks to the false inference, they are applied to the *me*, as they now supposedly qualify the *me* substantially. To Kant, the 'I' (= x) is tautologically speaking as 'simple' and 'unified' as it looks like; it is, on all appearances, substance, simple, unified, etc. However, from an appearance we cannot infer anything

---

[195] I take for granted that an inner-mental image of oneself cannot be constructed from within the enclosure of the mind itself; it cannot emerge out of nothing, as it were. It must adopt its form, however shadowy and unconsciously, from something 'outside.' I then furthermore take for granted that the most obvious 'image' available to the subject will have to be the subject's own mirror-image. We do not identify ourselves with other species or other people; we identify with a unique image of ourselves. (Similar – but more elaborate – arguments about imaginary identification can of course be found in Jacques Lacan.)

[196] When a dialogue evolves between the 'I' and the 'me' – according to the formula, 'I' say this to 'me' – I am addressing myself as something both outside me ('another'), and still as belonging to me (myself); stronger, I am addressing myself as 'another,' which at the same time *is* me. Since sane and normal, when I talk to myself, I certainly do not believe I talk to some stranger. Rimbaud's much-quoted, "I *is* another" – as a formula for schizophrenic alienation – does not apply (perhaps better: I *are* another).

about it as thing-in-itself, we cannot know it; therefore, 'I' is at best Kant's anonymous x. However, applied to the *me*, substance, simplicity, unity, etc., are predicates that have objectivity (of which we can therefore produce knowledge).

Whether it is *me* who thinks or *I* who thinks, both entail thinking. There is therefore, in any case, a split between a subject and its thinking, a doer and a deed, an agent and an action. We saw that in Descartes, this split was merely surfacing thanks to his application of the formal cause-effect relation, and it gave him no cause of concern, because he did not envision the possibility that there could be a substantial and qualitative rift between a subject's *intention* to think something and the *actualization* of this intention in the thinking. In Kant, this particular problem does not even emerge, because the 'I' is not an intentional subject in the first place; it is not something that can have a will, since it is merely a formality or ideality (also, it is neither a conscious nor an unconscious subject, in Freudian terms). Still, there is in Kant a split between the 'I' as a unifying, synthesizing agent, of which we cannot form any synthetic judgments, and the 'thinking' manifold, i.e., the synthetic judgments, that becomes the resulting 'action' of this 'agent.'

3.3. A Glassy 'Rational Subject'

In Kant, the split is often thematized as a distinction between the 'logical' and the 'empirical' subject,[197] where the paralogism confounds logical and empirical subject. The paralogism presupposes the logical subject, applies it to the empirical subject, and believes that it can recover in the empirical subject the logical subject. Consequently, it is falsely believed that the empirical subject has a substance, is simple, etc.[198] Thanks to the paralogistic

---

[197] See also Schlimgen: "Kant differentiated between an empirical 'I' as object of the perceptions of the inner meaning (= a determined 'I'), and a transcendental or pure 'I' as the subject of thinking (a reflecting 'I'), which is, as the unity of consciousness, the condition of the possibility for the objectivity of knowledge." Schlimgen, Erwin: Nietzsches Theorie; loc. cit., p. 43.

[198] In the second paralogism (of simplicity/unity), Kant's argument runs largely parallel to the one from the first paralogism. The 'I' is merely a logical subject, and offers us no insight into its underlying constitution. This 'I' we presuppose in all thought, and we represent it to ourselves as a principle which holds our manifold of thoughts together. "We require, in order to have any thought, the absolute unity of the subject only because otherwise we could not say *I think* (the manifold in one presentation). For although the

3. Kant and Nietzsche: Deconstructing the Cartesian Cogito

confusion Descartes is able to construct his master-argument: 'I think, therefore I must exist as a thinking thing,' where the 'thinking thing' is supposed to be identical to a self, which as thing-in-itself underlies *thoughts*.

Nietzsche is repeating Kant's criticism, when, in the passage above, he corrected Descartes: "Something is being thought: consequently something thinks': this is the outcome of Descartes' argument. But that means that we posit our belief in the concept of substance as 'true a priori' – that, when something is being thought there must be something 'that thinks'." (Nachlaß 1887, KSA 12, 10[158]). – Nietzsche is here implying, that when something is being thought, there is not necessarily something that thinks. So far, Kant and Nietzsche are in agreement.

In these discussions, we structurally employ a total of three concepts of subjectivity: (i) *the logical subject* of the empty-formal 'I think'; (ii) *the*

---

whole of the thought could be divided and distributed among many subjects, still the subjective *I* cannot be divided and distributed, and yet we presuppose this *I* in all thought." (KrV; A 354). The 'I' in the *I think* necessarily has to be simple. The 'thoughts' in the 'I think' represents a manifold, but the 'I' must relate to this manifold as the one and same. Thinking cannot be distributed between several independent parts like single words cannot constitute a verse. Self-consciousness is "logically simple." *I think* means nothing more than *I am simple*: as thinking, I represent myself as the same thinker; as thinking, I bind together a manifold of thoughts in the unity of my own apperception. "The proposition, *I am simple*, already lies in every thought itself. The proposition *I am simple* must be regarded as a direct expression of apperception. [. . .] But *I am simple* means nothing more than that this presentation *I* does not comprise the least manifoldness, and that it is [thus] absolute (although merely logical) unity." (A 355). Still, this simplicity of the subject is a logical representation, and it gives us no right to conclude anything about the simplicity of the subject in itself: "The *I* attached to this thought designates the subject of the inherence of thought only transcendentally; and through this *I* we do not indicate in this subject the least property, nor are we acquainted with or know anything about this subject at all. [. . .] The simplicity of the presentation of the subject is not therefore a cognition of the simplicity of the subject itself." (KvR; A 355). In the third paralogism (of personality/self-identity) Kant addresses the self-identity of the thinking self. Self-identity comes in Kant in the expression the "numerical identity of self," indicating that in all its representations, it is the same identical self doing the representing. Kant's criticism is identical to that in the preceding paralogisms. From the identity of the apparent thinking self, we cannot conclude anything about the identity of the self as thing-in-itself. The reasoning self as a logical subject must assert itself as self-identical, and we must represent ourselves as self-identical, but from this representation we can know nothing regards the constitution of the underlying self.

empirical subject of its manifold of representations; and (iii) the result of the paralogistic confusion, the substantive self as thing-in-itself underlying the empirical self: *the noumenal subject*. Accordingly, we may suggest the following condensation of the positions in Kant's explanation of rational psychology's 'I think':

Logical Subject	'I think' as formal substance, simple, and self-identical
Empirical Subject	Totality of self's empirical representations/thoughts
Noumenal Subject	The unknown underlying self = x; substantive self as thing-in-itself

According to this table, 'thinking' has unity thanks only to the unity and self-identity of the *logical* subject; the *empirical* subject is disparate and fluctuating; the *noumenal* subject is unknown. Therefore, from the mere unity of the thinking performed by the logical subject, we cannot justify any statement regarding the unity of the self as such, which is beyond our comprehension, and in front of which we must therefore exercise Kant's particular epistemological modesty: that of which we cannot speak, we have to stay silent. The gulf separating 'thinking' and the 'x' cannot be transgressed, and 'x' remains therefore an unknown thing-in-itself. Kant has therefore said nothing about the *nature* of our selves; he has instead left the problem *irresolvable*.[199]

'Thinking' has *formal* unity only, and a certain 'glassiness' seems already to characterize the Kantian 'rational subject.'[200] This 'glassiness' will be even stronger emphasized by Nietzsche, since he underscores the empirical aspect of the self. Nietzsche still regards the 'I' as a necessary "fictional" unity, but his analysis is usually focused on the empirical self, and this self is determined as in almost exact contrast to the attributes Kant

---

[199] Kant also has not rejected the possibility of an unconscious self, but since a putative unconscious self would be located beyond the bar, as the enigmatic x, it still has the status of something of which we cannot speak.

[200] German philosopher and authoritative Kant-commentator, Dieter Henrich, has in a number of essays argued, from Kant's positions, for a return to the 'rational subject' (from a too frivolous contemporary post-Modernism). It is to Henrich impossible not to accept a fundamental 'unity of reason' as stipulated by Kant (in, Henrich, Dieter: *The Unity of Reason: Essays on Kant's Philosophy*. Cambridge; Harvard University Press, 1984). Henrich's arguments are detailed and weighty, and are not easily dispensed with, and we shall in the following remark not so much contest his basic claim, as we shall qualify it. It seems correct that Kant argues for a 'unity of reason,' but he does not necessarily argue for a unity of the self. In his essays, Henrich gives a meticulous analysis of the unity of reason, but seems to me to ignore the Kantian limitation: the fact that unity of reason has no consequences for the self.

attaches to the unifying reason in 'rational psychology.' Nietzsche's self is (i) no longer substance and permanent but flowing and chaotic; it is (ii) no longer simple and unified but complex and manifold; and it is (iii) no longer 'numerically identical' or self-identical, but heterogeneous and fragmented. Nietzsche's chaotic self is now seen as interfering with what previously had been regarded as serene and impartial reason, and its functioning belies the supposed unity of reason, and reduces 'reason' to a secondary and derived manifestation. A chaotic, power-driven, mind inserts its irrational imperatives and desires within reason itself; it contaminates what was understood as reason; now, "all our conscious motives are surface-phenomena: behind them stands the struggle of our drives and conditions, the struggle for power." (Nachlaß 1885-86, KSA 12, 1[20]).

4. The Linguistically Constituted 'I' in Benveniste

In the present section, we shall interpret the Kantian 'I' discussed above specifically as an *utterance-subject*, or a *subject of enunciation*, accompanying all statements. It is still no more than an ideal 'logical' entity, but now it is seen as constituted in discourse and on sentence-level. Applying contemporary linguistics to Kant's thinking, the logical subject appears in numerous simple sentence-constructions. In a sentence like "I think that it will rain tomorrow," the 'I think' is not an object of thought; the 'I think' is not self-reflexively thematizing itself while enunciating the sentence; it is only a so-called "vehicle" (cf. KrV, B 399) for the utterance. In this application, Kant's *logical* subject is identical to the *subject of enunciation*, and emerges now as a linguistic convention: namely the grammatical convention that as *first person present indicative, a subject always precedes a predicate*. By contrast, the *empirical* subject becomes a *referent*, and is accessed through introspection – or through observation in empirical psychology – as the totality of thoughts. In the first sense, the logical subject is simple and self-identical as the necessary conventional condition for every uttered thought of the form: 'I think *p, q*, and *r*' (where the 'I' 'synthesizes' *p, q*, and *r*); but we bear in mind that the subject is constructed merely as a pragmatic surface-rule, and is as such empty of any determinable content. In the second sense, the empirical subject is identical to its flow of representations; that is, to its *thoughts*, but not to a thinking substance 'behind' or 'beneath' these thoughts. In the empirical subject, it is impossible to access a thinking substance behind thoughts; in the empirical subject, Hume's observation from above applies: "When I enter most intimately into what I call *myself* [. . .] I never can catch *myself* at any time without a perception, and never can observe any thing but the perception."[201]

The understanding of the 'I' as 'subject of enunciation' ('utterance-subject'; 'subject of discourse') has been advanced by linguist Emile Benveniste in particular.[202] In Benveniste, the linguistic shifter, 'I,' is as empty of essence as is Kant's logical 'I' and Nietzsche's grammatical 'I'; however, this 'logical,' 'grammatical,' 'discursive' 'I' is in all three cases nevertheless understood as fundamental in constituting a sense of identity. One may now ask oneself the pressing question: how is something as superficial as a *sign* able of constituting something as profound as a sense of identity? More precisely: how does it come about that a *sign*, with no substantive referent – and/or with a referent that is merely defined through its own instance of use (as the performative situation itself) – constitute something as pervasive as a sense of identity? Since we believe that Benveniste – among Kant, Nietzsche, and himself – has the best theoretical grasp of the implications of the linguistic formality of the 'I,' we shall retrace and develop his argument.

First and most crucially, the 'I' has no referent outside its use. This means that 'I' is any person who *says* 'I,' and that 'I' cannot be defined outside the situation of enunciation; as Benveniste states below, "'I' is the individual who utters the present instance of discourse containing the linguistic instance 'I'":

> The instances of the use of *I* do not constitute a class of reference since there is no 'object' definable as *I* to which these instances can refer in identical fashion. Each *I* has its own reference and corresponds each time to a unique being who is set up as such. [. . .] *I* cannot be defined except in term of 'locution,' not in terms of objects as a nominal sign is. *I* signifies "the person who is uttering the

---

[201] David Hume: A Treatise of Human Nature. (London: Penguin Classics, 1984), p. 300.

[202] See Benveniste, Emile: Problems in General Linguistics. Coral Gables (The University of Miami Press), 1971. Especially the following three articles are of relevance: "Relationships of Person in the Verb," "The Nature of Pronouns," and "Subjectivity in Language." Also Austin and Searle's introduction of the 'performative' is relevant in this context (see Austin, J. L.: How to do Things with Words. Cambridge, MA (Harvard University Press) 1962; and Searle, John: Speech Acts. Cambridge (Cambridge University Press), 1969. One may find other relevant discussions of 'enunciation' in Ricoeur, Paul: Oneself as Another. Translation K. Blamey. Chicago (The University of Chicago Press), 1992; and in Todorov, T. & Duclot, O: Encyclopedic Dictionary of the Sciences of Language. Translated by C. Porter. Baltimore (The Johns Hopkins University Press), 1979.

present instance of the discourse containing *I*." This instance is unique by definition and has validity only in its uniqueness. [. . .] It is thus necessary to stress this point: I can only be identified by the instance of discourse that contains it and by that alone. It has no value except in the instance in which it is produced. But in the same way it is also as an instance of form that *I* must be taken; the form of *I* has no linguistic existence except in the act of speaking in which it is uttered. There is thus a combined double instance in this process: the instance of *I* as referent and the instance containing *I* as the referee. The definition can now be stated precisely as: *I* is the individual who utters the present instance of discourse containing the linguistic instance *I*."[203]

Thanks to the 'I's lack of reference to any object (not despite of), the 'I' *in use* becomes now as unique as a fingerprint. Every uttered 'I' fits, or refers back to, only one person, the person speaking. Exactly because the 'I,' as a non-referential pronoun, is completely anonymous and general, it is well designed to fit everybody uttering 'I.' It is because of its general emptiness, that it is uniquely applied whenever it is uttered. Thus, language has, by introducing a set of pronouns like 'I,' 'you,' 'we,' created a number of 'empty' signs that have no meaning in themselves, but becomes 'filled' with meaning only through their use. They make up like a small reservoir lying dormant in language, springing to life only when pronounced. These signs are necessary for communication, or for – as Benveniste puts it – "the conversion of language into discourse." In order for the individual to assign language to him or herself, and for her to direct language to another, she must use the empty 'I' and 'you.' Starting to communicate, the individual takes possession of the 'I' as transmitter and the 'you' as recipient of her discourse. Even if not actually pronounced, the 'I' is implied in every utterance addressed to a 'you'; in each discursive instance, the person speaking is referring to him or herself as 'I' – that is, positing herself as *subject* opposed to an object.

When the empty 'I' posits the speaker as subject, it gives him a "feeling of his irreducible subjectivity." As such, through an empty *sign*, the person speaking constitutes a first sense of subjectivity. However, since empty, the sign cannot in any way substantiate or qualify this sense. As Benveniste states, if there were a distinct personal pronoun for every speaker, "there would be as many languages as individuals and communication would become absolutely impossible." We believe we have here found a solution to the paradox, introduced by Kant and Nietzsche, that although the 'I' refers to the unique individual, and establishes a first sense of identity, it is nothing but a logical formality (in Kant), or a "fiction" (in Nietzsche).

---

[203] Benveniste: Problems in General Linguistics; loc. cit., p. 218.

> Language has solved this problem [the problem of inter-subjective communication; PB] by creating an ensemble of 'empty' signs that are nonreferentia with respect to 'reality.' These signs are always available and become 'full' as soon as a speaker introduces them into each instance of his discourse. Since they lack material reference, they cannot be misused; since they do not assert anything, they are not subject to the condition of truth and escape all denial. Their role is to provide the instrument of a conversion that one could call the conversion of language into discourse. It is by identifying himself as the unique person pronouncing *I* that each speaker sets himself up in turn as the 'subject.' [. . .] If each speaker, in order to express the feeling he has of his irreducible subjectivity, made use of a distinct identifying signal [. . .] there would be as many languages as individuals and communication would become absolutely impossible. Language wards off this danger by instituting a unique but mobile sign, *I*, which can be assumed by each speaker on the condition that he refers each time only to the instance of his own discourse.[204]

> We hold that 'subjectivity,' whether it is placed in phenomenology or in psychology, as one may wish, is only the emergence in the being of a fundamental property of language. 'Ego' is he who *says* 'ego.' That is where we see the foundation of 'subjectivity,' which is determined by the linguistic status of 'person.'[205]

Ego is he who says 'ego'! This is the "foundation of 'subjectivity'" – 'subjectivity' in scare-quotes, because 'subjectivity' has become a concept empty of content. Incidentally, this definition was almost verbatim anticipated by Descartes (although with conclusions radically different from those of Benveniste) when he stated: "we must come to the definite conclusion that this proposition: I am, I exist, is necessarily true *each time that I pronounce it*, or that I mentally conceive it" [italics added]. It is "necessarily true" that *I am* each time I say so (at least because the truism, insofar as I am speaking, I must exist); still, this discursive confirmation of identity cannot be substantiated. The utterance-subject may assert *that* it is, not *what* it is.

The subject constitutes itself as *individual* in contrast to another through the utterance, and simultaneously, produces a first sense of identity. We shall now suggest a slight change in vocabulary (already anticipated above): we shall say that the 'I' of the utterance, always refers to a 'me' as a structural position of the subject; the structural equivalent to the "feeling of subjectivity" is the 'me.' However, because the 'I' is a mobile and generally applicable *nonreferentia*, the 'me' which it represents has also no particular

---

[204] Benveniste: Problems in General Linguistics; loc. cit., p. 219-220.
[205] Benveniste: Problems in General Linguistics; loc. cit., p. 224-225.

content, whose attributes and qualities we could possibly investigate. "Sense of identity" is no more than a "sense." As a structural position, the 'me' is established as the core of this sense, but since the 'I' is incapable of giving the individual a hint of the substantive content of this sense, the individual also remains in the dark as to how to determine his or her identity in the name of 'me.' The individual only knows, as "necessarily true," that *I am me*, and that suffices.

So-called 'identity' is established thanks to communicative 'customs and habits': one refers to oneself as 'I' a sufficient number of times, and eventually 'I' designates the self-identical 'me.' A bond and a relation have been created between 'I' and 'me,' and the two positions can consequently start a 'dialogue' (as a *self-self* relation), which we suggest imitates the dialogical situation between 'I' and 'you.' For example, the 'I' talks to 'me' *as if* it talks to another; or it sees 'me' *as if* inserted into certain imagined scenarios. Thanks to this transfer of the dialogical situation into inner life, the *individuum* has become *dividuum* (cf. Nietzsche, MA 57); that is, a divided subject to which we return in more detail below. Thanks to this new split, we also have a first explanation of phenomena like self-contradiction, inconsistency, or incompatibility as frequently being the normal-average condition of the subject. Since 'I' and 'me' are just empty forms, their contents consist of internalized positions, which structurally may be organized as extreme opposites in a struggle for power in the psyche. It was always a difficult task to bring the 'me' in line with the 'I' in the pursuit of a 'rational' subject; it can be done, but it requires first and foremost *discipline* (so Nietzsche).[206]

Communication emerging from *soliloquy*, as 'silent dialogue' between an 'I' and a 'me,' we will call *self-reflective*; whereas communication emerging from *dialogue*, carried out between an 'I' and a 'you,' we will call *pragmatic*. In pragmatic communication, the 'I' posits itself in opposition to the 'you' in its address according to an interior/exterior opposition. This contrast is instrumental in producing a consciousness of self (cf. "consciousness of self is only possible if it is experienced by contrast"). So, if

---

[206] Thus we do not see 'rationality' as the natural state of man like Descartes will have it; nor do we see it as a potential set of principles latent in 'communicative action,' as Habermas will have it. 'Rationality' is rather a most unnatural addition to man's self-education, a fact which does not rule out is possibility (and maybe even its desirability), but in our Nietzschean inspired conception, we emphasize that it requires *education, training*, and *discipline*; at least as much *training* as it does to become an accomplished piano-player. Neither our stubborn fingers nor our stubborn minds have evolved for the purpose of mastering such delicate manipulations of the world.

the subject of self-reflective communication is a *dividuum*, the subject of pragmatic communication is necessarily an *individuum*, setting itself apart from the 'you' it addresses.

> Consciousness of self is only possible if it is experienced by contrast. I use *I* only when I am speaking to someone who will be a *you* in my address. It is this condition of dialogue that is constitutive of *person*, for it implies reciprocally *I* becomes *you* in the address of the one who in his turn designates himself as *I*. Here we see a principle whose consequences are to spread out in all directions. Language is possible only because each speaker sets himself up as a *subject* by referring to himself as *I* in his discourse. Because of this, *I* posits another person, the one who, being, as he is, completely exterior to 'me,' becomes my echo to whom I say *you* and who says *you* to me. [. . .] Neither of the terms can be conceived of without the other; they are complementary, although according to an 'interior/exterior' opposition, and, at the same time, they are reversible. If we seek a parallel to this, we will not find it. The condition of man in language is unique.[207]

Hence, to repeat the major idea, we suggest that the model for pragmatic communication is taken over by and imitated in self-reflective communication, so that the 'I' and 'me' carry on a soliloquy that is essentially 'inner dialogue' ('I' addresses a 'you,' which happens to be *me myself*). We assume here, as often before, that our inner life can only constitute itself from *appearances*; i.e., from models or patterns that are constituted in the *exterior*; never from the *interiority* of a mysterious inner life, derived from nowhere. The 'I' – 'me' opposition is as such an internalization of the 'I' – 'you' opposition. This analysis we will continue below and further elaborate in what we call the "Special Theory" of the split subject.

---

[207] .Benveniste: Problems in General Linguistics; loc. cit., p. 224-225.

Part II:

*Nietzsche's Theories of
the Split Subject*

5. Nietzsche's "General Theory" of the Split Subject

5.1. Spir and Nietzsche's Interpretations of the Kantian Double-Determination of the Subject

The paradox and riddle, the self is both *one* and *many*, did, thanks to Kant, find a solution: the self was considered *one* as a formal principle, but *many* regarding its representational contents.

This ambivalent determination of the subject continues in the neo-Kantian African Spir; and through Spir, in Nietzsche.[208] The unity of subject is seen as an ideal principle, whereas the multiplicity is seen as the real content. In Spir, it is still strongly emphasized that the ideal unity of self is indispensable.

> What arguments could steal from me the consciousness of my own identity? What could make me doubt that I am not the same as I was five, ten or twenty years ago? The denial of a self-identity would be tantamount to a denial of one's existence as such [*seines Daseins überhaupt*] [. . .] To experience oneself as a thing or a substance simply implies that one does not experience oneself as a part of, or a moment of, another.[209]

However, Spir also accepts the empiricist contention that in introspection we only encounter ourselves as a multiplicity of representations: "That we experience and must experience ourselves as things, as substances, i.e., as real unities, is quite self-evident. [. . .] But equally self-evident is it that we in truth are not things, not substances, not real unities."[210]

To account for this double-determination of the subject, Spir applies the distinction, Ideal and Real [*Ideale und Reale*] (equivalent to Kant's *logical*

---

[208] For a book length account of the relationship between African Spir and Nietzsche, see Green, Martin Steven: Nietzsche and the Transcendental Tradition. Urbana, Chicago (University of Illinois Press), 2002.

[209] African Spir: Forschung nach der Gewissheit in der Erkenntniss der Wirklichkeit. Leipzig (Förster und Findel), 1869; p. 220-21.

[210] Spir: Forschung nach der Gewissheit; loc. cit., p. 221.

and *empirical*), as Spir maintains that the 'Ideal' is in no way less important, than is the 'Real.'

> It is also obvious, that the unity of our self [*Ich*] is not real, but merely an ideal [*ideelle*], based on our self-consciousness, and conditional upon the opposition between subject and object of our self-knowledge. The real content of our self is by contrast always multifarious and changing. Our existence is consequently in truth no being [*Sein*], but rather utter occurrence [*blosses Geschehen*].[211]

> The self is really both different and one, both changing, flowing, and identical to itself. [. . .] The different and flowing is the object of inner perception, it is the immediately given in the self, the real content itself; in contrast is the unifying, the unity of self, something ideal and formal, and is thus the sole object of thinking.[212]

In what we here call Nietzsche's "General Theory" of the split subject, Nietzsche continues and radicalizes Spir's Kantian position. If in Spir, there is an equal emphasis on the formal and the empirical aspect of the subject, Nietzsche refocuses and relocates his emphasis increasingly toward the empirical aspect of the subject, and will typically adopt and favor the second part of Spir's description: the real content of our self as being always multifarious and changing; as having no *Sein*; and as being merely a *blosses Geschehen*. In several different instances, Nietzsche declares that there is no 'I' understood as origin, cause, and substance:

> As for the I! It has become a fable, a fiction, a play on words: it has completely given up thinking, feeling, and willing! . . . What is the result? There are no mental causes at all! (GD, "Die vier grossen Irrthümer"; KSA 6, p. 91). [. . .] There are no Subject-"Atoms" [*Subjekt-"Atome"*]. The sphere of a subject is constantly g r o w i n g or d e c r e a s i n g – the midpoint of the system is constantly being displaced – ; (Nachlaß 1886-87; KSA 12, 9[98]). [. . .] The subject is just a fiction; an ego does not exist at all (Nachlaß 1887, KSA 12, 9[108]).

In Nietzsche, the formal and ideal aspect of self becomes a fictional unity, an "article of faith" (Nachlaß 1888; KSA 13, 14[79]). Still, it is in Nietzsche an important article of faith, because it establishes our belief in identity *as such*. For example, thanks to our fictional *sense* of self-identity, our fictional sense of ourselves as unities, we are able to generate our notions of

---

[211] Spir: Forschung nach der Gewissheit; loc. cit., p. 222.
[212] Spir: Forschung nach der Gewissheit; loc. cit., p. 223.

'thing' (a unity) and of 'atom' (another unity – Nietzsche's so-called "*Klümpchen-atom*"[213]). We as such project our false sense of self-identity into the world as the identity of the 'thing' and of the 'atom'; from our false sense of self emerges our false beliefs in individuals and singularities as such.[214]

> When one has grasped that the 'subject' is not something that creates effects, but only is a fiction, much follows.
> It is only according to the model of the subject that we have invented the t h i n g - n e s s [*Dinglichkeit*] and projected it unto the medley of sensations. If we no longer believe in the e f f e c t i v e subject, then belief also disappears in e f f e c t i v e things, in interaction, cause and effect between those phenomena that we call things.
> Equally disappears, of course, the world of e f f e c t i v e a t o m s : the assumption of which always depended on the supposition that there has to be subjects. (Nachlaß 1887, KSA 12, 9[91])

> We need unities, in order to calculate: this does not mean that such unities exist. We have borrowed the notion of unity from our "ego" concept [*"Ich"begriff*], – our oldest article of faith. If we had not regarded ourselves as unities, we would also never have formed the concept of "thing". Nowadays, rather lately, we have been abundantly convinced that our conception of an ego-concept [*Ich-Begriff*] does not confirm a real unity. (Nachlaß 1888, KSA 13, 14[79]).

One assumes this important "fable," "fiction," or "article of faith" for the sake of self-preservation. In order to survive, the human being must necessarily simplify a world too complex and chaotic in its immediate display. As a minimal requirement for being able to orient themselves, humans simplify, thus 'falsify,' the world around them, including the inner world. But

---

[213] From Roger Boscovich (see also fn. 68) and Fr. Albert Lange, Nietzsche takes over the notion that there is no smallest unit in form of an indivisible atom, the so-called 'clump-atom.' This view is of course completely verified in modern physics, where in the last century there has been an ongoing investigation into still smaller dimensions of our universe – investigations, which are, if anything, only gaining momentum today, where new particle colliders make it possible to look into the unfathomably small; down to the frontier for hypothesized 'strings,' which have no mass in a conventional sense.

[214] See also Schlimgen: "The belief in the 'I' as a substance is, according to Nietzsche, also 'projected as 'being' [*Sein*], which is equal to saying that there is a fixation of things [*Fixation von Dingen*] as stable discriminate unities. The thing-ontology corresponds thus to the I-ontology, and is understood thanks to the same categories: Unity, Identity, Durability, Substance, Cause, Thingness, Being." Schlimgen, Erwin: Nietzsches Theorie, loc. cit., p. 44.

moreover, we learn that the most rudimentary mechanism for simplification is the 'invention' of the formal notion of self as such (cf.: "It is only according to the model of the subject that we have invented t h i n g - n e s s "). If we translate back this formal notion of self to the utterance-subject, we can conclude that the rudimentary sense of identity and unity emerges thanks to a subject being able to refer to itself as 'I.' Thanks to this self-reference, the subject develop an *ego-consciousness*. The subject that develops *ego-consciousness* constructs simultaneously a world to itself; it develops a first sense of thing-hood.

The 'I', the self, or the subject *understood as unity* therefore still have a unique position in Nietzsche's thinking.[215] It is granted that the subject in

---

[215] Both Alexander Nehamas in *Nietzsche: Life as Literature* [loc. cit.] and Henry Staten in *Nietzsche's Voice* [loc. cit.] have interesting discussions of the fragmented subject in Nietzsche. Now we can weigh in on these discussions, and from within our paradigm make further clarifications. Nehamas states correctly that "our thoughts contradict one another and contrast with our desires, which are themselves inconsistent and are in turn belied by our action. The unity of the self, which Nietzsche identifies with this collection is thus seriously undermined." [Nehamas, ibid. 180]. Nehamas, however, sees subjective unity emerge thanks to the sense we have of a unified/unifying body. "On a very basic level the unity of the body provides for the identity that is necessary, but not at all sufficient, for the unity of the self. [. . .] Because it is organized coherently, the body provides the common ground that allows conflicting thoughts, desires, and actions to be grouped together as features of a single subject" [Nehamas, ibid. p. 181]. In our reading of Nietzsche, it cannot be the body that accounts for the unity of self; it is rather the other way around, the sense of self accounts for the unity of bodies. We should here recall the fact that the perception of one's own body is seriously flawed; it presents one with a fragmented image of the body, insofar as one sees only a torso, legs, and parts of arms, but nothing else above. Admittedly, this fragmented image is supplemented with the 'intellectual' conjecture, that the fragmented body of representation has unity like the surrounding bodies in which one mirrors oneself. Thanks to these 'intellectual' conjectures, one adds to the fragmented representation of one's body the overriding 'interpretation' of the body as unified. The unified mirror-image of the body is thus an *intellectual* achievement that requires that the subject is capable of organizing its fragmented body-representation under *the concept* of a unifying self. Henry Staten has also expressed his doubt about this interpretation of Nehamas: "Nehamas seems inconsistent in exempting the body and the self from the otherwise universal ontological indeterminacy of objects," Staten, however, sees another problem arising . . . "but the utter dissolution of the unity of the self leaves us with the problem I am raising, of how it would then make any sense to speak of the feeling of increased power." (Staten, loc. cit., p. 127.) If

5. Nietzsche's 'General Theory' of the Split Subject

reality is fragmented, but the subject understood as unity becomes, genealogically speaking, nevertheless a kind of super-concept from where all other concepts of unity derive, such as, substance, thing, atom, etc.[216] If in the philosophical tradition (for example as in Descartes) 'substance' is the general concept (the so-called 'super-concept'), the self or subject becomes, in Nietzsche, a hierarchically over-determining super-concept. If in Descartes, the substance-accidence and cause-effect distinctions are seen as the general conceptual frameworks applied to the subject as subject-thought, subject-action, or subject-will, this hierarchy is turned around in Nietzsche. Now, the 'subject' is the general matrix, from where we are able to derive the concept of 'substance.'[217] The idea relates to Nietzsche's 'anthropomor-

---

Nietzsche's mind is a power-struggle of wills, increasing or decreasing in intensities, Staten sees a contradiction in the idea that one state A can change into another state B, because this would presuppose individual unities ("*Einheiten*" he says) in the psyche, namely in the form of states A and B. This objection I happen to find irrelevant. A model of the psyche as changing states cannot compromise or contradict the notion of a multiform empirical subject, because the model *itself* expresses the *very structure* of fragmentation. 'Forces' must necessarily be thought as transmitted and distributed between 'points.' It can therefore serve no purpose to discuss whether 'points' (as mathematical devices asserted in an abstract model) are themselves 'fragmented.' Thus, it seems to me that Staten are confusing *means of representation* with *represented*. Conclusively, there is a theoretical superiority in reiterating Nietzsche's own distinction between formal self and empirical self. The self can as such be understood as respectively uniform or multiform, although its possible uniformity is of course *formal*, therefore *ideal*, therefore *fictitious*. Staten is therefore still be quite right in criticizing poststructuralist writers when they take for granted that "Nietzsche utterly shatters the unity of the self." (Staten, loc. cit., p., 127.)

216 Cf. Schlimgen: "For Nietzsche the I becomes a fundamental article of faith [*Glaubensartikel*] in Western metaphysics: it is fundamental because from the notion of self [*Ich-begriff*] all other essential notions in the philosophical tradition can be derived, so for example, the substance-concept, the thought-concept, the atom-concept, the notion of subject, and the notion of cause and effect; it is an article of faith because the representation of an idea of I [*ich Vorstellung*] is a necessary substantial unity, while also a fictive representation. Schlimgen, Erwin: Nietzsches Theorie; loc. cit., p. 43.

217 We notice that Heidegger is adamantly opposed to this Nietzschean reversal of subject and substance, and believes that Nietzsche is here misunderstanding Descartes and the metaphysical tradition. Both Descartes and Nietzsche interpret, so Heidegger, the subject *as* the unique 'modern' substance; however, according to different interpretations: Descartes as *cogito*; Nietzsche as *will-to-power*. Thus, it is not the case that one believes in *substance* as foundation,

phism' (discussed in *Chapter 1*, and therefore not repeated in great detail at this point). Our thinking is necessarily intimately tied up to ourselves, and we ultimately interpret things in the image of ourselves. Consequently, concepts like 'substance' and 'thing' also derive from the fictional and imaginary subjective core. Nietzsche gives an entirely explicit account of this hierarchical reversal of substance and subject in the following:[218]

> The concept of s u b s t a n c e [is] a consequence of the concept of the s u b j e c t : n o t the other way around! [*Der Substanzbegriff eine Folge des Subjekts-begriffs: nicht umgekehrt!*]. If we give up the soul, 'the subject,' then there is no foundation at all for the assumption of a 'substance.' [. . .] S u b - j e c t : this is the terminology of our belief in a u n i t y behind all the different moments of the highest feeling for reality [*Realitätsgefühls*]: we understand this belief as t h e e f f e c t of a single cause, – we believe in our belief to such an ex-

---

the other in *subject*; because they both believe in a *substantial subject* as foundation. Heidegger criticizes: "The following sentence makes it clear just how far Nietzsche was thrown off the path of an *original* metaphysical meditation: "the *substance*-concept a consequence of the *subject*-concept: *not* the reverse!" (WM 485). Nietzsche understands "subject" here in a modern sense. The subject is the human "I." The concept of substance is never, as Nietzsche believes, a consequence of the concept of the subject. But neither is the concept of the subject a consequence of the concept of substance. The subject-concept arises from the new interpretation of the *truth* of the being, which according to the tradition is thought as *ousia, hypokeimenon,* and *subiectum*, in the following way: on the basis of the *cogito sum* man becomes what is properly foundational, becomes *quod substat*, substance. The concept of the subject is nothing other than a restriction of the transformed concept of substance to man as the one who represents, in whose representing both what is represented that one representing are firmly founded in their cohesion. Nietzsche mistakes the origin of the "concept of substance" because [. . .] he stakes everything on the priority of man as subject." Heidegger, Martin: Nietzsche v. 4. Translated and edited by D. F. Krell. San Franscisco (Harper Colllins), 1991; p. 130.

[218] The chaotic self has been exposed to unification and simplification, which now generate the false belief that the subject is a unified 'I' in possession of will, and able to produce effects. The originally chaotic self becomes as such an image of unity and consciousness. It is as mirroring itself in this image that the self becomes substance, simple, and identical. It is as this image that the subject experiences itself as a conscious and intentional actor in the world. This division between a real chaotic subjectivity, and an imaginary unified subjectivity, has in another vocabulary been emphasized also by Jacques Lacan in his theories of the "order of the Real" and the "order of the Imaginary."

tent, that in order to will its existence [*um seinetwillen*], we imagine 'truth', 'reality,' or 'substance'.

"Subject" is the fiction, that several s i m i l a r states in us are the effects of one substratum: however, it is us who first constituted the 'similarity' of these states; the a s s e r t i o n of similarity and arrangement is the f a c t, n o t the similarity. (Nachlaß 1886-87, KSA 12, 10[19]).

Man has projected out of himself his three 'inner facts' – the things he believed in most firmly, the will, the mind, the I – he first derived the concept of Being from the concept of the I, and posited the existence of 'things' after his own image, according to his concept of the I as cause. It is no wonder if later on he only rediscovered in things what h e h i m s e l f h a d p u t i n t o t h e m . – The thing itself, to say it again, the concept of thing, is just a reflection of the belief in the I as cause. . . . And even your atom, my dear mechanicians and physicists, how much error, how much rudimentary psychology still remains in your atom! (GD, "Die vier grossen Irrthümer"; KSA 6, p. 91).

A further consequence of our belief in a fictitious unitary subject, is that we believe also our thinking to be unitary and consistent. In this case, the subject-predicate logic is re-fashioned into a logical relationship between antecedent and consequent; and human thinking is understood to imitate a logical schematics, where statements can be divided into majors and minors, and conclusions are true in all circumstances.[219] This logical schematics has been extrapolated as such from the more fundamental subject-predicate, cause-effect, matrix, and then projected backwards to explain or illustrate human thinking. "We believe that thoughts, as they follow one another in us, stand in some causal interconnection; in particular, the logician, who apparently talks about pure cases which never occur in reality, has got used to the presupposition, that thought c a u s e s thoughts, – he names it – thinking." (Nachlaß 1887, KSA 13, 14[152])

---

[219] We notice that this understanding of thinking is today pursued most explicitly in Analytic Philosophy: philosophy is supposedly constructed like a long syllogism; one can isolate some of its parts, and start to analyze them with respect to their logical consistency. The subsequent discussions in Analytic Philosophy are usually concerned with whether this or that part is consistent with this or that other part (etc.). Since it is generally assumed that the mind is a logical machine, they *ought to be* consistent; the mind is not allowed to make errors. (– *En passant*, there are lots of 'hidden morality' in Analytic Philosophy . . . not mention the 'hidden self-congratulation' of the Analytic philosopher, who has elevated him or herself into an ever-alert logical machine, to which the entire line-up, Kant, Hegel, Nietzsche, Freud, Husserl, etc., must now capitulate.)

5.2. The Fictions of 'I' and 'Will' versus the Reality of 'Thinking' and 'Wills.'

5.2.1. Chaos and Becoming in the Empirical Subject.

In the so-called "General Theory" of the split subject, Nietzsche's subject as 'I' becomes a unity in name only. If Kant's 'I' was formal and transcendental, something whose content we could not penetrate into, but still a subject of apperception accounting for the unity of perception, Nietzsche's 'I' becomes a unity in name only. Like in Kant, it has no content; the attempt to investigate it as a 'thing-in-itself' would be as futile in Nietzsche as in Kant.

As in Benveniste, the 'I' is a non-descript pronoun since 'I' defines nobody in particular, but simply anybody who says 'I.' Nietzsche's 'I' becomes a grammatical 'I'; we adopt it because we imitate a matrix introduced to us through language, namely the linguistic convention adopted in Indo-European (and most other, if not all other) languages: a *subject* always precedes a *predicate*. As speaking, we *practice* subject-predicate logic unconsciously, and we now transfer this familiar logic to ourselves as human beings, erroneously assuming that, (i) we are subjects of our thinking, (ii) we are subjects of our action, and (iii) we are subjects of our speech. In the subject, we place 'will' and 'intention,' while 'thinking,' 'action,' and 'speaking' become *products* of the intentional subject. When we apply this matrix to ourselves, we (in what indeed *also* could be seen as a *paralogistic confusion* of the notion *subject*) take the *subject* from grammar, and transfer it to ourselves as *subjects* of thinking or action. 'Subject-predicate' in thought as 'cause-effect.'

Grammar becomes "language-metaphysics" when the elementary subject-predicate logic is 'fetishized' into something supposed to explain ontological issues as well. In this fetishization of language, the *grammatical subject* is applied onto the *existential subject*, and as the erroneous result of this mix up, the existential subject is now assumed to have a localizable 'I' and 'will,' which, in collaborate effort, release a chain of effects and consequences.

> We become entangled in a crude fetishism [*Fetischwesen*] when we make ourselves conscious of the basic premises of language-metaphysics, in plain words, of reason. This is what sees a doer and a deed everywhere; it believes in the will as cause in general; it believes in the 'I', in the I as Being, in the I as substance, and p r o j e c t s the belief in the I-substance onto all things – only then does it c r e a t e the concept of 'thing' . . . Being is thought into, imposed on everything as cause, only following from the conception 'I' is the concept 'being' derived. (GD, "Die 'Vernunft' in der Philosophie" 5; KSA 6, p. 77).

Since the subject-predicate model is thought as a cause-effect model, it reinforces the supposed *uni-directionality* of the *'I'* → *thinking/action/speech* model. That is, the 'I' is being seen as *doer, first, causing, moving*, and *one*; its product as *deed, second, effect, moved*, and *complex*.

Nietzsche's General Theory of the split subject we can now understand according to this simple structure: we have two simple positions or localities, 'I/Will' and 'thinking/wills.' We imagine the position of the 'I' and 'Will' as empty of content; and the side of 'thinking' and 'wills' as filled with content. If we let this model guide own thinking, the subject is now 'split' only thanks to a misunderstanding, since we erroneously believe in an 'I' or a 'Will,' which, as Nietzsche reiterates, is nothing but a "fable" and a "fiction" taken over from grammar (merely a *label*, but nonetheless important, since it gives us our narratives about a world of substances, things, and unities). However, the 'real subject' – to use Spir's term – is found in the position of 'thinking' or 'wills,' and is nothing but complex and random power-struggles, so-called 'will-to-power-processes' (it's *full* of representations). In this position, the subject is not even 'split' strictly speaking (if we suppose that a 'split' divides a known unity into two identifiable pieces), it is more correctly *fragmented*. It becomes the subjective equivalent to Boscovich's force-point universe;[220] a kind of particle-subject broken into pieces exerting forces in various directions. It is a subject of so-called 'becoming' [*werden*], a subject in flux, with no fixed unities, but rather composed of 'particles' or 'force-points' – appearing and disappearing, aggregating and disaggregating, increasing and decreasing – in ever shifting relationships and organizations.[221] This is the deepest 'truth' of and under-

---

[220] A number of commentators have demonstrated Nietzsche's influence from physicist and philosopher Roger Boscovich; for example Whitlock, Greg: "Roger Boscovich, Benedict de Spinoza, and Friedrich Nietzsche: The Untold Story." In Nietzsche-Studien bd. 25. Berlin/New York (Walter de Gruyter), 1996: "As the centerpiece of the dynamic worldview, *Boscovich's theory of a force-point-world counts as the parent theory to that of the will to power* [. . .] Nietzsche still holds the boscovichian legacy that *there is no matter, there is only force*. But now Nietzsche has made his own autonomous addition, for *all force is will to power*." Whitlock: loc. cit., p. 216 & 217. See also Stack, George J.: *Nietzsche and Lange*. Berlin, New York (Walter de Gruyter), 1983. Also Abel, Günter: *Nietzsche: Die Dynamik des Willen zur Macht und die Ewige Wiederkehr* (Berlin/New York: Walter de Gruyter, 1998.

[221] Cf. Müller-Lauter: "The multiplicity of power quanta must therefore be understood not as a plurality of quantitatively irreducible ultimate givens, not as a plurality of indivisible 'monads.' Power-shifts within the unstable organiza-

ground for our subjectivity; and as such, it will never reveal or illuminate itself. In this position, we live in a kind of indigenous wilderness. Only thanks to language, we find a means by which to tame patches of these barren and wild wastelands.

This chaotic underground for subjectivity cannot regulate itself, but in language, we find a superficial means by which to regulate the inner turmoil. Language becomes a *necessary supplement* to chaos and wilderness; it becomes a *secondary*, but artificial, *elaboration* of this abundance of stuff. Language, with its limited dictionary, is as such a "simplification-apparatus" and a "scheme" applied to an abundance of material, thereby 'simplifying,' 'abbreviating,' 'organizing,' and 'interpreting' a whirl of emotional clusters into something identifiable, communicable, and memorable. As well as we name our external world, we also name our internal world, in this, enabling us to reason about it, fostering the belief that we know it. Language, with its subject-predicate logic, becomes a "schema" that gives us elementary reason; it may be an artificial addition, but we are nevertheless unable to discard it:

> We stop thinking when we no longer do so according to the linguistic compulsions [*Sprachliche zwange*], we arrived here to the doubt that here we were seeing a boundary as boundary. Reason [*vernünftige Denken*] is an interpretation according to a scheme, that we cannot discard [*abwerfen*]. (Nachlaß 1887, KSA 12, 5[22]).[222]

To provide an example, which is not Nietzsche's, we may think we know what it is "to fall in love," although so-called 'love' involves a *cluster*, a *net* of emotional processes that are often incomprehensible and often self-

---

tion allow one power quantum to become two or two to become one. If we use numbers in a fixating and conclusive sense, it must be said that the 'number' of being always remains in flux. There is no 'individual,' there is no ultimate indivisible quantum of power, that we can reach." Müller-Lauter, Wolfgang: Über Werden und Wille zur Macht: Nietzsche-Interpretationen I. Berlin, New York (Walter de Gruyter), 1999; p. 42.

[222] See Josef Simon: "All our thinking is thus controlled by the *concept* of language, from where our present language has already developed itself. One could also say: "Thinking" is according to Nietzsche an "interpreting" *translation backwards* [*Ruchübersetzung*] to an idea of language, that would correspond to the universal grammar of the concept of language." Simon, Josef: "Grammatik und Wahrheit. Über das Verhältnis Nietzsches zur spekulativen Satzgrammatik der metaphysischen Tradition," in Nietzsche-Studien bd. 1. Berlin, New York (Walter de Gruyter), 1972; p. 12.

contradictory: love should be attraction, but then it regularly involves fear; love should be affection, but then it easily generates hatred; love should involve generosity, but then it habitually becomes possessive, etc. The emotional complex or cluster, 'love,' is 'truly,' and as will-to-power-process, indescribable; only reduced to the four-letter word 'love' does it give us the deceptive feeling that we know what we are talking about, the soothing sense of familiarity, and at the same time enables us to communicate this emotion, or rather, communicate the *skin* of this emotion. (Compare to Nietzsche's passage from *Götzendämmerung*: "Psychological explanation. – To trace something unknown back to something known is alleviating, soothing, gratifying and gives moreover a feeling of power. Danger, disquiet, anxiety attend the unknown – the first instinct is to eliminate these distressing states. First principle: any explanation is better than none." (GD, 'Die vier grossen Irrthümer' 5, KSA 6, p. 93).)[223]

The subject 'full' of representational content is equivalent to Kant's *Empirical Subject* and Spir's *Real Subject*. When Nietzsche situates 'wills' or 'thinking' in this position, will and thinking cease to be formative singularities in (self-)control of their impact and consequences; they become instead semi-random results of complex processes. '*The Will*' becomes now '*many wills*,' and is now seen as multiple forces dragging the confused subject in multiple directions until finally one force is able to drown the noises of the rest.

Genealogically speaking, the fragmented subject of power-processes is seen as an early form, and the artificial 'I' as a later addition to this early form (cf. FW 110, 111, & 354). Genealogically speaking, the subjective split must occur in early prehistory. An early ability to set up a division between *me* 'thinking,' and this same *me* being able to identify itself and refer to itself as 'I,' must announce the progression from an animal consciousness to a human consciousness.[224] This 'I' is the condition of the possibility for

---

[223] See also Nietzsche's statement from *Die fröhliche Wissenschaft*: "What do they [the common people] want when they want 'knowledge'? Nothing more than this: Something strange [*Fremdes*] is to be reduced to something familiar [*Bekanntes*]. And we philosophers – have we by knowledge ever understood anything different from this? [. . .] Is it not the instinct of fear that bids us to know? [. . .] What is familiar, is known [*was bekannt ist, ist erkannt*]." (FW 355, KSA 5, p. 594).

[224] We know no example of animals being able to refer to themselves as 'I' or being able to make a distinction between their 'mental activity' and themselves as agents for this 'mental activity' – although we believe that a few higher mammals are able to recognize themselves in a mirror, and identify themselves as body-selves.

the subject's appropriation of a language; only in making myself a reference-point for discourse, can I make a discourse mine. Thus, the development of the 'I' would have to be concurrent with the development of language, and thus of a consciousness that we can identify as human. A subject saying 'I' must minimally have a language able to distinguish between 'I' and 'you' as subject and object; and further, distinguish 'I' and 'you' as present persons from 'he' or 'she' as absent persons; and still further, distinguish 'I,' 'you,' and 'he/she' as living from 'it' as dead; a language, therefore, that starts making fundamental distinctions between *subject and object, presence and absence, life and death*, and as the master-distinction hovering above all the rest, *self and other*. (The effort to understand the simple statement 'I think' is ultimately an attempt to explain what it is to be human.)

5.2.2. On Willing: A Reading of JGB 19:[225]

We recall, "There is [*es gibt*] no Will; only will-punctures [*Willens-Punktationen*], which continuously expand or reduce their power." (Nachlaß 1887–88; KSA 13, 11 [73]).

If Nietzsche's 'I' is form only, constituted thanks to a pragmatic surface-rule, it can as form not harbor complex mental contents like 'will' and 'intention.' As form and label only, it cannot imply a psychological subject, since a psychological subject has contents. In Nietzsche's so-called "General Theory" of the split subject, we always find what we call 'will' in the second position of the equation, doer → deed, I → think, etc.; that is, in the position of 'thinking,' 'action,' and 'speaking.' What we call 'will' is consequently entirely redefined, and at odds with most of the philosophical tradition. 'Will' is no longer collaborating with the 'I' in creating a subject in control of and completely transparent in its thinking and action. 'Will' is no longer a mover and motor for a logical chain of consequences.[226] In this

---

[225] In a strong hermeneutical reading of the aphorism in question, Günter Figal arrives in several instances to conclusions similar ours. See Figal, Günter: Nietzsche: Ein Philosophische Einführung. Stuttgart (Reclam) 1999; chapter IV.4 "Etwas Complicirtes."

[226] It was Müller-Lauter, who first noticed that Nietzsche was not, despite his concept of *will*-to-power, defending a *Will*, understood as singular, but rather a complex of wills, in the *plural*. The idea has since been generally accepted in recent Nietzsche-research; also here, I take it for granted (see Müller-Lauter: "The world Nietzsche is speaking of reveals itself as a play and counter play of forces, or respectively, wills to power. If we recall first that the

sense, will is "something complicated" "that is a unity only as a word." Aphorism 19 from JGB gives us a condensed argument for this particular notion of 'will.'

> Willing seems to me to be above all something c o m p l i c a t e d, something that is a unity only as a word. [. . .] In all willing there is, [1] first of all, a plurality of sensations, namely the sensation of the condition we l e a v e, the sensation of the condition towards which we g o, the sensation of this 'leaving and 'going' itself, and then also an accompanying muscular sensation which, even without our putting 'arms and legs' in motion, comes into play through a kind of habit as soon as we 'will.' As well as feelings, and indeed many varieties of feeling, can be recognized as an ingredient of will, so, [2] secondly, can thinking: in every act of will is there a commanding thought [*commandirenden Gedanken*]; – and one should not imagine that thought could be separated from 'willing,' as

---

accumulations of power quanta are constantly increasing or decreasing, then we can speak only of continually changing unities, but not of the one unity." Müller-Lauter Wolfgang: "Nietzsches Lehre vom Willen zur Macht"; in Nietzsche-Interpretationen I, loc. cit., p. 40. Also Abel, Günter: Nietzsche, loc. cit.; and Schlimgen, Erwin: Nietzsches Theorie; loc. cit.). The Will (in the singular) that Nietzsche rejects may indeed come in two forms: first, it may be understood as Schopenhauer's metaphysical concept of Will; a Will supposedly permeating organic as well as inorganic nature, as a drive or force that never manifests itself as such; this is Schopenhauer's 'improved' version of Kant's thing-in-itself. This metaphysical notion of Will is rejected throughout Nietzsche's writings. Or secondly, it may indicate the supposed unitary Will that should precede human action. The first example that comes to mind here is Kant's "Good Will" as the standard by which we may judge whether actions qualify as morally worthy or not. The concept of 'will' fuses here with the concept of 'intention.' It is assumed that humans have singular, and determinable, intentions preceding their actions, thoughts, and speech. Since they are believed to be determinable, we judge human action according to these 'intentions' (i.e., our interpretation of them). Court cases often progress as prolonged proceedings meant to determine, or interpret, the 'intention' behind an act; justice is metered out according to how one ends up determining the defendant's 'intention.' (Cf. "One interpreted the origin of an action in the most decisive sense as the origin of an I n t e n t i o n [*A b s i c h t*]. One agreed on the belief that the value of an action was inhabited in the value of its intention. The intention as the entire origin and prehistory of an action: under this prejudice, lasting almost to this day, one has issued moral praise, censure, judgment, and philosophy. [. . .] All [the action's] intentionality, everything about it that can be seen, known, or become 'conscious,' belongs only to its surface and skin – which, like every skin, reveals something but c o n c e a l s even more. In short, we believe that the intention is only a sign and symptom that first needs to be interpreted." (JGB 32, KSA 5, p. 51).)

if only will would then remain! [3] Thirdly, will is not only a complex of feeling and thinking, but first of all an a f f e c t [*Affekt*]: and in fact the affect of command. What is called 'freedom of will' is essentially the feeling of superiority [*Überlegenheits-Affekt*] in respect to him who must obey: 'I am free, "he" must obey' – this consciousness adheres to every will, as does every tension of the attention, every straight look fixing itself exclusively on one thing, every unconditional evaluation 'this and nothing else is necessary now,' every inner certainty that one will be obeyed, and whatever else pertains to the state of him who give commands. A man who w i l l s – commands something in himself which obeys or which he believes obeys.

We interrupt Nietzsche at this point in order to recapitulate. We learn that will involves a complex of sensations; it (i) includes many "varieties of feeling." The example Nietzsche gives to elucidate this thesis is simply an *analysis* of the concept 'will': there must in 'will' be a sense of *moving toward* something together with a sense of *leaving behind* something, since 'will' is *directional* (when you move from one point to another, you leave something behind and move toward something else). The combined sense of *moving toward* and *leaving behind* triggers a physiological response insofar as one makes oneself ready to make the move: we put '"arms and legs' in motion." Will (ii) also includes 'thinking,' and the two concepts cannot be separated (cf. "one should not imagine that thought could be separated from 'willing,' as if only will would then remain!"). 'Will' is as such not understood as some independent and anonymous substance preceding, causing, and determining a content in the form of thinking. When 'thinking' always-already participates in defining 'will,' it follows (since 'thinking' is always a sign-process[227]) that 'will,' in order to have an effect,

---

[227] We find in Nietzsche the following explicit reference to thoughts as signs in the Nachlaß material: "The thought is in the form, in which it comes, an ambiguous [*vieldeutiges*] sign, which is in need of interpretation, or to be more precise: of random limitations [*Einengung*] and restrictions [*Begränzung*], in order to become unambiguous. [...] It arrives, independently of any will, usually surrounded and obscured [*verdünkelt*] by a multitude of feelings, desires, and aversions, by other thoughts as well, often hard to distinguish from a 'willing' or a 'feeling' [. . .] The origin of thoughts remains hidden; the probability is great that it is only a symptom of a far more extensive state. [. . .] For our consciousness, the thought acts as a stimulant – ; in all this, there is something regarding our total state-of-being [*Gesammtzustand*] which expresses itself in signs." (Nachlaß 1885; KSA 11, 38[1]). The latter quote seems to contradict the passage we are discussing in the main text: one says that "thought [cannot] be separated from 'willing'"; another says that "[thought] arrives independently of any will." I propose that one resolves the

has to be *articulated*. A linguistic pre-figuration is necessary for expressing a 'will.' When a so-called "commanding thought" prefigures and formats *will, will* is becoming *expressed will*. It is only possible to act decisively on an *expressed will*; i.e., to respond to a so-called *command*. A will, not expressed, not articulated, not 'commanded,' is not 'will' at all, but is rather an instinct: it exists as a drive or an impetus directed toward something, but executed without subjective awareness.[228] We must therefore believe that Nietzsche's 'will' is always understood as *expressed will*;[229] that is, it has linguistic form (*therefore*, it cannot be separated from thought). Finally (iii), will is not only a fusion of feeling and thinking, but first of all, "an affect," an "affect of command." It is not completely clear how Nietzsche is using the word 'affect' [*Affekt*] in this context. The affect can be either the feeling accompanying the will, or it can 'influence,' 'have an impact on,' or 'move' somebody as in *affect somebody/something* [*jemanden/etwas auswirken*]. In the first sense, will is affecting the commander; in the second sense, it is affecting the one who obeys.[230] In 'willing' something, one *commands* something of someone (or of some other part of oneself), which is now expected to *obey*.

The affect of the command (of the self) on the obedience (of the other) – the feeling of being in control – gives a sense of increased freedom, and thus a sense of superiority, a sense of power, since 'freedom' is now manifesting itself in the contrast to the obvious subjection of the other (cf. "I am free, 'he' must obey").

---

apparent paradox like follows: 'willing' cannot be independent of thoughts (they are already linguistically pre-figured), but thoughts arrive independently of willing (because otherwise, they would derive from a pre-linguistic substance named will).

[228] Cf. Figal: "When one wills, something has to be willed, and whereas this cannot be immediately experienced, it can only be comprehended in the form of a thought. It is in thinking one articulates the aim in willing." Figal, Günter: Nietzsche, loc. cit., p. 226.

[229] Cf. Figal: "However, in Nietzsche' sense, it is not possible to understand will as something isolated. It is only possible to talk about it, when it comes in something like a commanding thought – a thought which articulates the order 'you must' [*"Du sollst"*]. [. . .] Orders are guidelines for action [*Handlungsvorgaben*], to which one must take a stand: one must fulfill or refuse them, one must obey or oppose them – either 'I will' or 'I will not.'" Figal, Günter: Nietzsche, loc. cit., p. 227.

[230] In the second sense, Nietzsche's universe is not identical to Beckett's, where there is "nothing to be done"; 'Will' actively intervenes in events, and changes *status quo*.

However, whereas Nietzsche starts out discussing the command/obedience dialectics applied to the relationship between self and other (interior/exterior), he quickly turns the discussion into what seems to be his true concern: the relationship between self and self (interior/interior) (cf. "A man who wills, commands something in himself which obeys"). The dialectics of command/obedience is now applied to the auto-affective subject, and this subject does not command something of itself as it would from another person. Whereas the distinction between 'self' and 'other' is posited clearly and unproblematically along the axis, interior/exterior, there is no clear distinction between 'self' and 'self,' since everything happens in the interior. Therefore, in the interior, the act of command and the act of obedience must be seen as interwoven. It is indeterminable what 'happens' first, what is the cause and what is the effect.

> But now observe the most peculiar thing about this will – about this multifaceted thing for which people have only one word: inasmuch as in given circumstances we are at the same time the commander and the obedient, and as the one who obeys know the sensations of constraint, compulsion, pressure, resistance, motion, which usually begin immediately after the act of will; inasmuch as, one the other hand, we are in the habit of disregarding and deceiving ourselves over this duality by means of the synthetic concept 'I'; so a whole chain of erroneous conclusions and consequently of false evaluations of the will itself has become attached to the will as such – so that he who wills truly believes that willing s u f f i c e s for action. Because in most cases willing takes place only where also the effect of the command, that is to say obedience, that is to say the action is to be e x p e c t e d, that a p p e a r a n c e has translated itself into the sensation, as if there were here a n e c e s s i t y o f e f f e c t. [. . .]

Again, we are reminded that 'will' is merely an abbreviation, a single word, for a complex process, characterized by the basic structure, command-obedience. Will as such is not organized under the unifying and synthesizing 'I.' To express 'willing' as in 'I will' is merely our conventional linguistic means by which to indicate the command-structure in 'will,' but the subject-predicate construction deceives us into believing in the singularity of the commanding agent (the synthesizing 'I'), and disguises the complexity of 'willing.' The command-obedience dialectics disappears, because the willing of the commanding agent now "suffices for action." Thanks to the subject-predicate logic from where we start, we have erroneously organized 'willing' under a simple linear and uni-directional cause-effect logic, as described above: 'I will' initiates, or causes, my actions.

If, on the contrary, we insist on the dialectics between command and obedience, there is simultaneity between the commanding self and the obeying self. In the first place, there is no effectual command not followed up by (or believed to be followed up by) obedience; a command shouted out in a vacuum is nothing. In the second place, the 'obedient self' already senses, before any command is issued (before any *expressed will*), a number of pressures and resistances which it is up against and which restrain it. It already sees the obstructive wall before the 'commanding self' instructs it to tear down the wall; therefore, "the action is to be expected." In this case, the linear and uni-directional cause-effect structure collapses, because if the obedient self already sees a wall, before it hears the commanding self's instructions, it already 'knows' (as unexpressed, unconscious knowledge) that this instruction is to follow upon its seeing. When thereupon the instruction is put into so many words, we are dealing with the genuine 'will,' which we call 'expressed will.' Now language has stepped in and helped the subject understand what needs to be done, what action needs to be taken.

> [He who wills] also enjoys the triumph over resistances involved but who thinks it was his will itself which overcame these resistances. He who wills adds in this way the sensations of pleasure of the successful executive agents, the serviceable 'under-wills' or under-souls – for our body is only a social structure composed of many souls – to his sensations of pleasure as commander. L'effect, c'est moi: what happens here is what happens in very well-constructed and happy commonwealth: the ruling class identifies itself with the successes of the commonwealth. In all willing it is absolutely a question of commanding and obeying, on the basis, as I have said already, of a social structure composed of many 'souls.' [JGB 19, KSA 5, p. 32-33].

If 'willing' was 'Will' (that is, if willing started out and derived from the unifying willful 'I' as a singularity), there would be a linear and uni-directional cause-effect relationship between command and obedience. The 'I' would be a cause, and the following action or thinking would be effect. As cause, the 'I' would be seen as a substance, open to further investigations (as in so-called "Rational Psychology," as criticized by Kant). It would remain a mystery why it so stubbornly resists centuries of persistent probes into its hidden essence. Accordingly, our mind would be constructed like layers connected as in a 'chain of being' *en miniature*, willing starting out from the self-identical and self-present 'I,' and then through a unidirectional chain of consequences becoming manifest in action. In Nietzsche, however, willing is an interaction between several "serviceable 'under-wills' or under-souls," in a mind that is likened to a "social structure composed of many 'souls'."

When the subject eventually succeeds in *doing* something; that is, when some agent sets him/her/it-self up as commander, and subjects the many 'under-souls' to his command, there is an increased "sensation of pleasure." In a subject fundamentally ignorant about its value, meaning, and purpose of existence, something has been accomplished; the subject has arrived at an opinion; it has adopted an opinion; and it is almost bursting with pride. In its constitutional emptiness, the subject walks a tight-line on the edge of madness, and as a remedy giving its existence a sense of meaning, it defends 'opinions.' That these 'opinions' often are as 'mad' as the individual is as subject, change nothing in the consequent "sensations of pleasure" over having them (we shall be more explicit about implications of this view in the two following chapters).

> The Greatest Danger [. . .] The greatest danger that always hovered over humanity and still hovers over it is the eruption of madness – which means the eruption of arbitrariness in feeling, seeing, and hearing, the enjoyment of the man's lack of discipline, the joy in human unreason [*Menschen-Unverstand*]. Not truth and certainty are the opposite of the world of the madman, but the universality of the universal binding force of a faith; in sum, the non-arbitrary character of judgments." (FW 76, KSA 3, p. 431).[231]

Let us illustrate Nietzsche's notion of 'willing' by a simple example taken from everyday life and familiar to everybody. Some early morning, a student ponders, should I go to class, or should I stay in bed and continue sleeping. There is so far no 'command' and no 'obedience,' but merely two thoughts engaged in a struggle, which we call a will-to-power struggle (however modest it may seem).[232] On one hand, there is the thought of going to class; on the other, the thought of staying asleep. Undoubtedly, to the two main thoughts an entire complex of justifications and rationalizations are being attached for each position, rapidly parading by the mind's eye, while being tacitly assessed and discussed. As such, from the beginning, the struggle takes on a unique linguistic form. The student also 'senses' the *resistances* against going to class (which the example construes as her 'duty'); and she 'senses' the *pressures* to stay in bed (which the example construes as her 'pleasure' or 'inclination'). As such, there are

---

[231] We will say, in our analysis, that madness is always present, ready to overtake the subject, because the means to secure subjectivity are flimsy and fragile. It does not take much newspaper reading to confirm the thesis.

[232] My example of will-to-power is deliberately minimalist; it is no match for the will-to-power of Napoleon Bonaparte, bent on defeating and conquering Europe; but exactly because it illustrates an everyday situation, it may provide a better understanding of Nietzsche's will-to-power, than do the grandiose examples that he himself often introduces in order to illuminate his notion.

"feelings" of resistances and pressures, before there is any clearly expressed will. She also 'knows' that she is supposed to obey something before she (or one of her "under-souls") has issued a command; she knows she is supposed to break down the resistances against going to class, and resist the pressures to stay in bed. Her expected observance of 'duty' (her expected 'respect for the law,' as it were[233]) will eventually prompt her to issue to her obedient self the command that she must rise from bed, and go to class. When this moment occurs, she has *expressed* a will; but *before* this moment, she has *already recognized* what resistances she has to break down.

The eventually articulated thought, "I must go to class," is the *expressed will*, and thought and will are as such *manifestly* intertwined; as are feelings and will. Before issuing this command, the student is engaged in a struggle between thoughts, and since one craves a resolution to a struggle, a victory for one of the positions, it is only fitting to call the struggle, a will-to-power-struggle (and the processes implied in the struggle, will-to-power-processes).[234] Eventually, when the student *obeys* the command, she re-

---

[233] The student in the example is a true Kantian; despite all her struggle, she obediently follows Kant's maxims: "duty is the necessity of an action done out of respect for the law. [. . .] The will can be subjectively determined by the maxim that I should follow such a law even if all my inclinations are thereby thwarted." Kant: Grounding for the Metaphysics of Morals. Translated by J. W. Ellington. Indianapolis (Hackett Publishing Company), 1981; p. 13

[234] Cf. Werner Stegmaier: "Thought-processes are in themselves already power-processes, which arrive in our consciousness as signs, and which we can only see as such. As such, signs are not *means* of thinking, signs do not *determine or direct* [*verfügt*] thinking. Thought-processes *are* always already sign-processes, and sign-processes are interpretations, stabilizations [*Festsetzungen*], but first and foremost, abbreviations of power-processes; whose complexity vastly exceeds our ability to observe and calculate. Their abbreviation into the sign makes possible observations and calculation as such. [. . .] The abbreviation itself does not follow logic in the traditional sense, but is rather an art, an "abbreviation-art" [*"Abkürzungskunst"*]. It is thus the art to simplify and arrange an infinitely complex reality in order to orient ourselves in it; a reality, which is always something other than what we conceive when we try to think it in even our most refined concepts; a reality which is always, as Nietzsche usually says, "unutterably more complicated". Stegmaier: *Nietzsches 'Genealogie der Moral'*, loc. cit., p. 80-81. Stegmaier distinguishes here between three processes: power-processes, thought-processes and sign-processes, where he sees thought- and sign-processes as co-dependent or interwoven (cf. "thought-processes *are* always-already sign-processes"), and sign-processes as 'interpretations' of power-processes. *First*, this means that thought will always announce itself in signs (most typically as language, but

solves the struggle; she now "commands something" of herself, and enjoys the "triumph over resistances involved" in going to class, in the belief that it was her "will itself which overcame these resistances." The end to the inconclusiveness of the struggle will give her an elementary "sensation of pleasure." This also ends her original 'ignorance' – or, as we may say less politely – her original 'stupidity.'

The struggle of wills/thoughts/feelings is, at the point when they are resolved, being translated into one *Will*, organized under the auspices of the synthesizing 'I.' One *Will* becomes the explanation of her great accomplishment of overcoming resistances and resisting pressures. The student therefore projects backwards the idea of one *Will*, as the *actual cause* of her decision. The original struggle of many 'wills' is quickly forgotten, and a supposed "freedom of the Will" is instead explaining her action.

In this insistence on one *Will* controlling action, the student, however, is deceiving herself. This is partly because of, as already described, the entire complexity of the process of willing, but furthermore because it is granted that she will eventually, and necessarily, resolve the struggle between her many "under-wills and under-souls." She will eventually arrive at *some* decision, and paradoxical as it may sound, this implies that there would be *Will* in *any which* decision; more precisely, she would procure and see a *Will* in any which decision. If she goes to class, then this is projected backwards as her *Will*; but if she continues sleeping, then this is also projected backwards as her *Will*. Willing is *truly* only a culmination of processes of power-struggles carried out in inner-mental life, but as *Will*, it is *constructed* after-the-fact in order to explain action, and *interpreted* as something directing action. It is added to the actual processes (now forgotten) retrospectively or *nachträglich*. This aspect of *Will* is better illuminated in the following passage from GD (what Nietzsche here calls 'will,' is what we accentuate as '*Will*' – the *origin* and *cause* of a unidirectional chain of effects):

---

in my reading, possibly also as other symbolic images, such as formulae, diagrams, abstract structures or schemas). *Secondly*, thought and their co-dependent signs are always power-processes; I my reading, this does not imply that the two processes are identical, but that the thought and sign-processes are 'abbreviations' of the power-processes, are as such a smaller material included in the general sphere of power-processes, which is therefore allowed to include several other processes as well (to do with, for example, sense of reality, perception, drives, desires, etc.). *Finally*, while we can know the thought/sign-processes, since they announce themselves "on the table" as something relatively simple, the power-processes *as such* we cannot know, since they are "under the table" as an inaccessible complex reality.

We believed that we ourselves were causes for the act of willing; we thought that at least we were catching causality in the act. Likewise one did not doubt that all antecedentia for an action, its causes, had to be sought in consciousness and would be recovered there, when sought – as 'motives': otherwise, one would not have been free, responsible for it. Finally, who would have disputed that a thought is caused; that the 'I' causes the thought? Of these three 'inner facts', by which causality appeared to be confirmed, the first and most convincing one is that of will as cause [*Wille als Ursache*]; the concept of a consciousness ('mind') as cause and later, of the 'I' (the subject) as cause, is only invented after-the-fact [*nachgeboren*], after the causality of the will had been established as empirical. [. . .] Since we have thought better of all this. Nowadays we no longer believe a word of it. The 'inner world' is full of illusions and will-o'-the-wisps [*irrlichter*]; the will being one of them. The will no longer moves anything, and therefore no longer explains anything – it simply accompanies events, and can even be absent. (GD, "Die vier grossen Irrthümer" 3; KSA 6, p. 90-91).

In conclusion, any kind of struggle requires the termination in a *decision*, a *conclusion*, and an *outcome*; in any kind of struggle, decisions have to be made, and actions have to be taken. Although *any action* implies that a process arrives to a conclusion, it is the belief that this inevitable, but in fact random, conclusion is the effect of a sovereign self's *Will*. Thanks to this metaphysical construction, the subject is essentially congratulating itself. It now acquires a sense of sovereignty, of power, and thus of pleasure. It is understanding itself as independent and free; it feels that it can do what it wants, and consequently infers that what it does was always what it wanted. In other words, 'Doing' is mistranslated into 'Willed.'

6. Nietzsche's "Special Theory" of the Split Subject

6.1. Nietzsche's 'Dividuum' as Foundation for the Moral Subject

It had been noticed before Nietzsche that man has a 'twofold' life, an ability to split himself into two, and thus to converse with himself. This observation introduces for example Feuerbach's analysis of Christianity in *The Essence of Christianity*: "Man thinks, that is, he converses with himself. [. . .] Man is himself at once I and thou; he can put himself in the place of another, for this reason, that to him his species, his essential nature, and not merely his individuality, is an object of thought."[235]

In Feuerbach, this observation justifies the claim that only man, not animals, can have a religion. Only man executes self-reflection; he has both an outer life and an inner life, whereas animals only have an outer life. Man can perceive himself, whereas animals can only perceive their surroundings. As such, man becomes in Feuerbach what Nietzsche below calls a *dividuum* (although Nietzsche and Feuerbach's humans are split according to different fault-lines, and although their arguments serve different strategic purposes in their texts). In Feuerbach, man sees himself both as *specific* and *general*, as *individual* and *universal*; in the latter case, he develops an essential concept of his nature as human being. In Feuerbach's words, he comes to understand himself as *species*. It is this essential and general concept of *mankind*, man will project into God as his vision of the divine.

When Nietzsche in *Menschliches, Allzumenschliches* (aph. 57) introduces a so-called *dividuum*, in apparent contrast to the more familiar *individuum* (the English translation would turn out as *dividual* versus *individual* in the adjective form; and *dividuality* versus *individuality* as noun), his explicit intention is to introduce a condition fundamental to the emergence of the 'moral' subject.

When we say that the 'self-division' of the *individual* into a *dividual* becomes a foundation for understanding the moral subject, let us first emphasize that 'moral' is understood in the broadest sense; as any kind of rule, norm, or value a human might adopt, comply by, and conform to. 'Moral' is not narrowly defined as what Christianity (or Kant) describes as moral duty, but is any 'self-dividing' 'duty,' which an outside agency might impose on the subject (one could for example imagine as a 'moral act' a very un-Kantian duty to *kill* – in order to prove oneself worthy of the society; to defend the country; as a ritual initiation-act; etc.) The 'moral subject' we take as such to be anybody who *internalizes* a system of norms and values, imposed by society, community, family, or any other outside agency. In brief, we understand 'moral' to be *any ideology*, and the 'moral subject'

---

[235] Feuerbach, Ludwig: The Essence of Christianity. Translated by G. Elliot. Amherst, New York (Prometheus Books), 1989; p. 2. Considering that Feuerbach, in writing an analysis and investigation of Christianity that at least regarding its *thematic content* is close to Nietzsche's project, his near-total absence in Nietzsche's writings is a peculiar omission. One wonders why Nietzsche seems to avoid reading peers (Hume on Identity, Feuerbach on Christianity) who could have provided him, if not with ammunition for his own arguments, then with inspiration to develop them in different polemical directions, whether positive or negative.

to be *any ideologically infected* subject. In an allusion to psychoanalysis, which in general it is impossible to ignore when addressing Nietzsche's theory of morality,[236] the subject internalizing a moral (ideological) command is anybody who develops a 'super-ego' opposing his or her 'ego.'

The theory of the *dividuum* is therefore also different from what we hitherto have been discussing as the 'split subject.' The fault-line of the split does not go between a formal 'I' and actual 'thinking'; the fault-line goes between something in the thinking subject and something else ('something' to be determined below); or, as other commentators and philosophers have preferred to put it, between *voices* within the self.[237] Thus, we encounter two very different 'splits' along two very different 'fault-lines,' what has prompted us to introduce two equally different theories, a so-called "General" and a so-called "Special."

We get a first idea of what Nietzsche understands by the *dividual*, this "self-division of man," from the following passage[238]:

> Morality as self-division [*Selbstzertheilung*] of man. – A good author, whose heart is really in his subject, wishes that someone would come and annihilate him by presenting the same subject with greater clarity and resolving all the questions contained in it. A girl in love wishes that the devotion of her love could be tested by the faithlessness of the man she loves. A soldier wishes that he falls on the battlefield for his victorious fatherland; for in

---

[236] Even though we do not intend to carry out a Psychoanalytic reading of Nietzsche in the following, there are several unavoidable and striking 'family-resemblances' between Nietzsche's theory of the moral subject, and Freud's theory of the 'super-ego.' We shall not here try to follow this particular line of research (except in the following *Essay 4*, where I juxtapose Nietzsche's model of the subject to some of Freud's pre-Psychoanalytical writings), but other commentators have thorough accounts of the relationship; most importantly: Gasser, Reinhard: Nietzsche und Freud; loc. cit.; also, Assoun, Paul-Laurent: Freud and Nietzsche. Translated by R. L. Collier. London (The Athlone Press), 2000.

[237] Most prominently, Staten, Henry: Nietzsche's Voice; loc. cit.; and Derrida, Jacques: The Ear of the Other: Otoboigraphy Transference Translation. Translated by P. Kamuf. Lincoln, London (University of Nebraska Press), 1988. A good discussion of the lack of unity of self in Nietzsche, we also find in Nehamas, Alexander: Nietzsche: Life as Literature; loc. cit.

[238] Also in this case, Günter Figal anticipates my discussion of the above aphorism in his *Nietzsche: Ein Philosophische Einführung*; loc. cit.; chapter III.6: "Selbstzertheilung des Menschen." Also Gianni Vattimo has a reference to this passage; see Vattimo, Gianni: Nietzsche: An Introduction. Stanford (Stanford University Press), 2001; p. 67-68.

the victory of his fatherland is his highest desire triumphant. A mother gives to her child that which she deprives herself, sleep, the best food, if need be her health, her strength. – Are these all unegoistic states? Are these deeds of morality m i r a c l e s because they are, in Schopenhauer's words, 'impossible and yet real'? Is it not clear that in all these instances man loves s o m e t h i n g o f h i m s e l f, an idea, a desire, an offspring, more than s o m e t h i n g e l s e o f h i m s e l f, that he as such d i v i d e s his nature and sacrifices one part of it to the other? Is it something e s s e n t i a l l y different from when some obstinate man says: 'I would rather be shot down than move an inch out of that fellow's way?' – T h e i n c l i n a t i o n f o r s o m e t h i n g (wish, drive, demand) is present in all the above-mentioned instances; to give in to it, with all the consequences, is in any event not 'unegoistic'. – In morality man treats himself not as individuum but as dividuum. (MA 57, KSA 2, p. 76).[239]

In the cases here mentioned, all the subjects have some immediate 'egoistic' self-interests – the author wants success, the girl wants love; the soldier wants life; and the mother wants health – which are nevertheless contradicted and annihilated by some subsequent action, done in the name of something else. The immediate 'inclinations' are now thwarted because of a 'sense of duty,' as Kant might say; and we may at first be inclined to think that Nietzsche has provided a number of felicitous examples of Kant's maxim for the categorical imperative. This, however, is obviously not Nietzsche's intention: "Are these all unegoistic states?" he asks, and we are supposed to answer, 'No, they are not,' because Nietzsche presupposes that the subject is no longer whole and unified. When it is the assumption that the subject is split, it is perfectly possible for an *egoistic* interest to develop in *each* of the divided parts. That is, one egoistic interest can develop in naked contradiction to another egoistic interest; in a split subject *A* and *non-A* may exist side by side.[240]

---

[239] Also in *Morgenröte,* Nietzsche introduces this idea of conflicting and competing drives within the same subject. "That one wants to combat the violence of a drive at all is not within our power, neither the choice of method nor whether that method will succeed. Rather, in this whole process our intellect is clearly just the blind tool of another drive that is a rival of the one that is torturing us by its violence: whether it be the drive for peace and quiet, or fear of disgrace and other evil consequences, or love. So while 'we' think we are complaining about the violence of a drive, it is basically one drive that is complaining about another; that is: the perception suffering from this kind of violence presupposes that there is another drive that is just as violent or even more violent, and that there is going to be a struggle in which our intellect is going to have to take sides. (M 109, KSA 3, p. 98).

[240] We notice that when these divided parts develop contradictory interests, it can

Some of Nietzsche's cases are outdated (when is the last time anybody heard about a girl who desires to see her love tested by the faithlessness of her lover?), but others still apply: the soldier is ready to sacrifice himself for the victory of his country; the mother is ready to sacrifice her own health for the health of her child. Something, which we may label a 'voice,' tells the subject that he/she *ought to* pursue an interest, which contradicts the subject's immediate interest of self-preservation. The body has immediate needs; the body wants life and health; but an *idea* overrides these pressing concerns, and imposes upon the subject another urgency. This *idea* must represent something dear and precious to the subject, something "man loves of himself," for example the idea of one's country or of one's child. It is the introduction of this idea into the subject that generates the division. The soldier or the mother are split in the same sense as our student above was split between a 'pleasure' and a 'duty,' but now the 'sense of duty' in the soldier and the mother is so pronounced that pursuing 'pleasure' would entail intolerable 'pain.' Like the student, the soldier/the mother is also involved in a will-to-power struggle, which first and foremost is a struggle between thoughts (therefore, is always-already linguistically pre-figured): the soldier can either live (for the sake of self-preservation), or he can die (for the sake of preservation of his country); the mother can either stay healthy (for the sake of self-preservation), or she can become sick (for the sake of preserving the health of her child).

6.2. The Unique Formula for the Commanding Voice

It is as if a *voice* within the soldier/the mother commands: 'you ought to . . .' – a voice that consequently splits the subject into an 'I' talking, and a 'you' listening, but where the 'I' talking is the internalized 'voice' of another, and where the 'you' listening is never a real 'you,' but 'me' myself taking the place of the real 'you.' As we noticed above, the 'I' – 'you' dialectics from the familiar speech-situation has been internalized as an 'I' – 'me' dialectics; where the 'I' speaks to 'me,' as if a 'you,' only because the subject has adopted the habits of communication. The fundamental formula for the *lonely dialogue* (or *soliloquy*), which above we called *reflective*

---

no longer entail a 'self-contradictory,' 'self-defeating,' 'inconsistent,' etc., subject-theory on Nietzsche's part, since this could only apply within the paradigm of the old subject-theory. This kind of pseudo-logical criticism of Nietzsche starts from the false assumption that the subject is unified, that 'will' derives from the 'I' as a synthesizing core of the unified subject, that the 'I' therefore cannot endorse contrary 'wills.'

communication (in contrast to *pragmatic communication*), is now: *I say to me this*. The modality of the 'this' in the formula determines whether the message expresses an inclination, a cognition, or a morality. If the 'this' means: *(I say to me) that I want/wish/desire this* . . . , then the message is inclinational. If the 'this' means: *(I say to me) that this is the case/a fact/the state-of-affairs* . . . , then the message is cognitive. If the 'this' means: *(I say to me) that I must/should/ought to do this* . . . , then the message is moral.[241] The moral message is thus a special case of lonely dialogue; it must compete with *fantasies* (wishes) and *facts* (perceptions and states-of-affairs). The fundamental formula is in all cases, 'I say to me this,' but the 'this' in the moral message is specified as representing an *idea* understood as proper, just, virtuous, righteous, noble, or the like. It is an idea, therefore, of something the subject has internalized and appropriated as a precious component of his self-identity; an idea that has now become something man "loves of himself."

We notice now that what Nietzsche describes as the individual's *dividuality* must be a general pre-figured form without which the *special dividuality* of the *moral* subject could not develop. It is not the moral judgment *per se* that constitutes *dividuality*; *dividualtiy* is already constituted as an 'I' – 'me' dialectics imitating of the 'I' – 'you' dialectics from discourse. The 'I' – 'you' dialectics is constituted as soon as the subject starts to communicate; thereupon it is transferred into inner life as possible and potential dialogue – as 'lonely dialogue' or 'soliloquy.' The subject first sets itself up in contrast to a 'you,' by doing so constituting the fundamental *self-other* opposition that defines its imaginary 'I' as reference point and addressee of its discourse. This fundamental *self-other* opposition is thereupon internalized and transferred to inner life as an 'I' – 'me' opposition, splitting the subject in an 'inner' *self-other* opposition. As such, the distinction must be a proto-form necessary for any further variations over the subject's *dividuality* – therefore we claim that the 'General Theory' must precede the 'Special Theory.'

---

[241] Such a tripartite division of communicative purposes bears a, at least, superficial resemblance to Habermas' theory of communication. It would be an intriguing future undertaking to compare in more detail a theory of 'reflective communication' to what is Habermas' main concern, 'pragmatic communication' – to settle for example the question whether, as one would suspect, the existence of a 'reflective communication' would not 'cut into' and start undermining the rational promises of 'pragmatic communication,' which is so much at the heart of Habermas' philosophy.

6.3. The 'Perverse' Soliloquy of the Moral Judgment

What is added in the 'special theory' is essentially that the 'I' is setting itself up as a "categorical imperator" (as Nietzsche says in the Nachlaß-material), subduing its 'me' to its commands – it becomes a *categorical imperator* commanding its subjectivity to conform to its *categorical imperatives*.[242] Thus, the 'I' makes its 'me' a 'slave' to an idea that contradicts the subject's original self-interests and self-preservation. Doing so, the strict 'I' (now on behalf of something else but itself) generates Nietzsche's *Slave*. In the moral judgment, the commandments of the 'I' as 'categorical imperator' alienate the subject from its 'total state' [*Gesammtzustand*], its presupposed 'healthy natural instincts.' We witness the destruction of aristocratic values, and the introduction of herd values: exit the *Master*; enter the *Slave*.[243]

If we think about the simplicity of the state-of-affairs in *pragmatic communication*, the 'I' says something to a 'you,' and asserts simultaneously itself as sender and the 'you' as receiver of the discourse according to an unproblematic self-other (interior-exterior) opposition, we notice that this simplicity is jumbled in *reflective communication*; and even more so when *reflective communication* turns *moral*. In *pragmatic communication*, we said that the subject constitutes itself as *individual*. In *reflective communi-*

---

[242] Cf. "An authority speaks – who speaks? – One may forgive human pride if it sought to make this authority as high as possible in order to feel as little humiliated as possible under it. Therefore – God speaks! One needed God as an unconditional sanction, with no court of appeal, as a 'categorical imperator.'" (WM 157). From God as the 'categorical imperator,' Kant deduced the 'categorical imperative.' With this descent into rational inner life, not only God is devising laws, the same laws already exist inside us as rational principles. Kant internalizes God – the categorical imperator becomes the categorical imperative. 'You shall not steal,' 'you shall not kill', 'you shall not lie' are not only laws pronounced by God, they are rational principles, which, if not followed, causes human existence to become illogical: a human cannot want to lie, because then he sanctions lying as justifiable, and then everybody is allowed to lie; but if everybody lies, then he cannot effectively lie even when he tries, because nobody is duped – a logical conundrum! Nobody wants to entangle themselves in a logical conundrum!

[243] By contrast, we notice that in the cognitive judgment, the 'I'/'me' dialectics has no restraining purposes. When 'I say to me that this is the case,' the typical purpose of my soliloquy is to achieve conscious awareness of an impression or a fact. The 'cognitive judgment' would thus equate the 'judgment' in Kant's sense – the purpose is essentially to organize a perception under a concept. We detect no *repression* or *self-repression* in cognitive activity. Still, the cognitive subject is no less divided than the moral subject.

cation, it constitutes itself as *dividual* (to the extent we in this context can talk about 'constitution') according to its imitation of the *self-other* opposition, which, transferred to inner-life, is in reality a *self-self* opposition. In the *moral* judgment, the alienation and estrangement continues: the subject is becoming still further entangled, ensnared, and complicated in oppositions that no longer represents itself (i.e., its supposed background of 'natural instincts'). In its soliloquy, the moral subject still follows the rudimentary dialectical structure of a purported 'I' talking to a purported 'you' (it cannot throw off its fundamental communicative habits, and must continue to execute inner dialogue according to the fundamental *self-other* opposition). However, in the moral judgment, the *self-other* opposition suffers a perversion. The 'I' that speaks has become the voice of *another* (a father, a mother, a commander, a teacher, a priest, etc.) and the 'you' that listens, has become a passive and impotent 'self,' a 'me' conforming itself to this commanding voice in the self, talking as an authoritative *Other*. The *self* as an autonomous and autarchic entity has in effect disappeared from the subjectivity of the moral subject: as 'I' it is eclipsed by the authoritative Other; as 'me' it is impoverished and demoted to apathy and passivity. The subject has become a "hollow barrel," a "windbag," a confused battleground for interests that could or should not concern it.

6.4. Formal Consciousness and Spatialization of Self

With these theoretical deliberations in mind, let us read some of Nietzsche's detailed descriptions from *Die fröhliche Wissenschaft*, *Jenseits von Gut und Böse*, and *Zur Genealogie der Moral* on the nature of the moral subject.

> Considering that obedience so far has been best and longest practiced ad cultivated amongst humans, it is easy to suppose that by now the average person has developed an innate need to obey, a kind of f o r m a l   c o n s c i e n c e [*f o r m a l e n   G e w i s s e n s*] that commands: 'you shall unconditionally do something, unconditionally not do something,' briefly, 'you shall.' This need tries to satiate satisfy itself and to fill its form with a content; like a crude appetite, it indiscriminately grabs up, according to its strength, impatience, and tension, whatever is shouted into its ear [*in's Ohr gerufen wird*] by some commander – parent, teacher, law, class prejudice, public opinion. The strange limitation of human development – its hesitance and slowness, its frequent regressions and reversals – is due to the fact that the herd instinct of obedience has been most effectively inherited, and at the cost of the art of commanding. (JGB 199, KSA 5, p. 119).

We notice again that Nietzsche's description only makes sense under the assumption that the subject is divided. We encounter explicitly a description of *reflective communication* turned moral; i.e., a lonely dialogue where (i) a self addresses a self, ('*you shall unconditionally do something*, etc.'); and (ii) where the self addressing itself speaks in the imperative mood ('*you shall*'); and finally, (iii) where the self addressing itself, does so as an 'I' commanding something of a 'you' ('*you*'), which is in actuality a 'me.' The 'I' and the 'me' thus stand opposed to each other as 'active' and 'passive,' as 'commander' and 'obedient,' or as 'voice' and 'ear.' This structure has now been internalized, throughout millennia, and to such an extent that it has become a kind of "formal conscience." More precisely, the 'I'-position – the one speaking or rather "shouting" – has developed itself into this 'formal conscience.' The conscience is "formal," implying that it is, as Nietzsche explains, first and foremost 'form'; it is in-itself empty, and precisely because it is empty, it *can be filled*; precisely because it is empty, it *craves to be filled*.

At this point in Nietzsche's description, we encounter another actor on the stage. We have been introduced to an (implicit) 'I' shouting its commands to an (explicit) 'you' (which is actually a 'me') – 'I' and 'you' thus interacting in a *self-self* relation. This *auto-affective circuit* between self and self is not sufficient to explain *alienation*; a subject cannot 'self-alienate.' Nietzsche consequently introduces a third actor on his stage, the 'Other' or the 'They,' described as "some commander" represented for example by "parent," "teacher," "public opinion," and one might add, "priest." It is this third actor that injects its imperatives into the subject, as it enlists and takes over the 'I' to fulfill this purpose. *First*, the 'I' becomes an 'ear' for the 'voice' of the Other, the They; *second*, the 'I' now imitates this communicative situation as it transforms itself to a 'voice' shouting the commands into the 'ear' of the 'me.' The subject is therefore submitted to the moral command in two stages: *first*, the 'they' shouts into the 'ear' of the 'I'; *then*, the 'I' shouts into the 'ear' of the 'me.' This mechanism of course also describes 'internalization' in the psychoanalytical sense;[244] it is the mechanism by which some outer repression becomes inner repression.

We notice furthermore from Nietzsche's description that the 'They' can take on many different shapes. What is shouted into the recipients 'ear' is not something already pre-determined. In all forms, the 'They' is a "commander," but it issues 'commands' according to the interest of the

---

[244] Although internalization is a famous concept from psychoanalysis, Nietzsche introduces in fact the concept 'internalization' [*Verinnerlichung*] before Freud; see quotation from GM below.

institution it represents: family, school, church, public opinion, etc. Consequently, the 'I' must necessarily re-represent the same diversity of interests as originally the 'They.' Again, as *form*, it *commands*, but as *content*, it issues *a wide variety* of commandments. It *shouts into the ear* of the 'me,' but it shouts a diversity and multiplicity of instructions, depending on the 'commander' it has internalized. This implies that the subject as *dividuum* – that is, divided between *commander* and *obedient*, *active* and *passive*; or between *"something man loves of himself"* and *"something else man loves of himself"* – is at bottom *fragmented* in both of the implied positions. The *commanding self* is a confusion of imperatives adopted from the outside; and correspondingly, the *obedient self* is submitting itself to this confused variety of different instructions. Thus, the subject is even more 'divided' than Nietzsche makes theoretically explicit: 'dividuality' is branching out like rhizomes from its main moral self-division.

In order for the moral operation to succeed, the subject must be subservient to the commanding 'They,' and be prepared to carry out the commandments, while sacrificing its own self-interests. It must abandon all commanding itself, and instead fill ("with an insatiable *appetite*") its empty inner space (its empty *stomach*) with the commands (the already half digested *food*) of the Other. The more empty the subject (the more *starving*), the more eagerly does it "grab up" exterior imperatives. The 'slave' is permanently *hungry* in Nietzsche's metaphor – with no sense of good diet, the slave indiscriminately gobbles up everything put on the table. This economy of reverse proportionality (the *less* full . . . the *more* hungry; the *less* independent . . . the *more* subservient, etc.), we often see reiterated; e.g., in FW:

> The believers and their need for beliefs. [...] Faith is always coveted most and needed most urgently where will is lacking; for will, as the affect of command, is the decisive sign of sovereignty and strength. In other words, the less someone knows how to command, the more urgently does he covet someone who commands, commands severely – a god, prince, class, physician, father confessor, dogma, or party conscience. (FW 347, KSA 3, p. 582)

The slave lives with a permanent deficit on his ideological account, which he tries to cover by supporting any idea that comes his way.

In *Chapter 5*, we will in more detail return to the particular economy of the so-called 'master' and 'slave.' Here, we will therefore just briefly intimate one psychological consequence of "moral self-division." We have seen that 'moral self-division' is a result of internalization of the moral judgment (something *not mine* becomes *mine*, in competition with something else that is *mine*). However, this internalization does more to the

6. Nietzsche's 'Special Theory' of the Split Subject

subject than simply making an exteriority interior; ultimately, it alters the *form* of the subject. Not only does internalization split the subject, but it also expands the subject's inner space; it hollows out the subject. The inner world, "originally as thin as if stretched out between two membranes," acquires "depth, breadth, and height" (cf. below). The moral subject carves out of itself a cavity that now needs to be filled. This cavity or hollowness has a dynamics much like the famous 'black hole' in contemporary astronomy: it pulls in all kinds of stuff, but at no point is it ever satiate, and at no point is there any creative return.

If superficiality characterizes the pre-moral and post-moral subject (the master/the noble), the moral subject becomes *deep*. However, *depth* (to be 'deep') is not a distinction in Nietzsche; it usually means that the subject is un-whole and unwholesome. We are referring to the following description of the process from GM:

> All instincts that do not discharge themselves outwardly turn inward – this is what I call the internalization [*Verinnerlichung*] of man; it was thanks to this that man first developed what was later called his 'soul.' This entire inner world, originally as thin as if stretched out between two membranes, to the extent they effect one another, acquired depth, breadth, and height, as the outward discharge was inhibited. Those fearful bulwarks with which the state apparatus [*staatliche Organisation*] protected itself against the old instincts for freedom – first and foremost punishments belong amongst these bulwarks – brought about that all those instincts of the wild, free, prowling man turned backward, turned against man himself. Hostility, cruelty, joy in persecuting, in attacking, in change, in destruction – all this turned against the possessors of such instincts: that is the origin of the 'bad conscience.' (GM II 16, KSA 5, p. 322).

As such, thanks to 'self-division' man develops a spatial self, a self where now there is room for different agencies opposed to each other. We notice that *difference* makes possible *spatialization*; it is self-division that expands and extends the self. In a self-identical self, there would be no space, but only mass. We also notice, that Nietzsche's descriptions are foreshadowing Freud's later models over the spatial self; especially Freud's famous 'topographical' model over a subject divided between an Id (Nietzsche's 'instincts'), and the Superego-Ego complex (the 'moral self-division' in Nietzsche). In both Nietzsche and Freud, the self has become spatial thanks to a civilizational process; room has been created for different agencies, standing over and against each other, engaged in permanent struggles for power.

6.5. The Metaphor of the Ear:
To Hear the Differences in the Same

In the passage from JGB above, we read that someone is 'shouting' his commands into the 'ear' of the subject. The 'ear' receives, is in fact only all too receptive to, this moral shouting. This metaphor of the 'ear' as recipient of moral commandments is not coincidental; it transpires in different other contexts. In Nietzsche's work, one finds the metaphor elaborated into a distinction between two 'kinds' of ears: either the very *big*, or the very *small*. So, we find in *Also Sprach Zarathustra*, a description of a perversely big 'ear' grown out of all proportions, impoverishing the bearer of this ear, who has lost his body and all healthy instincts for self-preservation and self-augmentation. In this context, the so-called 'big ear' is not an advantage, and a so-called 'small' a disadvantage (assuming that the big ear would make one a better listener; and the small, a poorer listener). In Nietzsche, this reflex translation of the metaphor is reversed to its opposite.

> When I came out of my solitude and crossed over this bridge for the first time, I did not believe my eyes and looked, and looked again, and said at last: 'That is an ear! An ear, as big as a man!' [*"das ist ein Ohr! Ein Ohr, so gross wie ein Mensch!"*] I looked even more closely: and actually, under the ear something was moving, something that was pitifully small and miserable and frail. And in truth, the enormous ear sat upon a little, thin stalk – the stalk, however, was a man! [*– der Stiel aber war ein Mensch!*] By the use of a magnifying glass, one could even discern a little, envious face, as well as a swollen little soul dangling from the stalk. The people told me, however, that the great ear was not merely a man, but a great man, a genius. But I have never believed the people when they talked about great men – and I held to my belief that is was an inverse cripple [*umgekehrter Krüppel*]. (Za II "Von der Erlösung", KSA 4, p. 178)

In *Ecce Homo*, we find a contrasting description of the 'small,' the 'fine,' and the 'delicate' ear, which happens also to be Nietzsche's ear.

> All of us know, even know from experience, which beast is long-eared [*Langohr* ('*Meister Langohr*': the *Esel*)]. Well then, I dare to say that I have the smallest ears. This is interesting not least to the little ladies – it seems to me that they feel I understand them better. . . . I am the anti-donkey [*Antiesel*] par excellence and thus a world-historical monster. (EH "Warum Ich so gute Bücher schriebe" 2, KSA 6, p. 302).

Jacques Derrida refers in his essay, *The Ear of the Other*, to these passages, and adds the following commentary:

The hypocritical hound whispers in your ear through his educational systems, which are actually acoustic or acroamatic devices. Your ears grow larger and you turn into long-eared asses when, instead of listening with small, finely tunes ears and obeying the best master and the best of leaders, you think you are free and autonomous with respect to the State. You open wide the portals of your ears to admit the State, not knowing that is has already come under the control of reactive and degenerate forces. Having become all ears for this phonograph dog, you transform yourself into a high-fidelity receiver, and the ear – your ear which is also the ear of the other – begins to occupy in your body the disproportionate place of the 'inverted cripple.'[245]

The 'big' and the 'small' ear function differently. If the 'big' ear is like a megaphone that only amplifies the moral noise of the priest screaming his moral ideology to the subject, the 'small' ear is rather like a processor of the moral noise of the priests. The small and fine ear isolates for example foreground from background; it discriminates between important and unimportant, active and reactive, and retrieves what is important and active. A subject with megaphones for ears becomes a 'donkey'; he or she hears only noise, and transports only 'noise' into his/her inner self (to the 'me' so-called); while the subject with small ears processes the noise, and listens for a background that may have been rendered almost inaudible in the decibels of the noise itself. The subject with small ears listens with – as psychoanalysts say – a "third ear"; assuming that to our two 'conventional' ears is added a so-called 'third' ear that becomes like an inner labyrinth processing and isolating the desires or interests or purposes with which an ideological message was composed. With this 'third ear' one listens to a discourse with "distracted attention"; i.e., one does not necessarily hear whole sentences; one skims over the logic that presents itself in the discourse – all the excuses, the justifications, the rationalizations – and listens instead for *motives* that are uniquely attached to an *interest* or a *desire* of the subject. However, if the psychoanalyst listens for the desire of the individual, Nietzsche's "anti-donkey" tends to listen for the desire of *the ideologue*. Nietzsche's "anti-donkey" is a subtle *Critic of Ideology*. The purpose of the keen ear is, as Derrida states, to "perceive differences" "between apparently similar things."[246] For example, a sentimental appeal made by a political

---

[245] Derrida, Jacques: The Ear of the Other, loc. cit., p. 35.
[246] In a roundtable discussion attached to the English translation of the essay, Derrida makes the following clarification: "A keen ear is an ear with keen hearing, an ear that perceives differences, those differences to which he was very attentive. And precisely to perceive differences is to pass on the distinction between apparently similar things. Think of all that was said yesterday

candidate is never spoken with the intention it pretends to vindicate; its 'deeper' purpose is to seduce the electorate into believing that their political candidate is ardently supporting the same sentimental values as they are. To a 'donkey,' the politician becomes a 'megaphone' for his/her own idiosyncrasies. The 'donkey' sees no 'difference in the same,' but amplifies instead the professed sentimentality; the noise of the inane becomes almost total. The keen and discriminating ear, by contrast, *hears the seduction*; hears all too crisply the background of party-politics and electoral calculations. As such, the keen and discriminating ear hears *the difference in the same*.[247]

7. From a Theory of the Split Subject to a Theory of Ideology

7.1. Why Re-Introducing Nietzsche's Notion of a Split Subject?

As we have stated before, there is in itself nothing new in introducing a Nietzschean notion of a 'split' (a heterogeneous, decentered, fragmented, multiform) subject. But (i) there may be something new in refusing to see this 'split' merely as some kind of quasi-ideological formation that resigns us to the thrilling *terra incognita* of the irrational. We take the 'split' seriously as an inescapable subjective condition that is partly to blame for the need of ideology in the first place. To take the 'split' seriously, in its linguistic-ontological nature, means that it is objectively always *there*. 'Siding with' or defending a new dogmatic irrationalism does not escape the fundamental condition, because the position would be exactly as

---

about political discourses and about stereotypes that seem to resemble each other. Here, precisely, is where the keen ear must be able to distinguish, the active from the reactive, the affirmative from the negative, even though apparently they are the same thing." Derrida, Jacques: The Ear of the Other, loc. cit., p. 50.

[247] In other contexts in Nietzsche, the ear has been cultivated by one's experiences. That which one cannot 'hear' is also that which one has never experienced: "For what one lacks access to from experience one will have no ear. Now let us imagine an extreme case: that a book speaks of nothing but event that lie altogether beyond the possibility of any frequent or even rare experience – that it is the first language of a new series of experiences. In that case, simply nothing with be heard, but there will be the acoustic illusion that where nothing is heard, nothing is there." (EH "Warum ich so gute Bücher schreibe" 1, KSA 6, p. 300)

ideologically contaminated as old-fashioned Rationalism. In the context of the 'split,' there can be no gain in understanding oneself as 'irrational,' and no loss in understanding oneself as 'rational'; in both cases, self-deceptive ideological positions permeate the opinionated subject. This comes about because, in any case and whatever you do, everything is a *response* to the empty formality of your subjectivity. Immanuel Kant is as 'adequate' or 'logical' or 'healthy' a response to this empty formality as is Marquis de Sade – its nature cannot be captured by surface-distinctions like rational and irrational. (ii) It may also represent a novelty to theoretically differentiate between the levels on which Nietzsche discusses this well-known 'split' or 'fragmented' subject. There is a categorical difference between his criticism of the unity of the 'I' in 'I think,' and his introduction of a subject lacking unity thanks to moral self-division. In the first case, the fault-line of the division runs between a formal 'I' and empirical 'thinking'; in the second, it runs between 'voice' and 'ear' – more specifically, between a commanding 'I' and a subservient 'me.' In the first case, the 'I' is a "fable" and a "fiction"; in the second, the 'I' is as 'actual' as it can possibly become. There is nothing fictitious about the moral 'I' 'shouting' its commands to the subject – this is rather the all-too real outcome of Christianity's long-lasting supremacy in Europe. Finally (iii), there may be novelty in taking Nietzsche's insights into a contemporary linguistic territory. Here, we move into untrod land and we navigate with greater difficulty, because we take Nietzsche's insights beyond his own explanations. In the logical nature of things, beyond Nietzsche, we can not expect much help from Nietzsche. We still believe, however, that it is in the spirit of Nietzsche to expand his own explanation of the emergence of a unitary 'I.' To Nietzsche, we are 'seduced' by language, meaning its grammar; we suggest that even more fundamentally, the subject internalizes the unitary 'I' from a formative communicative 'habit,' the dialogue. When in one of the epigraphs for the present chapter Hölderlin stated that we are "signs, un-interpretable," we can now determine *which* sign exactly, namely "the I." The 'I' is now the *un-interpretable sign*, which nevertheless fills us with a sense of identity. Man's self-understanding is short-circuited by the contradiction: as *active* and in *use*, the 'I' is unique, designating 'me'; as *passive* and *dormant*, it is general, empty of content, and un-interpretable. Man does not grasp the contradiction: something, which is nothing, represents me, which is everything.

7.2. A Theory of Ideology

One of the best prospects of the theory we have extracted from Nietzsche is its superior ability to explain the phenomenon of ideology. Thus, as indicated above, we interpret Nietzsche's criticism of the moral subject and moral discourse as a *critique of ideology*; we read Nietzsche's 'priest' as a label for *any ideologue*; we see Nietzsche's 'slave' as the *ideologically infected* subject; and we finally read Nietzsche's 'master' as the promise of an *ideologically emancipated* subject.

We now understand (i) that the fundamental conditions of possibility of ideology is the empty formality of the subject (the subject craves ideology, and anything will do provided it fills up these empty positions of the subject. We understand (ii) why the ideologically infected subject constantly involves him or herself in blatant self-contradictions, and especially, why the subject rarely detects such self-contradictions. In our revised theory of 'moral self-division,' the subject internalizes *several* positions according to their emotional appeal (not according to their coherence), that is, according to the intensity of desire and hatred invested in the positions. The subject therefore encompasses several positions or *clusters, configurations*, or *groups*. In the fragmented subject these groups exist in relative independence of each other; that is, one group expressing one view may exist comfortably next to another group expressing another view.[248] We finally understand (iii) why ideological positions often override and annul realities and facts. Simply put, the ideological infected subject falls in love with an idea, we might even say, makes love to an idea. Given the empty formality of his or her subjectivity, "any explanation is better than none," as Nietzsche has it. The ideologue instills in the receptive subject certain images of high emotional intensity; it is often something the subject is being told to desire, but is prevented from fulfilling by an antagonist social group,

---

[248] In the ideologically infected subject, we encounter a logic not unlike the logic Freud described was governing dreams: "The governing rules of logic carry no weight in the unconscious; it might be called the Realm of the Illogical. Urges with contrary aims exist side by side in the unconscious without any need arising for an adjustment between them. Either they have no influence whatever on each other, or, if they have, no decision is reached, but a compromise comes about which is nonsensical since it embraces mutually incompatible details. With this is connected the fact that contraries are not kept apart but treated as though they were identical, so that in the manifest dream any element may also have the meaning of its opposite." Freud, Sigmund: An Outline of Psychoanalysis. Translation J. Strachey. New York, London (W. W. Norton), 1969; p. 43.

class, race, or the like, on which the infected subject can now legitimately unload its hatred. The subject is now so desperately in love with the idea, that it ignores whether at all it is realizable, or whether the imaginary hate-group has any responsibility for its suppression. Instead, the imaginary hate-group, which supposedly prevents fulfillment, is by its sheer existence fueling the desire of the infected subject, in creating imaginary resistances to, and setting up obstacles for, the fulfillment of the beloved idea.

One could give numerous examples illustrating the basic structure; the following two has a certain contemporary resonance. The jihadist wants to include present-day Spain in his imaginary Caliphate. He has fallen in love with this idea, and now he makes love to it. He therefore does not comprehend how absurd its realization is in the present geo-political environment; he also does not comprehend that the Spaniards have not chosen enmity to Islam, since Spain's possible inclusion in a new imperialistic Islamic super-power never crossed their mind. Opposed by the resentful and envious, the innocent are always taken by surprise. It never occurred to them that they owed somebody an unpaid debt.[249]

Certain writers have in the last few decades engaged themselves in fighting the perceived hegemony of the natural sciences in the Academy – a struggle that in the United States has been labeled the 'science war.' This is almost always carried out as either an attempt to argue for the social constructiveness of natural science (as such, castrate its claim to truth, and reduce it to a field within History of Ideas), or by arguing for its articulation of a supposedly suppressive logo-centric or phallo-logocentric discourse; meaning that 'rational' or 'masculine-rational' ideals permeate its discourse. The following passage from Luce Irigaray makes this latter claim:

> Is $E = Mc^2$ a sexed equation? Perhaps it is. Let us make the hypothesis that it is insofar as it privileges the speed of light over other speeds that are vitally necessary to us. What seems to me to indicate the possibly sexed nature of the equation is not directly its uses by nuclear weapons, rather it is having privileged what goes the fastest.[250]

---

[249] The modern Jihadist is the fanatic par excellence; he fulfills perfectly Nietzsche's diagnosis: "For fanaticism is the only "strength of the will" that even the weak and insecure can be brought to attain, being a sort of hypnoticism of the whole system of the senses and the intellect for the benefit of an excessive nourishment (hypertrophy) of a single point of view and feeling, that henceforth becomes dominant. [. . .] Once a human being reaches the fundamental conviction that he must be commanded, he becomes 'a believer.'" (FW 347, KSA 3, p. 583)

[250] Irigaray quoted from Nagel, Thomas: "The Sleep of Reason" in *Theory's*

According to Irigaray, Einstein's equation and his prediction of a speed of light are 'masculine' propositions. With Irigaray, we assume that Einstein, like any small child, was originally fascinated with what is *strongest, biggest, greatest,* and *fastest,* and thinking within this masculine-infantile paradigm, he suggested a speed of light that "goes the fastest" in disregard of other speeds that are "vitally necessary to us." That the formulation makes no sense (how are speeds "vitally necessary"?), we will here ignore; the point is that these "necessary speeds" are feminine. We therefore arrive to the revelatory conclusion: Einstein's famous equation, $E = Mc^2$, is in fact a sexist ("sexed" one says today) proposition, it privileges the masculine over the feminine. Modern physics is not just a social construct, it is a *masculine* social construct.

That Alan Sokal and Thomas Nagel, from who I have borrowed the enjoyable example, object that these theories are all verified "to a high degree of certainty," is all correctly pointed out (the speed of light has obviously no gender, and we can be sure that it existed also before humans started to inhabit the world). In my context, however, the point is to illustrate the techniques of the new *ideologue/priest*. We see some of the steps already mentioned above repeated: First, the ideologue always presumes to reveal ideology, here the 'ideology' of the theory of relativity (a nonsense, surely!). Second, the ideologue suspends all commitments to realities and facts, here the fact of the speed of light. Third, the ideologue positions herself on behalf on a supposedly suppressed group, in this case women (again a nonsense – how could women be suppressed (discriminated against?) by the speed of light?). Fourth, the ideologue finds herself an imaginary hate-object (an alleged transgressor of the ideology she is preaching), here Einstein. Finally, the ideologue accuses the transgressor of a transgression that never occurred to himself, in this case, sexism. In this, the ideologue makes the completely innocent guilty. Against the cleverness of the resentful, not even Einstein stands a chance.

Empire: An Anthology of Dissent. Edited by D. Patai and W. H Corral. New York (Columbia University Press), 2005; p. 542. See also Sokal, Alan & Bricmont, Jean: Fashionable Nonsense: Postmodern Intellectuals' Abuse of Science. New York (Picador), 1998.

CHAPTER 4

Theory of Knowledge as 'Neuro-Epistemology'

Toward a Biological-Linguistic Subject in
Nietzsche and Contemporaries

>Through the long succession of millennia, man has not known himself physiologically: he does not know himself even today. To know, e.g., that one has a nervous system (– but not a 'soul' –), is still the privilege of the best informed.
>— Nietzsche: *Der Wille zur Macht*.[251]

>The actual brain-process [*Gehirnprozeß*] producing a thought is something essentially different from what we are aware of in thinking: the representations [*Vorstellungen*] that we know about, is the smallest and most inferior part of what we have.
>— Nietzsche: Nachlaß 1880-81.[252]

>The world, insofar as we can know [*erkennen*] it, is only our own nerve-activity, nothing else.
>— Nietzsche: Nachlaß 1880-81.[253]

>The ignorance about physiology – Christ has no nerve-system – the contempt for and the arbitrary desire-to-avoid-seeing [*Wegsehen-wollen*] the cravings of the body –
>— Nietzsche: Nachlaß 1888.[254]

---

[251] Nietzsche, Friedrich: Der Wille zur Macht, # 229. Stuttgart (Kröner Verlag), 1996.
[252] Nietzsche, Friedrich: Nachlaß 1880-81, KSA 9, 5[44], p.191
[253] Nietzsche, Friedrich: Nachlaß 1880-81, KSA 9, 10[E95], p. 436.
[254] Nietzsche, Friedrich: Nachlaß 1888, KSA 13, 15[89].

0. Introduction

As we saw in the previous chapter, in Hume's stream of consciousness, we find no centering self, no 'I think,' but only a flow of distinct impressions. His inner world is a world in flux, a world, as it were, of constant becoming. If or when the subject ascribes identity unto this flux, this ascription is artificial, and the result of associative processes that are in themselves infinitely more complex than the unity, which is assumed in the ascription. The ascription of identity belongs to the so-called 'ideal world,' not to the 'real world,' where impressions remain distinct and disconnected.

Much in this conception reminds us of Nietzsche. Nietzsche too envisions our inner world as a world of movement and fluctuation of forces, as ever-changing becoming. In Nietzsche too, various different predications of the mind have no actual existence as *identifiable* entities. If or when identity and unity is created in the mind, it is fictitious, belonging to an 'ideal world,' but not to the 'real world' of fluctuation and becoming. In Nietzsche too, the subject is a multiplicity, not an entity.

From Hume to Nietzsche, vocabulary and concepts have evidently changed. In Nietzsche, it is 'wills' and 'forces' rather than 'impressions' and 'ideas' that fluctuate. In Nietzsche, these 'wills' and 'forces' exist *before* the subject is conscious about them, whereas in Hume, the notion of 'unconscious' impressions would make little, if any, sense. Ideas and impressions have in Hume always-already arrived in consciousness as perceived (an 'impression' not perceived becomes a contradiction in terms). If or when wills and forces are eventually perceived in Nietzsche, it is because they have undergone a rudimentary interpretation-process, which allow them to enter consciousness as experienced material. This implies that not only is the subject de-centered in Nietzsche, which it also is in Hume, but before any of these rudimentary interpretation-processes start to take effect, it also leads a secret life, which would be inaccessible to empirical introspection in Hume's conception.

To summarize two of the most apparent differences in their positions: (1) in Hume, the subject is de-centered in its *conscious representations*; in Nietzsche, the subject is de-centered in both its *conscious and unconscious representations*. (2) Although Nietzsche can be seen as setting up a distinction between 'ideal' and 'real' like Hume, the fault-line, and the dichotomy it distinguishes, has changed. In Hume, 'ideal' and 'real' distinguish between a fictitious unified self and an actual empirical stream of consciousness. In Nietzsche, the 'ideal' would instead correspond to the material that in inner-mental life has found expression and form (i.e., has undergone an interpretation-process), while the 'real' would correspond to the still-unexpressed chaos of forces and drives living their secret and unconscious life in the subjective underground.

The idea of the subject as an *unconscious web* of a *multiplicity of forces* or of *'wills to power,'* is repeatedly emphasized in Nietzsche's thinking; especially as it takes form from the mid-eighties:

> The nervous system and the brain is a conductive system [*Leitungssystem*] and a centralizing apparatus [*Centralisationsapparat*] consisting of numerous individual spirits [*Individual-Geister*] of different range. (Nachlaß 1884, KSA 11, 26[36]).

> The assumption of one single subject is perhaps unnecessary; perhaps it is just as permissible to assume a multiplicity of subjects, whose interaction and struggle is the basis of our thought and our consciousness in general? A kind of aristocracy of 'cells' [*Eine Art Aristocratie von 'zellen'*] in which dominion resides. Nachlaß 1885, KSA 11, 40[42].

> My hypothesis: the subject as multiplicity (Nachlaß 1885, KSA 11, 40[42]).

> The human being as a multiplicity of "wills to power": each of them with a multiplicity of expressions and forms. The distinct so-called "passions" (e.g., the cruelty of man) are only fictive unities, insofar as that which are different basis-drives [*Grundtrieben*] arrive equalized in consciousness, as synthesized into an "essence" [*"Wesen"*] or a "capacity" [*"Vermögen"*] – as such creatively condensed [*zusammengedichtet*] into a distinct passion. It is much similar to how the 'soul' is in itself an expression for all conscious phenomena. (Nachlaß 1885-86, KSA 12, 1[58])

> The subject: this is the terminology for our belief in a unity underlying all the different impulses of the highest feeling of reality. [. . .] The 'Subject' is a fiction, as if several similar states in us were an effect of a single substratum. (Nachlaß 1887, KSA 12, 10[19]).

> There is [*es gibt*] no Will; only will-punctures [*Willens-Punktationen*], which continuously expand or reduce their power. (Nachlaß 1887-88, KSA 13, 11[73]).)

As such, Nietzsche's 'subject,' in its 'true' chaotic underground, has strictly speaking not yet constituted itself as subject. (The term 'subject' becomes a misnomer given this lack of subjective constitution – however, we are forced to call things by a name, and provisionally we will use this inaccurate term, because it undeniably has certain connotations to the 'what' we are describing.) So far, the 'subject' is no more than a sensitive 'blind' organism, shooting out its tentacles in order to sense the pains and pleasures of an inner and outer world. It is so far no more than an indefinite number of nerve-endings scanning the world for information. Nietzsche's unconscious 'subject' operates as such before the threshold to subjectivity. It is like a net of rhizomes, sucking nourishment out of the ground around it, to feed the tree above; and like the rhizomes have no awareness of the tree above, the tree does not take any notice of the rhizomes.

We notice already here that Nietzsche's *unconscious* has another structure than the *unconscious* we encounter in Psychoanalysis. In Psychoanalysis, the unconscious belongs to the subject as the subject's *innermost own*. It is made up of material accumulated from a long life of disappointments; disappointments now hidden away as painful wounds to the personal pride; disappointments that cannot be accepted, and oftentimes cannot be remembered. In Freud, we recall that the unconscious is drawn as a big ungainly sack at the bottom of his topographical model, stuffed full — we imagine — of compromising and embarrassing material. Freud reiterates often enough what a delicate operation it is to open up for this 'sack.'

This is not Nietzsche's unconscious 'subject'; Nietzsche's unconscious 'subject' is situated before any subjectivity, properly speaking, is constituted. It is the net of rhizomes receiving impressions, which have still not transgressed the threshold to subjectivity. It is consequently not made up of 'repressed' material, because it has never encountered a repressing agent. It has never had the chance to take the crucial round-trip from unconsciousness to consciousness and back again to the unconscious underground. In Nietzsche, our physiological mechanisms for receiving information are *unconscious*. This is a thought, which theoretically Nietzsche would have known from certain of Schopenhauer's writings (most obviously from SzG), but also from writers such as Herman von Helmholtz, Friedrich A. Lange, Gustav Fechner, and Eduard von Hartmann. It is a thought also with strong affinities to the young (*neurological*) Sigmund Freud. In these writers, we are *unconscious* before we start to sense.[255]

Let us start the present chapter by outlining a few of the theories about our biological origin that begin to take form in some of Nietzsche's contemporaries. We refer to contemporaries that we know had an influence on Nietzsche, such as Schopenhauer, Helmholtz, Lange, and Fechner, and will include as well, and most crucially, Sigmund Freud — although it is certain

---

[255] In his late Nachlaß material, Nietzsche has acquainted himself with scientific writings, related especially to physio-psychological research. Cf . Gasser: "In the late phase Nietzsche discovers eventually a physio-psychological, as well as a strongly scientific oriented point of view, which he attempts to synthesize with his revolutionary Power-philosophy." Gasser, Reinhard: Nietzsche und Freud. New York, Berlin (Walter de Gruyter), 1997; p. 612

that Nietzsche did not know Freud, since he first started to publish his research a few years after Nietzsche terminated his activity.²⁵⁶

Whereas the affinities between Nietzsche and orthodox Psychoanalysis have been frequently pointed out, but often seem exaggerated and artificial,²⁵⁷ the affinities between Nietzsche and the neurological Freud has

---

²⁵⁶ If Freud helps us to understand problems related to stimulus, sensation, memory, and cognition, this is sufficient justification for juxtaposing him to Nietzsche, regardless of Nietzsche knowing him or not. As stated in the Introduction, the present work is not and does not pretend to be neither a philological nor a historicist work, but a philosophical. Its ultimate purpose is not to trace Nietzsche's statements to different stages of his writing, nor to unveil his sources of inspiration as a self-sufficient aim in itself (like some of the newest Nietzsche-commentators (e.g., Christian Emden, Gregory Moore, and Torben Brobjer), quite laudably, have been doing). The work rather endeavors to understand Nietzsche's *conceptuality*, the *structure of his thinking*; but surely with the help of the scientific paradigm of his day. In a sense, it is a *phenomenological analysis of conceptual structure* read within what appears to be the *most pertinent intellectual context*. On some counts, methodologically, it has certain family-resemblances to the *Deconstruction* of the early Derrida. Even if I might prefer *Reconstruction* of conceptual structures to Derrida's *Deconstruction*, the theoretical effects of the two strategies are often the same (whether the 're-' or the 'de-' – in the last analysis, this may be an idle battle over two equally appropriate prefixes). (There are good reasons why re- and de-construction often turn out to be the same thing – it has to do with the nature and structure of the concept – but I will refrain from trying to explain the logic at this point).

²⁵⁷ Recently, Paul-Laurent Assoun's work on Freud and Nietzsche appeared in English (Assoun: *Freud and Nietzsche*. Translated by R. L. Collier (London: The Athlone Press, 2000). In many respects, an admirable and erudite work, on almost all counts, it differs from my own approach, and from my personal theoretical convictions and interests. First, in his comparison of Nietzsche and Freud, Assoun does not address the early Freud, but the traditional Freudian concepts like drives, dreams, sexuality, unconsciousness, therapy, etc. Secondly, Assoun sets out to write a comparative analysis where allegedly he posits neither Nietzsche as "the law of Freud" nor Freud as "the law of Nietzsche." However, comparing Freud and Nietzsche on a background of the traditional Freudian inventory would seem tacitly to construe Freud exactly as the "law of Nietzsche" (in what consists, for example, Nietzsche's 'therapeutics'?). In contrast to Assoun's exposition, it is here the argument that on crucial psychoanalytical issues, Nietzsche does not have any obvious equivalents to established psychoanalysis, and is likely to would have opposed Freud had he known him. For example: (a) Nietzsche's theory of the subject is *not* corroborated by Freud's later topographical and structural models of the psyche (for example, his well-known Superego-Ego-Id models); also the 'It,'

hardly received any attention in Nietzsche-commentary, although we believe that they are both infinitely more illuminating and much better related to Nietzsche's cognitive project.[258] When it is sensible to juxtapose Nietzsche and the young Freud, although Nietzsche had no knowledge of Freud, it is because that at this closure of the 19th century, they both belong to the same paradigm, and they both think within this paradigm. To a large extent, they even use the same 'library' (Schopenhauer, Helmholtz, Hartmann, Herbart, Fechner, Wundt, etc.) to substantiate their views.[259] At this

---

Nietzsche says – foreshadowing Freud's *Es* (Id) – is a construction (cf. BGE; see *Chapter 3*)). (b) Although Nietzsche has remarks on sexuality and childhood, he does not have a sexual 'metaphysics' according to which sexuality becomes the universal essence of human behavior, nor does he advance any deterministic understanding of the importance of childhood. (c) Nietzsche never contemplates a 'therapeutics.' In Nietzsche's discourse, 'therapeutics' is likely to appear rather to be just another attempt to cultivate the *herd-idea*, being merely another disciplinary practice imposed on the modern human; designed to nurture, what Nietzsche calls, "the toleration of life" (cf. GM III; see *Chapter 5*). Nietzsche's Super-human [*Übermensch*] certainly does not come about as a result of 'therapy.'

[258] See most prominently, Paul-Laurent, Assoun: Freud and Nietzsche, loc. cit., and Gasser, Reinhard: Nietzsche und Freud, loc. cit. An exception is Gasser, who predominantly juxtaposes Nietzsche and the classical Psychoanalytical theory, but still includes precise descriptions of Freud's notoriously difficult early *Project for a Scientific Psychology*.

[259] To appropriate Nietzsche (traditionally understood as the designate 'poet-philosopher' at the beginning of the 20th century, and – with little substantial difference – as a post-modernist 'poet-philosopher' toward the end) as relevant to scientific inquiries, may be an untypical but not entirely absent strategy in especially the newer Nietzsche reception. Already Walter Kaufmann refers, in his *Discovering the Mind*, to Nietzsche's (and Freud's) interest in the natural sciences: "Freud was [. . .] among other things, a biologist, while Nietzsche came to regret his lack of training in the natural sciences. None of these men was a materialist, but Nietzsche, like Freud after him, hoped that physiology might hold the key to some of the mysteries of "the mind," or "the spirit," or "the soul." Kaufmann, Walter: *Discovering the Mind: Nietzsche, Heidegger, Buber* vol. II. New Brunswick, London (Transaction Publishers), 1980/92; p. 68. Babette E. Babich pursues Nietzsche along this track in Babich, Babette E.: Nietzsche's Philosophy of Science. New York (State University of New York Press), 1994, as well as in the anthology, Babich, Babette E. (ed.): Nietzsche, Epistemology, and Philosophy of Science: Nietzsche and the Sciences. Dordrecht (Kluwer Academic Publishers), 1999. Both Gregory Moore and Christian Emden give an abundance of references to Nietzsche's readings of the scientific literature in his days in

juncture, they both investigate the biological-neurological origins of the subject, and try to understand the following trinity of relationships: *stimulus and sensation, sensation and cognition*, and *cognition and language*. It is this trinity of conceptual relations, if properly accounted for, that promise a full understanding of subjectivity. One inquires, on one hand, what the human animal is before it becomes subject (as '*biological*'); and, on the other, what it is after it has established itself as subject (as '*linguistic*'). Thus, the *biological-linguistic subject* becomes our catch-phrase and label for this new, gradually developing, concept of subject, this interest in thinking a subjectivity, which is neither 'rational' in Descartes' sense, nor 'empirical' in Hume's.[260]

---

their respective: Moore, Gregory: Nietzsche, Biology, and Metaphor. Cambridge (Cambridge University Press), 2006; & Emden, Christian: Nietzsche on Language, Consciousness, and the Body. Urbana and Chicago (Illinois University Press) 2005. See also Moore, G, & Brobjer, T. (eds.): Nietzsche and Science. London (Ashgate), 2004. Erwin Schlimgen has very precise and pertinent descriptions of Nietzsche's theories of mind and consciousness in his, Schlimgen, Erwin: Nietzsches Theorie des Bewußtseins. Berlin/New York (Walter de Gruyter), 1998.) Müller-Lauter has in a number of articles pointed out what an avid reader Nietzsche was of the scientific literature of his day (see Müller-Lauter, Wolfgang: Über Werden und Wille zur Macht – Nietzsche Interpretationen I. Berlin/New York (Walter de Gruyter), 1999.) Günter Abel, in his *Nietzsche*, juxtaposes him regularly to contemporary scientific theory. See Abel, Günter: Nietzsche: Die Dynamik des Willen zur Macht und die Ewige Wiederkehr (Berlin/New York: Walter de Gruyter, 1998). However, to introduce Nietzsche explicitly as of relevance for neuroscience and theory of mind is completely new, and has very little precedence. Schlimgen is surely trespassing into the field of theory of mind, but otherwise, I know of only two previous works explicit in this pursuit: Günter Abel's essay, "Bewußtsein – Sprache – Natur. Nietzsches Philosophie des Geistes." *Nietzsche-Studien*, Band 30, 2001 (Berlin/New York: Walter de Gruyter, 2001), pp. 1-43, and an article by Abraham Olivier: "Nietzsche and Neurology," in *Nietzsche-Studien,* Band 32, 2003 (Berlin/New York: Walter de Gruyter, 2003), pp. 124-141.

[260] In investigating this 'biological-linguistic subject,' we suggest a much broader conception of Nietzsche's notion of subjectivity, than offered in several of the commentaries in the post-Structuralist and post-Modernist traditions, where oftentimes 'language' seemed to be the only existing attribute of the subject in its relations to a surrounding world (much Continental, followed up by North American, Nietzsche-reception in a period of a good forty years, from the sixties to the beginning of the new millennium). In this theory, one assumed that there is 'language' from top to bottom: if ever one talked about stimuli and sensations, stimuli were a form of language, and so were sensations, before

When we super-expose Freud's neurological model on Nietzsche's more tentative efforts, we find that Nietzsche's exploratory thinking attains a much clearer theoretical structure and expression. With the introduction to Freud's neurological notion of the subject,[261] we notice that the theory of a fragmented subject (as already discussed in the previous chapter) is taken into new, foreign, and esoteric territories. With Freud, we will begin to understand in more detail, and from another perspective, the inner dynamics of the subject as introduced in Nietzsche's often-quoted statements about subjective multiplicity. We will from Freud's neurological perspective understand, for example, what exactly enables the subject to experience *identity*; or, what accounts for Nietzsche's *simplification*; or how – from a biological-neurological perspective – the subject acquires a *sense of reality* and a *sense of value* (i.e., the origin of *valuations* such as 'true' and 'false' and 'good' and 'bad'); or how and why conscious perception necessarily is *delayed*; or, finally, get a beginning understanding of the *principles* according to which the subject is *fragmented*. At this final point in the exposition, we have left behind us all traditional, pre-theoretical, commonsensical notions of the subject. We have at this point accustomed ourselves to perceiving the 'subject' – instead of behaving like a *lighthouse*, from its unified interior projecting a beam of light toward an exterior world – behaving rather like a *chessboard* on which pieces are incessantly moved around according to inner mental rules ('drives') that must seem forever arbitrary and mysterious (see also *Section 5.1* below).[262]

---

they entered language properly speaking, which was now without distinguishing features. Language was everywhere, and could be comprehended neither as phylo- nor ontogenetically constituted, because any possible constitution was *already a kind of language*. At any arbitrary point of beginning, language was always-already *there*. While we dismiss this ideological fetishization of language, we also *do not* espouse any contrary position; we still assign a prominent role to language in the development of subjectivity.

[261] We will turn our attention to Freud's earliest expositions of these issues as we find them in for example the brief essay, *On Aphasia* [1891], in a letter to Fliess from 1896, and more fully developed in the *A Project of Scientific Psychology* [1895], *Studies on Hysteria* [1895], and chapter 7 of *The Interpretations of Dreams* [1900]. Many of these early considerations of Freud's will impact his later work, and we see them resurface under other labels in especially late metapsychological writings such as *Beyond the Pleasure Principle* [1920], *The Ego and the Id* [1923], and *A Note upon the 'Mystic Writing Pad'* [1925].

[262] We find several interesting parallels between some of Nietzsche's conclusions on the mind, and some of the conclusions arrived at by contemporary neuroscientists, cognitive scientists, and neuro-psychoanalysts. See for example,

0. Introduction

In the *first part* of the present chapter, we therefore give a detailed account of Freud's neurological thinking; along the way, we will relate to main notions in Nietzsche's thinking, which, in the *second part* of the chapter, we will more fully elaborate. The program is the following: we intend to give an account of the trinity, *stimulus-sensation, sensation-cognition, cognition-language*; we intend to understand the role and constitution of *memory* and *language* in Freud and in Nietzsche (– we return to Nietzsche's question from *Wahrheit und Lüge* (cf. *Chapter 1*), 'what is a word,' and suggest new answers to this question); we will explain our notions of *ego-cluster* and *subjective fragmentation*, as introduced already in the previous chapter, and we will continue to elaborate on how this new subject-structure is eminently well designed to explain *ideology* and the *ideological subject*; and how and why, in this new context, *aggression* is in inner-mental life a stronger motive than Freud's famed 'sexual drive.'

After an introduction to some of the influential sources of Nietzsche's, the theoretical program of the present chapter is therefore the following:

1) Introduction and explanation of the trinity, stimulus-sensation, sensation-cognition, cognition-language.
2) Explanation of the role and constitution of memory and language.
3) Explanation of the notions, ego-cluster and fragmented subject.

Solms, Mark and Turnbull, Oliver: The Brain and the Inner World. New York (Other Press), 2002, and for an overview, the article by Solms, Mark: "Freud Returns" in *Scientific American* vol. 290, Number 5 (May 2004). See also the work of Damasio Antonio: Descartes' Error: Emotions, Reason, and the Human Brain. New York (HaberCollins), 1995; & Damasio Antonio: Looking for Spinoza: Joy, Sorrow, and the Feeling Brain. New York (Harcourt), 2003; LeDoux, Joseph: The Synaptic Self: How our Brains Become Who We Are. New York (Viking Press), 2003; Pinker, Steven: The Blank Slate. The Modern Denial of Human Nature. New York (Penguin), 2003. Especially Daniel Dennett's two works, Dennett, Daniel C.: Consciousness Explained (Boston (Little, Brown, and Company), 1991), and Dennett, Daniel C: Darwin's Dangerous Idea (New York (Touchstone Books), 1995), seem in their combined theoretical aspirations and interests (cognition and evolution) to repeat, in a contemporary language, what was also Nietzsche's theoretical interests and aspirations. Dennett does not see himself as a "Nietzschean thinker," but his program has much resemblance to Nietzsche's exploratory thinking on cognition and evolution. Two earlier works I was reading for a number of years ought also to be mentioned: Hofstadter, Douglas: Gödel, Escher, Back. New York (Baisc Books), 1999 (rev. ed.); and Penrose, Roger: The Emperor's New Mind: Concerning Computers, Minds, and the Laws of Physics. Vintage (London), 1990.

4) Suggestion of an original aggression as a structural feature in a subject 'frenetically defending' 'truth.'

5) The role of ideology, the ideologue, and the ideological subject in the context of a Nietzschean 'biological-linguistic subject.'

Part I:

*Nietzsche's Contemporaries on
Sensation, Cognition, and Language*

1. Schopenhauer, Helmholtz, and Lange on the Retinal Image

As previously mentioned in *Chapter 1*, Kant's thing-in-itself is already in Schopenhauer's early essays, *Über die vierfache Wurzel des Satzes vom zureichenden Grunde* (SzG) and *Über das Sehn und die Farben*,[263] inserted in a new epistemological-cognitive framework, and re-interpreted as a nerve-stimulus, impressing itself upon our sensory organs, without us being conscious of these processes. Schopenhauer gives several examples from the scientific literature of his day to substantiate this view. We shall here refer only to what becomes his most illustrative example, as this example is extensively discussed in the 19th century – above all, by Johannes Müller and Hermann von Helmholtz, but taken up also by Friedrich A. Lange.

Helmholtz, with his detailed inquiries into human vision, is the one who in the 19th century gives the most thorough empirical explanations of the mechanics of the eye. Lange largely inserts these empirical investigations into his neo-Kantian context, the philosophical purpose of the discussions always being to substantiate the view that understanding (*Verstand*) is needed for sensations to make sense.[264] We are referring to the discovery that the retina of the eye receives an impression that is different from the image of which we become conscious in proper perception. The retina for example receives an inverted image of the world; still, we do not see the world turned upside-down; or our two eyes receive two slightly different

---

[263] See Schopenhauer: SW III.

[264] Gregory Moore has the following assessment of the relationship between Helmholtz, Lange, and Nietzsche, similar to my own: "Though Nietzsche obviously arrive at radically different conclusions, his own extensive writings nevertheless owe something to the preoccupation of mainstream German philosophers, following Helmholtz's resurrection of Kant, with the conditions and limits of knowledge. This ought not to be surprising given his familiarity with the works and ideas of early neo-Kantians such as Otto Liebmann and, more famously, Friedrich Lange, who, in his History of Materialism (1866), appropriates and develops Helmholtz's physiological Kantianism in the service of a critique of vulgar materialism." Moore: Nietzsche and Science, loc. cit., p. 8.

images of the world; still, we conceive the two images as a single perceptive image.²⁶⁵

In SzG, Schopenhauer had already called attention to the fact that on the retina, an object is depicted in the reverse and upside-down; and furthermore, that the object is depicted inside the eye, as if painted on the retina. However, in the actual perception of the object, we have managed to turn the object back on its feet, so to speak, and to project it outside the eye as a thing existing independently of us. "If vision consisted in mere sensation, we should perceive the impression of the object reversed and upside down because we receive it in this way [. . .] we should also perceive it as something existing within our eye."²⁶⁶ Schopenhauer illustrates his example by the following well-known figure, where an object, A-B, thanks to the convex lens within the eye is inverted and depicted on the retina as b-a.

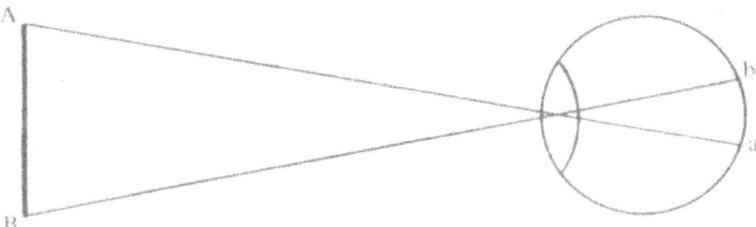

Mere sensation can as such not explain how we see the world: neither is the world depicted upside-down, nor is it experienced as if inside the eye. In order to avoid the sensation-chaos of simple sense-impressions, the understanding (*Verstand*) with its causal laws has stepped in and aided our vision. Thanks to the principle of sufficient reason, it has referred back the received

---

²⁶⁵ We notice that Nietzsche was aware of these discussions, and apparently – according to a letter to Carl von Gersdorff – regards Schopenhauer as the forerunner of what he labels the "Young-Helmholzsche Farbentheorie." In this letter from 1870, Nietzsche reports how he has come across an article by Czermak, which to his satisfaction provides an account of the theory supporting Schopenhauer's earlier essay: "[Czermak] notices, that Sch.[openhauer] independently and in original ways has arrived to the insights of what one today designates the Young-Helmholtzian color-theory: between this and Schopenhauer's is the most wonderful and detailed correspondence. The entire point of departure, that the color first and foremost is a physiological creation of the eye, was first put forward by Sch.[openhauer]." (Nietzsche to Gersdorff, 12 December 1870, KSB 3, No. 111).

²⁶⁶ Schopenhauer: SzG, SW 3, p. 75

impression to its *presumed* cause, namely to an object "that presents itself, upright and outside, as an object in space."[267]

Thanks to this reference to a presumed cause, we are *seduced* into the misunderstanding that there is a world 'outside' the eye imprinting itself as a picture 'inside' the eye – this misunderstanding constituted the nature of the 'Materialist' misapplication of the principle of sufficient reason, which Nietzsche criticized in his early WL above (cf. *Chapter 1: 3.1*).[268] In contrast to Materialism's misunderstanding, the world '*out-there-outside-us*' is still under complete annulment in Schopenhauer's example. Schopenhauer's figure must be read as follows: in two crucial stages, we have *first* a sensation of an object turned upside-down, showing itself on the retina at the right side of our figure; *thereupon* we have perception proper, showing itself as empirical reality *as if outside* our eye on the left side of the figure. The left side of the figure looks like outside reality, as verily it should; it has, however, been through an interpretation-process, thanks to the causal laws of our understanding (*Verstand*). It is constructed after-the-fact. The correct chronology is therefore: *first*, we receive a sensation impressing itself on our retina; *second*, we interpret this sensation as outside reality in proper perception. Consequently, our proper perception of an empirical world is an effect of an interpretive activity. Proper perception arrives only *after* the interpretive activity.[269]

---

[267] Schopenhauer: SzG, SW 3, p. 75.

[268] The logic of Schopenhauer is that the world cannot and must not become a cause for sensations, since it is under radical erasure. Not even as a reticent Kantian thing-in-itself, as the unknown quantity 'x', can the world become a cause. That this exactly would save the day for Kant, becomes now to Schopenhauer Kant's most serious mistake. The Kantian answer, that the world as thing-in-itself 'causes' itself to be perceived, insofar as it provides the matter for what the mind will endow with its forms, is bitterly criticized in Schopenhauer. This is Kant's most basic self-misunderstanding. In this Kant allegedly 'forgets' (Schopenhauer believes, deliberately) that his law of causality is after all not *a priori*; i.e., is not a form the mind imposes on perception, but becomes confusedly a law that *makes possible* perception. Since to Kant, the world is not entirely under erasure, but is in-itself, it is still assigned a locus from where to effect perception, whereas to Schopenhauer, the world is entirely crossed out and annulled.

[269] Although it cannot be the place here to go into detail with this discussion, Schopenhauer's idealist view is of course problematic. It remains for example unanswered in Schopenhauer, how, and from where, we in the first place receive the primitive sensation. In his conception, it is as if sensations originate *ex nihilo*. Applied to our concrete example, his thinking is: first a figure appears on the retina of our eye upside-down, then we turn it around and place it

Helmholtz's explanation is identical to Schopenhauer's except for the fact that he does not appeal to the principle of sufficient reason, but to learning-processes under which the subject will eventually learn to distinguish the invented, inside, and double image as the proper "sensible sign" signifying an object conceived as upright, outside, and one. The sensible impression is therefore arbitrary relative to that which it signifies, the important point being here that the sensible impression should not be taken at its face value (inverted, inside, and double), but merely as *an arbitrary sensible sign* for a singular object. Accordingly, any possible or impossible impression could as such count for the perceptive image of a 'dog,' the only condition being that learning-processes must have associated the possible or impossible sign with 'dog.' As well as (less than half a century later) the *linguistic sign* is arbitrary in Saussure, the *sensible sign* is arbitrary in Helmholtz. This theory, which Helmholtz calls the "Empirical Theory," supposes "that the actual sensible 'sign,' whether it be simple or complex, is recognized as the sign of that which it signifies."[270] The upshot is that the perceiving human being is at no point troubled with retinal images being inverted or double, because it has learnt "the signification of the local signs which belong to our sensation of sight, so as to be able to recognize the actual relations which they denote."[271]

---

securely back on his feet; – but this begs the questions: 1) from where does the figure emerge, and 2), why would we turn it around? Why would we not continue to see the world as upside-down, instead of rectifying this matrix? And how does one 'rectify,' when the standard according to which one supposedly 'rectify' is nonexistent insofar as the world as 'really outside' is annihilated? C. Janaway seems to share these objections when he writes: "The account has a certain ingenuity, but is troubling. For one thing, where do bodily sensations come from? They must surely be originally caused in the body by something prior to the operation of the intellect, but Schopenhauer does not discuss what that prior cause might be." Janaway, Christopher: Schopenhauer. Oxford (Oxford University Press), 1994, p. 18.

[270] Helmholtz: "The Recent Progress of the Theory of Vision," in *Science and Culture*, loc. cit., p. 179.

[271] Helmholtz: "The Recent Progress of the Theory of Vision," in *Science and Culture*, loc. cit., p. 179. Helmholtz repeats this view in the essay "The Facts in Perception": "Our sensations are precisely effects produced by external causes in our organs, and the manner in which one such effect expresses itself depends, of course, essentially on the type of apparatus which is affected. Insofar as the quality of our sensation gives us information about the peculiarity of the external influence stimulating it, it can pass for a sign – but not for an image. [. . .] A sign, however need not have any type of similarity with what it is a sign for. The relations between the two are so restricted that the same

Friedrich Lange gives this discussion of the inverted image received on the retina an extra twist. The inversion is not experienced as such because our supposed reference-frame, i.e., our body, is as 'optical image' inverted as well – like people do not experience themselves walking with their heads upwards on one half of the globe and downwards on the other half, because the reference-frame is in any case the surface of the earth. Lange quotes physiologist Johannes Müller for proposing this view: "For the image of all objects, even of our own limbs, in the retina are equally inverted, and therefore maintain the same relative position. Even the image of our hand while used in touch is seen inverted. The position in which we see objects we call, therefore, the erect position."[272] Our body is therefore also experienced as a phenomenon, and it is perceived under the same conditions as the images of external objects. We see external objects relative to our body-image; if this body-image is inverted in our perception, inverted images on the retina exist in a proper upright position relative to our body-image.

As we saw in *Chapter 1*, according to the 19th century's "corrected Kantianism" (Lange), the nether epistemological limit becomes a sense-impression, producing in Nietzsche's vocabulary a nerve-stimulus [*Nervenreize*] still unconscious to the subject. The retinal image is also a nerve-stimulus; we do not know it as such, because we only know it as *presented* for-us, that is, when it is *presented* as a proper perceptive image.[273] The upshot of these investigations is the realization that the subject has a biological background or underground, which one can infer, but not fully know.

For theorists thinking within the paradigm, some of the crucial questions become: 'What are we, before we sense?' 'What happens on the threshold where a stimulus (as unconscious) is turned into a sensation (as con-

---

subject, taking effect under equal circumstances, produces the same sign, and hence unequal signs always correspond to unequal effects." Helmholtz: "The Facts in Perception" in *Science and Culture*, loc. cit., p. 347.

[272] J. Müller quoted from Lange: The History of Materialism, 2nd book, 1st section, p. 208.

[273] In modern neurological research, one has been able to reconstruct the impressions actually imprinting themselves on the retina of the eye. When for example we 'receive' the impressions of a face, we acquire no clear 'picture' of the face on our retina. We 'receive' instead a blur of colors and shadows, which with some leniency one can recognize as the outlines of a face (it looks somewhat similar to the artistic expressions of faces we know from painter Francis Bacon). The face, which we 'recognize,' that we are familiar with, and actually *see*, is consequently *reconstructed* by the mind, according to later processes, from this blur of received impressions.

scious)?' It is on this threshold the subject encounters the object, and at the same time gains a consciousness of itself as entity. It is on this threshold, the subject opens its eyes and starts to *see*; and not only does the subject in this decisive moment opens its eyes to the object, it simultaneously opens its eyes to itself as seeing subject. Not only does it *see*, it *sees itself seeing*. In this crucial moment not only is *objectivity* constituted, but also *subjectivity*. It is no wonder that the 19th Century theorists, immersed as they are in Kantian thinking, becomes preoccupied about determining this threshold.

2. Gustav Fechner's Analysis of Sensations

2.1. On the Threshold for Subjective Sensations

It is essentially this problem, Gustav Fechner sets out to examine in his own eminently practical fashion. He and fellow researchers to who he refers (especially his mentor E. H. Weber), have run a series of tests to see at which point an individual is able to sense the difference in sensational input. The results of the tests belong in experimental psychology, and we do not need to go into detail with them in a work on Nietzsche's thinking, but the nature and the set-up of these tests draw on general epistemological assumptions that can help us understand the scientific paradigm of the day.

One assumes in this paradigm that the human being is an *open receptor* of an *infinite number of stimuli*. However, not all stimuli are apparently registered; that is, not all stimuli will actually be sensed by the individual. They as such exist *below threshold*. The experiments of Weber and Fechner are now designed to test when a stimulus is sufficiently strong to be registered. They assume that the increase of force of a stimulus will trigger a corresponding increase in sensation; and as they measure the intensities of different stimulus and sensation, they aspire to set up tables accounting for the proportionality between the strength of a stimulus and the strength of a sensation. In the tests they carry out in respect of touch, sight, and sounds, they want to account for, so Weber, "the smallest difference in weight which we can distinguish by touch, the smallest difference in length of lines which we can distinguish by sight, and the smallest difference of tones which we can distinguish by ear."[274] In a classical experiment, Weber has engaged a number of test-subjects to lift weights. Gradually, and without

---

[274] Weber quoted from Fechner: *Elements of Psychophysics*. New York/Chicago (Holt, Rinehart and Winston), 1966. Translated by H. Adler. Edited by D. Howes and E. Boring; p. 114.

their knowledge, he increases the weights, until the test-subjects notice a difference. ("I repeated the same experiments on the same people, this time having them lift up their hands and compare the weights in them. After this was done, when I discovered by how much the weights had to differ for their discrepancy to be recognized with certainty, again I made a note, and calculated the difference in weight."[275]). Fechner repeats the experiment, and this procedure allows now Weber and Fechner to write up tables for what they call, the "smallest perceived difference of touch" for different test-persons. The general interest of the experiment is to determine the *threshold* for sensibility.

It is Fechner, who draws the general conclusions from this and similar experiments (Freud will draw even more wide-ranging conclusions, as we shall see shortly). The experiments have proved, somewhat unremarkably, that "in general, a sensation or a difference between sensations increases with the magnitude of the stimulus or stimulus difference which gives rise to it."[276] In other words, the stronger the stimulus, the stronger the sensation! However, this proportionality does not hold for all values. When a stimulus is sufficiently weak – although being applied to the test-subject – the corresponding sensation remains zero. And conversely, the ability to register a stimulus disappears before it has sunk to zero.

> It can be shown that every stimulus as well as every stimulus difference must already have reached a certain finite magnitude before it can be noticed at all – that is, before our consciousness is aroused by a sensation or before a difference between sensations becomes apparent. Conversely, the ability to notice a stimulus or a stimulus difference disappears before its value has diminished to zero. The zero-point of sensation or sensation differences is therefore found to lie above that of the occasioning stimulus or stimulus difference.[277]

This implies that there is a "threshold" below which the subject does not sense and registers stimuli; a "threshold" below which the subject never becomes conscious about them. This holds true for both Fechner's "intensive" and "extensive" stimuli; that is, for stimuli caused from the inside and the outside of the organism (or what we today label, endogenous and exogenous stimuli). The human organism must therefore live in a world, of which it is largely unconscious. The majority of the stimuli reaching the organism will never be noticed; but when they are, it happens in *qualitative* jumps from a zero-sensation response to a sensation-response. At one arbitrary

---

[275] Weber quoted from Fechner: loc. cit., p. 115.
[276] Fechner: loc. cit., p. 199.
[277] Fechner: loc. cit., p. 199.

point, the mind is affected, and it starts to become aware. Sensation is a function of stimuli, and as Fechner explains, "when y is a function of x, y can vanish at certain values of x or change into the negative or become imaginary. We know that it suffices to increase x beyond this value to see y again reach positive values."[278]

Fechner calls this theory of stimulus/response "the mathematical point of view," and according to this "mathematical point of view," unconscious sensations have a *negative value* (that is, they are stimuli too weak to be felt), whereas the "threshold" has exactly the *value zero*, and conscious sensations have a *positive value*. The organism has a certain excitability-level, determined as the 'threshold,' from where a sum of nothing suddenly adds up to a positive value. This "mathematical point of view" makes sense, Fechner contends, because if it did not apply, the organism would be inundated in an ocean of impressions that it could not process.

> The fact that each stimulus must first reach a certain limit before it arouses a sensation assures to mankind a state undisturbed to a certain degree by external stimulation. It is not necessary to bring the stimulation down to zero, something man is not capable of doing, in order for him to remain undisturbed by them. All that he needs to do is to move far enough away from those stimuli that are weakened by distance, and in general to bring stimuli down below a given limit. Besides the fact that we are saved from disturbances by unwanted and strange perceptions, because any stimulus escapes notice when it fall below a certain point, there is also the fact that a uniform state of perception is assured because stimulus differences cannot be noticed below their threshold.[279]

As such, this constitution of the organism secures it its peace of mind. The organism is relatively indolent, and wants to remain so; it wants to maintain a state of relaxation, and it does so by keeping the preponderance of impressions down below zero. This also implies, conversely, that below zero, a flurry of activity goes on that the subject does not register; i.e., does not know.

It is this idea, which is translated into Nietzsche's notion of consciousness as a "simplification-" or a "filtration-apparatus" (cf. *Chapter 2*). The 'threshold' works as a filter for stimuli; only stimuli above a certain level and with a certain intensity are allowed to pass through. The world as we consciously perceive it has therefore been through a simplification-process. As consciously perceived, it is infinitely more 'simple,' than the world we receive as a multiplicity of impressions "below zero." If this is the case,

---

[278] Fechner: loc. cit., p. 205.
[279] Fechner: loc. cit., p. 208.

there is now reason to believe that the world we receive as impressions below zero is a disorganized chaos of stimuli – a chaos, which we cannot as such process, and which we therefore have to ignore.

2.2. The Psychophysical Energy-Subject

Behind and supporting Fechner's assumptions about the interaction between stimuli and sensitivity stands a physical theory about the distribution of energy. His assumptions are as such supported by the scientific discoveries of *kinetic* and *potential* energy, and the theory of *conservation of energy*, proposed by a number of 19th century contemporary scientists, for example Hermann von Helmholtz and Ernst Mach.[280] Fechner's subject is essentially an 'energy-subject.' The same laws that in general applies to the universe, supposedly applies also to the subject in its various manifestations. Even immeasurable mental activities, such as thinking, obey the law of conservation of energy and the reverse proportionality between kinetic and potential energy.

We notice that an 'energy-subject' has strictly speaking no privileged center; if one part of the subject engages in an activity, it is because another part provides the necessary energy; if the mind thinks, it is because the metabolic processes provide the energy necessary for the mind to think; if the subject engages in a strenuous physical activity, it is because the mind concentrates energies toward this activity; etc. An 'energy-subject' is like a microcosms mirroring the universe in total, in which – after Copernicus and beyond – there is also no privileged center, but merely a balance between kinetic and potential energy, keeping the energy of the total system constant.

Stimuli are now understood as small packets of energy. As they affect the body, they transfer energy to activities that will evoke or change sensations: "stimuli evoke or change sensation only by causing or changing some kind of activity within our body. Their magnitudes are therefore representative of the extent of the physical activities that are related to sensation dependent on them in some manner."[281] What particular processes stimuli start, and what exactly they effect when they impact the sensory body, re-

---

[280] Both von Helmholtz and Ernst Mach published a "Popular Lectures"; and in both of these two collections do we find seminal essays on the conservation of energy. See Helmholtz, Hermann von: Science and Culture: Popular and Philosophical Essays. Chicago (The University of Chicago Press), 1995; and Ernst Mach: Popular Scientific Lectures. La Salle (Open Court) 1898.

[281] Fechner: loc. cit., p. 19.

main an unsolved riddle, but the input of the stimulus is measurable, and the output, in form of a sensation, is also measurable.

Kinetic energy becomes the general force in psychophysical processes; it is the force that permeates both dead and living systems:

> In conclusion, as far as we can tell, not merely all creation of kinetic energy, but also its transmission, propagation, and modification depend on the interaction of its components. [. . .] The whole of nature is a single continuous system of component parts acting on one another, within which various partial systems create, use, and transmit to each other kinetic energy of different forms, while obeying general laws through which the connections are ruled and conserved. Since in exact natural science all physical happenings, activities, and processes [. . .] may be reduced to movement, be they of large masses or of the smallest particles, we can also find for all of them a yardstick of their activity or strength in their kinetic energy, which can always be measured, if not always directly, then at least by its effects, and in any case in principle.[282]

Fechner therefore assumes that stimuli are transmitted in the form of kinetic energy. Whether stimuli are understood as waves, as particles, or as packets, their effect is always a combination of *mass* and *velocity*; i.e., they have a *momentum*; and it is this momentum that starts a chain-process whose outcome is a sensation. Stimuli therefore follow the general physical law, mv^2 (kinetic energy equals mass, m, multiplied with the square of its velocity, v). Ideally, one should now be able to measure the momentums for all stimuli causing a sensation in order to arrive to the total kinetic energy effecting the system:

> The kinetic energy of a whole system is then the sum of the kinetic energies of its parts, and therefore in a system of three or more particles with masses, m, m', m'' . . . and velocities v, v', v'' . . .[. . .] kinetic energy = $mv^2 + m'v'^2 + m''v''^2$ . .[283]

Such a measurement of the sum-total of particles is at least what should be possible "in principle"; however, it is not *practically* possible to measure particles (especially not in cases where no particles seem to be involved; like in touch), and measurements must therefore rely only on the *effects* of these general laws: i.e., the input of the stimulus (which is measurable) and the output in the sensation (which is also measurable).

---

[282] Fechner: loc. cit., p. 23.
[283] Fechner: loc. cit., p. 20.

2. Gustav Fechner's Analysis of Sensation

One consequence of this theory of kinetic energy is that everything is always and forever the same – at least, insofar as we talk about energy. In respect to energy, one can say in an entirely stringent sense that everything is 'eternal recurrence of the same.' According to the law of conservation of energy, energy is *constant*; energy cannot emerge from nothing and it cannot disappear into nothing. When potential energy is being released, it is released as an equivalent amount of kinetic energy; and conversely, in order to build up potential energy, one must exert a 'work' in kinetic energy equivalent to the potential energy. A stone, dropped from the height of a meter, releases its potential energy as heat; the potential energy is equal to the work it took as kinetic energy to lift the stone one meter. (If the example is not intuitively evident, one may replace the stone with a large meteorite hitting Earth; the release of energy in form of heat would be catastrophic, and would be equivalent to the meteorite's mass times the square of its velocity.)

Now we suggest that Nietzsche's determination of the subject as a 'chaos' of 'wills' and 'forces' in perpetual strife for 'mastery' is a adumbrated, a 'creative' and 'poetizing,' interpretation of the energy-subject introduced in the 19th century by contemporary scientists, such as Fechner. Structurally speaking, he introduces the same model of the subject: (i) a subject without privileged center; or where provisional 'centers' combat for power; (ii) a subject where different bodily processes – traditionally devalued in a Christian anthropology – such as the digestive system and the sexual drives are given new prominence; processes that are often valued higher in Nietzsche than intellectual processes, and/or are contributing to the outcome of these 'intellectual' processes; and (iii) a subject where the majority of these processes occur below the threshold for subjective awareness, i.e., unconsciously and instinctively.

A famous and often-quoted passage from Nietzsche's Nachlaß-material may now be interpreted within this psycho-physiological context. The passage has always been taken to evidence Nietzsche's eternal-recurrence-thought in its cosmological version, but seems in the present context rather to represent the world of becoming as a non-centered and chaotic 'energy'-world. If the world is ultimately *energy* (and not matter), and if its final law is the law of the conservation of energy (as such certifying the world's eternal *status quo*), the description of the universe, which Nietzsche gives in the passage, would seem to constitute an adequate metaphysical description of this 'new' universe.

> If the movement of the world [*Weltbewegung*] had an end-state, then it would have already reached it. The single fundamental fact is however that it d o e s

not have any end-state: and every philosophy and scientific hypothesis (e.g., mechanism), for which such a thesis is necessary, is contradicted through this single fact. . . . I seek a conception of the world, where this fact is justified; where becoming is explained without one is seeking refuge in such final purposes: Becoming [*das Werden*] must appear justified in every moment. [. . .] It is necessary to deny [the existence of] a total-consciousness [*Gesammtbewußtseins*] for becoming, a "God," in order to avoid bringing the occurrences under the perspective of a pitying, sympathizing and still not desiring creature: "God" is useless, if and insofar as he does not want something.
[. . .]
1) Becoming has no end-state [*keinen Zielzustand*], results not in a "being" [*Sein*"].
2) Becoming is no state of appearance [*kein Scheinzustand*]; maybe the existing world [*seiende Welt*] is an appearance.
3) Becoming is value-neutral [*Werthgleich*] in every moment: differently expressed: it has no value. (Nachlaß 1887-88, KSA 13, 11[72]).

As 'energy-world,' the world is still a kind of 'eternal recurrence of the same,' but that which recurs in this context is not life, not history, and not even the universe itself. That which recurs is the fundamental elements of the world; or more strictly – since the paradigm prevents us from talking about *elements* – that which remains the same is the sum-total of the action and re-action of forces. Therefore Nietzsche must conclude that the 'energy-world' is just such a 'soup' of the same, with no conceivable beginning or end, since it is to Nietzsche's mind, as well as to the mind of any 19th century scientist, inconceivable that energy could simply come into existence out of nothing or spontaneously cease to exist. (One recalls that the so-called "Big Bang" theory, explaining the creation of the universe as an expansion from nothing, was unknown in the 19th century, and met considerable resistance far into the 20th century.)

The new Conception of the world. 1) The world exists; it is not something, which come into being, and not something, which cease to exist [*sie ist nichts, was wird, nichts, was vergeht*], but it has never started to become, and it never stops passing away – it preserves itself in both . . . it lives from itself: its excrements are its nourishment. (Nachlaß 1888, KSA 13, 14[188]).

In such a 'soup' of energy and forces, there is no room for a 'God.' Any assumption of a *Gesammtbewußtsein* overlooking it all becomes extraordinary naïve. There is no super-creature who *wants* something, or arranges *designs* and *purposes* into something. The world has been leveled to a substance of the same; that is, it is value-neutral regarding moral values, but value-neutral also ontologically; it has been leveled hierarchically; that is, there is no room for a hierarchical discrimination between something 'apparent' and something 'real' or 'in-itself.'

3. Freud's Analysis of Sensation, Memory, and Consciousness

3.1. A Neurological Distinction between Stimulus and Sensation, phi and psi

Freud takes many of the insights discussed above further, as he endeavors to construct a systematic neurological model of the mind in its processing of stimuli and production of sensations.[284] In *Project for a Scientific Psychology*, Freud proposes a mental system that distinguishes between impressions, memory, and conscious perceptions in the form of three different systems in a neurological model: a *phi*, a *psi*, and an *omega* neuron system.

The *phi*-neurons have the task simply to receive impressions or stimuli (they are identical to Fechner's 'stimuli,' or what in *Chapter 2*, we called 'empty perception,' since we are talking about perception not yet conscious). The *psi*-neurons 'store' some of these impressions or stimuli – but only conditionally upon their intensity – in or as a system of memory traces. Finally, the *omega*-system interprets the received stimuli, with this making the subject conscious of and attentive to stimuli. Thus, consciousness or attentiveness is in Freud's early model achieved only *after* impressions/stimuli have passed through a memory system. We do not *see* with attention in empty perception, but only *after we remember* what we see.

In introducing the first two systems, a *phi*- and a *psi*-system, Freud was solving a problem that throughout his life would continue to occupy him: how could the mental apparatus stay both infinitely open to ever-new impressions and retain an infinite amount of material. A model of mental functioning would have to be able to account for both *infinite receptivity* and *infinite retention* or *storage*.

It would seem, therefore, that neurones must be both influenced and also unaltered, unprejudiced. We cannot off-hand imagine an apparatus capable of such

---

[284] We are in the following referring to Freud's earliest expositions of these issues as we find them in the essay, *On Aphasia* [1891], in a letter to Fliess from 1896, and more fully developed in the *A Project of Scientific Psychology* [1895].

complicated functioning; the situation is accordingly saved by attributing the characteristic of being permanently influenced by excitation to one class of neurones, and, on the other hand, the unalterability – the characteristic of being fresh for new excitations – to another class.[285]

Freud's solution was the suggestion of the two classes of neurons mentioned above, *phi* and *psi*, or with his Greek notations, φ and ψ, which, in an attempt to ease the reading, I shall describe by their main functions as respectively, the *phi-receptor-neuron* and the *psi-memory-neuron*.[286] The two systems must necessarily be qualitatively different. One system must be *permeable*, allowing excitation to pass through neurons not offering resistance to excitation. This system must be capable of receiving new stimuli, but without stimuli being imprinted into the system. The other system must be *impermeable*, offering *resistance* to stimuli, which are therefore being 'imprinted' into the system; as such being retained and stored as memory traces. A simple example might illustrate the idea: we can imagine a single ray of light passing through a windowpane offering no 'resistance' to the beam of light, which 'imprints' itself as a white spot on the wall behind, since the wall offers 'resistance.' On this illustration, the window is the *phi-receptor-neuron* and the wall is the *psi-memory-neuron*. The two neuron-systems are described as follows:

> (1) Those which allow $Q\eta$ to pass through as though they had no contact barriers [*Kontaktschranken*] and which, accordingly, after each passage of excitation are in the same state as before, and (2) those whose contact-barriers make themselves felt, so that they only allow $Q\eta$ to passes through with difficulty or partially. The latter class may, after each excitation, be in a different state from before and they thus afford a *possibility of representing memory*. Thus there are *permeable* neurones (offering no resistance and retaining nothing), which serve for perception, and *impermeable* ones (loaded with resistance, and holding back $Q\eta$), which are the vehicle for memory.[287]

---

[285] Freud: Project, SE 1, p. 299; GW N, p. 391.
[286] The text of the Project is so dense and esoteric that it threatens the exposition of any commentator. On the one hand, it is necessary to remain attentive to detail, but on the other, it is desirable to avoid putting unnecessary strains on the reader. The challenge is well met by commentators like Richard Wohlheim (in: Freud. London: Fontana/Collins, 1971) and Jean Laplanche (in: Life and death in Psychoanalysis. Baltimore: Johns Hopkins University Press, 1985). I shall try to follow their example, albeit with other interests invested in my exposition of the text.
[287] Freud: *Project*, SE 1, p. 299-300; GW N, p. 392.

The *phi-receptor-neurons* immediately unload received stimuli, and thus stand ready to receive new information. As such, they account for a *first* perceptive layer of the mental apparatus – the above 'empty' perception. The *psi-memory-neurons* retain received stimuli in order to build up a memory bank of information.

But what exactly is 'memory' in Freud's model? – Freud explains it by the two notions, *contact-barrier* [*kontaktschranken*] and *facilitation* [*Bahnung*]. *Contact-barriers* account for the *resistance* offered to new stimuli, but broken down by sufficiently intense stimuli. This can be seen as identical to, and merely another term for, Fechner's 'thresholds.' *Facilitation* accounts for the traces created within and between the *psi-neurons*, granted sufficiently forceful stimuli. Thus a 'memory bank' is not created as some kind actual storage capability in the nucleus of the neuron; neurons do not 'stack' material. Instead, on this model, memory is 'stored' qua *facilitating passages carved as differentiating traces* throughout the neurological network. On this neurological level, memory is not an *image*, but a mesh, a web, or a grid of traces (when memory becomes *conscious*, then of course, it manifests itself to the subject typically as an *image*). 'Memory' is a question of sending off freshly received quanta of excitation along already facilitating pathways [*Bahnungen*]; like we might metaphorically say that the American interstate highway- and road-system provides the car with a 'memory' of how to get from New York to California. (Without such an interstate road-system there would be little traffic across the United States and the society would collapse in paralysis, like a mental system would.)

In Freud's quantitative approach, an impression is thus understood as a quantum of energy. Logic requires that both *phi-receptor-neurons* and *psi-memory-neurons* are transporting *something*. Freud sees this *something* as quantities of energy, and supplies two kinds, so-called Q and Qη. It is not possible in Freud's text to establish a clear distinction between the two kinds, since occasionally he confuses them himself (i.e., "If we think of a neurone filled with Qη – that is, cathected – we can only assume this Q [*sic.*] is uniform over all the . . ." [288]) As a first approximation, one is tempted to think of Q-quantity as representing *external*, Qη-quantity as representing *internal*, excitation. However, since Q-quantity can have also an *endogenous* source (e.g., hunger), the better distinction is to understand Q-quantity as of first-order, while Qη-quantity is of second-order. Q-quantity I shall therefore see as 'raw' energy, while Qη-quantity is 'processed' – that is, 'raw' Q-energy converted into 'processed' Qη-energy. For example, Q-quantity emerges from the *periphery* of our mental system,

---

[288] Freud: *Project*, SE 1, p. 301; GW N, p. 394

and is now carried into the interior of the mental system as Qη-energy. If we understand these quantities in relation to the *phi-receptor-* and the *psi-memory-neurons*, Q-quantity would reach the *phi-receptor-neuron* as 'raw' *external or internal* stimuli, but as it would be unloaded to the *psi-memory-neuron*, it would continue as 'processed' internal stimuli. It is typically the case that Freud refers to Q-quantity when he describes primary processes, while referring to Qη-quantity when describing secondary.[289]

Evidently, facilitating pathways have to be constructed in the first place. In 'empty' perception, we see everything and discriminate against nothing, while in 'perception proper' we remember the seen; we see *again* what has already been seen before. We cannot require our sensory organs to choose to see, hear, or smell according to preconceived patterns before these patterns have been conceived. The facilitation of passages for Qη-quanta depends on partly the force and partly the frequency of the stimulation (that is, *intensity* and *repetition*) with which quanta of Qη energy is passing through the *psi*-system. Freud therefore speculates that, *first*, an impression must be forceful enough to break down the 'contact-barrier' and produce a trace (my ray of light must be forceful enough to pass through my 'window,' and imprint itself on my 'wall'), and *secondly*, when repeated, it must reinforce an already formed trace; it will thus be traversing the same path [*Bahnung*], and as such evoke the same memory. (In the last case, my 'window'/'wall' model is less felicitous; – in order to adjust the model, the beam of light would have to be something in the order of a laser-beam etching a trace into the wall. Another model might better clarify the idea: a trail in a forest is hardly perceptible if used only a few times, but if the same trail is being used frequently, it forms a track that is both easy to recognize, and furthermore, continues to *attract future traffic*. Similarly, not all smells triggers a response, but the smell of food inevitably triggers the expectation

---

[289] There is in the literature on Freud considerable confusion about these two forms of energy. Even in acute commentators like Jean Laplanche (*Life and Death in Psychoanalysis*, loc. cit.); Paul Ricoeur (*Freud and Philosophy—An Essay on Interpretation*. New Haven: Yale University Press, 1970); and Richard Wohlheim (*Freud*; loc. cit.), I have found no clear explanation of the supposed difference between the two types of energy. James Strachey, the authoritative editor of the Standard Edition, is equally baffled: "Last of all among these alphabetic signs come Q and its mysterious companion $Q\eta$. Both of them undoubtedly stand for 'quantity'. But why this difference between them? And, above all, why the Greek *ēta* with the smooth breathing? There is no question that the difference is a real one, though Freud nowhere explicitly announces it or explains it." ("Editor's Introduction" to *Project*, SE 1, p. 289).

of – that is, the memory of – food, since it has been repeated frequently and in compelling circumstances (i.e., when hungry).)[290]

According to Freud's mental apparatus, the subject learns stimuli-response patterns according to a Humean formula, by means of *custom and habit*. However, in Freud's model, to 'learn by habit' implies that the system must be able to store and represent memory according to certain relevant functions of the system. It must be able to *cathect* memory-traces with greater or lesser amounts of energy, which can then be discharged along already pre-formed traces when a specific action is called for. Certain excitations form these passages, and subsequent excitations of the same kind will follow the same passages; they will trigger an associative chain already molded (– phenomenologically speaking, they will evoke the same memories). I see a chocolate bar in the supermarket, and it triggers the memory of the taste of chocolate, not of smoked salmon. Freud concludes his discussion of memory with two statements: "(1) *Memory is represented by the facilitations [Bahnungen] existing between the ψ [psi] neurons*" . . . "(2) *Memory is represented by the differences [Unterschiede] in the facilitations between the ψ [psi] neurons.*"[291]

---

[290] We tend to envision facilitating passages in the mental apparatus as *engraved* thanks to frequent repetition of impressions. If passages are breached and pathways facilitated, we resort to metaphors like *engraving*, *inscribing*, or *etching*. We conceive the process of breaching implying a certain measure of violence committed to a yet virgin system, like Freud's own representation in his note on the *Wunderblock*: If a hard instrument like a stylus inscribes something directly on the delicate surface of the flimsy wax paper, it tears the paper/the surface apart. In the *Project*, however, it seems expedient to abandon various metaphors for *engraving*. Breaching facilitating passages is not as much a question of etching, as of creating layers of conductive traces. The metaphors that come mind here are rather that facilitating passages result from the production of rails or bars or dikes; that is, from depositing layer upon layer of material upon a blank surface until a pattern emerges. In the *Project*, Freud's facilitating passages (*Bahnung*) – instead of being seen as 'openings' – should perhaps rather be seen as hardening traces able to conduct electrical charges. This 'hardening' consists in creating conductive traces that can transport the frustrating rise in excitation in safe directions. In a virgin system, traces have to be laid down, and the system repeats this labor until facilitations are constructed – it is difficult to image this process being performed in any other way than by *repetition*. As such, traces are impressed, painted, or printed, much similar to how an inkjet printer sprays fine layers of paint on the same spot of a blank piece of paper until a readable letter emerges – better still, similar to how conductive traces of silicon are laid down on a microchip.

[291] Freud: *Project*, SE 1, 300; GW N, p. 392-93.

We understand now from this new neurological angle what Nietzsche's important notion *simplification* implies. We have said that the simplifying subject is defending itself against *too much reality, too many stimuli*. Now, according to Freud's model, it is the so-called 'contact-barriers' [*kontaktschranken*] (Fechner's 'thresholds') that allow only stimuli above a certain intensity to pass through the system. The simplifying subject, furthermore, learns to understand reality through *custom and habit*, exercised in the neurological system as the *repeated imprint* of 'facilitating passages' [*Bahnungen*], conditional upon the intensity and frequency of stimuli. Thus, as its first defensive layer, its first buffer against *too much reality*, the mental system sets up these two mechanisms in order to filter material according to *intensity* and *repetition*. In this process, the mental system 'simplifies' – that is, 'falsifies' and 'interprets' – reality. It 'takes in,' becomes conscious of and memorizes, only a fraction of possible impressions.

Nietzsche's 'simplification' implies that a super-abundance of impressions have too low an intensity to overcome the resistance of the contact-barriers; or they are too abundant or too minute to imprint themselves in the psychical system; consequently, they never enter consciousness. This is why we do not see a tree in its minute manifold and its infinitely changing shapes. The manifold of impressions of the 'detailed' tree simply never overcomes the threshold of the contact-barriers, and never imprints itself. This manifold never 'enters' consciousness, it 'stays outside,' and is as such, in Nietzsche's sense, unconscious. What we see is the 'simplified' tree, because the detailed tree would overwhelm us with an information-overload we could not possibly process. Our natural defense against 'too much reality' is to 'abbreviate' and 'truncate'; that is, to 'interpret.' We create 'forms' that are easier to conceive, but remain approximations to the information that was potentially available.

We recall from *Chapter 2* that this was what Leibniz and Nietzsche had been saying before Freud. Leibniz would say that we usually encounter the environing world without attention; it just passes us by as an empty horizon. In order to see *attentively*, one must, besides having the visible impression, *remember* the impression,[292] and Nietzsche followed up on this Leibnizian insight (cf. FW 354 & WM 479) by suggesting that an impression had to be 'seen' as if in an inner-mental *mirror*, before it could be consciously seen; i.e., before it could be *perceived* in the proper sense. In Nietzsche, we

---

[292] "Memory is needed for attention," Leibniz had said (G. W. Leibniz: New Essays on Human Understanding. Translated & edited by J. Bennett and P. Ramnant, Cambridge (Cambridge University Press) 1982, p. 54.) This was, according to Nietzsche, Leibniz's "precocious insight" (cf. KSA 3, FW 354).

would understand and see only something we had already understood and seen beforehand:

> Understanding is an amazingly fast accommodating [*entgegenkommendes*] fantasizing and conjecturing [*Schließen*]: out of two words we render a sentence (when we read): out of a vowel and two consonants we render a word when we hear; yet, there are several words we n e v e r hear, and still we c o n s i d e r them as heard. [. . .] I suppose that we only see what we k n o w ; in their handling of numerous forms our eyes are continuously being put into practice: —The greatest parts of images are not sense-impressions [*Sinneneindruck*] but f a n t a s y - c r e a t i o n s. It only extracts a few reasons and motives from sensations [*Sinnen*] and these are then further creatively elaborated [*ausgedichtet*]. (Nachlaß 1881, KSA 9, 11[13]).

Therefore, what in the 'living self-presence' of the subject would be *experienced* as first (the proper perception of this or that object), was *actually* the *conclusion* of a process. What seemed to be first, was last. The 'living presence' of the conscious sensation was constituted in *delay* [*Nachträglich*] (we will return to this notion of 'time-reversal' below).

Now, with Freud, we have a simple model envisaging these insights of Leibniz and Nietzsche: a system of memory traces is simply inserted between impressions and perceptions. Consequently, impressions (*phi-*) must pass through a memory system (*psi-*) before they can become conscious (*omega-*).

3.2. A Neurological Explanation of the Sense of Reality

In the *Project*, Freud assumes that the *principle of inertia* [*Trägheit*] (in later writings, the *principle of constancy*) governs the mental system. This implies, that the mental system strives to "keep itself free from stimulus," it strives toward a zero-tension resolution of all stimuli, Freud says, in an early formulation of what in later writings will resurface as his 'death-drive.' Freud understands transference of Qη-quantity from the *phi-receptor-system* to the *psi-memory-system* as an increase of the general energy-level in the system, impelling it to restore the original level of equilibrium (therefore the "principle of *constancy*"). Motor reaction (movement, bodily activity, etc.) itself is seen as such a 'discharge' of excess Qη-energy. For example, the recognition of mother's well-known face *arouses excitement* in the infant, causing a *motor discharge* involving the infant's giggling and kicking about arms and legs, as such felt as *pleasure*. The motor reaction of the infant *discharges excess energy*, thus restores *equilibrium*, which is finally felt as *pleasure*. So-called 'pleasure' is therefore discharge of excess Qη-energy; it reestablishes a zero-tension condition in the psyche. (We must as such assume that in 'empty perception' there is no rise of excitation, since there is no penetration of the mental system. However, in perception 'proper,' perceptive stimulus increases the level of excitation, thus causing 'unpleasure,' and impelling a discharge in order to restore the original equilibrium – the reestablishment of which is felt as 'pleasure.' (We will return to this idea in our explanation of certain aspects of Nietzsche's Eternal Recurrence in our last *Chapter 6*.)

Now, it is possible to flee from *exogenous* stimuli prompting a rise in excitation, and thus restore equilibrium. However, flight from *endogenous* stimuli (e.g., hunger or sexual desire) is impossible, and the system is consequently forced to abandon the "original trend to inertia [*Trägheit*], that is, to bring the level [of Qη quantity] to zero [*zum niveau = 0*]."[293] That is, when the individual is hungry, it cannot just passively disappear into its own cozy fantasies about food and eating; fantasies do not satisfy. The individual is *forced* to confront reality (it has to consult Freud's later 'reality-principle') in order to reduce the rising tension. What happens is that the *endogenous excitation* (hunger) creates in the mental system a 'wish,' that is, a *mnemic image* [*Erinnerungsbild*] of the fulfilling object; or more precisely, the individual *cathects* memory-traces storing the satisfying resolution to a tension, and produces thereby a *hallucination* that directs the subject toward a *corresponding object* in reality. First then, the subject can carry out adequate motor reaction. A raise of endogenous stimuli results in the emergence of *mnemic images of satisfaction*. These 'mnemic images of satisfaction,' we will call 'desire.' We now understand that desire starts in *hallucinations*; these hallucinations propel the subject to overcome its intrinsic inertia and seek out resolutions in reality, which finally ends in *alterations* of the external world, in the subject's fulfillments of desire. (E.g., the endogenous sensation of hunger triggers the *mnemic image* of a possible fulfilling object, a sandwich. The sandwich is so far a *hallucination*, but it propels the subject to seek out a corresponding object in reality. Visiting the refrigerator, the subject overcomes its intrinsic inertia, addresses the rising tension caused by the hallucination of food, and by alternating reality (by making and eating the sandwich), it fulfills its desire, and brings back its mental system to its zero-tension condition. What is here described as 'intrinsic inertia' and 'zero-tension condition' is what in Freud's later writings will emerge as the *pleasure-principle*.)

This, however, creates a new problem concerning the interrela-

---

[293] Freud: *Project*, SE 1, p. 297; GW N, p. 390.

tionship between subject and object, individual and reality. Not only does the subject need to screen external reality, it also needs to screen the *presentations* in internal reality of external reality. Not only does the subject suffer under 'too much' external reality, it suffers also from 'too much' internal reality. It crucially has to learn to distinguish between hallucination and reality, otherwise the *mnemic image* of a frightening object would prompt superfluous flight reactions, and the *mnemic image* of the fulfilling object would prompt purely imaginary satisfactions. The subject has to learn that *mnemic images* are not real and offer no satisfaction in and of themselves.

The last neuron in Freud's system, the so-called *omega*-neuron (ω), has this important function. It provides the mental system with differentiating principles preventing the suicidal confusion of hallucination and reality. It gives the subject so-called "indications of reality" [*Realitätszeichen*]. In general, the *omega*-neuron-system accounts for consciousness, that is, functions like attention, judgment, thought, and finally language (Freud's *word-presentations*; more below). Thus, it is the *omega*-system that *interprets* Qη excitation, and introduces to consciousness something that hitherto has been understood merely as physical quantities. Since "consciousness knows nothing of quantities and neurons,"[294] there must in the mental apparatus exist an agency that *translates quantities into qualities*, that is, translates force and energy into images and feelings.

This corresponds to Nietzsche's insight, as frequently expressed in the Nachlaß material, that we can only perceive *qualities*. Qualities have to be, says Nietzsche, "our insurmountable limit" (cf. Nachlaß 1886-87, KSA 12, 6[14]), although he always surmises that a reality of *becoming* impresses itself on our sense-apparatus as minute gradations in *quantities*. In Nietzsche, the external world *beyond* or *before* conscious perception is explicitly conceived as *a world of becoming*, or as a world of *quantities* and *interrelations* between quantities, which is then eventually stabilized as a *qualitative* world in conscious perception.

> Quantities in-themselves [*an sich*] do not occur in our experience; our world of experience is a qualitative world." (Nachlaß 1886-87; KSA 12, 6[14]). [. . .] The p h e n o m e n a l is therefore: the interference of the notion of number, the notion of subject, the notion of movement: we always have our e y e s, our p s y c h o l o g y, immersed therein. If we eliminate these additions [*zuthaten*]: then there is no thing left, except dynamical quanta, in a relation of tension [*Spannungsverhaltniß*] to other quanta, whose essence in their relation to other

---

[294] Freud: *Project*, SE 1, p. 308; GW N, p. 400.

quanta consists in their effect on them – the will to power is not being, and not becoming, but rather a P a t h o s as the most elementary fact from where becoming and effect arise. (Nachlaß 1888; KSA 13, 14[79]).

This distinction between quantities and qualities is reiterated in Freud's *Project*. Consciousness can only give us quality-sensations, although quantities would characterize the "external world" – that is, a world independent of the human psyche: "Consciousness gives us what are called quality-sensations, which are different in a great multiplicity of ways and whose difference is distinguished according to the relations with the external world. Within this difference there are series, similarities, and so on, but there are in fact no quantities in it. [. . .] Where do qualities originate? Not in the external world. For out there, there are *only masses in motion and nothing else*." (*Project*, SE 1, p. 308; GW N, p. 401; italics added). These "masses in motion" are equivalent to Nietzsche's world of becoming; these "masses in motion" will necessarily have to be translated into conscious perception, as such into qualities.

Since Nietzsche never offered a systematic model of the mental apparatus, he did not explain how, when, or where in the system quantities are transformed into qualities. This transformation has now a locality in Freud's typographical models, insofar as it is located in his *omega*-neuron-system. Since the main function of this neuron-system seems to be to interpret, I shall consequently label it, the *omega-interpreter-neuron* (– 'interpretation' understood here both in the narrow sense, as 'translation'; and in the broader sense, as 'explicating,' 'construing,' or 'giving meaning to'). It is thanks to this third neuron-system that we become conscious of perceptions. The *omega*-interpreter-neuron translates quantity into quality, and finally gives these sensuous qualities a certain value, determining whether they are hallucinations or real – it essentially assigns the value 'true' or 'false' to impressions.

Freud introduces the *omega-interpreter-neuron* (ω) tentatively, after he rules out that the *phi*- (φ) and the *psi*- (ψ) systems can be creating 'qualities,' i.e., can be the seats for consciousness. Qualities cannot be originating from the external world, which is only the above-mentioned "masses in motion"; and the two systems that transport stimuli can consequently not be responsible for 'qualities.' Freud therefore suggests his third system.

> Where do qualities originate? Not in the external world [*Außerwelt*] . . [. . .] In the φ system perhaps? That tallies with the fact that the qualities are linked with perception, but it is, contradicted by everything that rightly argues in favour of the seat of consciousness being in the *upper* storeys of the nervous system. In the ψ system then. Against this, however, there is a weighty objection. During

3. Freud's Analysis of Sensation, Memory, and Consciousness

perception the φ and the ψ systems are in operation together, but there is one psychical process which is no doubt performed exclusively in ψ – reproducing or remembering – and this, speaking generally, is *without quality*. Remembering brings about *de norma* [normally] nothing that has the peculiar character of perceptual quality. Thus we summon up courage to assume that there is a third system of neurons – ω perhaps [we might call it] – which is excited along with perception, but not along with reproduction, and whose states of excitation give rise to the various qualities.[295]

From these considerations, we can now construct a first schematic model of Freud's mental apparatus. We have a mental apparatus circumscribed by an 'outer' and an 'inner' periphery, receiving exogeneous and endogeneous stimuli, transporting these stimuli as quantities through three different kinds of neuron-systems (the *phi-receptor-neuron*, the *psi-memory-neuron*, and the *omega-interpreter-neuron*), according to the following model.[296]

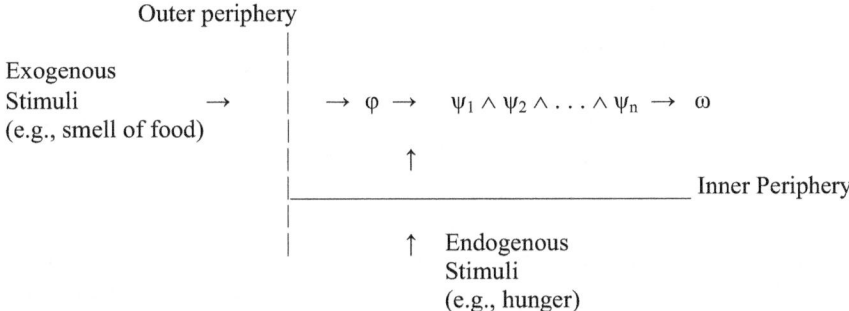

The permeable *phi*-neurons (φ) and the impermeable *psi*-neurons (ψ) are equipped, respectively, *without* and *with* so-called 'contact-barriers' [*kontaktschranken*]. We notice from the hand-drawings of Freud that he conceives a '*psi*-neuron' as a combination of nucleus, antennas, and synapses. We have a nucleus from where several antennas radiate, and where each of the antennas ends in a contact-barrier, a synapsis, drawn like a hammerhead axon at the end of the antenna. If each of the *psi*-neurons connects to its neighbor qua one of the synapses at the end of the antennas, even a relatively small bundle of neurons is forming a complex net of traces. (In Freud's drawings we notice, in conformity with contemporary neuroscience,[297] a minor gab between each connecting synapsis. Possibly

---

[295] Freud: *Project*, SE 1, p. 308-09; GW N, p. 401.
[296] The model has structural similarity to models R. Wollheim introduces in *Freud*, loc. cit., p. 52, and J. Laplance in *Life and Death in Psychoanalysis*, loc. cit., p. 58.
[297] See for example, J. DeLoux: *The Synaptic Self; How our Brains Become Who*

Freud conceives their connection as electrical impulses being fired off from one synapse to the next.) Freud suggests, furthermore, that only a fraction of these traces are 'cathected' [*Besetzt*]. Of a potentially infinite number of traces, only a small fraction is being utilized to store 'memory.' (Also this assumption conforms to contemporary neuroscience; only a tiny fraction of the neurological network is being utilized, while the major parts 'atrophy.'[298]) Thus, when several *psi*-neurons transmit stimuli along their connected antennas, facilitating passages are being formed through the repeated transmission of impulses. These especially well-cathected traces now constitute the memory of the system (cf. our forest-metaphor above: out of a potentially infinite number of possibilities for tracking the forest, only a few well-proven trails are being used, attracting the most of all future traffic, while potential alternative possibilities are wasting away without husbandry and cultivation).

3.3. Ego-Clusters and Will-to-Power-Formations.

It is from Freud's *omega-interpreter-system* an *ego* will eventually emerge. This ego is in Freud's writings introduced in the singular, but as a consequence of the logic of his thinking, it must be thought rather as a multiplicity of *egos* – or, of so-called 'ego-clusters,' as we shall say.

The value that is impressed upon a certain sensation – whether 'good' or 'bad,' 'friendly' or 'hostile' – can only be "biologically taught," says Freud. But when it has been taught, it will result in an external object being seen as either attractive or repulsive. From then on, the mnemic image [*Erinnerungsbild*] of an *attractive object* is inclined to be cathected, i.e., invested with psychic energy; while the mnemic image of a *repulsive object* will be de-cathected, i.e., divested of psychic energy.

> The wishful state results in a positive *attraction* towards the object wished-for, or, more precisely, towards its mnemic image [*Erinnerungsbild*]; the experience of pain leads to a repulsion, a disinclination to keeping the hostile mnemic image cathected [*Besetzt*]. Here we have primary *wishful attraction* and primary *defense* [*Abwehr*].
> Wishful attraction can easily be explained by the assumption that the cathexis of the friendly mnemic image in a state of desire greatly exceeds in Qη the cathexis which occurs when there is a mere perception, so that a particularly good

---

We Are. (New York: Viking Press, 2003). Or Steven Pinker: *The Blank Slate: The Modern denial of Human Nature.* (London: Penguin Books, 2003).

[298] See for example Solms and Turnbull: *The Brain and the Inner World*, loc. cit.

facilitation [*Bahnung*] leads from the ψ nucleus to the corresponding neurone of the pallium.
It is harder to explain primary *defense* or *repression* [*Abwehr oder Verdrängung*] – the fact that a hostile mnemic image is regularly abandoned by its cathexis [*Besetzung*] as soon as possible. Nevertheless, the explanation should lie in the fact that the primary experiences of pain were brought to an end by reflex defense. The emergence of another object in place of the hostile one was the signal for the fact that the experience of pain was at an end, and the ψ system, taught *biologically,* seeks to reproduce the state in ψ which, marked the cessation of the pain.[299]

The mind is thus doing its best in furnishing itself with everything that *feels good*. It creates particularly well-facilitated passages [*Bahnungen*] between attractive mnemic images (ψ) and consciousness (ω). It does so by repeatedly cathecting attractive mnemic images. The mind likes to surround itself with, so to speak, backslappers, and expel party-poopers. The problem with backslappers, however, is that they quickly degrade the sense of reality in the subject. In an 'ideal' narcissistic mental condition, the mind would be employing only backslappers to bolster its fragile ego; it would give in to the temptation to live in an inner world of hallucinations without having to trouble itself with reality; this would indicate an *ultimate* pleasure (equivalent to Freud's later conceived notion of the *pleasure-principle*). However, we cannot live entirely according to the pleasure-principle; that would introduce into the subject self-destructive delusions regarding reality.

In order to avoid this *temptation-to-hallucinate*, the inner mental system consequently needs an *Ego*, says Freud; an Ego with the important job to *inhibit action* on basis of hallucinations. It cannot allow Qη excitation to travel unhindered along the most direct paths from ψ to the ω-system, as such, impulsively prompt discharge of the wishful image into activity. The straight and uninhibited path is necessarily inhibited, otherwise mere *ideas* ('hallucinations') are cathected setting in motion illusory action. Action prompted by a wishful image would be delusive, and satisfaction would fail to occur (fantasies of food do not satisfy); action prompted by a repulsive image would mean to adopt disproportionate defenses against illusory dangers (like in delirium). The individual would be fighting hallucinatory lions and hunting hallucinatory deer. Consequently, *inhibition is necessary*. This necessary inhibition is now by Freud explained by means of the notion, 'side-cathexis' [*Seitenbesetzung*].

So, what is 'side-cathexis'? – First, the 'side-cathexis' must be situated in the *omega-interpreter-system*; it may even be seen as the fundamental

---

[299] Freud: *Project*, SE 1, p. 322; GW N, p. 415.

modus operandi of this system. In explaining 'side-cathexis,' we are *zooming in* on the mechanism of the *omega-system*. Freud envisions a 'side-cathexis' as the *redirection* and *diversion* of a neuron traveling from *a* toward *b*, where '*a* toward *b*' designates the most straightforward route of the neuron; the route chosen according to the 'pleasure-principle.' Now, instead of traveling from *a* to *b*, the neuron is redirected into a neurological 'net' or 'cluster'; more precisely, major amounts of its $Q\eta$ energy is absorbed into (cathected by) this 'net' or 'cluster' of alternative facilitations [*Bahnungen*]. So instead of *a* traveling directly to *b*, *a* gives off only small amounts of $Q\eta$ energy to *b*, and travels instead along a new path leading into a 'net,' a 'cluster,' described as a grid of interconnected locations: from α to β to γ to δ, etc. If the so-called direct path of '*a* toward *b*' is described as a *psychical primary process*, the indirect and diverted path is described as a *psychical secondary process*. In Freud's own words.

> A *side-cathexis* [*Seitenbesetzung*] thus acts as *an inhibition of the course of $Q\eta$*. Let us picture the ego as a network of cathected neurones well facilitated in relation to one another. If we suppose that a Qn enters a neurone *a* from outside, then, if it were uninfluenced, it would pass to neurone *b*; but it is so much influenced by the side-cathexis α – *alpha* that it gives off only a quotient to *b* and may even perhaps not reach *b* at all. Therefore, if an ego exists, it must inhibit psychical primary process.[300]

– And Freud adds the following model in his manuscript[301]:

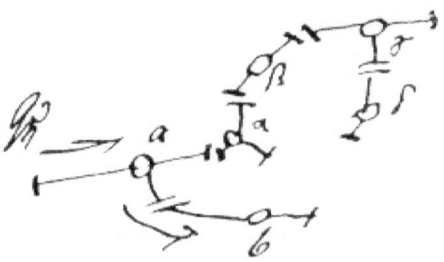

We notice that in the model $Q\eta$-energy travels along 'antennas,' spreading out from nuclei, with synapses in their end, rendered as the hammerhead axons mentioned above. The starting point in the drawing is $Q\eta$-energy entering *a*. If 'uninhibited,' the energy proceeds to *b*. However, exposed to

---

[300] Freud: *Project*, SE 1, p. 322; GW N, 415.
[301] Freud's drawing: SE 1, p. 324; GW, Nachtragsband, p. 417.

'side-cathexis,' it is distracted from its original course, and guided into the net of neurons (designated α, β, γ, and δ in the drawing). It is this 'net,' we call an 'ego-cluster'; and we will see it as equivalent to Nietzsche's enigmatic 'will-to-power-formation' ('-complex' or '-configuration').

'Side-cathexis' is prompting the mental system to *control* and *delay*; two functions, without which the subject would self-destruct in impulsive action, based on hallucinations. In the primary versus secondary processes, we encounter two contrary processes accounting for respectively *uninhibited wish-fulfillment* and *inhibited wish-fulfillment*. It is the side-cathexis of the ego-cluster that brings about a *moderation* of the cathexes of the original wish.[302]

Furthermore, it is the side-cathexis that is responsible for 'indications of reality,' or 'reality-signs,' implying in the subject an ability to distinguish between *idea* and *perception* (between 'false' and 'true,' as described above), enabling as such the subject to act on only ('true') perceptions. We notice again that the *origin* of this celebrated dichotomy, *true—false*, is the basic ability to judge what is real against what is unreal; the subject must perforce learn what is *Real*. In biological terms, the subject needs to acquire an ability to distinguish between 'false' and 'true,' where *hallucinations* are always 'false,' while *perceptions* are always 'true.'[303] (Since this ability is

---

[302] Freud is of course here introducing a distinction that will later become known as the distinction between 'pleasure-principle' and 'reality-principle' – as developed in later essays like *Two Principles of Mental Functioning* [1911], *A Metapsychological Supplement to the Theory of Dreams* [1917], *Beyond the Pleasure Principle* [1920], and the posthumous, *An Outline of Psychoanalysis* [1940].

[303] We notice that an adumbrated manifestation of this origin of true and false has survived in commentators insisting on the 'truth of the real' on every possible, and often impossible, occasion, and in an often rather unspecified manner – e.g., against the perceived threat of Nietzsche! We notice that their insistence will regularly be accompanied with certain physical expressions such as stamping in the floor, or knocking on the table. (Like Dr. Johnson's famous refutation of Bishop Berkeley: "I refute you thus!" – and he kicks a stone in the direction of a devastated Bishop Berkeley (or whatever!)). These physical expressions in fact make up *the entire argument*; and a powerful one too, albeit not particular sophisticated, because with our original animal consciousness, nobody (that is, nobody!) can deny that this floor or this table or this stone is *Real*. By stamping in the floor the dedicated 'Realists' are saying, 'this is not my hallucination'; they stamp in the floor so that we can know that this, in the original biological sense, is true. Pre-reflectively, they take for granted that the correlate to 'truth' is a perception. (We notice that if or when people are *obsessing* about the truth of the real, then one inevitably gets the

understood to be *acquired*, it is almost as if the subject is pre-programmed to live in hallucinations, but by biological necessity is forced to unlearn that programming. To a delirious or schizophrenic subject, this unlearning has not been successful, and the 'indications of reality' have broken down; but normally, hallucinations will not be allowed to run their predestined course and discharge in futile action. Instead, they are absorbed into well-consolidated ego-clusters.)

The job of ego-clusters is thus to *interpret* to the subject what is *Real*, but according to interpretive principles that remain unconscious to the subject.

> It is accordingly inhibition by the ego [*Ichhemmung*] which makes possible a criterion for distinguishing between perception and memory. Biological experience will then teach that discharge is not to be initiated till the indication of reality [*Realitätszeichen*] has arrived. [. . .] During the process of wishing, inhibition by the ego brings about a moderated cathexis of the object wished-for, which allows it to be cognized as not real.[304]

By virtue of the interpreting 'ego-clusters,' the subject will eventually adopt a relatively fixed set of responses to various external circumstances. This adoption may well be seen as a defense against a psyche that is flooded with mental material, as the attempt to fight off this superfluity, given the biological necessity of confronting the external world. It introduces into the psyche a 'secondary process' able to override and revoke unchecked primary processes, and is necessary for survival. Instead of acting impulsively on inner stimuli, the mental apparatus delays action. It guides the stimulus into a cluster of particularly well-facilitated memory-traces that are able to recognize, judge, and evaluate the stimulus before discharging in motor reaction.

Freud calls the *totality* of these well-facilitated clusters of memory traces, "*the ego*," and talks about the ego as "a network of cathected neurones": "The ego is to be defined as the totality of the *psi* cathexes, at the given time, in which a permanent component is distinguished from a changing

---

suspicion that the *Real* is precisely their greatest problem – in other words, that they are predisposed to psychosis. We probably get this suspicion because we intuitively understand that the language, which is compulsively energized to remedy the perceived lack, is always too flimsy a medium, and never quite up to the task. We then sense that it cannot restore something that was never sufficiently internalized in the first place; that it cannot restore this originally lost sense of solidity in the reality-obsessing subject.)

[304] Freud: Project, SE 1, p. 326-27; GW N, p. 421-22.

one. [...] Let us picture the ego as a network of cathected neurones well facilitated in relation to one another."³⁰⁵

If 'the ego' is a network, we must consequently be talking about several different ego-*clusters*; well-facilitated *densities, concentrations,* or *configurations* in a neurological net of memory traces infusing the psychic system. We are therefore inclined to understand Freud's *'ego'* (in the singular) as an indefinite number of clusters (in the plural); as small islands of 'knowledge' in a vast neurological net. *The* 'ego' becomes an *indefinite* number of configurations within a 'net' providing an *infinite* number of possibilities for additional configuration. They as such emerge as power-configurations and -concentrations that most expediently and economically help the subject to realize desires without self-destructing. However, since we are talking here about not a single uniform ego, but of several *ego-clusters*, we must assume that they are without 'supervision' (*a fortiori*, without *rational* supervision); we assume that there is no central cluster governing the rest.³⁰⁶ Furthermore, we assume that they are subject to change, and often exist in conflict and competition with one another. If as such competing, we finally assume that some ego-clusters are eventually wasting away while others are being cultivated, according to the relevant learning processes that an individual undergoes.

It is these ego-clusters that we understand as the neurological correlate to Nietzsche's 'wills' or 'cells.' We mentioned earlier that Nietzsche's *will-to-power* comes about as a result of a competition between forces engaged in a perpetual struggle. Nietzsche's 'will' is therefore never a singularity, but implies several *wills*. As the opportune constellation of forces, Nietzsche's 'wills' materialize as local and temporary orders of rank; they materialize as 'organizations' of quanta of forces. The Ego, now understood as the organization of multiple ego-clusters, is accordingly 'made up of' the co-existence of multiple units or 'cells,' some of which will emerge as superior at given times (the so-called "aristocratic cells"). These multiple ego-clusters are responsible for the interpretation-processes that continuously goes on in the individual; Nietzsche's 'wills-to-power-processes' are responsible for elementary interpretation of the environing world. to substantiate, we reiterate here some of the *Nachlaß* passages, with which we started this chapter: "The nervous system and the brain is a conductive system [*Leitungssystem*] and a centralizing apparatus [*Centralisationsappa-*

---

³⁰⁵ Freud: Project, SE 1, p. 323; GW N, p. 416-17
³⁰⁶ This is also in conformity with contemporary cognitive science, see Dennett, Daniel C.: Consciousness Explained. Boston (Little, Brown, and Company), 1991.

rat] consisting of numerous individual spirits [*Individual-Geister*] of different range." (Nachlaß 1884; KSA 11, 26[36]). "The human being as a multiplicity of "wills to power": each of them with a multiplicity of expressions and forms." (Nachlaß 1885–86; KSA 12, 1 [58]). "The assumption of one single subject is perhaps unnecessary; perhaps it is just as permissible to assume a multiplicity of subjects, whose interaction and struggle is the basis of our thought and our consciousness in general? A kind of aristocracy of 'cells' [*Eine Art Aristocratie von 'zellen'*] in which dominion resides." (Nachlaß 1885, KSA 11, 40[42]).

The "subject" is a multiplicity of selves whose inner struggle is the basis of thinking. Still, against the backdrop of this inner chaos, the subject tries to exert a certain measure of control. The subject is described as a multiplicity of "cells" in which some cells try to dominate other cells. In Freud's language, these 'cells,' 'wills,' or 'ego-clusters' are responsible for attracting into their well-facilitated network Qη-energy (quantities or forces) that would otherwise float along the most perspicuous pathways in the neurological system. As such, certain particularly powerful (so-called "aristocratic") ego-clusters inhibit impulsive reaction to stimuli. They 'distract' and 'attract' Qη-energy, as they exert Freud's so-called 'side-cathexis' [*Seitenbesetzung*].

If now we see will-to-power-formations as identical to the organizations of these ego-clusters, it becomes clearer what will-to-power is actually doing in the psyche; what kind of job it has. We have said that its elementary function is to 'interpret,' in order to distinguish (in the biological sense) the real from the unreal, the true from the false. The unreal primarily manifests itself as a hallucination, and represents the ultimate pleasure in inner mental life, the so-called zero-tension resolution of all conflict. Consequently, since a will-to-power formation screens off the unreal, its main function must be to *inhibit pleasure*. Or to put it differently, *the pleasure of a will-to-power-formation is to inhibit a pleasure*. Will-to-power-processes are thus the ultimate 'party-poopers.' They put a freewheeling psyche under a permanent restraining order. This is exactly what we understand as 'power.'

In this fundamental restraint as self-restraint, will-to-power-processes are in themselves able to evolve into a 'pleasure' – but neither a sexual pleasure nor a pleasure of repose and tranquility in the absolute nirvana, instead a 'pleasure' of another and different order, a 'pleasure' of control, command, and management understood primarily as *self*-control, *self*-commandment, and *self*-management. This is the will-to-power as pleasure, and what Nietzsche understands as the ultimate pleasure.

3.4. The Psychological Origin of Entity and Identity

We have now learnt how crucial it is to develop in the psychic apparatus the ability to distinguish between image and perception, or more precisely, between *mnemic image* and *perceptive image*, since otherwise the subject would react on mere hallucinations. We have learnt that the ego must inhibit its reaction to *mnemic images*; and in Freud's explanation, it does so by moderating the *cathexis* of the mnemic image, as such lowering the intensity of the cathexis – the actual effect being that the image is recognized as non-real. We now understand that when a subject wishes for an object, the wished-for-object first has to be recognized as *absent*. An "inhibition by the ego brings about a moderated cathexis of the object wished-for, which allows it to be recognized as not real."[307] The subject therefore has to learn to distinguish between *presence* and *absence*. Recognition of *absence* is at least as important as is recognition of *presence*, possibly even more important.

Freud's now speculates that the subject's ability to make this crucial distinction (between *presence* and *absence*) comes about thanks to cathexes of different chains of neurons. When the subject desires a certain object, that is, evokes a *mnemic image* of an absent object, it cathects a chain of neurons, let us say, $a + b + c$. As the subject thereupon searches reality for the fulfillment of the wished-for object, it cathects certain *perceptive* images equivalent to the *mnemic* image. However, in the perceptive image only certain components in the neuron-chain may be present, while others may be missing; let us suppose that in reality $a + b$ is found and cathected, but c is lacking. Now, the 'mnemic chain' ($a + b + c$) is compared to the 'perceptive chain' ($a + b + \ldots$), and the absent c becomes an 'indication of reality' or a 'reality-sign.' It is in Freud's terminology, the *precathected*, but non-existing component in the chain; it becomes the gab in a memorized series. "If a perception arrives which is identical with the *idea* [the wished-for object] or similar to it, it finds its neurones *precathected* by the wish. [. . .] The difference between the idea and the approaching perception then gives occasion for the process of thought."[308] Two chains are compared, and

---

[307] Freud: *Project*, SE 1, p. 327; GW N, p. 422. Later in the *Project*, Freud has another formulation of the same idea: "Tension due to craving prevails in the ego, as a consequence of which the idea of the loved object (the *wishful* idea) is cathected. Biological experience has taught that this idea should not be so strongly cathected that it might be confused with a perception, and that discharge must be postponed till the indications of quality appear from the *idea* as a proof that the *idea* is now real." (*Project*, SE 1, p. 361).

[308] Freud: *Project*, SE 1, p. 361; GW N, p. 421.

insofar as the perceptive chain indicates absence, so-called 'biological experience' (i.e., custom and habit achieved through learning processes) have taught us not to respond with motor discharge. "Biological experience will teach here [. . .] that it is unsafe to initiate discharge if the indications of reality do not confirm the whole complex but only a part of it."[309]

If we have the two chains above, $a + b + c$, as the model on *mnemic* (*phantasmatic*) plenitude, and the model, $a + b + . . .$, as the model on *perceptive* (*actual*) deficiency, the subject will in thinking be searching for the missing c (and/or will in thinking initiate a likely course to take toward obtaining c) in order to restore plenitude. It will as such continue to cathect several possibilities until the missing c has been obtained, in which case thinking terminates. As long of this process endures, the memory of the wishful object remains cathected, and the energy quantity, $Q\eta$, travels various associative paths radiating from the memory of c, in order to obtain a pathway towards its realization, propelling the desiring subject into a search for the missing wished-for object. Non-coincidence of cathexis of a *mnemic* image (a 'wishful cathexis') and cathexis of a *perceptual* image "gives the impetus for the activity of thought, which is terminated once more with their coincidence."[310] Thus, the mental system aims to find a way back to the missing neuron (in my example, c), and *establish identity* between *mnemic* and *perceptual* image, in which case the thought-process terminates. Hunger is the obvious case: our tribal ancestor is starved, *remembers* various sources of nourishment, starts *thinking* about how to obtain the wished-for object, *initiates* literally a search for the remembered object, food, in order to establish *identity* between the *phantasmatic* and the *actual* object. Once this *identity is established*, the thought-process stops.

Freud's explanation-model has the fascinating implication that it gives us a first hint as of what the neurological origin is for such important human activities as judging and thinking. According to the model, judging and thinking start in *deprivation*, in *absence*; namely in the recognition of the non-existence of a wished-for object. More precisely, absence is noticed as the dissimilarity between the two chains of cathexis, the cathexis of the plenitude of the mnemic image, and the cathexis of the insufficient perceptive image. (We notice in this that absence is nothing *in-and-for-itself*; i.e., it could not be felt *as such*, but only in comparison to an already remembered series.) Consequently, thinking is originally an attempt to restore presence in absence, and to establish identity into a state of difference and dissimilarity (– before it would be biologically safe to discharge in activity). As

---

[309] Freud: *Project*, SE 1, p. 328; GW N, p. 423.
[310] Freud: *Project*, SE 1, p. 328; GW N, p. 423

Freud briefly indicates, this pattern applies to thinking in general: "The process can, however, *make itself independent* of this latter aim [discharge in activity] and *strive only for identity*." [. . .] "The aim and end of all thought-processes is thus to bring about a *state of identity*."[311] So, we must be able to conclude that thinking originates in *desire*; that thinking is an activity performed to *fill a gap*, and it strives to *establish a state of identity*.

Freud also manages to explain the phenomenon of *understanding* by this model (by *understanding* Freud implies here *sympathetic* understanding; i.e., understanding of the passions and emotions of a fellow human being). A subject 'understands' another human being by relating to its own body the impressions it receives in the visual field of the other: "His features [the features of the fellow human being] in the visual sphere [. . .] will coincide in the subject with memories of quite similar visual impression his own, of his own body."[312] If for example the fellow human is screaming, screaming can be 'understood' by the perceptive subject as a pain-expression, because screaming "will awaken the memory of his own screaming, and at the same time of his own experiences of pain."[313] Again, identity is established by relating a *perceptual* image to a *mnemic* image (below, we shall see how a 'scream' as a first primitive word-representation also helps to inform the subject of the memory of pain).

Both in the case of 'thinking' and 'understanding,' Freud is addressing a question that also occupied Nietzsche. How is self-identity established; how is *something* being recognized *as something*, as *such and such*. By self-identity we imply here the identity of the self-same, often expressed by the equation: $A = A$. Like Freud, also Nietzsche will suggest an explanation of the *psychological* origin of this equation, as we shall see below. Within Nietzsche's perspective, we are talking about how a world of *becoming* is constituted as a world of *being*. Self-identity is established in the world of chaos; but how is such a floating 'phenomenal complex' constituted as 'thing,' and how it is comprehended as the self-identically same thing?

---

[311] Freud: *Project*, SE 1, p. 330 & 332; GW N, p. 425 & 427; italics added.
[312] Freud: *Project*, SE 1, p. 331; GW N, p. 426.
[313] Freud: *Project*, SE 1, p. 331; GW N, p. 426.

3.5. Toward a Theory of Language: Three Variations over a Theme

3.5.1. Word- and Thing-Presentation.

We know from Structural Linguistics that the sign is a two-part unity consisting of *signifier* and *signified*, sound-image and concept. This two-part unity, the *sign*, has a *referent*; a thing to which it refers. However, this last reference is typically not the concern of Structural Linguistics, since it is regarded as an epistemological issue, and it is often deliberately suspended in order to maintain formal purity in the investigations of linguistic meaning.

Freud, writing before the breakthroughs of Structural Linguistics, suggests a different language-theory. In *On Aphasia*,[314] it is a language-theory revolving around the two entities, *word* and *thing*; more precisely, *word-presentation* and *thing-presentation*. Let us start by remarking on some differences in Freud and Saussure's view.

Ad. 1: thing-presentation. First, we notice that the *thing-presentation* is not identical to the *referent* in Structural Linguistics; in Freud we are always talking about the *thing-as-represented* rather than a *thing itself.* (The thing-as-represented might better correspond to Kant's *for-us*, but with the following important caveat: the Freudian *for-us* would be a *for-us as private individuals*, not Kant's *for-us* supported by his universal conditions for experience.) The *thing* is also not identical to the linguistic signified/concept, since in Structural Linguistics, the *signified/concept* is conventionally determined by the signifier, delineated only in its arbitrary relationship with the signifier, and representing thus an artificially selected slice of reality (as discussed in the previous *Chapter 2*). By contrast, Freud's thing-presentation is neither arbitrarily nor conventionally determined; rather, it refers back to a *perceived thing, a represented reality*, and especially (albeit not exclusively) to a *visually perceived thing* as its necessary *nodal point*. However, there is no one-to-one relationship between *thing-presentation* and *perceived thing*; the thing-*presentation* is not simply a copy or a mirror-image of the thing (it is not like a projection into the mind of the real 'thing'), since to Freud, the *thing-presentation* is open-endingly referring to all possible *associations* emanating from the 'thing' as a nodal point. A *thing-presentation* then consists of an indefinite number of atomic impressions stored as memory in or as memory-traces, existing in some non-

---

[314] Freud, Sigmund: Zur Auffassung der Aphasien. Leipzig und Wien (Franz Deuticke), 1891.

specific more or less loose connection with the apparent actual thing. Moreover, before a word is attached to the thing-presentation, it lives a rather uncertain and flimsy existence in the mental apparatus as an association of naked impressions stored as memory-traces. Since as yet there is no language to describe the *thing-presentation*, it is pre-dominantly unconscious.[315]

Ad 2: word-presentation. As well as the Freudian 'thing' is different from both linguistic signified and referent, the Freudian *word-presentation* is different from both the linguistic signifier and signified, as well as from their association in the sign. In *On Aphasia*, Freud's 'word' is a four-part unity, consisting of, 1) writing-image, 2) reading-image, 3) sound-image, and 4) motor-image.[316] The *writing-image* and the *reading-image* represent the written or graphical image of the word as rendered in respectively handwriting and print (– I see no difference in so-called 'writing' and 'reading' image, and shall therefore treat them as a single unity). The *sound-image* is equivalent to Saussure's sound-image: the image of the sound of the word as uttered forth in speech. The *motor-image* adds a new component to the word, which Structural Linguistics never included in its investigations. Deciphering Freud's dense writing to the extent possible, it seems to represent *the image of what the word can do*, or, *the image of the action suggested by the word*. This new component would thus seem to anticipate Austin and Searle's speech-act theories of language; it adds a performative dimension to language. Given this four-part unity (which I condense into three), the sentence, 'please, close the door,' has, first, a written (graphic/printed) image; second, a sound-image as uttered forth; and third, a motor-image as the image of what the sentence can do, the image of a door being closed.

As an important distinction between word- and thing-presentation, Freud points out that the word-presentation contains a *closed*, and the thing-presentation an *open*, complex of presentations. In its three-fold rendition – as graphical-image, sound-image, and motor-image – the word is seen as a unit, which cannot extend its associative links beyond a certain conventional limit (– except when exactly the *word* is transformed into and being treated like a *thing*, as for example in dreams or schizophrenia). However, while the *word-presentation* represents a closed and limited set of associa-

---

[315] Lacan talks about the 'Freudian thing' as a 'thing of nothing,' but the Freudian thing is not nothing, it is only not verbalized. Lacan superimposes half a century of developments in Structural Linguistics on Freud's 'thing'—and is therefore not in entire conformity with *Freud's* linguistics.

[316] See Freud, Sigmund: Zur Auffassung der Aphasien. Loc. cit., p. 79.

tions, the *thing-presentation* remains open; it is made up of an indefinite variety of visual, acoustic, tactile, and kinesthetic presentations, which in the instance of perception, it is impossible to enumerate and restrict.

> The thing-presentation itself is once again a complex of associations made up of the greatest variety of visual, acoustic, tactile, kinesthetic and other presentations. [. . .] The thing-presentation is thus seen to be one which is not closed and almost one which cannot be closed, while the word-presentation is seen to be something closed.[317]

Freud now believes that *the meaning* of a *word* is established when it is connected to a thing-presentation. The word is then as sound-image linked to a visual presentation; meaningful speech is thus conceived as a linkage between acoustic and visual components, sound and sight.

> A word acquires its *meaning* by being linked to an 'thing-presentation,' at all events if we restrict ourselves to a consideration of substantives. [. . .] The word-presentation is not linked to the thing-presentation by all its constituent elements, but only by its sound-image. Among the thing-presentations, it is the visual ones, which stand for the object.[318]

Shortly, we shall return to Freud's development of the notions of thing- and word-presentation, but we already notice how the notions so far correspond well to Nietzsche's conception of language. Also to Nietzsche, before humans crucially encounter language, inner experiences are regarded as an originally unstructured chaos. Upon this chaos, we eventually superimpose language, and as such shape, organize, and fashion a certain material consisting of what may be well described as 'thing-presentations' to fit the garments of this new linguistic medium. While 'inner experiences' ('thing-presentations') are in principle open-ended and infinite, language as consisting of closed and unitary linguistic 'word-presentations' is in principle simplifying and generalizing. As such, the translation from *inner experience* into *language* (from 'thing-presentation' into 'word-presentation') implies an inevitable distortion. Language simplifies, thus falsifies, inner experiences. Notwithstanding this falsification, Nietzsche realizes that language introduces us to the "only inner

---

[317] Freud, Sigmund: Zur Auffassung der Aphasien. Loc. cit., p. 78-79. *On Aphasia*, p. 221-22.

[318] Freud, Sigmund: Zur Auffassung der Aphasien. Loc. cit., p. 78. Attempting to reduce reader confusion, I have translated Freud's original '*Objektvorstellung*' in the quotations from his *Aphasia* essay to 'thing-presentation' [*Dingvorstellung*], since in later writings, the term *Dingvorstellung* replaces the early *Objektvorstellung*, and since throughout the present essay, I am using the former term.

3. Freud's Analysis of Sensation, Memory, and Consciousness

world of which we can become conscious." We become conscious only of a simplified and falsified inner world. We are conscious only of a "surface and sign world" (cf. FW 354).

3.5.2. The Replacement of Thing with Word.

In a letter to Fliess [1896], Freud suggests an elaboration of his model on the relationship between thing- and word-presentations. The model anticipates the topographical models from chapter 7 in *The Interpretations of Dreams*. Freud suggests the following line:

```
   W            Wz            Ub            Vb           Bews
x  x———————x   x———————x  x----------x  x———————x   x
x              x x           x  x          x             x
```

The abbreviations, *W, Wz, Ub,* etc., represent the various agencies in the mental system; the *x*'ses are not explained, but they would seem to indicate sensational elements differently registered under the disparate agencies. Let us quote in its entirety Freud's commentary on this line:

> *W* [*Wahrnehmungen* (perceptions)] are neurons in which perceptions originate, to which consciousness attaches, but which in themselves retain no trace of what has happened. For consciousness and memory are mutually exclusive.
> *Wz* [*Wahrnehmungszeichen* (indication of perception)] is the first registration of the perceptions; it is quite incapable of consciousness, and arranged according to associations by simultaneity.
> *Ub* [*Unbewusstsein* (unconsciousness)] is the second registration arranged according to other (perhaps casual) relations. Ub traces would perhaps correspond to conceptual memories; equally inaccessible to consciousness.
> *Vb* [*Vorbewusstsein* (pre-consciousness)] is the third transcription, attached to word-presentations and corresponding to our official ego. The cathexes proceeding from this Vb become conscious according to certain rules; and this secondary thought-consciousness is subsequent in time, and is probably linked to the hallucinatory activation of word-presentations, so that the neurons of consciousness would once again be perceptual neurons and in themselves without memory.[319]

Wahrnehmungen (*W*) indicates a first encounter with the world in what in previous chapter we have called 'impression' or 'empty perception.' (It may

---

[319] Fliess Papers, letter 52, 1896, in Freud: "Extracts from the Fliess Papers," *Standard Edition*, vol. 1 (London: The Hogarth Press, 1966) p. 234-35.

be a bit confusing that Freud here talks about 'perception,' since is our use, 'perception' is consistently seen as *conscious*; nonetheless, in this particular context, Freud's *perception* is equivalent to what we label *impression* or *empty perception*.) As yet, nothing is penetrating, nor being registered by, the mental system (we are here addressing what in the *Project for a Scientific Psychology* was described as the *phi-neuron* system). In this primary encounter with the human organism, the world is still chaotic and disorganized, and would correspond to Nietzsche's 'chaos' or 'world-of-becoming,' our 'hyper-reality,' or what we also determined as the 'human ground' in *Chapter 2*. In this encounter with the organism, 'empty' perceptions are *not nothing*; rather, they are super-abundant as a continuum of stimuli, which in wave upon wave impinges themselves upon the mental system. In the *W*-system, the impinging impressions are still not remembered, nothing is recognized, the world still lingers as surface and absolute presence, and approaches us as such – we also assume that an awareness of temporal dimensions has not yet developed. However, this impinging world is not for a second understood as a Kantian *an-sich*; it is merely a 'world' seen as in an *unblinking stare*, as by a *virgin eye* that knows no discrimination and prejudice. We might label this world, the *Real*,[320] although I have already indicated my preference for the neologism, the *hyper-real*, describing thus a reality of absolute presence.

Wahrnehmungszeichen (*Wz*) and *Unbewusstsein* (*Ub*) represent two different strata or levels of registration (we are addressing here what in the *Project* becomes the *psi-neuron* system). The difference between the two strata is not completely obvious, but it is clear that they represent a 'lower' and a 'higher' organization of material. It is interesting that Freud describes the 'lower' stratum as operating according to '*association*' and '*simultaneity*' and the 'higher' as operating according to '*causality*.' This brings us back to David Hume's suggestion that originally we perceive only *association* and *simultaneity*, which subsequently, we *interpret* as *causality*. In these early formulations, we notice that the *Wz*-system seems to operate according to what is subsequently conceived as the *Unconscious*-system from *The Interpretations of Dreams*. Like this system, Freud's early *Wz*-system has not yet introduced notions of causality and chronology into the mental system, and operates predominantly according to association and simultane-

---

[320] The "Real," after Lacan, as it were. However, I want to avoid entangling myself in Lacanian subject-philosophy for different reasons; but first and foremost because it seems to me counterproductive to add to an already difficult exposition yet another level of complexity. It is always better to keep an investigation as pure as possible, instead of distracting matters by filling in and dropping names at every possible and impossible occasion.

ity. According to the line, it is first in the *Ub*-system that the subject is introduced to a rudimentary sense of temporality and chronology – in order for the subject to experience causality, it necessarily needs a sense of *before* and *after*, and *past* and *future*. Both of the two strata would account for the *thing-presentation* above, the thing presented as a superfluity of visual, acoustic, tactile, and kinesthetic associations in the memory system – and of which the actual, chiefly visual, *thing* is the nodal point. Given Freud and Breuer's dictum that *consciousness and memory are mutually exclusive manifestations*, the two systems are unconscious.

Finally, the *Vb* [*Vorbewusstsein*] and *Bews* [*Bewusstsein*] systems: it is not before the entry of word-presentations that thing-presentations are capable of becoming conscious; this happens in the pre-conscious- or *Vb*-system (a system that corresponds to the *omega-neuron* system from the *Project*). As thing and thing-presentation, *the world presents itself to us*; but as word-presentation, *we present the world to ourselves*; in other words, *we re-present the world* (cf. Nietzsche's "mirror," cf. *Chapter 2 & 6*). As thing and thing-presentation, the world presents itself as presence, while the word-presentation replaces the absolute presence of the thing with the word, which becomes now the universal, timeless, and generic stand-in for the thing. As such the word *re*-presents the thing, but in its new cruder linguistic garments; – a veil has been thrown over the splendor and dazzle of the presence of the self-present. As we noted above, it is while contemplating this operation that Nietzsche interjects his critical question, what do we need the *re*-presentation for, why the 'mirror'? Now, Freud gives us an answer! *Re-presentation* helps us retrieve from unconscious memory the world as *a thing of the past*, strictly, as a *no-thing*. As the word facilitates this retrieval, it re-activates past perceptions, in such a way that unconscious memories of past perceptions become conscious as *present hallucinations*: assisted by the word, we 'see' the absent past. This particular 'seeing' of the past is what conventionally we call 'remembrance,' while in Freud's stricter vocabulary, and granted the mutual exclusivity of memory and consciousness, it represents 'consciousness,' since we are seeing, in *conscious presence*, the absent past. We note that since we are never consciously engaged in contemplating our totality of linguistic competencies, the conventional replacements of words for things are mostly pre-conscious. However, pre-conscious material surfaces without distortion as conscious thought-processes. Therefore the two strata are separated by a bar that offers virtually no resistance to the ego's attempt to cognize pre-conscious material (we recall that in *The Interpretation of Dreams* the two systems are regularly represented as a single Pre-conscious/Conscious-system; the so-called *Pcs/Cs*-system). The conscious-system (the *Bews*-system, according to Freud's line) is therefore merely an extension of the pre-conscious (*Vb*).

3.5.3. From Ego-Cluster to Semantic Ego-Cluster.

We understand that in Freud's three neuron-systems (*phi, psi,* and *omega*) language-acquisition would belong in the *omega-interpreter-system*. It is first with the development of an 'Ego' (which we believe is in fact the development of a 'cluster' of egos) that language emerges.

Ego-clusters are seen here as accounting for the individual's first appropriation of the world, the individual's first *interpretation*, insofar as the ego that evolves makes the world, always, *mine*. However, this *my-world* is *private* and cannot be communicated before conventional signs are attached to ego-clusters, in this giving them linguistic meaning, and therefore transforming them into, what we may call, *semantic* ego-clusters. When language attaches itself to *ego-clusters* and transforms these into *semantic ego-clusters*, the human animal becomes conscious and self-aware.

The semantic ego-cluster is a *word-presentation* for a *thing-presentation*. When it represents a *thing-presentation*, rather than a *thing*, it does not represent the thing merely in the thing's own concrete thing-like appearance – like a mirror (or a photo) represents a thing – it instead represents the thing as existing in inner-mental life, that is, in its totality of *associative aspects*. That is, it represents the thing (as the nodal point) plus all the associations it gives off to me personally (as radiating from this nodal point). The difference between an apple as a thing and as a thing-presentation could be something like this: whereas the apple *as thing* is merely an entity (with extension, solidity, size, color, smell, etc.), the apple *as thing-presentation* would involve also my knowledge of, and my associations related to, the apple: as an edible substance; as the texture of its meat; as tasting better when ripe than not; as rotting quickly without skin; as Adam and Eve's apple; as Newton's apple subject to the laws of gravity; as in a recipe for that apple-cake; as picking apples that summer-day many years ago . . . etc. So, the thing plus the associations it gives off is what we call a *thing-presentation*, and it is equivalent to Nietzsche's inner world of becoming. As such, a *thing-presentation* is a multitude and multiplicity, or, as we have said all along, a cluster, a net of interrelated locations.

Now, the *word* is the simplification of this cluster. With the introduction of language, the multiplicity becomes *as if* a singularity. The nodal point, plus the totality of its associations, becomes *as if* wrapped up in a single word. The relationship is best rendered if one simply pictures a cluster as a complex net, and then above the net a label naming it. This attachment of a word to the thing-presentation, we now call a *word-presentation*. We see it as equivalent to Nietzsche's stabilization of the inner world of becoming.

With the emergence of word-presentations, we are able to communicate, but without being able to communicate our deepest and most private selves, since the word has truncated our private lives into some crude average. More precisely: when the word as *signifier* is attached to the ego-cluster, it *deflates* the cluster, and in its place we get a new artificial and fictitious entity called a *signified*, some rough *idea* often conceived to be related to the signifier in a one-to-one (denotative) relationship. The relationship between *signifier* and *signified* is arbitrary, says linguistics, but so is the relationship between *signified* and *thing-presentation*. (E.g., we have the signifier 'love'; as *thing-presentation* nobody knows what it is; but as the *fictitious signified* everybody knows what it is; 'everybody knows' the fictitious signified because they know the sign it is bound up with; 'everybody knows' what the four-letter word 'love' *conventionally means*, its *denotation*, or what it *stands for* in the conventions of our language. However, this does not contradict that they have virtually no idea of what a complex of private associations, emotions, feelings, desires, etc., that this four-letter word *connotes* to the subject in its instance of enunciation, i.e., what is the *private meaning* of the speaking subject.)

Because of these states of affairs, it is often also difficult to understand what people (or we to ourselves) *genuinely mean*. The word does not reveal this *private meaning* (although it is supposed to give us some direction), because *private meaning* floats around as unspoken associations under the Teutonic plates of our language. And here, no word or sentence is sufficiently refined or multifaceted to hit the exact right nerve or nuance. In some sense, we seem to live our lives in an *excess of inner meaning*, but with *a deficit of words*, always unable to *explain* ourselves. Paradoxically, language enables us to communicate between ourselves, but disables us in communicating ourselves. The cataclysm of the Tower of Babel, the confusion of tongues, starts as early as in any single individual's language-use. It emerges from the rift and chasm between *private, 'inner,' meaning* and *conventional meaning*; it emerges because we do not have a *private language* corresponding to our *private meanings*.

Language is like the crust of our earth. It appears solid, but it is only skin-deep. On closer inspection, our 'Teutonic plates' are merely a number of shallow sheets floating about on a fluid core; a core so extremely hot, that we cannot touch it.

Part II

Toward a 'Biological-Linguistic' Nietzschean subject

4. Fundamentals in the Constitution of a Biological-Linguistic Subject[321]

4.1. On the Constitution of the Experience of Identity.

After this introduction to Freud's neurological writings, we now understand that the perceived identity of a *thing* is conditional upon the coincidence of *memory* and *impression*. Granted that the impression does not arrive in our mind as something absolutely novel, the *impression* will always activate or recall a *menmic image*, which – at least in its main components, its 'gestalt' or 'schema' – will match the impression, and as such secure that the impression will be *recognized* and *identified* as this or that, as such *perceived* as this or that.

In Nietzsche too, it is explicit that identity cannot be established without the *aid of memory*, cf., "an identical case . . . presupposes comparison with the aid of memory":

> Judgment – this is the belief: "This and this is so." Thus, there is in every judgment the assertion of having encountered an 'identical case': *it therefore presupposes comparison with the aid of memory*. The judgment does not produce the appearance of an identical case. It rather believes it perceives one; it works under the assumption that identical cases exist. (Nachlaß 1885, KSA 11, 40[15]; italics added).

In producing identical cases like in logic, one freezes the moment, renders the world as still-life, and recognizes *unity* in the world of flux. In general, humans cannot know a world of *becoming*, they can only know what *is*.

---

[321] We find several introductions to Nietzsche's theory of consciousness and subjectivity. Already mentioned are Abel, Günter: Nietzsche, loc. cit.; Schlimgen, Erwin: Nietzsches Theorie, loc. cit., and Emden, Christian: Nietzsche on Language, loc. cit. Very readable is also the earlier work of Grimm, Herman Rudiger: Nietzsche's Theory of Knowledge (Berlin/New York: Walter de Gruyter, 1977), and the two first volumes of Müller-Lauter's *Nietzsche-Interpretationen*: Müller-Lauter, Wolfgang: Über Werden und Wille zur Macht, loc. cit., and Über Freiheit und Chaos: Nietzsche-Interpretationen II. Berlin, New York (Walter de Gruyter), 1999.

4. Fundamentals in the Construction of a Biological-Linguistic Subject

They can therefore only know the image of this frozen world. This knowable world that *is*, will now appear as an aggregation of *things* (not as ever-changing forces and processes floating about in eternal becoming).

It is this *thing*, we *recognize* or *judge* to be *self-identical* (applying the meta-logical law, $A = A$) thanks to our rapid and spontaneous unconscious comparisons between *perceptive* and *memorized* images. If a perceived series of impressions, $a \ldots b \ldots c$, corresponds to a memorized series, $a' \ldots b' \ldots c'$, we *judge* that they are *identical*. This theory of the constitution of entity/identity makes three important assumptions: We assume (i) that we encounter 'stuff' (not yet constituted as 'thing') as a complex of impressions; thereupon (ii) this complex is nested in memory; and finally (iii) when the same complex of impressions are repeated in a new encounter as the same, the psyche has a comparison-background thanks to its memory-traces, and the new encounter results in some kind of pre-conscious *'Aha!'* experience ('Aha, I have seen this before!'). The psyche has compared the complex nested in memory with the complex encountered, and notices identity – consequently, a 'thing' has been constituted. In is as such we stabilize the world, and this stable and unchangeable world becomes now our matrix for what eventually we will come to call *truth*, where *truth* in this rudimentary biological sense is that which *is* (i.e., that which is identical to itself), contrary to the sensation-chaos that impresses itself upon us (both from the outside and the inside).

This drive to posit things as equal and self-identical is the precondition for logic as explicitly stated in Nietzsche:

> Let us suppose that there were no self-identical [*sich-selbst-identische*] A, such as every proposition of logic (and mathematics) presupposes, and the A were merely a p p e a r a n c e, then logic would have a merely a p p a r e n t world as its condition. In fact, we believe in this proposition under the influence of an endless empirical world which seems continually to c o n f i r m it. The 'thing' – that is the real substratum of A: o u r b e l i e f i n t h i n g s is the precondition for our belief in logic. The A of logic is, like the atom, a reconstruction of the 'thing' . . . If we do not understand this, but make logic a criterion for true being, we are already positing as realities all those hypostates: substance, attribute, object, subject, action, etc.; that is, conceiving a metaphysical world, that is, a "real world" (– b u t t h i s i s o n l y t h e a p p a r e n t w o r l d once more). (Nachlaß 1887, KSA 12, 9[97], p. 389-90).

In a logical statement, we presuppose that something is A (therefore is a *substance*); and that A is identical to itself (therefore is *self-identical*); and that A and non-A cannot be asserted in the same proposition (therefore is *consistent*). These are founding rules for logic, without which logic would not exist. Without asserting an A understood as identical to itself, it would for human beings be *impossible to think* – but that means: *impossible to live, to advance, and to excel*. The invention of the self-identical is therefore life-preserving, and it is so-called 'true' *because* it is life-preserving. Logic, as "will to equality," is therefore also *will to power*:

> The Spirit w a n t s equality; that is, to subsume sense-impressions under an already existing series. [. . .] Toward an understanding of L o g i c : t h e w i l l t o e q u a l i t y i s t h e w i l l t o p o w e r . – The belief, that something is so and so, this is the essence of j u d g m e n t, it is a consequence of a will that as much as possible o u g h t to be equal. (Nachlaß 1885/86, KSA 12, 2[90]).

> One should not understand this need to form concepts, classes, forms, purposes, laws – "This world of Identical cases" – as if this fixation of the true world is the state of affairs; but rather see it as a need to arrange a world, whereby our existence becomes possible – we create as such a world, which is predictable, simplified, comprehensible, etc., for us. (Nachlaß 1887, KSA 12, 9[144]).

> Will to power a s k n o w l e d g e : Not to know" [*nicht "erkennen"*], but to schematize, to impose as much regularity and form on chaos as necessary for our practical needs. In the image of reason, logic, and categories this requirement has become decisive: the need, not to "know" [*"erkennen"*], but rather to subsume, to schematize, to aim the understanding, to calculate . . . to arrange, to produce something similar and equal – the same process that permeates all sense-impressions, also develops reason. (Nachlaß 1888; KSA 13, 14[152])

> There is in us a power to order, simplify, falsify, artificially distinguish. 'Truth' is the will to be master over the multiplicity of sensations – to classify phenomena into definite categories. [. . .] The character of the world in a state of becoming as incapable of formulation, as false. Knowledge and becoming exclude one another. (WM 517).

In Nietzsche's genealogical analyzes of the origin of knowledge from FW (cf. FW 110, 111, & 354), we can isolate three distinct stages in human evolution. At a *first stage*, Nietzsche presupposes a prehistory where the hominid is still more animal than human; it does not yet know how to abstract, classify, categorize, or schematize. We assume that to this early human everything is foreground; flowers, livestock, predators, etc., are not yet identified as belonging to *generic categories*. Each time behold, flora and fauna appear in their own wondrous individuality. However, in this hypothetical prehistory, the lack of scheme and concept gives the early human an evolutionary *disadvantage*, and those humans that eventually develop an intellectual capacity for abstraction will get a selective *advantage*. This up-

4. Fundamentals in the Construction of a Biological-Linguistic Subject

graded hominid would thus occupy Nietzsche's *second stage*. At a certain point in prehistory certain humans – the quick-minded, the shallow, the superficial, those who paint the world "with the broadest brush" (FW 354) – start to schematize, that is, falsify. They presuppose that "there are enduring things; that there are equal things; that there are things, substances, bodies; that a thing is what it appears to be; that our will is free; that what is good is good in itself." (FW 110, KSA 3, p. 469).

In his analysis, Nietzsche takes for granted that originally humans are not rational or logical beings. Logic comes about because of evolutionary expediencies. Our hypothetical humans were originally living adhering only to immediate instincts (and – to Nietzsche's mind – they were living a happier, more wholesome, existence; marveling at this never-ending sensation-overflow). Still, out of necessity, our early hominid had to adopt a conceptual and logical perspective on the world.

> The Origin of the Logical. – How did logic develop in man's head? Certainly from the illogical, the realm of which must originally have been immense. [. . .] He, for instance, who did not know how to find 'identity' often enough, both with regard to nourishment and to hostile animals, he who subsumed too slowly and was too cautious in subsuming, had a slighter probability of survival than he who in all cases of similarity immediately guessed that they were identical. (FW 111, KSA 3, p. 471).

Paradoxically, these superior survivors are better at producing falsehoods about their surrounding world than are their kin. They simplify and narrow down the world "in order for the concept of substance to originate, which is indispensable to logic though nothing real corresponds to it in the strictest sense. It was necessary that for a long time changes in things not be seen, not be perceived; the beings who did not see things exactly had a head start over those who saw everything 'in a flux.'" (FW 111, KSA 3, p. 471).

Logic can as such be seen as resulting from certain basic *errors*, which nonetheless the human species necessarily had to cultivate for the sake of survival. To see the world roughly, without much sense of detail, as a crude approximation, *this was rewarded* with survival. In Nietzsche's universe, it is the quick and superficial who survive, while the cautious and conscientious die out. Although these shallow-minded 'falsify' the world by throwing a net of crudity over the world of becoming, they become superior in this early world. Their truths narrow down the world, but their truths are needed; their superficiality and shallowness make strong; they liberate themselves from the contingencies of reality; they take control over a world in fluctuation.

It is only at the *third stage*, we encounter the Nietzschean crisis. Here we find the entry of metaphysics and religion: the beginning of a *self-conscious belief* in truth. In this later stage, pursuit of truth becomes an intellectual occupation, reserved for philosophers and priests. The last two stages are summarized in the following passage.

> It was only very late that truth emerged – as the weakest form of knowledge. It seemed that one was unable to live with it: our organism was prepared for the opposite; all its higher functions, sense perception and every kind of sensation worked with those basic errors which had been incorporated since time immemorial. [. . .] Gradually, the human brain became full of such judgments and convictions, and [. . .] every kind of impulse took sides in this fight about 'truths.' The intellectual fight became an occupation, an attraction, a profession, a duty, something dignified – and eventually knowledge and the striving for the true found their place as a need among other needs. (FW 110, KSA 3, p. 470-471).

In this conception, the emergence of 'truth' and the opposition 'true versus false,' is in all cases dependent on an evolutionary prehistory. 'Truth' is originally equivalent to what preserves and advances life, and this original content is preserved in modern concepts of truth, albeit in adumbrated forms. In Nietzsche, 'true' and 'false' are no longer abstract and universal qualities: instead, what preserves and advances life *is called* 'true,' and what obstructs and impedes life *is called* 'false.' Some of our strongest theoretical disciplines (like mathematics and physics) are therefore *called* 'true,' not because they are true in a universal and absolute sense, but because they are indispensable for our life-preservation and life-advancement.

> The valuation "I believe, that this or that is like this" is the essence of truth.
> In valuations, *we express preservations- and growth-conditions*.
> All our cognitive and sensual organs *have evolved with regard to preservations and growth conditions*.
> The faith in reason and its categories, in dialectics, that is, *the valuation of logic only proves its utility for life, evidenced through experience*: but not its "truth". (Nachlaß 1887, KSA 12, 9[38]; italics added).

> The world, which is of any concern to us, is false; that is, it is no fact, but rather a poetic invention [*Ausdichtung*] and rounding up from a meager amount of observations; it is "in flow" [*"im Flusse"*]; as something becoming; as an always novel moving falsity, which never come closer to the truth: therefore – there is no "truth". (Nachlaß 1886-87, KSA 12, 2[108]).

4. Fundamentals in the Construction of a Biological-Linguistic Subject

To see identity, equality, substance in that which is fluctuation and becoming: this is the foundation for logic. "Without granting as true the fictions of logic, without measuring reality against the purely invented world of the unconditional and self-identical, without a continual falsification of the world by means of numbers, mankind could not live." (JGB 4, KSA 5, p. 18).[322] When Nietzsche states that we must "grant as true the fictions of logic"; that "mankind could not live" without the fictions of logic, the statement (superficially read) appears to be paradoxical. We apparently read, 'the fictions of logic are true!' – and it is only natural to ask, 'so, are they *true* or are they *fictions*?' However, the statement makes sense because Nietzsche presupposes two different comparison-backgrounds for the statement: against the background of chaos, *logic is fiction*; but against the background of human survival and advancement, *logic is true*. His concept of 'truth' is, as we tend to say in the 20th century, *pragmatic*; it is not an absolute value, but is designed to fit different social, historical, and intellectual circumstances.[323]

In the following passage, logic is for example understood as 'fiction,' because in this particular context, logic is judged against the comparison-background of *chaos*.

> The logical thinking, which logic talks about, is a thinking where one thought is seen as the origin [*Ursache*] of a new thought – , this is the image of a complete fiction: a thinking of that kind does in fact never occur; it is instead coming about through form-schemas and filtering-apparatuses, by the help of which we water down and simplify the actual, incredibly variegated, event through think-

---

[322] Also in Freud, logic derives from biological necessity: "In what do *logical faults* consist? Stated briefly, in the non-observance of the *biological rules* for the passage of thought. These rules lay down where it is that the cathexis of attention is to be directed each time and when the thought-process is to come to a stop. They are protected by threats of unpleasure, they are derived from experience, and they can be transposed directly into the rules of logic – which will have to be proved in detail. Thus the intellectual unpleasure of contradiction, at which the passage of testing thought come to a stop, is nothing other than the [unpleasure] accumulated for the protection of the biological rules, which is stirred up by an incorrect thought-process. *The existence of biological rules of this kind can in fact be proved from the feeling of unpleasure at logical faults*." Freud: *Project for a Scientific Psychology*, loc. cit., p. 386.

[323] We find this pragmatic-perspectival-historicist notion of truth not only in Pragmatism in the thinking of the 20th century, but also in Hermeneutics, in some Theory of Science (notably Thomas Kuhn; and to some degree, Karl Popper), and in much post-Structuralism, most obviously in Michel Foucault.

ing: so that we herewith make our thinking comprehensible in signs, apparent and communicable. (Nachlaß 1885, KSA 11, 38[2]).

Nietzsche's basic assumption is that originally, we live in something we may call a *chaosmos*; however, out of this *chaosmos*, we create a *cosmos*. In the original *chaosmos*, identity does not exist; but we necessarily 'invent' something as identical to itself (according to the mechanism above); and this self-identity becomes a foundation for logic – since otherwise, we cannot assert *propositions, cannot think.*

In these statements about the genesis and origin of the equal and self-identical, it is obviously not Nietzsche's recommendation that we should try to dispense with this falsified world (not that we actually could, even if we wanted). Our historical 'will-to-truth,' 'will-to-order,' 'will-to-equality,' is, firstly, too deeply ingrained and rooted, and, secondly, these wills are all variations over the all-pervasive 'will-to-power.' We *will* truth and knowledge, because we *will* power over reality. We *crave* control, and we *subject* reality to our will, because we want to *take possession of*, to *appropriate*, reality as *our own*.[324] When reading Nietzsche, one must never underestimate, nor explain away, his affirmation of this fundamental human aggression in every of its projects.

4.2. On the Constitution of the Sense and Evaluation of Reality.

We have sufficiently explained above how our sensory system *filters* and *falsifies* received stimuli; per biological constitution, it screens an always too abundant external reality. These 'falsifying filters' make up a *first defensive layer* against too many stimuli – against 'too much reality,' as we say.

As a *second defensive layer* against *too much reality*, we saw above that Freud introduced his so-called *omega-interpreter-system* (ω). The *omega-*

---

[324] We go about our being-in-the-world-as-becoming much like when, in a typical IQ-test, we are asked to find identical forms imbedded in a number of images, which superficially seem to be only a confusion of lines. First, we see nothing, but soon we start noticing a pattern imbedded in and repeated as the same in all the images. In what is originally chaotic, we have found *identity* and *repetition* of identity. This is how we re-create a *world of becoming* as a *world of being*. We gaze at an original confusion of 'lines' and start gradually to detect a structure; we gaze into nothingness and start seeing patterns; we gaze at a cloud, and start recognizing human shapes – although the cloud, *in-and-for-itself*, is both in-human and shapeless.

interpreter-system had several functions in Freud, all of which were in some way or other related to *consciousness*; but although we can establish this much, the different functions often seemed type-different, without their differences being sufficiently elaborated by Freud. In relation to Nietzsche, its three most important functions seem to be the following: (i) When the system interacts with the *psi-memory-system* (ψ), it establishes *something as something*; in this capacity, a current sensation is cross-checked against the memory of a similar sensation, and is thus being established as *so and so*; it is being recognized and *seen*. This recapitulates how we above explained the precondition for *recognizing identity*. In this capacity, the *omega-interpreter-system* is a reformulation of Nietzsche's 'mirror,'[325] and his contention that identity "presupposes comparison with the aid of memory" (cf. Nachlaß 1885, KSA 11, 40[15]). The conception also implies a criticism of the projection-theory, according to which an *impression* simply arrive into the mental apparatus in order to nest itself there as *idea* (according to, most obviously, John Locke). (ii) Besides being accountable of what is consciously seen, the *omega-system* also has the job to provide, says Freud, 'indications of reality' (or 'reality-signs' [*Realitätszeichen*]). Not only does the subject need to screen external reality, it also needs to screen the *presentations of internal reality*. Not only does the subject suffer under 'too much' external reality, it suffers also from 'too much' internal reality. The subject has to learn that *mnemic images* are not real and offer no satisfaction in and of themselves. It must be able to distinguish *between reality and hallucination*, i.e., between representations that are real and representations that are false. Nietzsche's *chaos*, applied to inner-mental life, is identical to Freud's *hallucinations*. In order for this inner chaos to be subdued, the system must be able to establish a basic distinction between *true* or *false*. However, in this neurological context, the 'true' is simply determined as what is not my hallucination, while the 'false' is my hallucination. Like in the section above, we can still see 'the true' as a correspondence between a perceived series, *a . . . b . . . c*, and a memorized series, *a' . . . b' . . . c'*. However, in inner-mental life 'the true' must see itself as in perpetual *competition* with the un-true, the hallucination, when particularly well-cathected memory-traces (for example in the form of *desire* or *hatred*), without any corresponding 'indications of reality,' take over the control of perception.[326] (iii)

---

[325] Cf., Nietzsche: FW 354.

[326] Our perceptions are often under the direction of what we desire or hate. One does not need to be psychotic in order to perceive 'falsely' the world around. For example, I desire this woman, and now I desire her desire; I believe I see 'indications of reality' of this desire; I believe that a certain behavior, e.g., a smile, on her part, is an indication of the reality of her desire. But there was

Finally, the system has the task to impress upon representations a value, either *good or bad*. Since these processes are still pre-linguistic, we notice that our psychical system starts to *interpret* the world *before* language is introduced into the system. In Freud, as in Nietzsche, the *interpretive processes* are always primary, and the *linguistic processes* secondary.[327] In this neurological explanation of the important and celebrated dichotomies, *true versus false* and *good versus bad*, everything comes down to self-preservation: 'true' is what aids my perception of the real, and 'good' is what aids my personal survival (– or as Nietzsche sometimes paraphrases the view, "what is good for me, is good"). In this biological context, the 'good' and the 'bad' derive from the evolutionary earlier distinction between 'friendly object' and 'hostile object.' It was necessary for survival to establish the sight of a lion quickly as *true (= real)*, and then quickly as *bad (= hostile)*, in order for our prehistoric ancestor to flee from and escape its claws. 'True' and 'false,' 'good' and 'bad,' were originally merely distinctions necessary for survival.

If senses *simplify*, and if they assert something as *true and false*, and something as *good and bad*, they originally do so out of evolutionary neces-

---

[327] really nothing. I was deluded. My desire lead me on. It constructed an illusory memorized series that only too readily and eagerly took over the control of my perception, and I started to 'see' things that were not really there.

Notice that this view is fully compatible with the way we understand animals. Also animals have to screen the world for what is important for their survival benefits and what is not. Also animals have a sense of reality, and do not confuse imaginary prey and real prey, but start charging only when something is *real*. Also animals have a sense of 'good' or 'bad' – they distinguish quickly predator from prey; and discern quickly a rival in the hierarchical order of their pack. Animals, in other words, *interpret* the world in *pre-linguistic processes*; we do not believe that they *articulate* this interpretation and understanding in a propositional language. This is extremely strong evidence for our general contention: *interpretation-processes precede linguistic processes*. The view is corroborated by Günter Abel. Like myself, Abel is not diminishing the importance of linguistic processes, but he emphasizes the primacy of interpretive processes: "The interpretive functions form the foundation of the sign-functions, not the other way around. [. . .] Linguistic and propositional symbols are far from the only means available for mental, imaginary [*vorstellungsmäßigen*] representation and presentation. A general theory of human consciousness, mind, thinking, and action must require the inclusion also of *non-linguistic* as well as *non-propositional sign- and interpretations-systems*. [. . .] Interpretation is the condition for successful linguistic and non-linguistic uses of signs, not an option." Abel, Günter: "Bewußtsein – Sprache – Natur. Nietzsches Philosophie des Geistes,." loc. cit., p. 38-39

4. Fundamentals in the Construction of a Biological-Linguistic Subject

sity. It was never necessary for humans to build up a memory-system retaining all possible data of the outside world; it was necessary to evolve a much simpler system that could for example crudely distinguish between trees that yielded edible fruits and trees that did not. It was also necessary to learn what is *real*, subduing and restraining a mental (*hallucinatory*) system, having a tendency to wander off, and escape into its own cozy world of fantasies. The subject needed to acquire an ability to distinguish between 'false' and 'true' – *hallucinatory* representations and *perceptive* representations. The subject needed to learn to fight off its inner chaos, and evolve a psyche under the auspices of *will-to-power*. Under the rule of *will-to-power*, hallucinations were no longer allowed to run wild and unchecked, in order to discharge in futile action. Instead, they were absorbed into well-consolidated ego-clusters; configurations of knowledge essential for survival.

We notice in passing that on such an evolutionary theory of knowledge, the classical distinction between Materialism and Idealism – and the aporetic problems it over several centuries has generated in the theories of knowledge – have evaporated. If "our cognitive and perceptive organs have evolved only in regard to conditions for preservation and growth" (Nachlaß 1887, KSA 12, 9[38]), then the human system has evolved to *respond to*, and *adjust itself to*, an *external* world, whether or not the human system has an exact 'corresponding' perception of this external world. The human system evolves to take control over a *real and tangible* reality, because, as well as animals did not (see footnote above), humans did not and could not have evolved in a 'world of ideas' (see also *Section 5.2* below). In the form of will-to-power the human being, "makes itself master of [reality], in order to appropriate it in its service":

> The usefulness [*nützlichkeit*] of preservation [...] is the motive behind the development of the cognitive organs [*Erkenntnißorgane*] [...] they developed in such a way that their attention were sufficient for our preservation. In other words: the degree of will to knowledge [*Erkennenvollens*] depends on the degree to which this sort of will-to-power grows: this sort comprehends as much reality as it takes to make itself master of it, in order to appropriate it in its service. (Nachlaß 1888; KSA 13, 14[122]).

It is as such value-tables are "necessary for life" – as Nietzsche keeps reiterating. In his genealogical analyses, Nietzsche arrives to a precise understanding of this origin of the two celebrated dichotomies: *true and false*, and *good and bad*.

4.3. On the Constitution of the Experience of Causality.

4.3.1. Causality as Humanization.

As an example of a causality-judgment, let us return to Nietzsche's, *lightning flashes* (cf. *Chapter 2*). In Hume, Kant, and Nietzsche we find significantly different explanations of how two concepts are combined or 'synthesized' in a causality-judgment like Nietzsche's example above, *lightning is causing flashing*.

In Hume, the combination is contingent and associative. This means that it is impossible to derive logically one concept from the other. If logical identity between the two concepts is excluded, but the two concepts are nonetheless presented as combined, the binding must come about for other reasons. This Hume sees as the empirical association of the two concepts. The binding of the two concepts is grounded in experience: *"What is the foundation of all our reasonings and conclusions concerning that relation* [the relation of cause and effect]? It may be replied in one word. EXPERIENCE."[328] So, repeated experience of the association of lightning and flashing teaches us that lightning is *always* associated to flashing, and impresses therefore upon the subject the erroneous belief that a causality-relation between lighting and flashing is an objectively existent nexus. However, Hume contends, the causality-relation comes about only because of the experiencing human, and not because of a supposed objective nexus between the lighting and the flashing; the causality-relation does not inhere in nature itself. Admittedly, two distinct concepts are combined, and the judgment is *synthetic*, but since the combination is induced from contingent experiences and therefore never implies universality and necessity, the judgment is only *a posteriori*, never *a priori*.

Although Kant agrees with Hume that the binding between lightning and flashing cannot be logically inferred, and furthermore, that the causality-relation is also not constituted in the world understood as thing-in-itself, he will argue that on the level of phenomena, the relation is still objective, universal, and necessary; i.e., *a priori*. Thanks to his tribunal of transcendental categories, the judgment is not merely constituted contingently in the experiencing human, but is endowed with universality and necessity. The predicate of the judgment (*flashing*) adds a knowledge to the subject (*lightning*), according to a transcendental rule (*causality*), which transgresses the merely contingent, and makes the judgment universally valid in the world of phenomena. From now on, we can know with certainty that in

---

[328] David Hume: An Enquiry Concerning Human Understanding, loc. cit., p. 20.

4. Fundamentals in the Construction of a Biological-Linguistic Subject

the world of appearances (the only world we know) flashing always follows lightning.

Nietzsche's analysis of the causality-judgment has a first immediate family-resemblance to that of Hume's. Also to Nietzsche, it is *habit or convention*, rather than categories, that creates the impression that some event follows from another. However, the experience of causal relationships, and the inclination to ascribe causality relations to things, is not simply generated because events are repeated in a given order and with a certain regularity, but because they are always understood as *human*, and thus being *humanized*; that is, they are interpreted *as if* following from a will or an intention. The idea is explicit in the following passage (where Nietzsche also pays homage to Hume):

> In every judgment is presupposed a fundamental belief in subject and predicate or in cause and effect; and this last belief (that is, the claim that every effect is an activity, and every activity presupposes an actor) is even an exceptional case of the first, so that the fundamental belief left over is: there are subjects [*es giebt Subjekte*].
> I notice something and seek a ground/reason [*Grund*] for it: this means originally: I seek an intention in it [...] in all activities we see intentions, all activity is a doing [*Thun*]. This is our oldest habit [...].
> Therefore, Hume is fundamentally right, habit (but not only the habit of the individual) makes us expect that a certain often perceived succession follows from another: nothing else. What gives us extraordinary belief in causality is not just the habit of seeing a repetition of events, but our inability to interpret an event as anything but an event from intentions. (Nachlaß 1885-86, KSA 12, 2[83]).

To "see intentions in activities," this is "our oldest habit"; this is as such a habit older than Hume's 'habit.' Nietzsche agrees with Hume and Kant that humans *experience* causality-relations; however, their 'experience' comes about because of a fundamental falsification of the reality they experience. *In truth*, there is no causality-relation; no objective nexus between cause and effect; but humans can do no better than apply themselves and their standards on this foreign world. They apply their sense of subjectivity (which, as argued in the previous chapter, is always linguistically constituted) as it manifests itself in the subject-predicate logic of the language in which they are embedded. They take the grammatical structure of this language as their general explanation-matrix for activities in the world. From what is nearest to humans, their language, they deduce intentions and purposes in a world of indifferent events and activities. In-themselves, events are indifferent, indistinguishable, and continuous, but now they are, in a rudimentary sense, being separated into subject and predicate, actor and action, 'doer' and 'deed,' mover and moved, or first and second. In nature (*in truth*), there is no first and no second; there is a continuum, which is only as an after-effect being sequenced. The causality-relation is applied to the continuum, and events are now distinguished according to a subject-predicate, actor-action, matrix.

> On "Causality"
> It is immediately obvious that as little as things-in-themselves can form a relationship of cause and effect with each other, as little can appearances with appearances [form such a relationship. PB]: from which it follows that the notion "cause and effect" – in a philosophy that believes in things-in-themselves and appearances – is unusable [nicht anwendbar ist]. Kant's error –. Actually, the notion of cause and effect derives, examined psychologically, only from a way of thinking, which always and everywhere believes in will from an effecting will, – [a way of thinking. PB] which only believes in life and essentially only in "souls" (and not in things) [. . .] The continued succession [Aufeinanderfolge] of certain appearances proves no 'law,' but only a power-relationship between two or more forces. [. . .] The separation of "activity" from "actor", of the occurrence of something from something that brings about the occurrence, of processes from something that is not process, but rather endurance, substance, thing, body, soul, etc., is – the attempt to comprehend the occurrence as a kind of displacement and stand-in for something "existing" ["*Seienden*"], for something enduring [*Bleibendem*]: this old mythology has implanted a belief in "cause and effect" insofar as it has found a stable form in the grammatical functions of language. (Nachlaß 1885-86, KSA 12, 2[139]).

In Kant, the causality-sense comes about because of a 'category' – the category of causality. This category, as a part of human organization and constitution, is a form, which we cannot but apply to appearances. In Nietzsche, there are no such 'forms' in our subject-constitution responsible for the so-called causality-sense. If or when such a 'sense' emerges it is (1) thanks to our drive to humanize, and (2) thanks to the application of a grammatical logic immanent in language. Humans apply ideal linguistic rules to nature, *as if nature is also language*. The application is unconscious, and it has the effect that not only is nature pre-reflectively 'understood' as language, it has also pre-reflectively been endowed with intention, will, and even reason.

Therefore, in Nietzsche's analysis of our paradigmatic example, *lighting flashes*, his position is more radical than is Hume's. He agrees with Hume that there is (*in truth*) no cause-effect relationship between the two events; but moreover, he contends that *there are no two events* in the first place, no separation between a first and a second. His radical position is that '*lighting flashes'* is in fact *one* event, which only artificially has been divided into two according to subject-predicate logic. One and the same event – we might label it *'light-flashing'* – is now seen as first subject and then as predicate, and now reinvented as a cause-effect relation. One and the same deed becomes a "deed-deed" or a "double-deed":

> People essentially double the deed when they make the lightning flash; it is a deed-deed; it posits the same occurrence first as cause and then again as its effect. The scientists are no better, when they say 'the force moves, the force causes,' etc. (GM I, 13, KSA 5, p. 279). [. . .] When I say that the lightning flashes, then I have first taken the lightning as an activity, and then as a subject. (Nachlaß 1885-86, KSA 12, 2[84]).)

We shall allow ourselves to recapitulate the important consequences of this thinking (already outlined in *Chapter 2*). A world, which is only *one*, is interpreted to be *two*. One doubles the world in first, an *actor*, and then, an *action*, as the way and manner by which humans humanize an inherently inhuman world. Behind appearances, there is now supposedly a will, an intention, a reason, or a purpose. In any case, one assumes that the world must have a hidden double, something that gives it meaning and explains it.[329]

In the world as continuum or hyper-reality, there is only 'light-flashing'; that is, the zigzag exploding on the background of the black sky. When this zigzag is divided according to subject-predicate logic, as first an actor and then an action, we can in effect enter into a kind of *dialogue* with the zig-

---

[329] Also Lange, and other contemporary 19th century theorists, espouse the idea of scientific notions being 'personifications,' and explain the mechanism according to a logic that Nietzsche eventually adopts and reiterates, the subject-predicate logic: "Our 'tendency to personification,' or, if we use Kant's phrase, what comes to the same thing, the *category of substance*, compels us always to conceive one of these ideas as subject, the other as predicate." Lange: *A History of Materialism*, loc. cit., 2nd book, 2nd section, p. 379. We also find a reference to subject-predicate logic in Eduard von Hartmann. In general, one may find several of Nietzsche's insights in Hartmann's *Philosophie des Unbewußten*, but they are usually introduced haphazardly in his voluminous writing, as if he is not clear about their implications. They are usually also not developed in any systematic manner. "The notion of the judgment is unquestionably abstracted from the grammatical sentence by the omission of the verbal form. The categories of substance and accident are derived in the same way from subject and predicate; the discovery of a corresponding natural antitheses of substantive and verb is still an unsolved, perhaps a very fruitful philosophical problem." Hartmann, Eduard von: Philosophie des Unbewußtsen, Bd. 1. Berlin (Carl Dunckers Verlag), 1870; p. 240.

zag. Tacitly, the assumption of an intention has been introduced into the flash, and we can ask, 'what intention?' Now we believe that something must be 'doing' the flashing, and we determine this 'doer' as lightning. As 'linguistizised' and 'logicizised,' the world is therefore 'humanized'; it has become like a friend, with whom we can – with a little patience – conduct a conversation. It is possible for us to ask lightning the pertinent question: why are you doing such a flashing? The *why* can only be asked if there is more to the zigzag than the zigzag; language postulates this additional layer. Now, we also have the right to expect a reasonable answer (which would materialize as some scientific explanation of this particular behavior; as argued earlier, this doubling of the world is a formal requirement for the *foundation* of science).

The phenomenon on the sky is in other words no longer a randomized continuum, but a *rational behavior*. Nature is no longer blind, deaf, and mute, but loquacious. Suddenly, the zigzag has intention.[330] As such, the subject-predicate relationship generates and over-determines, as an unconscious background, the cause-effect relationship. It is as such, there is a much *older habit* behind Hume's *habit*.

In the world of chaos, on the so-called 'Ur-Ground,' there is no cause-effect relationships, but only a randomized continuum, a fluctuation of forces, determined as will-to-power. There is in this universe no hierarchy, no distinction between a first and second, no cause and effect, and, as it were, no 'master' and 'slave.'[331] In the following fragment, Nietzsche brainstorms himself on this idea and its immediate consequences.

---

[330] Müller-Lauter too refers to this Nietzschean example on subject-predicate logic. See Müller-Lauter, Wolfgang: "Whenever we say – to cite one of Nietzsche's favorite examples – 'lightning flashes,' we have within ourselves the "state" of flashing. Yet we don't stop at this, but rather invent an extra cause (the lightning) (KSA 12, 2[84]). Through this reification of the effect we bring about a linguistic 'doubling.'" "On Judging in a World of Becoming" in B. Babich (ed.): Nietzsche, Theories of Knowledge, and Critical Theory loc. cit., p. 168. Also Schlimgen: "In itself [*An sich*] *is* the lightning only *flashing*; but we are impelled infer as if there is an originator [*Urheber*]. This projection *creates* [*setzt*] the division [*Ur-Teilung*], which finds its formal expression in the schema of judgment [*urteilsschema*], S is P." Schlimgen, Erwin: Nietzsches Theorie, loc. cit. p. 124.

[331] Nietzsche's metaphysical vision of the universe seems to have some similarity to the universe of quantum- and relativity-theory. Klaus Spiekemann reads Nietzsche's epistemology in this context. (See Spiekemann, Klaus: Naturwissenschaft als subjektlose Macht? Nietzsches Kritik physikalischer Grundkonzepte. Berlin. New York (Walter de Gruyter), 1992). While it is not the endeavor in this work to compare Nietzsche's epistemology to different

> The Will to Power is in principle
> critique of the concept of "cause"
> I need as point of departure "Will to Power" as the origin of movement. Consequently is the movement not conditioned from the outside – it is not caused [*verursacht*] . . .
> I need movement-beginnings and movement-centers [*Bewegungsansätze und –Centern*], from where the will grasps around
> [. . .]
> Our "understanding of an event" consists in that we in it found a subject, which was responsible for that something happened and how it happened.
> We have condensed our feeling of will, our "feeling of freedom"; our feeling of responsibility and our intention with an action in the concept "cause."
> [. . .]
> There is no causality-sense, as Kant believed
> One wonders, one is anxious, one wants something familiar, which one can hold on to . . .
> As soon as something new is referred back to something old, we are calmed down.
> The so-called causality-instinct is only the fear of the unusual and an attempt to uncover therein something familiar
> A search not for causes but rather for the familiar. (Nachlaß 1888, KSA 13, 14[98])

While Nietzsche does not entirely discard Hume's explanation of causality, humans are in Nietzsche no longer seen as mere *passive recipients* of impressions (as in Hume); they take *active part* in *constructing* causal sequences. However, they do not do so because 'categories' dictate a certain necessary perception of the world (as in Kant), but because of "fear of the unusual." Nietzsche's explanation has turned biological and psychological. When humans have an *active desire* to find causes, it is because they out of "fear" search for the "familiar." Humans are engaged in *active interpretation* perpetually. If I experience an object move, I *actively* start to look for a cause for the movement, and do not put my mind to rest before I have found it – it is more than unsettling, if I cannot find a cause, and the object seems like moving itself (symptomatically, this scenario belongs in horror-movies). If someone displays an unusual behavior, I start to look for a 'cause' that might explain it. If someone utters an incomprehensible remark, I seek to restore the lost meaning, by supplying a plausible 'cause' for the remark. If something unfortunate befalls me, I start to look for a cause that could *explain* why this should happen to *me*, etc. In these and other cases,

---

trends in 20th Century physics, the endeavor still seems justified.

"something new is referred back to something old" and I am "calmed down." We read below, "The fear of the unpredictable is the background-instinct of science":

> What is "knowledge" ["*erkennen*"]? To lead something strange back to something well-known and familiar. First principle: that which we have gotten used to, counts no longer as enigma, as problem. [. . .] Therefore the first instinct in the knowing subject is to seek a rule: while obviously, with the ascertainment of the rule, nothing has been "known" – hence the superstition of the physicists: that which they have halted, that is, where the regularity of the phenomena allows the application of an abbreviating/reductive [*abkürzenden*] formula, that they believe is known [*Erkennt*]. They feel 'secure'; but behind this intellectual security stands the appeasement of their fear: they want the rule, because it disrobes the world of fearfulness. The fear of the unpredictable is the background-instinct of science. (Nachlaß 1886-87; KSA 12, 5[10]).

The bottom-line is that although the world is *in truth* (as we put it) a chaotic Ur-ground, it cannot resist the *interpretive desire of humans*, and it will – given this *relentless interpretive pressure* – eventually 'open' itself up to humans as 'meaning.' At a point, it is being constituted as Human ground: that is, as a falsified and simplified world, essentially obeying our desire to see ourselves *once more* in everything surrounding us.[332]

Let us recall that this idea of the world being 'humanized' is not exclusively Nietzsche's, and on the background of 19th century science, the discussion is far from esoteric. De Bois-Reymond makes the same observations, and Friedrich Lange introduces the discussion in a chapter on "Force and Matter" from his *Geschichte des Materialismus*.[333] In Lange, humanization is introduced under the concepts "personification" and "picturability." For the neo-Kantian, the situation is that something, which can essentially not be represented – which in other words exists as thing-in-itself – neces-

---

[332] It is no different than if one lies down, look up in the sky, and 'put an interpretive pressure' on a cloud above. Eventually, the cloud will 'open' itself, and one will start seeing it as something. As writer, one puts such an 'interpretive pressure' on a blank piece of paper, the result being that soon the paper starts to 'open' itself – as all writers know. One has the suspicion that great writers, writers 'full of confidence and healthy instincts' (if one may here imitate the tone of Nietzsche), always start writing from the blank piece of paper; whereas secondary and insecure writes start writing from the 'library.'

[333] An expanded discussion of Nietzsche's relationship to Lange and physics, one can also find in George Stack's *Lange and Nietzsche*, loc. cit. Especially the chapter "A Force-Point World" is relevant for the present discussion.

sarily must be *personalized* and *pictured* as a concept, familiar enough for the contemporary scientist to work with (therefore Lange's "personification" and "picturability").[334]

---

[334] In 19th Century physics, the concepts one has had of the world for millennia are increasingly becoming inadequate. The confidence one had established in the age of Bacon and Descartes of a mechanical world, existing in a stable state as 'matter' had been shaken in step with discoveries one made of still smaller units in forms of atoms, which one assumed were possibly composed of so-called 'under-atoms,' which again might be composed of even more elementary units, until one seemed to be left with nothing but extension-less 'points' exerting 'forces.' (In our day's contemporary physics, an 'under-atom' might be translated into a *proton, neutron,* or *electron*; and an extension-less 'point' would come close enough to a *quack*; a 'force' comes on atomic level in the three varieties, *electromagnetic, weak,* and *strong*.) The world in-itself (our so-called 'Ur-ground') became so conceived a *force-point world*, where matter in the classical sense had disappeared. However, even this force-point world is a 'picture' – that is, a *personification* of something that remains absolutely veiled as nature's mystery. Lange quotes physicist De Bois-Reymond for a view, which we notice closely resembles Nietzsche's: "Force [. . .] is nothing but a more recondite product of the irresistible tendency to *personification* which is impressed upon us; *a rhetorical artifice, as it were, of our brain*, which snatches at a figurative term, because it is destitute of any conception clear enough to be literally expressed. [. . .] What do we gain by saying it is reciprocal attraction whereby two particles of matter approach each other? Not the shadow of an insight in the nature of the fact. But, strangely enough, our inherent quest of causes is in a manner satisfied by the involuntary image tracing itself before our inner eye, of a hand which gently draws the inert matter to it." (De Bois-Raymond quoted from Lange: *A History of Materialism*, loc. cit., 2nd book, 2nd section, p. 378; italics added.) Nietzsche talks about similar issues when he makes the following observations: "The means of expression of language [*Ausdrucksmittel der Sprache*] is useless: it belongs to our inescapable need for preservation: constantly positing a cruder world of the enduring, the 'thing', etc. Relatively, we may speak of atoms and monads." (Nachlaß 1888, KSA 13, 11[73]) [. . .] "The presuppositions of Mechanism, the stuff, the atom, pressure, impact, and weight are not "facts as such" [*"Thatsachen an sich"*], but rather interpretations helped by psychological fictions." (Nachlaß 1888, KSA 13, 14[82]). Claudia Crawford too refers to the passage of Du Bois-Raymond, and comments: "Here we find that there are at bottom neither forces nor matter. Both are rather abstractions from things." Crawford: *Nietzsche's beginnings of Language*, loc. cit., p. 87.

4.3.2. Causality and Time-Reversal.

Let us for the last time return to Nietzsche's example 'lighting flashes.' In the reconstruction of a cause for the flashing, we notice that the explanation follows the steps in a model we already introduced in *Chapter 1*. Although Nietzsche never makes it structurally explicit, it is a figure or 'logic' that he often resorts to in explaining the constitution of cause-effect relations, and by extension, the nature of *all explanation*. It becomes also a good illustration on the ultimate (we emphasize, *ultimate*) superficial nature of all explanation.

Step 1: Phenomenon (the world is *one*; the *flashing* is alone; there is only a zigzag) →
   Step 2: Phenomenon is interpreted as effect (the *flashing* is not alone; the world cannot be superficial) →
      Step 3: A 'cause' is added to the 'effect' (Flashing results from a *doer*; the world is *two*; there is a subject behind *flashing* called *lighting*) →
Step 4: Cause is interpreted as preceding *Step 1* (there is a subject/an intention/a cause as *lighting* behind and producing *flashing*.)

The figure could be drawn as a square or a rhombus, and has as such four angles; in the interpretive process, the figure proceeds clockwise from angle to angle; from 'step 1' to 'step 4,' where the last *step 4* chronological precedes *step 1*, although *step 1* precedes the entire series. Progressively, during the progression from angle to angle, an issue is supposedly still better clarified and defined. As such, the figure illustrates the circle of explanation and interpretation, where the point of departure is a certain phenomenal pre-conceptual knowledge, and the terminal point is the supposed conceptual explanation of this phenomenal knowledge. As we said in *Chapter 1*, the figure illustrates Nietzsche's so-called "chronological reversal" or "time-reversal" of observation and explanation. In our logical reconstructions, we always conceive an explanation to be chronologically *first*, and an observation, *second*; but the process goes the other way around: the observation is always *first*, and it prompts an explanation that is *second* (we shall come back to this shortly).[335]

The model fascinates Nietzsche, because it makes obvious that the supposed explanation (*step 4* in our model) can never explain *more* than what

---

[335] Nietzsche anticipated the model in *Über Wahrheit und Lüge*, when he described the irony of looking for and finding something one had oneself just been hiding: "When somebody hides something behind a bush and then looks for it again at the same place and finds it there, there is in such seeking and finding not much to applaud. Yet, this is how we seek and find of 'truth' within our realm of reason [*Vernunft-Bezirkes*]." (WL, KSA 1, p. 883).

is already apparent.[336] In the last analysis and in the strictest sense, human explanation/interpretation is as such futile. Humans have the 'feel' that they understand an issue, thanks to the explanation, but at bottom, their 'understanding' is superficial and does not reveal the inner workings of things. Even in the strongest of cases – and that is in Nietzsche always *scientific explanation* – explanation can never be more that a laborious formalization and schematization of certain relationships between sets of particular data, which are *already fully self-present* in the apparent world, and which do not emerge into any kind of *fuller presence* by being formalized. We, who 'invent' a simplified word, cannot expect that this self-invented world should yield to us a *secret*; we can consequently not expect *to find a secret*; that is, to 'explain' that invented world in an absolute sense. We are confined to the surface, and consigned to making *descriptions* of *surface-relationships*. Simply put, we can only explain *observations*.

> Cause and Effect. [. . .] How could we also explain! We operate with nothing but things, which do not exist, with lines, surfaces, bodies, atoms, divisible time, divisible space —, how could explanation at all be possible, when we first make everything into an image, our image [*Bilde*]. It is sufficient to see science as the best possible and most faithful humanization [*Anmenschlichnung*] of the things, we learn always to describe ourselves still more precisely, when we describe the things and their succession. (FW 112, KSA 3, p. 472).

"How could explanation at all be possible," Nietzsche states, meaning, how could it explain the ultimate nature of things, when 'things' always reflect *our* world and horizon. (We notice in the passage that science is promoted to the "best possible" description, and that Nietzsche still believes that we describe "ourselves still more precisely" when we describe "things and their succession." For example, even the description of an occurrence like the Big Bang – happening 12-15 billion years before humans started to inhabit Earth, and therefore *in-itself* having nothing to do with humans – inevitably provides *us* with an image of *our origin*. As a 'metaphor' in the extended, non-literal, sense (cf. *Chapter 1*), Big Bang suggests that the *universe*, by implication *life*, by implication *us*, could have emerged out of *nothing*; and

---

[336] The model explains what is apparent only in the best of cases; for example when explanation is 'scientific.' In the worst of cases, the "explanation" becomes entirely fictitious, for example as when "God" is invoked as a last-resort explanation of incomprehensible existential or historical turn of events. We have in the latter case an example of a pseudo-explanation, where, as Nietzsche puts it, "a word is inserted, at the point where our ignorance begins, – where we cannot see any further." (Nachlaß 1886-87, KSA 12, 5[3]).

that *we* may return to *nothing*. However strictly the theory is based on observation and induction, it gives almost immediately rise to a spontaneous *metaphysics*, where *nothingness*, *immensity*, and *we* are related in new and fascinating ways.[337])

It is now this way of thinking Nietzsche applies to inner-mental life as well. That is, also in inner-mental life are we confined to describe surface-phenomena, and also in inner-mental life do we 'invent' cause-effect relationship according to the logic of 'chronological reversal.'[338] There is for example a 'time-reversal' between the moment of the inscription of an impression, and its conscious materialization as sensation. The 'time-reversal' concerns the following: a sensation is always by the subject felt as *spontaneous and immediate presence*; however, the sensation is the result of a *work*, and it emerges only *after-the-fact* of this work; i.e., after the conclusion of a sequence of processes that the impression must undergo before it materializes as sensation. At the exact moment of inscription, there is no awareness, because the impression, as Nietzsche says, "needs time before it is finished: but the time is so small." (Nachlaß 1885, KSA 11, 26[44]). The time may be "small," but still, the brain needs time to process the impression. Therefore, only when the inscription is processed, does it 'return' in the sensation, and start belatedly to have an effect. It is in this precise sense that the 'outer-world' is "our work" (implying that we do not *create* the *material* world; more about this in *Section 5.2* below).

> The reversal of time: we believe in the outer-world as causing an effect on us, but we have already initially changed the actual and unconsciously progressing effect i n t o o u t e r - w o r l d. That, which stands opposed to us, is already our work, which now effects us retrogressively [*zurückwirkt*]. It needs t i m e , before it is finished: but this time is so small [*diese Zeit is so klein*]. (Nachlaß 1885; KSA 11, 26[44])

> The reversed order of time.
> The "outer world" effects us: the effect is telegraphed to the brain, where it is prepared and developed and lead back to its cause: Thereupon the cause is projected and first then does the factum arrive to consciousness. That is, the world

---

[337] One of the major puzzles of the 'big bang' theory today is how 'big bang' generated a universe according to such precise parameters that it neither imploded nor exploded in its early stages (in the language of the physicists, why is $\Omega = 1$). That is, how did the universe generate a uniformity (a homogeneity and isotropy) that eventually became the condition of the possibility of life, the condition of the possibility of *us*.

[338] *En passant*, one may notice that this concept is closely related to Freud's notion of the so-called 'deferred effect' [*Nachträglichkeit*].

of appearance appears first as cause, after it has affected us. That is, we turn constantly the order of the happening around. (Nachlaß 1885; KSA 11, 34[54])

Nietzsche does not always present these complicated processes in completely clear and consistent concepts, and we oftentimes have to translate his thinking into what seems to make best logical sense. We shall translate his statements above as follows: (i) something (an impression) is "telegraphed to the brain" (a fortunate metaphor!); (ii) then it is "developed" and lead back to a possible cause (to a 'thing' causing a sensation); (iii) thereupon the cause is invented (a 'thing' is stabilized as the cause); (iv) finally something originally non-nondescript arrives to consciousness as "fact" (the stabilized object appears as intuitively self-evident as 'fact').

The same logic applies to activities. One has an activity, or is subjected to activities, and imagines that a 'will,' an 'intention,' has been causing this activity (cf. *Chapter 3*). However, in Nietzsche the 'deed' comes first, and the "cause is imagined [only] after the 'deed'":

> Like in dreams we at the outset seek the cause for a canon shot and first subsequently hear the shot (that therefore a reversal of time [*Zeit-Umkehrung*] has occurred: this time-reversal [*Zeitumkehrung*] always occurs, also in waken life. The 'cause' is imagined after the 'deed'; what I mean is that our means and purposes are consequences of a process?) (Nachlaß 1885; KSA 11, 26[35]).

4.4. On the Nature and Constitution of Language: Proposition, Word, Meaning

4.4.1. The Judgment and the Categories.

Nietzsche's discussion of propositional language, the Kantian notion of judgment in particular, is complex, and has no systematic form. Let us try to engage and defeat the complexity by organizing the issues under discussion in five distinct sections.

(a) If we take a brief look at the Kantian theory of 'judgment,' the *judgment* is the quintessential format for knowledge-formation, and the *categories*, in their different varieties, are supposed to be the empty forms that make possible and valid synthetic judgments. Judgments have the basic form, a predicate is added to a subject, S is P, and they come in the two varieties, analytic and synthetic. In the analytic judgment, the predicate is already

contained in the concept of the subject, and nothing new is being added to the subject. The analytic judgment therefore does not produce new knowledge, but expands only on knowledge already inherent in the subject. If true, there is identity between subject and predicate, and the judgment is tautological; for its verification, the analytic judgment relies on the principle of contradiction. The synthetic judgment, on the other hand, combines two distinct concepts that are inherently unrelated. In this combination, the synthetic judgment produces new knowledge; for its verification, the synthetic judgment relies on observation and experience.[339]

When in Kant we as humans have a "capacity to judge" it entails that we are able to form statements about states of affairs in the form of synthetic judgments. Thanks to this capacity, we produce knowledge; and production of knowledge has thus the simple structure: one adds a predicate to a subject in order to further augment one's knowledge of the subject. In sentences like, 'the car is expensive,' 'humans are mortal,' 'God is benevolent,' one asserts that an individual thing S (the subject) has the property P (the predicate), where the predicate as such adds some information to the subject that could not have been extracted from the subject itself. S and P are combined in the production of knowledge, and the rudimentary mechanism for forming judgments and producing knowledge becomes thus the *synthesis*, the *combination*, or the *binding*.[340]

In *Die Welt als Wille und Vorstellung I*, Schopenhauer gives a helpful graphic illustration of *synthesis* drawn in the form of circles. He lets a circle represent a concept or a concept-sphere. When two circles are combined, they partially overlap; and the overlapping area may now represent the synthesis. For example, God is represented by one circle, and benevolence by another; the two concepts are brought together, and the overlapping area

---

[339] Kant is almost uniquely interested is synthetic judgments that secure objectivity, that is, *synthetic a priori* judgments. It is the well-known endeavor of *Critique of Pure Reason* to argue for the existence of this class of judgments in addition to the already known classes David Hume had identified: *synthetic a posteriori* and *analytic a priori* judgments. To Kant's mind, it must be possible that the binding of two concepts be not completely random and associative, but be subjected to a rule that secures its objectivity. Some synthetic statements must be universally applicable and necessary true. Kant finds them in mathematics and the natural sciences, and it is his hope that he can remedy the current confusion of metaphysics, and find an application of the *synthetic a priori judgments* in metaphysics as well.

[340] Kant talks about this binding as sometimes *synthesis*, which represent no translation-problem, sometimes *Verknüpfung*, which I translate 'combination,' and sometimes *Verbindung*, which I translate 'binding.'

shared by the two circles would now represent the synthetic judgment, 'God is benevolent.' (There is no total overlapping of the two concept-spheres, because God is more than benevolent, and there are things other than God benevolent; two entirely overlapping concept-spheres would supposedly represent the analytic judgment.)[341]

In Kant, the categories make up the transcendental conditions for possible experience. Insofar as we experience a manifold of things and events in the world, we necessarily organize them under categories, as Kant states in a famous maxim: "Thoughts without content are empty, impressions without concepts are blind" [*Gedanken ohne Inhalt sind leer, Anschauungen ohne Begriffe sind blind*]. (Kant, KrV, B 76). Accordingly, our impressions or intuitions require the so-called 'concept' before we *see* anything with *noticing awareness* – that is, before we *experience* something we need to organize the material under the concept. The categories may as such be seen as the fundamental formal inventory necessary to make propositions about the world. In this interpretation, whenever we form propositions, we first apply the form, subject-predicate, S is P (e.g., "God is benevolent"), insofar as we in our statement always assert a substance, S, to which we add a certain property, P (we 'understand' the world as consisting of individual substances, endowed with certain properties). Furthermore, we give substances location and determination in relation to space and time; implying for example that a substance can occupy one, and only one, place at a particular time. Finally, we believe that substances have relations; that they may reciprocally effect one another, or may stand in causal relationships to one another. In order to form statements we typically need the following categories (and Kant lists include several additional): space, time, substance, property, relationship, and cause-effect. It is Kant's minimal contention that it is impossible to produce knowledge, form statements, without these (and other) categories. The categories become a kind of *elementary grammar of knowledge-formation*. (For example, in forming a sentence like, "the busy man had to travel to both Paris and London," we employ a number of categories: *substance* (man); property (busy); *event* (traveling); *space* and *time* (destinations Paris and London); the modality, *necessity* ('had to'); and the logical operator, *conjunction* (both Paris and London). Without these forms, we would instead of a meaningful sentence have only a bundle of discrete elements that would make no sense, and could convey neither experience nor meaning.)

In this sense, the so-called 'manifold' must be organized under *categories*, and according to a rule, in order for it to made sense. A perceptive

---

[341] See Schopenhauer: Die Welt als Wille und Vorstellung, bd. I, loc. cit., # 9.

content is arranged into one and the same world of experience; and consequently, subjective perception is objectified. Kant talks about this operation as the "synthesis of the intuitive manifold through concepts [*Synthesis der Anschuungmannigfaltigkeit durch Begriffe*]."[342] This 'synthesis' of the manifold seem to be a minimal requirement in propositional language. This reading of Kant's categories would to undersigned make the best sense, and also be best supported by Kant, insofar as he explicitly labels the categories of understanding a 'transcendental logic,' and deduces them from a logical table that is quasi-Aristotelian.

(b) Nietzsche does not question the fact that humans 'judge,' i.e., make propositions about states of affairs, and therefore 'bind together' concepts. On the contrary, Nietzsche understands judgments to be our "oldest beliefs," and he sees the judgment as essential to our being to the extent that we are defined as "judging animals." Nietzsche also follows Kant in understanding the judgment as *combination* or *synthesis* of subject and predicate:

> In the judgments are our oldest beliefs presented, all judgments convey a holding-for-true or not-holding-for-true [*Fürwahrhalten order für Unwahrhalten*], an affirmation or denial, a certainty that something is in this and not some other way, a belief, that one has really come to "know." (Nachlaß 1885-86; KSA 12, 2[84]).

> The human being is first and foremost a judging animal; in the judgments is hidden our oldest and most permanent beliefs, in every judgment there is essentially a holding-for-true and a conviction, a certainty, that something is this and not something else. [. . .] What is it, which in every judgment is believed to be true? That we have a right to distinguish between a subject and a predicate, between a cause and an effect." (Nachlaß 1886-87, KSA 12, 4[8]).

However, in a longer note from 1886-87, we see some of the discrepancies emerging between Kant and Nietzsche. In the note, Nietzsche summarizes Kant's theory of the synthetic a priori judgment, and inserts his own critical comments. The note appears like a private brain-storming session, where

---

[342] Kant goes further in his reasoning: it must be a condition for the synthesis of the manifold that one and the same consciousness carries out the operation. Synthesis requires a single agent, in this case the same perceiving consciousness. The same person must synthesize the manifold, and all elements must be part of that one person's world of experiences. A bunch of elements belonging to different individuals and synthesized by different individuals could not make up a single world of experience.

4. Fundamentals in the Construction of a Biological-Linguistic Subject

the first clause of a paragraph often is an axiom in Kantian thinking, and the following clauses represent Nietzsche's reservations.

> "Knowledge is judgment!" But judgment is a b e l i e f [*Glaube*] that something is so or so! And n o t knowledge!
> "All knowledge consists in synthetic judgment" – a necessary and universal combination [*Verknüpfung*] of different representations –
> It has the characteristic of universality (the matter is in all cases this and not something else)
> It has the characteristic of necessity (the opposite of the matter can never happen)
> [. . .]
> Therefore the conclusion is:
> 1) There exist assertions, which we hold to be universal and necessary.
> 2) The characteristics of necessity and universality cannot derive from experience.
> 3) Consequently, it must g r o u n d i t s e l f d i f f e r e n t l y without experience, it must have another source of knowledge.
> Kant concludes 1) there are assertions which are only valid under a certain condition; 2) this condition is that they do not derive from experience, but from pure reason [*der reinen Vernunft*].
> [. . .]
> He already presupposes, that there are not only "data a posteriori", but also data a priori, "before experience." Necessity and universality could never be given through experience: how is it then obvious, that they exist at all without experience?
> [. . .]
> Hume had declared: "there is no synthetic judgments a priori." Kant says, but yes! The mathematical! And if such judgments exist, then perhaps also metaphysics exists, a knowledge of things through pure reason! Quaeritur.
> Mathematic is possible under conditions, under which metaphysics never could be possible
> All human knowledge is either experience or mathematics.
> A judgment is synthetic: that is, it combines [*verknüpft*] different representations.
> It is a priori: that is, each combination is universal and necessary, which can never be given through sensual perception, but only through pure reason.
> If synthetic judgments a priori exist, than reason must be able to combine: the combination is a form. The reason must c o n t a i n f o r m - g i v i n g a b i l i t i e s. (Nachlaß 1886-87, KSA 12, 7[4] p. 264-66).

Clearly, Nietzsche accepts the fundamental mechanism of synthesis or combination (*verknüpfung*), but the over-determining problem is that when reason combines two representations in Kant, it appeals to a 'tribunal' in the form of the categories. This *tribunal* secures that the predicate in the judgment follows a rule that makes the judgment universal and necessary. This *tribunal* acts like a rational *super-subject*, which over and above individual subjectivity guarantees objectivity of syntheses. It is allegedly the sphere of *transcendental subjectivity*; it as such has the complicated and paradoxical role of being *both* situated in the individual *and* above all individuality.[343]

In Nietzsche's critical paraphrase of Kant, sensuous experience is in itself random and cannot carry with it absolute necessity. Only insofar as we go beyond experience, do we realize (says Kant) a *rule* that makes a cause-effect relation *necessary*. If such a rule cannot derive from experience, it must derive (says Kant) from 'pure reason' (cf. "they do not derive from experience, but from pure reason [*der reinen Vernunft*]." Ibid.); – it derives thus from our so-called rational super-subject, as the head of a tribunal of categories, which is now endowed with "form-giving capabilities." Kant therefore "already presupposes, that there are not only 'data a posteriori,' but also data a priori, 'before experience.'" (Ibid.). It is this tribunal 'before experience,' this super-subject with "form-giving capabilities," that Nietzsche questions in the passage above. It is the *'super-subject' 'before experience'* that especially bothers Nietzsche. This is even more apparent in another passage: "We have no categories, which allow us to separate a "world in itself" from a world as appearance. All our categories of reason [*Vernunft-kategorien*] are of a sensual origin: read out from the empirical world." (Nachlaß 1886-87; KSA 12, 9[98]). Thus, 'pure reason' cannot be a ground; the ground is rather an 'empirical world.'

(c) If the categories are understood as a 'tribunal' (or an 'inventory') employed under the auspices of a Kantian 'super-ego,' one can hardly think of them otherwise but as 'faculties' in the mind, something that must be a part of our cognitive make up; something like twelve busy dwarfs seated somewhere in the mind organizing our perceptions, with Santa Claus (the transcendental ego) as the ultimate supervisor. This, at least, is the direction in which Nietzsche takes his criticism.

Anti-Kant.
[. . .] Hume explained the causality-sense by habit. Kant, with great composure, said instead, "it is a faculty [*Vermögen*]." The entire world was happy,

---

[343] Cf. Stegmaier: "'Pure reason' and the 'pure, will-less, painless, time-less subject of knowledge [*Erkenntnis*]' are paradoxical, because on the one hand, they have to be purged from individuality, and on the other hand, they still have to belong to the individual – the individual should simply not as rational [*vernünftige*] subject have been an individual." Stegmaier, Werner: Nietzsches Theorie, loc. cit., p. 187.

4. Fundamentals in the Construction of a Biological-Linguistic Subject

especially because it also exposed a moral faculty." (Nachlaß 1885, KSA 11, 34[82]).

If Kant by his categories is referring to a 'faculty,' his explanation of the human capacity for judgment is unsatisfying. At best, he has, in Nietzsche's catch-phrase, "inserted a word where ignorance begins." Kant's reference to a certain *"Vermögen"* is to Nietzsche's mind no more than elaborate non-explanation. The criticism returns in the famous aphorism 11 from *Jenseits von Gut und Böse*. Again, Nietzsche refers to Kant's categories and his guiding question: 'How are synthetic *a priori* judgments possible?'

> How are synthetic judgments a priori p o s s i b l e ? Kant asked himself, – and what, really, did he answer? By means of a faculty [*Vermöge eines Vermögens*]: but unfortunately not in a few words, but so circumspectly, venerably, and with such an expenditure of German profundity and flourishes that one overlooked the comical niaiserie allemande involved is such an answer. [. . .] By means of a faculty [*Vermöge eines Vermögens*] – he had said, at least meant. But is that – an answer? An explanation? Or is it not rather a repetition of the question. (JGB 11, KSA 5, p. 24-25).

It is the emptiness of the concept of 'category' that is the object of Nietzsche's mockery. If we ask ourselves why we have a sense of causality, and Kant answers, 'it is because of a faculty,' this explains nothing. If we do not know why *synthetic a priori judgments* are possible, we know even less what is a *faculty*.

The answer becomes particularly trivial if we translate *vermögen* with 'ability.' [Note: *vermögen*, as transitive Verb, translates *capability, ability*; *Vermögen*, as substantive neutrum, translates *property, faculty*]. If we have a sense of causality, then, obviously, we have an *ability* to have such a sense. Nietzsche's mock-answer, *Vermöge eines Vermögens*, only underscores the repetitions pattern in Kant's answer: "By means of what ability/faculty do we know synthetic *a priori* judgments? – By the ability of that faculty!" To drive home his point, Nietzsche compares Kant's complex argument for the categories to the following scene from Moliere: an examiner asks a medical student why opium makes people sleepy; the student thinks long and hard on the question before he answers ponderously: *quia est in eo virtus dormitiva, cujus est natura sensus assoupire*. Opium makes people sleepy 'because it contains a certain dormant faculty that has the property of making the senses sleepy' (thus, 'by the ability of a faculty') – and the examiner passes the student in admiration of such a display of profound knowledge.

Similarly, in his answer, *Vermögen*, Kant has fooled himself and his audiences into believing that he has uncovered something profound, while his notion of an ability/faculty is already represented in the surface-manifestation of the phenomenon he investigates. The logic of the reasoning is similar to the circle we introduced above in explaining the time-reversal of cause and effect, applied to the example, 'lightning flashes.' Now, the circle of explanation/interpretation is invested as follows:

Step 1: Phenomenon = causality-sense →
    Step 2: Phenomenon is interpreted as effect of a *vermögen* (as ability) to experience the phenomenon →
        Step 3: The *vermögen* (as an *ability*) to experience the phenomenon is seen as a cause (as a *faculty*) →
Step 4: The *Vermögen* as cause (as a *faculty*) is interpreted as preceding Step 1

The point is the same as above. The explanation, 'ability/faculty,' is already inherent in the initially observed phenomenon. However, during the explanation, a property already determining the superficial phenomenon, i.e., an ability to sense causality, is re-invented as a cause for that same causality-sense. The re-invention of the faculty as cause provides now the illusion that a secret ground has been exposed, while, in truth, the 'ground' is nothing but reiterating the initial surface-observation. 'Pure reason' as ground is an invented ground. It is invented as *ground*, but it only repeats what is self-evident from observing the surface, the 'sensuous' and 'empirical' world. In this sense, there is no difference (because there can be no difference) between appearance and reality. So-called 'reality' is *always-already-only* the apparent manifestation; the 'reality' we refer to in order to *explain* the surface, is itself drawn from the surface.

If Nietzsche is right in this criticism, we notice that he has revealed a *paralogism* in Kant's argument for the categories. The *vermögen*, the ability to sense causality, becomes a *Vermögen* understood as category, ground, and faculty ('v' slides tacitly into capital 'V' – so to speak). This is a categorical mistake similar to Descartes' category-mistake regarding the *cogito* (cf. *Chapter 3*), which Kant so acutely analyzed in his "Paralogisms of Pure Reason." That which can never be more than a surface-phenomenon, constituted in and as activity (more precisely, in and as *interpretive* activity), is in the course of the argument endowed with objective existence. The alleged objective existence is an illusory construction. Drawing attention to this futility in Kant's explanation, Nietzsche can now re-phrase Kant's famous question, "How are synthetic a priori judgments possible?" into the ironic, "Why are synthetic a priori judgments *necessary*?"

(d) In Nietzsche's polemic directed against Kant's categories, he is not so much discussing their *existence*, as the *how* of their existence. As cognitive tools, they have evolved as practicable and useful; but only *utility* defines their existence. When Kant wants to see them as a super-subjective *tribunal* guaranteeing absolute and universal truth, Nietzsche believes that he has sneaked, what is in effect, a new set of *substances* into the mind through the back door of his transcendental Ego. If categories are 'faculties,' which it is only possible to think of as *substances*, Kant has entangled himself in a tacit self-contradiction. In his philosophy, *substances* can belong only in the world of appearances; his philosophy does not permit them to be something, which they themselves constitute.[344]

Instead of being grounded in 'pure reason,' categories derive from an evolutionary process; they have a biological-evolutionary explanation. Although Nietzsche does not work out this explanation out in any great detail, this seems to be the direction of his criticism: "The categories are 'True' only in the sense that they are life-conditioning for us: like the Euclidian space is such a conditional 'Truth.' [...] The necessity of the subject not to contradict oneself, is a biological necessity." (Nachlaß 1880-81, KSA 9, 5[44]).

What does is possibly imply that a judgment, and a 'capacity for judgment,' is biologically constituted? Nietzsche is, as said, not explicit, but his thinking might be reconstructed as something like the following. In a biological-cognitive context, we may understand the *synthetic judgment* as the formalization of what is asserted and being counted as *real*, and thus *true*;[345] while we may understand the *categories* as the formalization of various *as-*

---

[344] In his polemic engagements with Kant, Nietzsche often points out Kant's silent resorts to *substances* where they cannot and should not be. Both in the case of the thing-in-itself (as discussed in *Chapter 1*), and of the categories, he sees Kant's concepts as *substances*. The 'thing-in-itself' is seen as a thing-like 'thing' (thus a *substance*) hiding itself under a cover of appearances. The 'categories' are also seen as substances seated in the mind guiding our apprehension of the world of appearances; therefore again a set of substances *transcending* the world of appearance. In both what is deepest (the thing-in-itself) and what is highest (the categories), Nietzsche sees Kant re-inventing *substances* – a charge which is, if true, devastating to Kantian thinking.

[345] Truth must be the formal ideal inherent in the assertion of a synthetic judgment, although the logical form, S = P, admits a multiplicity of cases, that are not necessarily true, have no possible verification, and no correspondence to reality; e.g., "God is benevolent." In the speech-act, asserting something to be the case must involve an appeal to 'truth' as ideal requirement, as, for instance, John Searle and Jürgen Habermas have often been arguing.

pects of the things asserted as *real*. First, our biological subject identifies something as a *thing* (*substance*), according to the constitution of identity discussed above; then this *thing* is assigned certain qualities (*properties*), for example, hostile or friendly or edible or inedible (as also discussed above); furthermore, it is being located in *time* and *space*, and in certain *relations* to other things, such as *cause-effect* relations (again discussed above). The *synthetic judgment* now brings *knowledge* (the world interpreted according to elementary interpretation-processes) on propositional-linguistic form. As such; it (i) *abbreviates* knowledge necessary for survival (because it is easier to remember a short sequence, than a long); and simultaneously (ii), it *memorizes* knowledge (makes it easier to *retrieve* knowledge). It abbreviates an original sensation-overflow, labels it and brings it on formula, therefore making it retrievable. As such, it makes it possible for our ancestor to orient him or herself in a chaotic world.[346]

(e) Nietzsche' questions the *origin* of the categories. In Kant, this is pure reason itself; in Nietzsche, it is an evolutionary process. Nietzsche suggests that categories are a kind of survival-techniques; they have utility, but not necessity. This entails that seeking an *objective* and *a priori* grounding of the judgment is a futile endeavor. Humans certainly make judgments, and do so to a fault, but a judgment is an interpretation, and only as such do humans 'judge.' In this, the judgment does not carry with it necessity, and it guarantees no objectivity. The judgment is "belief," and if it appears to be so-called *a priori*, it is only because it is a particularly well-consolidated belief.

However, since Nietzsche still admits the existence of judgments and categories – since, as said, he does not so much question their *existence* as

---

[346] I will not develop the following comment at this point; but often, when one encounters Nietzsche's polemical encounters with Kant, one feels that Nietzsche exaggerates his "Anti-Kant." Often one finds differences so minor in their positions that one is never quite sure whether, under scrutiny, they would in fact hold up as differences. Are the categories biologically constituted or are they transcendental? – It would require an extremely agile mind to spell out why these two positions necessarily contradict and oppose each other! First of all, Nietzsche is sure, no less than Kant, that humans *judge*. Secondly, in both cases the categories are (or have become) *necessary*. Thirdly, in both cases they constitute a fundamental 'grammar of knowledge-formation.' Fourthly, if something evolves into *something*, is it not perfectly legitimate to study its present "synchronic" (transcendental) structure, instead of emphasizing its "diachronic" (biological) development? It has several advantages to study a *state*, rather than a *process* (– why the *either/or*)?

the *how of their existence* – he is compelled to give them a ground different form Kant's transcendental Ego and its twelve categories. This other ground cannot be the evolutionary process itself. Although judgments and categories come about *through* or *qua* an evolutionary process; it cannot be nature itself that *creates* judgment and categories. Nature cannot produce logic. Logic is a second-order *simplification* of nature, which humans is responsible for; it is not nature itself.

So, Nietzsche admits that we *judge*; that we have a *propositional logic*, that there are *categories*; but he rejects that categories derive from *pure reason* or the *transcendental Ego*. From where do these pure forms then derive? – Not *from* nature itself, although *during* an evolutionary process, but instead from *language*! As already discussed (cf. previous *Chapter 3*), Nietzsche finds an explanation of 'categories' in the form of the subject-predicate logic as a grammatical structure underlying all Indo-European Languages (and most other language-groups). As Josef Simon has asserted, in suggesting this new grounding, Nietzsche is turning Kant's transcendental philosophy into linguistic philosophy. Several of the antithetical relationships from Kant's symmetrical twelve-item table can now be seen as deriving from Nietzsche's subject-predicate logic; so, for example, the *subject-accidence* relationship, the *cause-effect* relationship, the *unity-plurality* relationship, and possibly the *necessity-contingency* relationship.

According to Nietzsche, all propositional thinking, and that is thinking as such, starts in a fundamental structural/logical, but non-essential, difference; namely in the subject-predicate relation (which might now represent a Nietzschean version of Derrida's *Différance*). From this fundamental root-difference, thinking disseminates and branches out in second-order differences, which are now, since deriving from this *fundamental root-difference*, unable to recover an essential singularity-principle, motivating their perpetual dissemination.

Summarizing, Nietzsche sees the *judgment* and the *categories* come about as (i) biologically conditioned; (ii) therefore, are crucially dependent of a 'sense' of *entity/identity* before becoming possible as relational logic (cf. discussion of biological constitution of *sense of identity*); (iii) thus, are emerging as products of an antecedent 'interpretative' activity, which cannot guarantee *a priori truth*; (iv) furthermore, interpret *entity/identity* as identical to grammatical 'I' and interpret consequently the 'world' in terms of subject-predicate, actor-action, or doer-deed relationships. (v) As such, humanize the world; makes it into a *for-us*.

4.4.2. The Emotional Word.

From *Über Wahrheit und Lüge* we learned that two so-called 'metaphors' contributed to the transformation of a nerve-stimulus into something recognizable by us: the *perception-image* and the *word/concept-image* (cf. *Chapter 1*). "What is a word?" Nietzsche asked himself in WL, and answered with the famous passage, "A moveable army [*Ein bewegliches Heer*] of metaphors, metonymies, and anthropomorphisms." (WL, KSA 1, p. 881). In the later theory, both perception and word still simplify an inner universe of chaos and becoming. As such simplifying units, they can still be seen as 'metaphors' in Nietzsche's generalized sense; that is, they 'translate' arbitrarily something from one sphere into an entirely different sphere. In this section, we shall elaborate our explanation of how and why the *word* is constituted in the mental apparatus.

That the word *simplifies* presupposes at least three things. First, we assume that we have a rich inner life consisting of an abundance of material. Secondly, when the word 'simplifies,' it necessarily becomes an *inaccurate* and *insufficient* representation of this abundant inner life. Thirdly, this *inaccurate* and *insufficient* word is, one the other hand, the only means we have to gain access to this our over-abundant inner-life – what is tantamount to saying that absolute access to our mental processes is denied us.

In Freud, we saw that inner-life was understood as *thing-representations*. It represented the memory of a 'thing' plus all the possible private associations emanating from its core. Recollection of things past transpired when some of these associations surfaced in consciousness. They might then surface as *thing-images* (images) of which the subject was not fully conscious because they floated by the mind's eye rapidly, continuously, without organization, and possibly perpetually (in waken as well as in sleeping life). They might also surface in linguisticized form, as *word-images* ('voices'), in which case, a *word-representation* had been attached to the thing-representation, and was now dividing, segmenting, and sequencing the flow of images into simpler and more stable word-images.

This thinking makes the 'word' (in both Freud and Nietzsche) the most important simplification-mechanism in inner-life; i.e., the mechanism with the greatest impact on the human subject. The word imposes itself on a network of associations that is complex in the extreme, as it necessarily simplifies this network, thus making it 'understood.' We shall now suggest that the ego-clusters discussed above represent certain significant clusters of associations that eventually, during upbringing, will be assigned certain significations and valuations. During these linguistic learning-processes, they will be transformed into *semantic ego-clusters*. When the individual again encounter the world, a given impression will consequently be guided or directed into the associated *semantic ego-clusters* or *networks*. In the process, the impression is being furnished with *meaning* and *value*; it will be *interpreted* according to these semantic networks. Thus, words label (mark, brand, classify) inner processes that are in themselves unknowable. Certain impressions prompt an activation of certain clusters that have been, through learning-processes, assigned certain words; as such, the impressions arrive to us as 'understood.' (Let us say that I in the present receive multiple impressions of a 'dog.' Thanks to learning-processes internalized as memory, not only do I perceive the creature as a 'dog,' I also 'understand' several of its qualities, for example its friendliness. The aggregate of dog-impressions is immediately *interpreted* in first *image* and then *word*.)

The dialectics between impressions and inner-processes described by Nietzsche is somewhat similar to the experience of writing on a computer. The keystrokes on the keyboard (the *impressions*) activate certain strings of formulas in my computer's microprocessor (*inner processes*), which I as subject know nothing about, because they manifest themselves only in the appearing word (*image* or *word*) on the screen. Keystrokes take a 'roundtrip' into the microprocessor before they 'come out' and manifest themselves as recognizable images on the screen. The 'inner experiences' of the microprocessor reads my keystrokes according to certain strings of formulas, our so-called *clusters*. Only when they are labeled by the word appearing on the screen do I 'understand'; now they have been transformed into *semantic clusters*. From the analogy, it also becomes clear that the appearing word is a simplifying representation of the original string of formulae. (In computer-science, the word 'meet,' as in 'to meet someone,' is derived from the following meaningless string, 001 388 002 544.) Finally, from the analogy, we also understand that the appearing word is the conclusion and termination of a process; it is that which manifests itself on my conscious surface (my computer screen) as the *last sequel* of a complex computation process. The surface is an end-result of processes that play themselves out beneath the surface ("under the table," Nietzsche says), and of which we know nothing.

If the word is a 'simplification-mechanism,' helping us to 'understand' inner processes that are in themselves inaccessible to consciousness; this insight has another important consequence. In Nietzsche, the word does not simply *express* a state of affairs already existing in inner mental life, as the label for this complex. Simultaneously, it *produces* a state of affairs. The word *processes*, *brings out*, and *intensifies* 'feelings' that were, before the word, only vaguely understood, if understood at all. The sound-image and motor-image of the word prompts motor reactions, and these motor-reactions intensify 'feelings,' they make us *re*-remember something primordial – should we have forgotten. In brief, words are not simply *expressions of emotions, words produce emotions too*. An emotion does not exist as a perfectly whole and rounded object; as a thing-in-itself; as an X corresponding to a label, as some kind of 'emoticon' corresponding to the emotion. Emotions are being produced in the linguistic process. (If I remember correctly, it was Bertrand Russell who once reported that when on one occasion he declared his love to a woman, it was not before actually pronouncing the sentence, 'I love you,' that it dawned on him that he loved her. The sentence brought out and intensified an emotion associated to something called 'love,' i.e., the emoticon made him *creatively remember*, even *produce*, an emotion called 'love,' which does not exist as such.)[347]

This 'productive aspect' of the word, Freud is aware of too in this *Project*. Freud's example of such a 'productive word' is the 'scream.' A scream helps the individual to identify a sensation as painful. The 'scream' becomes a catalyst for the sensation of pain; which, before the representation in the 'scream,' either had not yet presented itself in consciousness as felt, or was felt less intensely. The 'scream' interacts with an anonymous inner world of impressions, bringing identity to these impressions.

> [T]here are objects – perceptions – that make one scream, because they arouse pain; and it turns out as an immensely important fact that this association of a sound [...] with a perceptual image [...] emphasizes that object as a hostile one and serves to direct attention to the perceptual image. When otherwise, owing to pain, one has received no good indication of the quality of the object, the information of one's own scream serves to characterize the object. Thus this association is a means of making memories that arouse unpleasure conscious and objects of attention: the first class of conscious memories has been created. Not much is now needed in order to invent speech.[348]

The primitive proto-word, the scream, helps to "characterize the object." In the example, it helps the individual to see an object as 'hostile,' and as such capable of producing or intensifying pain. This means that the "information of one's own scream" interacts with old memory-traces, and makes one *remember* the hostile object as a generic cause of pain.

A *linguistic representation* helps the mind to *focus on sensation*.[349] As such, words start a chain-reaction of feelings that otherwise would remain

---

[347] We shall return to this 'productive' aspect of the word in more detail in the final part of this chapter.
[348] Freud: *Project*, loc. cit. p. 366-67; GW, Nachtragsband, p. 457.
[349] We are in Freud's example of the scream returning to the distinction between

dormant, like Russell's complex emotions regarding a woman might have remained dormant, but through the pronunciation of a word were transformed and abbreviated into the emotion, 'love.'

In his *Nachlaß* material, Nietzsche describes similar processes:

> All our conscious motives are surface-phenomena; behind them exist a struggle within our drives and dispositions [*Zustände*], a struggle for power. (Nachlaß 1885-86, KSA 12, 1[20]).

> Everything that becomes conscious is only the last link in a chain, a conclusion. That a thought is the immediate cause for another thought is only appearance. The actual associations of occurrences play themselves out beneath our consciousness: the series and successions of feelings, thoughts, etc., that appear on our stage are symptoms on what actually takes place. – Beneath every thought there is an affect. Every thought, every feeling, every will is not born out of a certain drive, it is rather a totality of all states [*Gesamtzustand*], the total surface of the entire consciousness, and results in an immediate fixation and positioning of power [*Macht-Feststellung*] in all our constitutive drives. (Nachlaß 1885-86, KSA 12, 1[61]).

> That a thought is a cause for another thought cannot be established. On the table of our consciousness, a behind-one-another [*hintereinander*] of thoughts appears as if a thought is the cause of the following thought. But actually, we do not see the power-struggle that is being played out under the table. (Nachlaß 1885-86, KSA 12, 2[103]).

"Under the table," says Nietzsche, things are played out that we know nothing about; we can only know what happens "on the table."[350] 'Under the

---

thing- and word-presentations that he makes early in his writings: the thing-presentation is here represented by the *hostile object*, the word-presentation by the *scream*. In his example, the *scream* becomes a signifier representing a rudimentary and embryonic word that rouses memories, thus making the subject conscious of the hostile object, detecting it as cause and reason for the pain. We notice that uttering a word induces a reversal of the chronology between cause and effect: *first*, there is an effect, *then*, the subject starts looking for a cause.

[350] Compare to Günter Abel: "One must here emphasize that consciousness never succeeds in suspending or distancing itself from the network of its own conditions. [. . .] The cause, the ground, or the tangle of conditions [*Bedingungsgeflecht*] for consciousness does not present itself within the field of consciousness, and none of the states and objects that enter consciousness recognize that they are determined from a network of non-conscious conditions." Günter Abel: "Bewußtsein – Sprache – Natur. Nietzsches Philosophie

table,' we thus find well-facilitated and well-cathected ego-clusters, combining numerous components (nuclei) and several strands of facilitated passages (antennas connecting via synapses) for the safe transport of Qη energy. However, we have no consciousness of the facilitation of 'Qη energies,' and we know nothing of 'nets,' 'clusters,' or 'concentrations.' These are all, 'under the table.' Only when these 'nets' are eventually marked, branded, or labeled – that is, when a word is assigned to a cluster – we see for a cluster a *word*. At that point, what was originally an incomprehensible complexity will now appear to us as a singularity. It is in this branding or marking that the *neurological cluster* is transformed into a *semantic cluster*. This is what we can become conscious of as our thoughts and feelings, not our biological or "bodily self": "behind your thoughts and feelings stand your body and your bodily self [*Selbst im Leib*]: the t e r r a   i n c o g n i t a. Why do you have t h e s e thoughts and these feelings? Your bodily self w a n t s something with this." (Nachlaß 1888, KSA 10, p. 225). The *terra incognita* "under the table" is nothing but our "nerve-activity": "The world, insofar as we can apprehend [*erkennen*] it, is only our own nerve-activity, nothing else." (Nachlaß 1880-81, KSA 9, 10[E95]).

If a word represents a complex of associations, it is representing much more, and a much richer material, than what the dictionaries establish as its definition. The word is in this conception much richer than simply being a *signifier* with a corresponding *signified*, established thanks to convention – as Saussure and followers envisions language. If a word is attached to a complex net of configurations, it may prompt all kind of *unconventional* significations and valuations with no place in a dictionary, because they belong to the individual's personal chain of associations.[351]

Herder once stated that language originates as "passionate sounds."[352] In Nietzsche, we return to the idea that words (insofar as they are alive, be-

---

      des Geistes." In *Nietzsche-Studien*, Band 30. Berlin, New York (Walter de Gruyter), 2001, p. 3.

[351] We notice that this idea anticipates Freud's later technique of 'free association.' In his analyses of dreams, Freud came to realize that the words represented in dreams very rarely represented what they represented in a conventional sense. A 'book,' a 'flower,' a 'theater ticket,' a 'beetle' could mean something completely different from what was their conventional meaning.

[352] We recall that Herder already had a sophisticated theory of the origin of language, on several counts anticipating Nietzsche and Freud's. One can compare to this passage of Herder's: "[Man] manifests reflection when, confronted with the vast hovering dream of images which pass by his senses, he can collect himself into a moment of wakefulness and dwell at will on one image, can observe it clearly and more calmly, and can select in it distinguish-

4. Fundamentals in the Construction of a Biological-Linguistic Subject

cause they can be dead too) represent 'passions.' But, whereas in Herder, 'passion' was a concept that he could not explain any further, in Freud and Nietzsche, we find a beginning and tentative explanation of the 'passionate' background of words. When we receive and react to the impressions deriving from out outer world, we not only characterize and identify objects, thanks to the words we pre-consciously attach to them; we also activate *mnemic images* associated to the identified object. This means that the object may provoke 'feelings' (feelings of hostility or friendliness) that materialize themselves in a 'motor discharge'; a bodily expression. Accord-

---

ing marks for himself so that he will know that this object is this and not another. He thus manifests reflection if he is able not only to recognize all characteristics vividly or clearly but if he can also recognize and acknowledge to himself one or several of them as distinguishing characteristics. The first act of this acknowledgment results in a clear concept; it is the first judgment of the soul – and through what did this acknowledgment occur? Through a distinguishing mark which he had to single out and which, as a distinguishing mark for reflection, struck him clearly." Herder: Über den Ursprung der Sprache. In *Frühe Schriften*, Werke bd. 1, (Frankfurt a/M: Deutscher Klassiker Verlag, 1985), p. 722-23. The slow recognition of a thing as distinctive – the gradual capability *to see something as something* – is also in Herder the precondition for the emergence of the word. Herder explains even better how this formation of language occurred, how the *origin* of language was conceived: "Let that lamb there, as an image, pass by under his eyes; it is to him, as it is to no other animal. Not as it would appear to the hungry, scenting wolf! Not as it would appear to the blood-lapping lion. [. . .] Not so with man! As soon as he feels the need to come to know the sheep, no instinct gets in his way; no one sense of his pulls him too close to it or too far away from it. It stands there, entirely as it manifests itself in his sense. White, soft, woolly – his soul in reflective exercise seeks a distinguishing mark – the sheep bleats! His soul has found the distinguishing mark. The inner sense is at work. This bleating, which makes upon man's soul the strongest impression . . . the soul retains it. The sheep comes again. White, soft, woolly – the soul sees, touches, remembers, seeks a distinguishing mark – the sheep bleats, and the soul recognizes it. And it feels inside, 'Yes, you are that which bleats.' It has recognized it humanly when it recognized and named it clearly, that is, with a distinguishing mark." Herder: Über den Ursprung der Sprache, loc. cit., p. 723. The lamb jumping past the perceptive subject is not recognized *as such* before the subject recalls from its memory the same 'white, soft, woolly' creature, identical to the creature jumping about in its visual field. When finally it "bleats," the subject understands, 'Ha, you are the one that bleats,' and it recognizes the lamb *as* lamb. The subject has recognized *something as something*; it has established identity, the $A = A$, and in the process reduced or simplified a world of becoming into a world of being.

ing to Freud, one of the components of the word was the so-called *motor-image*, implying that various expressions are accompanying the word in the form of *the images of motor reactions*, i.e., gestures, facial expressions, guttural exclamations, etc.

To feel disgusted by something is for example not simply to be able to pronounce the sentence, 'this is disgusting!' It is not only the *intellect* that reacts with disgust, the *body* reacts too, and probably far stronger. The body *enacts a violent de-cathexis* of the *mnemic image of the object*. The process is approximately the following: the object is *seen and identified*; it activates *mnemic images* of 'disgust'; then it activates *sound-images* and *motor-images* as reaction to the *mnemic images*. If the *mnemic images* signify 'disgust,' they are literally thrown out of the body. The sight of the disgusting object evokes the *mnemic image* of something *in* the body that is regarded as terrifying, horrific, dangerous, venomous, etc. – something the body wants to get rid of. It is *as if* thrown up or spit out (one makes spitting- or vomiting-gestures when one encounters something truly disgusting – illogical as this may be, because the object is of course *already outside*).

Thanks to this extra dimension of the word, its ability to activate *mnemic images* and discharge emotions, a 'language of disgust' is not reducible here to the monotonous and impassioned pronunciation of the sentence, 'it is disgusting!' (One may, for example, see 'language of disgust' well depicted by Woody Allen fighting a spider in *Annie Hall* – the panic, the anxiety, the bodily convulsions, the exclamations of fragmented language, the fear of the disgusting object he has to encounter and fight, etc. Another example, the sight of a cockroach produce in some cultures no significant response – cockroaches are not in themselves aggressive, menacing, poisonous, or dangerous, and no response need necessarily develop. In most Western Cultures, however, they are almost uniformly seen as 'disgusting.' So, if in some cultures, the sight of a cockroach evokes no particular memories, in the latter case, the sight of a cockroach is directed into a neurological network of complex associations of *mnemic images*. This complex is furthermore connected to linguistic sound-images and motor-images, originally installed through learning-processes, that all indicate something we simplifying call 'disgust.' So, the disgusting cockroach is never disgusting in-itself, and disgust is never derivable from the cockroach; however, disgust is *added* to the object, and the object is being *interpreted* as such. As such added, the interpretation as linguistic expression has motor-images that provoke motor-reactions; the expression effects the body; the body 'feels' disgusted. It is, however, all invention and creation. It is 'all in the mind,' as one says. A 'cultural world' has been invented where cockroaches have significance as repulsive. Now, they may return to haunt our dreams (or our B-movies), where in cultures where they are insignificant, nothing returns.)

4.4.3. The "Fluidity of Meaning."

Werner Stegmaier introduces, in his *Nietzsches Genealogie*,[353] a concept of something he calls 'floating meaning' [*'Flüssigen Sinns'*], or sometimes 'meaning-displacement' [*'Sinn-Verschiebung'*]. What we have been describing above is closely related to this concept, which most essentially asserts that the meaning of a word is never fix and never timeless.

Although we are able to communicate, implying that we stabilize meaning in specific well-known contexts, and understand signs as representing such stabilized meaning, the relationship between a word and meaning does *never* coagulate; meaning always *fluctuate*. In its two most immediate conceptions, the meaning of a word is fluid, *first*, because words may have, and often have, more than one conventional meaning. An example from the textbooks points out that 'bank' may as noun refer to a financial institution or to a riverbank (in the verbal form, one can *bank on*, rely on, somebody's support; or one can *bank*, deposit, a cheque, etc.). This commonplace characteristic has often been discussed, and is well-understood in linguistics and language theory. As such, a word's multiple meanings are not truly fluid or floating; they are fixed and well-defined within their *contexts*. *Second*, in another immediate conception, the meaning of a word is fluid because words changes meaning historically. This is another well-known 'fluidity,' having often been studied by diachronic linguistics, and is often exemplified by Saussure himself. As such, a word's multiple historical meanings are again not truly fluid or floating, since they are fixed and well-defined in their *historical contexts*. Both context-dependence and the historical development of language are facts well-understood and well-described by the linguist and the language-philosopher alike. Without questioning these insights, we shall suggest a deeper-rooted and more radical *fluidity of meaning*, as we return to our neurological or psychological perspective from above.

We can get a first, and maybe surprising, sense of *radical fluidity of meaning* when we read the pearls of wisdom in our daily newspapers. Here we often come across something common redefined in an adage or a maxim: 'what is life but a . . . ,' 'what is love other than . . . ,' and we read a definition that is usually a complete surprise and nobody has ever before

---

[353] Stegmaier: *Nietzsches 'Genealogie der Moral'*, loc. cit., p. 80ff.

contemplated, and nonetheless often produces a sense of familiarity. In the film *Forest Gump*, life was for example compared to "a box of chocolates." (The idea must be that when one selects a piece, one sometimes makes a good pick, sometimes not. In an expensive box of chocolates, the pieces are wrapped up, so one is not in control of what one chooses.) Now, we surely know that 'life,' as defined in the dictionary, has nothing to do with chocolates, and we may therefore ask ourselves: how is the adage possible; how is such a radically different 'meaning-addition' [*Sinn-hineinlegung*] possible? – And the *simple* answer we can now provide too: it is possible because words are always the flimsy stand-ins for something *that is not understood*!

Freud's 'thing-presentations,' and Nietzsche's 'chaos of inner experiences,' are what we above described as ego-clusters: small islands of 'knowledge' in the neurological net that determines individual reactions to impressions. These 'islands' are in-themselves complex, and the complexity increases exponentially into super-complexities insofar as they (via synapses) connect to other 'islands.' Language is our means to bring order into this chaos. We must assume that a generic and all-inclusive concept like 'life' finds cathected clusters in almost every corner of the network; consequently, somewhere in the net, it is also possible to find "a box of chocolates" (or what metaphorically it implies). The reader-response is therefore '*Aha!*' – As if the reader 'already knew' this 'obvious' connection or association! However, the reader is naïve, because she does not know that she 'already know' another couple of million possible connections.

In *Chapter 2*, we introduced a diagram formalizing the signifier-signified relation from Structural Linguistics as an a- and b-level, adding a c-level as a continuum of external reality that eventually is segmented and structured, thanks to the sign (the signifier-signified, or the a/b, level). The model was applied to external reality; but we can now apply the same model to internal reality, to 'inner-mental life.' We still have a sign, a signifier-signified relation, but now the c-level represents a reality of 'inner experiences' or 'memory traces' that in-themselves stay chaotic, but may surface in consciousness, that is, may be segmented, structured, and simplified, thanks to conventional signs. In the social use of language – insofar as we communicate and understand each other – the conventional sign *reduces* the fluctuation of meaning, whereas inner life represents a domain over which the sign never gains control. Here, we find an inner anarchy perpetually rebelling against conventions. The c-level, the continuum, is now like such a *rebellious signified*. It is '*Another Signified,*' we shall say, behind the conventionally established signified. It represents our so-called *fluid meaning* behind the *conventionally established meaning*. It becomes like *a signified of the signified*, in a complex model of the sign consisting now of *signifier, signified*, and *the Other Signified*. The 'Other Signified' is the chaos, that we either do not know, or we sink back into in dreams; and sometimes, in insanity.

Such a theory does not, and is not meant to, contradict the recognition from Structural Linguistics and Language Philosophy that, in our social practices, the signifier-signified relationship is *conventional* and *arbitrary*; and that the system of signs, as a *system of differences*, is independent of the referent. In our theory, dictionaries are still our linguistic law-books for prescribing how to use language correctly, intended as they are to root out any *private uses* of language. As social individuals, we comply with, and we rely on these conventional linguistic codes in communicative action. Non-compliance is indeed perceived and treated as pathology.[354] In summa, in social life we find something as relatively 'rational' and 'stable' as a *signifier-signified relationship.*[355]

However, this 'rational' theory of the sign does not include a dimension for the 'emotional word,' i.e., the dimension for a 'chaotic inner life,' where we find, not the conventionally established *signifier-signified* relationship, but the 'irrational' *signifier-signified-the Other Signified* relationship. In the latter case, the signifier is being tied up in a *double-bind trap*; it is designat-

---

[354] One of the manifestations of 'schizophrenia' (in itself a label for a psychological condition we do not fully understand) is the utter abandon of conventional language-use and other social-linguistic codes. It is as if the schizophrenic did not tolerate the social-linguistic codes, and 'chose' to ignore and bypass the 'conventional signified.' He consequently slipped back into what we here call *the Other Signified*; this his completely private world of millions of possible connections; this his cozy and safe world of private significations and hallucinations.

[355] Stegmaier has a similar conclusion: "That it cannot be definitely established what they [concepts] are and mean, does not imply that they cannot be mutually communicated, on the contrary. Only that which has no established meaning can be mutually communicated in signs. The stable, to everybody and forever, identical meaning has corresponding signs only if also the conditions of communications could be stabilized to everybody and forever. Stable meaning presupposes stable conditions of communication, if the context changes, then also the meaning changes. However, when different people communicate with one another, also the conditions of communication change. The signs that are used in communication, must therefore be restricted, when many are supposed to be using them. But then it must be possible, in our daily lives, to understand the same signs differently. . . . . "Meaning-addition" [*Sinn-hineinlegen*], as Nietzsche notes in his Nachlaß, "is in most cases a new interpretation added to an old interpretation that has become incomprehensible, which is in itself only a sign." (Stegmaier, loc. cit. p. 76.)

ing both the relatively simple *conventionally determined signified*, and the extremely complex *privately determined signified*, the inner continuum.[356] The 'emotional word' is now no longer simply identical to its agreed upon 'meaning,' it expresses a million other 'things' besides.[357] This inner continuum, these 'million other things,' is equivalent to something Nietzsche sometimes describes as the "music behind the words" and the "passions behind this music."

> The best understood about language is not the word itself, but rather the tone, force, modulation, tempo, in which a sequence of words are being pronounced – in brief, the music behind the words, the passions behind this music, the person behind this passion. This is therefore what cannot be d e s c r i b e d. Therefore, it has nothing to do with writing. (Nachlaß 1882, KSA 10, 3[1/296]).

A word without this music, without this passion, without this person, is also described as a dead word; cf. the poem, "Das Wort": "A dead word, a hideous thing // A skeleton-rattling cling, cling, cling" [*Ein Todtes Wort, ein häßlich Ding // Ein klapperdürres Kling, Kling, Kling*]. (Nachlaß 1882, KSA 10, 1[107]).

---

[356] In our daily communication, we are always caught up in these couple-bind traps. Any example will do! If a woman complains to her husband, "you don't like me any more," the man does not soothe her doubts and suspicions by responding, "but yes, I do like you," because 'like' is bound up in a double-bind trap. To use it according to dictionary helps nobody; the man has to activate a whole different battery of emotional manifestations if he wants to convince; manifestations that may have something to do with 'like' and may have 'like' at its core, but consists of sound- and motor-images that are not found in a dictionary under the entry 'like.'

[357] Returning to our example above: according to the dictionary, a 'cockroach' can obviously not be defined as "a disgusting insect," but more sobering as "any of numerous orthopterous insects of the family *Blattidae*, characterized by a flattened body, rapid movements, and nocturnal habits." The dictionary says that cockroaches have a 'flattened body, etc.'; and I surely believe in the dictionary. Nonetheless, my inner experiences tell me something different; they for example tell me that cockroaches, when turned around, look swollen and juicy, and (for good measure) just about to burst. Intellectually I know better, but time and again, when I come across the creature, my body overrules my intellect. According to certain 'rapid movements' and 'nocturnal habits' of my inner mental life (as I now may say, embracing a certain *fluidity*), *meaning floats*, and a word can come to mean just about anything.

Part III

*Reconciling Positions and
Drawing up Implications*

5. The 'Confused-Aggressive' Subject as the Condition of the Possibility for Ideology

5.0. Introduction.

In the present section, we shall reconcile different branches or aspects of Nietzsche's thinking. *First*, we will continue what we tentatively began toward the end of the previous chapter, namely, to see Nietzsche's criticism of morality and the moral subject as a *critique of ideology*, and with this combine two branches of Nietzschean thinking, *criticism of the unified subject* and *criticism of morality*, into an explanation of the nature and constitution of *ideology*. Accordingly, we read Nietzsche's 'priest' as a label for *any ideologue*, Nietzsche's 'slave' as the *ideologically infected* subject, and Nietzsche's 'master' as the promise of an *ideologically emancipated* subject. (In the following *Chapter 5,* we will return to and detail this interpretation, especially in a reading of the difficult third part of *Genealogie der Moral*). *Secondly*, we will reconcile another two aspects of Nietzschean thinking, namely his *epistemology*, as introduced in *Chapter 2*, and the *theories of split or fragmented subjectivity* as introduced in *Chapters 3 & 4*. We will continue to promote the view that Nietzsche in his epistemology is a *Realist*, rather than an *Idealist* (as often received), but that he is so in a qualified sense that takes into account his precocious neurological/cognitive theories of the subject.

5.1. Ego-Clusters as Competing Power-Configurations.

We have learned that the evolution of "cells" or "ego clusters" is a question of the self-preservation and survival of the individual. With the invention of an 'ego' (which is in fact *many egoes*), the subject is capable of judging and gaining control over reality (external as well as internal). The subject quasi-randomly evolves certain personality traits that ensure this control. In Nietzsche's language, it evolves certain "aristocratic cells" that will exert their control over more primitive and impulsive cells.[358] Although this signifies a condition present in every human being, Nietzsche's so-called "master" or "noble" represents the rare individual who to an exceptional degree succeeds in subordinating impulsive cells to more powerful aristocratic cells. The master creates him or herself out of original chaos; asserting out of multiple wills-to-power his or her own will-to-power; becoming thus the *relatively more homogeneous*, not heterogeneous, subject (see also *Chapter 5*).

In this particular context, Nietzsche's famous perspectivism is now not merely a question of different individuals imposing on the world different interpretations according to their different wills-to-power; according to cognitive, moral, political, or religious preferences and interests. Much more profoundly, we encounter in Nietzsche an *inner perspectivism* in every subject, insofar as the single subject is a multiplicity, made up of multiple "cells," and thus populated with several wills-to-power)[359]

---

[358] Cf. "[We] assume a multiplicity of subjects, whose interaction and struggle is the basis of our thought and our consciousness in general? A kind of aristocracy of 'cells' [Eine Art Aristocratie von 'zellen'] in which dominion resides." (Nachlaß 1885, KSA 11, 40[42]).

[359] Cf. "The human being as a multiplicity of "wills to power" (Nachlaß 1885–86; *KSA* 12, 1 [58]); "The individual contains far more persons, than he thinks. The 'person' is only an accentuation, a concentration of treats and qualities." (Nachlaß 1884, KSA 11, 25[365]). "We gain the correct idea of the nature of our subject-unity, namely as regents at the head of a communality" (WM, 492). Hales and Welshon label Nietzsche's theory of the self, *Nietzsche's Bundle Theory/No Self View*. As to what Nietzsche might mean by a 'self' that is, firstly, *a bundle* and, secondly, *not one*, they suggest the following answer: "The self is a confederation of drives and affects, an 'aristocracy' of them. Which drives and motivations may be uppermost at any time is mutable; the lead bird in the flock changes. This reveals the deep constitutional perspectivity of the Nietzschean self. Which goals are unified by any particular drive is a function of what pragmatically promotes power for that drive." (Hales & Welshon: Nietzsche's Perspectivism. Urbana (The University of Illinois Press), 2000, p. 171). In our vocabulary, 'ego-clusters' have been quasi-randomly internalized as preconscious strategies adopted for the (phantasmatic) resolution of pragmatic problems in the individual's life-world. In Nietzsche's intra-subjective perspectivism, however, we must be talking not so much of drives, but rather about the strategies by which drives find *expression*, are *redirected*, or are *repressed*. Nietzsche's *self* is an 'aristocracy' of drives and affects. Which drives have the upper hand at any time is changeable. Which goals are being

5. The 'Confused-Aggressive' Subject as the Possibility for Ideology

The self is seen as composed of quanta of forces organized into several units in perpetual competition. These quanta of forces do not exist in a state of stasis but are in perpetual change.[360] Our so-called ego is formed through a struggle between ego-units or ego-clusters, a struggle in which some go under, some survive, some expand, some merge, and some live harmoniously side by side, however stark is the contradiction between the respective imperatives informing their beliefs. In this conception of the subject, there is no rational supervision of the psyche, no overarching *logical super-self*.[361]

Our inner experiences exist primordially as unstructured chaos. However, upon this chaos we impose a certain order. This implies in the concrete that we, by means of language, impose our interpretations on a certain material, as such, shape, organize, and fashion that material to fit a new linguistic medium. Although inner experiences are in principle open-ended and infinite, language, consisting of conventionally locked linguistic signs, is in principle simplifying and generalizing. This implies that the translation from *inner experience* into *language* involves an inevitable distortion, falsification, and simplification of the inner experience. Notwithstanding this falsification, Nietzsche emphasizes that language introduces us to the *only* inner world of which we can become conscious. We become conscious only of this simplified and falsified inner world; we become conscious only of a "surface and sign world" (cf. FW 354). Were it not for language, we would not possess schemata or taxonomies through which to understand the chaos of inner life; we would not recognize an impression as being such-and-such, as being this and not that, belonging as this part to that whole, following this and preceding that, and so on.[362]

---

pursued by any particular drive is a function of what pragmatically promotes power for that drive. In Nietzsche's intra-subjective perspectivism, 'ego-clusters' adopt different strategies by which to realize phantasmatic objectives.

[360] cf.: "The sphere of a subject is constantly growing or decreasing, the center of the system constantly shifting; in cases where it cannot organize the appropriate mass, it breaks into two parts" (WM, 488)

[361] Cf. Schlimgen: "The total-organism [*Gesammtorganismus*] as human being is to [Nietzsche] a 'tremendous synthesis of living beings and intellects'; a multiplicity of 'consciousnesses.' [. . .] These many consciousnesses, this multiplicity of living beings, or, as he also says, 'subjects,' is situated as a 'governing multiplicity and aristocracy.' Schlimgen, Erwin: Nietzsches Theorie, loc. cit. p. 48.

[362] Cf.: "We stop thinking when we no longer do so according to the linguistic compulsions [*Sprachliche zwange*] [. . .] Reason

328   Chapter 4: Theory of Knowledge as Neuro-Epistemology

This predicament poses a dilemma at the root of our subjectivity. Inasmuch as language is the only tool we have at our disposal for expressing ourselves, it is obvious that this tool, being the *standard product* of the multitude, is incapable of expressing the richness and complexity of our inner selves. It can only express a simplified and conventionally acceptable version of our so-called inner self.

Language produces a knowledge of our selves by means of conventional symbols that simplify the material they are explaining. Still, this knowledge transforms the strange and the other into the familiar. Explanation is reassuring; it neutralizes and disarms the strange and the other by appropriating and assimilating it. As such, to Nietzsche, knowledge is power (as it was, but in an entirely different sense, to Francis Bacon), because it reassures us in our herd instinct; it reduces what is strange and other to what is familiar *for us*.

5.2. The Master-Analogy: Inner-Mental Life as a Game of Chess.

Nietzsche has replaced the Aristotelian notion of essence with his own notion of power. In contrast to essence, power is always up against some other power. In a subject, which is assembled as localities of power constellations, there is no essence in the sense of a single overarching and independent power.[363]

[*vernünftige Denken*] is an interpretation according to a scheme, that we cannot discard [*abwerfen*]." (Nachlaß 1887, KSA 12, 5[22]).

[363] The passage paraphrases Werner Stegmaier's more detailed description: "'Essence' [*Wesen*] was Aristoteles' notion by which to think identity; he thought identity, while subtracting from it, time. He subtracted time, since he conceived 'essence' as a power overpowering becoming, as the master over *its own* changes. Nietzsche, in order to think identity as temporal [*zeitliche*], is now returning from the notion of essence to the notion of power [*Macht*]. He no longer understands 'power' [. . .] as 'essence'. Power is for Nietzsche power up against another power, a power in play with other powers. It is in this we have the distinction: through the notion of essence, identity becomes independent from the other; through the notion of power, on the contrary, it is conceived as dependent of the other. However, in the dependency of the other, essence becomes in itself changeable [*veränderlich*]; in the power play, it is not stable, but it always has to be stabilized over again. In Nietzsche's sense, power is the power to bring to bear such stabilizations/fixations [*Festlegungen*]; it is in the organic world the power to organize the other within the meaningfulness of the self; and, insofar as human thinking and concepts are put in play, it is to create order through

Instead of a self-identical self, expressing or acting out itself in the world, we have a self, engaged in perpetual inner struggles; promoting some and demoting some others of these internalized positions. Since we as humans do not see 'forces,' 'energies,' and the like, we only perceive these positions insofar as they are linguisticized, i.e., turned into thought- and sign-processes. The processes are in themselves will-to-power-processes; and, as already suggested, in their most rudimentary form, they empower the subject to deal with reality. They fend off and neutralize the 'pleasures' of the inner world, the 'mad' pleasures of *hallucination* and *auto-affection*. On this essential level, will-to-power-processes are designed to avoid *ever-threatening madness*; they are *inhibitors* suppressing the impulsiveness of Freud's 'hallucinations' and Nietzsche's 'inner chaos.' They indicate to the individual what is *Real*.

However, will-to-power-processes penetrate the system also on higher levels. They also manifest themselves in the form of the local (ideological or quasi-ideological) formations and configurations in a subject. As such formations, they have been transformed into sign- and thought-processes, engaged in internal power-struggles, always competing.

As such, they can be compared to a game of chess (where, *mutatis mutandis*, the *board* becomes the *brain*, and the *game* becomes the *mind*) on three counts. (i) There are two armies, a black and a white, opposing each other, and engaged in perpetual struggle until the death of one of the kings. In the process, different pieces are moved around; now to attack and now to defend, as such creating, on the chess-board, strategic 'clusters,' different power-concentrations that constantly change – and may change radically with just a single move of a piece. Sometimes one 'group' or 'configuration' is in power, sometimes it loses it again, and transfers power to another configuration on the board, etc. (ii) We can take the analogy a step further: chess is essentially an *aggressive* game; the ultimate end of the game is after all 'to kill' the other king; all pieces of one's army participate in achieving this singular end. A group or a configuration on the board is therefore 'good' or 'bad' only to the extent it efficiently brings about this outcome. A configuration has *value* only insofar as it has *power*; it has no value in-itself; there is no 'good' or 'bad' (strong or weak) cluster in itself; there is just a continuous investment and divestment of power in some pieces in order to achieve the ultimate end. (iii) We can press the analogy still further: although the *raison d'etre* of chess is 'to kill' the other king, as the flipside of the same coin, equally important is it to defend one's own. The

---

concepts." (Stegmaier, Werner: Nietzsches 'Genealogie der Moral'; loc. cit., p. 74).

'good king' is up against the 'bad king,' as white against black. All clusters are lined up in order to attack the strange and unfamiliar (which is understood as 'evil'), and to defend the known and familiar (which is understood as 'good'). The 'good king' is here our designation for what one 'loves' and 'desires'; it is an overbearing ruling idea internalized in the psyche; it is a particularly well cathected semantic cluster, standing out as something special among multiple clusters; it is a 'master-signifier' around which the individual arranges his or her life.

At this level of subjectivity, will-to-power (which has several applications in Nietzsche) has entirely transparent connotations to power. If the psyche is a chess-game where every move is made in order to attack the foreign king, and defend one's own, then the psyche explicitly operates according to 'will-to-power-processes'; then the psyche is a *battleground* for defending its most cherished beliefs, and attacking anything threatening these beliefs; then the psyche is most essentially, *aggressive*; not, as in the psychoanalysis of early Freud, *sexual*. At this level, will-to-power is desire-for-power, or what we might describe as *power-desire* in contrast to Freud's *sexual desire*.

5.3. On Intrinsic Irrationality.

In such an aggressive psyche 'everything goes'; we cannot here expect to find a strong commitment to logic and reason. If or when incompatibility or contradiction between imperatives emerges, there is only a scant awareness of 'self-contradiction,' if any at all. There is no moral law, no moral imperative. Here, Nietzsche's catch-phrase applies, "what is useful to *me*, is something *good*" (M 102). In this confused psyche, the most immediate consequences of a position are not necessarily drawn; on the contrary, consequences defeating the position may well be defended alongside the position they defeat. Here, the psyche does not bother itself about solving contradictions, incompatibilities, irrationalities, or other logical tensions in inner-life. If a tension ever surfaces, the psyche does something much easier and faster. It creates a new way to see and understand; a new 'perspective'; a new inner-mental compartment, where something unacceptable can suddenly be seen as acceptable. This *perspectival 'method'* by which to solve contradictions overrides the methods of formal logic. Thanks to this 'method,' it is now possible to mean both A and non-A, and (if at all the contradiction surfaces as such) with only the skimpiest of explanations.

A man may consider himself a 'good man,' from what normally follows that he treats fellow human beings benevolently; and then, he may on a reg-

5. The 'Confused-Aggressive' Subject as the Possibility for Ideology 331

ular basis be beating up his wife. As an unreflective subject, this would create no inner conflict in his aggressive-confused psyche, and he would be living the conflict with a clear conscience (as psychologists and social workers, dealing with such cases on a daily basis, will tell us is often the case). A subject, just a notch more reflective, might invent a law, a rule, or a principle according to which he, as a 'good man,' and of no fault of his own, is somehow forced to discipline his wife (e.g., "*women deserve . . .*"; "*she makes me . . .*"). According to Freud, he *rationalizes*. He creates an *ad hoc amendment to* (or an *ad hoc annulment of*) a general rule, meaning that he creates another perspective from where to see something old as something new. In the example of such a 'good wife-beating man,' we have at least two 'compartments' or 'configurations' standing over and against one another in stark contradiction; the only reason why this stark *contradiction* is not felt as *self-contradiction* is that the 'self' is not a unity. The self is like, as we had it in metaphor in the previous chapter, a cabinet with several drawers storing different articles: one drawer for shirts, one for socks, one for ties, etc. To store different articles in different places cannot be experienced as contradiction. The 'good man' is such a cabinet with several drawers. Although he offends our ethical standards and imperatives, he thinks that one drawer is as good as the next one. He has the agility of a cat; now, he jumps into one drawer, one into another. The 'good man' may realize that it is *wrong* to beat up his wife; but, he regretfully tells himself, it is also sometimes *necessary*. He is making the contradiction tolerable, because he is talking from two different places, two different compartments, two different 'drawers'; utilizing two different discourses, where in one of them, the action is his fault (and he congratulates himself for admitting so much), and in the second, the action is his wife's fault (and he blames her for making it necessary). Thanks to *perspectival conflict-resolution*, no contradiction emerges in inner-life; and the subject goes on living a life in complete inner harmony.

We notice that if the human being is a bundle of 'drives' – transformed into 'semantic clusters' – and engaged in perpetual infightings, it possesses an almost infinite flexibility and plasticity. It has in its *intrinsic structure* the ability to adopt and mean everything, if not at once and simultaneously, then under *rapidly shifting* perspectives, whose coherence and consistency is a small matter.

We notice that it is only *thanks to* 'logicization' and 'linguistication' that the psyche becomes an extremely *illogical* place. Chaos in itself cannot be 'illogical,' and cannot produce a contradiction. The fluctuating inner-life has to be stabilized into entities/identities, before something can be recognized with awareness, and as such can be seen as standing over and against something else. Therefore, linguistication of inner-life must be a condition *sine qua non* for detecting something like self-contradiction in the psyche; it is, however, not a *sufficient* condition, because it is easily overridden by what we labeled *perspectival conflict-resolution.*

5.4. On 'Irrationality' as Frenetic Defense of 'Truth.'

We said that the psyche was like a chess-game where every move is done in order to attack the foreign king, and defend one's own; the psyche was as such a *battleground* for defending an individual's most cherished beliefs, and attacking anything threatening these beliefs. The soliloquizing subject is now engaged in a perpetual war within itself to hold on to its 'truths,' its 'master-signifiers.' In this activity, the subject moves its different pieces around in an infinite number of constellations. Therefore, let us take our chess-analogy still another step. In its inner 'game of chess,' the soliloquizing self is necessarily engaged in a futile one-man chess-game, where, for example, the desire to 'defeat' a hostile truth-threatening position is merely one self's desire to defeat another self – but where the final and conclusive checkmate never occurs because, within a single ego, one partition of the multiple-self subject is quite incapable of outwitting another partition. The interior chess-game remains as such locked up in some inconclusive paralysis; pieces are continuously being moved around in order to protect now one, now another locality, but nothing decisive happens. On the Nietzschean chessboard, 'truth' seems at best to be only changing localities, changing semantic clusters, or changing will-to-power concentrations.

Thanks to this paralysis, the subject never finds a conclusive confirmation of itself; a final answer to the existential question, 'who am I, what should I do.' The subject remains a fragile construction because its self-interpretations are fragile; or, to put it more strongly, the subject is fragile because interpretations are *always* fragile. Like an overstretched rubber band, the subject is always in peril of slipping back into its own intolerable chaos. We now suggest that because the subject, unconsciously, knows this – but knows it as repressed knowledge that cannot and must not be admitted into consciousness – it also puts up a tenacious fight to keep its interpretations – its 'truths,' its dearest and most precious possessions – intact. It is because interpretations are the *always fragile* foundational network of the self that there is in Nietzsche a "will to truth." The fear of the chaotic, the changing, the random, and the contingent breeds its own contrary; it stirs up a kind of counter-hope and counter-promise erected on top of the void: there *must* be truth. The will-to-truth is thus the will to stabilize and fixate

5. The 'Confused-Aggressive' Subject as the Possibility for Ideology

that which is in itself never stable and fixed, and which the subject knows (unconsciously) is never stable and fixed. Will-to-power becomes a will-to-truth, where 'truth' here designates the individual's strongest beliefs – the so-called 'master-signifiers' of the individual, according to which he or she projects meaning into its universe.

Truth becomes a precious imaginary object; it promises a world which – according to the philosophical (Platonic) tradition – "does not contradict, does not deceive, does not change"; a world "in which one does not suffer"; a world which guarantees "happiness":

> Man seeks "Truth"; a value, which does not contradict, does not deceive, does not change, a true world – a world in which one does not suffer: contradiction, deception, change – causes of suffering! He does not doubt that a world, as it should be, exists; he wants to find a way to it. [. . .] Happiness can only be guaranteed in what is existing [*im Seienden*]: change and accident rules it out [. . .] In summa, the world, as it should be, exists; but this world in which we live, in only an error, – this our world should not exist. (Nachlaß 1886-87, KSA 12, 9[60], p. 364-5).

'Truth' is equated with 'happiness'; we therefore suggest that this 'defense of imaginary happiness' is the background-motive for the frenetic defense of truth in the individual.[364]

Moreover, we notice that on this internal chessboard, the individual's 'truths' do not exist only as ideal objects of *desire*; they also exist as ideal objects of *hatred*. Humans do not simply cathect positions they like, they also anti-cathect positions they do not like. A 'defense of imaginary happiness' involves automatically an offensive on what threatens this image. Anti-cathexis of hate-objects might even exert a stronger influence over the subject than the cathexis of love-objects; to hate, to live for revenge, gives life a unique purpose and urgency. This implies that anti-cathected hate-objects exist in the subject as internalized positions that have to be attacked incessantly.

---

[364] It is perhaps not necessary to spell out that nearly any kinds of semantic objects may promise this imaginary 'happiness.' The image of a Germany cleansed of Jews makes the fascist 'happy.' To the devoted catholic, the thought of the 'virgin Mary' – who has no actual appearance, and is truly imaginary – makes 'happy.' It is in these, and numerous other cases, difficult to see how the self actually benefits; and it what the 'happiness' consists. Nevertheless, these purely imaginary ideological constructions have all-too real consequences to the reality of the subject.

We understand the implications: if in Freud's early psychoanalysis, everything in the psyche works according to the so-called 'pleasure-principle' – meaning that in the last analysis, everything is expression of wants or desires[365] – in Nietzsche's so-called 'confused-aggressive' subject, we suggest that we instead find something we may neutrally designate, *intensities*; but not necessarily *desires* (although a *desire* is also an *intensity*; i.e., the psyche hyper-cathects love-objects as well as it hyper-cathects hate-objects; *intensities* include both). The Nietzschean subject constructs itself around *intensities*, positions that designate its particular 'truth,' and help articulating its particular will-to-truth. A subject's use of language will ultimately be referring to these intensities, implying that it will be serving, and revolving around, whatever 'truths' are cathected. In a will-to-power-to-truth-subject, busy defending its 'truths' (and attacking truth-threatening positions), there is no inbuilt rationality underpinning its use of language; rather, language is always first and foremost used *expediently*. The hyper-cathected position, the *intensity*, is like a hot inner core, and every semantic cluster coming into 'touch' with this core, changes value and color accordingly.

If for example a hostile object has been intensified in the psyche, all discourse is now directed at attacking it. We notice the mechanism at work all the time and everywhere; for example during political elections. Some people do not simply disagree with a political candidate, they *intensify* their disagreements, and recreate the candidate as a hostile object, who from then on can do nothing right, even when he or she suggests policies that are identical to those of the candidate they support. It is as if they have staked their existence and personal well-being on the outcome of the election. Hatred is now *nurtured, protected,* and *defended* at every possible opportunity. Anti-cathexis of the hostile object has become the subject's private obsession. Aggression is ignited and destruction is the aim.[366] When 'power' in a

---

[365] The dream is a manifestation of a desire, whether emerging from hunger, thirst, sex, or the simple wish to stay asleep. One of Freud's first laws of psychoanalysis is that the dream realizes a wish or desire. Psychoanalytic therapy is designed to secure the realization of these unilaterally positive desires; presupposed is it that the human being first and foremost wants *love*, but for all kinds of reasons has made the realization of this want impossible to itself; therapy is designed to lift the repression that desires have been subjected to. The assumption (which was of course modified in Freud's later Psychoanalysis by the introduction of the so-called 'death-drive') presupposes that desires are always aiming toward a love-object; that the psychical apparatus only hyper-cathects, or intensifies, love-objects.

[366] Whereas anti-cathexis is to be expected in political discourse, one might be slightly more surprised to see it exercised in discourses on woman and sexual-

5. The 'Confused-Aggressive' Subject as the Possibility for Ideology 335

fragmented subject has been turned into anti-cathexis, we have a psychological economy that Nietzsche diagnoses as resentment and envy. He designates it 'slave-morality,' in an attempt to establish a contrast to a supposedly less malevolent and venomous 'master-morality.' As we shall suggest in the following chapter, the 'slave' typically anti-cathects, whereas the 'master' typically only cathects.

A theory of irrationality starts to emerge. As paradoxically as it may at first glance seem, 'irrationality' does not emerge from any misapplication or misunderstanding of 'truth,' as traditionally understood. Rationality does not reside in man as his ideal form, and irrationality is not the deterioration of this idea form. Irrationality is not emerging, for example, because 'desires' invade and subjugate the otherwise rational subject, only to replace the otherwise neutrally judging subject with its own infantile spontaneity. In the first place, 'irrationality' *is belief in 'truth.'* In Nietzsche, 'will-to-truth' is always will-to-the-idea-of-truth; the *idea* of truth is never truth itself in any absolute and universal sense, as we have sufficiently seen in previous chapters. It is merely 'idea,' that is, interpretation; or, as we say, it is a hyper-cathected position, an intensified 'master-signifier,' providing the subject with 'existential meaning.'

Irrationality is now the *frenetic defense* of these hyper-cathected truth-positions (and the complementary attacks on truth-threatening positions). It is when language comes into 'touch' with this hot core of the subject that logic breaks down. Now, the subject's language deteriorates: conventional meaning turns into private meaning; formal logic turns into personal 'logic.' The tone and rhythm of speech changes; in frenetic defense, we often expe-

---

ity. Especially if one has been leaning heavily on the early Freud, one might ask in incredulity: could there really be a desire for not desiring sex? The answer is a clear and unambiguous, Yes! In a will-to-power-subject, everything is possible; sexuality has no privileged position; there is even nothing particularly unusual about anti-cathexis of woman and sex. We are suffused by a long tradition of writings where these two issues, oftentimes intertwined, are anti-cathected. 'Sexuality,' we recall, is typically anti-cathected in theological (Christian) discourse, implying that woman, as the temptress, is anti-cathected as well. In nineteenth century thinking, one of the most intense manifestations of anti-cathexis of woman we find in Schopenhauer's essay *Über die Weiber* (Schopenhauer, Arthur: Parerga und Paralipomena bd. II, SW bd. V. Frankfurt (Suhrkamp), 1986). A manifestation of anti-cathexis of sexuality we find in Kierkegaard's *Forførerens Dagbog* (Kierkegaard, Søren: *The Diary of a Seducer*; in Either/Or bd. I. Princeton (Princeton University Press), 1987). We recall that Kierkegaard's seducer does not seduce for the sake of sex (best is it if avoided), but for the sake of something called 'the interesting.'

rience a broken language, a stammering; we almost literally see the 'body' materializing in the subject. The aggression is apparent; and the reason is precisely that the 'truth' that has to be defended is merely interpretation, is *truly* 'a thing of nothing.' We believe that the stammering subject tacitly knows this all too well, although trying to drown the noise of doubt, and trying to convince itself and its audience of the opposite.

For the neutral observer of humans, a bleak picture emerges. Humans are incapable of acting and speaking with any degree of consistency. Formal knowledge of the rules of logic is certainly no guarantee for coherent dialogue. The pull downward toward randomly hyper-cathected positions, whether of 'love' or 'hatred,' is too strong, and overrides immediately the agent's whatever superficial awareness of existent rules for argument. As soon as the mind is no longer under extreme discipline, no longer occupied with the formal organization of x, y, and z, the surface cracks, and the mind slips immediately back from these acknowledged rules; rules it only kept extended for a brief moment and with too great an effort. The logical mind is like extended in free air with no support, why therefore it only sustains itself with an enormous effort, and only for brief moments of time.[367] The logical mind is without strength, and it is only too happy to slip back to its initial and much more comfortable positions, the old well-known hate and love objects.

5.5. On Ideology as Imaginary Repair of the Subjective Sense of Loss.

In the previous chapter, we referred to Nietzsche's notion of a *command-structure*, where a commander 'shouts' a command to the receptive subject, as essentially a description of the *ideologue* disseminating his *ideology*. The subject was receptive to this 'shouting' because of its cravings for meaning. Ideology became the artificial attempt to 'fill in' the empty positions of the subject with 'existential meaning.' This subjective emptiness was as such the fundamental condition of possibility of ideology. When a subject 'falls in love with an idea,' as we had it (or, not without a heavy dose of scorn, 'makes love to an idea'), it is because the idea has become an imaginary repair of loss. As such, ideology is imposed on the subject from without, and

---

[367] See also Schlimgen: "Logic serves, to Nietzsche, only as simplification, but to think so simple requires an enormous effort [*kraftanstrengung*]: affects, feelings, and contents associated or combined with the sign, must ("with a firm hand" ["*mit fester Hand*"]) be forced back [*zurüchgedrängt*]." Schlimgen: Nietzsches Theorie, loc. cit., p. 128.

is like *the fast foods* of 'existential meaning': it is ready-made and conveniently packaged; it is certain to contain all the flavors that our taste-buds find most agreeable; the subject needs only to engage in a minimal effort for its assimilation.

Ideology always repairs *a loss*; it also always appeals to the *original aggression* of the subject; it is like a virus infecting these two original subjective deficiencies, confusion and aggression. Ideology creates hyper-cathected love-objects as well as hyper-cathected hate-objects; its aim is to create a group of self-righteous individuals, who can legitimately unload their hatred on other groups. In all grand ideologies we notice how essentially important *hatred* is for the ideological appeal to the confused individual. By means of language and rhetoric, one intensifies and hyper-cathects certain positions, certain semantic clusters, in the individual as the means to win him or her over for the political cause. In the major ideologies, the cultivation of hatred is always essential. In Fascism, in the 30ies Germany, one hyper-cathected the Jews as favorite hate-group; in McCarthyism, in the 50ies United States, one hyper-cathected the 'communists'; in Stalinism, in the 50ies Soviet Union, one hyper-cathected a hate-group vaguely defined as renegades, dissidents, reactionaries, and contra-revolutionaries; and in the Ku Klux Klan, in the 60ies United States, one hyper-cathected the African Americans as favorite hate-group. The mechanism is always the same; on the subjective chess-board, one singles out a white king (oneself) against a black king (the other).[368] Always *oneself* against the *other* (possibly a residual valuation of the world deriving from our evolutionary prehistory: it was necessary to protect and defend one's habitat against incoming and migrating groups). In any case, the 'white king' becomes the 'truth' of the ideological subject, and a *frenetic defense* of this position, which is supposed to guarantee the subject and its society unity and integrity, is inaugurated.

In especially ferocious-aggressive ideologies, that which is 'truth-threatening' is interpreted as 'life-threatening' too. The metonymical gliding from the *loss of truth* to the *loss of life* is relatively minor, since that which is understood as truth-threatening, threatens the unity and integrity of the subject – implying that as well as *the inner core* of the subject *disintegrates* in the *loss of truth*, *the outer shell* of the subject *disintegrates* in the *loss of life*. The metonymical gliding from *loss of truth* to *loss of life*, from *inner core* to *outer shell* is slight; in the first case, the subject's inner semantic core *disintegrates*, in the second case, its body *disintegrates*. In both

---

[368] In Ku Klux Klan – a particularly primitive ideology – our metaphor, white versus black, has materialized as literal.

cases, the effect is a feeling of extreme danger, and we should not expect the confused subject to be able to draw any fine distinction between one disintegration and another. The *ideologue* consequently has an easy game to stir the subject into an ideological frenzy aimed at destruction of all those who allegedly threaten the subject's life (best and most recent example, the genocide in Rwanda in the mid-nineties).

Especially in GM, Nietzsche introduces the notion of the 'priest'; an entity, which becomes an object of Nietzsche's furious attacks. No language seems forceful enough to describe his disdain. The rhetoric is puzzling if a 'priest' is seen as the average small-town clergyman serving the spiritual needs of his congregation – is he or she not too insignificant to deserve Nietzsche's unrelenting philosophical attention in the first place; but if so, why the fury; is such a priest not rather entirely harmless? Since this literal understanding of Nietzsche's priest does not make good sense, we interpret the *priest*, not as the small-town clergyman, but as a completely different, and much more dangerous, creature, the *consummate ideologue*.[369] Under the label of Nietzsche's concept of 'priest,' we must (as always) allow for considerable *fluctuation of meaning*. As *ideologue*, the 'priest' enrages Nietzsche, because, as we now understand from above, he exploits and

---

[369] In current debate, we have recently been experiencing a certain 'anti-religion war,' started by Daniel Dennett and Sam Harris, and continued by Oxford biologist Richard Dawkins (see Dawkins, Richard: The God Delusion. London (Mariner Books), 2008). In our language, Dawkins is criticizing the 'priest' literally; to Dawkins, there is nothing harmless about the clergyman; all said and done, religion is "nonsense." A divine creature that could read "millions of humans simultaneously," and communicate to them its demands – but how, by means of "spiritons"! – such a creature would indeed have to be extremely complex, raising the problem of how it came into existence in the first place. That is all well and good, and we are not questioning Dawkins' basic assumption, 'religion is nonsense.' We question Dawkins' conviction of the urgency of his atheistic mission (a conviction propped up by, as I learned from a lecture of his, the impressive sales-figures of his book). I am not convinced. Religion was already 'nonsense' to Schopenhauer and Marx, not to speak of Nietzsche, and launching the insight yet again seems like a strange obsession; coming approximately one hundred and fifty years too late; knocking down already wide open doors. It is also not a mission I find particularly urgent; in our Western secularized societies, the church has a dwindling influence on political issues, if any at all; why kick a man already down? What *is* urgent, on the contrary, is a criticism of the *'priest' as ideologue*. Here, with unfortunate irony, Richard Dawkins comes across as an *ideologue* for his atheistic mission.

5. The 'Confused-Aggressive' Subject as the Possibility for Ideology

abuses the constitutional weakness of the subject, the subject's always-present lack of or always-threatening loss of existential meaning. A subject, which is already sufficiently confused as it is, is now persuaded – by promises of meaning, promises of an imaginary repair of its original lack – to serve even more confused purposes. The 'priest' as *ideologue* becomes the nadir of dishonesty.

5.6. Two Brief Applications.

If our so-called 'ego' consists of several ego-clusters – several positions or partitions – we notice that this understanding of the psyche, makes possible a new (and rather straightforward) interpretation of Søren Kierkegaard's famous *either-or*. Has in fact this formula, which Kierkegaard believes suspends everything important in life, anything to do with the famous 'existential choice,' as traditionally asserted? When Kierkegaard suggests that whether we do this or we do that, we regret it either way, he is only 'speaking his mind,' so to say (his 'partitioned' mind). He is only articulating a condition always present: there is always some partition of the self looking with envy on the choices of some other partition of the self. Is this famous formula not rather a formula for the utter futility of the so-called 'existential choice'?

> Marry, and you will regret it. Do not marry, and you will also regret it. Marry or do not marry, you will regret it either way. Whether you marry or you do not marry, you will regret it either way. [. . .] Hang yourself, and you will regret it. Do not hang yourself, and you will also regret it. Hang yourself or do not hang yourself, you will regret it either way. Whether you hang yourself or do not hang yourself, you will regret it either way.[370]

Since there is no *central supervision* of the self, 'it' speaks from several different places; voices are sounding their opinions from several different locations, creating a competition between multiple selves, where it is now the case that one self wants to get married, while another opposes it. The human self is this struggle between several different positions that may be, as single positions (and at best) *locally* rational, but granted their plurality, constantly collide, thus introduce into the subject different and conflicting imperatives.

---

[370] Kierkegaard, Søren: *Either/Or*, vol. I. Translation H. V. Hong & E. H. Hong. Princeton (Princeton University Press), 1987; p. 38.

The dream too we may see as a 'game of chess,' where inner mental struggles are being acted out with even less reservation than in waken life – with all their original passion and violence. Re-reading Freud's dream-interpretations in the light of Nietzsche's power-processes, we notice that they often thematize such collisions of conflicting imperatives. However, while Freud understands these collisions in the light of a single mechanism, the *desire* in one end of the system ('Id' controlled) versus the *censorship* in the other end of the system ('super-ego' controlled), in a Nietzschean re-formulation we instead imagine that we deal with several localities in mutual conflict. Furthermore, we notice that Freud's dream interpretations are not as often about 'sex,' as Freud invariably claims. They are as often about *aggression*: 'ambition,' 'control,' 'power,' 'jealousy,' or 'revenge.' Several commentators of Freud have noticed that Freud's own dreams, as interpreted by himself in *The Interpretation of Dreams*, are usually revolving around his professional aspirations and ambitions; they tend to thematize triumphs or frustrations related to his career; in their wishfulfillments, they promote himself and demote his colleagues. Freud, however, remains curiously oblivious to this aspect; or more precisely, if or when he *does* notice these aspects, they have no role to play in his further explanations. When power or revenge are obvious motives in a dream, then they are always *too* obvious to Freud's mind, and he breaks off immediately, locating instead a *far less obvious sexual motive* for the dream (one gets the suspicion that Freud may be too ambitious to spend time on *the too obvious* – this, notwithstanding his great merits, does not make him a neutral observer of the psyche).

In Freud's *Traumdeuting*, power is trivial; in a Nietzschean *Traum(um)deutung,* power is at the root of a dream's attempt to articulate an inner struggle. We could provide several examples from Freud's interpretations of dreams to substantiate this thesis; I shall here limit myself to a single. The dream is known as *The May-Beetle Dream*. A younger woman has consulted Freud about her marital problems with a much older husband. She reports to Freud that in one of her soliloquies, a few days before consulting Freud, she caught herself expressing a death-wish directed against her ailing husband, "I wish you would hang yourself." Uncovering various 'day-residues,' Freud learns that the woman a few day before had been reading old love-letters from a lover with whom she had been in love years ago. She had also the day before visiting Freud found a dead insect in a bucket of water. She also remembers that her daughters, one summer they had suffered from a plague of May-beetles, had collected them and squashed them "mercilessly," or killed them with arsenic. The woman had the previous night had the following dream:

5. The 'Confused-Aggressive' Subject as the Possibility for Ideology   341

> She called to mind that she had two may-beetles in a box and that she must set them free or they would suffocate. She opened the box and the may-beetles were in an exhausted state. One of them flew out of the open window; but the other was crushed by the casement while she was shutting it at someone's request.[371]

She has two may-beetles in a box; she opens the box (there are two beetles and they are "exhausted"); one beetle escapes through the open window; the other is also about to escape, but is squashed by the casement as the woman closes the window.

Now, this would seem to say it all. The woman is thoroughly unhappy about her husband (she is 'exhausted'), she thinks back on happier and more innocent days, and – at least in *one* of her *will-to-power configurations* – she wants her husband dead. The dream gives her what she wants: he is squashed by the window-frame, while she escapes into free air. *In summa*: "Why don't you hang yourself"?

However, to Freud's mind, this analysis is much too obvious. As always, Freud must do something difficult and reveal something secret. He therefore starts pondering the secret meaning of one of the dream's so-called 'nodal points.' The *squashed beetle* is such a nodal point. Curiously, Freud takes for granted that this image cannot mean that the unhappy woman wants to see her husband squashed. Instead, Freud approaches the meaning of this nodal point, cautiously and patiently, by reconstructing a long chain of associations, which – without here tracing all the elements – eventually establishes that 'squashed beetles' constitute the essential ingredient in one of the popular aphrodisiacs of the day, the so-called *Spanish Fly* (another popular aphrodisiac was *arsenic*). Now Freud has his interpretation. The dream is a concealed sexual wishfulfillment. The woman's imagery conceals an association to aphrodisiacs that could cure her ailing husband's impotence. That she the previous day caught herself in expressing a death-wish against her husband is open to analysis too. Hanging a man is known to give him a powerful erection, therefore also a form for 'cure' of impotence. The dream thus expresses the woman's wish to restore her husband's sexual prowess.

Thanks to this restoration or revelation of an unconscious underground for meaning, in Freud's interpretation, the woman approximately wants the opposite of what she is expressing: she does not want her husband dead, she wants him instead very much alive. It does not occur to Freud that she could *de facto* want her husband dead – perhaps out of sheer 'exhaustion,' per-

---

[371] Freud: The Interpretation of Dreams, loc. cit., p. 395.

haps in a gnawing regret over her lost opportunities, perhaps in order to be able to re-enter a sexual market of younger and more attractive partners.

6. In Defense of a Cognitively Modified Nietzschean Realism.

6.1 On the Reception of Nietzsche's Philosophy of Mind as Idealism.

One passage from the *Nachlaß* material has been particularly important for the discussion of Nietzsche's alleged idealism. The passage was made famous by Paul de Man, after in the seventies he read it as an analogy on deconstructive method[372]; it was used for similar purposes by Jonathan Culler in his influential introduction to deconstruction, published a few years later.[373] In these readings of de Man and Culler, they both notice a 'reversal' of cause and effect in Nietzsche's thinking, but they do not indicate any awareness of the *content* of which Nietzsche is talking: becoming *conscious* of a *sensation* with a certain *time-delay*, thanks to the work of our *mind*. This cognitive dimension of Nietzsche has disappeared entirely. Instead, we are introduced to the pure formal structure of two binary positions, called 'outer/cause' and 'inner/effect,' which are now said to be "arbitrarily interchangeable" (Paul de Man). We get the impression that Nietzsche wants to 'deconstruct' the cause-effect, outer-inner, relation *as such* (i.e., for the sake of *deconstructing*; or for the sake of *playful interchangeability* of terms), and that he is, through this example, arguing that the positions, outer/cause and inner/effect, can be "substituted for each other at will."[374] We even get the impression that de Man and Culler mean that when Nietzsche, in some qualified sense (cf. below), describes the 'inner' as *causing* the 'outer,' he champions classical Idealism; implying that Deconstruction – since endorsing his example as method – is a kind of Idealism too. The readings as such start a problem that has been plaguing American Deconstruction ever since,

---

[372] See the essay "Rhetoric of Tropes" in de Man, Paul: Allegories of Reading. New Haven (Yale University Press), 1979.

[373] Culler, Jonathan: On Deconstruction: Theory and Criticism after Structuralism. Ithaca, NY (Cornell University Press), 1982, p. 86. For another de Manian commentary, see also Klein, Wayne: Nietzsche and the Promise of Philosophy. New York (State University of New York Press), 1997.

[374] "The two sets of polarities, inside/outside and cause/effect, which seemed to made up a closed an coherent system (outside causes producing inside effect) has now been scrambled into an arbitrary, open system in which the attributes of causality and of location can be deceptively exchanged, substituted for each other at will." (de Man, loc. cit., p. 108).

and repeatedly it has had to defend itself against: its apparent affinity to Idealism.[375]

However, not just among deconstructionists has this particular passage (to which we return shortly) inspired commentators to see Nietzsche's philosophy as Idealism. In an expert commentator of Nietzsche like Erwin Schlimgen, we find a similar position. Not a deconstructionist, and not interested in 'playful interchangeability,' Schlimgen reads Nietzsche's passage in the context of philosophy of mind and consciousness (– like undersigned[376]). However, Schlimgen sees Nietzsche adopting the indefensible positions of Solipsism and radical Idealism identical to (. . . if anything, even more radical than . . .) Berkeley's.

> Nietzsche adopts in these discussions the extreme position of solipsism, which claim that reality only consists of the prevailing subject and its sensations, presentations, ideas, and so on. All data of a presumed spatial-temporal reality are data of a consciousness, and the acceptance of an objectively existing external world is based on a projection, which is always a mind-phenomenon [*Bewußtseinsphänomen*]. [. . .] The sense-impression [*sinnesempfindung*], which is regarded as if arriving from the outside, is in reality a purely (intrinsic) phenomenon, and has its foundation in consciousness. The projection, that brings about that a cause is believed to come from the outside, is a consequence of an

---

[375] One may find such a defense in Martin McQuillan's introduction to Paul de Man: "One would understand nothing of deconstruction and de Man's work if one thought of it as merely an extension of the so-called 'linguistic paradigm' (the idealist belief that reality is merely a linguistic construct). Rather, de Man wants to free the study of literature from naïve opposition between texts and 'the real world' and from uncritical conceptions of art. Literary theory does not deny the relation between literature and the real world but suggests that it is not necessarily certain that language works in accordance with the principles of the supposed 'real world'. Therefore, it is not at all certain that texts are reliable sources of information about anything other than their own uses of language." McQuillan, Martin: Paul de Man. London, New York (Routledge), 2001; p. 52-53. That is probably a fair reflection of Paul de Man's views; but what in the last sentence does not imply 'idealist belief'? – Whether one is locked up in ideas, in language, or in texts, one is always in the Idealist paradigm encapsulated in the self-same, in a solipsistic cage (a "prison-house" Frederic Jameson once said), from where there is no escape.

[376] Although I disagree with Schlimgen on this particular issue, and suggest an interpretation different from Schlimgen's interpretation of Nietzsche as Idealist, this does not change my assessment of Schlimgen's work, to which I frequently refer, as a superior presentation of Nietzsche's theories of mind, consciousness, and knowledge. See Schlimgen, Erwin: Nietzsches Theorie. Loc. cit.

impression that has become conscious for us; that is, we have for something changing in ourselves found a cause. According to Nietzsche, in the constitution of the external world a 'reversal of time' happens, insofar as we understand it a 'a cause of an effect in us.'[377]

In a footnote, Schlimgen presents his most explicit interpretation of Nietzsche's passage as classical Idealism.

> Locke's formula: *Nihil est in intellectu, quod non sit prius in sensu* – is in contrast an expression for an foundation of knowledge free of intellect in sense-experience. Berkeley dictum, *esse est percipi,* agrees better with the core of Nietzsche's thesis, although it does not quite reflect the radicalness of Nietzsche's positions. Although Berkeley excludes a thought-independent external world, he nonetheless appoints a divine spirit as the guarantor of reality.[378]

My reading of the passage is significant different from both deconstructionist, Paul de Man's, and philosopher of mind, Erwin Schlimgen's. In the first case, I am interested in the *content* of which Nietzsche is speaking; not in 'playful interchangeability' – that is, the futility of turning *A to B* around into its opposite, and then turning *B to A* around once more, etc., until the mind gets tired. This exercise is after all a simple mind-game that yields no insights (what a consummate deconstructionist might argue is exactly the very purpose: the theoretical lightheartedness, the frisky and cheerful philosophizing, the 'Homeric laughter' – isn't there already too much superficial Nietzsche in these positions to make anybody comfortable?) In the second case, to see Nietzsche's philosophy, and the passage in question, as classical Idealism, I see as contradicting, and being irreconcilable with, Nietzsche's philosophy on several fundamental levels.[379]

---

[377] Schlimgen, Erwin: Nietzsches Theorie, loc. cit. p. 88.
[378] Schlimgen, Erwin: Nietzsche s Theory, loc. cit., p. 90.
[379] Although as little as Nietzsche, I do not like to resort to labels – these artificial tools of schematization that always carry in them the germs of misunderstanding, because they are conceived by minds that want to tidy up Nietzsche, and out of him create a dogma – Nietzsche's philosophy can better be identified as, in some of its aspects, a Realism; in other of its aspects, a Pragmatism; and in still other aspects, a Cognitive Science.

6.2. The Mind Creates Perception, not Matter.

Let us, after these preparatory remarks, turn our attention to the passage in question. We first notice that is a coherent philosophical reflection on epistemological matters introduced by Locke and Hume, but developed and modified by, prominently, Kant, Schopenhauer, and Friedrich A. Lange. It starts by rehearsing and summarizing some of these well-known positions.

> The phenomenalism of the 'inner world.'
> The chronological reversal [*die Chronologische Umdrehung*], so that the cause enters consciousness later than the effect.
>   we have learned that pain is projected to a part of the body without being situated there
>   we have learned that sense impressions naively supposed to be conditioned by the outer world [*Außenwelt*] are, on the contrary, conditioned by the inner world [*Innenwelt*]; that we are always unconscious of the real activity of the outer world . . . The fragment of the outer world of which we are conscious is born after an effect [*nachgeboren nach der Wirkung*] from outside has impressed [*geübt*] itself upon us, and is belatedly projected [*Nachträglich Projiziert*] as its 'cause.'
>   In the phenomenalism of the 'inner world' we turn around the chronology of cause and effect.
>   The fundamental fact of 'inner experience' [*"Innere Erfahrung"*] is that a cause is imagined, whereupon an effect follows . . .
>   The same applies to the progression of thoughts . . . we seek a reason [*Grund*] for a thought, before it has become conscious for us: and first then enters the reason [*Grund*] and its result in consciousness . . .
>   All our dreaming is the interpretation of our complete feeling [*Gesammt-Gefühlen*] from possible causes: and so much so, that a condition first becomes conscious when the related chain of causality has entered consciousness.
>   The entire 'inner experience' comes about because the excitation of a nerve-center seeks and imagines a cause – and first then does the discovered cause enter consciousness: this cause is simply not adequate as the real cause, – it is an exploration [*ein Tasten*] thanks to our former 'inner experience' – that is, our memories. But the memory contains also the habits of old interpretations, that is, the erroneous causalities . . . so that the 'inner experience' carries with it all the results from formerly erroneous interpretations.
> [. . .]
>   'Inner experience' [*"Innere Erfahrung"*] enters our consciousness only after it has found a language the individual understands . . . i.e., a translation of a condition into a condition more familiar [*bekanntere*] to him – 'to understand'

means merely: to be able to express something new in the language of something old and familiar. (Nachlaß 1888, KSA 13, 15[90]).[380]

In the passage, we are – and of this there is no doubt – introduced to a criticism of the so-called 'projection-theory,' the empiricist idea that (i) sense-material travels from the outside (of the world) to the inside (of the mind) along a linear trajectory; (ii) that there is a one-to-one relationship between the inside images and the outside objects, and (iii) finally, since the trajectory is linear, that chronology and causality are firmly established between the outside and the inside: the outside is first, the inside second; the outside is the cause, the inside is the effect.

In Nietzsche, every sense-perception is instead – of this there is also no doubt – *preceded* by a judgment: the inner world is "conditioning," or at least *participating* in defining, the outer world. This is explicitly stated, and if one stops one's reading at this point, it might indeed seem to indicate a traditional (Berkeleyan) Idealist position (cf. "we have learned that sense impressions naively supposed to be conditioned by the outer world [*Außenwelt*] are, on the contrary, conditioned by the inner world [*Innenwelt*].)" But from who have "we learned"? – Most obviously from Kant and Schopenhauer, and their numerous followers in the 19th century. If there is any affinity to Idealism in Nietzsche's position, we must be looking in the direction of Kant's 'transcendental idealism.'[381] Nietzsche must be seen as closer

---

[380] We find identical formulations in *Die fröhliche Wissenschaft* and *Götzendämmerung*: "What do they [the common people] want when they want 'knowledge'? Nothing more than this: Something strange [*Fremdes*] is to be reduced to something familiar [*Bekanntes*]. And we philosophers—have we by knowledge ever understood anything different from this? [. . .] Is it not the instinct of fear that bids us to know? [. . .] What is familiar, is known [*was bekannt ist, ist erkannt*]." (FW 355, KSA 5, p. 594). "Psychological explanation. – To trace something unknown back to something known is alleviating, soothing, gratifying and gives moreover a feeling of power. Danger, disquiet, anxiety attend the unknown – the first instinct is to eliminate these distressing states. First principle: any explanation is better than none." (GD, 'Die vier grossen Irrthümer' 5, KSA 6, p. 93).

[381] Kant defined in his *Prolegomena* 'true Idealists' [*echten Idealisten*] as follows: "The doctrine of all true Idealists, from the Eleatic school to bishop Berkeley, is contained in the following formula: 'All knowledge [*Erkenntnis*] through sense and experience is nothing but mere appearance, and only in the idea of pure mind and reason [*reines Verstandes und Vernunft*] is there truth.'" (Kant: Prolegomena zur einen jeden künftigen Metaphysik, in WA V. Frankfurt (Suhrkamp Verlag), 1977, p 253.) In contrast to the doctrine of the 'true Idealist,' Kant explains his own idealist doctrine (often labeled 'tran-

to Kant's Idealism than to Berkeley's. We perceive things as 'objects' thanks to a certain formative power of our 'inner world' – in Kant, the transcendental categories. If our perceptive apparatus influences how we see 'reality,' the simple linear trajectory envisioned by Locke and Hume must be conceived as something far more complicated. Now, the perceived world is constructed *belatedly*, or *after-the-fact*. From the passage, it is clear that the *instance* of inscription of an impression we do not perceive; we only perceive the result of the 'processing' of this impression.

The crux of this thinking is that a perception "needs time before it is finished" (Nachlaß 1885, KSA 11, 26[44]), before it becomes aware of itself. The passage is a statement about our cognitive make-up; it says that our *perception* needs our *mind*. As such, Nietzsche is not saying that mind or consciousness creates *matter* after-the-fact; he is only saying that the mind creates *perception* after-the-fact; our minds do not create the world; but they *do* create our *perception of the world*. This thesis corresponds well to Nietzsche's general claim that our minds are 'simplification-apparatuses.' Nietzsche generally supposes that we are immersed in a sensational manifold that cannot be grasped in its complexity. Immersed in this sensational manifold, our minds have to 'choose' and 'select' what to see, since we cannot assimilate and process everything; since we cannot perceive it all. This 'selection' of what to perceive is done according to our immediate needs; on a *neurological* level, it becomes a kind of 'natural selection' 'for the sake of survival.' As such, our cognitive apparatuses are involved in our interaction with the world as we see it. The world is necessarily *there*, but, as we put it, there is always 'too much' of it. The human solution to this potentially paralyzing condition is to *simplify*. The mind has this task: it *simplifies, falsifies, interprets*.

Let us explain the same idea by means of an example. If I need to pass the street, I need only to look out for the oncoming and passing cars, and in the moment of passing the street, I virtually see nothing but oncoming and passing cars. I am immersed in the world, but I am never assimilating all possible visual impressions that the street could provide; only a minor fraction. My 'mind' adjusts my perception according to my immediate needs. In this utterly pragmatic sense, my 'inner world' is 'causing' the 'outer world.' I am bombarded with impressions, but I 'invent' only a few 'causes' for

---

scendental Idealism') as follows: "The doctrine that through and through directs and determines my Idealism is in contrast: 'All Knowledge [*Erkenntnis*] about things, from simple pure mind, or pure reason, is nothing by mere appearance, and only in experience is there truth.'" (Kant: Prolegomena, ibid., p 253).

these impressions (those I need for survival); and consequently, I see the world in which I am immersed *as something*, and not as something else. I always-already select what to see in my horizon; I always-already 'interpret.' This reading is far removed from any hint of Idealism, because nobody denies the actual existence of the street or the cars; and nobody claims that street and cars are figments of our imagination, 'caused' by our inner world. On the contrary, the claim is that street and cars are perceived according to need, and ultimately for the sake of survival. As such, a horizon of all possible impressions undergoes a selective processing, which now transforms them into perceived objects within my horizon. So, we do not create *matter* after-the-fact (the street and the cars), but we do create *perception* after-the-fact (the street and the cars) – a crucial difference, we would like to contend.

6.3. Nietzsche's Master-Axiom: the World is Language-Independent

If, according to Schlimgen, Nietzsche is a *Solipsist* and a *Berkeleyan Idealist*, there is, *first*, no thought- and language-independent world 'out there'; and, *second*, it becomes impossible (as it always was in the History of Philosophy) to explain how we share experiences; how we constitute an objective world.

Addressing the *first point*, we suggested above that Nietzsche has the exact opposite position. The problem about 'interpreting' and 'explaining' the 'world' (which includes the biological organisms that we are) is never that it is not there ('is only language,' etc.), but rather that there is always 'too much' of it, and that this abundance and profusion of material is radically language-*independent*. No language is a natural fit. The 'world' and 'human language' have undergone two different evolutionary processes; the 'world' in its complexity has been designed neither *in* human language, nor in order to *correspond to* human language. The 'world' has developed *chaotically* (it has no design, no arrangement, no structure). Therefore, any language (scientific or natural) trying to 'explain' grapples in the dark, and must undergo numerous trials and errors (that is, numerous 'guesses,' surely based on observation, deduction, tests, etc.), before producing just a limited understanding of a single aspect in this ocean of multiplicity – which is now, through the linguistic 'metaphor,' eventually counted as understood.

We find numerous examples in Physics of the soberness of this thesis. For example, (i) *the universe*. The deeper we penetrate into the universe, the better do we understand what a complete 'mess' it is. There is no intrinsic order, and there are surprises at every corner, when we with our improved technologies are able to observe something new. We are surely able to 'classify' various objects in the universe, for example the stars. We classify them according to mass, size, luminosity, and other parameters, but such classification does not reveal an intrinsic order of stars, it only applies the capacities of our visual perception to distinguish between large and small, bright and dimmed, etc., to a group of objects we call stars. Another example, (ii) *the speed of light*. We now know from experiment that light travels with a certain speed, and we have a value for its velocity. However, the value looks completely *random*; it is 'unaesthetic' and follows no logical or mathematical index (approximately 299,792,458 meters per second). It could never have been inferred by even the acutest Aristotelian or Cartesian thinker. The value is a physical constant, which is also identical to the speed at which electromagnetic radiation propagates in a vacuum. We do not question this number, and it is a great achievement that the physicists have been able to determine it, but why is the number so random? – Because nature never arranges itself in order to please our language or our mathematics; because nature is radically language-*independent*!

The only reason why it is a human predicament to have to *'interpret'* the *'world'* is that the 'world' in-itself is language-*independent*. If in-itself, the 'world' were language-*dependent*, it would present itself to us as already interpreted, already understood. In interpreting, we always interpret an *abyss*, something that withdraws itself. In the serene self-present and self-presenting *surface* of appearances, we assume that something is unknown, and although this self-present surface-world is our only entry-point, we set about to reconstruct the unknown. We give that which has in-itself no language, the abyss, *a language*. The 'world' (for example as 'inner experience') enters, so Nietzsche, "our consciousness only after it has found a language the individual u n d e r s t a n d s" (ibid.); thus, it is not *already language*, before it has found this language.

Addressing the *second point*, Schlimgen offers the following explanation of how we share experiences (and the explanation we see often reiterated in the post-Structuralist/-Modernist paradigms):

That we believe that sense-impressions have been caused from the outside, and *what* we perceive as sense-impressions, are mind-controlled [*Bewußsteinsgesteuerte*] processes. The assumption that we refer to a common objective external world finds its origin in our sign-mediating [*Zeichenvermittelten*] consciousness – it is not the external world that we share, it is the consciousness of the external world and what it is supposed to be. That is, we sense similar excitations as unities for which we have words or concepts: the belief in a common outer-world is language- or sign-mediated.[382]

"It is not the external world that we share, it is the consciousness of the external world" – it is a strong and well-formed statement, but is the situation not the exact opposite? We do share an external 'world,' but not the consciousness about it; not the interpretations we produce about it, or the perspectives from which to see and understand it? Exactly because the 'world' – insofar as we start describing and communicating this 'world' – is "sign-mediated," it can be *linguistically constructed* in an indefinite number of ways. In this explanation-process, we *do share*, and this might be what Schlimgen means, *language* understood as the *language-system* (Saussure's *langue*); still, we *do not share* the numerous possibilities of activation of this language-system as *parole*. 'Consciousness' could only emerge as an *activation* of the language-system; it cannot be identical to the language-system itself.

When Schlimgen writes, "the belief in a common outer-world is language- or sign-mediated," it is impossible to disagree because the statement is a truism; we always assume that a 'belief' has to be *articulated*, and is as such *necessarily* sign-mediated. A *belief* in an external world is thus *articulating* the existence of the external world, and this *articulation* is linguistic, and part of a communication. Schlimgen's 'belief' seems, however, to have been inserted as a 'buffer,' in order to, exactly, make the statement irrefutable. What the passage does *without* this 'buffer' is to demote the world as existent, and promote the view that the world is language-dependent or sign-mediated.

We shall instead reassert that the world is language-*independent* rather than language-*dependent*, and it is this language-*independent* world we share. Reiterating ideas already proposed in *Chapter 2*, we (i) share a 'world' as *Ur-ground*, that is, an *Environment* that is *there* and which we share with all other organisms. This world is open to an indefinite number of ways of perceiving it; for each perceptive system, we assume that it must be 'looking' different. Perceived through enhanced smell, through enhanced hearing, through echolocation, through chemical signals, through visual perception,[383] this open world looks differently in each case. However, why

---

[382] Schlimgen, Erwin: Nietzsches Theorie, loc. cit. p. 89.
[383] Even animals favoring 'visual perception' see the world differently, that is, through different 'optics' and different organizations of their visual capacities. Some animals do not perceive dimension, but only movement. Some mammals do not perceive color, while birds perceive a far broader color-palette than the human being, and live as such in a world of unimaginable splendor.

would this acknowledged difference in perceptive systems imply Idealism? Why would it nullify the world's fundamental *openness*, its radical *self-presence*. Only if the world is *there*, can it be seen differently. Furthermore, (ii) as human beings, we share a world as *Human Ground*, that is, we share a perceptive system by which to see the world. Our system strongly favors visual perception (as organism, we have evolved a 'Human Optics'). On the Human ground, we share essential parameters for perceiving the *Ur-ground*, such as dimension, space-time, cause-effect, color, warm-cold, near-far, up-down, front-behind, and right-left (several of these parameters, we share with other animals too). Finally, (iii) we share a *Language*, in which to express ourselves, and make conscious to each other and ourselves various pertinent decisions necessary for survival. The *Human Ground* has evolved as a *response* to the environment, the *Ur-ground*, the 'world' as such; *Language* has evolved in order for humans to communicate their *Human ground*; ultimately in order for them to *orient* themselves on this ground.

6.4. Reconciling Realism and Cognitive Theory.

Language is in Nietzsche always seen as the last and latest development in these processes – we recall, first metaphor is the image, second metaphor is the sound (cf. WL: *Nervenreiz* → *Bild* → *Laut*; see *Chapter 1*). The Ur-ground, the 'in-itself,' we do not access *as such*, because we have evolved perceptive and cognitive apparatuses that process information as needed.[384]

---

[384] Other animals, like many insects, perceive the world through multiple eyes, and must have a kaleidoscopic, non-dimensional, perception of a world with no up and down, etc. One can only wonder what kind of 'objective science' such creatures would have developed, if they had had the intellectual capacity and a language in which to articulate their 'science.'
Especially in recent years, several works have emerged on Nietzsche's relation to the evolutionary paradigms of his day. Book-length introductions are, Richardson, John: Nietzsche's New Darwinism. Oxford (Oxford University Press), 2004; and Moore, Gregory: Nietzsche, Biology, and Metaphor. Cambridge (Cambridge University Press), 2006. Two articles also discuss Nietzsche and evolution: Stegmaier, Werner: Darwin, Dawinismus, Nietzsche. Zum Problem der Evolution" in Nietzsche Studien 16. Berlin, New York (Walter de Gruyter) 1987; and Müller-Lauter, W.: "Der Organismus als Innerer Kampf" in Über Werden und Wille zur Macht, loc. cit. Already Hans Vaihinger understood how important the evolutionary paradigms were for Nietzsche; in Vaihinger, Hans: Nietzsche als Philosoph. Porta Westfalica (Gerhard Bleick), 2002 reprint.

The Ur-ground, the Environment, is therefore *there*, and it drives our evolution, including the evolution of a brain; however, the evolved brain does not see the Ur-ground as such, it only sees what it has evolved into seeing. Instead of the empiricist 'projection-theory' – an image travels from the outside into the inside, where it lodges itself as idea – Nietzsche envisions the self as an *apparatus*, which has an input, a processing, and an output. The input is what he calls a 'nerve-stimulus.' In his cognitive model, we do not access the Ur-ground as such, but we still have an *Encounter* with this Ur-ground: necessarily something stimulates and excites our perceptive apparatus; the 'nerve-stimulus' is this *Encounter*. This interpretation is explicit in Nietzsche's passage: "The fragment of the outer world of which we are conscious is born after an effect [*nachgeboren nach der Wirkung*] from outside has impressed [*geübt*] itself upon us, and is belatedly projected [*Nachträglich Projiziert*] as its 'cause.'" (Ibid.) – Something 'from outside' is 'impressing itself' upon us (this is what we call the *Encounter*) – then the processing starts, and first thereupon is the processed material sent back to where it came from, and now seen as a *cause* for an *effect* in us; at this point, we perceive in the proper sense. Our perceptive apparatus is therefore like a *machine*; it needs an input from an environment, but it also needs to process this input, and after this processing, the output is differently formatted than the original input. The original input we call impression, the output we call perception.

We understand now that we necessarily *perceive* with a certain 'time-delay' whenever we *experience* perception (I will have to say *experience perception*, because previously, I included the possibility of so-called 'empty perceptions,' that is, perceptions that are not experienced), because a process precedes the experience, and the perception consequently materializes as an after-reconstruction – an 'after-image,' as it were.

In the passage above, Nietzsche applies this general idea of 'time-reversal' also to inner-mental phenomena such as thoughts, pain and pleasure sensations, or dreams. As in the case of perceptions, we can for example 'have thoughts' that we do not experience. The requirement for experiencing a thought is that we find a reason for having it (cf. "we seek a reason [*Grund*] for a thought, before it has become conscious for us"). We invent causes as interpretations of this or that sensational complex, in order to objectify and fixate a certain feature within the complex, which, at that point, we become conscious about as *this* feature.

If the world was constituted merely as Berkeley's 'ideas,' or as post-Structuralism's 'language,' we could not have evolved. We do not evolve in *a world of ideas*, because there are in fantasy no exigencies, no struggle for survival, no competition, and no adjustment. Without an environment, we would in the first place not have evolved a perceptive apparatus selecting the most important information from its surroundings, in order to survive. Without an environment, we would also not have evolved a brain able to process and communicating ideas in a language; a precondition, which from the outset must be neutralizing the possibility of Idealism. That there is an *Ur-ground*, on top of which a *Human ground* evolves, on top of which a *Human language* evolves, are now not three irreconcilable positions; these are merely stages in a process. At the end-stage of the evolutionary process, all three grounds exist simultaneously, and in perfect harmony[385]: *Ur-ground* (or Environment), *Human ground* (or Human optics), and *language*. There is no conflict; world and individual were never arranged as according to a *simple disjunctive binarism*, presupposing that *either* there is an 'in-self' *or* a 'for-us,' either a *world* or a *subject*, but not both! (This binarism is in-itself language-metaphysics and logicization.) Therefore we defend, as the better alternative, a so-called "cognitively qualified Nietzschean Realism," where a subject is always adjusting itself to a world, which is *there* as 'the outside,' while *at the same time* producing perceptive images of this world, which *cannot* be understood as exact replicas or photographic imprints of this outside, but are the results of our perceptive systems processing of, or our *Encounters* with, this material world.[386]

6.5. The Dubious Evolutionary Value of 'Explanations.'

When language is added to these processes, we experience a radical simplification and falsification of the world; language offers an 'interpretation' of

---

[385] This is true in principle; but it is not true as actual fact, where today the human being has evolved up to a point where it is able also to destroy its environment. For urgent political reasons (to invoke completely different sets of argument), it does not seem very reasonable in the 20th and 21st centuries to evoke and defend something like Kant's 'dreamerish Idealism.' Under the pressures of environmental disasters looming, it comes across as whimsical intellectualism.

[386] From another research background, we note that the suggested theoretical association of cognitive theory and evolutionary theory, has been eloquently presented by Daniel Dennett in his two major works: Dennett, Daniel: Consciousness Explained, loc. cit., and Dennett, Daniel: Darwin's Dangerous Idea: Evolution and the Meaning of Life. New York (Touchstone), 1995. Another work relevant for these discussions is, Tetens, Holm: Geist, Gehirn, Maschine. Philosophische Versuche über ihren zusammenhang. Reclam (Stuttgart), 1994.

the world infinitely less subtle and refined than our more original perceptive interpretations. Our 'bodies' interpret far better than our 'intellects.' Therefore, language is never fetishized in Nietzsche, and it is not a 'rescuing' concept, promising transparent knowledge of the world and ourselves. For that matter, it is rather the villain than the hero of his philosophy. When people start to 'explain' themselves, Nietzsche hardly manages to disguise his contempt (cf. "one constantly confuses the explanation with the text – and what 'explanation'!" (Nachlaß 1888, KSA 13, 15[82])).

In a note preceding the passage we are discussing, Nietzsche provides the following example of such superficial 'explanation': "Women, well brought up, on old oatmeal and grains, with temperaments of a cow, little moved by misfortune: and then, they ascribe this to their 'faith in God' [*Gottvertrauen*]. They don't understand that their 'faith in God' is merely an expression of their strong and unwavering total constitution [*Gesammtverfassung*] – an expression, no cause . . ." (Nachlaß 1888, KSA 13, 15[83].) The crux of the somewhat blunt description is that we have a woman of a healthy constitution, and brought up on a healthy diet (we remember how important diet was to Nietzsche). She is, however, also a traditional woman, so she *explains* her health by her 'faith in God'; this is what she understands as the *cause* of her robust constitution. Looking for *causes*, she chooses the one most tempting, seductive, and sentimental. She invents a false cause, and she is confusing effect and cause. This sort of confusion is what Nietzsche generally calls "the essential fact" of the "inner world": "The 'inner world' and its famous 'inner sense' [*innerer Sinn*]. The inner sense confuses the effect with the cause. The 'cause' is projected, after the effect has taken place: the essential fact of 'inner experience.'" (Nachlaß 1888, KSA 13, 15[85].) The 'effect' is her healthy body; the 'cause,' the linguistic/ideological *Gottvertrauen*, projected backwards from the immediate perception of health, as pseudo-explanation, as 'false cause.' It should have been unnecessary, except for the fact that, in Nietzsche, *explanation* often becomes a *catalyst* making the subject consciously aware of a condition; implying that woman not necessary has any clear awareness of her own healthiness *before telling herself* that so she is, and *before offering herself an explanation* on why she is so (– as in the section of the "emotional word" above, it is as if the *word* becomes a ray of light in this dark, unenlightened psyche). That is, not before inventing "old and familiar language" (ibid.) in which to fit the new, following Nietzsche's dictum that "any explanation is better than none" (GD, 'Die vier grossen Irrthümer' 5), and trusting that *"was bekannt ist, ist erkannt"* (FW 355), does the woman 'understand' her healthy condition.[387]

In the concept of 'chronological reversal' in perception and cognition, Nietzsche is in a sense pointing out a well-known fact (and one must expect that all scientists agree, and maybe even, unbeknownst of themselves, are committed Nietzscheans). He notices that we must always *encounter* an effect, *before* we can start looking for a cause. The cause-effect relation presents itself in an order reverse to actuality: in the *logical reconstruction* of events, the cause will always be seen as the first mover or motivator for whatever is the effect. However, in the phenomenology of our perception and cognition, the cause is necessarily imagined *after* the encounter of the effect; as *interpretation*, the cause emerges *always after* the effect. For this reason too, we cannot see inverted chronology, "time-reversal," as a regression to Idealism; quite on the contrary: the thinking implies that *we can always only react to an apparent surface-world* (respond *to an Environment*), which necessarily has to *manifest itself* in events, occurrences, or happenings before we bother looking for causes.

The 'reversed chronology' has the further consequence that we never *know* causes in and for themselves; we may at best think that we know a cause, by observing an effect. This uncertain situation is partly to blame for our historical and existential predicaments: our propensity, time and again, to invent false and fictitious 'causes.' Exactly because we never *see* causes in-themselves (because they do not lie around inertly and passively), humans, historically and individually, have often explained events by causes that had no relation to the explained event.[388] In other words, they have ob-

---

[387] If we can extrapolate this idea from the example, we learn that *false* causes are exactly as *effective tools of self-understanding* as are *true* causes. For 'true' or 'false' causes alike, the processes in inner life are exactly the same – paraphrasing Nietzsche: in "inner experience," we "seek and imagine a cause"; now it "enters consciousness," but not necessarily as "the real cause"; instead as a "memory" with all "the habits of old interpretations"; that is, "erroneous causalities" relying on "translations of a condition into . . . the language of something old and familiar." *Gottvertrauen* is such old and familiar language; it is part of the woman's internalized ideological discourse, and therefore easy for her to grasp.

[388] It is only if a car moves, that I perceive movement, and believe something must be causing the movement. If the car does not move, I also don't look for a cause (we don't search around for causes of nothing). Again, if the car moves, and somebody happens to be pushing the car, then I will tend to believe that the pushing of the car is the cause of its movement; but the nexus could never, to Hume and Nietzsche's mind, be established *a priori*. It could be that the engine of car is running and causing the movement, and the man

served an *event*, then taken it to be an *effect*, then again inferred a presumed *cause*, and finally explained the *event* by the *cause* (according to the circular inference from *Chapter 1* and as well from the present chapter above). Later observations may then have demonstrated that there was in fact no nexus between what had been interpreted as cause, and what as effect. The so-called 'cause' worked only as perhaps ideological, perhaps religious, perhaps existential, consolation. (All areas of science offer examples of such flawed explanations; but perhaps none more so than the Medical Sciences, with their rich history of outlandish diagnoses and exotic treatments of diseases.[389])

A fortiori, if we are at risk of inventing false causes when observing the apparent world, the risk is only augmented manifold as soon as we try to explain phenomena that are not part of the observable world, i.e., "inner phenomena." In these cases, we only 'experience' rapid and chaotic 'inner movements,' and to these 'movements' we add some more or less random 'causes,' 'explanations' (– and what godforsaken 'explanations'). Hence, the causes or interpretations, by which we explain 'inner movements,' are second-order-constructions; they are not truly related to the 'inner movements' as such, but emanate rather from *the discourse* in which the subject is imbedded and with which the individual is most *comfortable*. In this sense, inner life remains "absolutely hidden" for us, and everything we become conscious about is "through and through arranged, simplified, schematized, and selected":

On Psychology and Theory of Knowledge [*Zur Psychologie und Erkenntnisslehre*]
   I insist on the phenomenon and the *inner* world: *everything, which becomes conscious* is through and through arranged, simplified, schematized, and selected – the *real* processes of inner 'perception,' the *causal connections* between thoughts, feelings, desires, as well as between subject and object, remains absolutely hidden for us – perhaps they are completely imaginary. The "*apparent inner* world" has been adapted exactly according to the same forms and procedures as the outer world.
   [. . .] To suppose an immediate causal connection between two thoughts, as it is done in logic – this is only a consequence of the crudest observation. Between two thoughts, *all kinds of affects* are playing their game, but the

---

pushing it only engages in some make-believe act for the sake of my entertainment.

[389] Michel Foucault has better than anybody written the history of 'false causalities'; especially his two early works come to mind: *Madness and Civilization* [*Histoire de la Folie*, 1961] and *The Birth of the Clinic* [*Naissance de la Clinique*, 1963].

movements are too quick, therefore we mis-*recognize and disclaim them*. [. . .] "Thinking," as the theorist of knowledge prescribes it, does not occur: it is a quite arbitrary fiction. (Nachlaß 1887-88; KSA 13, 11[113])

CHAPTER 5

The Meaning of *Master*, *Slave*, and *Priest*: From Mental Configurations to Social Typologies

> Whatever they may think and say about their 'egoism', the great majority nonetheless do nothing for their ego their whole life long: what they do is done for the phantom of their ego which has formed itself in the heads of those around them and has been communicated to them; – as a consequence they all of them dwell in a fog of impersonal, semi-personal opinions [. . .] a strange world of phantasms. [. . .] This fog of habits and opinions lives and grows almost independently of the people it envelops [. . .] No individual among this majority is capable of setting up a real ego, accessible to him and fathomed by him, in opposition to the general pale fiction.
>
> — Nietzsche: *Morgenröte* 105[390]

0. Introduction: Servile and Assertive Configuration

In Nietzsche's combat against a *servile configuration* labeled the 'slave,' the 'herd,' or the 'ascetic,' he proposes an *assertive configuration* labeled the 'master,' the 'noble,' or the 'sovereign.' The two well-known positions of Nietzsche we describe here as 'configurations,' with this suggesting that they are different possible formations of the psyche: the 'slave' is thus the label of one mental formation, the 'master' the label of another. The human being *as such* is a blank slate, but, like a hard disc on a computer, it can be differently configured.

Nietzsche sees two distinct and antagonistic historical configurations of the human being having developed through the history of civilization. In the name of 'master' and 'slave,' the two configurations are invested with contrasting valuations: one is despised, as it appeals to weakness, death, and self-pity; another is celebrated, as it appeals to strength, life, and indiffe-

---

[390] M 105, KSA 3, p. 93.

rence. Nietzsche's project is to foster the idea of an assertive configuration that could defeat the servile configuration. His project is a speculation on how we could get rid of a certain servility that from the inside contaminates modern man (contemporary European *'man'* – as Nietzsche usually underscores; not forgetting the sarcastic quotation marks[391]), how we might 'think' or 'cultivate' a true and full subjectivity. When Nietzsche observes contemporary European (so-called) 'man,' the assertive configuration seems to have been either utterly defeated or reduced to a merely embryonic existence; the task it to develop this embryo into a fully grown system.

It is in Nietzsche always an arduous task to combat the servile configuration, since it behaves like a cancer infecting all the cells of the assertive configuration – paradoxically, the servile configuration is always more assertive than the assertive configuration. Instead of being servile, as it is supposed to be, and subordinate itself to the assertive configuration, it is tirelessly and infinitely resourceful in its ways of circumventing its counterpart.[392]

However, are we allowed to interpret 'master' and 'slave' as *configurations*, with this implying that they are different aspects of a personality-structure that one must now expect have the potential for breeding and sustaining them both? – Traditionally interpreted, and regularly indicated in Nietzsche's own texts, the opposition 'master' and 'slave' is a *fait accompli* that either indicates two distinct types of human beings or labels two diverse races: strong human beings or strong barbarian races asserting their power over weaker more peaceful ones. (– Although regarding *race* Nietzsche never singled out any particular ethnic group as having a birthright to the master-position: at different periods in history, the Greeks, the Romans, the Vikings, the Japanese, the Arabs, the Incas, etc., would be 'master-races.') If we interpret 'master' and 'slave' as aspects of the same personality-structure, these distinctions are obviously blurred; if there is a potential for a 'master' in every 'slave,' and the potential for a 'slave' in every 'master,' what happens to the famous distinction?

---

[391] See for example JGB 239, KSA 5, p. 177.

[392] It is never the case in Nietzsche that only the 'master' but not the 'slave' has will-to-power, or that 'masters' have a stronger will-to-power than 'slaves.' The will-to-power of 'masters' respectively 'slaves' is identical in *quantity*, but different in *quality*. Compare to Tracy B. Strong: "Master morality is not equivalent to a strong will to power, nor is slave morality a weak will to power. Both kinds of morality are will to power, but in different ways." Strong, Tracy: Friedrich Nietzsche and the Politics of Transfiguration. Urbana, Chicago (University of Illinois Press), 1975/2000, p. 257.

The distinction *as such* would obviously not disappear (as opposition it continues to be semantically invested), but its extension and externalization into the form of a homogenous, distinct, and independent subject who is through and through displaying an identity as either 'master' or 'slave' – that externalized and ideal form disappears; the fiction that in the social world we are actually able to distinguish between 'masters' and 'slaves' – that fiction evaporates; the narcissistic self-comfort that, by reading Nietzsche, we could somehow learn to become 'masters' – that self-comfort is frustrated. But if this is the effect of our interpretive strategy, it is not something for which we need to be overly apologetic; it could only have the desirable effect that the discriminatory overtones reverberating from the often abused distinction disappear.

Moreover, in at least a few passages, Nietzsche himself supports the possibility of the proposed reading. In *Jenseits von Gut und Böse*, we read:

> There is a m a s t e r   m o r a l i t y and a s l a v e   m o r a l i t y ; – I will immediately add that in all higher and more mixed culture, attempts to mediate between these moralities also appear, although *more frequently the two are confused* and there are mutual misunderstandings. *In fact, you sometimes find them sharply juxtaposed – even inside the same person, within a single soul.* (JGB 260, KSA 5, p. 208; italics added).

Although we "in fact" may find the two positions "within a single soul," setting off from the passage above, Nietzsche goes on describing the two positions as *externalized forms*, as independent subjects, for the good reason that it is impossible to describe the *in-itself* of our psychological organization of the positions, the complex circuits of forces and energies that make up our inner selves. What Nietzsche possibly *can* describe is two external and ideal positions (for example in the figures of 'noble' and 'herd') engaged in a millennia-old battle, where, at least regarding the slave, every dirty trick is permitted, and where Nietzsche often rages against the lack of sportsmanship and fair play in the servile configuration.

So, Nietzsche has *rules* for this combat, imperatives that all in vain bid the servile configuration to give the assertive configuration a fair chance of asserting itself. What are Nietzsche's 'rules for fair play'? And how does the servile configuration circumvent these rules? – We shall address and try to answer these questions in the following.

Part I

*The Incredible Profundity
of the Truly Superficial*

1. Superficial and Profound Subjectivity

1.1. Defending Superficiality.

In almost all contexts, it is in Nietzsche a mark of excellence to be superficial – not, however, in all. A German nationalist with no learning and no sense of philosophy, chanting his *Deutshland, Deutshland, über Alles*, is also superficial, without depth, but is in this context the impersonation of a fool.

> It is increasingly clear to me that we are not sufficiently shallow/superficial [*flach*] and naïve [*gutmüthig*] [. . .] to sing along to the hate-wheezing stupidifying refrain [*Verdummungs-Parole*], *Deutschland, Deutschland über Alles*. (Nachlaß 1885-86, KSA 12, 1[195]).

> The Nationality-insanity and homeland-idiocy never cease to marvel me: *Deutschland, Deutschland, über Alles* clangs painfully in my ears. [. . .] The honest politician, who in his head unifies the daring mix of Royalism and Christianity with a purposeless politics of the moment [*Augenblicks-Politik*], who is concerned with philosophy no more than a peasant or an undergraduate student, stimulates my ironic curiosity. (Nachlaß 1885-86, KSA 12, 2[10]).[393]

---

[393] Toward the end of *Zur Genealogie der Moral*, Nietzsche returns to this explicit contempt for German nationalism, interwoven, in the passage, with his equally explicit contempt for anti-Semitism: "I also do not like these latest speculators in idealism, the anti-Semites, who today roll their eyes in a Christian-Aryan-bourgeois manner and exhaust one's patience by trying to rouse up all the horned-beast elements in the people by a brazen abuse of the cheapest of all agitator's tricks, moral attitudinizing (that *no* kind of swindle fails to succeed in Germany today is connected with the undeniable and palpable stagnation of the German spirit; and the cause of that I seek in a too exclusive diet of newspapers, politics, beer, and Wagnerian music, together with the presuppositions of such a diet: first, national constriction and vanity, the strong but narrow principle *Deutschland, Deutschland über alles*." (GM III, 26, KSA 5, p. 407-8). In recent Nietzsche commentary, much have been written about Nietzsche's criticisms of nationalism, anti-Semitism, and his often expressed admiration for the Jewish people; positions that indeed appear more like precocious anti-Fascism than the opposite. Quite uncompromising in this

The German nationalist is a fool because his superficiality does not 'touch' or 'react to' his core; his superficiality touches merely a surface: German nationalism as advanced in newspapers and by public opinion. The nationalist is therefore merely an extension of the public surface. Superficiality is only excellent when it is deep; it is only noble when it 'touches' an unconscious or instinctual core; when it is, as it were, a *reaction to* an empty core. A 'horizontal' superficiality that blends in with and merely extends the opinion of the crowd is despicable, while a 'vertical' superficiality that seems to spring from the empty abyss of the individual is admirable. Superficiality is good when it reacts to *human in-essentiality*. Then the superficial human being seems to have become doubly in-essential: adding in-essentiality in its performance to in-essentiality as its given condition. If the human reacts to own belief in *essentiality*, it is appalling, and indicates a major delusion on part of the subject. That is why the German nationalist and anti-Semite to Nietzsche is an abomination: the idiot actually *believes* in his political mission; he believes in a truth that is always *the other's truth*; a *truth* he has adopted as his own essential truth.[394] Also John Stuart Mill is to Nietzsche a superficial fool, while Napoleon Bonaparte, by contrast, is a superficial ge-

---

regard, we note how Nietzsche lashes out at contemporary anti-Semites, even when they profess their appreciation of and sympathy for his work. Theodor Fritsch – prominent anti-Semite at the turn of the century (and still, during the raise to power of the Nazi-party in the thirties, regarded as a one of its ideological fathers) – is completely brushed aside; it is indeed difficult to imagine a more blunt and emphatic rebuff: "Recently a certain Herr Theodor Fritsch from Leipzig wrote to me. There is in Germany no more shameless and stupid gang than these anti-Semites. As my brief thanks, I have dealt him a serious blow. This riffraff dare to take the name of Zarathustra in their mouths! Disgusting! Disgusting! Disgusting! [*Ekel! Ekel! Ekel!*]." (Nachlaß 1886-87, KSA 12, 7[67]). Beyond this note, I am not here repeating these discussions, but for a recent account, one might consult Allison, David B.: Reading the New Nietzsche. Lanham, New York (Rowman and Littlefield), 2001, especially Introduction & Chapter 4. See also the anthology, Golomb, J. and Wistrich R. S. (eds.): Nietzsche, Godfather of Fascism? On the Uses and Abuses of a Philosophy. Princeton (Princeton University Press), 2002.

[394] A fragment from Nietzsche's Nachlaß corroborates this interpretation; significantly the fragment juxtaposes the cleverness of the Jude with the ignorance of the Anti-Semite: "What constitutes the actual difference between the Jude and the Anti-Semite: The Jude knows t h a t he lies, w h e n he lies: the Anti-Semite does not know that he always lies – " (Nachlaß 1888, KSA 13, 21[6]). In other words, the Anti-Semite *believes* in his lies as his truths; while the Jew knows that he lies. It is clearly better to "know" that one lies, than to "believe" in one's lies.

nius. Stuart Mill *believes* in his essential humanity and essential reasonableness, whether he talks about liberty, the utilitarian principle, or the liberation of women. Bonaparte raises himself above his in-essentiality, ignores it, and by an iron fist casts *his* truth as in rock.[395] So, how do we best react to *essential human in-essentiality*? – By the double operation of (i) rejecting all notions of essentiality and (ii) creating on top of our *original lack* a *semblance* of the essential! Nietzsche's recipe on superior style: One first denounces the notion of *self*, thereupon one creates one's self. "Active, successful natures act, not according to the dictum 'know thyself', but as if there hovered before them the commandment: w i l l a self and thou shalt b e c o m e a self." (MA II/1 366, KSA 2, p. 524).[396]

When in *Zur Genealogie der Moral* (GM), Nietzsche sets out to analyze the etymological origins of words like 'good' and 'bad,' the crux of the analysis is always to demonstrate how *superficially* the words were originally conceived, and how this original superficiality gradually declined into a false abyss of hidden essences and intentions. Originally the words merely referred to an appearance; 'good' would thus refer to what everybody could *see* was good. 'Good' was simply what 'the good ones' called themselves; 'the good' were the noble, the superior, and the powerful. Out of an inno-

---

[395] There are numerous references to the supremacy of Napoleon in Nietzsche's work, for example: "Napoleon: to understand the necessary correspondence between the higher and fearful human being. [. . .] 'Totality' as health and superior activity; to rediscover the straight line, the great style in activity; the most powerful instinct, which affirms life itself as dominance." (Nachlaß 1887, KSA 12, 10[5]).

[396] In the *Die Fröhliche Wissenschaft* the operation of achieving the great style is further explained: "To give style to one's character – a great and rare art! He exercises it who surveys all that his nature presents in strength and weakness and then moulds it to an artistic plan until everything appears as art and reason, and even the weaknesses delight the eye. [. . .] It will be the strong, imperious natures which experience their subtlest joy in exercising such control, in such constraint and perfecting under their own law." (FW 290, KSA 3, p. 530). Next to Napoleon, Goethe is Nietzsche's best example of such a self-creating, strong, life-affirming nature: "What he [Goethe] aspired to was t o - t a l i t y ; he strove against the separation of reason, sensuality, feeling, will. [. . .] he disciplined himself to a whole, he c r e a t e d himself. [. . .] A spirit thus e m a n c i p a t e d stand in the midst of the universe with a joyful and trusting fatalism, in the f a i t h that only what is separate and individual may be rejected, that in the totality everything is redeemed and affirmed – h e n o l o n g e r d e n i e s ." (GD, "Streifzüge eines Unzeitgemässen," 49, KSA 6, p. 151-52).

cent and uncorrupted feeling of sheer superiority, they established themselves and their values as 'good.'

> Rather it was 'the good' themselves, that is to say, the noble, powerful, high-positioned and high-minded, who felt and established themselves and their actions as good, that is, of the first rank, in distinction to all the low, low-minded, common and plebeian. It was out of this pathos of distance that they first seized the right to create values and to coin names for values: what had they to do with utility! (GM I 2, KSA 5, p. 259).

And as well as 'good' had originally no ethical-psychological connotations, 'bad' also had no such connotations. 'Bad' simply designated the class that was by all considered common, plebeian, and low in contrast to the noble class. The German *schlecht* (bad, evil) has its etymological origin in the German *schlicht* (plain, simple), and were originally merely a designation for the plain, common man, Nietzsche explains.

Another opposition like pure versus impure, which today has inevitable Christian-moral implications (– pure as chaste, innocent, untainted with evil, 'pure in heart'), was again merely referring to an appearance. "The 'pure one' is from the beginning merely a man who washes himself, who forbids himself certain foods that produce skin ailments, who does not sleep with the dirty women of the lower strata." (GM I, 6, KSA 5, p. 265).

Gradually, however, the words themselves acquire something tantamount to a 'soul.' As values, they will be inverted: they will no longer refer to appearances, but to hidden essences. 'Good' will in later developments refer to the unselfish and non-egoistic action; a reference that culminates in Kant's dictum of the 'good will' that is good 'in-itself' – no longer 'good' as appearance.

If before, there were only self-affirmation and innocent surface-existence, the priests invent a false human depth. With this, the *possibility of evil* is for the first time conceived; the human being can be weighed and measured according to a scale residing in its false depth. A purely superficial human has the capacity of neither doing 'good' nor 'evil,' because there is no scale on which to weigh actions as either one or the other. Two assumptions are necessary before an act becomes 'evil': (i) one must assume that the act has been performed out of an evil *will*; (ii) one must assume that the individual has had the *freedom* to act otherwise, but desisted.[397] In both

---

[397] Compare to *Menschliches, Allzumenschliches*: "The evil acts at which we are now most indignant rest on the error that he who perpetrates them against us posses free will, that is to say, that he could have chosen not to cause us this harm." & "We do not accuse nature of immorality when it sends us a thun-

of these assumptions, it is taken for granted that in every action there is a *doer* before there is a *deed*, that is, a conscious and responsible agent. Qua this *doer*, depth has been applied to the individual; it is the supposed *doer* that is responsible for the action of the individual. "It was on the soil of this essentially dangerous form of human existence, the priestly form, that man first became an interesting animal, that only here did the human soul in a higher sense acquire depth and became evil." (GM I, 6, KSA 5, p. 266).

With the invention of this false depth, it is now possible to invert the formerly so innocent and healthy value equation of the good: good = noble = powerful = beautiful = happy = beloved by God. Instead of identifying 'good' with the powerful, 'good' is evaluated according to the new depth, the supposed *doer* behind and controlling action.

True innocence is always to be unconscious; true innocence is never to be conscious of own innocence; however, perversely, according to the new emerging paradigm, innocence is no longer to be unconscious, it is to be conscious of own innocence. Suddenly, *innocence* becomes a quality comparable to *harmless*, and it is the most *powerless* that are seen as the most *harmless*. Innocence becomes the preeminent quality of the new *doer*, who can now have the intention, or not have the intention, to inflict harm. Innocence becomes equal to not having the intention to inflict harm; 'good' is equal to *intentionally harmless*, and those *conscious of their intentional harmlessness* are consequently the most 'Good.' The slave-revolt in morality has started – according to Nietzsche, a specific Judaic revolution that was cleverly extended into Christianity. A new value equation is established: good = low = weak = ugly = unhappy = beloved by God. "The wretched alone are the good; the poor, impotent, lowly alone are the good; the suffering, deprived, sick, ugly alone are pious; they alone are blessed by god." (GM I, 7, KSA 5, p. 267).

1.2. The Magnificent Shallowness of Woman.

Why is the noble admirable in his superficiality? – As said, partly because his superficiality 'touches,' is a reaction to, his empty core; but moreover – adding to his excellence – because he exercises a willing and deliberate looking-away-from himself. If at all he is aware of reacting to his own ab-

---

derstorm and makes us wet: why do we call the harmful man immoral? Because in the latter case we assume a voluntarily commanding free-will." (MA I, 99 & 102, KSA 2, p. 96 & 99).

ysmal emptiness, he forces himself – with intuitive sophistication and refinement – to ignore this fact. He implements an active forgetfulness of own sentiments and emotions. He is (in some non-humanistic sense) 'deep,' but he intuitively understands the necessity of becoming shallow. This shallowness and superficiality might thus be understood as 'second nature,' as something acquired through meditation and self-reflection, but in the true noble, it is 'first nature'; it either is or has become instinct. If the true noble 'forces' himself to become superficial, it is best if he uses as little force as at all possible. A large expenditure of force would immediately be suspicious; it would indicate that there is something inherently wrong with his instincts.

In his writings, Nietzsche overwhelmingly describes the 'noble' as *he*. We have so far been so lax as to follow Nietzsche's precedent; but it is now the place to emphasize that insofar as the 'noble' emerges as a *figure* and an *economy*, the 'noble' is typically *feminine*. Intuitive refinement, instinctual superficiality, we repeatedly find in Nietzsche's 'woman.' By contrast, Nietzsche's 'man' is typically clumsy and importune, and consigned to the position of the 'slave.' By understanding Nietzsche's descriptions of the dialectics at work between man and woman, we therefore gain a unique insight into the dialectics between Nietzsche's 'master' and 'slave.' Without being fully aware of his displacement of object, Nietzsche descriptions of women (of *femininity* in general) are also his most incisive psychological portraits of the 'master.'

The dialectics between woman and man (i.e., master and slave) is for instance described in the preface to JGB. Here we are introduced to the less than perfect man – an example on the 'dogmatic' (i.e., metaphysical) philosopher – and his naïve idealizations of, and attempts at seducing, woman (i.e., truth).

> Suppose that truth is a woman [*Weib*] – and why not? Aren't there reasons for suspecting that all philosophers, to the extent that they have been dogmatists, have not really understood women? That the grotesque seriousness of their approach towards the truth and the clumsy advances they have made so far are unsuitable ways for capturing for themselves a lady [*ein Frauenzimmer für sich einzunehmen*]? What is certain is that she did not let herself be caught – leaving dogmatism of all types standing sad and discouraged. If at all it still stands! [*Wenn sie überhaupt noch steht!*]. (JGB Preface, KSA 5, p. 11).

Philosophers relate to truth like clumsy men relate to women. Woman is in the possession of truth, but only because of a masculine misunderstanding, namely that *she has what he is lacking*.

1. Superficial and Profound Subjectivity

In passing, it may be worthwhile noticing that the relationship between masculine and feminine in Nietzsche is typically 'matriarchal' in contrast to Freud's 'patriarchal' relationships. In psychoanalysis, man has what a woman lacks, a penis, which gives rise not only to the notorious 'penis-envy' in women, but equally notoriously also to her sense of inferiority, and her incapacity to engage in grand projects. She has no fear of losing what she has already lost – has no 'castration-anxiety' – and has therefore no motivation to engage in projects much beyond the concerns of the household. In Nietzsche by contrast, woman is in possession of the 'phallus,' namely as *man's interpretation of her as truth*. It is literally inscribed in the quotation above that the man that grants her the phallus of truth, in the process loses his. Today all dogmatism (i.e., belief in truth) stands sad and discouraged . . . "If at all it still stands." It just lost its erection!

Now, we must not forget that woman does not have the phallus that man inscribes in her as the *truth* that he is lacking, but because of her infinite subtlety she acts *as if* she had it. She is even more 'potent' in her deceptions than if actually she possessed truth. This interpretation is not clear in the passage from JGB, but when Nietzsche in more detail describes the operations of the feminine women in his notebooks, her deception explicitly grants her the 'master' position. Now we see how it is further substantiated that the feminine woman becomes 'master,' the man 'slave,' in Nietzsche's sexual economy.

> Woman, conscious of man's feeling concerning women, assists his effort at idealization [*kommt dessen Bemühen nach Idealiserung entgegen*] by adorning herself, walking beautifully, dancing, expressing delicate thoughts: in the same way, she practices modesty, reserve, distance – realizing instinctively that in this way the idealizing capacity of the man will grow. (– Given the tremendous subtlety of woman's instinct, modesty remains by no means conscious hypocrisy: she divines that it is precisely an actual naïve modesty [*eine naïve wirkliche schamhaftigkeit*] that most seduces a man and impels him to overestimate her. Therefore woman is naïve – from the subtlety of her instinct, which advises her of the utility of innocence. A deliberate keeping-one's-eyes-closed-to-oneself [*die-Augen-über-sich-geschlos-sen-halten*] – Whenever dissembling produces a stronger effect when it is unconscious, it becomes unconscious.) (Nachlaß 1887, KSA 12, 8[1]).[398]

---

[398] In the context of these notes, Nietzsche believes he is describing the economy of the artist. The artist idealizes his object, as man idealizes woman. Man's idealization of women is in this context (*as artist*) not as 'clumsy and importune' as when the dogmatic philosopher in JGB idealizes woman. Here 'idealization' is 'love,' and art is a kind of love too. Both artist and lover 'encrust' their object. "The demand for art and beauty is an indirect demand for

We notice again that 'truth' is not something that woman *has*; it is an addition attributable to masculine idealization and overestimation. The woman 'knows' (unconsciously) that man believes that she has what he lacks, and she 'knows' (unconsciously) that if, in her modesty and delicacy, she disguises that which man believes *that she has as what he lacks*, she will fixate his eternal interest and become the exclusive object for his idealizations. In this game, man is more stupid than woman, because he wants that of woman, which she does not have, but only simulates she has.

In this quotation, the opaqueness of the game of the woman becomes total when she *die-Augen-über-sich-geschlossen-halten* – by virtue of her delicacy and because she knows the utility of innocence. Now she does not even dissimulate any longer, granted that dissimulation presupposes a conscious operation in which the subject knows that she is dissimulating (implying that the subject would know the truth of her operation, namely that there is no truth). Instead, the woman closes her eyes to her *lack of truth*, lack of 'content' or 'essence.' Not only does man overestimate woman, she overestimates herself as well. She believes that she is exactly as ideal as man thinks she is. She is as guilty in self-deception as man; however, in her *healthy repression* of her deception, she actively looses any awareness of deceit. Here, she actively forgets her deception. What the woman represses here is therefore not *truth* (– what was always contended in Freud and Breuer's well-known analyses of hysterical women[399]), what is

---

the ecstasies of sexuality communicated to the brain. The world becomes perfect, through 'love.' [. . .] In art, as the 'embellishing' power: as man sees woman and, as it were, make her a present of everything excellent, so the sensuality of the artist puts into one object everything else that he honors and esteems – in this way he perfects an object ('idealizes' it)." (Nachlaß 1887, KSA 12, 8[1]). So far, art is a kind of love. There is the same sexual energy, there is the same falsification, qua 'idealization,' of the object; both activities make the object stronger, more perfect, more beautiful. The lover makes a woman 'beautiful,' as an artist makes an 'object' beautiful. So far, woman is an example of the art object. But at this point Nietzsche seems to forget himself, or is he still talking about an analogy between art-object and woman, when he starts speculating about how the woman on her side reacts to the lover's idealization of her – the art-object does not have any reaction to the idealizations of the artist in any obvious sense?

[399] In *Studies on Hysteria* (New York (Basic Books), 2000), in famous cases like *Anna O* and *Emma von N*, Freud and Breuer invariably trace the hysterical symptom back to an original scene, which, as the truth of the symptom, also has the power to cure insofar as the patient is helped to recall the scene. The patient famously 'suffers from reminiscences,' which it is the job of the analyst to make conscious to the patient.

1. Superficial and Profound Subjectivity

repressed by the woman is *lack of truth*, i.e., her self-deception regarding her possession of truth. Thus, if man's self-deception implies deficiency in his being, the woman's *repressed self-deception* does not imply any deficiency in her being. On the contrary, she deceives herself only out of the subtlety of her instincts. Her deception makes her stronger than man; she becomes the superior, he the inferior. She becomes 'master' (notice, the *master of reserve*); he becomes 'slave.'[400]

Furthermore, we notice that in this game of seduction, the woman not only assumes the *superior* position, ultimately she also assumes the *active* part, and assigns to man the passive. It is the woman who *seduces man into seducing her*; she "*assists* [or *invites*: *kommt . . . entgegen*] *his effort at idealization* by adorning herself, walking beautifully," etc. This characterizes the paradoxical movement of seduction: the woman *kommt* masculine desire *entgegen* by increasing the distance man has to traverse in order to

---

[400] The pattern is repeated later in JGB. A contemporary feminist would not be convinced by Nietzsche's rhetoric and argument, but when Nietzsche in *Our Virtues* (JGB 239) attacks Feminism, it is not – as commonly believed – from a misogynist position. Woman is *seduced* into Feminism by weak men because the feminine woman represents a danger to the weak, the *European, 'man.'* This slave-creature who himself has lost all healthy instincts, is now engaged in *defeminizing* woman by tempting her with 'equal rights.' Feminism is therefore essentially a *masculine* conspiracy, devised by demasculinized 'men': "Emancipation of woman [. . .] turns out to be a strange symptom of the increased weakening and softening of the most feminine instincts [*allerweiblichsten Instinkte*] of all. The stupidity in this movement, an almost masculine stupidity, is enough to make any woman who has turned out well [*wohlgerathenes Weib*] (which always means a clever woman) thoroughly ashamed." (JGB 239, KSA 5, p. 176). Feminism is defeminization, or masculinization, of woman. Woman becomes equal to man, but to *European 'man,'* that is, to this parody of a man, to an already feminine and demasculinized man. "Of course, there are plenty of idiotic friends and corrupters of women [*blödsinnige Frauen-Freunde and Weibs-Verderber*] among the scholarly asses of the male sex who recommend that women defeminize themselves like this and copy all the stupidities that the 'man' in Europe, that European 'manliness,' suffers from – who would like to bring women down to the level of 'general education,' and maybe even of reading the newspapers and taking part in politics." (JGB 239; KSA 5, p. 177). Here, 'man' is again occupying the position of the resentful slave who cannot endure the Other, the Different, the Autonomous, and the Powerful in form of truly feminine instincts, and therefore engages himself in dragging down the woman to his own cozy mediocrity. An educated guess would suggest that the 'scholarly ass of the male sex' referred to would be John Stuart Mill – among else famous for his essay, *The Subjection of Women*.

catch her, knowing very well that his desire grows with increasing distance. At the culmination of this logic, she would have become a purely imaginary object of desire. From her emptiness and lack, she 'refashions' in the imaginary herself as *Truth*. She performs what we call, a 'good reaction' to her empty core. Woman becomes the model-example of a metaphysical operation par excellence, operating in a fashion not fundamentally different from Aristotle's 'unmoved mover'; the Aristotelian god that moves only as a *final cause*, i.e., only as an object of desire and 'love' – except that in Nietzsche, in contrast to Aristotle, the object is fundamentally absent; or, is merely a projection.

In this game of deception, and deception upon deception, the 'feminine' must be seen as a *position*, resulting from a certain masculine idealization of woman, *adopted* by woman in order to augment masculine idealization. Thus, the 'feminine' is *not* essence or nature, not an *Ewig Weibliche* that would essentially characterize the biological woman. It is a position that might be adopted by the biological man as well. – But why and how? Here it is not the intention to invoke the purely ideological claim that 'there is a feminine side to every man' – and even less to introduce some late variation over C. G. Jung's old distinction between 'anima' and 'animus.' However, as a *consequence* of Nietzsche's theory of the subject (as introduced in *Chapters 3 & 4*), it must be possible in inner-mental life to adopt a variety of feminine and masculine *positions*. Consistently, we are in Nietzsche's notion of subjectivity addressing a heterogeneous and fragmented subject; a subject composed of multiple so-called 'ego-clusters' or 'ego-configurations'; that is, multiple *positions* or *identities* in the subject, some of which will be *conventionally* and *culturally* defined as 'masculine,' others as 'feminine.' As such, the so-called 'masculine' and 'feminine' are nothing but *semantic ego-clusters* within the subject; clusters that are played out against each other, some being repressed, others being allowed to surface in the subject's manifest action and speech. Thus, the biological man may surely display 'feminine' behavior, because feminine behavior is internalized as part of his *multiple identities*; and ditto the biological woman may display masculine behavior.

For example, the feminine basis-operation, to close one's eyes to one's lack of truth – and we suggest that this exhibition of modesty, tact, and delicacy in the downcast eyes is uniquely 'feminine' – is, we learn in a later passage, Nietzsche's own stylistic practice, and is being acknowledged as such. "There are realities that one may never admit to oneself; after all, *one is a woman*; after all, *one has a woman's pudeurs*." (Nachlaß 1888, KSA 13, 17[5]; italics added). 'One' (who is here Nietzsche) is a woman; 'one' writes as a woman; 'one' closes one's eyes to one's lack of truth. One is tactful enough to speak and write *as if* one speaks and writes the truth; one assumes the 'phallus' of truth, also as man.[401]

2. Two Economies: Hyper-Cathected and De-Cathected Self.

A 'will to ignorance,' an 'active forgetfulness,' a 'healthy repression,' is

---

[401] The view of women here presented is obviously challenging many of the facile accounts of Nietzsche as the feeble and revengeful misogynist in his relation to women (cf. note above). This view has never been as glibly advanced as in Bertrand Russell's *A History of Western Philosophy*. Now, it is fair to say that nobody takes Russell's introduction to Nietzsche seriously any longer. Russell is in fact so degraded (both here and there) that one could just as well relax one's defenses and start enjoying his quips, but I believe that there are still some need to respond to one of his most persistently recurring readings: the conventionally accepted cliché-interpretation of Nietzsche's notorious precept, "Are you going to Women? Do not forget your whip!" (Z I, "Of Old and Young Women"; KSA 4, p. 86). Russell comments: "His opinion of women, like every man's, is an objectification of his own emotion towards them, which is obviously one of fear. "Forget not thy whip" – but nine women out of ten would get the whip away from him, and he knew it, so he kept away from women, and soothed his wounded vanity with unkind remarks." (Bertrand Russell: A History of Western Philosophy. New York, London (A Touchstone Book), 1972, p. 767. We notice that in Russell's complacent reading, the *old woman's advice to Zarathustra* is perfunctorily read as *Nietzsche's advice to himself*. So, if Zarathustra is advised to remember his whip, Nietzsche is according to Russell's reading instructed by himself to discipline the women he visits (– however unsuccessful he may be, because 9 out of 10 women would bereave him of his whip, says Russell, evoking an "unkind" image on impotence and castration). The old woman's advice, however, suggests that Zarathustra/Nietzsche needs a whip not as a weapon of attack, but as one of defense. He visits women as an animal trainer enters an animal's cage. Animal trainers need a whip out of respect of the animals, such as (the most obvious association) the big cats (– Nietzsche often compares the woman to a cat!). In the big cats instincts kick in without much warning, and knowing that, the trainer must consequently approach them cautiously, and equipped with some kind of defense, such as a whip. He needs a minimum of protection, because they are so much stronger, so much more formidable and intense in their enigmatic and self-absorbed narcissism than he. Nietzsche's sentence does not indicate disrespect of woman, but rather some inordinate *respect*.

implemented by the noble and the woman, in order to disregard the fact that she does not have the truth (the 'phallus') on which authority she acts. She becomes innocent because she believes in her truth. *Innocence* is paradoxically to be unconscious about the existence of an Unconscious. If Freud prescribed, *Wo Es war soll Ich werden*, Nietzsche response could have been the brief, *forget it/Id!*[402] In its unconscious abyss, the human being is *nothing*. Absence and lack is fundamentally inscribed in the human constitution (Nietzsche and Freud seem to agree so far). The master, the noble, however, actively forgets this lack, and acts out a power, which fundamentally he/she does not have. Active forgetfulness is to forget *nothing* (i.e., that one *is nothing*). Will-to-power is therefore not an essence (and certainly not an essence endowed particular fortunate human beings); will-to-power emerges from nothing, and is therefore nothing but *will* – 'will to will' as Heidegger from a different analytical position says, but a 'will to will' that does not reflect itself. Napoleon Bonaparte exercises will-to-power because he assumes a truth that he does not have; by assuming this truth, he becomes it – i.e., he becomes truth, and acts with resolute conviction in himself as truth. To maintain himself as truth, he practices 'active forgetfulness' concerning his human limitations. Active forgetfulness is therefore what we describe as a *good reaction to* the essential absence in the subject; as such, it 'touches' an empty core.

Active forgetfulness helps the master to forget *nothing*, that is, the inner chaos of incoherent opinions, valuations, drives, voices, etc. It is as such a way of avoiding *contamination*: contamination from the inside, but contamination from the outside as well. First, it is a way of avoiding contamination from the outside, for example, avoiding the superficiality of public opinion, or the vengefulness of the slave – the noble pinches her nose, looks away, and forgets. Secondly, it is a way of avoiding 'contamination' from the inside. An individual is never a unity, in its unconscious abyss, the individual is a chaos of inconsistent and contradictory valuations and drives. The *inside* is as much a domain for incoherent babbling as is the *outside*, the public sphere for the babbling that is exercised as public debate. "A single individual contains within him a vast confusion of contradictory valuations and consequently of contradictory drives." (WM 259). The 'noble' and 'great' tames this inner *or* outer incoherent babbling, and syn-

---

[402] It is doubtful that Nietzsche would have embraced the later preoccupation with the psychoanalytic 'talking-cure.' He is likely, rather, to would have joined the many voices insisting on the failures of psychoanalytic therapy. This intense narcissistic interest in looking-into-oneself would not have been to his taste. Nietzsche's anti-analytic stance is as pertinent as ever, and worthwhile, at some appropriate time and day, a closer analysis.

chronizes his/her 'voices' (or 'drives') into expressing a single harmonic accord (his/her 'truth,' or 'phallus' so-called). This is achieved by forgetting, by shutting off, everything within the self that is foreign to and disturbs one's 'will,' one's adopted innermost purposes.

Thus, the 'noble' and 'great' has a unique relationship to itself; in contrast to the 'slave,' the 'noble' *hyper-cathects* the self. He or she lives from within; that is, his 'force' is always moving in a trajectory from within to without. As such, his force imposes itself on the outside, forming the outside; it is so-called 'active' (– what does not contradict its description as a *reaction to* the innermost core of *nothing*, a *good forgetfulness of nothing*; it is precisely in the *good reaction to the inner core of nothing*, one is enabling oneself to act in the outer). In contrast, the 'slave' *hyper-cathects* the outside, and his inside becomes thus a mirror of the outside, implying that he has no true 'inside.' The slave always has to find himself in the other, whereas the master finds himself in himself. The trajectory of the 'force' of the slave is a *circular confusion*, moving from the outside to the inside in order to impose itself on the outside as identical to what is outside in the first place.

> For all their apparent egoism, most people do nothing for their ego but only for the phantom of their ego that has been formed in the heads of those around them and communicated back to them – as a result of which everybody lives in a mist of impersonal, semipersonal opinions and arbitrary, and, as it were, poetic evaluations, each one always in the head of the other, and that head in turn in other heads: a wonderful world of phantasms, that yet manages to appear so sober! (M 105, KSA 3, p. 92).

This circular confusion is for example seen in the *sentimental appeal* to an outside that already endorses the appeal; an outside that is by the 'slave' (crucially) always-already recognized as endorsing the sentimental appeal, which, otherwise, would never have been made. The first rule of the slave: never take a risk; always repeat what is already regarded as 'correct.' (As when amiable colleagues on the occasional teaching symposium benignly appeal to us all – themselves included, of course – that we ought to do a better job *helping* and *understanding* students; the suggestion is not likely to meet objection, but is it too arrogant to suggest that some of us *help* and *understand* students without being conscious of doing so? One asks with Nietzschean suspicion, *who* does such a magnanimous display of good-will serve?) Since thus the 'force' of the slave is mimetic, it is necessarily uncreative and re-active.[403] It is essentially conservative and reactionary.[404]

---

[403] The 'slave' is the typically moral human, and the moral attitude he or she

adopts will always necessarily have to be a copy of something outside him or herself, as often indicated: "The moral man [. . .] is a type in regard to morality, only not his own type; a copy, a good copy at best – the measure of his value lies outside him." (WM 382).

404 In contrast to Deleuze's analysis of Nietzsche's *forces*, I see the *trajectories* of the forces as determining them as respectively 'active' or 'reactive'; if a trajectory is 'straight,' forces 'unload' themselves in a great gesture of generosity; if it is 'circular,' nothing is 'unloaded'; everything is taken back. It is thus not the *forces in-themselves* – as Deleuze has it – that are 'active' respectively 'reactive'; Deleuze suggests the distinction between 'noble' and 'slave' as informed by the 'active' and 'reactive' *forces* (see Deleuze: Nietzsche and Philosophy, loc. cit.). Deleuze builds up his entire argument around this famous distinction; the *active* forces being defined as "going to the limit of what they can do," the *reactive* as "separating" the active forces from this their own optimum. In Deleuze, 'nobility' versus 'servility,' 'generosity' versus 'resentment,' becomes, ultimately, biological distinctions. In this fundamental active-reactive distinction, Deleuze is therefore from the beginning sneaking metaphysical assumptions into his axiomatic. He tacitly presupposes 'good' versus 'evil' in the formative active-reactive distinction, in order to make a case more persuasively for the 'good,' the 'active,' the forces that "go to their limit." We understand why, if we superimpose on the distinction what is Deleuze's ideological concern in the beginning of the sixties. We then understand that with this distinction, Deleuze is producing a *strong metaphysical* argument *for* a transgressive, uninhibited, non-neurotic, emancipated personality-structure, *against* a conformist, inhibited, neurotic, and controlling. As politicized, Nietzsche's 'forces' are designed to fight Deleuze's fight. Inscribing within themselves the good versus the bad, they already side with the emancipative-'nomadic' project of Deleuze. My objection to Deleuze's distinction is therefore that *forces* cannot be qualified in any which way; that *forces* are *beyond* good and evil, active and reactive. When Nietzsche introduces a 'master' and a 'slave' morality – which may well be described as respectively 'active' and 'reactive' – it comes as an after-effect of 'forces' in themselves *neutral* in formatting this distinction. Forces are *always* will-to-power complexes, and are not, qua their own impetus, inscribing 'activity' or 'reactivity' into the subject. – Like I can use the perfectly neutral medium, *money*, for 'active' or 'reactive' purposes without having to ascribe 'activity' or 'reactivity' into two distinct classes of money. For example, I can hand money out in a great gesture of generosity; but I can also cling to them; horrified of the prospect of letting go. It is clear that it is not *money* (in deterministic fashion) that would be responsible for my 'active' or 'reactive' choices. This position finds support in Nietzsche when he writes: "There is only one type of force [*es gibt nur Eine Art Kraft*]." (WM 815). Deleuze's misunderstanding is also precisely addressed by Marco Brusotti: "The expression 'reactive force' does not occur in the *Genealogy*. Deleuze has in-

2. Two Economies: Hyper-Cathected and De-Cathected Self

In the quote below, Nietzsche seems on a first reading to confuse the two suggested positions; the slave *both* says 'no' to what is outside, what is different, *and* needs to direct his view outward instead of inward. The 'essence of ressentiment,' we learn, is the need of a hostile external world, but why direct oneself outward toward what is experienced as hostile?

> While every noble morality develops from a triumphant affirmation of itself, slave morality from the outset says No to what is 'outside,' what is 'different,' what is 'not itself'; and t h i s No is its creative deed. This inversion of the value positing eye – this n e e d to direct one's view outward instead of back to oneself – is of the essence of r e s s e n t i m e n t : in order to emerge, slave morality always first needs a hostile external world [*einer Gegen- und Ausserwelt*]; it needs, physiologically speaking, external stimuli in order to act at all – its action is fundamentally reaction. The reverse is the case with the noble mode of valuation: it acts and grows spontaneously, its seeks its opposite only so as to affirm itself more gratefully and triumphantly. [. . .] 'We noble, we good, we beautiful, we happy!' [. . .] The 'well-born' f e l t themselves to be 'happy'; they did not have to establish their happiness artificially by examining their enemies, or to persuade themselves, d e c e i v e themselves, that they were happy (as all men of ressentiment are in the habit of doing). (GM I 10, KSA 5, p. 271-72).

We seem to have in Nietzsche's slave a character that is busy placating a threatening outside world, while in the noble we have a character that with self-confidence acts himself out in it; his slogan could have been Shakespeare's: "The world's mine oyster, which I with sword will open."[405] Thanks to the self-investment (the hyper-cathexis of self) of the noble, the world is divested of importance. It is not perceived as a threat; or with suspicion, envy or ressentiment, as a dangerous outside. It is certainly 'interesting,' but it no longer overwhelms. It is no more than a playground for the nobles who are now eternally affirming this outside because it is merely an extension of themselves, a mirror to their own happiness. The slaves, by contrast, have hyper-cathected the outside world, which must

---

vented it: He misunderstands the opposition 'active'-'reactive' as an opposition between active and reactive *forces*. The idea of a 'reactive force', where the reactivity is an inner quality of certain forces is, however, foreign to Nietzsche's thinking. According to Nietzsche, the force as will-to-power is originally active. [. . .] Reactive manifestations are not derivable from certain reactive forces." Brusotti, Marco: "Wille zum Nichts, Ressentiment, Hypnose – 'Aktive' und 'Reaktive' in Nietzsche's *Genealogie*." Nietzsche Studien, Bd. 30. Berlin, New York: Walter de Gruyter, 2001. p. 111-12.

405 Shakespeare: The Merry Wives of Windsor (II, ii).

now appear overwhelming and dangerous, and which must therefore always have to be taken into account before any action is possible. As a result, the 'slave' no longer has any spontaneous sense of happiness; they have to 'persuade,' 'deceive' themselves into being happy by mirroring themselves in the world: they check themselves against the Other in order to decide whether they are 'happy' according to the Other's definition of happiness. There is thus no contradiction: the slave directs himself outward to an inherently hostile outer world in order to, in the Other, find confirmation of his weak, de-cathected, self.

We have in the *assertive configuration* and the *servile configuration* two contrary economies: in the *assertive configuration* the inside is hyper-cathected, and the outside de-cathected, while in the *servile configuration* the inside is de-cathected and the outside hyper-cathected. When in the *assertive configuration* the outside is de-cathected, it can also not constitute a threat to the assertive agent, while in the *servile configuration* it is hyper-cathected, therefore constituting a potential threat.

	'Noble' Assertive Configuration	'Slave' Servile Configuration
Inside	Hyper-cathected	De-cathected
Outside	De-cathected	Hyper-cathected

Since the nobles hyper-cathect their inside, they become fountains of energy; energy that needs an outlet. The spontaneous deed – the deed that cannot but be acted out – springs from this overflow. This deed is pure activity; it springs unhindered from the inside to the outside; it is inspirational in the purest sense – without having been mediated through a divine will, as in Romanticism.[406]

---

[406] In his rigorous study of Nietzsche's *Genealogy*, Werner Stegmaier as well draws attention to this 'unbroken' will of the noble; a will that acted out will appear as a straight trajectory of force, as it is impressed upon the world; contrary to the 'circular confusion' of the will of the slave: "If we understand the formulae, 'will to power,' 'pathos of distance,' and 'nobility' in relation to one another, then the pathos of distance is the mode according to which will to power manifests itself as will to power. Psychologically, it designates an individual confident about his action; who as such does not need somebody else's standards, nor any general standards; who needs no 'principles' to justify his actions. Knowing that he is different from others, he acts according to own standards, and is *able*, moreover, to act as such." Stegmaier, Werner: Nietzsches 'Genealogie der Moral'. Darmstadt (Wissenschaftliche Buchgesellschaft), 1994, p.102.

When the noble feels contempt, he does so, not out of hatred and impotence, but with such a stance of distraction that he soon forgets his contempt. Since he has super-invested himself, he has also divested the fellow human being of significance; consequently, negative sentiments like contempt, resentment, and hatred cannot become lasting impressions. "To be incapable of taking one's enemies, one's accidents, even one's misdeeds seriously for very long – that is the sign of strong, full natures in whom there is an excess of the power to form, to mold, to recuperate and to forget. [. . .] Such a man shakes off with a single shrug many vermin that eat deep into others." (GM I, 10, KSA 5, p. 273). Anger, hatred, or contempt in the noble is like a cloud on the wide blue sky; it evaporates instantly in the blazing sun without leaving a trace.

Whereas the noble is without depth; without, more precisely, a subjectivity separating intention from deed, thus reluctant to interrogate motives and purposes for actions, the slave has de-cathected his inside. As we saw in *Chapter 3*, he has hollowed out himself, created within himself a cavity that is waiting to be filled by values and voices that are no longer his own. He is now constituted as a double self, where the cavity within him – this his hollow and false self – can be filled only from the outside. His de-cathected inside will therefore inevitable be re-cathected, but with inauthentic values and voices. It will be filled by the voices of outside authorities, or *presumed* authorities, which now have – qua his subjective hollowness and 'lack' – free and unhindered access to him (this was described in *Chapter 3* as a 'command-structure' where an outside 'commander' were 'shouting' his commands into the 'ears' of the receptive slave[407]). Nietzsche's de-cathected subjective cavity becomes like a hole in the subject that attracts and needs to be filled with authority. In this structure, it does not matter who is 'shouting' his commands into the 'ear' of the slave, or what the nature of the command might be, as long as the slave has something, *just something*, to obey.

We are here attempting to give a description that would be most faithful to Nietzsche's renditions of these matters – faithful to the characteristic economy, structure, architecture, and metaphoricity of Nietzsche's own discourse – but it should be obvious that Nietzsche is foreshadowing identical speculations of Freud on the formation of the Super-ego. In his characterizations of the *servile configuration*, Nietzsche is describing an ego-split. In

---

[407] Cf. JGB: "the average person has an innate need to obey as a type of f o r m a l c o n s c i e n c e [*eine art formalen Gewissens*] that commands: 'Thou shalt unconditionally do something, unconditionally not do something,' in short: 'thou shalt' [*du sollst*]." (JGB 199; KSA 5, p. 119).

the figures of *noble* and *slave*, we have, respectively, a first-case scenario in which there is harmony between the ego and its instinctual reservoir – a noble and 'full' subject, and a second-case scenario, where the ego deepens, producing a cavity within the subject that finally splits away from the subject, implying that the resulting 'vacuous' and 'confused' subject is obedient to whatever is filled into this new extension of itself. Whether in the name of Freud's 'super-ego' or Nietzsche's 'formal conscience,' this new extension of the self is the structural underground of the servile configuration. (We may notice as well that what is here described as a *servile configuration* roughly is identical to what Theodor W. Adorno – in part inspired by Nietzsche and Freud – would describe as an *authoritarian character*.[408])

Thus, it is accurate to say that the slave creates within himself a *crypt*; a hollow and secret space where he can cultivate all kinds of poisonous plants.[409] A further consequence of the creation of this cryptic self is that the slave can now withdraw himself to this hollow and secret space in order to ruminate, calculate, reflect on consequences of potential actions not yet carried out.

> While the noble man lives in trust and openness with himself [. . .] the man of resentment is neither upright nor naïve nor honest and straightforward with himself. His soul s q u i n t s; his spirit loves hiding places, secret paths and back doors, everything covert entices him as h is world, h is security, h is refresh-

---

[408] See Theodor W. Adorno: Studien zum autoritären Charakter. Frankfurt a/M (Suhrkamp Verlag), 1995.

[409] Compare to Deleuze: "The Nietzschean typology brings into play a whole psychology of 'depths' or 'caves.' In particular the mechanisms which correspond to each moment of the triumph of reactive forces form a theory of the unconscious which ought to be compared to the whole of Freudianism. We must nevertheless be careful not to give Nietzschean concepts an exclusively psychological significance." (Deleuze, loc. cit., p. 145). I imagine Nietzsche's *servile configuration* as something that might resemble certain of Piranesi's etchings, or perhaps the architectural scenarios described in Kafka's novels and short-stories, rather than Freud's neat and well-ordered topographical models of the psyche: – i.e., a dark chaos of chambers, cellars, attics, false walls, and staircases leading nowhere. These scenarios are not entirely without order, but they are so sufficiently disordered that the minute humans inserted into these scenarios are always lost in their attempts to find a way out of these claustrophobic universes. In Piranesi as well as in Kafka, it is as if humans have been inserted into their own brain – from there, there is obviously no escape.

ment; he understands how to keep silent, how not to forget, how to wait, how to be provisionally self-deprecating and humble. (GM I, 10, KSA 5, p. 272).

Man today, as Nietzsche sees it, is this sick animal. It has become deep instead of superficial; self-conscious instead of unconscious; guilty instead of innocent; envious instead of content; unhappy instead of happy, etc. It has turned around the value hierarchy, good vs. evil; what was before good, innocent cruelty and happy egotism, is now evil; what was before bad, jealous resentfulness and unhappy ressentiment, is now good. However, the *outcome* of the process is that man inevitably has become more intelligent, calculating, clever, and crafty. There is in Nietzsche no doubt that the slave became victorious in the history of civilization. Who won the battle, Rome or Judea?

> Which of them has won for the present, Rome or Judea? But there can be no doubt: consider to whom one bows down in Rome itself today, as if they were the epitome of all the highest values – and not only in Rome but over almost half the earth, everywhere that man has become tame or desires to become tame – for three Jews, as is known, and one Jewess (Jesus of Nazareth, the fisherman Peter, the rug weaver Paul, and the mother of the aforementioned Jesus, named Mary). This is very remarkable: Rome has been defeated beyond all doubt. (GM I, 16, KSA 5, p. 287).

Thus, the so-called 'slave,' or in our adopted vocabulary, the *servile configuration*, has become the undisputed *master* of the earth. Our once upon a time 'full subjectivity' has been replaced with a crazy, confused, and vacuous 'ego' without unity, integrity, and straightforwardness; an 'ego' that can no longer confirm itself, but needs confirmation from the outside; an 'ego' split in two; an ego which can now only *deliberate* on its own 'happiness,' but not *be* happy; much as in a certain conversation between Vladimir and Estragon (– rendered with Samuel Beckett's superhuman sense of humor): "You must be happy, too, deep down, if you only knew it. / Would you say so? / Say you are, even if it's not true. / What am I to say? / Say, I am happy. / I am happy. / So am I. / So am I. / We are happy. / We are happy. (*Silence.*) What do we do now, now that we are happy? / Wait for Godot."[410]

---

[410] Samuel Beckett: Waiting for Godot. London (Faber and Faber), 1956, p. 60.

3. The Dialectics Between Forgetfulness and Memory

3.1. Necessary Forgetfulness; Impeding Memory.

In Nietzsche's narrative about our assumed origins, the human has a certain psychic make-up characterized by 'forgetfulness.' Nietzsche believes that originally the human animal is incapable of keeping promises, since there is too much forgetfulness in the human constitution. This original forgetfulness – which on a later civilizational stage will be redressed – gives the early individual a certain happy and cheerful attitude to life, an ability to live and enjoy the immediate present, which is later lost. If thus in the philosophical tradition, forgetfulness has been determined negatively, it is in Nietzsche a positive quality belonging to the active order. It belongs to the *assertive configuration* as a healthy and indeed necessary repression of memorized material. So far, forgetfulness is once more a *good reaction to* too much material; it forces the mental system to close down, shut out, discriminate against superfluous material, and with this, make room for new things:

> Forgetfulness is no mere *vis inertiae* as the superficial imagine [*sic!* the 'superficial' don't understand the necessity of exercising superficiality (P.B.)]; it is rather an active and, in the strictest sense, positive capacity for repression. It is responsible for the fact that what we see and experience enters our consciousness as little, while we are digesting it, as does the thousand-fold process related to physical nourishment – so-called 'incorporation' [*Einverleibung*]. To close the doors and windows of consciousness for a while; to remain undisturbed by the noise and struggle of our underworld of utility organs working with and against one another; a little quietness, a little tabula rasa of the consciousness, to make room for new things, [. . .] that is the purpose of active forgetfulness [*aktiven Vergesslichkeit*], which is like a doorkeeper, a preserver of psychic order, repose, and etiquette. So it becomes immediately obvious that there would be no happiness, no cheerfulness, no hope, no pride, no p r e s e n t , without forgetfulness. (GM II 1, KSA 5, p. 291).

Just to check our understanding of Nietzsche's reasoning: Why is there no *present* without forgetfulness? – Because without forgetfulness, the subject would hang on to past experiences without letting them go. Memories would inundate the psychic system; present experiences would be interlaced with past experiences, without the subject being able to sort out the tangle. The result would be a "dyspeptic" human that could not "digest" experiences, unable to live in the presence of the present, but only in a presence informed decisively by the past. Forgetfulness introduces necessary *tabula rasa* in the psyche; it "makes room for new things."[411]

Nietzsche's implicit model is similar to a model Freud, almost half a century later, would explicitly describe in his *Notiz Über den 'Wunderblock'* [1925].[412] As we already saw in the previous *Chapter 4*, Freud was in the early *Entwurf* [*Project for a Scientific Psychology*, 1896] addressing a problem that continued to occupy him: how was it possible for the psyche to be capable of both receiving ever-new impressions and infinitely storing them, without being saturated? Freud attempted to solve this problem in the *Project* by introducing two different neurological systems with two different functions in the psyche, the *psi* and the *phi*. In his *Notiz*, Freud presents a new and more elegant solution to this problem in the form of the analogy of his 'mystic writing pad' – a writing-apparatus composed of three layers. Topmost is a sheet of transparent celluloid; beneath, a thin and fragile layer of waxed paper, under which, finally, there is a wax slap. One writes with a pen or a stylus on the transparent celluloid layer. Under the pressure, the waxed paper sticks to the wax slap and creates a trace. When the waxed paper is raised from the wax slap, the trace disappears, and the apparatus is ready to receive new imprints. Impressions are 'permanently stored' in the wax-slap while the celluloid surface stays always ready to receive new impressions.

So, when receiving impressions, we are so to speak writing with the right hand, while erasing with the left. Nietzsche is emphasizing the operation of the left hand: the introduction of *tabula rasa* in the psyche, the exercise of active forgetfulness. Living completely in the presence of the present would imply erasing impressions with (almost) the same speed as they imprinted themselves on the system; every impression would be 'fresh' and 'alive.' Living with a 'long memory' (which is, as we shall see shortly, in some other contexts *also* a virtue in Nietzsche) would imply a slow left-hand-operation; a failure to forget; an accumulation of material; a ruminat-

---

[411] As early as in *Unzeitgemässe Betrachtungen II*, Nietzsche is explicitly aware of the necessity of forgetfulness: "Imagine the extemest possible example of a man who did not possess the power of forgetting at all and who was thus condemned to see everywhere a state of becoming: such a man would no longer believe in his own being, would no longer believe in himself, would see everything flowing asunder in moving points and would lose himself in this stream of becoming: like a true pupil of Heraclitus, he would in the end hardly dare to raise his finger. Forgetting is essential to action of any kind." (UB II, KSA 1, p. 250).

[412] Freud, Sigmund: Notiz über den 'Wunderblock', in Gesammelte Werke bd. 14.

ing, inactive subject weighed down under the burden of own memories; ultimately, a subject paralyzed in action, because it has to take into consideration all values, voices, or opinions in its inundated, saturated psyche.[413]

---

[413] Freud's 'Notiz' has fascinated also Jacques Derrida, and prompted him to produce a reading of this 'magical' apparatus (see Derrida, Jacques: "Freud and the Scene of Writing" in: Writing and Difference. Chicago (The University of Chicago Press), 1978). As Derrida understands this apparatus, imprints *happen in the reverse*, not from top to bottom, from stylus to wax slap, from exterior world to psyche, but from bottom to top, from wax slap to celluloid, from the psyche to the exterior world. We are being 'written' from within. Perception is now no longer the primary source of consciousness, consciousness 'occurs' from a differential net of traces – symbolized by the wax slap. In this interpretation, Derrida means to deconstruct a 'linear temporal' model according to which present impressions form consciousness. Freud's 'writing-apparatus' becomes an illustration on Derrida's *différance* or "generalized writing," the idea that an unconscious trace, an absolute past, structures a conscious system. Now, Derrida can effectively ignore the 'living presence' represented in this model as the stylus. Without rejecting Derrida's emphasis on the importance of the memory trace (cf. my exposition above), I see his interpretation as vulnerable to two objections. First, although memory-traces help perception becoming aware of itself (as we have emphasized in *Chapter 4*), there is still no trace produced were it not for the stylus, that is, the so-called 'living presence' (in *Chapter 4* (5.2.), I argued that there always is and must be an *Encounter* with the outside). Secondly, Derrida falsely makes-believe that he can properly determine the chronology of the cause-effect relationship between wax paper and wax slap. Since Derrida prefers that consciousness is 'written' from bottom upwards, the wax slap becomes the cause and the trace the effect in Derrida's rendition. This is a sleight of hand in Derrida's interpretation. Adhering to the model, we must instead resign ourselves to a far less conclusive and decisive interpretation, and accept that it is impossible to ascertain whether the wax slap sticks to the wax paper before the wax paper sticks to the wax slap. The best we can say is that there is (again) an 'Encounter' between slap and paper. Derrida's interpretation is thus born out of his specific deconstructive desire, out of a specific Derridian idiosyncrasy, requiring that as subjects, we are entirely unaffected by the 'living present' (i.e., reality), and are affected only by the 'old traces' of an 'absolute past.' According to Derrida, we live exactly like the heroes in the recent science-fiction cult movie, *Matrix*: we live purely imaginary lives within our own private cocoons. By an alien force, our experiences are being entirely 'written' from within.

3.2. Nietzsche's Chiasma:
Reversed Valuations of Forgetfulness and Memory.

Ability versus inability to forget emerges again as the central opposition characterizing the assertive versus the servile configuration. Forgetfulness is a mental faculty characterizing the positive and healthy system; memory is a mental faculty characterizing the resentful slave, brooding on taking revenge for past or imaginary slights.[414] Deleuze would therefore seem to have understood Nietzsche exactly right when he writes: "The type of the master (the active type) is defined in terms of the faculty of forgetting. [. . .] The type of slave (the reactive type) is defined by a prodigious memory." (Deleuze, loc. cit., p. 117).

Right, and then again! – When in the same aphorism, Nietzsche starts discussing the opposite mental quality, *memory*, also memory/memorization becomes a mark of distinction, a mark of the higher and sovereign human being. And as we continue our reading, the confusions seem to pile up, since now *forgetfulness* becomes a mark of the dull-witted, the poor and the wretched; those who cannot be trusted, who cannot repay a debt, who cannot requite in friendship or enmity. Memory is suddenly a quality the forgetful have to acquire, and since they cannot acquire it by impressing it on themselves, it has to be impressed upon them by the cruelest means. They must learn to remember by means of pain and torture. Into this originally so forgetful animal, civilization has to impress the opposite faculty, memory. The man, who learns to remember, is now the *sovereign* individual.

> The man [the sovereign individual] who has his own independent, protracted will and the right to make promises – in him a proud consciousness, quivering in every muscle, has at length been achieved and become flesh; a consciousness of his own power and freedom, a sense of the completion of mankind. This emancipated individual, with the actual right to make promises, this master of free will, this sovereign man [. . .] looks out upon others he honors or despises, and just as he is bound to honor his peers, the strong and reliable (those with the right to make promises) (– that is, all those who promise like sovereigns, reluctantly, rarely, slowly, who are hesitant in trusting, all those whose trust is a mark of distinction, who give their word [*sein*

---

[414] See also Werner Stegmaier: "Understood in Nietzsche's sense, forgetfulness is no longer an incapacity of the intellect, but rather a force necessary for life and enabling life. As Nietzsche recognizes, it is necessary for life to hold back information from consciousness, not only in order to focus our attention, but also to fade down concerns that are always bound to paralyze action." Stegmaier, Werner: Nietzsches Genealogie, loc. cit., p. 135.

Wort giebt] as something that can be relied upon because they know themselves strong enough to maintain it in the face of accidents), [. . .] he is bound to reserve a kick for the feeble windbags who promise without the right to do so, and a lash for the liar who breaks his word [*sein Wort bricht*] in the very instance he utters it. (GM II 2, KSA 5, p. 293).

Nietzsche's analysis produces a complete *chiasma* (two positions are converted into their opposites, crossing over each other as in an X). In the first position, forgetfulness marks the excellence of the master, while in the second position, it marks the mediocrity of the slave. In the first position, prodigious memory marks the vengefulness of the slave, while in the second position, it marks the trustworthiness of the master. There are those with the 'right to make promises,' and those without this 'right.' There are those who promise like sovereigns, and those who promise like windbags, breaking their word as soon as it is pronounced. The sovereigns promise "reluctantly, slowly, hesitant in trusting"; when finally they give their word, it can be relied upon. *To give* and *to break* one's word emerges as the new distinction marking respectively the master and the slave. To 'give one's word' means that the sovereigns do not forget, they operate with exceptionally long memories. It is in Nietzsche's economic system no longer 'forgetfulness' and 'memory' that, respectively, assign value or withdraw it. We must be talking about another economy, either competing with or overriding the first.

Forgetfulness was first characterizing the *assertive configuration*, now it is characterizing the *servile configuration*. Memory was first characterizing the *servile configuration*, now it is characterizing the *assertive configuration*. In our attempt to understand – and aspirations to resolve – this seeming inconsistency, three strategies seem available. *First*, one might simply dismiss Nietzsche's analysis, and pronounce Nietzsche guilty in yet another of his famous or infamous self-contradictions; case closed; the easiest solution, and also – if one dare say so – the most *superficial*. *Secondly*, one might argue that there is a significant distinction between the (forgetful) *noble* and the (memorizing) *sovereign* (and correspondingly, between the (memorizing) *slave* and the (forgetful) *windbag*). Nietzsche has in other words *two* master positions and *two* slave positions: a strategy intimated (but not elaborated) by Deleuze in a table he provides over affirmative and negative qualities after a crucial chapter on master and slave morality (see Deleuze, loc. cit., p. 146). Here we read that the principle of the noble consists of the "faculty of forgetting" and the principle of the sovereign of the "faculty of memory" (since the apparent inconsistency is not addressed any further, it does not seem to trouble Deleuze). This strategy poses, however, several problems. Apart from the fact that we find no indications in

Nietzsche's work that impels us believe that he generally envisioned two different types of masters and two different types of slaves, the solution is complicated by the fact that one of the slave-positions would have to be identical to the one of the master-positions, and vice versa. The 'solution' to the problem would be more convoluted and complicated than the problem. *Thirdly*, one might argue that there are different kinds of forgetfulness, as well as different kinds of memory, or that forgetfulness and memory are differently applied in different contexts. There might thus be a 'good' forgetfulness and a 'good' memory in one context, in contrast to a 'bad' forgetfulness and a 'bad' memory in another. This resolution-attempt surely begs the questions, what is *good* memory, what is *bad*? What is *good* forgetfulness, what is *bad*? How does one establish the 'right' to make promises, how does one lose this right? But the resolution-attempt has the advantage that *forgetfulness* respectively *memory* is established within the contexts of a varying psychological and/or libidinal economy; within an economy where we allow for a certain 'fluctuation of meaning' (cf. *Chapter 4*, sect. 4.4.3).

3.3. Justice and the Institution of Law.

Let us start by pointing out that although active forgetfulness belongs to the assertive configuration of the 'master,' *forgetfulness* cannot imply that the master erases everything from memory. Surely, the master creates "a little *tabula rasa* in consciousness," but he does not become completely blank. He for example 'remembers' his will-to-power. He may forget everything else, but he does not completely erase his will-to-power, his so-called 'truth.' When now Nietzsche talks about the memory of the sovereign, he precisely notices that in this context *memory* is *memory of the will* – involving a *desire* for the continuation of something that has been willed once before:

> This – out of necessity, forgetful – animal [the human being], for whom forgetfulness represented a power, a kind of fortified health, did now breed in itself an opposing capacity, namely a memory, with the aid of which forgetfulness is annulled in certain cases – namely in those cases where promises are made. This involves no mere passive inability to rid oneself of [*Nicht-wieder-los-werden-können*] an impression carved into the psyche, [. . .] but an active w i l l *not* to rid oneself, a will for the continuance of something willed once before, a r e a l m e m o r y o f t h e w i l l. (GM II, 1, KSA 5, p. 292).

Forgetfulness is only active if it creates room for something else, which is, in logical consequence, now *remembered*. Thus, active forgetfulness implies tidying up the psyche, cleaning out superfluous material; but something is left over after this spring-cleaning of the psyche. In the case of the promise, the leftover is the *word*, the word which the sovereign *gives* and *keeps*. The sovereign *remembers his word*. From the abyss of his psyche – originally nothing but a chaos of opinions, valuations, drives, and voices – the sovereign impresses upon himself responsibility and accountability by forcing himself to remember a word, a signifier, as a mark of his excellence. Deleuze draws the following distinction between the memory of the sovereign and the memory of the slave: the sovereign, says Deleuze, "memorizes a word," the slave "memorizes traces." Sharing with Deleuze his background in Freud's neurological writings, I find this a brilliantly precise distinction. The sovereign memorizes self-imposed Law in form of a signifier, the slave memorizes past emotions associated to pains and insults suffered in the past – i.e., 'traces' but no 'word,' no *Law*. The slave is despicable exactly because he is lawless – 'lawless' meaning here, he does not impose Law on himself. Without *Law*, he has 'no right' to promise, as Nietzsche time and again repeats. The sovereign, by contrast, had "the right to make promises," he was the "emancipated individual, with the actual right to make promises"; a "master of a free will [. . .] aware of his superiority over all those who lack the right to make promises." (cf. GM II, 2).

The sovereign is identical to the master, who recognizes Law, and imposes Law upon society and its members (ergo: sovereign and master are not two *different* master-positions). The sovereign starts by imposing Law on himself and ends by imposing Law on society. Law is thus also not a reaction of the slave, it is not revenge or ressentiment directed against the activity of the strong individual.

> From a historical point of view, law represents on earth [. . .] the struggle against the reactive feelings. [. . .] Wherever justice is practiced and maintained one sees a stronger power seeking a means of putting an end to the senseless raging of ressentiment among the weaker powers that stand under it. [. . .] The most decisive act that the supreme power performs and accomplishes against the predominance of grudges and rancor [. . .] is the institution of law. (GM II 11, KSA 5, p. 311-12).

As one consequence of this view, the 'master' is not simply – as numerous commentators has it – the playful, anarchistic individual, while the 'slave' is the restricted, conformist individual.[415] In this context, the 'master' institutes law in order to restrain the anarchism of the 'slave.' We have a 'stronger power' that dams up the anarchistic and indiscriminate rage and vengefulness of the 'weaker power' by instituting 'justice.'

Heidegger is therefore not right when he writes: "In his last years, Nietzsche is completely silent about what he calls justice."[416] On the contrary, one important faculty of the assertive configuration of the master, is its ability to meter out 'justice.' Justice is again a *good reaction* to human chaos. The slave does not *react to* his inner chaos, he *is* chaos. His opinions are nothing but incoherent, confused babble, enriched with his current hate-projects. Since he cannot forget (since he cannot forget Deleuze's so-called 'memory traces'), he is always immersed in too much material; as such immersed, he cannot step out of himself, thus cannot see himself with a measuring gaze. He is condemned to live his irrational psychobabble as a crazy, confused, and vacuous subject.

Emerging from the human abyss of nothingness, justice becomes a universal standard measuring human action. The master applies this universal standard as much to himself as to fellow human beings.

> The last sphere to be conquered by the spirit of justice is the sphere of the reactive feelings! When it really happens that the just man remains just even toward those who have harmed him [. . .] when the exalted, clear objectivity, as penetrating as it is mild, of the eye of justice and judging is not dimmed even under the assault of personal injury, derision, and calumny, *this is a piece of perfection and supreme mastery on earth.* (GM II 11, KSA 5, p. 312; italics added).

The mastery of the just individual consists then again in his/her ability to close one's eyes to one's lack of truth. Justice is never Truth essentially, nothing is Just *a priori* and in-itself, but it is a standard impressed upon and bringing order into original chaos. Justice is to set up a rule for human relationships. Justice is thus another name for an interpreting Will-to-Power;

---

[415] In Deleuze's sympathetic readings of Nietzsche, this dichotomy is underlying his analysis of master and slave, active and reactive economy. In another, less sympathetic reading, the view is adopted by Habermas in *The Philosophical Discourse of Modernity*. (Translated by F. G. Lawrence. Cambridge, Mass.: The MIT Press, 1996). Nietzsche becomes the 'irrational' philosopher promoting the playfulness of a purely aesthetic dimension, which, in Habermas diagrams of communicative action, is only a single component in communication, and certainly not the over-determining.

[416] Martin Heidegger: Nietzsche, vol. III. Translation: D. F. Krell (San Francisco: HarberSanFrancisco, 1987) p. 137.

the sovereign individual brings order into the disorder of human relationships; while the slave merely lives his disorder.[417]

The four emerging positions regarding forgetfulness and memory are now:

> (1) *Forgetfulness of the slave*: Forgetful regarding promises; unaccountable and irresponsible regarding Law; inability to requite in friendship and enmity; dull-witted.
>
> (2) *Forgetfulness of the master*: Forgetfulness as an art of showing reserve and keeping distance; forgetfulness applied to avoid saturation and thus contamination of psyche from the outside as well as the inside; a deliberate looking-away-from what displeases; an art of re-acquiring a little of the cheerfulness of the pre-historical hominid.
>
> (3) *Memory of the slave*: Memory of traces, i.e., of imaginary slights and insults; a ruminating memory in which revenge and envy germinate.
>
> (4) *Memory of the master*: Memory of one's word; memory in order to requite in friendship and enmity; memory of Law.

We notice, regarding the master position, that whether masters 'forget' or 'remember,' they are engaged in fighting off contamination, chaos, and disorder; that is, the contamination and chaos of 'voices' – irrational and spiteful psychobabble. They are engaged in establishing within themselves a master-voice, a master-discourse that guarantees Law in whatever material they decide to mold – Law in nature, Law in society, Law in human relationships, or Law in art. In order to establish this 'master-discourse' – what above we described as their 'truth' or 'phallus' – they have to hyper-cathect themselves, and de-cathect the outside 'contaminating' influences. Simply put, they have to *forget* in order to *remember*.

We notice that the structure applies to woman as described above: she has to forget that she is *nothing*, in order to remember that she is *everything* – although in this case, Nietzsche's woman is so enormously delicate that she forgets this as well: she unconsciously 'knows' that she is *everything*. This is the zenith of perfection: to *unconsciously 'know'* that one is everything. In the perfect individual, in Nietzsche's *super-personality*, self-knowledge of superiority is always *unconscious*. (But why? – Because *tact*, the femininity of the downcast eyes, is very much an integral part of the super-personality.)

---

[417] "The Will to Power interprets. [...] In truth, interpretation is itself a means to become master over something." (Nachlaß 1885-86; KSA v. 12, 2[148]).

Part II

*On the Ideological Formatting
of the Servile Configuration*

4. The Institution of Guilt

4.1. 'Schuldig' as Being Indebted and as Being Guilty

Let us return to the problem of the inscription of guilt in the individual, since this inscription becomes the pre-condition for the emergence of the slave in Nietzsche. In its first and primordial form, 'guilt' does not have the same destructive power as it gets later. In its primordial form, it is just another superficiality; and punishment of guilt is just another healthy manifestation of original cruelty in our ancestral human.

In the early inscription of 'guilt,' we are again (as so often in Nietzsche's foundational narratives) situated within the parameters of a hypothetical prehistory where human existence is still overwhelmingly characterized by forgetfulness. Into this forgetful animal civilization has to impress a sense of accountability and responsibility. The prehistoric human has to learn how to remember.

We recall how according to Kant's categorical imperative, it is self-contradictory to made a false promise, because the so-called maxim of the action, 'false promise-making' or 'lying,' cannot be promoted to universal law. If everybody makes false promises, the very institution of promise-making breaks down. Since, given our rational constitution, we cannot accept this contradiction, we are impelled – our 'duty' toward rational law impels us – to keep the promises we made.

In Nietzsche's explanation of the requisites for promise-making, we originally do not have the capacity of keeping promises; and when in later developments, we acquire this capacity, it is not because we realize that we have a 'duty' toward something as abstract as 'universal rational law.' A much stronger medicine was needed before the human being could advance to this stage. Before the feeble humans with their short attention-spans could finally learn to obey a few commandments, certain 'mnemonic techniques' had to be implemented. In order to learn to remember, the feeble-minded humans had to have even brief commandments literally drilled, inscribed, or burned into them. (In Nietzsche's narrative, inscription of Law is just about as concrete and physical as in Franz Kafka's short-story, *The Penal Colony*.)[418]

---

[418] Our ancestors, says Nietzsche, would express judgments on 'good' and 'evil' with absolute conviction in the truth of their own perspective: I am good if I kill my enemy, my enemy is evil if he kills me; I am good if I rape my enemy's wife; my enemy is evil if he rapes my wife, etc. In short, what is good for me, is good; what is evil for me, is evil. With the emergence of a disinterested and universal moral code in Christianity and Kant, this arbitrary subjective judgment of 'good' and 'evil' would seem to disappear, but it is in fact only disguised. Disinterested and universal morality is no less perspectival than primitive self-interested morality. It is still the case that what is good for me, is good; what is evil for me, is evil, except for the fact that Christianity and Kant cover up this perspectivism. In Kant's modern, disinterested, universal perspective, morality still poses itself against a common enemy, namely the strong, the healthy, and the exceptional, according to Nietzsche. The only reason why this self-interest is difficult to discern, is that now, it is a single homogeneous group, the weak, the suffering, and the mediocre, that are taking control over the moral judgment – and doing so, never in the name of themselves, but in the name of God. In the name of God, they exert their specific will-to-power in their moral evaluations. In this modern, Christian-Kantian-European, will-to-power three interests are hidden. "Three powers are hidden behind it: 1) the instinct of the herd against the strong and independent; 2) the instinct of the suffering and underprivileged against the fortunate; 3) the instinct of the mediocre against the exceptional." (WM 274). In these three interests, we see a common motive at work, the will to equality. There is a desire to level all difference, because *envy hurts*; and since one does not want to be hurt, one sets out to eradicate the cause of envy, namely distinction and difference. "The problem of 'equality,' while we all thirst after distinction: here, on the contrary, we are supposed to make exactly the same demands on ourselves as we make on others. This is so insipid, so obviously crazy." (WM 275). "Hatred for the privileged in body and soul: revolt of the ugly, ill-constituted souls against the beautiful, proud, joyous. Their means: inculpation of beauty, pride, joy." (WM 283). Thus, the birth of a universalized 'good' and 'evil' is fundamentally related to *envy*. Since envy is a pain, anybody causing envy is evil, while anybody that makes envy go away, is good. Good is now somebody who is judged equal to *me*, while evil is somebody excelling *me*. In order to achieve an existence of peace and quiet, contemporary Christian-Kantian-European man surrenders everything life-confirming. Instead of creating a world of evaluations himself, he surrenders himself to an abstract authority. He does not surrender himself to a real authority, which would only make him feel unimportant and therefore envious, but instead to someone, something, extra-human, namely God. God has devised the laws of the herd-instinct. "An authority speaks – who speaks? – One may forgive human pride if it sought to make this authority as high as

4. The Institution of Guilt

'If something is to stay in the memory it must be burned in: only that which never ceases to h u r t stays in the memory.' [. . .] Man could never do without blood, torture, and sacrifices when he felt the need to create a memory for himself; the most dreadful sacrifices and pledges (sacrifices of the first-born), the most repulsive mutilations (castration, for example) [. . .] all this has its origin in the instinct that realized that pain is the most powerful aid to mnemonics. [. . .] With the aid of such images and procedures one finally remembers five or six, 'I will not's' [*"Ich will nicht"*] in regard to which one had given one's p r o m i s e so as to participate in the advantages of society. (GM II 3, KSA 5, p. 295-97).

By these cruel techniques, the individual was *trained* to *make* and to *keep* promises. By cruelty, one disciplined the early human, and taught it to feel a sense of 'guilt.'

However, we are still talking here of an *early* 'feeling of guilt'; a feeling of guilt not yet internalized; not yet taken over by the individual and directed inwards; because the ego has not yet formed the spilt-out formation of itself that Freud would describe as *super-ego*, and Nietzsche as *formal conscience*. Since the agency called 'super-ego' or 'conscience' is still embryonic and under-developed, in these early days, to be punished for being guilty [*Schuldig*] leaves no permanent mental scar on the individual; and it does not hurt *as much* or *as long* as when later the individual becomes guilty in the eyes of himself and God. Exactly because punishment is less likely to have lasting effects, exactly because the individuals have feeble and fleeting memories, early society devises all kinds of harsh and cruel penalties in order to fix their attention. The degree of cruelty of the punishments is commensurate to the degree of amnesia of these early individuals. The more forgetful a human, the more cruel the penalties.

As Nietzsche argues, the German *Schuld* may signify both *guilt* and *debt*, from where we derive the adverbial form, *Schuldig, being in dept* or *being guilty*. The identical etymological origin of guilt and debt gives

---

possible in order to feel as little humiliated as possible under it. Therefore – God speaks! One needed God as an unconditional sanction, with no court of appeal, as a 'categorical imperator.'" (WM 275). God becomes the *categorical imperator*, and from there – as the rational principle for the categorical imperator – Kant deduced the *categorical imperative*. After Kant, not only God devises the laws outside us, the same laws exist already within us as rational principles. Kant internalizes God – the *categorical imperator* becomes the *categorical imperative*. 'You shall not steal,' 'you shall not kill', 'you shall not lie' are no longer simply laws pronounced by God, they are rational principles we are obliged to follow unless we make existence absurd and illogical.

Nietzsche the opportunity to argue that the psychological concept *guilt* derives from the legal concept *debt*. Therefore, to be guilty [*Schuldig*] in these early days is to be in debt [*Schuldig*]. This early 'sense of guilt' is more precisely a 'recognition of debt.' So far, it manifests itself as a subject's recollection of certain legal obligations, and indicates no more than a debtor's *recognition* of being indebted to a creditor. In Nietzsche's foundational narrative, we assume that at this stage, trading between societies has become widespread, and being *Schuldig* and feeling *Schuld* is a question of being able to recognize certain legal obligations.

Trading partners enter a contract, which, if broken, gives the creditor the right to "inflict every kind of indignity and torture upon the body. For example, cut from it as much as seemed commensurate with the size of the debt" (GM II 5, KSA 5, p. 299). The debtor-creditor relationship is entirely practical and mercantile. When punishment is executed, it is done in all good conscience because the debtor has failed to recognize a debt. He consequently owes the creditor something else; somehow he must recompense the creditor; and his compensation becomes to give the creditor the satisfaction of inflicting pain upon his body. Failing to pay his debt, he has given the creditor the right to take 'his pound of flesh' (as we recall from Shakespeare's *The Merchant of Venice*). In these early days of civilization, humans embrace cruelty more innocently; cruelty, indeed, 'makes happy.'

First much later does *Schuld* become a psychological-moral concept. This transformation from *Schuld as debt* to *Schuld as guilt* will eventually produce the tamed and caged individual in Nietzsche's narrative. The transformation is indicated, rather than being completely explicit, in the change of direction of Nietzsche's analysis, insofar as he tacitly displaces the discussion of *guilt ~ debt* with a discussion of *guilt ~ self-aggression*. When the society develops, and the environment becomes 'narrow' and 'oppressing'; when the human animal is no longer allowed to prowl around in the wild, stimulated by danger and the exigencies of survival, it becomes a caged animal, and start to internalize 'guilt' from the inability of acting out aggression.

> The human, who, from need of exterior enemies and resistances, is squeezed into an oppressive narrowness and regularity of customs, restlessly ripped apart, gnawed at, and frustrated, this animal who has been rubbing its wound on the bars of its cage when one wanted to 'tame' it; this deprived creature, which is consumed by longing for the wild; this creature has turned itself into an adventure, a torture chamber, has produced an uncertain and dangerous wasteland – this fool, this yearning and desperate prisoner became the inventor of 'bad conscience' ['*schlecthen Gewissens*']. He introduced the gravest and most uncanny of diseases, which humankind has hitherto suffered from, the human suf-

fering from the human, from itself [*das Leiden des Menschen am Menschen, an sich*]. (GM III 16, KSA 5, p. 323).

The 'sense of guilt' is re-directed from the external to the internal. From recognizing that one is indebted to a trading partner, the new 'sense of guilt' deepens, and is finally turned around and directed into the debtor's own self. All of a sudden, one is indebted to an agency within oneself; an agency that still has the right to "inflict every kind of indignity and torture upon the body," or more adequately, after the transition, the *soul*. Guilt/debt is internalized as aggression turned inwards. Transformed into this new psychological-moral concept, 'being guilty' is now self-aggression, and the penalty for 'being guilty' is no longer physical punishment, but spiritual self-punishment. The original 'enjoyable' and 'happy' cruelty is turned into forlorn and unhappy shame.

4.2. Internalization of Guilt

4.2.1. From Proto-Sadism to Proto-Masochism.

As long as the creditor-debtor relationship was purely mercantile and external, as long as *Schuld* was no more than being in debt, and punishment was simply to vent one's anger on an unreliable debtor, life was still good, and existence still uncomplicated and free. However, when the relationship became *moral* and *internal*, when modern man started to include within himself both *creditor* and *debtor*, we encounter the emergence of the Nietzschean scandal. Now, the image of the creditor inflicting pain on the hapless debtor becomes Nietzsche's intuitively brilliant representation of an inner psychological conflict: an aggressive agency punishes another, guilt-ridden, agency; or in Freudian vocabulary, the creditor, as strict *super-ego*, punishes the debtor, as weak *ego*.

When the relationship is internalized, the 'debtor' owes the 'creditor' a debt that can never be paid back – for the failure of which he is now punished to his death. Internal guilt is *perverse guilt*, like aggression turned inward is *perverse aggression*. As the creditor-debtor relationship is internalized, healthy active and primary *aggression* is turned inwards as passive and secondary *self-aggression,* as an unhealthy and perverse *masochism*.[419]

---

[419] In the essay, *Group Psychology and Ego Analysis*, Freud also makes this connection to Masochism. Freud lists three forms of *identification*: (A) an identification with an object one wants to be like; typical case, the child identifies with the father, and copies certain treats of the father during its

The human being, instead of enjoying inflicting pain on others, learns to enjoy inflicting pain on itself. Instead of the original joy in seeing others in pain, modern man, perversely, enjoys seeing himself in pain. "The second inquiry [of GM] offers the psychology of the c o n s c i e n c e – which is not, as people may believe, 'the voice of God in man'; it is the instinct of cruelty that turns back after it can no longer discharge itself externally." (EH "Zur Genealogie der Moral", KSA 6, p. 352).

The most unnatural in this inversion is perhaps the re-direction of the orientation of the senses. In the first (let us call it . . .) *proto-sadistic* position, senses are directed outwards; the eye scans the exterior world, and the human is healthily pre-occupied with the outside, impressing its own inside on the outside; the subject is conceived as undivided and unified. This corresponds to our *assertively configured subject*, transforming its outside into its own play-ground. In the second (let us call it . . .) *proto-masochistic* position, senses are directed inwards as they become unhealthily pre-occupied with the subject's own interior. In the masochistic position, the subject, as *servile configuration*, starts *examining itself*; questions motives and intentions of actions before they are carried out. The subject splits up itself into two conflicting positions, creates *one position* from where it is able to look at and examine itself in *another position*. With the emergence of this *moral (proto-masochistic) subject*, the subject is no longer an *individuum*, but (as described in *Chapter 3*) a *dividuum* (cf. "[Man] divides his nature and sacrifices one part of it to the other? [. . .] In morality, man treats himself not as i n d i v i d u u m but as d i v i d u u m. (MA I, 57, KSA 2, p. 76)).

---

development. (B) A strong identification with an object that is lost, but whose loss cannot be endured; resulting in the pathological reaction: one 'introjects' the object, buries it in one's unconscious, as such keeps it safe within oneself (safely locked up inside, it cannot die); one *becomes* the object. (C) Finally the identification with, and followed by introjection of, a strict and demanding other, e.g., father, priest, commander. The strict authority figure is introjected as ego-ideal, splitting the psyche in Nietzsche's 'dividuum': the strict ego-ideal praying on the defenseless ego. To Freud, this also becomes the origin of depression and self-punishment, since the ego can never satisfy the strict ego-ideal: "The melancholic shows us the ego divided, fallen apart into two pieces, one of which rages against the second. This second piece is the one which has been altered by introjection and which contains the lost object. But the piece which behaves so cruelly is not unknown to us either. It comprises the conscience, a critical agency within the ego. [. . .] We have called it the 'ego ideal.'" Freud, Sigmund: "Group Psychology and Ego Analysis. Translation J. Strachey. New York, London (W. W Norton) 1959; p. 52.

What provokes Nietzsche is the emergence of so-called *proto-masochism*, the perverse and paradoxical situation that the modern subject is formatted to *enjoy* and *prolong* its own pain, by turning it around as inner pain. In contrast to this redirection of cruelty, this complication and convolution of basic instincts, there is more innocence in the *proto-sadistic* position, the celebration of cruelty. Therefore, *cruelty as primary aggression (proto-sadism)* becomes a counter-image to the modern 'sense of guilt.' Here, there is no shame in "man being man." Celebration of cruelty belongs to the economy of (to speak with Deleuze) 'active forces' 'going to the limit of what they can do.' Whereas 'sense of guilt' belongs to the economy of (again Deleuze) of 'reactive forces' 'separating active forces from what they can do.'[420] In the execution of cruelty, the *trajectory* of 'forces' is wonderfully *straight*. Nothing is bended, turned around, or unnecessarily complicated. In the 'sense of guilt,' the *trajectory* of 'forces' is broken, turned around into what they came from, as in a *circular confusion*, before they have had a chance to reach the limit of what they can do. In the modern 'sense of guilt,' forces have been turned around, but without losing any of their original intensity, which they are now acting out *against* the individual. As such, they have become reactive. From now on, everything the individual *wants*, in an outburst of active energy, first have to overcome the blockades of reactive energy.[421] In this sense, the modern human has been paralyzed and 'crippled.' Reactive forces block all natural outlets for active energy; the subject has to find back-roads and side-roads in order to unload energy. Its 'forces' or 'energies' must take upon themselves artful guises in order to unload themselves, they become *sublimated* and *subtilized* [*subtilisiert*].

---

[420] "No longer being able to act a reaction, active force are deprived of the material conditions of their functioning, they no longer have the opportunity to do their job, *they are separated from what they can do*. We can thus finally see in what way reactive forces prevail over active forces: when the trace takes the place of the excitation in the reactive apparatus, reaction itself takes the place of action, reaction prevails over action." Deleuze, Gilles: Nietzsche and Philosophy; loc. cit., p. 114.

[421] Self-aggression is easy to understand. In caricature, it is pictured in the well-known cartoon-images of a figure knocking himself on his head, or pulling out his hair. In frustrated rage, he cannot act out punishments on the one who deserves it, and turns therefore his hand 'inwards'; and lets this hand do to himself what it wanted to do to the other.

4.2.2. Identical Positions on Conscience and Guilt in Nietzsche and Freud.

In the narratives of both Nietzsche and Freud, *primary aggression* is turned around and directed inwards thanks to the civilizational process. The two narratives are almost identical. In Nietzsche's narrative, man became measurable and accountable when he became a city-dweller. As soon as humans were enclosed within city-walls, instead of prowling around in nature using their instincts for hunting and survival, they were forced into the restricted life of thinking, calculating, and reckoning. Instincts that were meant to be discharged in outward action were necessarily turned inward, since society did not permit spontaneous aggression. Man was from now on forced to turn natural aggression back upon himself. Instead of aggressing against his enemy, he started to aggress against himself. Because of this self-aggression, he developed his *bad consciousness* and *feeling of guilt* in the modern sense.

> All instincts that do not discharge themselves outwardly t u r n i n w a r d : this is what I call the i n t e r n a l i z a t i o n [*Verinnerlichung*] of man: Thus it was that man first developed what was later called his 'soul.' The entire inner world, originally as thin as if it were stretched between two membranes, expanded and extended itself, acquired depth, breadth, and height, in the same measure as outward discharge w a s i n h i b i t e d . [. . .] Hostility, cruelty, joy in persecuting, in attacking, in change, in destruction – all this turned against the possessors of such instincts: t h a t is the origin of the 'bad consciousness. (GM II 16, KSA 5, p. 322).[422]

Freud is presenting us with the essentially same narrative. Civilization [*Kultur*] restricts man's original aggressiveness, as it forces aggression back into the mind from where it originated. Aggression is thus *internalized*, and transforms itself into an aggressive super-ego aggressing against the ego. With the formation of this strict super-ego, society controls humans more

---

[422] Nietzsche has here added a new aspect to his analysis of the formation of a 'formal conscience' that we already introduced in *Chapter 3*: the "inner world acquires depth, breadth, and height, in the same measure as outward discharge was inhibited." The servile configuration, we said above, forms a crypt within itself; it deepens the self and provides the self with a false interior that eventually splits away from the self. Now Nietzsche provides a phylogenetic explanation of this development: the servile configuration is formed *because* aggression is prohibited and turned inward. Thus, it is *self-aggression* that is responsible of the transformation from *assertive configuration* to *servile configuration*.

efficiently. Society disarms man by setting up an agency *within him* to watch over him. It does not need to assign a guardian to watch every social individual, because social individuals are more efficiently controlled through an inhibiting agency within themselves.

> What means does civilization [*Kultur*] employ in order to inhibit the aggressiveness which opposes it, to make it harmless, to get rid of it. [. . .] What happens in the [individual] to render his desire for aggression innocuous? Something very remarkable, [. . .] his aggressiveness is introjected, internalized [*Verinnerlicht*]; it is, in point of fact, sent back to where it came from – that is, it is directed towards his own ego. There it is taken over by a portion of the ego, which sets itself over against the rest of the ego as super-ego, and which now, in the form of 'conscience' is ready to put into action against the ego the same harsh aggressiveness that the ego would have liked to satisfy upon extraneous individuals, the tension between the harsh super-ego and the ego that is subjected to it, is called by us the sense of guilt [*Schuldbewußtsein*], it expresses itself as need for punishment. Civilization, therefore, obtains mastery over the individual's dangerous desire for aggression weakening and disarming it and by setting up an agency within him to watch over it.[423]

When fear of punishment is generated *externally*, the individual can dispose of it by either abstaining from performing the incriminating act, or when he has received his punishment. However, when fear is generated *internally*, nothing gets rid of it; now it infects the individual like a cancer for which there is no cure. As internalized, the 'feeling of guilt' punishes constantly and continuously, also when there is no *material reason* for guilt, as Nietzsche understood before Freud:

> *Nietzsche*: That someone f e e l s 'guilty' or 'sinful' simply does not prove that he is right, any more than a man is healthy merely because he feels healthy. Recall the famous witch trials: the most acute and humane judges were in no doubt as to the guilt of the accused; the 'witches' t h e m s e l v e s d i d n o t d o u b t i t – and yet there was no guilt. (GM III, 16; KSA 5, p. 376).

> *Freud*: Originally, renunciation of instinct was the result of fear of an external authority: one renounced one's satisfactions in order not to lower its love. If one has carried out this renunciation, one is, as it were, quits with the authority and no sense of guilt should remain. But with fear of the super-ego the case is different. Here, instinctual renunciation is not enough, for the wish persists and cannot be concealed from the super-ego. Thus in spite of the renunciation that has been made, a sense of guilt comes about.[424]

---

[423] Freud, loc. cit., GW XIV, p. 492-83.
[424] Freud, loc. cit., GW XIV, p, 487.

In Freud, the restrictions imposed by society had the beneficial purpose to restrain the destructive *Thanatos*, the death-drive. However, by restricting one set of instincts, civilization would by default restrict another set too. It would regulate not only aggressive instincts but erotic as well. Since the restrictive super-ego did not discriminate, to the super-ego, an unbridled *Eros* would appear to constitute as much danger as an unbridled *Thanatos*. Therefore Freud's final pessimistic assessment of civilization: what could it possibly offer mankind except *necessity* and *work*; or to stay in his own Greek terms, *Ananke*? *Ananke* against *Eros* & *Thanatos*: the tamed against the untamed; work against freedom; linear time against cyclical time; a *servile configuration* against an *assertive configuration*. We see the parallel to Nietzsche, who had already in *Morgenröte* introduced the disciplining effects of work:

> The eulogist of work [...] One essentially always feels at the sight of work – one always means by work that hard diligence from dawn to dusk – that work is the best policeman, that it keeps everyone in bounds and can mightily hinder the development of reason, covetousness, desire for independence. For it uses up an extraordinary amount of nervous energy, which is thus denied to reflection, brooding, dreaming, worrying, loving, hating; it sets a small goal always in sight and guarantees easy and regular satisfactions. Thus a society in which there is continual hard work will have more security." (M 173, KSA 3, p. 154).

Nietzsche and Freud are narrating a story that (phylo-genetically) starts in our prehistoric past, and presupposes the existence of an original freedom, which is gradually restricted, finally resulting in the psychological crippling, the systematic destruction, of contemporary man. Also onto-genetically, they are narrating similar stories. When Freud explains the installment of the super-ego in the individual onto-genetically, the story starts in how the child in early childhood internalizes the demands and ideals of its parents. Parental commands that starts in the precept: 'that is how you ought to be,' or in the prohibition: 'that is how you may not be,' is gradually adopted by the child. It is internalized as an unconscious part of the psyche controlling first the child from within, and later the grown up, since the early imprint of these precepts and prohibitions would continue to produce unconscious self-criticisms and guilt-feelings. The child would become, as Freud famously phrased it, *the father of the adult*. Nietzsche does not put the same importance on childhood as Freud, and he did not presage anything like Freud's Oedipus-complex, but as for the early internalization of imperatives, he has a conception identical to Freud's.

4. The Institution of Guilt

Conscience is installed thanks to the "belief in authorities"; it is "not the voice of God in the heart of man but the voice of some men in man."

> Content of the conscience.— The content of our conscience is everything that was during the years of our childhood regularly demanded of us without reason by people we honored or feared. It is thus the conscience that excites that feeling of compulsion ('I must do this, not do that') which does not ask: why must I? – In every case in which a thing is done with 'because' and 'why' man acts without conscience; but not yet for that reason against it. – The belief in authorities is the source of the conscience: it is therefore not the voice of God in the heart of man but the voice of some men in man. (MA II/2, 52, KSA 2, p. 576).

During these phylo- and onto-genetic developments, it is both Nietzsche and Freud's claim that in the history of civilization a *servile configuration* has been formed out of the malleable human psyche. The human psyche has been deepened and hollowed out, in order to finally split the human into two: a supervisor and a supervised. Since the supervisor supervises the supervised according to ideals imposed from the outside, the modern human has *hyper-cathected* the outside and *de-cathected* itself (its self). To Nietzsche's dismay, modern man is forced into re-covering itself in the other – a recovery that is all in vain, since the gap between self and other is irreparable. The modern human has become fundamentally alienated from its self.

In these several parallel conceptions of Nietzsche and Freud, we notice that not only does Freud in several cases employ the exact same vocabulary as Nietzsche – 'feeling of guilt' [*Schuldgefühl*], 'conscience,' 'aggression,' 'internalization' [*Verinnerlichung*] – also the plot-structure of his foundational narratives is in several cases the same.[425]

---

[425] When we read Nietzsche's genealogical analysis of the emergence of the sense of guilt and bad conscience; the analyses of the 'priest' and the evils of mass-psychology, it is hard to believe that Freud was never directly influenced by Nietzsche in writings such as *Massenpsychologie und Ich-Analyse* [GW XIII, 1921], *Das Ich und das Es* [GW XIII, 1923], and *Das Unbehagen in der Kultur* [GW XIV, 1931]. As Derrida has originally noticed (in Derrida, Jacques: La Carte Postale, loc. cit.), Freud would maintain that he deliberately abstained from reading Nietzsche in order to *avoid* influence: "In later years I have denied myself the very great pleasure of reading the works of Nietzsche, with the deliberate object of not being hampered in working out the impressions received in psychoanalysis by any sort of anticipatory ideas." Freud, Sigmund: "The Psychoanalytical Movement" in: *The Pelican Freud Library*, vol. 15 (London: Penguin Books, 1986), p. 73. Whether Freud maintained that

4.3. The Unstable Opposition Between 'Good' and 'Evil'

The modern subject is always too complicated to Nietzsche's taste; it lives in a confused wilderness of valuations that never have any clear definition. It often dishonestly assigns to itself values whose actual meaning is the opposite of the meaning, which the value nominally signifies. For example, the self-declared 'good man' is always to Nietzsche's mind a loathsome creature, because not only is he not particularly 'good,' but worse, he has taken upon himself a mask of false good-will. The 'good man' is always an *actor* and a *mask*; he is as 'evil' as any other human being, but he has had the indecency to make a show out of his *seeming* goodness. The 'good man' becomes the impersonation of deceit, duplicity, and underhandedness. In Nietzsche, the 'good man,' in his religious personification, is often like a *true Satan* – Satan as a man of the cloth, quoting the Bible.

But how could such an arbitrary execution of a supposedly solid distinction like *good and evil* be possible? – *First*, we must always remember that to Nietzsche, the distinction between *good* and *evil* is never as solid as we tend to think. It is, as all oppositions, a *vibrating opposition*. The unstable positions of an opposition are never more than different *degrees* of the same; the unstable positions of an opposition may swap meaning, and reverse their assigned values without warning. *Secondly*, the *good/evil* opposition is also 'simplification' – it simplifies inner-mental processes, drives, or valuations, too complex in-themselves to be understood. *Thirdly*, the positions in an opposition are mutually dependent on each other for their definition. In the *good/evil* opposition, the two positions are complementa-

---

> position during the twenties and thirties is questionable, but it is clear that this deliberate attempt to forget Nietzsche is an attempt to rid his mind of a potential rival psychologist. Freud aspires to establish a 'master-discourse,' and it is all-important to avoid influence – although it seems difficult to entirely avoid influence from a rival who, in the very instance of being dismissed, is recognized to have had the same insights as psychoanalysis. How does one decide to suppress something without first recalling that which is to be suppressed? In his study on Freud and Nietzsche, Assoun reiterates Freud's claim that he never read Nietzsche: "If we take Freud at his word, he has never read more than a half-page of Nietzsche." Assoun, Paul–Laurent: Freud and Nietzsche, loc. cit., p. 11. But Assoun also reports that according to the minutes from the meetings that the *Vienna Psychoanalytical Society* held from 1906 to 1918, there were several meetings dedicated to the discussion of Nietzsche – Nietzsche as the philosopher and Nietzsche as the psychoanalytical 'case' – one of these meetings were specifically dedicated to *The Genealogy of Morals*. Also Reinhard Gasser is completely explicit about the influence from Nietzsche to Freud. See Gasser: Nietzsche und Freud, loc. cit.

ry. There may be anthropological reasons why it is impossible in the human being to eradicate 'evil,' but there are also pragmatic-linguistic reasons. In the attempt to eradicate one of the positions, one destroys the entire value-system. That is, 'good' does not exist without a pre-knowledge of what is 'evil,' and vice versa, 'evil' does not exist without a pre-knowledge of the 'good.' As values, they come in pairs: "One is good on condition one also knows how to be evil, one is evil because otherwise one would not understand how to be good." (WM 351).

Thus, our *good/evil* distinction is an unstable and relative opposition, which in touch with the original processes it signifies, consists of interrelated and codependent positions. The so-called 'good' may turn out to be a mere *euphemistic re-labeling of something originally 'evil.'* What has happened is that at one point a 'semantic cluster' is labeled *good*, and *instantly* it splits away from the greater cluster it was once a part of. As an *identifiable* split-off formation ('identifiable' thanks to the *label* 'good'), the new semantic cluster, which is never more than *a different degree of the same*, now sees the old cluster as its opposite, as *evil* ("It is easier to think opposition, than gradation" cf. below). As such, the opposition 'good' versus 'evil' may well be of the same origin, and the *good will* of the self-righteous may easily be merely a refined and sublimated derivation of something that originally was, perhaps still is, annexed to original cruelty.

> There is in g o o d w i l l / b e n e v o l e n c e [*Wohlwollen*] refined lust for possession. [. . .] As soon as the refinement emerges, the earlier phase is no longer felt as a phase, but rather as an opposition. It is e a s i e r to think opposition, than gradation. [. . .] When a complex drive gets a n a m e, and is considered a u n i t y, it starts tyrannizing all thinkers, who are now seeking its definition. (Nachlaß 1881, KSA 9, 11[115]).

> When a drive becomes i n t e l l e c t u a l [*intellektueller wird*], then it assumes a new name, a new stimulus, and a new value. It will often be o p p o s e d to the drive of the old stage, as if it was its contradiction (cruelty, for example) – Many drives, for example the sexual drive, is capable through the intellect of great refinements (altruism; worship of the Holy Mary; artistic enthusiasm). (Nachlaß 1881, KSA 9, 11[124]).

As our first example: our contemporary Western legal system looks back in horror on how one penalized in the Medieval Ages. In ancient days, one would inflict all kinds of torture and indignity on a suspect in the public of the town-square; while today we imprison and 'put away' a criminal for a number of years. This new regime of punishment is regarded as more humane, and sees itself in *opposition* to the old regime; but it is only a new form of cruelty (a *new split-off formation*), no longer aiming at punishing the body, but at punishing the mind. That is, the purpose of punishment is to awaken the gradual realization of guilt in the criminal. The seriousness of the crime is commensurate with the years of imprisonment one believes are necessary before a genuine realization of guilt awakens in the criminal.[426] As our second example: the Christian 'good man' (cf. above) believes that the distinction *good and evil* is a solid distinction of opposing values. He consequently thinks that he can reject evil, – in himself and in others crossing his path. He believes that he can create a *pure will to goodness*. However, in pursuing his ideal, he develops new sensitivities to sniff up evil. Pursuing his obsession, he discovers evil everywhere: in mankind, in human nature, in life as such, or in his own dreams and desires. Paradoxically, the 'good man' is now consumed *by hatred*: he *hates* sin, and he *hates* sinners; he even *hates* the 'evil' in himself. Ultimately, it becomes his desire to be relieved from this 'evil' world, and – in a paroxysm of revengefulness ('what *I* cannot enjoy, *nobody* should be allowed to enjoy') – his most ardent longing becomes to see the world destroyed in an eagerly awaited Apocalypse.[427] Eventually, the so-called 'good man' begins to long for *nothingness*, for that *darkness*, which once ruled the world "before man whence light was born" – his agenda has become indistinguishable from that of Goethe's Mephistopheles.[428] "'The Good Man' sees himself as if sur-

---

[426] Cf. Foucault, Michel: Discipline and Punish, loc. cit.

[427] The 'good' becomes a paradoxical ideal, because, first, not even the greatest moralist is able to follow it; and, secondly, the ideal posits life as such, as evil. In Nietzsche, the great moralist is often the greatest immoralist; he claims to be virtuous, but his actions are not necessarily so. If virtue is the end, then the means to reach this end have traditionally been soaked in blood. A great moralist is thus, as Nietzsche says, a great actor. "A great moralist is, among other things, necessarily a great actor. [. . .] While it is his ideal to keep his *esse* and his *operari* in a divine way apart; everything he does must be done *sub specie boni* – a high, remote, exacting ideal! A divine ideal! And indeed, it is said that the moralist imitates in that no less a model than God himself: God, the greatest of all immoralists in practice, who nonetheless knows how to remain what he is, the *good* God – " (WM 304). The moralist is so by name only; he has in fact only re-named his immorality; as such he has beautified and legitimized immorality: "*By which means does a virtue come to power?* – By exactly the same means as a political party: the slandering, inculpation, undermining of virtues that oppose it and are already in power, by re-baptizing them, by systematic persecution and mockery. Therefore: through sheer 'immorality.'" (WM 311).

[428] Cf. Goethe's *Faust*: "I am the spirit of perpetual negation; / And rightly so, for all things that exist / Deserve to perish, and would not be missed – / Much

rounded by evil, and under the continuous onslaught of evil his eye grows keener, he discovers evil in all his dreams and desires; and so he ends, quite reasonably, by considering nature evil, mankind corrupt, goodness an act of grace (that is, as impossible for man). *In summa*: he denies life." (WM 351). As Nietzsche comments, "perhaps there has never before been a more dangerous ideology." (Ibid.). This ideology breeds the self-righteous man, the bigot, who sees evil everywhere. The 'good man' has become *a masochist* to himself, a *sadist* to others.

In life itself there is no good and evil; affirmation and negation are intertwined; yes and no, love and hate, exist side by side. When the Christian dreamer dreams about purifying the world, eradicating the negation, the no, he does the opposite. His life has become a *performative self-contradiction.* He *performs* a position opposite to the position he believes he has *adopted*; in his life, the positions in the *unstable* opposition, *good and evil*, have tacitly swapped meaning: "The good man who has renounced evil [. . .] in no way ceases to wage war, have enemies, say No and act No. The Christian, for example, hates 'sin.' Precisely because of his faith in a moral antithesis of good and evil, the world has become for him overfull of things that must be hated and eternally combated." (Ibid.).

4.4. Nietzsche's Affirmation of Cruelty as 'Primary Aggression'

It cannot be too hazardous to suggest that it is partly because so-called 'evil' covered up in false 'goodwill' is clouding everything on the human horizon that Nietzsche believes there is more health, fresh air, and straightforwardness in the ancient *celebration of cruelty*.

The issue of Nietzsche's affirmation of cruelty is contentious, and is often by Nietzsche's commentators either explained away or politely ignored.[429] 'Original cruelty' is nonetheless defended in the most explicit terms throughout Nietzsche's work:

---

better it would be if nothing were / Brought into being. Thus, what you men call / Destruction, sin, evil in short, is all / My sphere, the element I most prefer. [. . .] I am part of that part which once, when all began, / Was all there was; Part of the Darkness before man / Whence light was born, proud light, which now makes futile war / to wrest from Night, its mother, what before / Was hers, her ancient place and space." Goethe, Johann Wolfgang: Faust I. Translation D. Luke. Oxford (Oxford University Press), 1987) p. 42.

[429] For example Henry Staten: "Nietzsche still clings to the grotesque sentimentality that it is healthier and more noble to inflict suffering on others than to turn it inward." (Staten: *Nietzsche's Voice,* p. 53). Clearly, aggression has no

Will there be many honest men prepared to admit that causing pain gives pleasure? That one not seldom entertains oneself – and entertains oneself well – by mortifying other people, at least in one's own mind." (MA I, 50, KSA 2, p. 71).

To see others suffer [*Leiden-sehen*] does one good, to make others suffer [*Leiden-machen*] even more so. [. . .] Without cruelty there is no festival: thus the longest and most ancient part of human history teaches – and in punishment there is so much that is festive! [. . .] Let me declare expressly that in the days when mankind was not yet ashamed of its cruelty, life on earth was more cheerful than it is now that pessimists exist. The darkening of the sky above mankind has deepened in step with the increase in man's feeling of shame at man. (GM II, 6-7, KSA 5, p. 302).

To want-to-harm [das Wehethunwollen], the appetite for cruelty – has a long history. The Christians in their relation to the heathens; a

---

place in Staten's universe. In Peter Berkowitz, cruelty becomes a means to an end – the end being 'human excellence': "Blood and cruelty of course do not guarantee the production of human excellence. Cruelty in itself is neither good nor bad, but rather good or bad with respect to the end it serves. [. . .] For Nietzsche the primary end for which cruelty must be exercised is the attainment of human excellence." Berkowitz, Peter: The Ethics of Morality. Cambridge, Mass. (Harvard University Press), 1995. It is clear from several passages that Nietzsche never regarded *original cruelty* as a means to an end (and therefore excusable and justifiable according to a Utilitarian economy), but as an end in itself, namely as 'good entertainment' (see quotations below). Walter Kaufmann gets around the contentious issue essentially by collapsing agent and patient, spectator and participator. *'Man' as such* applies cruelty to himself for educational purposes; in order for him to adopt 'rational ideals': "Nietzsche's valuation of suffering and cruelty as not the consequence of any gory irrationalism, but a corollary of his high esteem of rationality. The powerful man is the rational man who subjects even his most cherished faith to the severe scrutiny of reason and is prepared to give up his beliefs if they cannot stand this stern test. [. . .] Nietzsche considered the mortification of the flesh a radial cure to which only the weak had to resort because they lacked the power to master their impulses and to employ them well. At the same time, Nietzsche realized that, before such power and perfect mastery could be attained, man generally had to harsh with himself." Kaufmann, Walter: Nietzsche: Philosopher, Psychologist, Antichrist. Princeton (Princeton University Press), 1974, 4th ed.; p. 244-45. In Nietzsche, it is certainly not for 'rational' purposes that humans are entertained by cruelty, and cruelty is certainly not something "the weak" must "resort to" in order to control himself; it is a spectacle in which "the weak" becomes a very unwilling participator. The authoritative Kaufmann has here an almost completely misunderstood interpretation of Nietzsche.

population against its neighbor and opposite; philosophers against people with other opinions; all freethinkers; the daily commentators; all living in abstinence, like the holy. . . . But is man therefore evil?" (Nachlaß 1881, KSA 9, 11[89]).[430]

Obligated to follow Nietzsche's text, we must thus affirm his view that there is pleasure in cruelty, that cruelty 'makes happy,' that cruelty is 'good entertainment' (cf. "to see others suffer does one good, to make others suffer even more so." Could it be clearer? Here, we find no wriggle-room for creative interpretations).

In this suggestion of a pleasure in cruelty, we believe that Nietzsche is foreshadowing Freud's later theories of a destructive drive, which in the name of *Thanatos* is locked as in an eternal struggle with *Eros*. In Nietzsche, as also in Freud, this destructive drive would eventually be contained by society, and was eventually turned inwards; as described above. However, in the process, society deprived man of the former joy of simply acting out aggression. Originally, there was (still is) joy in inflicting pain. Especially in *Das Unbehagen der Kultur*, Freud corroborates Nietzsche's insight.

> If civilization imposes such great sacrifices not only on man's sexuality but on his aggression, we can understand better why it is hard for him to be happy in that civilization. In fact, primitive man was better off in knowing no restrictions of instinct. [. . .] Even where it [*sadism*] merges without any sexual purpose, in the blindest fury of destructiveness, we cannot fail to recognize that the satisfaction of the instinct is accompanied by an extraordinarily high degree of narcissistic enjoyment, owing to its presenting the ego with a fulfillment of the latter's old wishes for omnipotence. The instinct of destruction [. . .] must when it is directed towards objects, provide the ego with the satisfaction of its vital needs and with control over nature.[431]

We shall suggest that Nietzsche envisions two kinds of aggression: a simple and original kind (we call it *primary*, or *proto-sadistic*) that fulfills *instincts* and therefore makes 'happy,' and a complicated and convoluted kind (we will call it *secondary*, or *proto-masochistic*) that derives from the ressentiment of the "suffering" individual, and has therefore 'gone sour' by being revengeful; thus enacted by an impotent individual (as we shall shortly explain).

---

[430] We notice that 'philosophers' and 'daily commentators' also *want-to-harm*; cruelty penetrates deeply all nooks of life.
[431] Freud: "Das Unbehagen in der Kultur"; GW XIV, p. 474 & 480.

Such a distinction we also find in Freud's psychoanalysis. We have, in one scenario, a derived aggression in the form of the pathological sadist, who identifies with his victim, and in the identification derives satisfaction. He has to 'feel the other's pain' in order to feel satisfaction himself. In another scenario, aggression is an *independent* drive impelling destructive behavior, as the so-called *death-drive*. In this scenario, the "inclination to aggression is an original, self-subsisting instinctual disposition [*Triebanlage*] in man."[432] Primary aggression, as derivative of the instinctual 'death-drive,' therefore cannot be *perverse* or *pathological*: nothing has been turned around and directed away from its natural course. On the contrary, if one assumes an *original aggressive disposition* in man, one will have to adopt Nietzsche's view that there is an original joy in inflicting pain, that cruelty "makes happy" and is "festive."[433]

It is typically this *primary aggression* Nietzsche refers to when he describes the predilection for cruelty in our ancestors. What we have labeled Nietzsche's 'proto-sadist' is thus not a 'sadist' in the pathological sense. Nietzsche's 'proto-sadist' is merely expressing his strength – or speaking with Freud, indulging in "narcissistic enjoyment"; enacting "old wishes for omnipotence"; "satisfying his vital needs." This kind of infliction of pain is by Nietzsche regarded as *innocent*: it is how an eagle kills a mouse, a cat toys with its prey, or a child tortures animals. "If one does not know how painful an action is, it cannot be malicious; thus the child is not malicious or evil to an animal: he examines and destroys it like a toy." (MA I 104, KSA 2, p. 101).

---

[432] Freud, loc. cit., GW XIV, p. 481.

[433] The existence of an original aggression is often evidenced in modern Ethnology and Anthropology. We know for example that native Indian tribes often arranged their festivals around the torture of an enemy as the evening's main event and festive climax. We know that our nearest ancestor on the evolutionary ladder, the Chimpanzee (which we therefore often compare to ourselves), is not the cuddly and peaceful animal we thought it was just ten years ago. Newer studies show that Chimpanzees often act with extreme brutality against out-cast group members, who are hunted down, beaten, bitten to death, and cannibalized. We must even guard ourselves against the false consolation that we find only this raw cruelty in the animal kingdom or in our ancestral past. Today, it thrives and proliferates in several war-torn regions; and in the many clandestine prisons around in the world (basically, it seems, it is reactivated whenever law breaks down, and the human being gets the opportunity to inflict pain).

5. Exploiting "Suffering": On the Meaning of the Ascetic Ideal and the Ascetic Priest

5.1. The Ascetic Ideal as a Will-to-Nothing

In the third part of GM, Nietzsche develops a criticism of something he labels *the ascetic ideal*, and its agent, *the ascetic priest*, who he believes is responsible for promoting this ideal. It is in either case not completely clear what Nietzsche means by this conceptual pair, partly because they have no precedent in philosophical discourse, and partly because, during Nietzsche's exposition, they are inflated.[434] They seem to include *too much*, if not *every-*

---

[434] Nietzsche's third inquiry from GM is in many ways his most difficult. Whereas it is relatively easy to follow Nietzsche's thinking in his first and second inquiry from GM, the third presents us with unusually fluid concepts. One experiences an unusual rapid fluctuation of meaning of various concepts, or, to put it in other words, an unusual diversity of meaning-investments [*sinnhineinlegungen*] of apparently identical concepts. The result must necessarily be reader-confusion, and the perception that Nietzsche is contradicting himself. If at all the third essay is commented about (the first and second essay have universal appeal; the third is often glossed over), we often experience in commentators this perplexity and confusion. Therefore, we will start with a remark on our own 'method' of reading this third inquiry. We may start by saying that *we always give Nietzsche the benefit of doubt*. That is, we like to take for granted that there is 'method in the madness,' and it is up to us to reconstruct this *method*. We find it uninteresting to point out obvious apparent contradictions in Nietzsche's application of nominally identical terms; and we do not see it as an intellectual achievement to identify such contradictions (we do not find 'nominal contradictions' interesting; that is, contradictions that emerge because a term is used with one meaning in one context, and another meaning in another context (we do, however, find 'structural contradictions' interesting)). We attempt instead to reconstruct the *cognitive motive* behind seeming contradictions, inconsistencies, incompatibilities, etc. This may be seen as essentially Freud's method; it is the method of psychoanalysis (the method is also akin to Phenomenology's reconstruction of 'essences'). One believes that beneath a seemingly incomprehensible and nonsensical manifestation, one is able to reconstruct *a meaningful sentence*. In our attempt to reconstruct Nietzsche's cognitive motives behind seeming inconsistencies, we essentially reconstruct *meaningful sentences* – and when not *sentences*, then *arguments*. The method is deliberately *reconstructive* and *rationalistic*. However, it is a different rationalism than the one promoted by Analytic and Anglo-Saxon philosophy during the best part of the 20th century. It is a rationalism that does not look for the contradictions in an argument, but for a rational core ('a meaningful sentence') in a thinking. It is perhaps surprising

thing. The latter poses a problem, because if a concept within its range includes *too much*, it is neither a very good nor a very clear concept. It loses its intrinsic purpose; it does not do what concepts are supposed to do: differentiate, distinguish, identify, circumscribe a material within a manifold; it does not assert meaning in the meaningless; it does not institute itself as Rule and Law within a continuum; it does not make a *clearance* in the wilderness of meaning. A concept that includes 'too much' or 'everything' *is* the manifold, the continuum, or the wilderness.

Both in GM and in Nietzsche's summary of GM in *Ecce Homo*, we encounter this *inflation* of the concept of the 'ascetic ideal.'

> The ascetic ideal expresses a will: w h e r e is the opposing will that might express an o p p o s i t e   i d e a l? The ascetic ideal has a g o a l – which is so

---

> that it has not been more often applied by commentators taking pride in calling themselves 'rational.' It is also a reconstruction/rationalism overriding some easy pseudo-deconstructions of Nietzsche. So, for example, Henry Staten's in his reading of the third essay in *Nietzsche's Voice* (see Chapter 2: "Transcendental Ressentiment"). Instead of attempting to understand Nietzsche, Staten (who one believes is a sympathetic reader of Nietzsche) presents the essay as a confused and pointless collection of nominal contradictions (now the ascetic priest is 'strong,' now he is weak; now he says 'No' to life, now he says 'Yes'; now Nietzsche is attracted to him, now repelled by him, etc.). And as if Nietzsche does not produce enough nominal contradictions himself, Staten helps him along by artificial and forced interpretations of some of his positions. For example: "Nietzsche is drawn by the ascetic will, and repelled by it. He says no to the ascetic because he wants to *say yes to the body* – the animal, senses, change, becoming, death. But what he rejects in the ascetic is his sickness and decay, which means that in saying no to the ascetic Nietzsche *says no to the body*, change becoming, death. Sickness and decay are precisely what is bodily about the body. [. . .] Nietzsche thus also *says yes to the ascetic will*, insofar as the ascetic priest, who is in one sense an expression of sickness and decay, is in another sense the only one how knows how to become master 'over life itself'." (Staten: Nietzsche's Voice, loc. cit., p. 60-61). Staten is in general a strong reader of Nietzsche, but this particular analysis is hardly convincing: Sickness is something bodily, and since Nietzsche says yes to the body, he must also say yes to sickness'; formally, *sickness infects the body :: Nietzsche says Yes to the body :: ergo, Nietzsche say Yes to sickness!* If we relax our intellects from that kind of artificiality, it is easy enough to understand that Nietzsche cannot be saying yes to the sick ascetic, simply because the ascetic has a body – as well as Holberg's Mother Karen is not a stone, simply because she cannot fly. The result of Staten's reading of the third essay is total incomprehension. If one is confused after having read Nietzsche, one is lost completely after having read Staten.

universal that all other interests of human existence seem, when compared with it, petty and narrow; [...] it permits no other interpretation, no other goal; [...] it submits to no power, it believes rather in its own predominance over every other power, in its unconditional d i s t a n c e   o f   r a n k [*Rank-Distanz*] regarding every other power. [. . .] Where is the o p p o s i t e to this closed system of will, goal, and interpretation? Why is the opposite l a c k i n g ? . . . Where is the o t h e r 'A Goal' ['*Eine Ziel*']? (GM III 23, KSA , p. 395-96).

The t h i r d inquiry [in GM] offers an answer to the question from where the ascetic ideal, the priest-ideal [*des Priester-Ideals*], derives its enormous p o w e r , although it is the h a r m f u l ideal par excellence, a will to the end, an ideal of decadence. Answer: n o t because God is at work behind the priests, as people believe, *faute de mieux*, – because it was the only ideal so far, because it had no rival. "For man will rather will n o t h i n g n e s s [*das Nichts wollen*] than not will [*als nicht wollen*]." . . . Above all, a c o u n t e r - i d e a l [*Gegen-Ideal*] was lacking. (EH "Zur Genealogie der Moral", KSA 6, p. 353).

The ascetic ideal is the "one goal" without opposite. It is the unconditional "only ideal"; it has "no rival"; no "counter-ideal." Since it has no *other*, and since we know no *other*, the 'ascetic ideal' must be *Ideal as such*. But if it is the *only ideal*, *Ideal as such*, the prefix through which it is always presented, 'ascetic,' seems superfluous. It at least begs the question, why would *Ideal as such* be 'ascetic'; what have asceticism to do with positing 'ideals'?

To be 'ascetic' is according to the dictionary to be abstinent, to practice self-discipline and self-denial; if something like an 'ideal' is 'ascetic,' we suppose that it imposes asceticism on the subjects following it. When asceticism has connotations to religious practices, what frequently is has, we think of certain monastery orders exercising abstinence, self-discipline, and self-denial in order to better serve God. In this sense, however, the 'ascetic ideal' is highly *specific* (since monasteries are small communities, living according to atypical social ideals), and it has several opposing 'counter-ideals.' This cannot resonate with Nietzsche's use of the conceptual pair, *ascetic ideal, ascetic priest*. It is obvious, that Nietzsche does not intend to deliver a criticism of the life of the monk. The concept of an 'ascetic ideal' being the "only ideal" has a far more universal range, and is a far more abstract description.

Several of Nietzsche's best commentators equate the *ascetic ideal* or *will* with the nihilistic will-to-nothingness promised as a religious *beyond*. The ascetic priest is as such identical to the Christian priest preaching a paradisiacal afterlife as a reward for denouncing this mundane and earthly life. The ascetic priest preaches *annihilation* of this life in return for a beyond that is also, but in a stronger sense, *nothing*. Thus, the doctrine produces an absurdity, a *double nihilism* that might read, *make nothing out of this life and you shall be rewarded with nothing in the yonder*. The irony of emptying this life for the sake of a promise of a life beyond, even more empty, is surely one of the intentions behind Nietzsche's criticism of 'ascetic ideal' or 'will.'

Since Christianity has been the master-ideology of Europe during two millenniums, this interpretation gives the concept a wide-ranging applicability. Yet, we shall argue that the conceptual range of 'ascetic ideal' or 'will' extends *still further* beyond this specific religious discussion of an afterlife. The afterlife-as-reward is part of the nihilism of the 'ascetic ideal,' and indeed, it gives us *a good image* on nihilism: the afterlife being a reward of nothing; the human being toiling for a reward of nothing; the individual suspending a life that could-have-been in the hope of this reward of nothing. But in these conceptions, the 'afterlife' is still only *one* image of the *Ideal as such*. Christianity is a good example, possibly the best example, on how the 'ascetic ideal' has been applied, but still, it is only an example.

Both Eugen Fink and Gilles Deleuze take their analyses in this direction, and suggest another universality of the 'ascetic ideal':

> All ideality of the historical ideals was ascetic. [. . .] [Man] cannot immerse himself in simple letting-live; he must have ideals suspended above himself; he must be able to see stars blinking above himself. All stars were so far yonder, they were priest-inventions; they were ideal in opposition to nature. [. . .] As such, Nietzsche brings will and ascetic ideal into an inherent relation. There is, in a certain sense, in all will asceticism. But what is it that the will has thus been wanting [*was hat dabei der wille gewollt*]. [. . .] The will was a will to nothing, a nihilistic tendency in life. [. . .] In the ascetic extended will the nothing is wanted, the nothing of the beyond, the afterlife, the moral idea. From where derives the fascination with nothing? Nietzsche says: "man rather will n o t h i n g n e s s than n o t will" ["*Lieber will noch der Mensch das Nichts wollen, als nicht wollen*"]. That means, hitherto there were on earth no other ideal than the anti-natural [*widernatürliche*] ascetic. [. . .] First with anti-nature [*Widernatur*] is the difference between reality and ideal possible.[435]

> The fiction of a world-beyond in the ascetic ideal [. . .] the will to nothingness needs reactive forces: it is not just that it only tolerates life in reactive form, but it need the reactive life as a means by which life *must* contradict itself, deny itself, annihilate itself. [. . .] the sense of the ascetic ideal is thus as follows: [. . .] to express nihilism as the 'motor' of reactive forces.[436]

---

[435] Fink, Eugen: Nietzsches Philosophie, p. 133-34
[436] Deleuze, Gilles: Nietzsche and Philosophy; loc. cit., p. 144-45.

5. Exploiting "Suffering": The Ascetic Ideal and the Ascetic Priest

The *Ideal as such* is what Fink describes as the "stars blinking above man"; since they are distant and unreachable, they are equated with nothingness. To *will* them is consequently to will nothing. Instead of being preoccupied on the horizon humans have been allotted, humans have made themselves busy with the unreachable dome of the sky.

Such a doctrine seems to inscribe an absurdity and contradiction into life itself. Werner Stegmaier has emphasized, especially, this self-contradiction of the doctrine:

> 'Ascetic ideals' are those, who require exertion, tireless exertion throughout life, and still, as ideals, they can never be fulfilled. 'Asceticism' means literally exercise, strict discipline, control of life. It gives life a meaning, insofar as it gives it a direction toward an aim, however, the aim is the ideal, [. . .] and as such the ideal has according to this scheme of meaning-investment [*sinngebung*] only the meaning that the asceticism gives to it. But when asceticism and ideal only give meaning to each other, when they only justify each other *reciprocally*, then they are both empty. The ascetic ideal thus requires a permanent violation of life, and is even in itself only a reflex of this violation; in the last analysis, it is a reflection of a pure will to self-violation [*Wille zur Selbstvergewaltigung*] – a will to nothing. The Will to Power, which came to power in the ascetic ideal was therefore '*a Will to Nothing*,' and the life it controlled, became nihilistic.[437]

When in Christianity the will-to-nothing is articulated as a 'double nihilism' (*make nothing out of this life, and you shall be rewarded with nothing in the yonder*), and expressed as Ideal – that is, when one is instructed to pursue this ideal – then human history has been guided by a self-contradiction. Life, which is Being (and, we think, should be a celebration of Being), has turned into a *will-to-Nothing*.

Not just the 'ascetic' Ideal, but all *Ideal* is a projected image or representation. When we 'pursue ideals,' we always pursue a *project*. We set up, as if in front of ourselves, an 'image,' the 'image' always being devised in the mind. Such an image we also call *idea*; but the *idea as Ideal* is now thrown forward into the shadowy world of the future. As such, we do not find *Ideals* in nature; they are never found in the self-presence of the empirical world, they cannot be observed, and they have no physical existence. The image of the mind, projected forward as the *aim* of the Ideal, is truly *a thing of Nothing*. Consequently, if we have turned life into a pursuit of *ideas as Ideals*, we have simultaneously dismissed the *world as Being*, and surrendered ourselves to a *will to Nothing*. This is also the meaning of Nietzsche's

---

437 Stegmaier, Werner, Nietzsches Genealogie; loc. cit., p. 171.

famous maxim: "man will rather will nothingness, than not will" ["*Lieber will noch der Mensch das Nichts wollen, als nicht wollen*"]. To 'will nothingness' is to will the false Ideals, unreachable in the first place, and therefore nothing. But 'not to will' is, in negation of the futile will-to-ideal, to will instead 'life' or 'being' in busy preoccupation, without letting oneself be distracted by false ideals. The misguided human being consequently constructs 'ideals,' rather than not. Simply, the human being *will rather will nothing*, than it *will not will nothing*.

We may now answer our initial query: what does it mean that the will-to-nothingness in the form of pursuit of Ideals is so-called 'ascetic'? We started by saying that 'ascetic' seemed an odd and unjustified prefix if Nietzsche were supposedly talking about *Ideal as such*. (We were quickly able to rule out that he was talking about something as highly specific as the religious ideals of abstinence, because it would be a simple matter to establish *opposing counter-ideals* for that kind of abstinence; over two centuries we have been inundated in 'counter-ideals' proposed as theories on emancipation and liberation. However, promoting a new liberation-theory is not a part in Nietzsche's agenda; he is, as he himself says, merely "describing.")

Therefore, we must understand what it *means* to *will an ideal*. When we will an ideal we always introduce discipline, severity, and seriousness into our existence. The introduction of *willing* into existence, transforms existence from being *indifferent* into being *involved*. When one starts to live according to ideals, starts to *pursue ideals*, the seriousness of purpose and urgency has been added to life. Life is no longer innocent letting-be, happy ignorance, and playful indifference, but a straining of oneself in the pursuit of distant, abstract, and absent ideals. We have "created a magnificent tension of spirit in Europe, the likes of which has never existed in the world before: with such a tense bow we can now shoot at the most distant goals." (JGB Vorrede, KSA 5, p. 13). Thanks to this tension of spirit, there is 'asceticism' in the will-to-Ideal; as well as there is 'asceticism' in the involved *re-direction* of the eye, the *looking-down-on Being*, and *looking-up-to Nothing*.

Nietzsche says that there has never been an opposing 'counter-ideal' to the ascetic ideal – but indeed there has! These 'counter-ideals' we often encounter in world-literature, when the protagonist is receiving the advice of a wise elder to give up his search for this or that – eternal life, meaning of life, his diseased beloved, his past, etc. – instead of just accepting and enjoying. An example, which even Nietzsche might have approved of, is the maid's advice to Gilgamesh in *The Epic of Gilgamesh*:

> Gilgamesh, where are you wandering?
> The life that you are seeking all around you will not find.
> When the gods created mankind
> They fixed Death for mankind,
> And held back Life in their own hands.
> Now you, Gilgamesh, let your belly be full!
> Be happy day and night,
> Of each day make a party.
> Dance in circles day and night!
> Let your clothes be sparkling clean,
> Let your head be clean, wash yourself with water!
> Attend to the little one who holds onto your hand
> Let a wife delight in your embrace.
> This is the true task of *mankind*(?)[438]

Remember to live, in order to make your short days full of that life you are bound to lose, the maid advices Gilgamesh. Do not waste precious time attempting to become something one cannot become, immortal. There is an immortality of sorts already in the simple pleasures, as they repeat themselves day after day, during a lifetime: food and drink, dance and play, bathing, children, and sex.

5.2. The 'Ascetic Priest' as Exploiting "Suffering"

The 'ascetic ideal' does not emerge by itself, and it does not emerge from nothing. It is always conditional upon, first, an agent able to articulate the ascetic ideal, and, second, an audience ready and willing to adopt the articulated ideal. The agent, Nietzsche describes as the "ascetic priest," and the audience, he describes as the "suffering" [*der Leidenden*]. The "suffering" is the "soil" on which the "ascetic priest" sows his seeds; but the "soil" is rotten, and the seeds are poisonous.

---

[438] Kovacs, Maureen Gallery: The Epic of Gilgamesh. Stanford (Stanford University Press), 1989; (ibid.), p. 85, fn. 1. *The Epic of Gilgamesh* is a reconstruction from the fragments of old Babylonian clay tablets written in the cuneiform alphabet. This fragmented existence of the poem presents the translator with extraordinary translations-problems, one of which we notice in the well-reconstructed passage above. The last word 'mankind' could also be translated 'womankind' in which case the message is no longer 'existential,' but refers to the duties of an ancient Mesopotamian woman; namely her "true task" to "delight" in a man's "embrace."

> On this soil of self-contempt, on such swampy ground, grows every weed, every poisonous plant, and everything is so petty, so hidden, so dishonest, so sugary. Here the worms of vengefulness and rancor are teeming; here the air stinks of secrets and concealment; here a web of the most malicious conspiracy is spun constantly, the conspiracy of the suffering against the well-constituted and the victorious; here the aspect of the victorious is h a t e d. (GM III 14, KSA 5, p. 369)

The ascetic priest and the suffering are codependent. If there were no suffering, there would be nobody for whom to preach, and nobody would have developed an ear for the sermons of the priest; and vice versa, if there were no priest, there would be no articulation of an ascetic ideal. The priest is therefore (as described in *Chapters 3* and *4*) the chief *ideologue* for the 'suffering' masses. He articulates the idea as Ideal, without which the masses would only live aimlessly on this rotten soil of theirs; a soil on which confusion, hatred, ressentiment, and envy germinate. The 'job' of the priest is to cultivate this soil. Therefore, originally, *there is* [*es gibt*] confusion; but the priest *articulates*, makes *distinct*, and thus *visible*, an idea in the confusion. He as such gives the masses a *direction*; now they see where they are going. Everything is better than confusion, so in that sense, the priest/the ideologue is a healer; or, rather, is *seen* as a healer – even as savior.

In Nietzsche, the priest exploits 'suffering,' as the capitalist in Marx exploits 'labor.' In Nietzsche's narrative, the priest is the most dubious of healers; he practices a kind of hocus-pocus medicine, where the cure makes the patient more sick than the illness.

> [The priest is] determined to sow this soil with misery, conflict, and self-contradiction wherever he can and, only too certain of his art, to dominate the s u f f e r i n g at all times. He brings salves and balm with him, no doubt; but before he can act as a physician he first has to wound; when he then stills the pain of the wound, h e a t t h e s a m e t i m e i n f e c t s t h e w o u n d. (GM III 15, KSA 5, p. 373).

As the chief ideologue of the sick, the priest is meant to give relief, but effectively he only pours more poison into their system; the drug he administers is venom. If anything, he only gives the knife of ressentiment an extra twist in an already festering wound. In Nietzsche's narrative, the priest is the nightmare physician that fractures an ankle that was only sprained, finally patching up the injury in a manner that will leave the patient permanently disabled. Thanks to the bungled up healing of the priest, the suffering will continue to come back to seek his help. The ascetic priest has made himself indispensable.

Less metaphorically, what is the priest doing? – As we will see in more detail below, the priest invents activities or strategies by which the individual is able *to make life tolerable*, i.e., to cope with suffering, depression, and boredom. The final purpose of these strategies is to make the individual *forget* suffering, depression, and boredom; and to *immunize* him or her against pain. However, the artificially introduced forgetfulness and immunization eventuates in an all-encompassing paralysis of life. As we shall describe later (cf. *Appendix III*), without pain, there is in Nietzsche also no pleasure (as without risk, there is no gain; without anxiety, no love, etc.) To dull the individual's capacity for pain results in a castration of the general capacity for life.

In the previous chapter, we used the phrase 'confused-aggressive' as a prefix to describe Nietzsche's slave. In GM, Nietzsche introduces a single term condensing this composite concept (confusion & aggression), namely 'ressentiment.' *Ressentiment* is, *first*, an aggression and a hostility directed at nothing in particular, because, *secondly*, is it also the inability and powerlessness to express these feelings of aggression. When one is unable to *express* aggression, it is 'confused aggression.' *Ressentiment* is thus the more abstract concept for 'confused-aggression' in its first and primary manifestation. It is the 'rotten soil' necessary for the priest to 'sow' his poisonous seeds. The Priest is exploiting the pre-existence of 'ressentiment,' 'confused-aggression,' 'suffering.'

However, the priest *re-directs ressentiment*; he articulates and gives it aim and object. His task is twofold. *First*, he directs ressentiment toward those who a 'healthy,' 'strong,' and 'happy.' The confused-aggressive, resentful, subjects 'learn' that the healthy and strong are obstacles to their own happiness. *Second*, the priest defends the herd against itself; he prevents their confused-aggression from boiling over into self-aggression and self-destruction.

> Dominion over the suffering is [the priest's] kingdom, that is where his instinct directs him, here he possesses his distinctive art, his mastery, his kind of happiness. [. . .] He has to defend his herd – against whom? Against the healthy, of course, and also against the envy of the healthy. [. . .] He also defends [the herd] against itself, against the baseness, spite, malice, and whatever else is natural to the ailing and sick and smolders within the herd itself; he fights [. . .] the most dangerous of all explosives, r e s s e n t i m e n t. [. . .] " The priest is the alternator of the direction [*der Richtungs-Veränderer*] of ressentiment. (GM III 15, KSA 5, p. 372-73).

We must now hold on to a new, crucial, distinction between *ressentiment* and *re-directed ressentiment*.

In the latter case, the priest gives ressentiment a direction; that is, he creates a determined crowd ready to obey orders. At this point ressentiment becomes so-called "creative." Ressentiment, from originally being an *aggressive confusion*, becomes an *aggressive project*.

> The slave revolt in morality begins when r e s s e n t i m e n t itself becomes creative and gives birth to values: the ressentiment of natures that are denied the true reaction, that of deeds, and compensate themselves with an imaginary revenge. Whereas every noble morality develops from a triumphant Yes-saying to itself, slave morality from the outset says No to what is outside, to its "other," to its "not-self": and this No is its creative deed. (GW I 10, KSA 5, 270-71).

When the priest gives ressentiment direction, he essentially *articulates*. As always in Nietzsche, in order for something to take effect, it must be linguisticized. It has no manifest existence before it is transformed into sign-processes. The priest is this necessary 'articulator' of 'suffering.' We also call such an 'articulator' an 'ideologue'; he gives 'reasons' and 'causes' for 'suffering'; suddenly 'suffering' has meaning and can be *understood*.

> Man, suffering from himself, in someway or other but in any case physiologically, is like an animal shut up in a cage, uncertain why or wherefore, thirsting for reasons – reasons relieve – thirsting, too, for remedies and narcotics, at last takes counsel with one who knows hidden things, too – and behold! He receives a hint, he receives from his sorcerer, the ascetic priest, the f i r s t hint as to the 'cause' of his suffering: he must seek it i n h i m s e l f, in some g u i l t in a piece of the past, he must understand his suffering as a p u n i s h m e n t. (GM III 20, KSA 5, p. 389).

The most sensational, the most cunning and daring, interpretation of 'suffering' offered by the priest is to 'find' a *cause* for 'suffering' as a transgression committed in the distant past, some betrayal of God in the past, some former sin committed by our ancestors that still reverberates as guilt in the offspring, and for which the offspring are now receiving their well-deserved punishment. Now the offspring suffers from a guilt that can never be appeased or repaired, since there is no going back and alter the development of events. Adam took a bite of the apple, and from then on, the world became a wail of tears.

However, the priest does not just give causes and reasons for suffering, he also invents 'methods' by which to overcome suffering. These are the so-called "salves and balm" he brings with him; they alleviate "the pain of the wound," while they at the same time "infect the wound" (ibid.). These "salves and balm" are his hocus-pocus- and pseudo-solutions; they are the 'fast food' of existential meaning, by which humans are supposed to justify their suffering existence. In offering this hocus-pocus medicine, the priest makes a suffering existence *tolerable*.[439]

5.3. Soft-Core and Hard-Core Strategies for the 'Toleration of Life'

We understand that the priest disseminates false ideals; we understand that he implements disciplining practices for taming and disarming individuals, in order to transform individuals into a controllable crowd. These practices have been particularly well cultivated in the master-ideology of Europe, Christianity; but they are exercised in all crowd-manipulation. The techniques of religious and political manipulation are the same.

Nietzsche charges the priest for an additional offense when he accuses him for *making life tolerable*. In "making life tolerable," the priest apparently offers relief, but what is the wrongdoing in offering *relief*? Moreover, in "making life tolerable," paradoxically, the priest says "Yes" to life.[440] ("This ascetic priest, this apparent enemy of life, this d e n i e r – precisely he is among the greatest c o n s e r v i n g and y e s - c r e a t i n g forces of life."

---

[439] The introduction of these strategies for the "toleration of life," general means to control the crowd (although they are not identical to what today we call 'crowd-control' – police-tactics we associate with tear-gas, water-cannons, and rubber-batons), seem almost entirely absent from all commentators of Nietzsche's *Genealogy* (an exception is Werner Stegmaier's *Nietzsche's Genealogy* (loc. cit.), p. 192). Although rarely commented on by scholars, the description of these strategies have been influential in 20th Century intellectual history, since they have been integrated and applied in the branch of historicism known as 'history of civilization' or 'history of mentality' [*Zivilisations-/Mentalitäten-Geschichte*] – represented by names such as Michel Foucault and Norbert Elias. In Elias Canetti's *Masse und Macht* as well, one find startlingly penetrating and original analyses reminding one of Nietzsche's *Genealogy* (see Canetti, Elias: Masse und Macht. Hamburg (Claessen Verlag), 1960.) In two new books on Nietzsche's *Genealogy*, consulted after I completed my manuscript, these strategies for the 'toleration of life' do in fact have the author's attention. So, Christopher Janaway produces a list of these strategies similar to my own below (See Janaway, Christopher: Beyond Selflessness: Reading Nietzsche's Genealogy. Oxford (Oxford University Press), 2007). Also Sverre Raffensoe describes these strategies in his excellent introduction to Nietzsche's *Genealogy* (see Raffensoe, Sverre: Nietzsches "Genealogie der Moral." Paderborn (Wilhelm Fink Verlag), 2007).

[440] See Nehamas: "Ironically, the ascetic ideal was life's ploy to make people continue to live." (Nehamas, Alexander: Nietzsche: Life as Literature, loc. cit., p. 133).

(GM III 14, KSA 5, p. 366).[441]) Now, we know from elsewhere that Yes-saying and affirmation of existence is the signature and emblem of the super-human in its ability to confirm existence – confirm existence to the point where one could want its *eternal recurrence* (cf. *Chapter 6*). How are we supposed to understand Nietzsche's apparent self-contradiction?

Let us suggest the following interpretation. To attempt to make life 'tolerable' is a perversion and negation of life, since according to Nietzsche's uncompromising life-affirmation, life is *intolerable* and should be affirmed as such. To 'make life tolerable' is to deny, and fail to confront, an intolerable life. More importantly (and *a fortiori*), since the 'tolerable life' is an *interpretation* of what *counts as* tolerable (that is, an evaluation with no objective foundation), the activity of the ascetic priest becomes a falsification of life. In other words, *we do not know* what we tolerate; we may be able to tolerate far more pain, than the priest think we may. Therefore, the priest prescribes his palliatives and drugs much too quickly, because in his *interpretation*, humans have a low threshold for pain. Instead of a human confronting pain and suffering, the priest provides anesthesia by which humans immunize themselves against what the priest falsely *interprets* as intolerable. Now, this new anesthetized condition eventually ends up being more intolerable than the intolerable life it was supposed to heal in the first place. (If this thought seems unnecessarily convoluted, an example might clarify the idea: if and when we modern/post-modern get bored, our easy remedy is to resort to the television set; television becomes our easy pallia-

---

[441] The context of the quote is the following: "The ascetic ideal springs from the protective instinct of a degenerating life, which tries by all means to sustain itself and to fight for its existence. [. . .] The case it therefore the opposite of what those who reverence this ideal believe: life wrestles in it and through it with death and against death; the ascetic ideal is an artifice for the preservation of life. [. . .] The ascetic priest is the incarnate desire to be different, to be in a different place, and indeed this desire at its greatest extreme, its distinctive fervor and passion; but precisely this power of his desire is the chain that holds him captive so that be becomes a tool for the creation of more favorable conditions for being here and being man – it is precisely this power that enables him to persuade to existence the whole herd of the ill-constituted, disgruntled, underprivileged, unfortunate, and all who suffer of themselves, by in going before them as their shepherd. You will see my point: this ascetic priest, this apparent enemy of life, this denier – precisely he is among the greatest conserving and yes-creating forces of life. [. . .] The No he says to life brings to light, as if by magic, an abundance of tender yeses; even when he wounds himself, this master of destruction, of self-destruction – the very wound itself afterwards compels him to live." (GM III 13, KSA 5, p. 366-67).

5. Exploiting "Suffering": The Ascetic Ideal and the Ascetic Priest

tive against boredom. Now, if life was felt to be 'boring' before, some might suggest that spending it in front of the television set eventually makes it even more monotonous and uneventful. Slowly days drip away into a pond of nothing, until the day of reckoning when the subject realizes that it spent a life on nothing. The TV becomes a false drug, infecting the wound it was meant to heal. (Recently, some American research-group reported that watching TV requires less brain-activity than dreaming.))

When Nietzsche draws up a list of means by which to combat suffering and depression, some are so-called "innocent" (we call them 'soft-core'), while others are so-called "guilty" (we call them 'hard-core'). The first strategy for the toleration of life is so-called 'innocent'; it is described as the "hypnotic muting of sensibility in general [*eine hypnotistische Gesammtdämpfung der sensibilität*], of the capacity to feel pain." (GM III 18, KSA 5, p. 382); it is also alternatively described as the "general muting of the feeling of life" [*Gesammt-Dämpfung des Lebensgefühls*] (GM III 19, KSA 5, p. 384).

> This dominating sense of displeasure is combated, f i r s t, by means that reduce the feeling of life in general to its lowest point. If possible, will and desire are abolished altogether; all that produces affects and 'blood' is avoided. [. . .] No love; no hate; indifference; no revenge; no wealth; no work; begging; if possible, no women, or woman as little as possible. [. . .] The result, expressed psychologically-morally, is 'selflessness,' 'sanctification'; expressed physiologically, hypnotization; one attempts to achieve for man an approximation to what in certain animals is h i b e r n a t i o n, [. . .] the minimum consumption and circulation of energy at which life still subsists without really entering consciousness. (GM III 17, KSA 5, p. 379).

Returning to our example above, it cannot be too hazardous to assume that had Nietzsche known the television, he would have singled out TV-watching as the ideal example of a 'soft-core' toleration of life running on the "minimum consumption and circulation of energy at which life still subsists without really entering consciousness" (ibid.)).

But whatever form this "general muting of sensibility" takes, it represents the first disarmament of the individuality of the individual; it is a first strategy for 'stupidifying' the individual; for reducing the individual to the lowest possible denominator.[442]

---

[442] Here it would be fastidious to limit one's critical comments to the role of the media, the television, the tabloids, etc. The combat against 'sensibility' is today regarded as such a self-evident end in itself that drugs have been and are being designed for the deliberate purpose of the 'hypnotic muting of sensibility.' The invention of drugs such as Valium, Prozac, and other so-called

If this strategy has been triumphant in especially 'developed' countries, the second strategy has had an almost universal appeal. It is by Nietzsche described as *mechanical activity* [*die machinale Thätigkeit*]. Again, the main aim is to avoid depression, or generally, to avoid the feeling of living and being-alive. However, this time, the means to achieve the aim is work, work, and still more work. Human behavior is being disciplined, regulated, and organized. The day is being arranged into predictable time-slots as a day full of activity, a day without spare-time. The individual makes itself 'busy'; he or she adopts a fully occupied schedule.

> Much more common than this hypnotic muting of sensibility in general, of the capacity to feel pain [. . .] is a different training against states of depression which is in any case easier: the mechanical activity [*die machinale Thätigkeit*]. That this regimen alleviates an existence of suffering to a not inconsiderable degree is beyond doubt: today one calls this fact somewhat dishonestly, 'the blessings of work.' The alleviation consists in this, that the interest of the sufferer is essentially directed away from his suffering, – that activity, and nothing but activity, enters consciousness, and consequently leaves little room for suffering: because it is small, this chamber of human consciousness. [. . .] Mechanical activity and what comes with it – such as absolute regularity, the punctual unreflective obedience, a once-and-for-all-fixed life, a fully occupied time, a certain permission of, indeed training for, 'impersonality,' for self-forgetfulness, for incuria sui [lack of care of self] – ; (GM III, 18; KSA 5, p. 382).

The rationale behind the strategy of 'mechanical activity' is simple: when one is busy, one is also too busy to think about oneself; there is no time for one's pain to surface, since, as Nietzsche puts it, "the chamber of human consciousness is *small*." Implied is it that this chamber is so small that it cannot simultaneously hold on to one's immediate duties, and to one's personal predicaments and sufferings. We notice that this disciplinary strategy is implemented from the very early years of human life in modern societies. The elementary school system socializes the child into accepting a linear time-schedule, punctuated by only brief 'breaks' – fortunately so brief that the child never gets a change to enjoy its childhood.

A third strategy amongst the 'innocent means' to combat suffering is the so-called *small* or *petty pleasure* [*kleinen Freude*]. A 'petty pleasure' is a 'pleasure' that has been 'de-intensified.' It has been detached from what might have counted as pleasure properly speaking, intense pleasure registered as such by the body. 'Petty pleasure' is a sublimated and

---

'mood-altering' drugs, is regarded as a triumph for Western medicine. Innocuously, they are precisely referred to as 'anti-depressants.'

intellectualized pleasure. It is predominantly pleasure only by name, receiving its gratifying effects thanks to the circuits of numerous social interpretations. 'Petty pleasure' comes most typically in the form of the *pleasure of giving pleasure* [*die Freude des Freude-Machens*]. As such, it is akin to the utilitarian pleasure of sacrificing one's own pleasure for the pleasure of the common good.

> An even more highly valued means of combating depression is the prescription of petty pleasure [*kleinen Freude*] that is easily attainable and can even be made into a rule; this medication is often employed in association with the previous one. The most common form in which pleasure is thus prescribed as a curative is that of the pleasure of giving pleasure [*die Freude des Freude-Machens*] (doing good, giving, relieving, helping, encouraging, consoling, praising, rewarding). Prescribing 'love of one's neighbor,' the ascetic priest prescribes fundamentally an excitement of the strongest, most life-affirming drive, even if in the most cautious doses – namely, of the will to power. The happiness of 'slight superiority,' involved in all doing good, being useful, helping, and rewarding, is the most effective means of consolation of the physiologically inhibited. (GM III 18, KSA 5, p. 383).

'Petty pleasure' is a derivative of the *will to power*, and, therefore, one still find traces of pleasure in its manifestation, since it attributes to the agent a sense of superiority (according to Nietzschean doctrine, *sense of power* is at the essence of pleasure; cf. *Appendix III*). It is individually rewarding to 'do good,' to 'help,' to 'console,' because it consigns the recipient to an inferior position, and oneself to a superior position.

The fourth way of combating depression, the *formation of the herd* [*Heerdenbildung*], is still included in one of Nietzsche's so-called 'innocent' methods, although it would seem to border on his so-called 'guilty.' In the 'formation of the herd,' the priest takes upon himself to defend the herd against self-destruction, since left to their own devices, the herd self-destructs. The priest therefore "defends it against itself, against the baseness, spite, malice [. . .] against anarchy and ever-threatening disintegration within the herd." (GM III, 18; KSA 5, p. 383).[443] This is how

---

[443] In the essay *Group Psychology and the Analysis of the Ego*, Freud has an analysis remarkably similar to Nietzsche's. Freud talks about how society appeases and ameliorates an original *envy* in the crowd by developing a 'group spirit' meant to secure that everybody in society are treated equally: "What appears later on in society in the shape of [. . .] 'group spirit', etc., does not belie its derivation from what was originally *envy*. No one must want to put himself forward, *everyone must be the same and have the same*. Social justice means that we deny ourselves many things so that others may have to do

the priest *protects life*; this is his "Yes" to life. He protects the slaves against their own malice and resentment by redirecting it toward the so-called 'healthy,' i.e., those posited *as different and other*. In this activity, *the priest even invents the other* – the other as different, foreign, unfamiliar, and potentially dangerous. In *Heerdenbildung*, the priest *invents the Other as Enemy* as the practical manner by which to re-direct resentment, spite, and aggression. As such, he achieves the coherence of group-identity. Were it not for the re-direction of ressentiment, the slaves would go about destroying each other in a perpetual war of everyone against everyone, as in some primitive Hobbesian dystopia. The consolidation of group-identity, in the clever invention of the *Enemy-Other*, is vital for the restoration of peace within the group, and it is a safe ventilation for aggression. Attentive to the slave's eternal lament, 'someone or other must be to blame for my feeling ill – but who,' the priest comes to the rescue, and invents this 'someone or other.' Aggression unloaded on this 'someone or other,' we will below describe as *defensive retaliation*.

Under the so-called 'innocent means' to combat suffering we have listed and explained these four main manifestations: the *general muting of the feeling of life*; the *mechanical activity*; the *petty pleasure*; and finally the *formation of the herd*. When Nietzsche introduces his so-called 'guilty' (his *hard-core*) means of defeating suffering and depression, it is introduced under the enigmatic label, to produce an '*excess of feeling*' [*eine Ausschweifung des Gefühls*].[444]

---

without them as well, or, what is the same thing, may not be able to ask for them. *This demand for equality is the root of social consciousness and the sense of duty*." (Freud, Sigmund: Group Psychology and the Analysis of the Ego; loc. cit., p. 57; italics added.) About the 'priest' Freud also has views similar to Nietzsche's: "Let us not forget, however, that the demand for equality in a group applies only to its members and not to the leader. All the members must be equal to one another, but they all want to be ruled by one person. Many equals, who can identify themselves with one another, and a single person superior to them all – that is the situation that we find realized in groups which are capable of subsisting." Ibid., p. 68. Also in Nietzsche, the 'herd' wants equality; it cannot endure anybody outstanding, and 'envy' is the emotion that drives the slave into a herd, demanding 'equal rights' for all. Also in Nietzsche, the leader, Nietzsche's priest, is exempt from this drive toward equality. The slaves identify with each other as equals, and everybody identifies with a single person superior to them all, the priest.

[444] Compare to Stegmaier's outline: "Psychological-moral means to alleviate physiological depressions in the broad masses: (1) Redemption [*Erlösung*] from suffering through immobilization [*ruhigstellung*]: a requirement in pessimistic religions. (2) Diversion [*Ablenkung*] from suffering through

5. Exploiting "Suffering": The Ascetic Ideal and the Ascetic Priest

> The means employed by the ascetic priest that we have discovered up to now the general muting of the feeling of life, mechanical activity, the petty pleasure, above all 'love of one's neighbor,' herd formation, the awaking of the communal feeling of power [*Gemeinde-Machtgefühls*] through which the individual's discontent with himself is drowned in his pleasure in the prosperity of the community – these are [...] his i n n o c e n t [*unschuldigen*] means in the struggle with displeasure; let us now turn to the more interesting means, the 'guilty' [*schuldigen*] ones. They all involve one thing: some kind of an e x c e s s o f f e e l i n g [*eine Ausschweifung des Gefühls*] [...] 'h o w can one produce an excess of feeling.' (GM III 19, KSA 5, p. 384-85).

The production of 'an excess of feeling' [Kaufmann translates 'an orgy of feeling'] is still one of the strategies for the toleration of life, but it takes these strategies to their dangerous limit- and peak-condition. Producing an *excess of feeling*, the priest makes the masses accept everything and engage themselves in anything.

> To wrench the human soul from its anchorings, to immerse it in terrors, ice, flames, and raptures to such an extent that it is liberated from all petty displeasure, gloom, and depression as by a flash of lightning: what paths lead to this goal? [...] Fundamentally, every great affect has this power, provided it explodes suddenly: anger, fear, voluptuousness, revenge, hope, triumph, despair, cruelty; and the ascetic priest has indeed pressed into his service indiscriminately the *whole* pack of savage hounds in man and let loose now this one and now that, always with the same end in view: to awaken men from their slow melancholy, to hunt away, if only for a time, their dull pain and lingering misery, and always under cover of a religious interpretation and 'justification.' (GM III 20, KSA 5, p. 388).

Producing 'an excess of feeling' might be best translated into the easily understood neologism, 'fanaticization.' The priest deliberately 'fanaticizes' the masses into raptures that make them forget themselves: make them 'tolerate life' to the point where they are ready also to tolerate death.

---

mechanical work and mutual doing-good [*wohltaten*]: requirement in the formation of the crowd. (3) Incitation [*anregung*] of excesses of feeling: requirement for great affects in the service of religion, the interpretation of suffering as guilt and sin." Stegmaier, Werner: Nietzsche's Genealogie, loc. cit., p. 192.

5.4. Strategies for Fanaticization of the Depressed Individual

Fanaticization always involves an original sense of guilt, and a thereupon introduced blame-shift. In fanaticization, the priest targets the self-blaming individual, offering this individual relief from its self-blame by re-directing it into blame of the other. The relief of having the old pain removed and its exhilarating re-direction toward an outside other, are important psychological elements for the successful fanaticization of the individual.

Thus, the priest "exploits the sense of guilt"; a sense of guilt, he himself – or rather his ancestors – have implanted, since it emerges as an interpretation of suffering; a 'cause' or 'reason' for suffering; some old explanation of suffering (often some past betrayal of God by one's ancestors, which still reverberates in the present). Nietzsche has two (at least) competing explanations for the origin of the sense of guilt. In the first explanation, one assumes that 'suffering' is like the chaotic ground of the subject, the so-called 'soil' which the priest 'cultivates,' among else by inventing reasons and explanations for suffering. In Christianity, the explanation becomes, 'you have yourself to blame for your suffering; you are born a sinner.' In the second explanation, sense of guilt is produced when aggression is turned inwards as self-aggression, in the process forming the subject as a *dividium*, a split subject dividing itself in an aggressive supervisor and a servile supervised. The supervisor represents the voice of the priest, reprimanding the supervised for all kinds of deficiencies. However, as we notice, the two competing explanations are not necessarily incompatible. The self-aggressing subject as *dividuum* reiterates essentially the mantra, 'you have yourself to blame.'[445]

---

[445] We recall from the previous sections that in the institution of the feeling of guilt, i.e., the implementation of aggression directed inwards, the subject created a 'cavity' within itself, ready to be filled with authoritative voices. The subject feels 'guilt' because it has internalized an agency aggressing against itself. This agency was never part of the (presumed) full and integral subjectivity of the so-called 'assertive configuration,' but a regrettable outcome of certain historical developments. This new agency is a mirror of an outside-Other (in the form of a commander), and can therefore be filled only from the outside. The so-called 'de-cathected' inside of the servile configuration would therefore inevitably be re-cathected, but necessarily with the voices of presumed outside authorities. The 'de-cathected cavity' of the servile configuration had become like a hole in the subject waiting to be filled with authority. It became like an abstract command-structure waiting for a commander, like a *formal conscience* preparing the subject to obey *something*, whatever that *something* might be. Because *feeling of guilt* is generated simul-

5. Exploiting "Suffering": The Ascetic Ideal and the Ascetic Priest

The priest first implants the sense of guilt; thereupon he starts "exploiting" it.

> The chief trick the ascetic priest permitted himself for making the human soul resound with heart-rending, ecstatic music of all kinds was, as everyone knows, the exploitation of the s e n s e   o f   g u i l t. (GM III 20, KSA 5, p. 389).

We must first understand the psychological-physiological system Nietzsche attempts to describe as fluid. He is not envisaging a binary conceptual system of locked positions; his positions are always able to transform themselves into new positions. A notion like 're-direction of ressentiment' is not a concept with a single, once-and-for-all decided, signification; it does not have a clearly definable fixed range. Ressentiment may be re-directed and then it may be re-directed once more, etc., in which case the new re-directed ressentiment becomes something new; that is, it becomes a new concept that assumes a new conceptual range. The *re-directed re-directed* ressentiment can also not be read, as in logic, like a double negation returning to the old position; it is an entirely new position.

Therefore, in a summary of some of the stages in the development of ressentiment, we notice a total of three positions: First, 'there is' [*es gibt*] ressentiment (confused aggression as the 'soil' and pre-condition). Then we experience the priest's re-direction of ressentiment in turning confused aggression into self-aggression: *'you have yourself to blame'*! Then emerges the priest's re-direction of re-directed ressentiment in "exploiting the sense of guilt" and instigating a blame-shift: *'someone must be to blame for your suffering'*! In the last transformation, we encounter one of the 'hard-core' (Nietzsche's 'guilty') tactics for the toleration of life. In order to succeed in this last transformation, the priest/ideologue produces an 'excess of feeling.' In this 'excess' (Kaufmann's 'orgy') of feeling, the priest/ideologue produces intensities in the subject, especially by hyper-cathecting hate-objects. on which the subject is given the right to unload aggression. The last transformation represents a blame-shift from the *old blame of self* to a *new blame of some other*; it unloads dammed-up feelings of self-blame in an explosion of aggression, and represents a relief to the subject.

In this most radical of the strategies for toleration of life, everything is 'noise.' The priest/ideologue 'shouts' his commands to the subject; and the receptive subject becomes like an enlarged ear reproducing and amplifying this shouting in his inner-mental self (cf. *Chapter 3*). All other voices are drowned in this amplified noise. All precautions are thrown aside; a gradual

---

taneously with an *insatiably aggressive super-ego*, the subject is especially susceptible to obey *something*.

century-old cultivation of Law – the rules for what humans can do and what humans cannot do – are suspended and replaced with a kind of *leader-regulated anarchy*.

When the subject internalizes the 'shouting' of the priest/ideologue, it obeys. It alleviates to obey *something*; and if in this *something* there is implied a justification for spreading death and destruction about, so much the better. Now the self-aggressive super-ego turn aggression around toward the outside; now the aggressive super-ego has found something to obey that as an added bonus also licenses destruction. The aggressive super-ego can in good conscience embark on a destructive course that is under divine jurisdiction and justification.

> The old depression, heaviness, and weariness were indeed overcome through this system of procedures; life again became very interesting: awake, everlastingly awake, sleepless, glowing, charred, spent and yet not weary. [. . .] One no longer protested a g a i n s t pain, one t h i r s t e d for pain; 'm o r e pain! m o r e pain!' the desire of his Disciples and initiates has cried for centuries. Every painful excess of feeling, everything that shattered, bowled over, crushed, enraptured, transported; the secrets of the torture chamber, the inventiveness of hell itself – all were henceforth discovered, divined, and exploited. (GM III 20, KSA 5, p. 390).

Above, we introduced a distinction between *primary aggression* and *secondary aggression*. Primary aggression we described as a 'disposition in man,' identical to Freud's 'death-drive.' To act on one's primary aggression was in Nietzsche understood as a 'healthy, unashamed' manifestation of natural instincts. We postponed the discussion of *secondary aggression*. Now we should be able to understand the difference. In Nietzsche, it comes down to a question of the 'trajectory of forces.' (1) Aggressive forces that express themselves as in a straight line from the inner self to the outside other, without unloading the individual's own pain on the other as an act of revenge, are generally understood as 'healthy' aggressive forces in Nietzsche. We might call this kind of aggression, 'superficial aggression' or 'innocent aggression,' because it is not given much thought; it has 'entertainment-value' only in the moment. When the child gets bored by tormenting the ant, it turns its attention to something new, happily forgetting the ant. (2) Aggressive forces that have taken a 'round-trip' from outer to inner to outer – from aggression being internalized, then internalized aggression being projected back to the outside as self-conscious aggression – are being understood as degenerate and 'sick' aggression in Nietzsche. The pain inflicted on the other is an act of revenge; this means, there is in the pain-infliction a constant comparison to oneself; it becomes a pleasure to see the other in pain, because one is able to make a psychological transfer of pain once suffered to the pain of the other. The other suffers the pain one once suffered oneself; one 'identifies with' the victim; i.e., one places oneself in the stead of the victim, who is now a vivid reminder of oneself. In this sick aggression, the 'trajectory of forces' has turned into a 'circular confusion,' because self-pain it projected out and now enjoyed as the other's pain, but then again taken back as a reflection of one's self-pain. The victim is a mirror of myself; I see myself hanging on the cross, when I see the victim hanging on the cross (the possible physiological reaction, a shameful, a nervous, a hysterical laughter, because I have to conquer my horror while 'enjoying'). In any case, Nietzsche's secondary aggression is a 'sick' and degenerate form of aggression.

We notice another distinction between primary and secondary aggression. While primary aggression is nature (and we cannot help our nature), secondary aggression is *formatted* and given *direction* thanks to *procedures* and *strategies* (of the priest/the ideologue) manipulating an always too easily *manipulatable* subject. Since the design of procedures and strategies for the sake of manipulation is always a political project, Nietzsche's obscure third inquiry has in our reading a new political relevance. In Nietzsche's peculiar homespun concepts and his often inconsistent logical narratives, we find an attempt to criticize the ideological exploitation of the easily *manipulatable* subject. The *re-direction of ressentiment* is identical to the *formatting* of a 'secondary aggressive' crowd, which is again identical to so-called *fanatization* of the crowd. Someone is responsible for this 'formatting,' this 'fanatization'! – Namely the priest/the ideologue – as the *articulator of ideas*. Nietzsche produces a *critique* of this priest/ideologue.

We have said that in three stages *confused aggression* is turned into *self-aggression* is turned into *aggression against the other*. The last position, *secondary aggression* and *fanatization*, we may finally introduce under a new label, *fascist aggression*. So-called 'fascist aggression,' as the execution of a particular psychological structure, surely has an affinity to the political ideology, Fascism, which historically has excelled in producing it. Still, under the label 'fascist,' we intend to describe, not so much one particular political system and its ideology, but rather the emotions produced and incited thanks to certain ideologies. We leave the description of Fascism as historical-political system to the historians and the sociologists, and emphasize instead *a certain manner of incitement* and the *emotions incited*, as something we legitimately may describe as Fascist in a generalized sense. We assume that it is a discourse which involves a kind of *leader-regulated anarchy*; which (1) is characterized by the breakdown of civil and natural Law (as described and cultivated, e.g., from Plato to Locke and

Kant); which (2) adopts a rhetorical style aiming at and licensing destruction of the *other* (producing *secondary aggression*); while (3) single-mindedly pursuing an *Idea* as an end justifying all means. In Nietzsche, Fascist ideology has two major poles, the 'priest' and the 'slave.' To the 'priest,' it is discourse or rhetoric; while to the 'slave,' it is psychology or emotion. The rhetoric of the priest becomes its *means of production*; the emotions of the slave become its *product*. There are as such *material means of production* behind the *production of emotions*. That is, one summons up discursive strategies and procedures meant to produce results in form of affects.

Contrary to Henry Staten, who in his chapter "Transcendental Ressentiment" (*Nietzsche's Voice*, ibid., cf. fn. 44) finds no merit in Nietzsche's third inquiry, we read it as essentially an analysis of fascist discourse, what gives it the status of an (albeit often obscure and sometimes self-contradictory) anti-fascistic statement.[446]

At always in Nietzsche, the subject has no 'intrinsic rational' buffer against the priest-interpretations that are imposed on it; it has no universal rational principle that could protect it against the nonsense of ideology. On the contrary, as we sufficiently described in *Chapter 3* and *4*, thanks to the

---

[446] When the third essay is enigmatic, and is often received as such, it is partly because Nietzsche takes it upon himself to analyze the fugitive emotions of fascistic discourse, its psychological pre-conditions and its physiological manifestations. This task is wrought with difficulties, first, because these 'emotions' have never before been catalogued; secondly, because it impedes Nietzsche's analysis that Fascism has not clearly manifested itself as a historical-political movement. To Nietzsche, 'Fascism' could hardly have been detectable as more than anticipation; perhaps as a *scent* of danger; a *scent* he tries to pick up and articulate. (It might be objected that Nietzsche, in such descriptions, may *actually* have had in mind some of the well-known totalitarian implementations of Christianity experienced in European History: the intolerance of dissent, the persecution of heretics, the witch-hunts, the cruelty of the means by which to make subjects 'confess,' etc. And one might object that Nietzsche could not have known Fascism since it had not yet emerged as a political system. This is probably correct. But, as described above, in our definition of Fascism as a psychological structure, the range of the concept is expanded. It is basically a manner of incitement aiming at and licensing destruction of the other. The Spanish Inquisition fits within this definition, as does German Nazism, as does the Stalinism of the old Soviet Union, the Khmer Rouge of Cambodia, the so-called "Lord's Resistance Army" of Congo, or the Al Qaeda-Taliban in Northern Pakistan. Fundamentally, whatever etiquette these movements glue on their nonsensical ideologies, they are all Fascist movements.)

inherent emptiness of the subject, it is both fully capable of and ready to adopt any interpretation and meaning whatsoever.

Given this constitutional emptiness of the subject, a series of social, institutional, and religious constructions have successfully, during the development of civilization, configured a *servile subject*. And yet – however victorious the configuration of a *servile subject* historically has been – Nietzsche reserves for himself the right to hypothesize on the possibility of another configuration: Nietzsche's 'noble,' my so-called 'assertive configuration.' In the 'noble,' Nietzsche envisions a subject, which in its happy self-contentment could not be exploited and manipulated. Satisfied with itself, the noble would see no need for adopting priest-ideals designed to compensate for a supposed lack and deficiency in his or her self.[447] It lives *ideologically emancipated*. Since it would not conceive itself as sinful, it would also not implement strategies for destroying itself (that is, self-destructive strategies developed in the super-ego designed to destroy the sinful ego), which would again imply that it would have no need to self-righteously impress its self-destructive strategies on those miscreants that still live in 'sin,' 'bad faith,' or 'false consciousness.'[448]

---

[447] Interestingly, Freud has a suggestion for an interpretation of Nietzsche's *Übermensch*; directly referring to Nietzsche (whom, we remember, Freud avoided reading; cf. fn. 36), the 'superman' is the ancestral leader of the pack: "He [the leader], at the very beginning of the history of mankind, was the 'superman' whom Nietzsche only expected from the future. Even today the members of a group stand in need of the illusion that they are equally and justly loved by their leader; but the leader himself need love no one else, he may be of a masterful nature, absolutely narcissistic, self-confident and independent. We know that love puts a check upon narcissism, and it would be possible to show how, by operating in this way, it became a factor in civilization." Freud, Sigmund, loc. cit., p. 71.

[448] Is there a 'priest' in today's liberal democracies? – Yes, in the form of the contemporary politicians. However, it would be a great shame and a gross mischaracterization to see the liberal-democratic leader to be implementing 'hard-core' strategies for the toleration of life (so-called Fascist aggressive strategies). In liberal democracies, power is exercised as 'soft-core'; for example in the form of Nietzsche's 'petty pleasure' (doing good for the sake of the common good), or as 'mechanical activity' (work, or in today's terms, 'employment'). A Nietzschean *Übermensch* would still be anathema to a modern Western politician, because he/she would signify a human politically un-exploitable and non-manipulatible; i.e., not *persuaded* into engaging him or herself in politics, or in some common plan necessary for the protection of *our* selves, *our* lifestyle, *our* economy, *our* nation, etc. Thus, to the modern politician, Nietzsche's 'noble' would look like a hopeless case of political illi-

6. Insight and Blindness in Nietzsche. On Defensive Retaliation

Daniel Conway has suggested that Nietzsche's descriptions of the ascetic priest are auto-biographical:

> In fact, virtually everything he [Nietzsche] says about the ascetic priest applies equally well to himself as a genealogist of morals. Like the ascetic priest, he 'alters the direction of *ressentiment*,' exciting in his readers and affective enmity for the institutions of slave morality. Like the ascetic priest, he aims to assuage the *horror vacui* of the human will by providing an interpretive context in which suffering is justified. [. . .] The *Genealogy* thus becomes its author's own priestly weapon for it reproduces and exemplifies the precise interpretative strategy that he imputes to the ascetic priest.[449]

Elsewhere in his work, Nietzsche himself suggests that there are auto-biographical connections between an author and his work; famously in a passage from JGB: "I have gradually come to realize what every great philosophy so far has been: a confession of faith on the part of its author, and a type of involuntary and unself-conscious memoir." (BGE 6, KSA 5, p. 20); and in more detail in the following passage from GM:

> One should guard against confusion through psychological contiguity, [. . .] a confusion to which an artist himself is only too prone: as if he himself were what he is able to represent, conceive, and express. The fact is that *if* he were it, he would not represent, conceive, and express it: a Homer would not have created an Achilles nor a Goethe a Faust if Homer had been an Achilles or Goethe a Faust. Whoever is completely and wholly an artist is to all eternity separated from the 'real,' the actual [*von dem 'Realen', dem Wirklichen abgetrennt*]; on the other hand, one can understand how he may sometimes weary to the point of desperation of the eternal 'unreality' and falsity of his innermost existence [*Daseins*] – and that then he may well attempt what is most forbidden to him, to lay hold of actuality, for once actually to b e . (GW III 4, KSA 5, p. 344).

The suggestion in the passage is *not* that the author mirrors himself in his work, but that the author is the negative image of the favorite character or figure he creates in his work. "A Homer would not have created an Achilles nor a Goethe a Faust if Homer had been an Achilles or Goethe a Faust" –

---

teracy and indifference.

[449] Conway, Daniel: Nietzsche's Dangerous Game. (Cambridge: Cambridge University Press, 1997), p. 131.

and Nietzsche, we suppose, would not have created an *Übermensch*, if Nietzsche had been an *Übermensch*.

Conway, as well as Staten, who also suggests auto-biographical connections between Nietzsche and the ascetic priest, see a positive connection, thanks to the fact that Nietzsche can be seen as 'preaching' no less than the priest. In this highly schematic reading, where content is ignored, Nietzsche is formally 'doing' what the priest is doing. We see another 'autobiographical connection' – a connection not particularly flattering to Nietzsche, because it re-introduces in Nietzsche's rhetoric a content that has been criticized re-directed ressentiment. It is as such not a simple nominal contradiction, which disappears when one ponders dissimilar contexts for similar terms, but a structural contradiction that indicates a serious confusion on Nietzsche's part (indeed, if anything, an 'aggressive confusion').

It is a connection surfacing because Nietzsche at some point in his third essay does not restrain himself from launching a diatribe, an explicit hate-discourse, a projected aggression against everything from weak, sick, priest, slave, to women.[450] In these passages, he is explicitly, and incomprehensibly, producing "an excess of feeling," projecting the other as dangerous in the extreme, and licensing destruction of this other. In these passages, he reproduces what elsewhere he has determined as the most 'dangerous' ('hard-core') strategy of the priest for 'toleration of life.' We refer to the following passages in particular:

> The s i c k are man's greatest danger; n o t the evil, n o t the 'beasts of prey.' Those who are failures from the start, downtrodden, crushed – it is they, the w e a k e s t, who must undermine life among men, who call into question and poison most dangerously our trust in life, in man, and in ourselves. Where does one not encounter that veiled glance which burdens one with a profound sadness, that inward-turned glance of the born failures which betrays how such a man speaks to himself – that glance which is a sigh! 'If only I were someone else,' sign this glance; 'but there is no hope of that. I am who I am: how could I ever get free of myself? And yet – I a m s i c k o f m y s e l f ! [*habe ich mich satt!*] [. . .] These failures: what noble eloquence flows from their lips! How

---

[450] Also in *Antichrist*, Nietzsche recommends the destruction of the weak and 'ill-constituted': "Pity on the whole thwarts the law of evolution, which is the law of s e l e c t i o n. It preserves what is ripe for destruction; it defends life's disinherited and condemned; through the abundance of the ill-constituted of all kinds which it r e t a i n s in life it gives life itself a gloomy and questionable aspect. One has ventured to call pity a virtue (– in every n o b l e morality it counts as weakness –); one has gone further, one has made of it *the* virtue, the ground and origin of all virtue. [. . .] Life is denied, made m o r e w o r t h y o f d e n i a l by pity – pity is p r a c t i c a l nihilism. (A 7, KSA 6, p. 173).

much sugary, slimy, humble submissiveness swims in their eyes! What do they really want? At least to r e p r e s e n t justice, love, wisdom, superiority – that is the ambition of the 'lowest,' the sick. [. . .] They walk among us as embodied reproaches, as warnings to us – as if health, well-constitutedness, strength, pride, and the sense of power were in themselves necessarily vicious things for which one must pay some day, and pay bitterly: how ready they themselves are at bottom to m a k e one pay; how they crave to be h a n g m e n . [. . .] The sick woman especially: none can excel her in the wiles to dominate, oppress, and tyrannize. The sick woman spares nothing, living or dead.[451] (GM III 14, KSA 5, p. 368-70).

Away with this shameful emasculation of feeling! That the sick should *not* make the healthy sick [. . .] should surely be our supreme concern on earth; but this requires above all that the healthy should be s e g r e g a t e d from the sick, guarded even from the sight of the sick. [. . .] Let us have fresh air! Fresh air! And keep clear of the madhouses and hospitals of culture! And therefore let us have good company, our company! Or solitude, if it must be! But away from the sickening fumes of inner corruption and the hidden rot of disease! (GM III 14, KSA 5, p. 371).

Nietzsche is here practicing, what he himself has been *criticizing*. In his own analysis, *projection of feelings*, as defense-mechanism, helps the subject ignoring that feelings projected outside belong to its own inside. The projecting subject expels, throws out, spits out, something belonging to its own body, often in the phantasm understood as rot or decay, threatening the life and health of this body. As such, the subject attributes to the outside-other qualities, which it repudiates and refuses to recognize in itself. This is the analysis of projection.[452]

---

[451] When one reads this diatribe against women, one is allowed to be puzzled, when in *Antichrist* we read: "All the things upon which Christianity vents its abysmal vulgarity, procreation for example, woman, marriage, are here [in the Law-Book of Manu] treated seriously, with reverence, with love and trust. [. . .] *I know of no book in which so many tender and kind remarks are addressed to woman* as in the Law-Book of Many; these old greybeards and saints *have a way of being polite to women* which has perhaps never been surpassed. 'A woman's mouth' – it says in one place – 'a girl's breast, a child's prayer, the smoke of a sacrifice, are always pure. Another passage: 'There is nothing purer than the light of the sun, the shadow of a cow, air, water, fire and a girl's breath.' A final passage 'All the openings of the body above the navel are pure, all below impure. *Only in the case of a girl is the whole body pure.*'" (A 56, KSA 6, p. 240; italics added).

[452] Although Adorno has a different analysis of ideology than the one we here propose, his analysis of the 'authoritarian personality' is often similar to our

However, we easily notice that the sick are doing exactly what Nietzsche is doing when he writes about what they are doing: they *project* their own suffering outside, and find in the outside a reason and a cause for their suffering. Now, they project their aggression unto these guilty outside-others, an operation Nietzsche describes as *defensive retaliation*. So, whom do they aggress against in their 'defensive retaliation'? – The healthy, the strong, and the well-constituted! This is the 'objective' analysis; however, we notice that the *difference* between the *defensive retaliation of the slaves* and the *defensive retaliation of the healthy* – whose task it is now to ward off the defensive retaliation of the slaves – is non-existent. What is outside the *other* is identical to Nietzsche's *inside* and *ideal self*, and what is outside Nietzsche's inside-self, is the aggressing outside-others. Nietzsche's 'healthy' inside-self has the same relationship to the 'sick' outside-other, as the outside-other has to Nietzsche's inside-self.

We notice that it is perfectly possible to view the following brief fictitious monologue as *projected*: "Someone or other must be to blame for my feeling ill" – the sentence is ostensibly uttered by one of the insufferably sick. The sentence refers to 'me'! – But 'me' *who*? 'Me' *who writes* the sentence (who would be Nietzsche) or 'me' *who utters* the sentence (who would be the sick)? We can of course not objectively settle such a question, but it is at least a textual fact that the insufferably sick make *Nietzsche* feel sick too (who is now most *sick*?); it is also beyond doubt that *Nietzsche* in the insufferably sick has found someone to *blame* for himself feeling sick. The sentence, "someone or other must be to blame for my feeling ill" is accurately summarizing his own situation, even if Nietzsche in his writing present forgets himself by assigning the utterance to the insufferably sick.

In his performative self-contradiction, Nietzsche is attributing tendencies to the slave and the ascetic that he refuses to recognize in himself. He turns away his attention from his own unconscious and redirects it onto the unconscious of the outside-other. In the process, he gains great insights into the *other*, while failing to generate any insight into his *self*. As such, it is *not* the case that Nietzsche analyzes of the ascetic are *incorrect or false* (at least not on this ground). *Projection* may be a *subjective deficiency,* but it is *not* mis-perception. It is rather *self-perception externalized and universalized.* (For example, a jealous husband, projecting his own desire to commit adultery onto his wife, may produce acute insights into feminine behavior from his vigilant observations of the behavior of his wife.) We therefore suggest that Nietzsche's analysis have validity, even if Nietzsche misapprehends and mis-recognizes himself. Nietzsche's inability to recognize a quality in

---

own.

himself may be in almost *equal proportion* his ability to recognize in others precisely that quality. What he cannot recognize in himself is what he recognizes in the other. Personal blindness becomes acute inter-personal insight.

The analysis of the ascetic, even if tainted by Nietzsche himself, may therefore have a kind of 'objective validity' (provisionally accepting such an entity), because the explanation of the ascetic as a paranoid figment of Nietzsche's mind, and the explanation of the ascetic as an diagnosis of a quasi-historical 'type' are not necessarily incompatible and rivaling explanation-models. At the highest level of *blind insight*, Nietzsche even seems to understand and analyze *the mechanism of projection* from himself. However, now it is of course projected onto the outside as an analysis of a defense-mechanism *they* (the sick, the weak, the women) employ; a defense-mechanism, consequently, that is not meant to apply to Nietzsche.

> Every sufferer instinctively seeks a cause for his suffering; more exactly, an agent; still more specifically, a g u i l t y agent who is susceptible to suffering – in sort, some living thing upon which he can, on some pretext or other, vent his affects [. . .] a desire to d e a d e n p a i n b y m e a n s o f a f f e c t s . [. . .] This cause is usually sought, in defensive retaliation. [. . .] 'Someone or other must be to blame for my feeling ill' – this kind of reasoning is common to all the sick. (GM III 15, KSA 5, p. 374).

He cannot recognize *his own* defense, but his analysis 'from himself' of *their* defense is still acute and has as such a kind of 'objective validity' (same proviso as above). It is not our intention here to expose Nietzsche to psychoanalysis (we merely reconstruct meaning, argument, and essence in his thinking), but it seems often to be the case that Nietzsche's analyzes of the sick (the slave, the weak, and the woman) are extracted, acquiring their depth and particular pathos, *from himself*. A psychoanalyst might well ask, who does Nietzsche *really* hate?

CHAPTER 6

Eternal Recurrence in Inner-Mental Life

Eternal-Recurrence as Describing the Conditions for Knowledge and Pleasure

> The hardworking artist desires to rest, he longs to get away from the demanding diversity of phenomena and take shelter in the bosom of simplicity and immensity; a forbidden penchant that is entirely antithetical to his mission and, for that very reason, seductive – a proclivity for the unorganized, the immeasurable, the eternal: for nothingness. To rest in perfection: that is what the striver for excellence yearns for; and is not nothingness a form of perfection?
>
> — Thomas Mann: *Death in Venice*[453]

1. Introducing Three Different Kinds of Return

1.1. A Brief Preliminary about Repetition and Joy.

The 'Song of Joy' from Joseph Haydn's *Die Jahreszeiten* introduces us to a celebration of the return of spring.

> See the lilies, see the roses, see all the flowers! / See the rivers, see the meadows, see all the fields! / O, how lovely it is to behold the fields now! Come, you young girls, let us wander over the spectacular scene / See the earth, see the water, see the light sky! / Everything lives, everything is hovering, everything so full of activity. / See the lambkins, how they spring about! / See the fish, how they are teeming! / See the bees, how they are swarming! / See the birds, how they flutter! / Everything lives, everything is hovering, everything

---

[453] Thomas Mann, Death in Venice and Other Tales. Translated by J. Neugroschel, New York (Penguin), 1998, p. 318.

so full of activity. / Oh what pleasure, what enjoyment, swells in our heart! / Sweet drives, gentle raptures, swell in our breast.[454]

Spring returns as if it had been traversing a circle. During one revolution, the year has been sapped of energy, but now, miraculously, it returns reinvigorated to begin a new rotation. At this entry to the return of spring, the chorus of revelers is pregnant with anticipation. Spring is the birth of a new year; at the birth of this birth, on the first day of spring, everybody sings out in joy.

Everything begins again and anew, but as the same. Life starts over, but as the same life. In Haydn, we have a simple example of 'eternal return'; an example of 'return' that is easy to accept. Besides the plain fact that seasons come and go, the 'Dionysian' celebration of the seasonal re-birth of the world has accumulated a vast number of cultural manifestations, and can be found in mythology, religion, anthropology, poetry, and music.

The celebration has a material basis – as Marx undoubtedly would have reminded us. A sense of joy kicks in when people experience that the difficult, dark, and cold winter-days are finally receding. The world is warming up, the flora is blossoming, and the fauna is proliferating. Survival becomes easier; one can finally again begin to eat well. (It is a joy so thoroughly incorporated, one dare suggest, that it still exists in the modern human as a repository from our pre-historical past.)

But a *sense* of joy is of course different from its ever-so sobering material conditions, and it needs another description. Whether the joy is triggered by the anticipation of abundance and fertility, it is described in Haydn as a joy in seeing the same again; of seeing what is utterly familiar; a joy, thus, of seeing again what is already known. This joy in the repetition of the same is marked in the incantation of the repetitious 'see the rivers,' 'see the earth,' 'see the flowers,' 'see the birds,' etc. It is a joy described by Kierkegaard as 'repetition's love' [*Gjentagelsens Kjærlighed*]: "Repetition's love is in truth the only happy love."[455]

Finally, we notice another source indicative of joy in Haydn, a source the ode itself is unaware of. It is explicit in Haydn that the subject-object relation is being simplified in the seeing of the seeing subject, as the subject

---

[454] From Joseph Haydn: "Song of Joy," *The Seasons*. Translated from the libretto included in the Karl Böhm & Wiener Philharmonic's recording of Haydn's Die Jahreszeiten. Deutsche Grammophon. The ode does not have a single author, but is a collaborative effort of a number of writers; in conformity with common practice in Haydn's days.

[455] See Søren Kierkegaard, Fear and Trembling & Repetition. Translation H. V. & E. H. Hong, Princeton (Princeton University Press), 1983, p. 131.

is prodded to "see" this, "see" that. As language tells its user to "see," it erases itself and its user in front of that at which it points. Language neutralizes itself as it is being reduced to simply a pointer. Language, obviously, is still being used to prod the seeing, but it forgets itself as a tool as well as the subject for whom it is a tool – we only "see." This seeing is joyful, even euphoric, because the subject forgets itself. The ode, however, disregards this 'seeing' – or, strictly, 're-seeing' – as a source of joy (exactly because 'seeing' is self-*un*conscious activity). Ostensibly, the ode posits the experience of the return of spring as joyful. But not only a year starts over as the same year; knowledge starts over as the same knowledge; and finally, moments start over and over as the same moments. There is joy in this repetitious return of the same. As Kierkegaard before Nietzsche (and Freud after Nietzsche) understood, *repetition* is a source of joy.

Haydn's celebration of the coming of spring calls to mind Nietzsche's descriptions of Dionysian festivals from the beginning of *Die Geburt der Tragödie* (GT).

> Whether under the influence of narcotic intoxicants of which all original humans and peoples speak in their songs, or because the powerful coming of spring penetrates all nature with joy, the Dionysian emotions are awoken, and as they grow everything subjective disappears in complete self-forgetfulness. Also in the German Middle Ages the ever-increasing crowd would be wheeling from place to place, singing and dancing under the influence of the same Dionysian force. [. . .] There are people, who from lack of experience or out of insensitivity, would turn themselves away from such phenomena as from a 'folk-disease'; in contempt and convinced of their own 'health.' These poor folks obviously have no idea of how corpselike and ghostly their own 'health' looks, when the Dionysian crowds roar past them in their radiant life. (GT 1, KSA 1, p. 28-29)

Haydn and Nietzsche could for that sake be describing the same Medieval German festivals. In Nietzsche, these festivals are understood under the label 'Dionysian'; explicitly, the *self-forgetfulness* they impress upon the participants is their most significant quality. Early on in Nietzsche's writings, self-forgetfulness is a positive quality. It will continue to return – in various disguises, more or less subliminally, more or less explicitly and elaborately – into his very latest writings; like (apropos) a Wagnerian leitmotif attached to certain characters, and frequently repeated.

This brief poetizing preliminary brings us straight to the pivotal argument of the present essay. Instead of classifying 'eternal recurrence' as either subjective or objective (as in many standard interpretations promoted over one hundred years of Nietzsche-reception; e.g., as 'anthropological' vs. 'cosmological' in K. Löwith), or as classifying it as either theoretical or ethical (as seen in more recent interpretations; cf. B. Magnus, W. Müller-Lauter, or G. Deleuze), I shall instead classify and categorize 'eternal recurrence' in three alternative main forms, where the first form includes most, if not all, of the standard interpretations. First, 'return' as *simple and mechanical return* of some-*thing*; in Haydn's example, the year. Secondly, 'return' of the same perception or knowledge (the subject appropriating and stabilizing knowledge in repetitious interpretive processes), as in *repetitive interpretation-processes*. Thirdly, 'return' of the self-same moment (indicating an over-joyful neutralization of subjectivity, of the *principium individuationis*, as Nietzsche following Schopenhauer puts it in GT), as *self-repetition of self-presence*.

1.2. Return as Simple and Mechanical Rebirth.

Spring returns with one-year intervals. We will therefore say that the recurrence in Haydn's example has a 'rate of return' of a year; or alternatively, it has a 'one-year frequency.'

However, not all occurrences have one-year frequencies or return-rates. When in *Die fröhliche Wissenschaft* (FW) Nietzsche introduces recurrence as the repetition of "every pain and every joy and every thought and sigh and everything unspeakably small or great in your life" (FW 341, KSA 5, p. 570), the frequency would be in the order of a life (ignoring for now that this particular passage from FW has a famous alternative interpretation). This 'one-life' frequency is also addressed, but less ambivalently, in the Nachlaß from 1884, as well as in *Zarathustra*:

> And when you once again are re-born, then it will not be to a new life or a better life or a similar life, but to the one and only selfsame life which you already now have chosen, in what is smallest and greatest. (Nachlaß 1884, KSA 11, 25[7]).

> I come again, with this sun, with this earth, with this eagle, with this serpent – n o t to a new life or a better life or a similar life: – I come back eternally to this same, selfsame life, in what is greatest as in what is smallest, to teach again the eternal recurrence of all things, – (Za III, "Der Genesende"; KSA 4, p. 276).

So, the 'rate of return' can be of a year or of a life. However, if the thought of recurrence is supposed to address the repetition of certain decisive historical periods and events, the 'rate of return' is again something different. In that case, the rate of return would be in the order of a few millennia. Although I have never seen the view of historical recurrence purported by Nietzsche himself,[456] one often sees it *applied to* Nietzsche. It is for example assumed in the commonplace comparison of Nietzsche's 'circular model of time' to Hegel's 'linear' – the comparison often implying a political critique. In Hegel, the famous *thesis, anti-thesis, synthesis* dialectics supposedly illustrates how conflicting positions in the history of consciousness are eventually resolved in a new overarching position including the old positions, but simultaneously becoming the steppingstone for new conflicts. As such Hegel's model, adopted and 'put back on its feet' by Karl Marx, represents history as a progressive linear development brought to a halt only in the Absolute Spirit (or the Communist Society), while by contrast Nietzsche's model suggests a circular and non-progressive history, being frustratingly in lack of telos.[457] This is understood as not only non-progressive, but also as inherently reactionary, by commentators taking for granted that 'world history' must be the object and 'rate of return' of eternal recurrence. (E.g., Nietzsche's nostalgic yearning for the Ancient Greek Dionysos-cult is projected forwards as the empty ideal for a new future for the resurrected Dionysos, as Habermas criticizes in a variation over the idea.[458])

---

[456] Nietzsche, on the contrary, has in various contexts been explicit about the *irreversibility* of time. In *Schopenhauer als Erzieher*, Nietzsche, adopting the persona of a 'traveller' (who seems for a moment to be his mouthpiece) explicitly rejects the possibility of re-living the same life: "Essentially, every man knows quite well that, being unique [*als ein Unicum*], he will exist in the world only once, and that not even the most strange accident will ever for a second time unify so wonderfully colorful a diversity as we are: he knows this, but hides it as a bad conscience." (UM III, 1; KSA 1, p. 337).

[457] Whereas Nietzsche does not advance the notion of an 'eternal recurrence' of particular historical events or periods, he is frequently advancing an 'anti-Hegelian' doubt in the historical process as *progressive* and *teleological*. Such 'anti-Hegelianism' is succinctly expressed in the following fragment labeled "**Progression** [*Fortschritt*]": "So that we don't deceive ourselves! Time moves forwards – we might believe that all what is in it, also moves forwards . . . that development is a forward-moving development [*Vorwärts-Entwicklung*] . . . This is an illusion, seducing the most sensible person: but the nineteenth century is not an advancement over the sixteenth century [. . .] 'Humankind' ["*Menschheit*"] does not progress, it does not even exist . . . The total aspect [*Gesamtaspekt*] is that of an enormous experimental workshop, where a few things succeed, and innumerable things misfire, where all order, logic, relation and relationships fails." (Nachlaß 1888, KSA 13, 15[8]).

[458] See Vorlesung IV: "Eintritt in der Postmoderne; Nietzsche as Drehscheibe" in Jürgen Habermas, Der Philosophishe Diskurs der Moderne. Zwölf Vorle-

Finally, we notice that according to the so-called 'cosmological interpretation' of eternal recurrence, the rate of the return would be in the order of millions or billions of years. The following is not exactly Nietzsche's model of the universe, but certain recent speculations in contemporary physics could support the idea of recurrence on a cosmological scale. Some physicists speculate that if our universe is a bubble that ultimately bursts or collapses, one must assume that another bubble will eventually emerge (or does already exists in parallel with our current universe) within which a solar system similar to ours will materialize, providing the conditions for life-forms similar to ours. Given sufficiently many 'bubbles,' one bubble will necessarily have the exact same composition as our current 'bubble.' In the realm of infinity, nothing is impossible. We note that the inherent presupposition in this contemporary 'bubble-theory' corresponds to Nietzsche's observation: "In infinite time every possible combination would at some point have been realized once; moreover, it would have been realized an infinite number of times." (Nachlaß 1888, KSA 13, 14[188]).[459] (The theory might also be seen as a variation of Leibniz's immortalized theory of 'the best of all possible worlds' – except for the fact that to Leibniz, the law of 'sufficient reason' would dictate that there could be only *one* such 'best of all worlds.' In other words, we may live in a multi-verse of infinitely many 'bubbles,' but God, in his wisdom, has arranged for only one to be inhabitable.)

Now, the circle of eternity can have different rates of return: a year, a life, a few millennia, or billions of years. Commentators of Nietzsche have typically asked, 'what is recurring in eternal recurrence?' – and have answered by choosing one of the possible 'rates of return.' In this, one has chosen one's object, and consequently, interpretation. Depending on the return-rate one assigns to the doctrine, it is for example interpreted as either 'subjective' or 'objective.' Assigning to the doctrine the return-rate of a year, as in the Haydn example, would give it 'objective' value; so would assigning to the doctrine a return-rate of billions of years. Assigning to the

---

sungen, Frankfurt am Main (Suhrkamp Verlag), 1988, p. 104ff.

[459] Astronomer and Physicist Max Tegmark introduces the bubble-theory in an article from Scientific American. Compare the following statement to Nietzsche: "In infinite space, even the most unlikely events must take place somewhere. There are infinitely many other inhabited planets, including not just one but infinitely many that have people with the same appearance, name and memories as you, who play out every possible permutation of your life choices." Max Tegmark, "Parallel Universes," in: Scientific American, May 2003, p. 41. See also Martin Rees, Our Cosmic Habitat, Princeton (Princeton University Press), 2001.

doctrine the return-rate of a life would give it subjective value; our life or particular 'intensified moments' in our life return.

In this spectrum of interpretations, we move from the cold dark blue to the hot dark red! At one end of this spectrum of interpretations, we thus find the cosmological interpretation as the most 'objective,' while at the other end, we find a 'subjective' interpretation applied to the single individual. There seems to be an interpretation to every taste! However, whatever return-rate we are discussing in the above, they are in all the interpretations addressing what we call 'simple and mechanical return.' Something (a year, a life, a cosmos) runs its course, as if in a circle. It starts in 12 o'clock position, traverses the circular orbit drawing still closer – exhausted and sapped of energy – to the same 12 o'clock position. Here it 'snaps.' Inexplicably and incomprehensibly, that which is dying, in the very instance of its death, is reborn; that which has imploded into nothing, starts over again in an explosion of new energy. The reversal is mechanical and self-propelled. No doubt, the thought is easiest to accept applied to the seasonal rejuvenation of the year. But the thought is also present is contemporary astrophysics as intimated above. If our universe (according to one theory) eventually implodes in a 'big crunch,' then – given that the total amount of mass never diminishes – one surmises that the 'crunch' will reverse itself in a new super-hot 'big bang' explosion, giving rise to a new universe. From birth in 12 o'clock position to death in 12 o'clock position, where everything 'snaps' and life is reborn out of death: a young tiny universe starts its new explosive life.

In one significant attempt to re-interpret recurrence, born out of frustration with the empirical rotation and the incomprehensible 'snap,' some have taken Nietzsche's doctrine beyond the old *objective–subjective* dichotomy, and re-applied it within a *theoretical–practical* dichotomy. Given this modification, the doctrine is no longer seen as *description*, but as a 'practical' or 'ethical' *prescription* of how to live and love one's life. It is submitted to Hume's famous principle that one cannot derive an 'ought' from an 'is,' nor an 'is' from an 'ought.' If the doctrine is 'practical,' it is no longer stating a fact. We can therefore effectively relinquish the circle as a model of empirical return, and with this, the idea of some-*thing* possessing a specific 'rate of return.' Recurrence is now *a question*: 'if you were given the chance, would you be willing to live this life again as the self-same life?' – a question or a suggestion proposed in the hypothetical conditional. It is no longer seen as a statement about material return, but appears rather as an *imperative* entreating the subject to inject into its life love and self-affirmation. It becomes in famous formulations an "existential imperative" for "the being-in-the-world of the Overman." The doctrine is Bernd Magnus and W.

Müller-Lauter's, who have most prominently defended the 'ethical' interpretation,[460] but Gilles Deleuze, and most recently Lawrence Hatab, as well have insisted on the interpretation.[461] Already Heidegger was in fact aware of this normative component of recurrence as introduced in FW 341.[462]

1.3. A Preliminary Introduction to Two Alternative Interpretations of Recurrence.

Over a century of Nietzsche reception, almost exclusively, the literature on Nietzsche's recurrence has been addressing the so-called 'simple and mechanical return.' From George Simmel to recent commentary in especially

---

[460] The formulations are almost identical in Magnus and Müller-Lauter. In Magnus it reads: "[Recurrence] is the emblematic of the attitude of *Übermenschlichkeit* and is the being-in-the-world of *Übermenschen*." Bernd Magnus, Nietzsche's Existential Imperative, Bloomington, London (Indiana University Press), 1978, p. 142. In Müller-Lauter it reads: "The Yes to eternal recurrence is the being-in-the-world of the overman." Wolfgang Müller-Lauter, Nietzsche: His Philosophy of Contradictions and the Contradictions of his Philosophy. Translation, D. J. Parent, Urbana, Chicago (University of Illinois Press), 1999, p. 100. For a critical discussion, see also Günter Abel, Nietzsche: Die Dynamik der Willen zur Macht und die ewige Wiederkehr, Berlin, New York (Walter de Gruyter), 1998, 2nd edition, p. 259 ff.

[461] So Deleuze: "The eternal return gives the will a rule as rigorous as the Kantian one. [. . .] As an ethical thought the eternal return is the new formulation of the practical synthesis: *whatever you will, will it in such a way that you also will its eternal return.*" Gilles Deleuze, Nietzsche and Philosophy. Translation H. Tomlinson. New York (Columbia University Press), 1983, p. 68. See also Hatab, Lawrence: Nietzsche's Life Sentence: Coming to Terms with Eternal Recurrence. London,. New York (Rouledge) 2005. For a critical but sympathetic review of Hatab, see Bornedal, Peter: "Different Kinds of Ecstasy" in Nietzsche Studien, bd. 35. Berlin, New York (Walter de Gruyter), 2006. .

[462] So Heidegger: " 'What would happen *if* one day . . .' The thought is introduced as a question and a possibility. [. . .] Imagine what would happen if in such loneliest loneliness a demon were to steal upon you and confront you with the eternal return of the same: 'The eternal hourglass of existence turning over and over – and you with it, speck of dust!' Nietzsche does not say what would in fact happen. He continues to *question* instead, and he uncovers two alternatives. Would you curse the demon, or would you perceive in him a god. [. . .] Nietzsche does not invoke 'being as a whole.' " Martin Heidegger, Nietzsche vol. II. Translation D. F. Krell, San Francisco (Harper and Row), 1979, 24-25.

1. Introducing Three Different Kinds of Return 443

the Anglo-Saxon tradition, its 'logical feasibility' has been and is still being appraised (generating lots of head-shaking and clever counter-argument). In this essay, we shall allow ourselves to treat it as the *least interesting*, the *least pervasive*, the *least persuasive*, as well as the *least 'scientific'*[463] interpretation of recurrence. The rough outline above of some of the standard manifestations of the interpretation we will therefore regard as sufficient, and we shall permit ourselves to leave them behind in order to concentrate on the two more 'interesting' and 'scientific' alternatives: (i) *Return as Repetitive Interpretation-Process* and (ii) *Return as Self-Repetition of Self-Presence*.

The two interpretations take Nietzsche's 'thought of thoughts' to a new, albeit more abstract, theoretical level. The two interpretations are not completely original. We find them, in various stages of development and introduced more or less self-consciously, in a number of commentators. To mention just a few such commentators – to use them as signposts, giving a first indication of the direction of our analysis – we notice that the first interpretation is anticipated in Heidegger's thinking of recurrence, but it is more fully developed, being carried beyond philosophy's self-reflection of Being, and given universal interpretation-theoretical significance, in Günter Abel's work (– from which work we take the following stipulation as emblematic for the suggested interpretation: "The Recurrence-Thought [*Wiederkunfts-Gedanke*] is essentially of *meaning- and interpretation-logical nature*"[464]). We see traces of the second interpretation in Klossows-

---

[463] We employ here the term with some leniency; approximately as follows: 'scientific' = *an in principle communicable, systematizable, and defensible theoretical position*. This re-application of the term is not, however, completely random and whimsical. We recall that the German *Wissenschaft* and the Scandinavian *videnskab/vetenskab* are broader concepts than the Anglo-Saxon *Science*, frequently applied also in the humanities. In Northern Europe, 'Comparative Literature' comes for example under the label, Literatur*wissenschaft* or Literatur*videnskab*.

[464] See Günter Abel, Nietzsche – Die Dynamik der Willen zur Macht und die ewige Wiederkehr, 2nd edition, Berlin, New York (Walter de Gruyter) 1998, p. 248. Heidegger understands Nietzsche's Will-to-Power and Eternal Recurrence as the latest interpretations of the world as respectively Being and Becoming, Nietzsche taking the interpretation of the world, as it originates with Parmenides and Heraclitus, to its final culmination point. In the early days of Greek thinking, philosophy took a deep breath, held it for over three thousand years, until finally, entering Nietzsche, it can exhale. As such, Nietzsche is thinking "the end" of metaphysics, but thinking still within the metaphysical tradition. His two key concepts are intertwined because "to say that being as a whole 'is' eternal recurrence of the same means that being as a

ki's work on Nietzsche's eternal return, here addressed as a phantasmatic so-called "high tonality of the soul."[465] It is persistently addressed in much of Joan Stambaugh's work; Stambaugh often introducing the interpretation under the label 'the innocence of becoming.'[466]

As I am applying the two sets of interpretation in the present essay, the first set purports to describe the conditions of possibility of *knowledge*, the second purports to describe the conditions of possibility of *pleasure*. Alternatively, if one position means to describe *knowledge-constitution*; the other means to describe *pleasure-constitution* (if Heidegger and Abel tend to focus on 'knowledge-constitution,' Klossowski and Stambaugh tend to focus

---

whole is, as being, in the manner of eternal recurrence of the same." (Heidegger, Nietzsche v. II, loc. cit., p. 199.) To Heidegger, during the 'History of Being,' philosophers have always been asking the question of Being. Their different answers have been formative for our history; our ability, for example, to manipulate nature, for our technological development, and for our essential understanding of our 'historical destiny.' As such, the answer to the question of Being has interpreted human history and self-understanding, but in an interpretation that has always concerned the human *as species* – 'species,' for example, in Feuerbach's sense. Günter Abel, also uniquely emphasizing 'will-to-power-processes' as 'interpretation-processes,' and also coupling these interpreting 'will-to-power-processes' with 'eternal recurrence,' has nonetheless a significantly different analytical project. Abel's 'referent' is not 'Being as a whole'; now the analysis has moved into the territory of the individual's cognitive interaction with the world. The individual certainly *interprets*, but not necessarily himself as 'species,' and not necessarily by articulating – in the form of interpreted Being – a single overarching interpretation formative for his 'historical destiny.' The *mind* interprets; it cannot but interpret, and Nietzsche's thinking becomes essentially a theory of mind. This latter perspective is adopted in the present essay, where the project is to reconcile a concept so 'mysterious' and 'enigmatic' (traditionally understood) as 'eternal recurrence' with insights on the verge of becoming generally accepted in the cognitive sciences and in neuroscience.

[465] The phrase is Klossowski's blanket expression for a psychical 'mood' that to Nietzsche requires articulation in the correspondingly intense thought on return. See Pierre Klossowski, Nietzsche and the Vicious Circle. Translation D. W. Smith, Chicago (The University Press of Chicago), 1997, e.g., pp. 56 & 60.

[466] See the following works by Joan Stambaugh, Nietzsche's Thought of Eternal Return. London, Baltimore (Johns Hopkins University Press), 1972; The Problem of Time in Nietzsche, Lewisburg (Associated University Presses), 1987; The Other Nietzsche, New York (SUNY Press), 1994; finally, the recent article, "All Joys Want Eternity," in: Nietzsche-Studien 33, Berlin, New York (Walter de Gruyter), 2004.

on 'pleasure-constitution'). Therefore, as the two positions are understood in this essay, they both describe certain inherent *cognitive and volitional conditions of possibility in the subject*. We are in other words talking about 'inner-mental-processes.' If 'eternal recurrence' is primarily an attempt to describe processes of knowledge- and pleasure-constitution, these processes would as their *referent* have certain inner-mental operations pertaining to perception, memory, knowledge, will, and desire – i.e., pertaining to *mind*. Pursuing this more discriminating interpretation, the understanding of 'eternal recurrence' as actual and empirical return of some-*thing* will necessarily recede as 'uninteresting' and 'unscientific'; in our context, as a *metaphor* at best.[467]

In the following, we shall suggest that the two aspects of the eternal-recurrence thought, rather than supporting one another, exist in a complementary relationship. As such, they exists as two *opposing* and *irreconcilable* parts, which nevertheless form a universal whole, like oppositions such as violet and yellow; night and day; man and woman; or yin and yang. They are intertwined opposites, existing together, but like the two different faces of the same coin, unable to see, or to 'touch,' one another. The interpretation introduced under the label *Return as Repetitive Interpretation-Process* stands opposed to, but complements, the interpretation under the label *Return as Self-Repetition of Self-Presence*, and vice versa. As a first approximation, one may say that if *Return as Repetitive Interpretation-Process* describes an *epistemological attitude* in the subject, *Return as Self-Repetition of Self-Presence* describes an *aesthetic attitude*; if *Return as Repetitive Interpretation-Process* is an essential will-to-power-manifestation, *Return as Self-Repetition of Self-Presence* is an essential will-to-nothing-manifestation. Will-to-power 'asserts' or 'generates' as its enigmatic counterpart a will-to-nothing. The subject is like encircled by this night and day of two different returns. Let us suggest the following image: the subject is like a rubber band; on the one hand, it stretches itself – far and way beyond itself – to stamp upon its existence an essential interpretation; on the other hand, it always exists under the temptation to slip back to its old essential zero-tension rest-position. (We recall: the subject is like a "camel" that in its final transformation desires to become a "child." (Cf. Za I, "Von den drei Verwandlungen"; KSA 4, p. 29 ff.)). Toward the end of the essay, we shall argue that the two complementary positions can be comprehended within *a*

---

[467] If this can be established, it will imply that some of Nietzsche's commentators have been guilty in 'literalness.' They have studied a metaphorical language as if it is factual and propositional. They have read *Zarathustra* as creationists read the *Book of Genesis*.

single theory of time-consciousness; with this, we hope to give the theory a *universal logical justification and foundation*.

It is probably fair to say that Nietzsche in the eighties was still in the *process* of becoming aware of recurrence as having universal theoretical significance beyond the idea of the simple and mechanical return. Thus, although assessments of Nietzsche's level of awareness must remain speculation, we will in the following assume that we are reconstructing two of the deepest intentions in Nietzsche's thought of thoughts; intentions that he (mostly in the unpublished *Nachlaß*) probes and investigates, but elliptically, and still without full lucidity and without absolute self-consciousness.[468]

One indication of this *maturing* awareness is Nietzsche's search for the adequate *model* for recurrence – was the *circle* in fact its most felicitous configuration? Let this question mark our starting point.

2. Recurrence as Circle or Loop

The standard idea that the formal configuration for Eternal Recurrence is best conceived as a circle finds obvious textual confirmation in Nietzsche's work. It is Nietzsche himself who in *Zarathustra* talks about 'everything coming back' and about eternal recurrence as a 'wheel' and a 'ring.' There is hardly anything more circular than a 'ring.'

---

[468] Many commentators would sympathize with Eugen Fink's frustration, when he observes that Nietzsche's "most profound intuition eludes a conceptual grasp"; that it "lacks a clear conceptual definition and form"; that it "defies the word": "This thought [eternal recurrence] is more implied than truly explicated. Nietzsche appears almost afraid to articulate it. In essence, his reflection defies the word. It is a secret understanding. Nietzsche hesitates and conceals his secret behind increasing walls because his most profound intuition eludes a conceptual grasp. The secret of the fundamental thought remains for itself in mysterious darkness. [. . .] The 'eternal return of the same', Nietzsche's most abysmal thought appears to be ambiguous. It seems that the thought lacks a clear conceptual definition and form. It rather resembles a somber prophecy or an oracular and mystical revelation than a rational conception." (Eugen Fink, Nietzsche's Philosophy. London, New York (Continuum), 2003, pp. 74 & 80).

2. Recurrence as Circle or Loop

> Everything goes, everything comes back; eternally rolls the wheel of being, Everything dies, everything blossoms again; eternally runs the year of being.
> Everything breaks, everything is joined anew; eternally the same house of being is built. Everything parts, everything greets every other thing again; eternally the ring of being remains faithful to itself.
> In every Now, being begins; around every Here rolls the sphere There. The center is everywhere. Bent is the path of eternity. (Za III, "Der Genesende"; KSA 4, p. 272-73).

However, in conflict with this terse and economical introduction of Eternal Recurrence, we are explicitly warned against thinking the time of recurrence as a circle elsewhere in *Zarathustra*. In the more detailed formulation of the Eternal Recurrence from the section, *Vom Gesicht und Räthsel*, the 'dwarf,' suggesting that time is to be thought as a circle, is mistaken and is being taken to task by an impatient Zarathustra. In this narrative representation, Zarathustra at first introduces in an image the three dimensions of time, as traditionally arranged on a line for the past, the present, and the future.

> See this gateway! [*Thorweg!*] Dwarf! I continued to speak: It has two faces. Two roads come here together: no one has ever followed them to their end.
> This long lane backward continues for an eternity. And that long lane forward – that is another eternity.
> They contradict [*widersprechen*] each other, these roads; they bang their heads together [*Stossen sich gerade von den Kopf*]: – and here, in this gateway, is it, they come together. The name of this gateway is inscribed above: 'Moment' [*"Augenblick"*]. (Za III; 'Vom Gesicht und Räthsel'; KSA 4, p. 199).

The dwarf now suggests that instead of conceiving time as two eternal lines pointing forwards and backwards, one should understand it rather as a circle, and it is this conception that Zarathustra angrily rejects as simplistic. Zarathustra instead describes a configuration that has all the attributes of a *loop*.

> Must not whichever thing c a n run, have run down this lane before? Must not whichever thing c a n happen. have already happened, been done, passed by, before?
> And if everything has already been there before: what do you think, dwarf, of this moment? Must not this gateway, too, have been there before?
> And are not all things knotted together so firmly that this moment draws after it a l l things that are to come? T h e r e f o r e – – itself too?
> For whatever of all things c a n run its course: also into this long lane o u t w a r d, – it m u s t run it once more. (ibid.)

Only in a loop can that which sinks back into the past, and that which runs off into distant future return to the self-same moment. The circle cannot fulfill this requirement. If we imagine that we bent the lines of past and future into a circle, they would indeed eventually 'meet' or 'bang their heads together,' but not in the moment – and this is required from Nietzsche's passage. If we bent these two lines into a circle, they would in fact meet 'opposite' the moment. This is easy enough to visualize: we imagine the *moment* in 12 o'clock position; to bend two lines over that pivoting point would eventually cause them to 'meet' ('bang their heads together') in 6 o'clock position. Therefore, we believe that the geometry that is in this context underpinning Nietzsche's 'thought of thoughts' must be the loop; i.e., an '8' tipped over; i.e., the following age-old symbol of infinity:

That which runs back into the past, and that which runs off into the future, comes back to the moment only when we bend the lines of past and future over and above themselves, to let them tack on to each other in the 'gateway,' the moment, the intersection of the model. The 'ring' of eternal recurrence is two rings; the 'wheel' two wheels.[469]

But does it make any difference? Does it matter whether we think eternal recurrence as a circle or a loop? – It seems that applying the adequate formal configuration to Nietzsche's thought effectively presents it with a new level of clarity, where oftentimes it is presented as an irresolvable and obscure paradox. In a perceptive commentator like Joan Stambaugh, the bafflement over this Nietzschean notion of time is explicit and acknowledged:

---

[469] In an article from a recent issue of Nietzsche-Studien, Michael Skowron comes precariously close to suggesting the loop as an immanent figure underlying Nietzsche's thinking, without ever taking his insights into explicit territory. Skowron compares the 'gateway' from *Zarathustra* with the 'hourglass' from *fröhliche Wissenschaft* (341), and comments: "The image of the hourglass with its two orbits [*Kreisen*] that are joined to each other in a narrow passage, corresponds to the two eternities, which in the gateway 'Moment' knock their heads together. As such also the gateway has "two faces." [. . .] The face of the moment is a Janus-faced two-face [*ein Janusköpfiges Doppel-Gesicht*]. If past and future are eternities, must not also the moment between them, simultaneously joining them together, be eternal?" Michael Skowron, "Zarathustra-Lehren: Übermensch, Wille zur Macht, Ewige Wiederkunf," in: Nietzsche-Studien 33, Berlin, New York (Walter de Gruyter), 2004, p. 78.

This gateway has two faces, one toward the long lane continuing backward for an eternity (the past), the other toward the long lane continuing 'outward' for an eternity (the future). These two roads come together in the moment. They bump into each other. No one has ever gone to the end of these two roads. When they meet in the moment, they "contradict each other," what is the meaning with this?[470]

Stambaugh first thinks *the line*, and according to this configuration, it is impossible for anything running off backwards and forwards to ever "bump into each other" or "contradict each other." This *is* truly impossible, as correctly emphasized! Stambaugh also understands that applying the circle to the gateway-image will not resolve the conundrum, because if one bent the lines of past and future into a circle they would indeed "bump into each other," but not in the moment – as we noted above, and Stambaugh concurs. Stambaugh must reject also this model: "For Zarathustra, time is *not* a circle. [. . .] Past and future come together in the moment, not out there (where?) in an eternal continuance directed *away from* the moment."[471] So far, so good! However, since Stambaugh never suggest any alternative formal configuration – which we now argue would have to be the loop – she also never gets beyond the conundrum. Consequently, her 'solution' becomes, significantly and symptomatically, a pseudo- or a non-solution. After correctly realizing that neither in the figure of a line nor in that of a circle, past and future could possibly "bump into each other" in the moment, she declares that the "meeting" of the three temporal dimensions *has* always-already happened, *is* always-already happening, in the self-same moment: "Past and future meet in the moment, and nowhere else. Past and future, and thus all time, thus the eternal return itself, are *in the moment*."[472] This reveals a fine understanding for the critical importance of the 'moment' in Nietzsche's thinking, but it does not explain the gateway-image, and it does not account for *how* three dimensions possibly *come together* in the moment. Three dimensions obviously do not 'meet' if they are in fact the same, and have been the same all along. The same certainly does not 'bump into each other.' Two balls may bump into each other, but one ball does not bump into itself.

Thinking *the loop*, the conundrum is solved, and everything appears simpler.

---

[470] Stambaugh, Nietzsche's Thought, loc. cit., p. 37-38.
[471] Stambaugh, ibid., p. 37-38.
[472] Stambaugh, ibid., p. 41.

3. Return as a Repetitive Interpretation-Process. Two Cases.

3.1. First Case: Sensation and Perception.

3.1.1. Knowledge as Familiarizing the Strange.

The loop is also the figure we sometimes see performed in figure skating, the skater being the apt metaphor for a quantum of force traversing the given path, fluently gliding from left to right back to left. This movement uniquely applies to the form of return we label a *repetitive interpretation-process*. Here the metaphorical movement 'from left to right back to left' illustrates the interpretive movement from internal to external back to internal. We experience in the interpretation-process how the internal becomes intertwined with the external in that very process.

In this context, we are talking about the subject-object relation. In the course of interpreting, the subject-object relation is obviously not suspended, but the object is being *appropriated* by the interpreting subject – *humanized* is Nietzsche's usual expression. So, the object as thing stays where is it as thing, i.e., *outside* the subject, but in the loop of interpretation, it becomes a thing with meaning, it can be 'understood.' An interpretation can therefore not touch a thing, it can only touch a subject. (An interpreted tree is not a new tree, and interpretation does nothing to the tree – the interpreted tree does not shake its branches and shiver in pride over its newly won meaning; only a subject can shiver in awe under the majestic crown of the tree.) Therefore, what in this logic 'returns as the same' is exactly not the thing-like object (this object goes nowhere); what 'returns as the same' is the subject, since it returns as itself in the interpreted thing. *As such* all interpretation is an 'eternal recurrence of the same.'

When we say that '*the subject* returns as itself' we are employing a shortcut-expression. 'The subject' is here the label of the relevant schemata and taxonomies that control the perception of the subject's outer world. These schemata and taxonomies are not exactly the subject's private depositories. Clearly, they must have been internalized and consolidated in the individual's ontogenetic past, but if, through genealogy, they can be traced back to an origin, that origin does not coincide with the subject's private self. The medium by which we storage such depositories, both transcending the individual, yet a part of individual immanence, is *language*. As such, they enable the subject to recognize an impression as being such and such, being this and not that, following this and preceding that, etc. Without such schemata and taxonomies, every impression would be what Nietzsche calls 'strange.'

> The Origin of our notion 'Knowledge' [*Erkenntnis*]. [. . .] What do they [the common people] want when they want 'knowledge'? Nothing more than this: Something strange [*Fremdes*] is to be reduced to something familiar [*Bekanntes*]. And we philosophers – have we by knowledge ever understood anything different from this? [. . .] Look, isn't our need for knowledge precisely this need for the familiar, the will to uncover under everything strange, unusual, and questionable something that no longer disturbs us? Is it not the instinct of fear that bids us to know? (FW 355, KSA 5, p. 594).

Nietzsche sums up his insight in the neat, *"was bekannt ist, ist erkannt"* (ibid.). Recurrence of the same is inscribed into this elegant phrase: only when the familiar [*bekanntes*] recurs as the same in the other, the other becomes known [*erkannt*]. Language is the medium by which we make the 'strange' familiar, and consequently known.

Already Francis Bacon would realize that 'knowledge is power'; however, knowledge is power in a manner entirely different for Bacon and Nietzsche. To Nietzsche, knowledge is power because it reassures us in our 'herd-instinct'; it reduces what is strange and other to what is familiar *for us*. It is ultimately a reaction to deep-seated fears.

> There is not, as Kant supposed, a sense of causality [*Causalitäts-Sinn*]. One is surprised, one is disturbed – one desires something familiar one can hold on to. As soon as something old is pointing us into the new, we are calmed. The so-called causality-instinct [*Causalitäts-Instinkt*] is merely the fear of the unfamiliar and the attempt to uncover in it something familiar [. . .] The calculability of an event does not consist in the fact that a rule is followed or a necessity obeyed, or that a law of causality was projected by us into all that happens: it consists in the recurrence of 'identical cases.' (Nachlaß 1888, KSA 13, 14[98]).

> Psychological explanation. – To trace something unknown back to something known is alleviating, soothing, gratifying and gives moreover a feeling of power. Danger, disquiet, anxiety attend the unknown – the first instinct is to eliminate these distressing states. First principle: any explanation is better than none. (GD, 'Die vier grossen Irrthümer' 5, KSA 6, p. 93).

This process of 'familiarization' is, first, *a process of interpretation*; second, *a will-to-power-process*, and third, *recurrence of the same*. We appropriate (i.e., make ourselves masters of) what is strange, dangerous, Other – in this appropriating will-to-power-process interpreting the *Other* as the *Same* (i.e., let the old return in the new), as a "recurrence of identical cases."

The thinking of 'familiarization' can be more precisely captured by the following three formulaic expressions, all of them suggesting the aspiration to humanize (i.e., *mastering by interpreting*) a hostile, dangerous, and inexplicable exterior world. The subject engaged in generating meaning is invariably: 1) *reducing the other to the same*; 2) *familiarizing the strange*; and, since these two expressions indicate the same process and operation, 3) *transforming some unknown 'x' into some known 'X'*.[473]

As we saw in the previous *Chapter 4*, the process is typically in Nietzsche applied to explanations of how we become conscious of sensations, bearing in mind that sensations can be both exogenous and endogenous. Sensations constitute everything from the perception of sunlight reflected in water, reading a page in a book, the smart of a bee sting, stomach ache, the taste of chocolate, the sound of water dashing upon the shore, the smell of meat being grilled, to . . . the list is of course endless. In all of these endless cases, we invariably *Reduce the Other to the Same, Familiarize the Strange*, or *Transform some Unknown 'x' into some Known 'X'*.

3.1.2. Time-Reversal and 'Delayed' Perception.

As we noted in *Chapters 3* and *4*, in the tradition of the British Empiricists, primarily Locke and Hume, our sensations travel as in a straight line from the outside to the inside where they are nested as 'ideas.' The senses are seen as entrances for material that will eventually fill up and furnish the mind. Once sense-material is inside, it can be manipulated and combined at our pleasure to form imagined objects. (We can imagine a 'golden mountain' even if no golden mountain exists, because we have had the sensory experiences of 'gold' and 'mountain' – as Hume argues.[474]) This conception is compelling in its simplicity; sense-material travels from outside to inside along a linear trajectory. Moreover, according to the conception, we suppose a one-to-one relationship between the inside images and the outside objects – and if inside images are 'complex,' the different parts of which

---

[473] For a brief history of 'X' in the philosophical literature, see the article, Werner Stegmaier, "Das Zeichen X in der Philosophie der Moderne," in: Werner Stegmaier (ed.): Zeichen-Kunst, Frankfurt am Main (Surkamp Verlag), 1999, pp. 231ff.

[474] "When we think of a golden mountain, we only joined two consistent ideas, *gold* and *mountain*, with which we were formerly acquainted." David Hume, An Enquiry Concerning Human Understanding, Indianapolis, Cambridge (Hackett Publishing Company), 1993, p. 11.

3. Return as a Repetitive Interpretation-Process

they are composed still have a one-to-one relationship with outside objects (cf. the 'golden mountain'). Finally, since the trajectory is linear, chronology and causality too is firmly established between the outside and the inside; the outside is first, the inside second; the outside is the cause, the inside is the effect.

In Nietzsche, this linear trajectory has been replaced with the loop. Nietzsche challenges the Empiricist conception in a number of aphorisms, for example in the following two notes from 1884 and 1888, which we already encountered in *Chapter 4*; now, we shall revisit them from the perspective of Eternal Recurrence.

> Like in dreams we look for the cause for a canon-shot and first then h e a r the shot (that therefore a time-reversal [*Zeit-Umkehrung*] has taken place: this t i m e - r e v e r s a l   a l w a y s   o c c u r s, also when we are awake. The 'cause' is imagined [*imaginiert*] a f t e r   t h e   ' d e e d.' I mean, our e n d s   a n d   m e a n s are consequences of a process?? [*Vorganges??*]) . . . We only a c c e p t the canon-shot when we have figured out from what possibility it originated. [. . .] Also every so-called sense-perception [*Sinneswahrnehmung*] is preceded by a j u d g m e n t, which – before the process 'enters' consciousness – is a f f i r m e d or d e n i e d [*bejaht oder verneint*]. (Nachlaß 1884, KSA 11, 26[35]).

> The phenomenalism of the 'inner world.'
> The chronological inversion [*die Chronologische Umdrehung*], so that the cause enters consciousness later than the effect.
> we have learned that pain is projected to a part of the body without being situated there
> we have learned that sense impressions naively supposed to be conditioned by the outer world [*Außenwelt*] are, on the contrary, conditioned by the inner world [*Innenwelt*]; that we are always unconscious of the real activity of the outer world . . .
> The fragment of the outer world of which we are conscious is born after an effect [*nachgeboren nach der Wirkung*] from outside has impressed [*geübt*] itself upon us, and is subsequently projected [*Nachträglich Projiziert*] as its 'cause.'
> In the phenomenalism of the 'inner world' we invert the chronological order of cause and effect.
> The fundamental fact of 'inner experience' is that the cause is imagined after the effect has taken place [*die Ursache imaginiert wird, nachdem die Wirkung erfolgt ist . . .*]. (Nachlaß 1888, KSA 13, 15[90]; cf. WM 479).[475]

As we emphasized in *Chapter 4*, it is critical here to read Nietzsche with some caution; it is not his postulate that we *create* or *invent* the outer world *from within*, implying that the outer world is nothing but our *idea* (in Berkeley's sense) or *Vorstellung* (in Schopenhauer's sense). If this were the case,

---

[475] See also Schlimgen's comments on the fragment: Erwin Schlimgen, Nietzsches Theorie des Bewußtseins, Berlin, New York (Walter de Gruyter), 1999, p. 134-135.

Nietzsche would be defending a model as simplistic as the model of the British Empiricists, but just in the reverse; i.e., a linear trajectory, where the line was simply conceived to travel from inside to outside. It is clear that Nietzsche tries to avoid this equally unattractive interpretation, when in the fragment from 1888 he continues: "The fragment of the outer world of which we are conscious is born after an effect from outside has impressed itself upon us, and is subsequently projected as its 'cause.'" (ibid.). In this passage, the outside world is not conceived as *idea* or *Vorstellung*. The outside world explicitly impresses itself upon our sense-organs as raw sense-material; thereupon the impression is interpreted, as such made 'familiar' [*bekanntes*] – enabling us to consciously perceive the material. The *interpreted perception* we see as 'outside'; however, it is intertwined with our 'inside.'[476]

It is the proposed '*Zeit-Umkehrung*' or '*Chronologische Umdrehung*' in this conception that we depict in the figure of a loop. Something is entering the loop's 'right' side, runs its course from 'right' to 'left' back to its point of origin, *before* it is fully *interpreted*. Given this *essential interpretive nature* of the loop of our selves, *some unknown 'x' is transformed into some known 'X.'* This process helps us to *characterize* a sensation (exogenous or endogenous) that is at first *uncharacterized*. As an illustration, let us here suggest an analysis of how the endogenous sensation 'thirst' is transformed from unknown to known.[477] *First*, thirst announces itself as blind and confused 'raw' sensation – it is so far an unknown x-sensation (or maybe it is a multifarious sequence of sensations extremely difficult, probably impossible, to decipher as such). *Secondly*, this announcement triggers an associative chain of images of, for instance, glasses of water, oneself drink-

---

[476] The fragment from 1888, included in *The Will to Power*, has been – together with Nietzsche's early essay "On Truth and Lies in an Extra-Moral Sense" – crucial in the formulation of American Deconstruction. It is cited by Paul de Man in *Allegories of Reading* (see Paul de Man, Allegories of Reading, New Haven, London (Yale University Press), 1979, p.107), and subsequently by Jonathan Culler in his influential *On Deconstruction* (see Jonathan Culler, On Deconstruction. Theory and Criticism after Structuralism, Ithaca, NY (Cornell University Press), 1982, p. 86); it re-appeared in Wayne Klein's De Manian commentary to Nietzsche's early work (Wayne Klein, Nietzsche and the Promise of Philosophy, New York (State University of New York Press), 1997).

[477] My example suffers from what examples usually suffer from, simplification and abstraction; it is unlikely that it describes the actual processes as they occur in the mind, but it does approximately represent Nietzsche's way of thinking these processes.

ing, etc. *Thirdly*, it evokes the silent thought depicting the *cause* of thirst, say, 'because I need water, I feel thirst.' *Finally*, it is pronounced in the fullfledged sentence 'I am thirsty' – as known X-sensation. In pronouncing the sentence, 'I am thirsty,' the unknown x-sensation is identified or 'characterized.' If one was not truly thirsty while having the blind x-sensation, one is after having *articulated* the sensation *positively thirsty*. The sensation has become *known* or '*characterized.*' Thus, even though Nietzsche usually suggests that the strange may be identified or 'interpreted' in any signsystem, the *word* has a unique ability to familiarize the strange; that is, to transform the unknown 'x' into some known 'X'.[478]

In the fragment, we find Nietzsche suggesting an example structurally similar to our own. A 'simple man feels unwell' – but only after he has figured our *why*! "'I feel unwell' – such a judgment presupposes a great an late neutrality of the observer; the simple man always says: this or that makes me fell unwell – he makes up his mind about his feeling unwell only when he has seen a reason for feeling unwell." (Nachlaß 1888,

---

[478] It is especially by means of language, but not exclusively, that humans acquire the ability to schematize inner experiences. It is required that the 'strange' is re-interpreted into something familiar and already known, but this re-interpretation could take place in any sign-system. In the following passage Nietzsche talks about '*a* language,' not '*language*' or '*the* language': "'Inner experience' [*"innere Erfahrung"*] enters our consciousness only after it has found a language the individual understands ... i.e., a translation of a condition into a condition more familiar [*bekanntere*] to him – 'to understand' means merely: to be able to express something new in the language of something old and familiar." (Nachlaß 1888, KSA bd. 13, 15[90]; cf. WM 479). We must assume then that when employing '*a* language' Nietzsche believes that we are engaging any available sign-system in order to familiarize the strange; possibly also pictorial sign-systems; possibly also associative chains of images, as in our dream and fantasy worlds. This assumption finds support in Günter Abel's observation: "There is no reason to adopt the thesis that we have to limit our concept of mental representation, as well as generally the question of the relationships between consciousness, mind, and world to linguistic systems and forms in a narrow sense. [...] Linguistic and propositional representation-symbols were never the only means for mental, imaginary representations and presentations. A comprehensive theory about human consciousness, mind, thinking, and action requires the inclusion also of non-linguistic, as well as of non-propositional sign and interpretation systems; (that is, e.g., graphical, diagrammatical, or pictorial systems)." Günter Abel, "Bewußtsein – Sprache – Natur. Nietzsches Philosophie des Geistes," in: Nietzsche-Studien 30. Berlin, New York (Walter de Gruyter), 2001, p. 39.

KSA 13, 15[90]). The simple man feels unwell, but he needs a reason, a cause, before he can be sure of feeling unwell. In our example, as well as in Nietzsche's, the sensation is first bind sensation, or so-called x-sensation, and is as such not yet recognized. Only when the subject has found a reason, blind sensation is transformed into recognized sensation, or so-called X-sensation.

We notice that blind sensation, or x-sensation, stands to articulated sensation, or X-sensation, as unconscious to conscious, as unstructured reality to structured reality, as multifarious super-abundant reality to simplified and interpreted reality. Furthermore, it is appropriate here to notice that x-sensation is *not identical* to the Kantian *Ding-an-sich*. It is *not* beyond our perceptive possibilities, it is very much *there* as being 'received,' albeit 'received' in a confused and distracted manner. Perhaps it is accurate to determine x-sensation as *received* sensation, and X-sensation as *perceived received* x-sensation; language gives us here a number of options; one might also evoke Leibniz's old distinction between 'perceived' and 'apperceived' reality.

3.1.3. Living in the Mirror of Consciousness.

In *Die fröhliche Wissenschaft* Nietzsche continues in aphorism 354 an insight that was originally Leibniz's. In the *New Essays on Human Understanding*,[479] Leibniz had observed that we do not perceive the world as consciously as we tend to believe. Due to either the habitualness or superabundance of impressions, we become conscious of only a fraction of our surrounding world. As mentioned in our previous chapters, reality is too abundant, too heterogeneous and multifaceted for the human to process, and the human being is therefore always subjected to an information-overload that it has to reduce and simplify in order to obtain any information at all. As said, in Nietzsche as in Leibniz, we suffer under *too much reality*.[480]

If now this was granted, according to what principle does our perception eventually 'lighten up' the world enfolding us? – Leibniz would say that at-

---

[479] G. W. Leibniz, New Essays on Human Understanding. Translated & edited by J. Bennett and P. Ramnant, Cambridge (Cambridge University Press), 1982.

[480] For a discussion of this simplification or 'abbreviation' of reality, compare to Werner Stegmaier, Nietzsches 'Genealogie der Moral', Darmstadt (Wissenschaftliche Buchgesellschaft), 1994; and Werner Stegmaier, "Weltabkürzungskunst. Orientierung durch Zeichen," in: Josef Simon (ed.), Zeichen und Interpretation, Frankfurt am Main (Suhrkamp Verlag), 1994. Also our previous *Chapter 2*.

tentive perception requires *memory*. In the history of metaphysics, the relationship had usually been conceived the other way round: memory would seem in some obvious sense to require perception; we seem to remember only what we have perceived; what else would there be to remember? This was how John Locke, whom Leibniz in his *New Essays* is responding to, had conceived matters. Now, Leibniz says instead: "*Memory is needed for attention*: when we are not alerted, so to speak, to pay heed to certain of our own present perceptions, we allow them to slip by unconsidered and even unnoticed. But if someone alerts us to them straight away, [. . .] then *we remember them* and are aware of just having had some sense of them."[481]

We know that when we are accompanied by someone, she needs to alert us to what she sees before we have the same perception as she. Now, we extend this observation to our solitary selves. Also when walking about without accompaniment, our inner self needs to alert us to perceptions. In both cases, someone (or something) must tell us 'look at that!' We are made aware of our perceptions only when alerted to them, even if the interval between the actual impression and the alert is infinitesimal. What alerts us is *memory*; it tells us 'remember, you just saw a car,' as the necessary precondition for seeing the car, even if the car is still there, passing me by in the same instance as I remember to look at it; I *remember to see*.[482] From the immediate past, memory informs present perception. This would be the first mental mechanism for stabilizing and fixating a world of becoming: I see, and become aware of, *something as something*.

In Leibniz as well as in Nietzsche, perception proper is therefore *delayed*; impressions have to traverse a path (which we here illustrate as a loop), before consciousness becomes fully aware of them. The perceived outer-world is therefore the *end-product of a process*. That which stands

---

[481] Leibniz: *New Essays*, loc. cit., p. 54; my italics.
[482] To some readers' mind, the phrase may sound paradoxical and absurd; but it is plain enough! I believe that everyone has had the experience of having had to *remind themselves to see*. If in the supermarket, I walk idle around, among an abundance of articles, I see explicitly only a small fraction. Only in a few cases does my perception interact with the memory of an object. Not always do I see with noticing awareness the chocolate-bar, but when eventually I do (besides 'seeing' it in empty perception), a process starts where I start recalling various qualities about chocolate, its taste, texture, etc. We notice, as a typical shopping experience, that oftentimes one has *to tell oneself to remember to see*. One has the hunch that one needs something in the section for dairy products, and not *until then* does one start to *remember to see* the abundance of dairy products, hopeful that one will eventually also see the product needed.

opposed to us – the *perceived* outer-world – is therefore, as Nietzsche states, "our work":

> The reversal of time: we believe that the outer-world [*Außerwelt*] is the cause of the effect it has on us [*ihrer Wirkung auf uns*], but we have t r a n s f o r m e d its actual [*thatsächliche*] and unconsciously processed effect i n t o outer-world [*zur Außerwelt verwandelt*]: that, which stands opposed to us, is our work, which only works on us retroactively [*zurückwirkt*]. It needs time before it is finished, but the time is so small [*klein*]. (Nachlaß 1884, KSA 11, 26[44]).

In aphorism 354 from FW, Nietzsche elaborates on Leibniz's observation. Referring explicitly to Leibniz, he remarks: "We could think, feel, will, remember, and also 'act' in every sense of the term, and yet none of all this would have to 'enter our consciousness' [*in's Bewusstsein zu treten*] (as one says metaphorically) [*wie man im Bilde sagt*]." (FW 354; KSA 3, p. 590). 'Enter consciousness' is here a metaphor, an image [*Bilde*]; something can either 'enter' our consciousness or 'stay outside.' If it 'stays outside,' it is in Nietzsche's sense 'unconscious.' In Nietzsche as in Leibniz, we talk about a sight that, although it is immediately *there* to be seen, is still not seen with awareness. In this 'unconscious' mode, we *see*, but oblivious to the seen – the *obliviously seen* is not an object of *reflection*.

Reflection, originally, is also a metaphor. It implies that the world is doubled in *original* and *image of the original* in such a way that the original is 'reflected' in consciousness as image. Consciousness is consequently like a mirror. Nietzsche's initial question is, what do we need the mirror for? "All of life would be possible without, as it were, seeing itself in the mirror [*Spiegel*]; and still today, the predominant part of our lives actually unfolds without this mirroring. [. . .] F o r w h a t do we need consciousness at all [*Wozu überhaupt Bewusstsein*] when it is basically superfluous?" (FW 354, KSA 3, p. 590). Nietzsche's question addresses the peculiarity that, being conscious, we seem to see *twice*. First, we see the world as it presents itself as appearance to our (so to speak) 'external' eyes; thereupon, we see the image of the world again with our (so to speak) 'internal' eyes. Accordingly, we assume that we have a set of eyes directed outwards toward the world as presentation, but, in addition, that we have a second set of eyes mounted at the inside of our skull, directed towards the images of the world we have received from external perception. Consequently, we see 'twice' when we see these images as in the internal mirror. "Consciousness always implies a double mirroring [*eine doppelte Spiegelung*] – there is nothing immediate [*Unmittelbares*]." (Nachlaß 1885, KSA 12, 1[54]).

But again, what would we need the mirror for? Why *re-flection* [orig.: bending back; throwing back]? In Nietzsche's Nachlaß from the years when

3. Return as a Repetitive Interpretation-Process

he starts working on *Die fröhliche Wissenschaft*, (1880-81), we find several attempts to provide a more detailed answer to this question. First and foremost, according to Nietzsche, it is always indispensable to human survival and self-perseverance to stabilize a world in flux; the *mirror of consciousness* is doing this important job.

> All relationships, which are so important to us, are m i r r o r - i m a g e s [*Figuren auf dem Spiegel*], not the truth. All distance is mirror-optic [*Optik auf dem Spiegel*], not the truth. [The statement,] 'There is no world where there is no mirror,' is nonsense. But all our relationships, however exact they may be, are human descriptions, n o t t h e w o r l d . [. . .] It is not appearance, not deception, but a cryptogram [*chifferschrift*] in which an unknown state of affairs expresses itself. (Nachlaß 1880, KSA 9, 6[429])

> We speak, as if there were e n d u r i n g t h i n g s, and our sciences speak only of such things. But an enduring thing exists only according to h u m a n o p t i c ; from this we cannot free ourselves. The becoming of something, a movement in-itself is completely incomprehensible to us. We c a n o n l y m o v e e n d u r i n g t h i n g s [*S e i e n d e D i n g e*] – in this, our world-image depends on the mirror. [. . .] If we now try to consider/look at [*betrachten*] the mirror in itself, then we discover only things. If we try to comprehend the things, they ultimately only come back in the mirror. (Nachlaß 1880, KSA 9, 6[433])

> For a s u b j e c t to exist at all, something enduring must exist and likewise there must exist equality and similarity. [Otherwise,] the a b s o l u t e l y d i f f e r e n t in perpetual change would not be arrested, and nothing would arrest it; it would flow away like rain on a stone. [. . .] The mirror always suppose [*setzt . . . voraus*] something enduring. – But now I believe: the subject could emerge simultaneously to the emergence of the error of equality. (Nachlaß 1881, KSA 9, 11[268])

In this 'mirror-stage' of Nietzsche's, the prehistoric hominid is transformed into a *subject*. In the inner mirror in which we see the world *again*, we see *something as something*; we commit the 'error' of equalizing a world in flux, a world of becoming, and emerge after the process as *subjects*, that is, as equalizers, falsifiers, simplifiers.[483]

Nietzsche's world of becoming, the world in its own self-presence, gives rise to no sense of time and space. Not until the world in flux is presented as entities arranged next-to- and after-one-another, does a world of identities and similarities emerge; a world that can be organized according to the three parameters, time, space, and causality.

---

[483] Since this 'error' is constitutional to our subjectivity, it is not an 'error' that we should desperately try to 'correct.' It is obviously part of our evolutionary history, and as such, as Nietzsche emphasizes time and again, an error 'necessary for life.'

> First the after-one-another [*Nacheinander*] produces the sense of t i m e [*Zeitvorstellung*]. Let us suppose that we did not experience cause and effect, but rather a continuum; in that case we would not believe in time. [. . .] A continuum of force is w i t h o u t a f t e r - o n e - a n o t h e r [*N a c h e i n a n d e r*] and w i t h o u t n e x t - t o - o n e - a n o t h e r [*N e b e n e i n a n d e r*]. Without after-one-another and next-to-one-another there is no becoming f o r u s, no multiplicity [*Vielheit*]. (Nachlaß 1881, KSA 9, 11[281]).

Nietzsche's mental mirror is thus doing more than just 'mirroring' – it does not produce an exact double of the world it mirrors, in which case it would do nothing but replicate the flow of impressions, which our sense-apparatus receive. Instead, Nietzsche's mirror is arranging, organizing, and equalizing the flow of impressions. As such, the 'mirror' is a metaphor for what Nietzsche in other contexts describes as a 'simplification-apparatus.' *Consciousness, mirroring, simplifying* are all attempts to describe the one and same fundamental operation: the necessity of bringing order into an abundance of received impressions. In the course of human evolution, the development of a 'mirroring' consciousness has become an advantage.

If we can extricate ourselves from the postmodernist understanding of language as a 'gray blanket' that covers up the world in its self-presence and transforms it into 'signifiers,' then Nietzsche's 'mirror' is language (or more precisely, a *sign-system*, which can be of either purely linguistic or general semiological nature). Nietzsche's 'mirror' is an excellent metaphor exactly because we in the mirror still see the reflection of the original – nothing is truly lost and it is definitely not 'hidden' in the mirror; and yet, we can accept that in the mirror-image an infinitely deep world has been captured within the 'simplifying' two-dimensional frame of the mirror. Nietzsche's mirror does not 'cover' the world; it sees it *again*, but through a linguistic/semiological apparatus that makes everything simpler, easier, and plainer – and finally, an apparatus that makes communication possible.[484]

---

[484] Originally, Nietzsche's prehistoric hominid would communicate thoughts, feelings, or perceptions neither to itself nor to anyone else. Gradually, however, in the course of evolution, this uniquely private creature develops a 'consciousness' in synchrony with its need for communication. For the sake of survival, the early human must learn to *name* impressions. Impressions would thus have to be 'taken in,' to 'enter consciousness' (they could no longer 'stay outside'). Furthermore, they would have to be *held on to* and *looked upon once and again* – i.e., 'memorized' and 'retrieved from memory' – until they stabilized as identifiable images that could as such be labeled, and finally communicated. In this process, the formerly so private self evolved into a social self. "It seems to me that the subtlety and strength of consciousness is always related to a person's (or an animal's) a b i l i t y t o c o m m u n i -

3. Return as a Repetitive Interpretation-Process 461

In this understanding of the mechanism of perception, perception has become *re*-interpretation; it sees again. The external world that is encountered in the impression of an object, is 'taken back,' 'held on to,' and 'looked upon' before it is properly perceived. The object is thus seen with a certain delay. We notice that as such the impression follows the path of our loop before it is properly perceived: it is first sensed and taken back into our memory-systems, where it is adjusted according to our inner mental mirror; thereupon it shoots out from these inner recesses, becoming finally a properly perceived object. From the right side of the loop it travels to the left side, and then back to the right side; in this itinerary 'repeating what already

---

cate [*Mittheilungs-Fähigkeit*]; and the ability to communicate, in turn, to the need to communicate [*Mittheilungs-Bedürftigkeit*]. [. . .] Consciousness in general has developed only under the pressure of the need to communicate; at the outset, consciousness was necessary, was useful, only between human and human. [. . .] Consciousness is essentially only a relations-net [*Verbindungsnetz*] between human and human. [. . .] The solitary and predatory person would not have needed it. [. . .] As the most endangered animal, he needed help and protection, he needed equal beings; he had to express his misery, to be able to make himself understood – and for all this, he first and foremost needed 'consciousness'; that is, simply to 'know' what distressed him, to 'know' how he felt, to 'know' what he thought. For to repeat: man, like every living creature, always thinks but does not know it; the thinking which becomes conscious is only the smallest part of it, let's say the shallowest, worst part – for only conscious thinking takes place in words, that is, in communication symbols; and this fact discloses the origin of consciousness. In short, the development of language and the development of consciousness [. . .] go hand in hand. (FW 354; KSA 3, p. 591-92). Originally, we would be "unknown to ourselves," and this would have bothered nobody; on the contrary, it would only indicate a certain measure of health and strength. Now – past the dazzle of these wonderful prehistoric days – modern man tries to 'understand,' tries to force an encounter with this his unique individuality, encouraged by the evident proximity with which he seems to be living with himself. Humans try to turn the tool of knowledge toward themselves; they try to appropriate themselves as the *Same*. They direct this tool toward their own subjectivity in an attempt of self-explanation, self-interpretation, and self-appropriation. However, the unique is never expressible by means of the average. Our individuality escapes us, because it is not expressible by means of a tool that everyone can take up. As well as in Wittgenstein, there is in Nietzsche no 'private language.' For an extended discussion of FW 354, see also Stegmaier, Werner: "Nietzsches Zeichen" Nietzsche-Studien 29. New York, Berlin (Walter de Gruyter), 2000, p. 52ff.

is.' The impression has as such been through an interpretation-process, and the properly perceived object emerges as the interpreted impression. Something as elementary as perception is an example of *eternal recurrence of the same*: "Memory maintains the habit of the old interpretations, i.e., of erroneous causality – so that the 'inner experience' has to contain within it the consequences of all previous false causal fictions. *Our 'outer world' as we project it every moment is indissolubly tied to the old error of the ground.*" (Nachlaß 1888, KSA bd. 13, 15[90]; cf. WM 479; my italics).

Understood in this way, 'eternal recurrence' in no longer a blind, mechanical, self-propelled rhythm (e.g., year follows year, and spring replaces spring, *ad infinitum*), it is rather a fundamental interpretation-mechanism. It is only after a circular interpretation-process, gaining its strength and definition from the memory-systems which we always-already are, that the object is perceived *as* something. We are still far removed from Idealism (cf. above, "'There is no world where there is no mirror,' is nonsense." (ibid.)). I still have the impressions of tree-stuff; I thereupon *take in* the tree-stuff and compare it to adequate memories of tree-stuff; I finally discover the tree as my perceptive image, being now able to also communicate my perception: "This is a tree"! As such, my memory *recurs* in the impression of the tree, re-forming it into the actually perceived (and communicable) tree. And together with this recurrence/repetition of what I am in what I see, I have interpreted the world.[485] It is as such we understand perception as repetition of 'what already is.'[486]

---

[485] Compare to Abel: "There is no in-itself of things, but only interpreting and interpreted processes of positing [*Fest-stellung*]. This does not imply that there is no reality, that interpretation is merely fantasy. But that something [*Etwas*], which appears as reality and is addressed as such, is not something given [*Gegebenes*] in an ontological sense. [. . .] Reality is always constructed reality. It is about production, not about reproduction." Günter Abel: Nietzsche, loc. cit., p. 183.

[486] As well as we are inundated with sensations, we are in our inner lives also flooded with thoughts, whether rendered linguistically or pictorially. However, like sensations, thoughts too live mostly 'unconscious' lives. As they occur, they are not reflected upon; they are not 'mirrored' and thus 'identified' by the attentive subject. Nietzsche suggests that we think unconsciously, until we need a reason for thinking about what we are thinking. *When* eventually we self-consciously 'think,' it is always as an after-effect to a question about what we are at present thinking. In the concrete: we may have been unconsciously thinking about something; suddenly someone asks us about what we are thinking; by this question, we are forced to take a step back and take another look at what we were thinking just a moment ago; but *without* the question – whether asked by an actual observer or ourselves – we do not think

3.2. Second Case: How One Becomes What One Is.

3.2.1. The Polemical Environment.

Even the recurrence implied in the formula, 'How One Becomes What One Is,' is most precisely understood according to the configuration of the loop; i.e., as an interpretation-mechanism and a recurrence of the 'old' in the 'new.'

When Nietzsche in *Ecce Homo* explains 'how one becomes what one is,' the dictum is applied to the creative economy of the writer. Nietzsche gives us, in *Ecce Homo,* a recipe on how he became what he is in his most important manifestation, a writer. We notice that when several commentators expound the enigmatic dictum, they do not refer to this self-explanation of

---

about what at present we are thinking. In much the same sense, we do not know what we have been dreaming before we begin re-telling to ourselves what we have been dreaming. We remember that in Freud, this 're-telling' of the dream was seen as a re-interpretation of the dream. If the censor-mechanisms in dreams exposed the original dream-thought to a so-called *primary elaboration*, we – telling the dream to ourselves – would expose the dream to an additional layer of interpretation, the so-called *secondary elaboration*. Now, in much the same sense, when we tell our thoughts to ourselves, our narratives are always, according to Nietzsche, *secondary elaboration*. (Digression: To these two layers of interpretation, we could add a third layer of interpretation, namely in the form of Freud's, the Doctor's, dogmatic interpretation of the dream. In the first layer of interpretation, 'drives' or 'forces' are cathected and given representation in primitive images and/or signs; in the second layer of interpretation, representations are given narrative, causal, and chronological form; in the third layer of interpretation, a narrative is being hermeneutically appropriated by an analyst, a critic, or a doctor; and is being situated within the reference-frame of a dogmatic (so-called 'professional') language. The suggestion of such three layers of interpretation corresponds to Günter Abel's proposal of the three interpretative layers: *Interpretation$_1$*, *Interpretation$_2$*, and *Interpretation$_3$*. These three layers proceed from a primary world-creating interpretation$_1$ to the dogmatic 'appropriating' interpretation$_3$ of for example the literary critic. Here, the point is that we cannot meaningfully access or recognize any creeds, ideas, or principles beyond or 'before' the primary interpretation$_1$. In the place of 'the before' primary interpretation$_1$, we construct at best only a heuristic and theoretical fiction; we construct the idea of a flow of un-knowable 'forces,' or 'drives,' or 'energies,' in themselves without representation, but in our fiction meant to represent the nether limit of our universe. See Günter Abel, "Was ist Interpretationsphilosophie?" in: Simon, Josef (ed.): Zeichen und Interpretation, Frankfurt am Main (Suhrkamp Verlag), 1994.)

Nietzsche. Neither Karl Löwith, Alexander Nehamas (who in their work on Nietzsche both devote a chapter to the interpretation of the maxim), nor Babette E. Babich in a recent article, refer to the relevant passages from *Ecce Homo*.[487] We notice that they substantiate their interpretations by copiously referring to Nietzsche's work, but doing so, they merely start an interpretive machine that on the inexhaustible energy-resources of Nietzsche-quotes runs in all possible directions – *except* in the direction of Nietzsche's self-explanation. In this oversight or evasion, they invariably view the *becoming self* as resulting from teleological and conscious operations. The *becoming self* becomes the *existent self's project*; it comes about as the existent self's intentional purpose. One unifies oneself with being as a whole (Löwith; cf. n. 43); creates oneself as an author creates a character (Nehamas; cf. n. 36); or teaches oneself how to love (Babich; cf. n. 39) – assuming, in these suggestions, that the one who unifies himself, creates himself, or teaches himself knows what he is doing![488]

---

[487] The works here referred to are the following: Babette E. Babich, "Nietzsche's Imperative as a Friend's Encomium. On Becoming the One Your Are, Ethics, and Blessing," in: Nietzsche-Studien 32, Berlin, New York (Walter de Gruyter), 2003. Karl Löwith: Nietzsches Philosophe der Ewigen Wiederkehr des Gleichen, Hamburg (Felix Meiner Verlag) 1978. (Translated by J. H. Lomax as Nietzsche's Philosophy of the Eternal Recurrence of the Same, Berkeley (University of California Press) 1997); and Alexander Nehamas, Nietzsche: Life as Literature, Cambridge, Mass. (Harvard University Press), 1985.

[488] In his important and influential *Nietzsche*, Nehamas addresses a "self-creation," which "in the ideal case" involves that we form from "everything that we have done" a coherent whole: "The creation of the self therefore appears to be [. . .] the development of the ability, or the willingness, to accept responsibility for everything that we have done and to admit that is in any case true. [. . .] The self-creation Nietzsche has in mind involves accepting everything that we have done and, *in the ideal case*, binding it into a perfect coherent whole. [. . .] To become what one is [. . .] is to identify oneself with all of one's actions, to see that everything one does (what one becomes) is what one is. *In the ideal case* it is also to fit all this into a coherent whole." (Nehamas, Alexander, Nietzsche, loc. cit., p. 188 & 191; my italics). Since *ideal cases* are not actualized in *all cases*; since they are by nature unique and exceptional, the interpretation has two moments: first, becoming oneself means *to accept oneself*; then, on top of this self-acceptance, it means *to create oneself*; i.e., 'one' creates a 'coherent self' out of 'everything that one has done.' In this conception, however, Nehamas seems ultimately to be reverting to the notion of a conscious agent, intentionally carrying out the requirement. Nehamas must be presupposing a confused self in a constant process of becoming, and then he must assume that hovering above this confused subject, we have "in the ideal case" a *super-self* arranging all the

However, Nietzsche does not know what he is doing! And it is about this fundamental ignorance, this essential lack of knowledge, that he sets out to express a theoretical rule (doing this – i.e., 'doing theory' – he is of course distinctly aware of what he is doing, but it is a different level of awareness). Since we will assume that Nietzsche's self-explanation must have a certain overriding authority, we shall in the following pursue it exclusively.

3.2.2. The Principle of Self-Development.

At one point in *Ecce Homo*, Nietzsche returns to the subtitle of his work in order to present us, the readers, with an explanation of his enigmatic maxim: "At this point we can no longer avoid to provide a real answer to the question, h o w o n e b e c o m e s w h a t o n e i s." (EH, 'Warum ich so klug bin,' 9; KSA 6. p. 293). We notice from the outset of this self-explanation that Nietzsche's becoming self is always involved in *unconscious* operations, and never according to a *telos* directing it. "To become what one is, presupposes that one doesn't have the faintest idea of w h a t o n e i s." (EH, 'Warum ich so klug bin,' 9; KSA 6. p. 293). *Consciousness* and *purpose* would immediately ruin the project. The becoming self must receive no direction from its conscious surface; the becoming self must not adopt any self-imposed purpose, agenda, or telos for its becoming. It cannot 'create' itself, as Nehamas's author creates a character. One can only become what one is, if the ego subjects itself to unconscious forces over which it has no control.

---

confused fragments into a coherent whole (– seemingly by default, reverting to the notion of a *doer* behind the *deed*). Nehamas seems to have been seduced by his own *model* – implicit in the subtitle of his work: the super-self creates a self *like* an author creates a character. Like the author is hovering above pen and paper creating on the empty surface of the paper a coherent character, the super-self is also (somewhere in the abstract) hovering above the chaotic self, creating out of an empty surface a coherent self. – The most pertinent problem being here that if conscious self-creation were an option there would be no need for a coherent self in the first place, because the conscious super-self would be several degrees more coherent that the self that it would be creating. We notice this contrast between Nehamas's conception and a fragment on 'becoming' found in *Der Wille zur Macht*: "Becoming must be explained *without recourse to final intentions*; becoming must appear justified at every moment (or i n c a p a b l e of being evaluated; which amounts to the same thing); *the present must absolutely not be justified by a reference to a future, nor the past by reference to the present.*" (WM 708; my italics).

So, there is a chance for the subject to become what it is, only, when unconscious wills and forces are allowed to do their work without interference from the conscious surface. Given this non-interference, and given that unconscious forces are left alone, a so-called 'organizing idea' begins to rule: "Meanwhile the organizing 'idea' [*"Idee"*] that is destined to rule grows and grows into still deeper depths – it begins to command; slowly it leads us b a c k from side roads and wrong roads; [. . .] it trains all s u b s e r v i e n t capacities before giving any hint of the dominant task, 'goal,' 'aim,' or 'meaning' [*"Ziel", "Zweck", "Sinn"*]." (EH, 'Warum ich so klug bin,' 9; KSA 6. p. 294). *Idea*, we notice here, is significantly placed in quotation marks because the unconscious forces to which Nietzsche is referring have no *actual ideational representative*; they are quantities that eventually, but in their own time, will become a quality. For the same reason, *goal, aim*, and *meaning* are placed in quotation marks: unconscious forces have no *representation* of goal, aim, or meaning.

Unconscious forces are in Nietzsche described as 'capacities'/'faculties' [*Fähigkeiten*]. These Nietzschean 'capacities' are not understood as potentialities, but as units in a net or a structure that do not 'develop' into actualities as such. They exist rather as a multiplicity of semantic condensations in our heterogeneous selves. As clusters of meaning or memory traces, they may be cathected or de-cathected. Nietzsche supposes that we have numerous of these 'capacities,' and according to unconscious processes, some are activated, some de-activated, until, eventually, *activated* capacities form a perfect whole. They are in Nietzsche's language 'wills' – not *one* Will – that perpetually increase or decrease in power. (We recall, "T h e r e is [*es gibt*] no Will; only will-punctures [*Willens-Punktationen*], which continuously expand or reduce their power" (Nachlaß 1887-88, KSA 13, 11[73]).)

As units in a net, 'capacities' or 'wills' are quanta of energy that live their unconscious existence in perpetual conflict and mutual contradiction. Now, according to the strategy of becoming oneself, Nietzsche requires that we let them exist undisturbed in their conflict. On a first reading, this may appear paradoxical: how create a whole out of chaos *by deliberately doing nothing*? – However, there is a *raison d'être* behind this politics of non-interference: if we want the *best force* to win the struggle between forces, then we cannot allow ourselves (i.e., 'us' as conscious surface) to interfere on behalf of *any* of the forces. If we, as conscious surface, interfere, we artificially effect the outcome of this inner contest, implying that we have no guarantee that it was actually the *best force* that came victorious out of the struggle. Rather, we have most likely given a *weaker force* an advantage. In the perpetual competition between unconscious forces, we would counter-productively have allowed *the survival of the un-fittest*.

Nietzsche, trying to give an account of himself in *Ecce Homo*, envisions himself as encompassing more 'capacities,' expressing more different 'voices,' than any other human being. He is, he believes, almost exploding from this superabundance of multiple voices. But Nietzsche, nonetheless, affirms them all, discriminating against none. Nietzsche never suffered from *solitude*, as he tells us, only from *multitudes*: "Suffering from solitude [*Einsamkeit*] is also an objection – I have suffered only from 'multitudes' [*"Vielsamkeit"*]." (EH, 'Warum ich so klug bin,' 10; KSA 6, p. 297).

To let a multitude of 'capacities' exist undisturbed implies, minimally, to be *indifferent* about their existence, and maximally, to be *ignorant* of their existence. The work of Nietzsche's instincts is *secret*. The strategy for becoming what one is therefore to stay unconscious about unconscious forces! – And then one day, they will have ripen, and – in a moment of spontaneity – they will *leap forth* in their own 'perfection.' "I never even suspected what was growing in me – and all my capacities, ripe, in their final perfection, will one day l e a p f o r t h / j u m p o u t [*hervorsprangen*]." (EH, 'Warum ich so klug bin,' 9; KSA 6, p. 294).[489]

Effectively, one has now handed over the control of one's self-development to the stage of the unconscious. Nietzsche's *ego* enacts no longer any desire on its own account, since desires are *secret*. The ego never knows what unconscious forces *really want*. But since unconscious forces are the secret underpinnings of the ego, the ego also does not know what *it wants itself*. In this fundamental *laissez-faire* of secret desires, the

---

[489] In his work on Nietzsche's theory of consciousness, Erwin Schlimgen arrives – without explicitly referring to Nietzsche's maxim – to conclusions similar to those we introduce above: "According to Nietzsche, everything becomes conscious through original corporeal processes. Only here, in the inspired case disappears the hesitation, and everything enters explosively, immediately, and perfectly formed as complete into consciousness. This again causes the feeling of absolute passivity (– "one does not see; one takes" –); it is as if a foreign trans-subjective power has taken over signs and images, so that the subject has become merely a 'mouthpiece' and a 'medium,' as such *desubjectivized* [*entsubjektiviert*]. [. . .] The feeling of happiness, introduced in the inspired state, and what Nietzsche obviously perceives completely consciously, is the happiness of the gifted/favored/blessed [*Beschenkten*]: without the exertion of the concept, without searching for the adequate poetic form, knowledge [*Erkenntnisse*], which is beyond the intellect, is given in evidence." Erwin Schlimgen, Nietzsches Theorie des Bewußtseins, loc. cit., p. 214.

ego gives up its own desires. The reasoning is that if we want to let secret desires do what *they want*, we cannot shackle their development by insisting on what *we want*. "I cannot remember that I ever tried hard [. . .] 'willing' something, 'striving' for something, envisaging a 'purpose,' a 'wish' – I know none of this from experience. [. . .] There is no ripple of desire." (EH, 'Warum ich so klug bin,' 9; KSA 6, p. 295).

Therefore, 'in becoming what I am,' I transfer my conscious will-to-power to these new forces which are in themselves will-to-power-processes, and which account for my real *Me*. These unconscious will-to-power-processes control me, in all their conflict, more surely than I could have controlled myself from my conscious surface. As I renounce directing and instructing myself, I also renounce my 'willing,' because all egoistic willing is nothing but aberration. I (*'I' as exterior surface*) now want *nothing*! But paradoxically, in wanting *nothing*, I (*'I' as interior absolute*) want *everything*. 'I want *nothing*' exactly in order to allow the *best forces* within me to survive well, to grow, to develop, and to realize themselves in the absolute.

3.2.3. Amor Fati as Anti-Narcissistic Love of the Inner Interpretation-Machine.

This becomes the psychological underground for Nietzsche's famous *amor fati*. The 'fate' one loves in *amor fati*, is the fate destined by one's unconscious forces. Therefore, it is crucially not a 'fate' predetermined by any agency (e.g., any divinity); this 'fate' does not exist *before* the struggle has been carried out; it exists *in* or *as* the struggle. If one loves one's 'fate,' one loves whatever results from an inherent will-to-power-struggle – an inherent will-to-power-struggle that operates as an inherent interpretation-machine churning out self-interpretations. One loves in *amor fati* the inherent *interpretation-machine* and its 'product' or 'spin off' in the form of one's interpreted self.

In two crucial definitions of *amor fati* from *Ecce Homo* Nietzsche emphasizes that in 'loving one's fate' one refuses *difference*:

> *I do not want in the least that anything should become different than it is: I myself do not want to become different*. But that is how I have always lived. I had no wishes. A man over forty-four who can say that he never strove for *honors*, for *women*, for *money*! [. . .] My formula for greatness in a human being is a m o r f a t i : *that one wants nothing to be different*, not forward, not backward, not in all eternity. Not merely endure what is necessary, still less conceal it [. . .] but l o v e it. (EH, 'Warum ich so klug bin,' 9 & 10; KSA 6, pp. 295 & 297; italics added).

On the exterior surface, one wants nothing, implying, in the context, that one suspends the most common objects of desire: *honor*, *women*, and *money*. On the exterior surface, desire is seen as a drive to obtain what one does not have; i.e., to fill *a lack*. As such, desire enacts itself as *a drive to become different*.

But, we might ask, different from what? – The obvious answer: different from the *interpretation-machine*! Everything is here about accepting the *machine*; indeed, it is about *becoming* a *machine*. The machine's machine-desire now overrides Nietzsche's superficial surface-desires: honor, women, and money. As he *refuses to be different*, he consequently *suspends his superficial surface-desires*. There is an essential correlation between *suspending surface-desire* and *refusal to be different from the interpretation-machine*, in the sense that the former facilitates and conditions the latter. In a series of propositions, the 'argument' could be reconstructed, at least *condensed*, as approximately the following:

- I want nothing to be different within myself (i.e., within my inner will-to-power-struggles)!
- Desire *projects me* beyond the enclosure (the envelope, the capsule) of myself!
- Desire thus introduces difference into the envelope of myself and interferes in *me being me*!
- I shall instead love myself as what I am in/as my interior machine, not as what I desire on my surface!
- I become what *I am* (i.e., my interior interpretation-machine) by suspending what *I will* (i.e., my superficial exterior)!
- Truly, I want nothing! – Except myself in the absolute!

(I merely want myself in the absolute! – Is that too much to ask?) With *amor fati*, Nietzsche declares his love for his inner machine. In this, he affirms that there is no agency controlling him, but only the relentless 'work' of the interpretation-machine churning out self-interpretations. As Günter Abel frequently emphasizes, there is (*es gibt*) only an *'Interpretations-Geschehen'* – implying that there is for this *'Geschehen'* no higher court of appeal whether in the form of metaphysical, theological, subjective, or other, principles. In these circumstances, the best we can say is that interpretations simply 'happen.'[490]

Given this lack of agency and identity, *amor fati* becomes a declaration of *love of one's self*, but crucially not of *love of oneself* (– and also not of

---

[490] See Günter Abel: Nietzsche, loc. cit.

'learning how to love'[491]). Nietzsche does not declare a love of his ego-ideal. Quite the opposite, he declares a love of the self that plays its secret games within him. In this economy, to *love one's self* is the opposite of *loving oneself*. If *love of oneself* indicates pathological *narcissism*, *love of one's self* indicates rather a radical *anti-narcissism*. If *love of oneself* indicates narcissistic absorption in the image of an ideal self, *love of one's self* indicates acceptance of one's unconscious underground. If *love of oneself* is to love a cartoon image of a *unified self*, *love of one's self* is to love a *fragmented self*.

This general acceptance of *one's self* as one's *fragmented self* implies an acceptance of one's many 'voices'; one's 'multitudes' or '*Vielsamkeit*.' As such, the acceptance finally also effects Nietzsche's *literary styles*. Nietzsche's 'styles' have become a theme for a number of perceptive commentators (so Alexander Nehamas, Henry Staten, and Jacques Derrida[492]); now, we notice that Nietzsche's many styles come about *as a consequence of* his *amor fati*. The variety of styles mirrors the superabundance of discourses that are being conducted in Nietzsche's fragmented self. As well as one must listen indifferently to these voices, one must also give them expression corresponding to their own individual 'pathos' and 'tempo.' The possibility of employing many styles grows out of *the indifference to differ-*

---

[491] In a learned article Babette Babich makes the latter suggestion: "To become what one is, one must take over one's own life as an invention; even more importantly and at the same time, one must learn love. The need for love, for learning how to love, and an active erotic deed or lived passion or expressed articulated desire expresses the importance of what Nietzsche calls benediction or yes-saying." (Babette E. Babich, "Nietzsche's Imperative as a Friend's Encomium," in: Nietzsche-Studien 32, loc. cit., p. 51). However, I see no indications that Nietzsche's teaching could involve a call on 'learning to love,' if by love we mean either 'romantic love' or 'sexual love' (cf. "an active erotic deed"). In structural terms, romantic love would topple the fragile economy of constructive auto-affection. Romantic love does not involve any cultivation of a becoming self, but rather of the mis-recognized ('beautified') self of the other. Romantic love, indeed, appears to be a *contradiction* to the affirmation of the 'machine.' We may recall in this context that the alleged remedial powers of love is a distinctly modern theme – discarded in no uncertain terms by the ancient Stoics and Epicureans, on this issue closer to Nietzsche's heart.

[492] See Nehamas, Nietzsche, loc. cit.; Henry Staten, Nietzsche's Voice, Ithaca, London (Cornell University Press), 1990; and Jacques Derrida, Eperons. Les Styles de Nietzsche. English/French version, Chicago (The University of Chicago Press), 1979.

ence in pathos and tempo between a multiplicity of inward states. To these many different inward states correspond many different styles.[493]

> This is also the point for a general remark about my art of style. To communicate a state, an inward tension of pathos, by means of signs, including the tempo of these signs – that is the meaning of every style; and considering that the multiplicity of inward states is exceptionally large in my case, I have many stylistic possibilities. (EH, 'Warum ich so gute Bücher schreibe,' 4; KSA 6, p. 304).

Ultimately, the employment of many styles comes about as an effect of the *love of one's self* and the *refusal to be different*. The two expressions have an overlapping content: 'love of one's self' means: *I love the differences in my self*; 'refusal to be different' means: *I am indifferent to the differences in my self.*[494]

---

[493] The abandonment of oneself to unconscious forces is another expression of what for shorthand we traditionally call 'inspiration.' This becomes clear when Nietzsche in *Ecce Homo* returns to the question of writing with great style, beyond self-control, as he explains the history of the conception of *Also sprach Zarathustra*. The experience of writing *Zarathustra* is an experience of being *indifferent* to voices, of letting them resonate in the subject, without exposing them to control. *To write Zarathustra* is therefore also *to become what one is.* " – Has anybody, at the end of the 19th century, a clear notion of what poets in strong times would call inspiration. [. . .] One hears, one does not seek; one takes, one does not ask what is given; as in lightning a thought is illuminated, with necessity, as form without hesitation, – I never had a choice. [. . .] Everything happens in the highest degree involuntarily [*unfreiwilling*], as if in a storm of feelings of freedom [*Freiheits-Gefühl*], of unconditionality, of power, of divinity. The spontaneity [*Unfreiwilligkeit*] of images and analogies is the strangest; one no longer has a concept of what an image or an analogy is, everything presents itself as the nearest, the most precise and simple, expression. It really seems, to recall here one of Zarathustra's maxims, as if the things arrived by themselves. [. . .] This is my experience of inspiration." (EH "Also sprach Zarathustra," 3; KSA 6, p. 339-40.)

[494] Nietzsche is articulating a writer-experience that is identical to an experience articulated in similar language in Kafka's *Diaries*. Kafka too talks explicitly about 'forces' that are, beyond his control, given voice without him discriminating against them; and without him interfering in the process. Kafka too suspends, 'sacrifices,' desire in order to engage a writing-process that is unconscious. Writing emerges from his 'organism,' not from his conscious 'surface': "It is easy to recognize a concentration in me of all forces on writing. When it became clear in my organism that writing was the most productive direction for my being to take, everything rushed in that direction and left empty all those abilities, which were directed toward the joys of sex, eating, drinking, philosophical reflection and above all music. [. . .] Natural-

3.2.4. To 'Become What One Is' in a 'Vertical Dimension' of Time.

The self one now becomes is a *repetition* of the self one always was. One does not 'create' oneself; and especially, one does not create a self *out of nothing*. One 'becomes' oneself from an abundance of possibilities always-already there. Becoming oneself must necessarily imply repetition and re-collection in the sense that in the repetitious becoming of oneself one re-collects a self among a number of possibilities, this re-collected self emerging – in the best of circumstances – as identical to one's innermost optimum. As such one becomes what one is, or, recurs as the same.

In this, one does not recur as a replica or duplicate of some former self. The recurrent self is not a reincarnation of some former self, and it is certainly not a reborn self. We are not talking about something in the order of the celebrated 'indiscernible' but 'numerically distinct' $self_1$'s and $self_2$'s. The self has not traversed the orbit of the circle from the introduction above, in order first to live, then to die, and finally, 'snap,' mysteriously, to live again.[495]

---

ly, I did not find this purpose independently and consciously, it found itself. [...] My development is now complete and, so far as I can see, there is nothing left to sacrifice." Franz Kafka, The Diaries 1910-1913. Max Brod (ed.); translation, J. Kresh, New York (Schocken Books), 1949, p. 211.

[495] If the self in our reading of Nietzsche's maxim is 'eternalized,' it is only so, insofar as it reverts to this absolute other language within itself. It is not eternalized as a *matter of fact*. So whereas to Karl Löwith, Nietzsche's eternalization of self becomes a *fact* (albeit a mystical one), played out as a conclusion of the entire 'History of Being,' the argument is here the more modest one, namely that it could never manifest itself as other than, strictly speaking, *pathology* (in the old sense: as what concerns the passions). In Löwith's interpretation, one becomes what one is as a transcendental-existential, so-called, 'cosmic child.' As such, one regresses deep back into world-history: "The activity of man does not begin only after his birth into self-being but already long before this time, in the generations of remote antiquity. With this view of preconscious and unconscious activities, the possibility arises of tying man back into the nature of all that is." (Löwith, Nietzsches Philosophy, loc. cit., p. 127). This becomes the project: to tie man 'back into the nature of all that is.' Accordingly, our personal histories do not begin in childhood, and we do not merely inherit family treats handed over in the process of socialization. As 'existential children' our 'childhood' starts in remote antiquity, and in becoming what one is, the human is now becoming unified with all there is. As specs of existence, we are fettered to the most remote corners of world-historical existence, mirroring – as the existential monads we are – the universal grand plan of history. Löwith's final metamorphosis into the *I am* of the 'cosmic child' is therefore to be translated into *I am*

3. Return as a Repetitive Interpretation-Process

The recurrent self *is* the self one *is and always was*. The difference between the recurring-self and the self-one-is-&-was is an almost invisible bar separating *inner* and *outer*. It is the outer that recurs as a repetition of the inner; or in the reverse, the inner recurs as a *manifestation* in the outer. To

---

the world. In paraphrase of Nietzsche, Löwith surmises that this necessarily must be Nietzsche's position. "*I*, Nietzsche-Zarathustra, *am* the truth of the *world* [sic.: *I am the world*], for I am the first over the whole history of the longest error to have rediscovered the world before Plato, I will nothing at all but this eternally recurring world, which is not longer alienated from me [sic.: *I am the world*] and is at the same time my ego and my fate. For I will even myself again eternally, as one ring within the great ring of the self-willing world." (Löwith, ibid., p. 98; my insertions). In this interpretation, there is no difference between *me* and *world*, and therefore, we have effectively defeated and conquered death, because *me* being identical to the *world* keep coming back as another identical *me* being identical to the *world* – *et cetera . . . ad infinitum*. Becoming what one is, is a becoming *one* with *the all*. The *me* is just one ring within the great ring of the *world*, but essentially my ring is identical to the ring of the world. Löwith's *Seins-mystique* is essentially a theory of fractals (before the invention of this mathematical language): the grand pattern of the world is copied over and repeated in any smaller dimension of itself; and conversely, any smaller dimension is merely a fractal repetition of the whole. As fractals we repeat ourselves/each other eternally as the same; being identical to both one another and the world as a whole. The objection that I am here directing against Löwith's interpretation of Nietzsche's playful 'cosmic child,' has precedent, I notice, in similar objections to Eugen Fink put forward by Mihailo Djurić. Addressing Fink's concept of 'play,' Djurić too objects to the universalization and 'transcendentalization' of the concept: "Instead of understanding the play of children and artists as empirical frames of reference for the Nietzschean thought of 'the great play of birth and death of all things,' Fink reverses this state of affairs. As if Nietzsche would comprehend the world-play as an objectively available [*vorhandenes*] occurrence, entirely independent of human play! [. . .] With this it is presupposed that the playing human is not simply a producer of an imaginary world of play [*Spielwelt*], but is rather 'a co-player [*Mitspieler*] in the play of the world,' such that his 'playing [*spielerische*] productivity' [. . .] can be comprehended and known only as the opposite side or re-appearance [*Kehrseite order Widerschein*] of an originally cosmic play." Mihailo Djurić, Nietzsche und die Metaphysik, Berlin, New York (Walter de Gruyter), 1985, p. 153. Löwith's interpretation could at best be only a *metaphor* for a 'pathological' operation; one might concede that within the enclosure of the self, the *languages* of three thousand years of Western Thinking has been, in Nietzsche's case, profoundly internalized. As such, but only as such, he lets them speak as the Other in himself, confident that his 'will-to-power-processes' by themselves will sort out the chaos, and let emerge a new system.

entertain the idea with a few examples: If the outer acts, it merely repeats an action already configured in the inner; as such, the inner *manifests* itself in the outer. If the outer is deceived in love, it merely repeats a deception already prefigured in the inner; as such, the inner *manifests* a secret anticipation in the outer. If the outer writes a book, it merely conveys to itself an interpretation-process that has already 'happened' in the inner; as such, the inner *manifests* an interpretation-process in the outer. In any case, the self recurs as the same; or one becomes (as outer) what one is (as inner). As such, it is never on some *horizontal dimension* of time that the self recurs (cf. traversing the circumference of a circular orbit); it is instead always in a *vertical dimension* that the self recurs. The self bops up and down on its fluid surface like cork on water. This movement is vertical, indicating that one becomes what one is *in every moment*.

As such, we live 'vertical' lives. The 'horizontal' life, lived on the traditional time-line of past, present, and future, is a mere epi-phenomenon. Now, to *accept* the 'vertical life,' this perpetual bopping up and down, *is to become what one is* in the strongest sense, but in a weaker sense, one cannot help but always becoming what one is, whether one accepts it or not. Repetition compulsion is inscribed into our vertical lives; however fast we try to outrun our fate, it will always catch up on us – in this we are all, as one might put it, sons of Oedipus.[496] We can make all kinds of arrangements in our lives, but we cannot outrun our personalities. There is now more grandeur in accepting what we have coming to us in any case, and not just accepting it 'as necessary, but love it': "Not merely bear what is necessary, still less conceal it . . . but l o v e it." (EH, 'Warum ich so klug bin,' 10; KSA 6, p. 297).

However, in this particular notion of fate, we emphasize again that the individual is subjected to the 'fate' of himself, not to a fate one traditionally would ascribe to a divinely prearranged world. Already in *Menschliches, Allzumenschliches*, Nietzsche introduces his specific (quasi-psychoanalytic) notion of 'fate' in juxtaposition to the traditional (theological) notion of fate, labeled *Türkenfatalismus*. In 'Turkish fatalism' all events, as prede-

---

[496] Oedipus, as a powerful image on Eternal Recurrence, is the character par excellence who keeps coming back to the *cross-road* – almost, if not exactly, a *gateway*. He starts fleeing from the cross-road/gateway as *prophecy*, runs at fast as he can in a circle that leads him back to the cross-road/gateway as *reality*; keeps running throughout the play until he in the end returns to the cross-road/gateway as *truth*. Finally, he sees that it was all the same: *prophecy*, *reality*, and *truth*. There is far more profundity in reading Eternal Recurrence into *Oedipus Rex*, than applying to the play that famous family-triangle Freud could not help but seeing whenever he opened a book.

termined by fate, are unchangeable and inevitable; accordingly, the world is prearranged by a deity, playing with humans an inscrutable game in which humans are only pawns.

> Turkish fatalism commits the fundamental error that it places man and fate opposite each other like two different things: Man, it says, may strive against fate, may try to defeat it, but in the end it always remains the winner, why the wisest thing to do is to resign, or just live in any which way. The truth is that every man in himself is a piece of fate [*ein Stück Fatum*]; when, as described, he thinks he is striving against fate, fate is in that very moment being realized; the struggle is imaginary, but so is resignation to fate. (MA II, 'Der Wanderer und sein Schatten,' 61; KSA 2, p. 580).[497]

Against the mistaken 'Turkish fatalism,' Nietzsche proposes a 'fatalism' emerging from the core of the single individual. Fate is not imposed on man by something *outside* man, like a deity. A man who is in himself "a piece of fate," is a man ruled by an unconscious underground over which he has no control. If this is the case, his struggle against his fate is merely an aspect of himself; and conversely, if he resigns to his fate, his resignation is merely an aspect of himself; whichever way, he walks into a ruse prepared by himself – precisely as Oedipus (cf. fn. 44), fleeing the horrific prophecy, only races straight toward its fulfillment.[498]

Let us now, from this new perspective, try to unravel an enigmatic passage that, on a first reading, would appear to support the so-called 'ethical' interpretation of recurrence.

> My teaching says: live in such a way as you may w i s h [*wünschen mußt*], to live again is the task – you will do so i n a n y c a s e [*jedenfalls*]! He for whom striving gives the highest feeling [*Gefühl*], he will strive; he for whom tranquility gives the highest feeling, he will be tranquil; he for whom obedience gives the highest feeling, he will be obedient. Only **must** he b e c o m e c o n s c i o u s o f

---

[497] For an extended discussion on 'Turkish Fatalism,' see also Joan Stambaugh, The Problem of Time in Nietzsche, loc. cit., p. 165 ff.

[498] Cf. note above. Nietzsche's particular 'fatalism' also reminiscences Kierkegaard's 'Enten-Eller' (which is, apropos Nietzsche's *amor fati*, introduced as "An Ecstatic Discourse"): do this or don't do this, it will make no difference, or, you will regret it either way. Kierkegaard, applying his doctrine to a number of cases ("Marry," "Trust a girl," etc.), gives the most radical case the following formulation: "Hang yourself, and you will regret it. Do not hang yourself, and you will also regret it. Hang yourself or do not hang yourself you will regret it either way." Cf. Søren Kierkegaard, Either Or v. I. Translation H. V. & E. H. Hong, Princeton (Princeton University Press), 1987, p. 38.

what gives him the highest feeling, and not shy away from any means. Eternity is at stake! [*Es gilt die Ewigkeit!*] (Nachlaß 1881, KSA 9, 11[163]).

On a first superficial reading, the passage seems to support the crucial 'ought' essential for the success of the 'ethical' interpretation of recurrence; and it might be translated into Deleuze's: "Whatever you will, will it in such a way that you also will its eternal return"[499]; or into Magnus's: "Live in such a way that you must wish to live again."[500] However, on a more rigorous reading, the presupposed separation of 'ought' and 'is' breaks down immediately in the passage: "live in such a way as you may w i s h, to live again is the task – *you will do so in any case*" (ibid.). First, the passage does not 'dictate' that we 'ought' to live as we wish, it merely suggests; second, it jumbles the celebrated Humean distinction between 'ought' and 'is.' On our interpretation of *Becoming What One Is*, we shall now argue that the passage does not assert an 'existential imperative' that can be constructed in parallel to Kant's 'categorical imperative.'[501] On our interpretation, we live

---

[499] Deleuze: Nietzsche, loc. cit., p. 68.
[500] Magnus: Nietzsche's Existential Imperative, loc. cit., p. 143.
[501] Kant's categorical imperative implies that actions whose maxims cannot be raised to universal law are contrary to reason. They can be rejected on logical grounds, since moral acts have to be in accordance with universal law. Kant offers this example, "when I am in distress, may I make a promise with the intention of not keeping it." (Immanuel Kant, Grounding of a Metaphysics of Morals, New York (Hackett Pub. Co.), 1993, p. 15). The maxim of the action, *insincere promise* or *lying* cannot be wanted as universal law, because if I *will* a universal law to lie, then all promise-making breaks down: "I immediately become aware that I can indeed will the lie but can not at all will a universal law to lie. For by such a law there would really be no promises at all, since in vain would my willing future actions be professed to other people who would not believe what I professed." (Kant, ibid., p. 15). If I cannot will a universal law to lie, I must admit that neither can I want to justify occasional lying. I would involve myself in a logical contradiction; wanting *lying* to become universal law implies that I can no longer lie, since universally everybody lie and are obligated to lie. In parallel, the existential imperative would imply that actions, which the subject could not want to relive in all eternity, would have to be rejected on logical grounds. The existential imperative would consequently prescribe: 'live is such a way, that you could want to live the same life again.' The following three objections come to mind: *First*, the parallel to Kant is not perfect, because it is not clear, what 'universal law' one would be violating, or what 'contradiction' one would involve oneself in, if one were living a life one refused to live again. *Secondly*, interpreted as an existential imperative, Nietzsche's "rule for life" (Deleuze) is simple hedonism advanced as a duty toward oneself. His proposal becomes identical to the age-old memento of

'vertical lives.' Now, in the weaker sense, we cannot help but always becoming who we are, whether we accept it or not; so, we will live again "in any case." But to *accept* this 'vertical life,' this perpetual bopping up and down, *is to become what one is* in the stronger sense. In the strong sense, "one *must* become conscious of *what* gives one the strongest feeling."

In the strong sense, one accepts one's *recurrence* – or rather, one's perpetual *recurrences – of the same* as a condition in one's life. Life is now not only lived vertically, which it is in both cases; furthermore, one has *actively accepted* that it is lived vertically. In this, one affirms that the outer is at every moment informed by the inner, and affirms it jubilantly, because it then seems *as if* the outer is re-living an eternity in every moment, namely the eternity existing in the inner. In this conception, *amor fati* becomes a teaching that *folds the ego back on the subject*, but crucially not a teaching that permits the ego *to escape from the subject*.

---

carpe diem: seize the day; enjoy the present; live and let live; forget heaven and fruitless metaphysical quests for meaning and immortality. However, it is redundant to dictate a human being to accept the promise of a life lived in pleasure. In general, we do not need to set up principles for what comes naturally; or, as G. E. Moore once said, we do not need to tell a red thing to turn red. (Eternity is not even inherent in this conception, because *carpe diem* was always the flip side of that other famous memento, the *memento mori*. They belong together as two different faces of the same coin, the most important stamp being the *memento mori*: if one 'remembers' death, one presumably starts 'remembering' life too; if life is short, a sense of economy dictates that one exploits every day to the full.) *Thirdly*, in aphorism 341 from FW, the proposal is suggested by a demon daring the persona of the aphorism to accept the proposition as if it represented the highest danger – the 'heaviest weight.' This supposed danger has disappeared in the existential imperative, "live your life in such a way that you could want to live it again," since there is no danger in being told that one should live as one wants; on the contrary, this would absurdly imply that *one is under the law to live as one pleases*. The interpretation does not give the persona any reason to feel crushed, throw himself down, or gnash his teeth. For a discussion of morality in Kant and Nietzsche, see also Josef Simon, "Moral bei Kant und Nietzsche," in: Nietzsche-Studien 29, New York, Berlin (Walter de Gruyter), 2000.

4. Return as Self-Repetition of Self-Presence.
Four Encounters.

4.1. Introducing the 'smallest possible loop.'

In the descriptions above, the subject does in both of our two cases, perception and becoming what one is, traverse the repetitious circuits of a loop, the loop being located, as our abstraction, in inner-mental life. After half a cycle, everything returns to the selfsame present, the intersection of the trajectories, the 'gateway.' It is an 'inner mental' loop where everything that shoots out from past and present in order to engage the future inevitably sinks back into the past. Since one cannot break free of the loop, one is bound to live one's repetitions. Repetition is the name and label of the loop; past being and future becoming repeat each other in never-ending cycles of overlapping, i.e., never-ending cycles of *being becoming* and *becoming being*. This structure is implying also the loop's essentially a-teleological structure.

Now, we imagine that we tighten the ribbons of the loop into a knot; consequently, we have something that appears like an eternal beginning. This is the *smallest possible loop*. Its 'rates of return' would be reduced to brief pulses, vibrating back-and-forth; pulses shooting out from the center of the loop, only to immediately sink back into its belly. Strictly speaking, the loop has disappeared; a so-called 'smallest possible loop' is an oxymoron. We are instead talking about what conventionally we call 'now,' 'instance,' or 'moment.' So, if we were to assign a return-rate to this 'smallest possible loop,' we may say that it has a return-rate of 'an instance.' If such instances are treated with absolute equality, i.e., as the same (and it is difficult to treat an instance otherwise), they repeat themselves as the same. Since, given their instantaneity, they must be repeating themselves as the same in complete self-presence, we can legitimately talk about this particular repetition as '*self-repetition of self-presence.*'

Given the instantaneity inscribed into the formula, it can no longer be addressing an interpretation-process. As demonstrated above, all interpretation-processes take time. They run through processes that involve the so-called *Zeit-Umkehrung* or *Chronologische Umdrehung*; i.e., something entering the system undergoes an interpretive transformation, is thus being translated – by an interpretation-machine – into a language *we understand*, before, finally, it announces itself as *interpreted-being*. However, in the case of sensations, it announces itself as *presence*; implying that *interpreted-being* disguises itself as *present-being*. Becoming-conscious take time, but this time is so "small" that we fail to notice. This entire process stands in contrast to our new formula: in *self-repetition of self-presence* nothing takes time; here we have only the pulses, the flashes, or the blips of nows emerging and disappearing.

To elucidate the contrast, we may say that that which through a *repetitious interpretation-process* 'announces' itself as presence, is always *false presence*; but that which in *self-repetition of self-presence* 'announces' itself as presence, is always *true presence* – a kind of *proto-presence*. In the first case, the 'announcement' is a scam; in the second case, there is no scam, but only because there is no 'announcement'.

In fact, we do not know *true presence*, because we cannot wrap our minds around it; the wrapping itself would take too much time. When, indefatigable, we nevertheless desire to force an encounter with the truly present (or the *proto-present*), we can paradoxically do so only in an *interpreting language*, an interpreting language replete with abstractions, examples, images, and metaphors. Therefore the paradox: we want to investigate the absolutely primordial, labeled *self-repetition of self-presence*, as the essential opposition to the *repetitious interpretation-process*, but we can do so only by educing, and within the frame of, a repetitious interpretation-process. (Cf. "The means of expression [*Ausdrucksmittel*] of language is incapable of expressing becoming" (Nachlaß 1887-88, KSA 13, 11[73]).)

The strategy can only be elliptical, i.e., we evoke a language that tries to 'catch a glimpse,' 'sneak a peek,' of the absolutely primordial from a variety of different perspectives or angles; the angles being, in this essay, of course Nietzsche's. We assume that the sum of the angles adds up to something that we, with a little benevolence and leniency, could call an insight.

4.2. First Encounter: The Environment Facilitating the Thought of Eternal Recurrence.

We shall begin by considering a *scenario* that seems to induce and facilitate the thought of eternal recurrence. In *Zarathustra* especially, but elsewhere in the total work, we are introduced to a lone wanderer (in *Zarathustra*, Zarathustra) in front of a mountainous scenery, starting to reflect on recurrence. The thought of recurrence, he experiences as its *involuntary medium*; it is a thought presumably deeper than anything he has ever before pondered.

In these scenarios, the thought of eternal recurrence is expressed by a subject *beholding the sublime* (in Kant and Schopenhauer's sense). It is to the mountaineer the thought appears when he is gazing into the sky, the night, or the distant horizon of mountain ranges and canyons beneath him. Under the impression of the immensity of the sublime, the individual seems to have shrunk into nothingness; and the immensity of the sublime juxtaposed to human insignificance seems especially conducive to the experience.[502] We will therefore start by proposing that the attitude, in which 'everything returns' in the specified sense, must be *aesthetic* (in the old sense) rather than *epistemological*: it is primarily related to *perception*, rather than to *knowledge*.

This preliminary observation coincides with Nietzsche's own reports of how he conceived the thought. In a letter to Heinrich Köselitz (alias 'Peter Gast'), Nietzsche describes how involuntarily he came upon this thought on his wanderings in the mountains near Sils-Maria, and the impact it had on him (the letter has a crucial place in Klossowski's exposition of recurrence).

> To Gast,
>
> Sils-Maria, 14 August, 1881.
> The August sun is overhead, the year is slipping away. The mountains and forests are becoming more quiet and peaceful. On my horizon, thoughts have arisen such as I have never seen before – I will not speak of them, but will maintain my unshakable calm. I suppose now I'll have to live a few years longer! Ah, my friend, sometimes the idea runs through my head that I am living an extremely dangerous life, for I am one of these machines which can explode. The intensity of my feelings makes me shudder and laugh. Several time I have been unable to leave my room, for the ridiculous reason that my eyes were inflamed – from what? On each occasion I had wept too much on my wanderings the day before – not sentimental tears, mind you, but tears of joy. I sang and talked nonsense. Filled with a glimpse of things which put me in advance of all other men.[503]

Although Nietzsche deliberately holds back the 'thought' that caused this explosion of feeling, the 'glimpse of things' that he saw can only be related to eternal recurrence. First of all, there are few other plausible candidates in

---

[502] A famous painting, often used as front-page to Nietzsche-literature, captures the idea, Casper David Friedrich's *Der Wanderer über dem Nebelmeer* (1818). In the foreground, a mountaineer stands on top of a mountain peak with his back on us. In the background, we see the same as he, a horizon of mountain ranges and canyons beneath him, partially clouded in fog. The painting is a good illustration on the Kantian sublime. It also captures the fascinations with mountains and canyons in Nietzsche's *Zarathustra*. When used, or overused, as front-page for much Nietzsche-literature, we are probably supposed to imagine that Nietzsche/Zarathustra is represented by the figure in the foreground.

[503] Nietzsche to Gast; cf. Curt Paul Janz, Friedrich Nietzsche. Biographie bd. II, 2nd ed., München (Carl Hanser Verlag), 1993, p. 76. See also Klossowski, Nietzsche, loc. cit., p. 55-56.

4. Return as Self-Repetition of Self-Presence

the Nietzschean repertoire; but in fact, we do not need to second-guess the content of Nietzsche's secret, since a few years later, in another letter to Gast, he confirms that the idea of *Zarathustra* and eternal recurrence was conceived in these early days of August 1881, on one of his wanderings in the mountains of Sils-Maria.

> 3. September, 1883
> Engadin is the birthplace for my 'Zarathustra.' I even found the first outline of the thought related to him. Underneath it says "Beginning August 1881; in Sils-Maria; 6000 feet above the sea, and even higher above all human things."[504]

The note Nietzsche apparently has found is included in the Nachlaß material from 1881; here we find an outline to a book called, Die Wiederkunft des Gleichen, and the following note: "Beginning August 1881 in Sils-Maria; 6000 feet above the sea, and even higher above all human things! – " (Nachlaß 1881, KSA 9, 11[141]). To leave no stone unturned, in *Ecce Homo* we find a similar account.

> The fundamental conception of this work [*Zarathustra*], and the Eternal-Recurrence-Thought [Ewige-Wiederkunft-Gedanke], this highest formula of affirmation at all attainable –, belongs in August 1881: it was penned on a sheet with the notation underneath, "6000 feet beyond man and time." That day I was walking through the woods along the lake of Silvaplana; at an enormous towering pyramidal rock near Surlei, I stopped. It was then that this thought [*Gedanke*] came to me. (EH 'Also sprach Zarathustra,' 1; KSA 6, p. 335).

So, there is no doubt that this 'thought of thoughts' belongs in a certain environment, and that this environment 'facilitates' the thought, although the nature of this 'facilitation' still remains of mystery. It is the environment of Nietzsche/Zarathustra's mountains, "6000 feet above the sea"; it is the environment of the sublime.[505]

---

[504] Nietzsche to Gast; cf. Janz: *Friedrich Nietzsche,* II, loc. cit., p. 79.

[505] Kant describes the sublime as follows: "The sublime is to be found in a formless object, so far as in it, or by occasion of it, *boundlessness* is represented. [. . .] As the mind is not merely attracted by the object but is even being alternately repelled, the satisfaction in the sublime does not so much involve a positive pleasure as admiration or respect, which rather deserves to be called a negative pleasure. [. . .] For the most part nature excites the ideas of the sublime in its chaos or in its wildest and most irregular disorder and desolation, provided size and might is perceived." Kant: The Critique of Judgment. Translated by J. H. Bernard, Amherst, (Prometheus Books), 2000, p. 102 & 104; Kant's italics. We emphasize here that the representation of the sublime is *not identical* to Nietzsche's eternal recurrence; but it is in these scenarios of

Going by the letter from 1881, there is also no doubt that this thought gives *pleasure* —and a particularly *intense,* even *ecstatic, pleasure*! After having encountered this thought, in front of this "enormous towering rock," Nietzsche spends several days in tears, "but tears of joy, mind you!"

Something gives *pleasure* in the perception of the sublime; the perception of the sublime must be able to facilitate a thought that gives *pleasure,* but *how*? – On a first, somewhat superficial answer, we may suggest that the *halt of time* does. We understand from passages in *Zarathustra*, that in this thought, facilitated by the perception of the sublime, time is felt as if suspended. "What happened to me? Listen! Did time perhaps fly away? Do I not fall? Did I not fall – listen! – into the well of eternity?" (Za IV, "Mittags"; KSA 4, p. 344) [. . .] "Woe unto me! Where is time gone? Have I not sunk into deep wells? The world sleeps." (Za IV, "Das Nachtwandlerlied"; KSA 4, p. 398). Time disappears; it 'flies away,' or is simply 'gone.' In this universe devoid of time, it is as if the world 'sleeps.' We understand that the individual, Zarathustra, is eternalized by this time-drop or -stop; he "falls into the well of eternity."

Time 'flies away'! Now, does time now 'fly away' from the world, or from the subject perceiving the world? The question implies, does Nietzsche assume that time is 'objective,' belonging to or attached to objects, or is he in this case adopting, rather, Kant/Schopenhauer's position, that time comes into existence in and as subjective presentation of sensations? It is most likely that Nietzsche is here following Kant and Schopenhauer in the belief that time is not a property of the world, that the world itself has no registration of time. In all contexts, especially in the Nachlaß material, Nietzsche's world of appearances is understood as simply *being-there*, as such, preceding all schematization and presentation; this world of appearances does not have a temporal presentation of itself. Time is then applied to the world by the perceiving subject, enabling subjective intuition of the world, being as such indispensable in subjective *presentation* of the world. As such, time would to Nietzsche as to Kant, be a "form of inner sense," a "subjective condition of our human intuition," but "apart

---

chaos, disorder, and desolation as experienced in a *boundless* and *formless* nature, Nietzsche's characters 'come upon' or 'encounter' the thought of eternal recurrence. On the other hand, between the universe as becoming and the representation of the sublime we notice a better affinity than, e.g., between becoming and the representation of the beautiful (providing a 'form' 'without a concept,' etc.). It is as if the representation of the sublime provides us with a rough sketch of what the universe as becoming would look like; in a flash of an insight.

from the subject," "nothing."⁵⁰⁶ If Nietzsche is following Kant and Schopenhauer, and time 'flies away,' it must then 'fly away' from the perceiving subject, the consequence of which is that the subject "falls" into the "well of eternity."⁵⁰⁷

---

⁵⁰⁶   These are all Kant's formulations: "Time is not something that is self-subsistent or that attaches to things as an objective determination, and that hence would remain if one abstracted from all subjective conditions of our intuition of it. [. . .] Time is nothing but the form of inner sense, i.e., of the intuiting we do of ourselves and of our inner state. For time cannot be a determination of outer appearances, because it does not belong to any shape or position, etc., but rather determines the relation of presentation in our inner state. [. . .] Time is no longer objective if we abstract from the sensibility of our intuition, and hence from the way of presenting peculiar to us, and speak of *things as such*. Hence time is merely a subjective condition of our (human) intuition (an intuition that is always sensible – i.e., inasmuch as we are affected by object); in itself, i.e., apart from the subject, time is nothing." Immanuel Kant, Critique of Pure Reason. Translation W. S. Pluhar, Indianapolis (Hackett Publishing Company), 1996, pp. 87-89.

⁵⁰⁷   In a recent article, Oliver Dier has expressed insights that have a resemblance to my own: "He [Zarathustra] suspects, in the 'thoughts and back-thoughts' that he himself fears, that our experience of time is dependent on the form of being of the self [*Seinsform des Ich*]. The dwarf's contempt for Zarathustra's sketchy time-analysis of recurrence derives from his ignorance of the correspondence between self [*Ich*] and time. The belief in an autonomous self confirms lived time-experience in the modus of separation. And reversibly, enforces in every separating time-experience the belief [*glaube*] in an autonomous self. In this interaction between time and self, the perception of world is formed. The thought of eternal recurrence is now a kind of time-experience, breaking through the circular reasoning [*Zirkelschluß*] by which perception of world establishes itself; and must in this eventually change the form of being of the self." Oliver Dier, "Die Verwandlung der Wiederkunft," in: Nietzsche-Studien 30. Berlin, New York (Walter de Gruyter), 2001, p. 153. I believe Dier is right in emphasizing the intimate correlation between time and self; and he is surely right in emphasizing how eternal recurrence would change the *Seinsform* of this self. One might add the following explanatory commentary, and I discern here the seed for a possible deviation from Dier's otherwise acute exposition: if an 'autonomous self' is a self that understands itself as different from the world, and vice versa (i.e., produces itself as 'independent'; i.e., a self constituting and living a subject-object relation), this self is not something one adopts as *belief* (in any meaningful sense of the term). It is constituted ontogenetically long before the subject starts adopting 'beliefs'; i.e., in the early formation of a neurological capacity for simply being in the world, and exist as an experiencing agency. It stands to reason that the 'autonomous,' the 'independent,' self constitutes itself temporally; i.e., in step with

4.3. Second Encounter: An Early Example of Self-Unconsciousness, the Forgetful Animal.

From early on in his writings, Nietzsche is fascinated with self-forgetfulness; the idea appears in his early work long before he tries to articulate it as one particular aspect of 'eternal recurrence.' It was, we remarked in the introduction, an explicit theme in *Die Geburt der Tragödie*, where it appeared in the defense of the Ancient and Medieval Dionysian festivals – Nietzsche being explicitly disdainful of the bourgeois renunciation of the uninhibited celebration of the Dionysian revelers.

In its early, still embryonic, form, the idea is expressed as a fascination with unconsciousness. It appears like a theme played in a very low key, hardly perceptible; or like a dream-thought given various representations because the thought cannot yet present itself. As such, it is also oftentimes – like all dream-thought – *displaced*; that is, Nietzsche does not necessarily bind the idea to himself (or to what would concern his own pleasures), he instead displaces it and cathects it to other figures in his thinking. This is what appears to happen in the second of the *Unzeitgemässe Betrachtungen*, where we encounter an early manifestation of the theme in the form of 'the forgetful cattle.'

Nietzsche addresses yet again the notion of self-forgetfulness, but we encounter it in the form of a fable applied to animal existence. The cattle are living in the presence of the self-present; they are not burdened with the typical human tribulations, especially consciousness, language, and reason.

---

an ability to *experience what is outside itself*. But as such, we must emphasize that the 'autonomous' subject has nothing to do with ideology, and cannot be seen as a concoction brewed together over, to paraphrase Derrida, 'three thousand years of Western Metaphysics.' We must also emphasize that as such, the 'autonomous self' is not identical to that other famous entity, 'the rational' or 'homogeneous' subject (which possibly *is* an ideological, or quasi-ideological, formation). The so-called 'rational subject' comes about as an ontogenetic later development than the autonomous/temporalizing subject. Temporalization is ontogenetically too primitive a capacity. This primitive capacity constitutes *the I – the world* as a subject-object relation, but in this, it does not co-constitute reason or rationality: *the ability to experience is not identical to an ability to reason* (cf. Kant). This, finally, must also imply that if Nietzsche 'deconstructs' this primitive capacity in his eternal-recurrence-experience, he changes the '*Seinsform des Ich*' in a much more radical and shocking sense than would be implied if he were simply reversing a 'belief in the autonomous self' (*as if* merely an erroneous ideology advanced by 'Western Thinking'). In comparison to Nietzsche's project, that fashionable project is almost nothing.

4. Return as Self-Repetition of Self-Presence

In the animal, Nietzsche finds a figure expressing this most fundamental and most fascinating possibility, which we label: *being-in-the-world-as-becoming* or *living-the-world-as-hyperreality*.

> Look at the cattle, passing you by grazing: they do not know what yesterday or today is, they leap about, eat, rest, digest, leap about again, and so from morning to night and from day to day, tightly fettered to their pleasure and pain [*angebunden mit ihrer Lust und Unlust*], namely to the pale of the moment [*an den Pflock des Augenblickes*], and thus neither melancholy nor bored. To see this is hard for man, [. . .] he cannot help looking on their happiness with envy – he precisely wants what the animals have, a life neither bored nor painful, yet he cannot have it because he refuses to have it like an animal. (UB II, KSA 1, p. 248)

In this passage, Nietzsche's persona wonders about the 'happiness' of the cattle living in the instance, thus, he presumes, in complete harmony with themselves, unconscious of past and future, concerned only with eating, resting, digesting, and leaping about. The cattle are "fettered to the pale of the moment," and now man, envious on their happiness, looks at them and asks: "Why do you not speak to me of your happiness but only stand and gaze at me?" The animal, we are told, would have liked to answer, but given its condition, it happily forgets what it is going to say: "'The reason is I always forget what I was about to say' – but then it forgot this answer too, and stayed silent: so that the human being was left wondering." (UB II, KSA 1, p. 248).

Since Nietzsche's cattle cannot retain the streaming now and fixate it (in a more rigorous language, since it cannot produce Husserl's 'retentional horizon'; cf. below, sect. 5), it is their predicament to live wholly absorbed in the present instance. They have no 'mirror' and cannot fixate their inner and outer perceptions in the interior mirror of consciousness. They do not have a consciousness that can be simultaneously turned towards the immediately experienced now and the immediately previous. Consequently, the animal cannot reproduce in consciousness what it was just thinking. It must necessarily forget, because in every instance it is always-already engaged in another perceptive now, a now irreversibly annihilating the previous now. Therefore, every one of its perceptive instances "sinks back into night and fog and is extinguished for ever" (UB II, KSA 1, p. 249). As such, the animal also lives innocently and honestly: "It is contained in its present, like a number without any awkward fraction left over. It does not know how to dissimulate, it conceals nothing and at every instant appears wholly as what it is; it can therefore never be anything but honest." (UB II, KSA 1, p. 249).

The animal forgets because it produces no 'retentional trace'; i.e., every current now is constantly replaced with some other now, *ad infinitum*. In this, we must be presupposing an *absolute flow of time*, and the animal's inability to *stop this absolute flow*: the animal would have liked to answer the inquisitive human, but as soon as it recalls a word, it is always too late; time has already passed by, and it forgets . . . has always-already forgotten. Differently put, and in better conformity with Nietzsche's language: the animal lives wholly absorbed in the world-as-becoming, unable to transform this world-as-becoming into a world-as-being.

If we take the logic of Nietzsche's fable a step further, the animal could strictly speaking not even *want* to answer the inquisitive human, since, living in the flow of time, it would be unable to remember, even to *hear*, the question. It would successively forget each word in the pronounced sequence of words. It might hear the noises of single words and syllables, but, in the flow of time, it could not construct any coherent sequence, and, consequently, it could not hear *sentences*. (Being pedantic, we notice that a paradox emerges. According to the tale, the animal has apparently a language, although, logically, this must be impossible. The animal hears a language, it thinks in a language, and it wants to answer in a language, and still, no word escapes it. However, this assigned 'language' is just a prerequisite for staging the fictional dialogue between animal and human; it is the outcome of the poetic license that Nietzsche permits himself, and according to which he is at liberty to override logic in order to produce the desired scene. Consequently, we get a thinking animal, but without a language to think *in*.)

In Nietzsche's tale, the cattle have memories of sorts, but the animal forgets them as soon as it tries to make them conscious: 'I would have liked to tell you about my happiness, but I always forget what I am just about to say!' So, while the animal has memories, but doesn't remember them, humans retain the past only all too well. Thus, humans are able to stabilize a vibrating world of becoming; they retain the immediately past in the presence of the now, with this *reproducing* the past. Humans are able to *make memory conscious*. Instead of sinking back into the past and disappear, the memorized moment comes back to man as "a ghost" disturbing "the peace of a later moment."

> He also wonders at himself, that he cannot learn to forget but always clings to the past: however far and fast he runs, the chain runs with him. It is puzzling: the moment [*Augenblick*], in a whoosh it is here, in a whoosh it is gone; before it, nothing, after it, again nothing; nonetheless it returns as a ghost and disturbs the peace of a later moment. Continuously, a leaf loosens from the wheel of time, falls away, floats about – and suddenly it floats back again into the lap of man. Then man says 'I remember' [*"ich erinnerte mich"*] and envies the animal, who forgets immediately and for whom every moment really dies. (UB II, KSA 1, p. 249).

4. Return as Self-Repetition of Self-Presence

The human predicament is to reproduce incessantly the trace of the past. Instead of living life as an uncomplicated line (like the animal), man folds the line back on itself, and then he folds it once more, and once more, etc., until it is a complex structure of multiple levels. Nothing seems to disappear, everything seems to come back, but as a shadow, a "ghost." As memory, the past flows along with the present, as such disturbing, distracting, corrupting, and polluting the experience of the present. In another fragment, past and future becomes like 'noisy women' disturbing the peace of the moment: "These two female characters [*Weibspersonen*], past and future, are making such noises, that the present runs away from them." (Nachlaß 1882, KSA 10, 3[1/396]).

Humans are bound to pronounce their "I remember." The "I remember" is the briefest expression of this 'double-flow' of consciousness: in the instantaneous enunciation of the sentence, the image of the past is back. In the celebrated moment of the self-presence of the present, the human recalls past memories, and recovers that which on its own was destined to flow away as it sinks back into the past.

The logic here derived form Nietzsche's description of the forgetful animal also applies to the child, as it is introduced both in *Unzeitgemässe Betrachtungen* and *Zarathustra*: "[The child] has nothing past to deny, playing between the fences of past and future in blissful blindness." (UB II, KSA 1, p. 249). "The child is innocence and forgetting, a new beginning, a play, a self-propelled wheel, a first movement, a holy yes-saying." (Za I, "Von den drei Verwandlungen," KSA 4, p. 31).[508]

Whereas animal and child (and later in UB II, the 'supra-historical man') possess the desired ability to live in self-forgetfulness and self-unconsciousness, the adult human has become annoyingly self-conscious; – this sense of person, self, and identity is typically being devaluated in Nietzsche's writing: "Self-consciousness is the last that is added to a fully functioning organism; it is a l m o s t something superfluous: consciousness of u n i t y. Anyhow, it is something highly imperfect and often-erroneous [*Oft-Fehlgreifendes*] in comparison to the real intrinsic incorporated [*eingeborenen einverleibten*] operating unity of all functions. Unconsciousness is the grand main activity." (Nachlaß 1881, KSA 9, 11[316]).

---

[508] In *The Other Nietzsche*, Joan Stambaugh quotes and comments on the same passages about animal and child. She labels the thought expressed in these passages, "the innocence of becoming," and gives it an Existentialist interpretation, very different from the 'cognitive,' 'psychological,' 'neurological' I am here promoting. See Joan Stambaugh, The Other Nietzsche, New York (SUNY Press), 1994, p. 95ff.

4.4. Third Encounter: Empty Perception of Hyper-Reality and the Celebration of the Super-Superficial.

It is impossible, and by Nietzsche being recognized as such, for the adult human being to return to animal existence. This avenue is closed off except perhaps under severe pathological conditions of which we in general have insufficient knowledge. Or it might perhaps be accessed by means of certain seriously hallucinogenic drugs – an option Nietzsche of course never allowed himself, radically averse as he was to any kind of stimulant.

Still, there is perhaps, in normal and sober life, an attitude in which we gain an intuitive insight into the attractive *conscious- and language-independent* existence; an attitude in which we, all by ourselves and intuitively, cast aside the vexations: consciousness, language, and reason. We have previously introduced this attitude as 'empty perception.' We described it the as a lingering speech-less state of mind in which the world is sensed and sensually 'seen,' but not in a proper, or stronger, sense consciously *perceived*.[509] It was a state, in which the inner monologue, that otherwise relentlessly continues its chatter within the human, seems for a moment suspended, insofar as for a short while the human being has been reduced to a glance and a stare. Waking up from this situation is like waking up from a dream one knows one has had, but can't remember, and it is difficult to recall what exactly happened (– probably because nothing happened!), and therefore difficult to express the situation adequately. Both in 'empty perception' and in the dream (which we recall is uniquely visual), we have returned to this primitive and rudimentary ('animal') way of seeing.[510] This so-called 'empty perception' seems to give us pleasure. So, following Nietzsche, we suggest that there is possibly a pleasure in *seeing*; something in the order of an 'eye-' or 'ocular' pleasure. It is a pleasure rarely given attention in the standard lists of human pleasures, but the fact that the dream, which uniquely deals in pleasure, inevitably sends us back to perception, seems a good first indication that *seeing* belongs to one of the most rudimentary and primal pleasures in human existence.

---

[509] See Chapter 2, "A Silent World."
[510] We recall that to Freud the dream was characteristically sending us back to elementary perception; it was regressing to his so-called 'perceptive apparatus.' The meaning of the dream was distorted, Freud would explain, exactly because it had been translated into images: a dream-thought had been translated into a dream-content; a sentence into a pictorial narrative. From the perspective of the analyst, dream-analysis was such a laborious process partly because it was difficult to extract the *meaning* from these *images*.

4. Return as Self-Repetition of Self-Presence

Nietzsche assumes that his cattle from UB are consistently involved in this unconscious seeing. Now we ourselves – in these fleeting instances that we typically don't remember – are also on a daily basis involved in 'unconscious seeing.' We too immerse ourselves in empty perception of a blank reality; in moments where we suspend consciousness and language.[511]

Let a compilation of passages serve to evidence that Nietzsche invariably expresses a fascination with the world of so-called 'empty perception'; a world I alternatively also address as, the *super-superficial surface-world*; and in which I describe subjective existence as *being-in-the-world-as-becoming*, or *living-the-world-as-hyperreality*. In a passage from *Morgenröte*, we get the impression of a world silent and at rest; the universe has stopped moving and, simultaneously, speaking. Nietzsche's super-superficial universe informs us of nothing. Instead it becomes like *a mirror* for the gazing subject: *silence is mirroring silence*.

> In the great silence. [...] Now all is still! The sea lies there pale and glittering, it cannot speak [*es kann nicht reden*]. The sky play its everlasting silent evening game with red and yellow and green, it cannot speak. The little cliffs and ribbons of rock that run down into the sea as if to find the place where it is most solitary, none of them can speak. [...] Ah, it is growing yet more still, my heart swells again: it is startled by a new truth, it too cannot speak, it too mocks when the mouth calls something into this beauty, it too enjoys its sweet silent malice. (M 423; KSA 3, p. 259).

In the mirror of the silent universe, the gazing subject finds an expression of itself. As well as the world is a surface, it too is a surface; as well as the world does not speak, it too does not speak.

In this interaction with the world as silence and surface, Nietzsche's persona is reduced to a gaze halting time to the same degree as time is already halted in the environing world. As the subject *identifies with* this silent, immobile, transfixed world, the world, on its part, *teaches him its own silence* – as explicitly stated: "I begin to hate speech, to hate even thinking; for do I not hear behind every word the error, the illusion, the delusion laughing. [...] O sea, O evening! You are evil instructors! You teach man to cease being human! Shall he surrender to you? Shall he become as you now are, pale, glittering, mute?" (M 423; KSA 3, p. 260). – Shall I, Nietzsche, become like you, O sea, "pale, glittering, mute"? (One may

---

[511] Following Nietzsche, we are, after all, animals, so why would not the absolutely primeval exist as a phylogenetic repository resurfacing from time to time. It seems more rational, more coolheaded, to give this fundamental irrationality a fair hearing, rather than shrugging it off as irrational.

compare also to this fragment: "Speech to the cliffs. I love that you don't speak. Your silence has dignity [*Würde*]." (Nachlaß 1882-83, KSA 10, 5[1/265]).)

The subject is, as Nietzsche has established on several occasions, in itself nothing: it has no essence, no substance, but is a chaos of drives and voices; its so-called 'intentions' are merely illusory after-reconstructions and rationalizations of this chaos. Now, in the perception of the super-superficial, one escapes from this chaotic, confused, noisy subject as the world "teaches" the subject its own silence. The world lies *there* in the presence of itself, stupidly and silently, revealing nothing but the surface of itself. Nietzsche's sensually seeing persona enters a unique relationship with this world, a relationship based on identification and sympathy. As he reduces himself to a gaze, he too becomes like the world, silent and stupid: "My brothers, nature is stupid [*dumm*], and insofar as we are nature, we are all stupid." (Nachlaß 1882-83, KSA 10, 5[1/262]). A poem from *Die fröhliche Wissenschaft* corroborates the interpretations (the persona of the poem is situated in Sils Maria and is thus directly associated with Nietzsche himself): "Sils Maria. / Here I sat, waiting – not for anything, / beyond good and evil, fancying / now light, now shadows, all a game, / all lake, all noon, all time without aim." (FW "Lieder des Prinzen Vogelfrei", KSA 3, p. 649).

In these passages, time has been ground to a halt, and all purpose and intention in the subject is equally suspended. We are introduced to the alluring notion that one could muffle oneself to a silence as complete as the silence of the things surrounding oneself, that one could absorb oneself in nature, put a halt to time, and by implication, to the incessant soliloquies in one's inner mental life. In the grand moment of transgression and transubstantiation, the eternalized recurrence-subject turns into the eternalized recurrence-universe, and vice versa.

So, the world without time, i.e., the world as *eternalized*, becomes *internalized*, but internalized in a peculiar sense, because it is never 'taken in' by the *conscious subject*, it is only hovering 'right-there-in-front-of' the subject. With the deconstruction of time-consciousness, the world has been reclaimed in its own original completion. As we explicitly read in another fragment, it is *time* that conventionally prevents us encountering this completion: "The world lies there complete – a golden shell/skin of benevolence [*eine goldne Schale des Guten*]. But the creative spirit wants to create also what is complete: so it invented time – and now the world rolled away from itself, and rolled together again in large rings." (Nachlaß 1882-83, KSA 10, 5[1/266]).

4. Return as Self-Repetition of Self-Presence

As this blank skin of a surface ('right-there-in-front-of'), the environing world is being (however peculiar the notion might be) *internalized by our eyes*. This thrilling, fascinating, passionate moment of *internalizing the eternalized external*, transforms us, and is by Nietzsche experienced as euphoric and ecstatic. In another passage from FW, we find once again an expression for this peculiar pleasure in "gliding over" the silent super-superficial surface-world.

> Here I stand amidst the breaks of the surf, whose white flames are licking at my feet: from all sides it is howling, threatening, screaming, shrieking at me, while the old earth-rattler sings his aria in the lowest of depths, deep as a roaring bull, while pounding such an earth-rattling beat that the hearts of even these weather-beaten monsters of the rocks are trembling in their bodies. Then, suddenly, as if born out of nothingness, there appears before the gate of this hellish labyrinth only a few fathoms away, – a large sailboat, gliding along silently as a ghost. Oh, this ghostly beauty! How magically it touches me! What? Has all the calm and silence of the world embarked here? Is my happiness itself sitting in this quiet place, my happier self, my second, eternalized [*verewigtes*] self? Not dead, but also no longer alive? As a spirit-like silent, watching, gliding, hovering middle-being [*Mittelwesen*]? Similar to the ship, which with its white sails moves over the dark sea like an enormous butterfly! Yes! To move o v e r existence [*Dasein*]! That's it! That would be it! (FW 60, KSA 3, p. 424).

Nietzsche identifies with, or *is*, the ship; the ship becomes a representation of his particular desire of just *gliding over existence*. In this attitude, the human no longer engage any mental activity; it is "not dead, but also no longer alive." Its immersion in sense-perception is introduced as a *possibility*, as in the hypothetical conditional: "Yes! To move over existence! That's it! That would be it!" If we could actually get into/onto that surface of the *super-superficial*, worries about death would be as irrelevant as worries about birth; we would truly be 'men without future'; everything would linger as one prolonged moment, as a *nunc stans*, and we would be nothing but diminutive specks sprinkled on the glittering surface.

The attraction is the surface-world, as this surface remains forever calm and silent. When this so-called 'sensual seeing' offers a sense of pleasure, it is, however, a remote pleasure. We are talking about an *aesthetic attitude* in the old sense; and the pleasure produced in such an attitude is traditionally of a tranquil nature. 'Aesthetics' was traditionally understood as related to the senses, specifically vision (so, for example, in Baumgarten and Kant, who also described his two forms of intuition, space and time, as 'aesthetic'). When the concept developed into a theory of the beautiful, the pleasures in contemplating the beautiful were typically understood as serene, calming, and soothing.[512] This original semantic value is retained in the present description of the 'aesthetic attitude.'

We remember that in the *epistemological attitude* introduced under the label *Repetitive Interpretation-Processes,* senses were in Nietzsche always 'nets' organizing, schematizing, and interpreting the world. In the epistemological attitude, we cannot hope to get beyond our 'nets,' our means of perceiving, simplifying, and interpreting the world. But in the *aesthetic attitude* introduced under the label *self-repetition of self-presence,* nothing is organized or schematized. Senses do nothing, and if perchance they do, we forget it so rapidly, that we could only *know* that they do nothing.

The surface of the super-superficial we also call the *hyper-real,* or the *world of becoming*. Here, the flow of time has stopped, and the passage, past – present – future, has become literally a thing of the past. In this context, 'eternal recurrence' appears to be a misnomer, because strictly speaking nothing recurs, everything stays the same on a surface frozen in time: the loop has been tightened into a 'knot.' Like in the example of the forgetful animal everything comes back to itself in Nietzsche's deconstructed subjectivity, because the 'now' is continuously being constituted as uniquely *new*. This *eternity in/of the now*, becomes Nietzsche's most fundamental 'formula' or 'matrix' for desire, for joy, or, as he says in this fragment, for *love*. "The love of life is almost the opposite [*Gegensatz*] to love of long-life [*Lang-Leben*]. All love thinks of the moment [*Augenblick*] and the eternity [*Ewigkeit*] – but not of 'length.' " (Nachlaß 1882, KSA 10, 3[1/293]). The continuously re-constitution of the now as the same, the *repetition* of the same, is joyful; and is the formula for joy.

4.5. Fourth Encounter: The Erotic Unification of the Eternal-Recurrence-Subject and the Eternal-Recurrence-Universe.

We have introduced the notion of a so-called pleasure of perception, as experienced in a so-called 'aesthetic attitude.' It involves a deconstruction of internal time-consciousness, and it suggests a certain unification of the deconstructed self and the environing sublime universe. At the very heights of

---

[512] Cf., Kant's *Kritik der Urteilskraft*, Schopenhauer's third book of *Die Welt als Wille und Vorstellung*, and the *Ergänzungen* in the second volume of the same work. The complicated relationships (here only intimated), between Nietzsche's eternal-recurrence-thought and the Kantian/Schopenhauerian notions of the aesthetic experience, and especially, the experience of the sublime, are deserving of far more thorough investigations, which must remain, however, beyond the scope of the present essay.

4. Return as Self-Repetition of Self-Presence 493

this unification, the world is reclaimed in its completeness, and ditto the subject. The subject *becomes* the world.

The unification itself is felt *ecstatically*, and is significantly described in sexual terms as unification between man and woman. Nietzsche has had to resort to what is conventionally our best *symbolization* of pleasure, namely sexuality, in order to describe this particular joy and rapture (we recall here that sexuality is merely a *symbolization*, a *representation*, of pleasure, which is in-itself a far more complex phenomenon).[513] In the following passage from *Zarathustra*, Zarathustra "trembles with desire" as he sees the deep sky; he "throws himself into the heights of heaven"; he "seeks only you" and "flies up into you" (the abysmal sky):

> O Heaven above me; you Pure! Deep! You abyss of light [*Licht-Abgrund*]! Seeing you, I tremble with godlike desires.
> To throw myself into your heights – that is m y depth. To hide in your purity – that is m y innocence.
> [. . .] You do not speak; thus you proclaim your wisdom to me. Today you rose for me silently over the roaring sea; your love and your shyness are a revelation to my roaring soul.
> [. . .] And when I climbed mountains, whom did I seek on the mountains, if not you?
> And all my wanderings and mountain climbing were sheer necessity and a help in my helplessness: what I want with all my will is to fl y , to fly up into y o u .
> [. . .] O Heaven above me; you Pure! Deep! That is what your purity is to me now, that there is no eternal spider of reason or spider-web of reason [*Vernunft-Spinne oder -Spinnennetze*]:
> — that you are to me a dance floor for divine accidents, that you are to me a divine table for divine dice and dice players! – (Za III, "Vor Sonnen-Aufgang"; KSA 4, p. 207-10).

In the so-called aesthetic attitude, the world has obviously become a very erotic place. While this eroticism is present in the passage above, as indeed in almost all passages related to eternal recurrence in *Zarathustra*, it becomes glaringly explicit in particularly one of the sections. (Paradoxical,

---

[513] We remark that in our approach to this aspect of Nietzsche's eternal recurrence, we revert to its *performative*, rather than to its *constative*, display of 'meaning.' That is, we do not listen too seriously to the theory presented in passages like, "I come again, with this sun, with this earth [. . .] I come back eternally to this same, selfsame life." And we certainly do not involve ourselves in theoretical quests to figure out how it is possible for human beings to live twice, and the like. We try rather to understand the pleasure *at the root of* the eternal recurrence experience; and try to explain the *pleasure* in conceiving the thought, as well as the *sexualization* of the environment in which it is conceived.

because the passage is repeated seven times, it is easily ignored as extravagant rhetoric.)

> O, why should I not lust after eternity [*nach der Ewigkeit brünstig sein*] and after the sacred ring of all rings. – the ring of recurrence [*Wiederkunft*]?
> Nowhere else did I find a woman, with whom I wanted children; unless it be this woman whom I love: because I love you, O eternity [*Ewigkeit*]!
> Because I love you, O eternity!
> (Za III, "Die sieben Siegel"; KSA 4, p. 287-91)

Zarathustra wants to marry, make love to, and have children with eternity, because he loves her emphatically. In fact, this is the only 'woman' he ever loved.

He could also, alternatively (. . . and as a modest proposal), have wanted to marry, make love to, and have children with *a woman*; but this is obviously not contemplated in the present context. We are situated, instead, in the space-time of Nietzsche/Zarathustra's mountains. This is his eternity; the eternity he lusts for, and wants to marry. Time has been grounded to a halt, and space seems like eternalized. In Nietzsche's space-time, the environing world has again become like a mirror, and it is this mirror he lusts after, —wants to marry. This mirror is the surface-world mirroring his own emptiness. This is his woman. When they marry, they become united; the world has become internalized, but as said, internalized by the eyes. In this 'empty gazing' we let the world be what it is, as we let it shine forth in its own self-presence. We are still seeing the world through our particular human optics (of course!), that is, according to the specific way and manner in which our eyes organize a visual field. And in this, we continue to 'falsify,' but we have reverted to the *skin* of our perceptive system.

At this point, we have *documented* from a number of Nietzsche's passages that allegedly, there is pleasure in this attitude, but still, we have not tried to *explain why*. Adhering to a model of the young neurologist Freud, we may give a very brief sketch in way of such an explanation.

In 'empty perception,' there is no rise of excitation in the psyche, since there is no deep-penetration of the mental system. Perceptive stimuli are sensed and sensually seen, but they are not *remembered*. They are as such not consciously perceived. In his *Project*,[514] Freud suggested that conscious perception would always increase the level of excitation in the psyche. It

---

[514] Sigmund Freud, "Project for a Scientific Psychology," in: The Standard Edition of the Complete Psychological Works of Sigmund Freud, vol. 1-24. Edited by J. Strachey, London (The Hogarth Press and the Institute of Psychoanalysis) 1966.

would in other words always cause 'unpleasure'; an 'unpleasure' the subject would deal with by bringing the rise in excitation-level back to equilibrium. This was for example done by consulting the difficult reality that had caused the rise of tension. In conscious perception, one would for example *see* an apple, *remember* it, and consequently see a *meal*; this would increase the excitation of the psychic system by producing a *wish* to possess and to eat the fruit. In order to fulfill the wish, one had to consult the reality of the tree. By contrast, in *empty perception*, the perceptive system was never deep-penetrated, memory not consulted, and there was no rise of tension. The apple was not *remembered*; it was only *seen*; consequently, it would exist merely in the 'innocent' self-presence of itself.[515] *Empty perception* of the *hyper-real* thus becomes a powerful model on what Freud called homeostasis, his zero-tension resolution of conflict in inner mental life.

In Freud's later writing, the notion was taken up again, and it became the model for what he would describe as (in a dramatic, somewhat misleading, formulation) the *death-drive* (– in *one* of its several interpretations!). In this interpretation, the Freudian 'death-drive' was conceived as absolute and ultimate pleasure, equivalent to the zero-tension resolution of conflict from his early neurological writings. This so-called 'death-drive' was not pleasure in the sense sexuality was pleasure; it was a 'deeper' pleasure equivalent to the tranquility, serenity, sublimity, and eternity Nietzsche experiences when he visually immerses himself in the panorama around Sils Maria.

As such we are suggesting that Freud and Nietzsche are trying to give name to a pleasure that reaches back to our primordial phylogenetic *animal* repositories. Freud describes his 'death-drive-pleasure' as *nirvana*; while Nietzsche describes his pleasure as an *eternal-recurrence-experience*.

In either description, the thought has oftentimes been presented as half-mystical. We assume instead that the two philosophers try to describe a pleasure extremely old, taking as an indication of the archaism of the thought that whenever these two master-writers try to describe and name it, their language breaks down; their eloquence fails them; at best, the thought is rendered in suggestive and poetic imagery. The thought therefore seems to reach back to an existence in the phylogenetic past before language entered the scene; the conceivable reason why it is near-impossible to retrieve.

---

[515] One might here adopt Stambaugh's phrase 'the innocence of becoming'; but re-applied within my neurological context, in contrast to Stambaugh's Existentialist.

5. Temporal Construction and Deconstruction of the Interpreted World

5.1. The Temporally Constructed World of Being.

The world, as we perceive it, is always constituted in time: I cross a creek; I then pick up a flower; I then rest on a mossy stone. The temporal order is, first, crossing the creek, second, picking up the flower, and third, resting on the stone; this is how I experience, and later remember, what I did. As such, *my-world* is always constituted temporally; i.e., in temporal sequences that can be retrieved in recollection in the order they were perceived. However, this temporal order obviously does not exist in *the-world*, the creek does not come before the flower, etc.; it is constituted subjectively. In *my-world*, I constitute even the stone as a temporal object. A simple example suffices: first I look at the stone; then I close my eyes, open them, only to look at the stone again; then I close my eyes, only to look at the stone again. The temporal order is: I look at the stone a first time, then I look at it a second time, and finally, a third time. This sequence of three periods also does not exist in *the-world* of the stone. But thanks to my temporal organization of my perception, I can ascertain that the stone persists as the same impression corresponding to the same object; consequently, I sense it as an enduring object. The temporal order of impressions, and in this, the sense of duration, is not a property of the stone itself. In *the-world*, the stone exists in the self-presence of itself.

We may formalize the two distinct 'worlds' – *my-world* and *the-world* – as follows. My perceptions of the stone constitute a sequence; where the first impression is prior to the second and third, etc.; like, $\alpha_1 \ldots \alpha_2 \ldots \alpha_3$. The stone itself does not constitute any sequence, since is what it is; like, a . . . a . . . a. In other words, something has happened between *stone* and *perception of stone*, between 'a' and 'α'. Not only has 'a' been transformed into 'α' (given our specific human sense-apparatus, our human 'optics'), more importantly in this context, to 'α' there is always and inevitably attached a temporal marker, the integer in subscript. It is thanks to this inner flow of time, that the universe is stabilized as *being* versus *becoming*. 'Becoming' is how the universe behaves from moment to moment without anybody building any order ('sequence,' 'sense of succession,' 'before and after,' 'cause and effect') into these moments. In contrast, the inner flow of time *stabilizes* the world as being. (To Heraclitus, who did not have an analysis of time-*consciousness*, time was therefore simply like the famous river one didn't step into twice. Time-*consciousness* is approximately doing the opposite of what that continuously flowing river is doing. The continuously flowing river is an image on the world of becoming; time-consciousness is the elementary prerequisite for constituting a world of being.)

In order to understand how the *inner flow of time* constitutes the universe as *being*, we have to make a digression to Husserl's analysis of time.

Husserl is always in his analyses concerned about how a temporal object is constituted in consciousness (what objective time may be, is not his concern). An object is understood a 'real' object with extension and duration, as perceived in sight or hearing; it may be something like a stone, a house, or a melody; but how is it temporally constituted? Impressions of such 'real objects' always arrive to us from the future along a line (in Husserl's conception); the line is open-ended because we are always open towards the future as receptive to the ever-new. The future (which cannot be part of time-*consciousness*) is always ahead of us, and then it arrives in the form of an object. It, so to speak, comes 'gliding down' Husserl's line, arriving eventually to us as impression, and after that point, it continues to 'glide back' as past. However, Husserl realizes that as it sinks back, it does not disappear altogether; it rather continues a 'pseudo-existence' in the next present as 'adumbrated'; in this, it co-constitutes subsequent impressions – Husserl's famous *retention*. This is for example how we hear a melody: first we hear one tone, it arrives to us from the future, then we hear another, it also arrives to us from the future, but 'in' the second tone, the first tone 'continues' to 'vibrate'; not as real, to be sure, but as a shadow-impression supporting our impression of the second tone. Music would be as such meaningless, if we were hearing only singular tones, forgetting them as soon as they disappeared as real. Instead, when hearing a melody, previous tones sink down 'behind' the currently present tone as a retentional horizon, co-constituting the currently present tone. Eventually, when the melody stops, the retentions attached to any current present also stop. The melody will now sink back into memory, and it may be retrieved from memory as *re-presentation* (or *reproduction*), but not as *retention*. (In this, the difference between retention and reproduction becomes clear: whereas *retention* attaches itself to an actually present now, *re-presentation* or *reproduction* is merely abstract recollection; it attaches itself to no actual now; it is a fantasy operation – as if I now reproduce to myself the beginning of Beethoven's *Pathetique*; I don't actually hear any music, but I can run through, *reproduce*, the first movement at will.)

Around in his work, Husserl describes inner time-consciousness as a comet: the now is the head, and the retention the tail of the comet. Like the head of a comet, the impression originally constitutes the object in inner time-consciousness; and like the halo of a comet, the retentions are the residue which is left over from the core/the present (and which to us observers make the comet visible in the first place). The original presence of the impression (the 'core') is always to Husserl indispensable in the constitution of the temporal object, but considering that the now is hardly anything in itself (it is understood, like in the classical analyses of time such as Augustine's, to be so brief an instant that it has no existence), what in actuality constitutes the temporal object is the 'halo,' the *retentional horizon*.

Now, we said above that in the world of becoming, the stone floats off like, a ... a ... a; and in time-constituting consciousness, like, $\alpha_1 \ldots \alpha_2 \ldots \alpha_3$. But the last model needs some help and modification before it can qualify as adequate, since as it is, it does not illustrate that in any 'α'-impression, the previous 'α'-impression is always retained. Adhering to Husserl, in consciousness, the world is stabilized as being thanks to retention, but this stabilization is not adequately represented in a diagram of a one-dimensional line. The world is temporally constituted because α_1 glides down behind α_2, and $\alpha_1 \ldots \alpha_2$ glides down behind α_3, in the succession of impressions. Impression 3 (α_3) is only understood as '3', because in its own presence, it has an awareness of '1' and '2'. The line looks consequently something like below, the vertical lines accounting here for the *sense* of succession and sequence; the *sense* of before and after, cause and effect (a more elaborate model follows below).

$$\begin{array}{ccc} \alpha_1 & \alpha_2 & \alpha_3 \\ & \alpha_1 & \alpha_2 \\ & & \alpha_1 \end{array}$$

Moreover, not only is the temporal object constituted as *being* thanks to the retentional horizon, it is also always-already *interpreted* qua this horizon being *thrown forwards as anticipatory*. When projected forwards as anticipatory, the retentional horizon is transformed into a *protentional horizon*. This, again, requires a brief explanation.

Husserl draws in the beginning of his investigations, and regularly returns to, a diagram of time-consciousness with its two essential dimensions, presence and retention. We imagine a temporal object having duration; it starts to run off in A_0 and ends in A_4; we may think of a melody fragment, where a first tone sounds in A_0 and the last in A_4. At A_1, the first tone-now, A_0, has sunk down beneath A_1, and the vertical line A_1-A'_0 represents now the retentional horizon of A_1. At time A_4, the vertical line A_4-A'_0 represents the retentional horizon of A_4. In A_4, the melody stops sounding; after that point we just have an unspecified future, not yet filled with nows (the punctuated line). Protention could now be drawn as the retentional horizon, A'_4-

5. Temporal Construction and Deconstruction of the Interpreted World   499

A'$_0$, being *projected forwards* as a horizon of meaning, *before* it has any actual now to attach itself to. This horizon constitutes therefore the now *ahead of* this now having come into actual existence. In other words, the world is *meant*, or with Nietzsche, *interpreted*, before it is consciously seen.[516] Husserl's diagram, with my modifications, is the following.

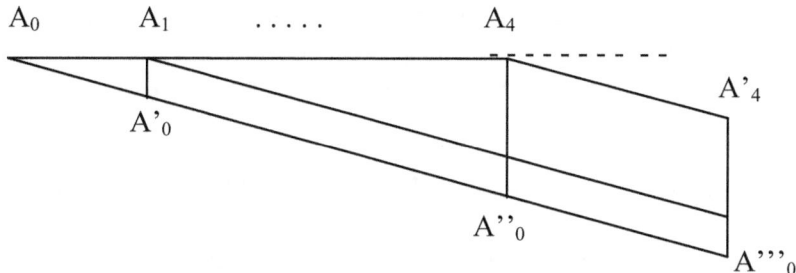

We now suggest the following hypothesis: much in Nietzsche's *intuitive* understanding of how inner time-consciousness constitutes the world as being, hinges on the combined effect of a 'retentional horizon' that primordially constitutes the object as meaning-full, and a 'protentional horizon' that always-already 'interprets' the object, ahead of this object being actually perceived in conscious perception. The importance of this protentional horizon to Nietzsche's epistemology is especially clear when Nietzsche, cf. above, talks about his 'chronological reversal' [*Chronologische Umdrehung*] in our perceptions of an external world; i.e., about the reversal of cause and effect in the constitution of the inner experience of an impression. As another example, but an issue with which I shall not concern myself at this point, we recall that pain- and pleasure-experiences to Nietzsche are always constituted in *delay*; this means that an impression has to be *interpreted* as painful before it is *perceived* as painful.[517] In general,

---

[516] It is not implied in this conception that the world has vanished as external reality – i.e., the conception is not an idealistic model transforming everything outer into our representations, or our interpretations. This becomes obvious when we account for the simple fact that it is always possible to be *surprised*. In the 'surprise' our immediate expectations are being rebutted and revised. I 'meant' to see this object as so and so, but no, it shows itself to be quite different. I 'meant' to hear the melody continue in this or that manner, but no, the composer has done something rather different. A general explanation of 'surprise' is perhaps exactly this: the 'surprise' comes about when reality 'bumps into' or 'collides with' a well-consolidated protentional horizon – and the better consolidated the protentional horizon, the greater the 'surprise.'

[517] Nietzsche's theories of pain and pleasure are rarely dealt with in Nietzsche

the *interpretation* is chronologically *slightly ahead of* the *perception*; or in other words, a protentional horizon is *projected forwards as anticipatory*. (Some readers may recognize this situation: the child starts crying *with delay*; it first needs to figure out whether the sensation it felt was caused by a hostile object, or by an innocent one. First when it has decided it was hostile, it starts crying; it has then decided to perceive the sensation as painful. Such decision-processes are, as Nietzsche emphasizes time and again, *intellectual*: the subject needs to find a *cause* for a sensation before it feels sure it has the sensation; cf. examples above, 'thirst' & 'feeling unwell.')[518]

5.2. Deconstructing the Temporally Constructed World of Being.

Let us suppose that we could now (somehow) subtract our temporal impressions of the stone from the stone, that we could ignore or 'forget' the stone as temporal object with duration, then – as we may well phrase it – time has 'flown back' into the stone, and we could see (supposedly) the stone for what it is. Time would have disappeared or evaporated. In the transformation from *my-world* into *the-world* – from 'α' to 'a' – 'everything' would have been regained as self-presence.

---

commentary, but Günter Abel has a fine exposition in his *Nietzsche*, loc. cit.; chapter IV.1. Also A. Olivier deals with the issue in an recent article, see Abraham Olivier, "Nietzsche and Neurology," in: Nietzsche-Studien 32, Berlin, New York (Walter de Gruyter), 2003.

[518] The notion of 'protention' is not being given analytical priority in Husserl. In the early notes on time-consciousness (notes from 1893 to 1901), before Husserl explicitly talks about 'retention' and 'protention,' the problem of an "*intuitive expectation*" or a "*forwards-directed intention*" gets the following formulation: "In the case of a given experience – in the case of familiar melodies, for example, or of melodies that are perhaps repeated – we frequently have *intuitive expectations* as well. Each new tone then fulfills this forwards-directed intention. We have *determinate* expectations in these cases. But we are not and we cannot be entirely without apprehension directed forwards. *The temporal fringe also has a future.*" (Husserl, The Phenomenology of the Consciousness of Internal Time, loc. cit., p. 172). The perception of a melody is therefore temporally extended, Husserl continues: something becomes objective as *now*, something becomes objective as *just past*, and then he adds, "perhaps also something or other is objective as "future."" (ibid.). We notice Husserl's discomfort about the latter case: 'perhaps' something becomes objective as 'future' – *future* in scare quotes; indeed a weird objectivity! An *objectivity* of the *not-yet*?

5. Temporal Construction and Deconstruction of the Interpreted World 501

As part of our inner time-consciousness, humans are sequencing the world incessantly and involuntarily, i.e., building temporal order into the world. If – and this I see as Nietzsche's thought-experiment – time-consciousness could be suspended, this sequencing would break down as well; there would be no temporal order, but only simultaneity. The creek would be simultaneous to the flower being simultaneous to the stone (the stone would be identical to itself). This simultaneity we would have to see as *more* 'authentic' than the 'artificial' temporal order we insert into the world, since we believe that *temporalization* is a first, a primordial, a rudimentary, *schmatization*. (We assume in this that *temporalization* is a first, primordial interpretation-process still language-independent; while language will eventually schematize the world according to another, more sophisticated, interpretation-process.) Without sequencing, every now would come back as the same. Not that it necessarily was the same, but we would not be able to recognize it otherwise, since we could not perceive anything but 'now.' We would not be able to recognize the before and the after, and could consequently not compare the present now with the past.[519]

---

[519] If I am beholding a landscape, taking in the first traces of the sun rising behind a mountain range, my now-perception of the first sunrays sink back as memory; time passes, and in what we will here call the 'next' perceptive now, the sun has now risen above the mountain range. Thanks to the inner-mental flow of time, something has happened between my so-called 'first' and 'second' perceptive now-phases. Thanks to my ability to reproduce my 'first' now-phase, I remember the difference between a mountain range imposing itself shadowy in the dawn, from the mountain range bathed in the glister of the first rays of the sun. Secondly, I have noticed that time has passed by, with this knowledge I also know, or am at least able to know, that I have grown a bit older, and even, that life (the world, the universe, cosmos) has grown older. But – to begin to understand Nietzsche's question of all questions – is this real? Or is this idea of things 'getting older' nothing but *us* imposing our sense of time on an in-itself indifferent universe? Is this just another example of Nietzsche's *Vermenschung*? Does the universe actually 'get older'? – And if not, now, do we? If now we apply Nietzsche's thought-experiment and imagine that we could effectively stop the inner flow of time, what essentially would happen to perception? First, let us emphasize yet again, we consider Nietzsche beyond Bishop Berkeley; there is therefore no question that the sun still rises above the mountain range, whether we are there to perceive it or not. Earth does not all of a sudden stop its orbit because we become extinct. However, as we hypothetically were suspending the inner flow of time, we would no longer be able to *perceive* any rise of the sun, since we would not perceive the sun's gradual ascent. Every perception would be perception of the now, and every now would therefore be the same, or in slightly different formula-

So, if on Nietzsche's though-experiment we hypothetically suspend the inner flow of time, it would most surely "change us," "transform us": "If you internalized this thought of thoughts, it would transform you." (Nachlaß 1881, KSA 9, 11[143]). In this, Nietzsche's hypothesis is radical, but it does not necessarily belong in a tradition of grand mysticism, because we could in fact imagine the possibility of 'stopping the flow of time' in the precise meaning of stopping *our sense* of this flow.

Absolute Time would continue to flow, but not in human consciousness. Nietzsche's self-*un*conscious human, living eternal recurrence, would *still* grow old and *eventually* die.[520] *Absolute Time* would wear out also the indi-

---

tion, every now would eternally come back as the same. There would be no way for us of comparing the first to the second now, and with this *constitute difference*. In this sense, every perceptual phase would be an 'eternal recurrence of the same.' In a universe perceived through no time-consciousness would be a universe of identities, not of differences. (This, I believe, was also the crux of what Jacques Derrida in *La Voix et le Phénomène* (Paris, Presses Universitaire de Paris, 1967) was trying to establish in his analysis of Husserl's phenomenology of internal time-consciousness: – Husserl's 'retentional trace' was *the institution of difference as such*; the 'now,' understood as origin of experiences that fade off into the past, could only have meaning within a structure of differences; this 'structure,' consequently, would have to be seen as even more 'original' than the original now; at least, as the condition of possibility of the 'now' being identifiable as such.) In the hypothetical identity-universe, time would have stopped counting, and there would be no sense of 'growing older.' In this respect, presence would have been eternalized. The human would no longer understand itself as a *Dasein* essentially determined through its 'being-toward-death,' since there would be no consciousness of death. Like the May-beetle, we would live our short summers as eternities. And now, returning to Nietzsche's question of all questions; if time is not 'real,' is not all sense of duration and time-span also delusory? Is not time now completely relative; does it for example make sense any longer to claim that the May-beetle has a 'shorter' life than a human being? Is a short summer not as much an eternity, as is a century? Is there not as 'much time' in a moment as there is in a life?

[520] We can be sure that to stop time is an impossible dream, something in the order of mysticism and religion. But let us immediately add a caveat to this commonsensical confidence: in the hard sciences, according to Einstein's special theory of relativity, the idea of a now 'inflated,' 'stretched out,' or 'dilated' is *a scientific fact*. This is how time behaves for objects close to the speed of light, or in the vicinity of dense and massive objects like a black hole. The phenomenon is known as 'time-dilation.' Humans, of course, do not move about with the speed of light, but if they did, their time from cradle to grave would be dilated. The closer to the speed of light they were moving, the

5. Temporal Construction and Deconstruction of the Interpreted World

vidual living eternal existence – like in Absolute Time eventually also the stone corrodes; therefore the stone, in its *actual empirical existence*, does not recur *eternally* as the same. (Cf.: "The actual movement of things has to correspond to an a c t u a l time, quite independent of the f e e l i n g of longer or shorter time-periods that the cognitive creature has. Actual time probably runs indefinitely much s l o w e r than we humans sense time." (Nachlaß 1881, KSA 9, 11[184]).)

However, Nietzsche's self-*un*conscious, eternalized individual would have no notion of its own (or the stone's) mortality. It would grow old and die like any other animal, but without knowing anything but its own eternal presence. – Even in its death-throes, it would know dying only as another eternal presence. The eternalized moment concerns the subject, not the world.[521]

If, according to Husserl's model of inner time-consciousness, the perceived world is continuously constituted as sequences with duration and temporal order thanks to his retentional horizon, Nietzsche's model of time in the *eternal recurrence of self-unconscious perception* is like Husserl's line, but detached from any retentional horizon. So, also in the eternal re-

---

longer would be their given span of life. This sounds most promising, and since it is a scientific fact, it might create the assuaging idea that we have finally found, at least in principle, the fountain of youth. There is, however, a catch. As much as, thanks to time-dilation, our life grew longer, everything *in* our life would grow longer, too. Everything we normally do in life would dilate in step with the dilation of our life span. If normally, one would read 100 books in a lifetime of 80 years, one would, close to the speed of light, still read 100 books in a lifetime of several hundred years, since reading would also dilate. In summa, one might live several hundred years, but one could not squeeze more 'life' out of these several hundred years, than what one squeezes out of the life one already has. Therefore, one might assume, that our perceptive apparatus would probably arrange things so cleverly, that a life of several hundred years wouldn't feel any different from a life of 80 years. See also Brian Greene, The Elegant Universe, New York (Vintage Books), 1999; especially Part II.

[521] See also Oliver Dier: "'You self' is the material that is the object in the thought of eternal recurrence of the same. [. . .] *The eternal recurrence of the same is a thought-concerning-self* [*Ich-Gedanke*]. [. . .] They [previous interpretations] overlook that the time-dimension of the moment [. . .] essentially always refer to the concrete I. [. . .] The I, as a "flash picture" [*"Blitzbild"*] of the eternal flow of becoming, carries – precisely because it is a picture – the same flow within itself. The self [*Ich*] *is* the moment, and vice versa." Oliver Dier, "Die Verwandlung der Wiederkunft," loc. cit., pp. 136 & 154.

currence of self-unconscious perception, now follows now; but one now is exactly identical to the next now, because the time-constituting consciousness is suspended. The *eternal-recurrence-subject* has reverted to Heraclitus' river, i.e., to the world of becoming. The perceiving subject is consequently not able to distinguish one now from the next. Although we maintain that this subject dies like other animals, it cannot know, and consequently, in-and-for-itself, i.e., in *own self-unconscious life*, it lives eternally.

In this attitude, there may be *succession*, but no *sense* of succession, no *sequencing*. Impression of stone follows impression of stone, but since there is no time-constituting consciousness, the subject no longer arranges its impressions of the stone in the before, the now, and the after. The stone is therefore not felt to be an enduring object, it is just felt to be; it is also not understood to be older than the flower, because there is no way of making judgments regarding duration and age; nor can it be established that the sun is causing the stone to warm (cf. Kant in *Prolegomena*), the stone is just felt warm, etc. Time has 'flown back' into the stone. We have finally gotten a glimpse of the *an-sich*; the world that "sleeps"; but *Nietzsche's an-sich*. And this *an-sich* does not hide itself; it is not even *an-sich* in the strictest sense because it is simply *there* as that which is, and always was, most immediately present.

When Nietzsche's eternal-recurrence-subject says 'Yes' to this universe, it is because 'No' has ceased to exist. A brief detour around an essay by Müller-Lauter about Nietzsche's "Yes-saying" is here helpful to clear up this suggestion. In the essay "Über das Werden, das Urteilen, das Ja-sagen bei Nietzsche," Müller-Lauter draws first a distinction between a so-called "primary yes-saying" and a "highest yes-saying."[522] While primary Yes-saying is simply evaluation, as requisite in, e.g., arts and sciences, Müller-Lauter's 'highest Yes-saying' is the yes of the decisive, self-transforming 'super'-human. "In our context, we understand Yes-affirmation [*Ja-setzen*] as the strong human being's saying yes to himself."[523] As such, Müller-Lauter's eternal-recurrence-thought comes about as a decision that the decisive subject impresses upon itself. "The eternal recurrence of the same is a thought, which can be learned, in order to be believed. The internalization of the thought is the 'aim' of Nietzsche."[524]

---

[522] See Wolfgang Müller-Lauter, "Über das Werden, das Urteilen, das Ja-sagen bei Nietzsche," in: Über Werden und Wille zur Macht. Nietzsche Interpretationen I, Berlin, New York (Walter de Gruyter), 1999.
[523] Müller-Lauter, ibid., p. 288.
[524] Müller-Lauter, ibid., p. 288.

5. Temporal Construction and Deconstruction of the Interpreted World

However, on the final pages of the essay – as Müller-Lauter takes his reflections to their pinnacle – he arrives at a conclusion that transcends the suggested distinction between "primary" and "highest," since he contemplates the possibility of a Yes-saying, which is, to put it squarely, *higher than even the highest*. This highest of high affirmations eclipses, in fact, all Yes-*saying*, – in this precise sense: it neutralizes all *pronounced* decisions on part to the 'super' human, and approaches the idea of the self-unconscious eternal-recurrence-subject as introduced above:

> The thought [of eternal recurrence] should not only be affirmed as thought, the Yes should be raised into a belief in the return. But this belief does not lead to a holding-for-true [*Für-Wahr-Halten*] in the theoretical sense. Belief is nothing but the 'life-condition' of the primary yes-saying.' [. . .] At the *highest level of internalization* [*Verinnerlichung*] of this thought, the *ultimate and all-encompassing yes-saying* would have been so strongly incorporated [*einverleibt*], that belief would perform a quasi-transcencental function. [. . .] A *creature* [*Wesen*], that had totally incorporated [*einverleibt*] this thought, would in every lived moment understand its existence as always 'eternal' [*Ewigen*].[525]

Precisely, we would here echo, beyond primary and highest yes-saying, we find a 'creature' 'believing' in affirmation without having the slightest knowledge of its belief. This kind of affirmation could consequently never come about as a conscious '*Ja-setzen*,' because there would be no conscious subject to *set down* or *set forth* anything. Any trace of belief would erase itself in the continuous flow of time, and the creature would live *as if* eternally. This 'creature' would be neither man nor 'super' man. We may describe this kind of 'belief' as 'unconscious' or as 'quasi-transcendental'; any of the two labels is adequate, because in any case, we are talking about something so deeply *internalized* that it becomes *incorporated*; as such, it is no longer available for conscious reflection and awareness. (That which is *incorporated* (*einverleibt*), becomes so integrally a part of me that it cannot be seen as distinct from me, and consequently cannot be seen *by* me; I can only see that which is distinct from me.)

We therefore suggest that when one says 'Yes' as 'creature,' in this the highest possible affirmation, it is because it is no longer *possible* to say 'No.' The 'yes' does no longer depend on personal decisiveness; instead, the *negation*, and the *possibility of negating*, has simply disappeared from the horizon of the affirmative eternal-recurrence subject. The *mind* can no longer negate, because it takes in every impression, discriminating against

---

[525] Müller-Lauter, ibid., p. 301; my italics.

none. The part of the psyche, which otherwise judges between true and false, good and bad, etc., is suspended.

As Freud observed, this was the case in unconsciousness and dreams: negation does not exist. Likewise in empty perception: perception reverting to the skin of our perceptive apparatus cannot see falsehood. Freud would claim that the dream could not think a negative condition, for example: 'I have not enough money to buy this nice car'; it could only think a positive condition: 'I already drive this nice car.' The situation is somewhat similar in empty perception: the subject cannot think, for example: 'the sun looks small, but this is false, because, really, it is enormous'; it simply sees a small sun. Nothing in the eternal-recurrence-universe can be false, and thus negated. Everything is 'just-there-in-front-of,' and is as such affirmed without further qualification.

Therefore, 'Yes-saying' in the strongest sense does not come about as a result of a personality-change in one's decisiveness; it is not the case that the person under the spell of eternal recurrence decides to become a more positive, generous, and affable personality. Instead, 'Yes-saying' comes about as a much more profound, essential, and constitutional cognitive condition *impressing itself upon* the self-unconscious eternal-recurrence-subject.

'Yes-saying' in its highest form, consequently, we therefore do not understand as a Nietzschean version of the categorical imperative, as a so-called 'existential imperative.' First, It cannot come about as an imperative, because – as Kant brilliantly demonstrated in *Grounding of a Metaphysics of Morals* – an imperative can only be thought as enacted according to 'duty,' according to 'respect of law,' as such enacted thanks to a fundamental *rational capacity* of the human being. This has no parallel in Nietzsche's highest affirmation-thought, since every rational capacity is destroyed in the eternal-recurrence-subject. Second, it is not enacted as an Existentialist 'choice,' because there is no subjectivity to do the choosing.

Appendixes

APPENDIX 1

Nietzsche and Ernst Mach on the Analysis of Sensations

1. Ernst Mach's Analysis of Sensations

1.1. Deconstructing the Cogito in Mach

Like Nietzsche, also Ernst Mach criticizes a model of a unified subject (a model of the subject, we discussed in detail in *Chapter 3*). Also Mach denounces the idea of intellectual processes as centrally seated in the 'soul,' which is again centered around a "point" in the brain – as according to a Cartesian model. This he regards as an ancient misconception, which has to yield to a new conception of the interconnection of physical and psychical.[526]

> The habit of treating the unanalysed ego complex as an indiscerptible unity frequently assumes in science remarkable forms. First, the nervous system is separated from the body as the seat of the sensations. In the nervous system again, the brain is selected as the organ best fitted for this end, and finally, to save the supposed psychical unity, a *point* is sought in the brain as the seat of the soul.[527]

---

[526] Whether Nietzsche knew Ernst Mach's work directly or indirectly is not easy to judge. Although they often use the same concepts, and largely have identical epistemological projects, we find no references to Mach in Nietzsche's correspondence. In the revised and later version of *The Analysis of Sensations*, Mach has references to Nietzsche, but not to Nietzsche as epistemologist (which at this point in time must have been a virtually unknown aspect of Nietzsche); rather to Nietzsche as typically received in the beginning of the 20th Century: Nietzsche of the 'super-man' and the 'aristocratic radicalism' that fascinated intellectuals like for example George Brandes. Mach's comments on Nietzsche in this context are only disparaging.

[527] Ernst Mach: The Analysis of Sensations and the Relations of the Physical to the Psychical. New York (Dover Publications), 1959; p. 26.

With approval Mach quotes Lichtenberg for the following observation, which also would have won Nietzsche's approved:

> We become conscious of certain presentation that are not dependent upon us; of others that we at least think are dependent upon us. Where is the border-line? We know only the existence of our sensations, presentations, and thoughts. We should say, *It thinks*, just as we say *It lightens*. It is going too far to say *cogito*, if we translate *cogito* by *I think*. The assumption, or postulation, of the ego is a mere practical necessity.[528]

The ego becomes a mere "practical" construction in Lichtenberg, Mach, and Nietzsche. Why is it "practical" to construct this limit, and what does it imply that it is merely "practical"? – Since we are talking about sensations or representations, some representations will appear to be independent of the ego, whereas others will appear to be dependent. The representation of a tree would appear to be independent, whereas the representation of a pain-sensation would appear to be dependent of the ego. These two modes of representation give rise to the distinction between what we call 'outer' and 'inner'; exterior and interior. The ego as a "practical" construction circumscribes the so-called 'inner' and interior representations. It seems to draw a line between that which belongs to body and mind, on the one hand, and that which belongs outside, on the other.

However, since we are talking about sensations, this border-line is vague and tentative. A pain-sensation may for example impress itself from the so-called 'outside,' but it is interpreted from the 'inside' as 'pain,' and as '*this* pain'; there is in other words no clear demarcation between whether the 'pain' belongs to the outside or the inside. The inside seems to help defining the 'pain' as much as the outside.

When the traditional 'membrane' circumscribing and confining the 'ego' become porous and permeable, the distinction between subject and object also start to disintegrate. The subject is no longer a clearly identifiable entity, standing over and against the world as object, but rather a filter for impressions, where the filtration screens material, and remove impurities that are deemed unsuited for the psychical apparatus; that is, it removes impressions unnecessary for the perseverance of the individual. This 'subject' does not so much see an object, as its sees what it *needs*, and maybe *wants*, to see. Its 'seeing' is no longer simply understood as an objective gaze di-

---

[528] Lichtenberg quoted from Mach: loc. cit., p. 29. Mach gives no references, but he is referring to Georg Christoph Licthenberg, 18th Century scientist and philosopher; and most likely the quote is from Lichtenberg's *Sudelbücher*.

rected toward the outside; it finds a secret motivation in the inside of the subject itself; a secret motivation, which Nietzsche labels 'power.'

> On the Theory of Knowledge: utterly Empirical
> There is neither 'Spirit,' nor reason, nor thinking, nor consciousness, nor soul, nor will, nor truth: these are all useless fictions. It is not about "Subject and Object," but rather about a certain animal species [*Thierart*], which flourish only under a certain relative correctness, first and foremost from the regularity of their perceptions. [. . .] Knowledge works as an instrument [Werkzeug] for power. (Nachlaß 1888; KSA 13, 14[122]).

1.2. The Dissolution of the World into Sensation-Elements, and the Introduction of Perspectivism as New Scientific Ideal

Conventionally speaking, we distinguish between three different sets of objects, or, as Ernst Mach has it, "elements." We believe in outside objects, existing outside ourselves and our bodies (such as a tree); we believe in objects that belong to our body (such as pain); and then we believe in objects that are merely imaginary belonging in our mind and thinking (such as fantasies). Mach formalizes these three sets of elements respectively: $A\ B\ C\ldots$ (outside, spatio-temporal, objects); $K\ L\ M\ldots$ (our body and related objects), and $\alpha\ \beta\ \gamma\ldots$ (imagination, memory-images, etc.). The border-line between world and ego, according to this formalization, is now drawn between the set $A\ B\ C\ldots$, one the one hand, and the two sets, $K\ L\ M\ldots$ and $\alpha\ \beta\ \gamma\ldots$, on the other:

> Let us denote the above-mentioned elements by the letters $A\ B\ C\ldots, K\ L\ M\ldots$ and $\alpha\ \beta\ \gamma\ldots$. Let those complexes of colors, sounds, and so forth, commonly called bodies, be denoted, for the sake of clearness, by $A\ B\ C\ldots$; the complex, know as our own body, which is a part of the former complexes distinguished by certain peculiarities, may be called $K\ L\ M\ldots$; the complex composed of volitions, memory-images, and the rest, we shall represent by $\alpha\ \beta\ \gamma\ldots$. Usually, now, the complex $\alpha\ \beta\ \gamma\ldots K\ L\ M\ldots$, as making up the ego, is opposed to the complex $A\ B\ C\ldots$, as making up the world of physical objects.[529]

In "naïve realism" – which implies here only the spontaneous and commonsensical view of the world – the complexes $A\ B\ C$ stand as physical objects over and against the Ego, as comprised of the complexes $K\ L\ M$ and $\alpha\ \beta\ \gamma$. The natural belief leads to the dualistic view that the 'world' consists of two radical separate domains, the physical and the psychical, the physical being

---

[529] Mach: loc. cit., p. 9.

tangible and concrete, the psychical being imaginary and ideational. It further facilitates the idea that the physical *effects* the psychical, i.e., produce a 'copy' of itself in the psyche, and we – since we have direct access only to these 'copies' – can know nothing about that physical world supposedly imprinting the 'copy'; that is, the concept of the physical world as a thing-in-itself has been created; and the universe is consequently divided into a 'real' and an 'apparent' world.

We are already acquainted with Nietzsche's criticism of this conception, and also in Mach it is regarded as a mis-interpretation of the universe sparking a host of philosophical pseudo-problems. To Mach (as to Nietzsche), there is only one sensational world, namely the world that appears (and as it appears) to the subject. Since it is not completely obvious what range of implications this contention may have, we shall elaborate and develop the thought through one of Mach's examples: *observing a green leaf*.

In only *one* sensational world there is no longer any radical distinction between the three domains described above (formalized: $A\ B\ C\ldots, K\ L\ M\ldots$, and $\alpha\ \beta\ \gamma\ldots$; defining approximately, the physical, the physiological, and the psychological). Instead, "elements" stand in a *functional relationship* to each other, gaining significance depending on the particular perspective from which one investigates them. Especially, in *one* sensational world, the canonical and classical 'master-distinction' between physical and psychical is suspended.

> There is no rift between the psychical and the physical, no inside and outside, no "sensation" to which an external "thing," different from sensation, corresponds. There is but one kind of elements, out of which this supposed inside and outside are formed – elements which are themselves inside or outside, according to the aspect in which, for the time being, they are viewed. The world of sense belongs both to the physical and the psychical domain alike.[530]

On this view, two epistemological master-distinctions have been suspended: the distinction between 'reality' and 'appearance' and the distinction between 'physical' and 'psychical' (or *outside* and *inside*). As such, the epistemology suggested must understand itself as in opposition to Kant's. The notion of a thing-in-itself will make no sense in a universe of sensational elements.

A world broken up in sensational elements corresponds to Nietzsche's *Relations-Welt*; a world of inter-connected surface-structures, without a deeper dimension in the form of a thing-in-itself: "The world, which we have not reduced to our being, our logic, and our psychological prejudg-

---

[530] Mach: loc. cit., p. 310.

ments, does not exist as a world "in-itself." A world-of-relations [*Relations-Welt*], has, depending on circumstances, from every point a different face/appearance [*Gesicht*]: its being is from every point something different." (Nachlaß 1888; KSA 13, 14[93]).

Now, what at a first glance seems to be a cumbersome designation of domains (the *A B C, K L M*, etc.), comes to good use as symbols for elements with in principle equal epistemological weight. The 'green' of the leaf is a sensation, experienced as 'green' under the light of our sun; but exposed to another light-source, the sensation 'green' might for example change into the sensation 'brown':

> Before me lies the leaf of a plant. The green (*A*) of the leaf is connected with a certain optical sensation of space (*B*), with a sensation of touch (*C*), and with the visibility of the sun or the lamp (*D*). If the yellow (*E*) of a sodium flame takes the place of the sun, the green (*A*) will pass into brown (*F*).[531]

Moreover, as well as the leaf could be observed in relationship to what we label, the physical world, it could with as much right be observed in relationship to what we label, the psychical.

> But the green (*A*) is also connected with a certain process of my retina. There I nothing to prevent me in principle from investigating this process I my own eye in exactly the same manner as in the previous cases, and from reducing it to its elements *X Y Z* . . . [. . .] Now in its dependence upon *B C D* . . . , *A* is a physical element, in its dependence on *X Y Z* . . . it is a sensation, and can also be considered as a psychical element.[532]

When the world is broken up in sensation-elements, it has therefore no meaning any longer to talk about the leaf as a 'body' with certain 'properties,' since the leaf changes so-called 'properties' according to its "functional relationships." The 'property' *color* – in the example above – depends on the given light-source. A so-called 'body' is now nothing more than a complex of sensations, and so-called 'properties' of this 'body' are no more that sensations that appear in the same relationship within this complex, and therefore seem to be fixed to the complex.

> Colors, sounds, temperatures, pressures, spaces, times, and so forth, are connected with one another in manifold ways; and with them are associated dispositions, of mind, feelings, and volitions. Out of this fabric, that which is

---

[531] Mach: loc. cit., p. 44.
[532] Mach: loc. cit., p. 44.

relatively more fixed and permanent stands prominently forth, engraves itself on the memory, and expresses itself in language.[533]

As such, Mach envisions a relativistic and perspectivist universe, where so-called 'bodies' are dispersed into sensational elements, and where the nature of one's scientific research depends on the perspective one adopts.

This, I suggest, is also Nietzsche's vision; and it makes up the crux of his often misunderstood 'perspectivism.' This notion for example does not simply signify that the same issue has multiple different interpretations because we prejudge issues from different hermeneutic horizons. (The sentimental and ideological: 'we are all different, and all opinions count' certainly has no role to play in this theory. Especially, the theory does not entail that we have a moral obligation to see an issue from as many angles as possible for the sake of objectivity and neutrality.) In a stronger sense, it means that when the world is broken up in sensational elements, it is possible to 'pair up' any number of diverse elements, not completely randomly, but according to the direction of the general interest of one's research (let it be scientific or ideological). A world broken up in sensational elements has lost its formerly two solid centers: matter and mind; traditionally understood as two entities standing over and against each other, with the task of the mind to arrest and interrogate a recalcitrant matter. 'Perspectivism' in the most abstract sense is to eradicate this classical theory of the two centers; it diffuses and dissolves these two centers into diverse elements with an indefinite number of functional relationships. On this view, scientific ethos and sobriety is neither challenged nor deconstructed. When the same complex can be seen from many different perspectives, it implies that we may investigate, for example, the green of the leaf as chlorophylic granules, or as color-impressions on the retina, or as a psychological mood-enhancer, or as something completely fourth, fifth, or sixth.

1.3. The Suspension of the Cause-Effect Relation

In a relativistic and perspectivist universe where elements stand in complex functional relationships to each other, there is also no simple cause-effect relationships as imagined in classical empiricist and realist theories. Since everything is tied up in complex relationships, there is not *one* thing effect-

---

[533] Mach: loc. cit., p. 2. Cf.: "My table is now brightly, now dimly lighted. Its temperature varies. It may receive an ink stain. One of its legs may be broken. It may be repaired, polished, and replaced part by part. But, for me, it remains the table at which I daily write." Ibid.

ing *one* other thing; or, such a conception is an idealization and "simplification" (Mach's term, adopted also by Nietzsche):

> The old traditional conception of causality is of something perfectly rigid: a dose of effect follows on a dose of cause. A sort of primitive, pharmaceutical conception of the universe is expressed in this view. [. . .] The connections of nature are seldom so simple that in any given case we can point to one cause and one effect. I therefore long ago proposed to replace the conception of cause by the mathematical conception of function, – that is to say, by the conception of the dependence of phenomena on one another.[534]

The conception of an *effective cause* has been created thanks to an analogy to human willfulness, Mach asserts. An unexpected movement in nature has been projected back to movements in humans, and explained as purposeful action. As such, the cause-effect relation is a result of "animism" or "anthropomorphism" (Mach's terms, also adopted by Nietzsche). Like humans engage in purposeful action, nature is also supposed to engage in purposeful action – albeit not consciously. Nature is as such interpreted as having a 'will' in the form of causality analogous to human willing.

> As soon as he [the savage] perceives unexpected but striking movements in nature, he instinctively interprets these movements on the analogy of his own. In this way the distinction between his own and someone else's volition begins to dawn upon him. Gradually, the similarities and differences between physical and biological processes stand out alternately with even greater clearness against the background of the fundamental scheme of volitional action.[535]

Nietzsche agrees with this analysis of Mach; also Nietzsche contends that the cause-effect comes about ultimately because we *project* a psychological condition into nature: namely, the conviction that we move and act because of *will*; the conviction that we as such *cause* the movement. However, Nietzsche will add that also the notion of human willfulness as a cause of action is an illusion. The real situation is that . . .

> We have absolutely no experience of a cause:
> : examined psychologically, the entire notion comes about because of the subjective conviction, and we are causes, namely, when we move the arm . . . but this is an error
> : we separate for ourselves the doer from the doing, and we use this scheme everywhere, – we seek a doer to every event . . .

---

[534] Mach: loc. cit., p. 89.
[535] Mach: loc. cit., p. 96-97.

: what have we done? We have misunderstood for a cause a sensation of force, tension, resistance, a muscle-sensation, which is always the beginning of an action (Nachlaß 1888; KSA 13, 14[98]).

The notion of causality is understood to be merely practical, as it serves our cognitive economy. When we perceive a complex of phenomena, we automatically look for a single feature that could explain, and would seem to generate, them all. This single feature tends to become their 'cause.' We automatically seek out in our explanations the highest abstraction and the plainest simplicity. In this, we abstract, idealize, and simplify a world, which in itself is composed of individual cases. In one of Mach's examples: Kepler's law of the elliptical orbit of the planets is only an approximation; if the orbits of individual planets were carefully measured, they would all be unique and distinct.

> The discovery of Kepler's laws depends upon a fortunate and fairly crude schematization. The more closely we consider a planet, the more individual does its movement become, and the less exactly does it follow Kepler's laws. Speaking strictly, all the planets move differently, and the same planet moves differently at different times.[536]

As in Nietzsche, this "simplification" of the world is also "schematization" (another of Mach's terms adopted by Nietzsche). It simplifies, abbreviates, and schematizes the world as it exists in its individual manifold, into an artificial abstraction and ideal. However, in this 'simplification,' the scientist has not uncovered a 'law' or a 'necessity,' as Nietzsche insists; the scientist has at best formalized regularity, or what appears to be regularity.

> When I bring a regularly occurring event on formula, I have facilitated, abbreviated, etc., the designation of the entire phenomenon. But I have not stated [konstatiert] a "law"; rather I have raised a question, How can it be, that something is here repeating itself: it is an assumption that the formula for the complex corresponds to, for the time being, unknown forces and force-cancelations [Kraft-auflösungen]: it is mythology to think that forces are obeying a law. (Nachlaß 1886-87; KSA 12, 7[14]).

> The regularity in the succession [Aufeinanderfoge] is only an imaginary expression, as if here a rule was being observed: no fact. The same applies regarding "lawfulness." We invent a formula in order to express an always recurring kind of succession: but in this we have not uncovered a "law," even less so, a force, as the cause to the recurrence of successions. That something always

---

[536] Mach: loc. cit., p. 336,

happens in such and such a way, is here interpreted as if a creature as consequence of obeying a law or a law-giver always act in this or that way: as if it, apart from the "law," had the freedom to act differently. (Nachlaß 1886-87; KSA 12, 2[142]).

The idea of something 'obeying a law' is now seen an another anthropomorphism; it is as if nature itself is a 'creature' that acts according to directives; as if nature itself as 'creature' has ultimately the 'freedom' to act according to law. In the last analysis, this view also sustain the myth that there is something enduring, lasting, and stable in nature behind all the activity; that is, that there is an actor behind the action, or a doer behind the doing.

> "Something changes" [*"Es Verändert sich"*]; there is no change without reason/cause [*Grund*] – this [view] always presupposes a something, which remains stable and steady behind the changes. "Cause" and "effect", examined psychologically, consist in the belief, expressed in the verb, active and passive, agent and patient [*thun und leiden*]. This implies that an event is divided into agent and patient, the assumption of an agent is presumed. The belief is that the doer remains in place; as if when all doing was subtracted from the doer, he would himself be left. (Nachlaß 1886-87; KSA 12, 7[1]], p. 249).

Alternative to these views, which derive from Mechanism, Nietzsche suggests his universe of "power-quantities," which in this context may be seen as a rephrasing of Mach's "functional relationships," and must be understood as the different strengths of the interconnections between "points" in Nietzsche's *Relations-Welt*:

> Powerquantities [*Machtquanta*]. Critique of Mechanism.
> Let us remove here the two popular concepts, 'necessity' and 'law': the first imposes a false compulsion, the second a false freedom into the world. "Things" do not behave with regularity, not according to a rule: there is no thing (– this is our fiction); it behaves a little under a compulsion from necessities. Here nothing is obeyed: when something is what it is, this strong or this weak, it is not a consequence of obedience, or of a rule, or of a compulsion . . . (Nachlaß 1888; KSA 13, 14[79]).

APPENDIX 2

A Theory of "Happiness"?

Nietzsche's Theory of Pain and Pleasure

> Suppose pleasure and pain were so linked together that he who w a n t s to have the greatest possible amount of the one m u s t have the greatest possible amount of the other also. [. . .] And perhaps that is how things are! The Stoics, at any rate, thought so, and were consistent when they desired to have the least possible amount of pleasure in order to have the least possible amount of pain from life. [. . .] Today, too, you have the choice: either a s l i t t l e p a i n a s p o s s i b l e, in short painlessness [. . .] or a s m u c h p a i n a t p o s s i b l e as the price of an abundance of subtle joys and pleasures hitherto rarely tasted.
> – Nietzsche: *Die fröhliche Wissenschaft*, 12.[537]

> What we call happiness in the strictest sense comes from the (preferably sudden) satisfaction of needs which have been dammed up to a high degree, and it is from its nature only possible as an episodic phenomenon. When any situation that is desired by the pleasure-principle is prolonged, it only produces a feeling of mild contentment. We are so made that we can derive intense enjoyment only from a contrast and very little from a state of things. Thus our possibilities of happiness are already restricted by our constitution.
> – Freud: *Civilization and its Discontents*, p. 25.[538]

1. Nietzsche's Pleasure Principle Reversing The Tradition.

We have seen that conscious perception is constituted in delay, as an aftereffect and a re-construction of original impressions not themselves conscious. This idea is applied also to perceptions of *pain and pleasure*, which

---

[537] FW 12, KSA 3, p. 383-84.
[538] Sigmund Freud: Das Unbehagen der Kultur. GW XIV, p. 434.

often are regarded as spontaneous and self-given sensations. In Nietzsche, pleasure and pain are sensations constructed after-the-fact too, and as such involving *interpretation*. However, the view begs the questions: if they are interpretations, what is the nature of the stimuli they are interpretations of, and how come that these stimuli eventually are being interpreted as pleasure or pain? We shall in the present appendix try to reconstruct Nietzsche's tentative answer to these questions.

We first notice that to Nietzsche, 'pleasure' is not primarily determined as a climatic conclusion of a prolonged desire. We notice that pleasure is often described also as *delay*, *frustration*, and even *resistance of* pleasure. In Nietzsche's theory of pleasure, we are introduced to something so apparently paradoxical as *a pleasure of resistance of pleasure*.

To avoid the seeming self-contradiction of the formula, the two pleasures referred to in the formula cannot be identical. The *pleasure of resistance* cannot be identical to the *resisting pleasure*. The latter pleasure must be a pleasure that withdraws itself, that retreats, that makes itself 'hard to get'; and the former a pleasure that exults in this retreat. The former pleasure becomes a 'drive,' and the latter becomes an 'aim.'[539] But since the former pleasure enjoys the resistance of the aim, it enjoys its own drive (its 'drivenness') more than the aim it is driven toward. And the more the latter pleasure retreats, the 'harder it is to get,' the more exultation in the former pleasure, the more driven the drive.

In the Nachlaß-material, we find the following explicit rendition of our paradoxical formula, *the pleasure of resistance of pleasure*:

> It is not the satisfaction of the will that causes p l e a s u r e [*Lust*] (I want to fight this superficial theory), . . . but rather the will's forward thrust and again and again becoming master over that which stands in its way. The feeling of pleasure lies precisely in the dissatisfaction of the will [*Unbefriedigung des Willens*], in the fact that the will is never satisfied unless it has opponents and resistance [*Grenzen und Widerstände*]. – 'The happy man': a herd ideal. (Nachlaß 1887, KSA 13, 11[75]).

The feeling of pleasure lies in "the *dissatisfaction* of the will"; in the fact that the will "*is never satisfied* unless it has opponents and resistance." The *resistance* of pleasure is now pleasure, not the "satisfaction of the will." Nietzsche's paradoxical view can thus be expressed in two other formulaic

---

[539] I shall here use these proven, even worn, philosophical concepts purely instrumentally. They serve, in other words, the purpose of expressing a thought, which – given the recalcitrant nature of thoughts – does not express itself.

expressions: (1) *there is no satisfaction in satisfaction* and (2) *there is satisfaction in dissatisfaction.*

We notice that a resistance *of* pleasure is not the same as a resistance *to* pleasure. In the first case, it is the pleasure doing the resistance, i.e., the object for pleasure is withdrawing itself; while in the second case it is the subject who resists pleasure, i.e., repress pleasure. The latter case would describe the Freudian equation, *pleasure = unpleasure*, namely in the particular instances where one part of our psyche (the super-ego) finds pleasure in punishing another part (the ego). Suffering is, according to that equation, a pleasure more often than not. However, in his pleasure theory Nietzsche is far from talking about the pleasure of suffering, in self-inflicted pain, humiliation, etc. Nietzsche is talking about a 'joy' (a 'self-joy' more exactly, to echo Henry Staten[540]) that is far more joyful than pleasure 'proper,' pleasure satisfied.

If there is pleasure in resistance *of* pleasure, we can start by noticing – permitting a brief digression – that in the history of literature nobody has misunderstood himself as profoundly as Faust. He was mistaken when he challenged Mephistopheles to provide him with an 'ultimate' pleasure so satisfying that he could pronounce to the moment: "beautiful moment, oh stay!" In other words, when Faust gave Mephistopheles the assignment to saturate his desires so completely that he could never want more, he was pursuing Nietzsche's 'superficial' theory of pleasure. At the point of absolute fulfillment, Faust would freeze the moment into everlasting eternity; his desire would be in effect dead; he would finally have no more projects to complete, no more opponents to defeat, no more resistances to prove his power against. This moment would, to Nietzsche's mind, represent the death of Faust's will to power, his complete capitulation to the herd ideal, namely, to the myth of contentment, the degeneration to the 'happy man.' On the contrary, and what Faust never understood, his perpetual striving, and Mephistopheles' attempts to introduce this difficult companion of his to the more shady parts of life, this 'golden tree,' these were his pleasures. These he could have indulged were it not because he was already clouded in his dream of complete rest.[541]

The lack of rest in the will-to-power is a recurrent theme of Nietzsche. The insatiable appetite in the will-to-power for more power, for growth and

---

[540] Henry Staten: *Nietzsche's Voice* (Ithaca: Cornell University Press, 1990).
[541] One is tempted to suggest that Faust might have served himself well by listening to Goethe in another context: "Everything in the world is bearable / Only not a succession of wonderful days." [*Alles in das Welt Lässt sich ertragen / Nur nicht eine Reihe von schönen Tagen*]. Here quoted from Freud: "Das Unbehagen der Kultur"; GW XIV, p. 434.

increase, is a defining quality of the will-to-power. The will-to-power wants, says Nietzsche, "more power" not "contentment"; it wants "war," not "peace": "What is good? – Everything that increases the feeling of power, the will to power, the power of the human being. What is bad? – Everything that derives from weakness. What is happiness? – The feeling that power grows – that an obstacle has been defeated. Not contentment, but rather more power; not peace, but rather war; not virtue, but rather discipline." (Nachlaß 1887-88, KSA 13, 11[114].[542]

Faust wants peace and not war, and in this, he is not an isolated case. Faust dreams a dream that philosophy has been dreaming for centuries, the dream of the standstill, the myth of the Elysian bliss where we after the vexations of this world shall live in perfect harmony and happiness. Since the world is painful, one has invented a world that is *not* painful, a world that would be better than this world, which consequently "ought not to exist."

> The sum of pain outweighs the sum of pleasure; consequently, the non-being [*Nichtsein*] of the world would be better than is its being [*Sein*]. [...]
> The world is something that quite reasonably ought not to exist, since it causes the feeling subject more pain than pleasure.
> Pain and pleasure are side-effects, not causes [*Nebensachen, keine Ursachen*]; they are value-judgments of a second order; they are derivation from a ruling value. (Nachlaß 1887, KSA 13, 11[114]).

Here, it does not matter whether the heavenly bliss is situated religiously, politically, or morally. In perpetuating this dream, philosophy has not only been inspired to elaborate descriptions of the beyond as in Augustine's *City of God*; also political eschatologies over the present society qualify. The Marxist dream of the end of history in the Communist society also emphasizes the standstill, the end of all social struggles, since social and economic equality is secured and, consequently, there is no oppressing class to provoke subsequent struggles. Perhaps most pertinently in Nietzsche's context,

---

[542] Compare to Günter Abel: "The human being seeks and wants an increase of power. His activity is not determined and explained by strive toward pleasure, respectively, by decrease of pain. Pleasure and pain are merely effects, "mere secondary-manifestation" [*Begleiterscheinung*], of the fundamental conatus, the power-struggle [*Machtstrebens*]." Abel: *Nietzsche – Die Dynamik des Willen zur Macht und die Ewige Wiederkehr* (Berlin/New York: Walter de Gruyter, 1998), p. 96. In general, Nietzsche's so-called 'pleasure-principle' seems to have been largely ignored by commentators. On this issue, one finds isolated remarks, but rarely any sustained discussion. The notable exception is Günter Abel.

the dream has been dreamt by moral philosophy as well. Plato and Aristotle have each of them different versions of how to achieve harmony in the soul. In Plato's *Republic*, the object of moral instruction is to achieve a state of harmony between the different departments of the soul; 'justice' Socrates calls it. The soul is likened to an unruly society, in which we find as the most unruly member, the appetite, the desire. In *Ethics*,[543] Aristotle explains how to achieve the ultimate good (the *summon bonum*) in contemplation. This is also the state in which the soul is closest to the thinking of god; and god, Aristotle taught, cannot have desires. Desire would introduce deficiency into his existence and thus reduce his perfection – a contradiction in terms, since perfection does not come in shades and degrees. The contemplating philosopher, most like god and therefore best loved by god, is like god at rest, thinking no longer on mundane matters, but on thinking itself.

It is helpful to first understand Nietzsche's paradoxical statements inserted into this historical-intellectual context. Traditionally, desire *as such*, has always been thought to be a burden rather than a blessing; to be a cause of dissatisfaction and insatiable cravings in an always-restless subject. Moral Philosophy has encouraged pursuit of the opposite ideal, a serene subject in rational control of its egoistic impulses. There is in this sense not much difference between Plato, Kant, Schopenhauer, and Stuart Mill; in each case, self-control, tranquility, and peace is at the core of their moral program. During the civilizational process, the chaotic and anarchistic individual has been instructed to internalize self-control for the benefit of society as a whole, and it is the various Schools of Moral Philosophy that provided the different *manuals* describing why and how this internalization was to be carried out.

Nietzsche is precisely reading moral philosophy as such *a manual* for the *construction* of a particular subject; and since this manual is designed to invent a self-restrictive subject, it stands to reason that one might get closer to the 'truth' of the individual by turning the instruction of three millennia around: i.e., that *drive* rather than *rest* provides, and has always provided, the subject with pleasure. We therefore see Nietzsche's paradoxical statements as addressing the philosophical tradition, by turning this tradition upside-down. Contrary to what traditionally philosophy has dreamt, the two oxymoronic expressions mean respectively: (1) *there is pleasure (satisfac-*

---

[543] Aristotle starts speculating about the 'ultimate good,' only after he has introduced us to his pragmatic good, his theory of the *medium*, where merely he outlines what counts as appropriate social behavior to an Athenian citizen.

tion) in drive (traditional 'dissatisfaction') and (2) *there is no pleasure (satisfaction) in rest (traditional 'satisfaction').*[544]

Seen in this context, Nietzsche's paradoxes make good sense. However, this by no means entails that we have completed our understanding of what we call *Nietzsche's pleasure-principle*; on the contrary, the above exposition indicates only a humble beginning.

2. A Relativistic Theory of Pleasure.

Immediately another paradox announces itself, already present in the quotation above. Even though, by and large, Nietzsche emphasizes the 'drive' rather than the 'aim' – that is, the driven-ness of the drive, rather than its rest – then, obviously, this cannot imply the entire suspension of the 'aim' of the drive. The 'aim' must still be present as something for the drive to conquer and master. This was explicit in the quote above when Nietzsche asserted that rather than satisfaction, pleasure is "the will's forward thrust and again and again becoming master over that which stands in its way" (ibid.). Implying is it that pleasure is not simply to bang one's head against a wall once and again, it is also to break through the wall.

On the one hand, Nietzsche emphasizes the 'again and again' – the lack of finality in the will to power, on the other, the project of the will to power is to gain mastery over an object – i.e., to secure finality in its strive.

The 'again and again' is better determined in two subsequent notes. In one note Nietzsche points out that dissatisfaction of our drives should not be seen as something depressing, but, on the contrary, as a "great stimulus of life" [*das große Stimulans des Lebens*], and then he adds a parenthesis, "One could perhaps describe pleasure in general as a rhythm of little unpleasurable stimuli [*einen Rhythmus kleiner Unlustreize*]." (Nachlaß 1887, KSA 13, 11[76]). The 'again and again' is in other words a 'rhythm.'

In another note, this 'rhythm' is still better determined. Here Nietzsche compares the rhythm of little unpleasurable stimuli to the "sexual tickling in the act of coitus" (WM 699). This example on 'rhythm,' the sexual act, is, if anything, an *exemplary* example; insofar as 'the sexual tickling' is the matrix on which the theory of pleasure as rhythm is formed in the first

---

[544] Nietzsche may be seen also to be challenging Freud's *constancy-principle*, the notion, which – according to Freud's economic theory of the psyche – asserts that 'pleasure' is 'reduction of tension,' that 'pleasure' consists in obtaining in the psychic system a state of psychological equilibrium or homeostasis.

2. A Relativistic Theory of Pleasure

place. The sexual act is the arch-typical model over sequences of small irritations and frustrations, small 'resistances' that are defeated in final victory.

Also Freud would eventually conclude that sex was the exclusive *metaphor for* and *symbolic representative of* pleasure.

After this exemplary example, Nietzsche can give us his best definition of pleasure as 'rhythm.' From the act of coitus, he generalizes:

> It seems, a little hindrance [*eine kleine Hemmung*] that is overcome and immediately followed by another little hindrance that is again overcome – this game [*Spiel*] of resistance and victory arouses most strongly that general feeling of superabundant, excessive power that constitutes the essence of pleasure [*Wesen des Lust*]. (WM 699).

> Many little hindrances, time and again defeated [*überwunden*], playfully and like in a rhythmic dance, resulting in a sort of tickling of the feeling of power! Pleasure as tickling of the feeling of power: always presuppose that something resists and will be defeated. All pleasure and pain manifestations are intellectual. (Nachlaß 1886-87, KSA 12, 7[18]).

The rhythm is a game of resistance and victory. As two immediate consequences of this pleasure-theory, it follows that pleasure as 'rhythm' (1) stands no longer opposed to pain, that there is pain in pleasure thanks to the to-and-fro movement of the rhythm, and (2) that pleasure, as a play of resistance and victory, is no longer determinable as a self-given, self-evident sensation, since it is entirely relative to the resistance opposing it. Traditionally, the two sensations, pain and pleasure, stand opposed as two clearly identifiable extremes. However, according to Nietzsche's logic, pleasure would not be registered if there were no resistance to oppose it.

> Suppose pleasure and pain were so linked together that he who wants to have the greatest possible amount of the one must have the greatest possible amount of the other also. [. . .] And perhaps that is how things are! The Stoics, at any rate, thought so, and were consistent when they desired to have the least possible amount of pleasure in order to have the least possible amount of pain from life. [. . .] Today, too, you have the choice: either as little pain as possible, in short painlessness [. . .] or as much pain at possible as the price of an abundance of subtle joys and pleasures hitherto rarely tasted. (FW 12, KSA 3, p. 383-84).

The idea of the entanglement of pain and pleasure finds its strongest formulation in a fragment from the Nachlaß. Here we read:

> Certainty, precaution, patience, wisdom, variety, all the fine nuances from light

to dark, from bitter to sweet – all of this we owe to pain; the entire canon of beauty, sublimity, and divinity is only possible in a world of deep and changing and multiple pains. [. . .] Friends! We must increase the pains of this world if we want to increase its pleasure and wisdom. (Nachlaß 1881, KSA 9, 13[4]).

If we cannot determine pleasure once and for all, as philosophical ethics has endeavored and still endeavors, then there is no Good that we as individuals or societies *ought* to pursue as *the* Good. Various Hedonistic philosophies are in error in their pursuit of these superficial notions of pleasure, and no philosophical ethics more so than the Utilitarianism of Bentham and Stuart Mill.

When for example Bentham describes pleasure and pain as quantifiable entities according to seven 'circumstances' – for example in respect to intensity, duration, certainty/uncertainty, or fecundity – it is the underlying assumption that pleasure as well as pain are given, constant, universal, and invariable qualities that we as humans already positively know.[545] Pain is *eo ipso* pain, pain; pleasure *eo ipso* pleasure, pleasure; neither pain or pleasure need further explanation. This underlying conviction permits the utilitarian to set up his balance sheet over pleasures and pains. Supposedly, we can add up pleasures and subtract pains in a so-called 'felicific' or 'hedonic' calculus, and thus compute relevant amounts of pleasures and pains in various hypothetical circumstances. The legislator – in this pseudo-scientific social utopia of Bentham and Stuart Mill – is in this 'felicific calculus' supposed to have a tool for the appraisal of various legislative alternatives according to their final 'hedonic' value. If such a social utopia were at all realizable, there would be no *resistance of pleasure*, and consequently no pleasure at all, to Nietzsche's mind. The social individuals would live in lazy contentment, soon turning into boredom, or, as Nietzsche would have put it, into general degeneration of their vital powers.[546]

---

[545] The notion that one could measure degrees of pain and pleasure of a certain activity in relation to 'seven circumstances,' in order to determine its ultimate 'hedonic' value, rests in all 'circumstances' on random subjective interpretation of the activity. What is the 'hedonic' value of drinking a bottle of wine – for example, in relation to 'fecundity' (the tendency of pleasure to produce more pleasure)? Some would think 'hangovers' and apply a negative value; some would think 'Dutch courage' and apply a positive value (or, indeed, a negative!). The values we apply to the activity in the different categories are nothing but the arbitrary result of our interpreting fantasy.

[546] We find an illustrative model of this society in the recent movie, *The Truman Show*. This movie precisely shows how the protagonist seeks resistance and challenge as alternatives more pleasurable than the given pleasures that are taken for granted and being devised by the utilitarian god of the movie, the

2. A Relativistic Theory of Pleasure

Before pleasure comes into existence, a frustration or an obstacle must exist as something the subject is impelled to overcome. The *impetus* toward this overcoming accounts for pleasure as much as the *overcoming* itself, and may even be more intense, insofar as the *overcoming* is immediately followed by an inevitable *fading of intensity*. The drive and impetus toward overcoming is the will to power, and is to Nietzsche the nature of desire: "The essential desire is Will to Power [*Die Grundbegierde ist der Wille zur Macht*]." (Nachlaß 1885-86, KSA 12, 1[59].[547]

When there is *pleasure in the resistance of pleasure*, the object of desire 'tickles,' tantalizes, and frustrates the subject by holding back itself from the conquering subject. Now, this logic introduces an economic calculus into desire: the more resistance the *object of desire* puts up against the *desiring subject*, the greater will also be the desire in the *subject* to repulse the resistance of the *desired object* (– and the more intense the sense of pleasure accompanying the actual victory). Hence, the value of the object grows with its inaccessibility; and the investments of the subject in the object increase with its inaccessibility. Thus, a 'clever object' (a 'clever woman' for instance) knows that the more it makes itself inaccessible, the more it increases its value. To put the logic simply: everybody wants what they can't get, and the more they can't get it, the more they want it.

Desire magnifies [*vergrößert*] that which one wants to possess; it grows by being unfulfilled [*durch Nichterfüllung*] – The greatest ideas are those, which are produced by the most intense and prolonged desires. We put into things *ever*

TV producer. In a Nietzschean reading of the movie, the protagonist gradually realizes that there is *no satisfaction in satisfaction*, but *satisfaction in dissatisfaction*.

[547] It is in the incessant drive to overcome obstacles, Nietzsche's subject become 'master'; but in a sense different from Hegel's 'master.' It is not here the place to go into a comparison between Hegel and Nietzsche's master/slave distinction, but one may note that Nietzsche's 'master' is typically not asserting his power as self over and against another non-self. Nietzsche's master is not bound up in a dialectical relationship, engaged in a war for recognition; significantly, he does not eventually *loose* this war, since he is not relatively determined in his dialectical dependence of the slave. More typically, Nietzsche's 'master' is master of himself and whatever constitutes his adopted existential project; implying that the pleasure involved in his will to power is enjoyment of self-improvement in respect to his project. There is for example power, and consequently pleasure, in such a solitary activity as thinking: "Pleasure in thinking. – Ultimately, it is not only the feeling of power, but the pleasure in creating and in the thing created; for all activity enters our consciousness as consciousness of a 'work'." (WM 661).

more value, in proportion to how our desire for them grows: that the 'moral values' have become the highest values, betrays that the moral ideal also always has been the most impossible to fulfill [*daß das moralische Ideal das Unerfüllteste gewesen ist*]. (WM 336).

We find in the *late* Freud a similar relativistic notion of pleasure (the young Freud, on the contrary, takes the *sexual metaphor* literally, and takes for granted that *pleasure* is identical to *sexual pleasure*). Pleasure is not understood as some one thing, but as a sudden release of pent-up drives, as the emancipation of frustrations that has thwarted the subject over a prolonged period of time.

> What we call happiness in the strictest sense comes from the (preferably sudden) satisfaction of needs which have been dammed up to a high degree, and it is from its nature only possible as an episodic phenomenon. When any situation that is desired by the pleasure-principle is prolonged, it only produces a feeling of mild contentment. We are so made that we can derive intense enjoyment only from a contrast and very little from a state of things. Thus our possibilities of happiness are already restricted by our constitution.[548]

It is in the context of this quotation that Freud pronounces his famous, "One feels inclined to say that the intention that man should be 'happy' is not included in the plan of Creation" (ibid., p. 25). – However, this pessimistic conclusion is far from shared by Nietzsche. The fact that frustration of desire is a pre-condition for pleasure, which as such only realizes itself in brief instantaneous bursts, does not give rise to pessimism in Nietzsche, and is not seen, like in Freud, as "constitutionally restricting our possibilities of happiness." The pain of frustration and non-fulfillment is understood, on the contrary, as the grand motivator and stimulus to life, therefore as something valuable and exclusively positive.[549]

---

[548] Sigmund Freud: "Das Unbehagen in der Kultur"; GW XIV, p. 434.

[549] Compare to G. Abel: "To Nietzsche it is crucial that every activity is "a defeat of difficulties and resistance." Pleasure evidences itself as a secondary manifestation of the perpetual overcoming of several kinds of resistance, which simultaneously "like in a rhythmic dance, results in a sort of tickling of the feeling of power! . . . Pain works, according to Nietzsche, as a "stimulus of life"; it strengthens the will-to-power." Abel: Nietzsche, loc. cit., p. 96-97.

3. The Rhythm.

We have indicated that Nietzsche emphasizes the pleasure of the drive rather than the pleasure of the aim in the project of securing pleasure. However, there is a tension in Nietzsche's thinking. On the one hand, he emphasizes the 'again and again,' the sequence of resistance and victory as an interminable rhythm, but, one the other, the logic he describes implies a halt of the will, namely in the will's mastery or victory over its object. Obviously, when the will becomes 'master' over an obstacle, a strife has ended – however local and provisional the ending. The will may immediately find itself a second obstacle, but still, it has ended its struggle to attain the first. However interminable *the process*, the *stages* on the way toward absolute fulfillment are gradually overcome. There is thus a tension between the *eternity* of the drive, and the *mastery* of the will.

Here, we notice that 'rhythm' is a notion that uniquely resolves this tension.[550] 'Rhythm' is a vibration that keeps the will both in movement and brings it to a halt (think for example on the rhythm of waves breaking on the seashore only in order to roll back into the sea beneath a wave that is bound to repeat the same movement). In the appearance of a single signifier, *rhythm* assimilates and reconciles the paradox. But although the contradiction has been internalized and digested by this small linguistic body, it still lives as a vibration inside this body of a single signifier. *Rhythm* may be the last word for Nietzsche's pleasure-principle, but it continues to inform the entire corpus of Nietzsche's theory of pleasure and desire. We can certainly say, and in more that one sense, that nothing stops in the rhythm.

As well as nothing stops in the rhythm, there would be no pleasure in a rhythm that stops. Although a rhythm of resistance and victory implies provisional victories, there has to be a drive to drive the rhythm toward new projects, new provisional victories. There has to be a drive for the drive. This second-order drive, the drive for the drive, tends by Nietzsche to be understood as life itself. If there were no drive for the drive, we would have a rhythm that stops, we would have a life satisfied, that is, no life, but a degeneration and a perversion of our vital instincts.[551]

---

[550] 'Rhythm' is, like Derrida's *Pharmakon* (Derrida, Jacques: "Plato's Pharmakon" in: Dissemination (Chicago: The University of Chicago Press, 1981), a notion that spans a paradox. In Derrida's reading of Plato, *pharmakon* is a drug both poisonous and remedial.

[551] The so-called 'life,' which Nietzsche with dismay observes is guiding his mediocre European contemporaries.

We can thus with some accuracy identify Nietzsche's 'slaves' as those for who the drive of the drive has stopped, for who there is no rhythm (i.e., for who the rhythm is no longer beating), for who there is satisfaction. They have drives, as everybody else, but only of the first order; they have no drive of the drive. However, as an immediate consequence of this logic, there is for Nietzsche's 'master' no real mastery; at least, there can be no absolutely 'satisfied' and 'gratified' master. Or, to put it in paradox, if the master became 'satisfied' as master, then he would immediately turn into a slave. Thus, in Nietzsche's writings, the master is far more ambivalent, far more difficult to determine than is the slave.

4. Beyond the Logic of Desire.
What if Desire is Nothing but Representation?

If we think the logic of desire according to tradition, then it is inconceivable to think of desire without aim, without object – especially as inspired by psychoanalysis, but by Western Thinking in general.[552] Desire cannot be blind; it beholds an 'image'; the 'image' being its aim. Desire implies an ideational representation (a *Vorstellungsrepräsentanz*, says Freud), a symbolic content without which it would not be desire, and toward which it is aimed. The ideational content is the fantasy-component of the desire, the yet-not-realized imaginary aim toward which the drive is driven. Thus, an imaginary 'aim' is always a part of the desirous 'drive'; it exists internalized in the drive as the 'yet-not-realized.' Nietzsche corroborates the view: "There exists no 'willing,' only a willing-something [*Etwaswollen*]: one must not detach the aim from the state, like the epistemologists do. 'Willing,' as they understand it, happens as little as 'thinking': it is a mere fiction." (Nachlaß 1887-88, KSA 13, 11[114]).

A *desire* without object and aim seems to be as well a logical as a semantic impossibility. In the psychoanalytical tradition, a *drive* with only an external aim, but *without internalized content* – that is, without a *symbolic representation* of the aim – is best characterized as *instinct*. As far as we know, the eagle has no *desire* to kill the mouse, but we believe it has an *instinct*. Thus, a desire without internalized fantasy-object has been either downgraded to instinct, or to a desire that desires only itself – a desire for

---

[552] For example by Hobbes to whom the main object of desire is self-preservation, laying the foundation for Hobbes' early version of a *will to power*.

only desire (whatever exactly that might be?).[553] In the latter sense, one may characterize desire as auto-affective. Without aim, bent in unto itself, it becomes like a circle, a ring – not like a line or an arrow, as we regularly represent desire.

Auto-affective desire becomes like the ancient symbol of the snake coiling around itself trying to devour itself. If for the game of it, one heeds this interesting image and elaborates the small narrative inherent in it, the aporia becomes manifest. What happens when the self-devouring snake (hypothetically) has consumed most of itself and arrives at its own head? Are there now two heads? What happens when it swallows up also its own head? Does the snake disappear altogether, or is there a head left? Like this ancient symbol, a desire without aim, a desire desiring only itself, is such an irresolvable aporia. The idea seems utterly impossible, and yet – although Nietzsche pronounces that "willing is always a willing-something" – *auto-affective desire* seems to be his ultimate *temptation*. Throughout the eighties, we notice in his work, and especially in the Nachlaß, a persistent questioning of the value of the internalized 'aim,' i.e., of the symbolic representation of the aim, the *Vorstellungsrepäsentanz*. The fascinating question engaging Nietzsche seems now to be, could there be something like a completely *auto-effective joy*, a joy involving suspension of the aim (the joy I here render as *the joy of desire of desire*)?

Before proceeding any further along this track, let us sum up some of the positions mentioned, but in abbreviated and formulaic from. We have been suggesting a dialectics between 'drive' and 'aim.' In the most primitive rendition of this dialectics, the drive is aiming toward fulfillment in an aim. According to this simple model, the drive is 'in' the subject, and the aim is 'in' reality. Therefore, our first and most simple model must be:

(1)   DRIVE → AIM

This model would describe the *instinct*, in which a mindless drive is driven toward realizing an aim in reality. While for millennia we have been convinced that this model characterizes animal drives, we believe that human drives are driven by the image of the internalized aim, the fantasy compo-

---

[553] Although Lacanians famously describe desire as the desire of the other's desire, the other's desire – implicating the other's love or recognition – is still a clearly delineated pleasure-object. And although we frequently talk of 'aimless desires,' we never mean that these desires are in fact 'aimless'; we mean on the contrary that such desires have several aims. By not being directed toward a single aim, such desires are confused, erratic, and drifting. Only in that sense are they 'aimless.'

nent, or the symbolic representation, in which case drives are transformed into *desires*. Therefore, a model on *human drives* (i.e., *desires*) must accommodate this complication. The aim is now 'in' the subject, and the complex below, (DRIVE ($\rightarrow$ AIM$_2$)), designates *desire*.

(2) (DRIVE ($\rightarrow$ AIM$_2$)) $\rightarrow$ AIM$_1$

Finally, we have asserted that in Nietzsche, there is a drive for the drive, a so-called 'second-order' drive, which secures that the first-order drive never puts itself to rest. There is no final satisfaction; there is an eternal rhythm of obstacles and defeats of obstacles. A final model must accommodate the inclusion of this second order drive. This formula may depict the will-to-power-process: will-to-power for more power.

(3) DRIVE$_2$ $\rightarrow$ (DRIVE$_1$ ($\rightarrow$ AIM$_2$)) $\rightarrow$ AIM$_1$

In several of Nietzsche's contemporary commentators, it is recognized that there is in Nietzsche a tendency to situate pleasure on the side of the drive, both in the sense of drive$_2$ and drive$_1$. The *drive* of the master is then becoming more fascinating than is his aim, his *reserve* more interesting than his decisiveness.[554]

Progressively in his thinking, Nietzsche tries still harder to think the circle, the ring of auto-affective desire, and in his last and most ecstatic endeavor, he gives his thinking expression in the notion of the 'eternal recurrence of the same.' The question Nietzsche seems to be asking himself in these endeavors is inspired, as well as his answer is dangerously clever – perhaps *too* dangerously clever.[555] Question and answer are motivated by a

---

[554]   Few are today thrilled by Nietzsche's references to the likes of Alexander the Great, Caesar Borgia, or Napoleon Bonaparte, while in earlier critics we notice a fascination with the prospect of this kind of military 'Mastery.' Nietzsche's writings became for earlier critics like an invigorating tonic; one injected oneself with a shot of Dutch courage by reading Nietzsche; one took Nietzsche literally, and 'philosophized with a hammer.' George Brandes, for instance, Nietzsche's first commentator and far from his worst, was convinced that he in Nietzsche's thinking had found the recipe for an 'aristocratic radicalism' by which he could denounce something as small and petty as the nascent democracy in Danish politics. The tendency today to see Nietzsche's 'master' as a far more complex figure (or simply to understand him/her as '*figure*') is adopted by several of Nietzsche's recent commentators.

[555]   As also Daniel Conway has noted, in thinking these affairs, Nietzsche is in his late thinking engaging himself in a "dangerous game." (See Conway, Daniel:

growing suspicion regarding what I have called the 'internalized aim,' or the 'ideational' (or 'symbolic') representation, or the *Vorstellungsrepräsentanz*.

In my free reconstruction, Nietzsche's soliloquy touching on these issues could have proceeded approximately as follows:

> N_1: What if that which drives us in our desires is nothing but a *Vorstellungsrepräsentanz*?
> N_2: In that case, our deepest and most impassioned engagements would be merely controlled by the illusion of a symbol! . . .
> N_1: They would be literally *nothing*, and the object of desire would be merely an elaborate hoax, an illusion, 'a thing of nothing,' which we could just as well do away with . . .
> N_2: If now we suspended all realization (and all *expectation* of realization) of the drive in the aim; if we bent desire unto itself, we would seem to live just as well, or even better, since in the first place the *Vorstellungsrepräsentanz* is 'a thing of nothing'!

We notice this tendency to suspend realization of the drive in Nietzsche's 'pathos of distance,' and, sometimes, in his descriptions of the operations of the 'feminine' woman. If we adopt our vocabulary above, situating pleasure 'on the side of the drive' means that Nietzsche emphasizes the pleasure of the fantasy-component, of the internalized representation, as more pleasurable than pleasure realized. The internalized aim preferably ought to stay internalized, while realization implies an immediate corrosion of satisfaction. The drive is surely driven toward an aim of which it wants mastery, but it wants mastery as fantasy rather than reality. (Although renowned for his philosophy of the master and the superhuman, we often get the suspicion that Nietzsche doesn't want mastery after all; as if he is too refined, too subtle, or too timid.)

We see this logic played out in several instances in Nietzsche's work, for example, in an aphorism from FW, explicitly named '*From a distance*' [*Aus der Ferne*].

> This mountain makes the entire region it dominates attractive and significant in every way; having said this to ourselves for the hundredth time, we are so unreasonably and thankfully disposed toward it that we suppose that it, the bestower of such delight, must itself be the most delightful thing in the region – and so we climb it and are disappointed. Suddenly the mountain itself and the entire landscape around us, beneath us, seem to have lost their magic; we had

---

Nietzsche's Dangerous Game. (Cambridge: Cambridge University Press, 2002).

forgotten that certain types of greatness, like certain types of goodness, want to be beheld only from a distance and always from below, not from above – only thus do they h a v e a n e f f e c t. (FW 15, KSA 3, p. 388).

Here, the object of desire is the mountain, the drive of the drive, climbing towards the peak, and the realization of the project of the drive, to reach the peak. (It is of course not accidental that mountain climbing is chosen as the image illustrating the logic of desire. Nietzsche's dialectics of resistance and victory is also such a 'climbing' toward 'peaks.' Nietzsche's image, mountain climbing, is an apt representation of 'drive.' To take a stroll on the British meadows, or being tossed around in a mountain river, etc., could not easily fit the bill.) Again, to reach the top promises only disappointment. There is *no satisfaction in satisfaction*. And in order to avoid the disappointment, we are recommended to keep our distance, to look at the peak from below, to endow it with 'magic' and desire, but not to conquer it. *Satisfaction is dissatisfaction.*

Another aphorism from FW repeats the same idea, here in relation to woman as the exclusive aim.[556] The persona of the aphorism is standing at the seashore, immersed in the noise of the surf breaking on the rocks. On the horizon, a sailboat glides past, calmly and silently, producing a contrast to the noise of the surf. While the noise is a symbol of our struggling existence, "our plans and projects," the sailboat is a symbol of the calm we long for in existence. "When a man stands in the midst of *his own* noise, in the midst of his own surf of projects and plans, he is also likely to see gliding past him silent, magical creatures whose happiness and seclusion he yearns for." (FW 60, KSA 3, p. 424). Abruptly follows an intersection, emphasized: " – e s s i n d d i e F r a u e n" [translated by Hollingdale simply "*Women*"]. So, the sailboat is a woman; she is the calm that the persona in the noise of his existence longs for. However, he is deluding himself. "He almost believes that his better self lives there amongst the women: in these quiet regions even the loudest surf turns into deathly silence and life itself into a dream about life. Yet! Yet! My noble enthusiast, even on the most beautiful sailing ship there is so much sound and noise, and unfortunately so much small, petty noise!" (ibid.). The object of desire, the sailboat gliding quietly past on the horizon, if actually one boarded it, it would also be noisy, namely from the chatter of women, which is "small and petty" noise. Therefore, Nietzsche's persona must finally recommend himself to keep distance. "The magic and most powerful effect of women is, to speak the

---

[556] The aphorism is quoted also in the beginning of Derrida's *Spurs* (Jacques Derrida: *Spurs/Eperons*. Chicago: The University of Chicago Press, 1979) for a somewhat different, but not necessarily conflicting, purpose.

language of the philosophers, action at a distance, actio in distans: but that requires, first and foremost – d i s t a n c e ." (ibid.).[557]

In the operations of the feminine woman, which is always a dangerous woman, the figure of distance, reserve, and withdrawal gets an even more complicated expression. In this play between man and woman, both achieve their respective 'mastery' only insofar as they understand the exigency of distance. The seductive woman retreats from the advances of the man, but the man too is recommended to disengage his advances; at least, to mistrust his idealizations of the woman. "Fortunately, I am not willing to be torn to pieces: the perfect woman tears to pieces when she loves. – I know these charming maenads. – Ah, what a dangerous, creeping subterranean little beast of prey she is!" (EH, "Warum ich so gute Bücher schreibe" 5, KSA 6, p. 306). The castration threat of the woman' is explicit, and man therefore has compelling reasons to avoid contact. We have two protagonists who are retreating from each other, *while* intensifying reciprocal desire. They engage in a dangerous erotic dance where they must be infinitely cautious not to touch.

---

[557] A brief digression: in *Beyond the Pleasure Principle*, Freud describes a simple play entertaining his small grandson, Ernst. The play is famously known as the *fort-da* game, and consists in Ernst throwing away (*fort*) and pulling back (*da*) a spool with a string attached to it. Freud speculates that one of the motives for the game might be that Ernst, in the symbol of this spool, is taking control over, *learning to master*, his mother's departures. By throwing away and pulling back the symbolic spool, he puts himself in the superior position of sending her away and pulling her back exactly as he pleases. Now, is Nietzsche not playing a *fort-da* game with the women on the sailboat (or, the woman *as* the sailboat) similar to Ernst's *fort-da* game with *his* significant (m)other? Nietzsche's persona first dreams himself on board of the sailboat, away from the noise of himself and his projects, comforted in the lap of a woman. The woman is *da*. Then he rejects her again, as he convinces himself that this sailboat is as noisy as he is to himself. The woman is *fort*. This is his final position, an infantile 'stay away' equivalent to Ernst's infantile 'go away' – Nietzsche's 'stay away' only intellectualized: 'a woman, *alas*, moves us from distance only; like God, her *modus operandi* is *actio in distans*.' They are both learning how to endure absence, – with only the minor difference that one-and-a-half year old Ernst still needs a spool with a string attached in order to play his game, while grownup Nietzsche no longer needs a toy in order to play. He plays just as well with an internalized toy-woman in pure thinking.

5. Pain-Sensation as Fantasy and Hallucination.

On the backdrop of these preparations, the critical question is now, what happens if we deliberately lost the *Vorstellungsrepräsentanz*? – It is granted that both pain and pleasure are *represented* to consciousness, and it is *as represented* they are identified as either this or that, as either pain or pleasure. If there is no ideational representative, consequently, there would be no pain, also no pleasure – but especially, as Nietzsche tends to emphasize, there would be *no pain*.

Pain gains its force and energy purely from a *Vorsellungsrepräsentanz*. It is thanks to this representative it is felt; but in itself, it is merely a fantasy and a hallucination. Pain is, as Nietzsche explicitly reiterates, "intellectual" or merely a "brain-phenomenon": "Measured intellectually, how full of error [*irrthumvoll*] is not the sense of pleasure and pain! How false does not one make judgments, when from the d e g r e e s of pleasure or pain, one draws conclusions about the value of life! . . . W i t h o u t i n t e l l e c t, there is no pain. . . . Pain is a p r o d u c t o f t h e b r a i n [*Gehirnproduct*]." (Nachlaß 1881, KSA 9, 11[319]). It is the ideational representative, stored in our memory systems, and reactivated as fantasy, that account for the perception of pain. Pain is consequently nothing in-itself. "Without fantasy and memory, pleasure and pain would not exist. [. . .] When a deprivation is not perceived by eye or touch, it is much less painful." (Nachlaß 1881, KSA 9, 11[301]).

Here, Nietzsche is extending this argument of the relativism of pleasures and pains not only to so-called 'higher' sensations, but also to so-called 'lower' physical sensations. Whereas it would be relatively easy to reconcile his argument to sensation of so-called 'higher' pleasures or pains, extending it to brutal physical sensations must seem contrary to common sense.

Regarding 'higher' sensations, it has always been difficult to establish the 'hedonic' value of intellectual activities such as, for instance, reading a book. Strictly speaking, we cannot know whether it is a pleasure or a pain to read a book because several different sensations fuse into the reading-experience, sensations for which we have no name and no value. If the self-comforting 'humanist'[558] asserts that reading a book is a pleasure (relaxa-

---

[558] Like for example John Stuart Mill who in *Utilitarianism* introduced the distinction between 'higher' and 'lower' pleasures, with this persuading himself of the superiority of intellectual, 'higher,' pleasures; – and if not in that essay, then with full force in his troubled *Autobiography*. See John Stuart Mill: "Utilitarianism," in, *On Liberty and Other Essays*, edited by J. Gray (Oxford:

tion after work, escape into another reality, education of the mind, etc.), he is merely *interpreting*. He makes a series of quick subconscious judgments that correspond to current ideology and self-understanding, but not to the reality of 'reading' *per se*. If innocently enough he suggests that reading is a freedom one indulges after work, a relaxation and an escape from burdensome reality, then according to this interpretation, he takes for granted that it is a relief to *escape* from reality; that reading is *freedom* and *relaxation*; while work is *exhausting*. Or if he goes further, reading also *educates* the mind, then he has immediately translated as 'good' what 'educates.' But in 'reality,' reading is a *terra incognita*, a Dark Continent populated with all sorts of bizarre and fanciful creatures. Therefore, so-called 'higher' pleasures are stamped with ambiguity; the so-called 'pleasurable' is no longer positively identifiable, what, on the other hand, by no means imply that it is a pain. The best we can say is that it is an ambiguous *pleasure-pain* (or a *sensational neutral*), and as such, it is left to the creative subject to specify its value. Thus, we shall say that watching a movie is a pleasure-pain, as is lying in the sun, taking a swim, listening to music, and dining at a five-star restaurant. We know with some certainty that *work* is a pleasure-pain that is typically interpreted as a pain, *because* also *being-out-of-work* is a pleasure-pain that is typically interpreted as a pain. We notice the following tendency in the interpretation of *pleasure-pains*. As a rule of thump, and in good accordance with Nietzsche's doctrine of the nature of pleasure, they are interpreted as pleasures whenever one has been barred from achieving them over a period of time – and reversely, as pains, whenever one has had them in abundance over a period. That is the reason why work is a pain for he who is employed and a pleasure for he who has been unemployed. The same logic applies to sexuality and generally – we appreciate scarcity, and depreciate abundance.

If now we are ready to accept Nietzsche's argument regarding 'higher' pleasures, what about so-called 'lower'? To Nietzsche's mind, there is no doubt; also palpable pain-sensations such as cutting one's finger, burning one's hand (– or what about debilitating attacks of migraine?) would be mere hallucinations; strictly speaking non-existent before they have been *characterized*, i.e., identified, in the *Vorstellungsrepräsentanz* and brought before consciousness. Pain is in itself nothing.

However, this position necessarily begs the question, how come that pain is *experienced* as unbearable? The *Vorstellungsrepräsentanz* must necessarily present consciousness with something unbearable. Even if we grant

---

Oxford University Press, 1991); and, *Autobiography* (London: Penguin Books, 1989).

that physical pain is nothing in-itself and is first experienced as pain when represented and characterized, then the *representation* itself must be 'painful' to consciousness. Otherwise, consciousness would not react with revulsion, and the individual would not withdraw from the pain-generating incident. The question is therefore, *what kind of representations could achieve this particular effect*? In some of his profoundest reflections from the Nachlaß, Nietzsche (who is acute enough, we notice, to understand that this question needs an answer) attempts an explanation. The suggestion is tentative and experimental since he is entering a field of which there is no concrete knowledge; and where even today, neuroscience is fishing around in murky waters.

> If we consider how pleasure o r i g i n a t e s ! How m a n y images/representations [*Vorstellungen*] do not have to come together, before they finally become a unity and a whole, which can no longer recognize itself as a multiplicity. As such, in e v e r y pleasure there could exist a pain! These are b r a i n - phenomena. But long ago they have become incorporated, and now present themselves only as wholes. W h y does it hurt to c u t a f i n g e r ? In i t s e l f [*an sich*] it does not hurt (although the person may experience a certain 'stimulus'); the one whose brain is anesthetized with chloroform feels no pain in his finger. Perhaps it is the j u d g m e n t of the loss of a functioning organ, on the part of the f a n t a - s i z i n g u n i t y, that is necessary? Is it only the unity that conjures up [/dreams up] the injury and – as it makes us feel pain – sends off the s t r o n g e s t possible stimuli to the place where the injury happened. (Nachlaß 1881, KSA 9, 11[303]).

First, pain or pleasure in-itself is a multiplicity of feelings. It is originally a cluster of different and contradictory sensations, which has eventually been simplified into the unity of a single cluster. The cluster replaces the multiplicity of several distinct traces within the cluster; instead of being a plurality of traces, it recognizes itself as unity. As such, different and distinct drives has from early on been 'incorporated' [*Einverleibt*] into our nervous system, presenting themselves now as an *identity*.

So, why does it hurt to cut one's finger, as Nietzsche pertinently asks? – Well, it does not hurt, but it is represented *as if* it hurts. It is *represented* as hurtful because it threatens the achieved unity of our system. It hurts as a result of a judgment on part of the so-called 'fantasizing unity.' This 'fantasizing unity' judges immediately that a wound threatens its unity, and consequently, it starts a hectic whirlwind of activity around, and sends off an abundance of stimuli to, the location where the injury happened. So, it is the threat of *fragmentation* and *disintegration* of the body that is represented to the mind as painful. While there is no pain in the wound it-

5. Pain Sensation as Fantasy and Hallucination

self, a pain is represented to the mind because of the reaction (which reads almost like a *hysterical over-reaction*) of the fantasizing unity (– as if a supremely heroic Nietzsche desires to tell himself that his migraine-attacks are merely hysterical over-reactions). "Intellectuality of p a i n : it does not relate to what immediately is harmful, but rather to the v a l u e the harm has in relation to the total individual." (Nachlaß 1886-87, KSA 12, 7[48]). Nothing is more horrific to the mind than the disintegration of the human body, and if this disintegration becomes a threat to the *total* individual, it is experienced as pain.

In another fragment, Nietzsche expands his explanation.

> Our h i g h e r pains, the so-called pains of the soul, whose dialectics we often do not realize since they introduce occurrences s l o w l y a n d m u t u a l l y i n t e r w o v e n [*auseinandergezogen*], in comparison to the l o w e r pains (for example in being wounded) whose character is sudden. But the latter is essentially as complicated and dialectical, and intellectual – . The essential is that several sensations all of a sudden break loose and p l u n g e s a g a i n s t o n e a n o t h e r [*losstürzen und aufeinanderstürzen*] – ; this sudden confusion and chaos is to consciousness identical to physical pain; pleasure and pain are not 'immediate facts.' A number of i m a g e s / r e p r e s e n t a t i o n s [*Vorstellungen*], incorporated in the drives, are suddenly engaged, with lightning speed, against one another. The opposite is pleasure, that is, when images/representations [*Vorstellungen*] are available equally quickly, but in harmony and balance – t h i s is now by the intellect felt as pleasure. (Nachlaß 1881, KSA 9, 11[314]).

Pain is experienced because of sudden disorder in the psychic system. A system that has achieved a certain equilibrium is suddenly disturbed, and 'drives' that have been incorporated as a unity – which have, in my reading, been collected and identified in and as a 'cluster' – break loose and react against each other. The ensuing disorder and chaos is identified as pain. Whereas the opposite tendency, the situation where a sequence of multifarious 'drives' suddenly comes together in harmony, is identified as pleasure.

Before a sensation can be identified as either pain or pleasure, the brain has to make up its mind (so to speak) about the quality of the sensation. This is done mainly by means of the symbolic representation (Nietzsche's *Vorstellung*; Freud's *Vorstellungsrepräsentanz*) that attaches itself to the sensation. Either it summons forth an image of disintegration and chaos or the opposite; in the former case, experience of pain ensues, in the latter, experience of pleasure.

There is in these reflections not much difference between Nietzsche's theory of pain and Freud's speculations on pain in his early neurological work, *Project for a Scientific Psychology*.⁵⁵⁹ Freud is not going quite as far as Nietzsche in claiming that the pain-sensation is nothing in itself, but it is clear that he believes that it is made more intense when characterized and represented.

We saw above (cf. *Chapter 4*) that to Freud, the *cause* of pain has to be identified as 'hostile' and how the scream helps in this process of identification. The 'scream' became a *catalyst* for the sensation of pain (cf. "The information of one's scream serves to characterize the object"⁵⁶⁰). As in Nietzsche, it is also in Freud the case that there is only a dull sensation before there is a *Vorstellung* to circumscribe and describe it. One first feels a certain discomfort, a certain disturbance, but it is the *representation* of this dull sensation in the *scream* that helps link the sensation to a *hostile object*, and thus help characterizing the sensation as pain. The point is not that there is no sensation before there is linguistic representation, but rather that there is no *mental focus on the sensation* before linguistic representation.⁵⁶¹ The representation of the pain in the scream helps us to distinguish a *cause*; it is *qua the scream* that an object is characterized as 'hostile,' and thus recognized as able to cause pain. In other words, the *information* of one's scream helps one *remember* the hostile object as a typical cause of pain. Moreover, through this characterization of the object, the pain is *emphasized* and *intensified*.

Compare these reflections to Nietzsche's profound remark: "The simple man always says: this or that makes me fell unwell – he makes up his mind about his feeling unwell only when he has seen a reason for feeling unwell." (WM 266). In other words, whether in the case of pain or feeling unwell, we can only read these exogenous or endogenous stimuli insofar as we have a language by which to connect the stimuli to the memory of certain hostile

---

⁵⁵⁹ Sigmund Freud: *Project for a Scientific Psychology* [1895]. In *The Standard Edition of the Complete Psychological Works of Sigmund Freud*, vol. 1-24. Edited and translated by J. Strachey (London: The Hogarth Press and the Institute of Psychoanalysis, 1966).

⁵⁶⁰ Freud: *Project*, loc. cit., p. 366-67.

⁵⁶¹ We are in Freud's example of the scream returning to the distinction between thing- and word-presentations that he makes early in his writings: the thing-presentation is here represented by the *hostile object*, the word-presentation by the *scream*. In his example, the *scream* becomes a signifier representing a rudimentary and embryonic word that rouses memories, thus making the subject conscious of the hostile object, detecting it as cause and reason for the pain. We notice that uttering a word induces a reversal of the chronology between cause and effect: *first*, there is an effect, *then*, the subject starts looking for a cause.

causes or objects. This is why children often start crying with delay. They first need to see what object caused the sensation, then remember the object as a hostile one, before they decide that the sensation is painful. First then do they start crying, therewith emphasizing the pain.

APPENDIX 3

The Fragmented Nietzschean Subject and Literary Criticism

Conflicting Images of Woman in Jacobsen's "Arabesque to a Drawing by Michelangelo"

> An artist is a sort of Sisyphus that is compelled to roll a stone to the top of a slope. But for himself the stone always escapes him near the top and rolls down again, although one would prefer to have an audience that believes that it has stayed at the top.
> – -J. P. Jacobsen, letter to Axel Helsted, 1880

1. On Severe Confusion and Fundamental Ignorance

Many of Nietzsche's insights on the subject have adopted by later theorists and applied in philosophical or literary criticism. The principle of analyzing the conflicting voices of a chaotic or fragmented self has formed the foundation for a theory that Jacques Derrida – in the brief programmatic essay "Otobiographies"[562] – has described as a new "autobiography." Elsewhere, Derrida has suggested the label hetero-biography, or even hetero-thanato-bio-graphy.[563] Closely following Derrida, Henry Staten has, in *Nietzsche's Voice*, introduced the theory under the label psychodialectics – Staten felicitously replacing the old "analysis" (implying a still deeper digging into the hidden compartments of the subject) with the new "dialectics" (implying

---

[562] Derrida, "Otobiographies," *The Ear of the Other*, loc. cit.
[563] Derrida, "To Speculate: On Freud," *The Post Card,* loc. cit.

interaction between configurations).⁵⁶⁴ In their critical projects, both Derrida and Staten are in effect analyzing Nietzsche's *voices* (or, as I prefer, ego- or semantic clusters) as these voices represent various interests, wills, or desires colliding within a multifarious and perspectival subject.

The Nietzschean insight that in our interpreting activities we necessarily appropriate what is strange, dangerous, and other, thus reducing the other to what is the same and familiar has been applied by Michel Foucault in his analyzes of the genealogies of social and institutional constructions – for instance, of the construction and appropriation of madness in the eighteenth and nineteenth centuries. It has also been applied by Edward Said, inspired by Foucault, in his analyzes of the appropriation of the Orient in an imperialist nineteenth century. In Derrida's essay *Eperons*,⁵⁶⁵ the attempt to understand, explain, or think the other has been explored in Nietzsche's thematization of woman; this is an especially relevant application in the context of the present appendix, as will become obvious shortly.

It is this Nietzschean thinking, and some of the critical strategies that have developed in its wake, that we will be exercising on a comparatively small text, a poem composed by the nineteenth-century Danish poet J. P. Jacobsen.⁵⁶⁶

In this poem, we experience how a self in perpetual conflict with itself, in a highly sublimated poetic language, tries to assimilate what in this specific poem is perceived as an enigma and a danger, namely, woman. Jacobsen has an inclination frequently seen among a number of late nine-

---

[564] Staten, *Nietzsche's Voice*. Staten describes "psycho-dialectical reading" as a "reading [that] treats the interaction between the libidinal economy of a text and its logical and dialectical structures" (2). He goes on to determine the method as a "form of deconstruction" and acknowledges the method's "family-resemblance" to Derrida's readings of Rousseau in *Of Grammatology*, or of Hegel in *Glas*. The method allows the critic, strictly within the formal boundaries of the text, to trace the connections between the protagonists of a work of art and the artist's voice.

[565] Derrida Jacques: *Eperons/Spurs,* loc. cit.

[566] In the context of late nineteenth-century Danish poetry, Jacobsen belonged to a group of prominent younger poets that gathered around the literary critic George Brandes. The group represented what is known as the Modern Breakthrough in Danish literature. Besides Jacobsen, it includes such names as Henrik Pontoppidan and Herman Bang. Inspired by Brandes, they reacted against the romanticism of the mid-century and wanted to introduce a stronger naturalistic and realistic element in poetry. Outside Scandinavia, Jacobsen is perhaps best known for providing Arnold Schönberg with the texts for his *Gurre-Lieder*. Next to these songs, the "Arabesque" stands out as the most remarkable and coherent poem in a relatively small collection of poems.

teenth-century poets, philosophers, and psychologists: to understand, to know, and to explain – in other words, to appropriate – "woman" or "the feminine." Unraveling his poem, we get the picture of a chaotic self trying to calm down its own inner turmoil, a self trying to neutralize a certain discomfort in the persistence of disturbing internal or mental concepts of women. Jacobsen seems to be engaged in a struggle within himself that is designed to defeat a truth-threatening position. But the struggle is carried out on his inner chessboard and consequently has no obvious solution.

As we read his poem – which carries the lengthy title "Arabesque to a Drawing by Michelangelo (Profile of a Woman with Downcast Eyes in the Uffizi"[567] – it is clear that it does not provide us with any obvious message. It merely depicts a movement and a glance. If reduced to a single sentence, its theme might be best described as the movement of an impersonal glance. However, there seems to be a question, a curiosity, behind this glance. When we read the poem together with its context (letters and drafts from the period), it dawns on us that the poem is self-reflexive; it seems to address the activity of writing poetry, as if Jacobsen is questioning the worth of this activity. Is this activity worthwhile? This is something Jacobsen cannot know and does not pretend to know; but the question's solicitation of knowledge seems to linger as the muted desire of the poem, represented as the curiosity behind or in the glance staged by the poem. The poem never provides an answer; its poetic value lies precisely in the fact that it never attempts to establish a concept, much less to formulate a message. It is sincere because it resists any artificial resolution of what appears to be a tumultuous inner conflict. We are left endeavoring to see an answer in a dreamlike glance, that is, to see it as image, not as language (although, obviously, language is used to conjure up the image).

A fortiori, the poem is not conscious of this deeper concern, which for now I label "the worth of poetry." It is not taking, in self-conscious or postmodern fashion, its own writing as object. There are hardly any images of writing in the poem. Instead, the images we repeatedly encounter are images of women. Thus, it seems that the question of the value of poetic activity is bound up with woman, as if the question of the worth of poetry has been translated into, "Do women have worth?" Woman has become the negation, the other, the utopia that could have been lived, were it not for a compulsive poetic activity. It is as if the antithesis is *poetry versus woman* – as if a choice must be made between the mutually exclusive, *either poetry or woman*. If this is the internalized opposition and conflict, it is only logical to turn the question about the worth of poetry around and ask, "Are

---

[567] Jacobsen, J.P.: "Digte," *Samlede Værker*, 4:149–152.

women worthwhile"? It is quasi-logical to establish the worth of something by interrogating the worth of its phantasmatic opposite. The compulsive poet suggests to himself, in a mode not completely conscious, that he is (perhaps) missing out on something, something that might (possibly) be women.

Now the poet lands in a situation where he can only hope that women are not worth pursuing, because that would justify his poetic activity. His secret desire: women are worthless; – but he is far from certain! The inner conflict is perpetuated and extended into another realm, the question of woman. Since in this poem he cannot know and does not pretend to know, he merely stages a glance that is infinitely curious about women and tries to read them and their secrets. The poet tries to understand a lack by means of meticulously constructed verses and to answer a question that he never explicitly formulates (and is not quite aware of in the first place). He listens to his own soliloquizing voices, and even when hearing things loud and clear, exulting in his rendition of particularly well formed verses, he does not understand what is being said by these voices, and even less who is speaking to whom in his soliloquy. He cannot see, for example, that he sometimes speaks to himself in the voice of his mother, and that he tries to free himself from the influence of that voice.

2. Me, on the Contrary . . .

When reading Jacobsen's correspondence, we notice that certain themes are repeated over and over: his loneliness, his lack of productivity, his unmarried status (while friends marry), his aspiration to immortality, his sense of resignation and (increasingly) of wasting his life, his illnesses (being a hypochondriac), and his careful evaluation of colleagues, his jealous appraisals and assessments of the responses they receive from reviewers and audiences.

A potpourri of citations will introduce some of these concerns:

Letter 114, 1876, to George Brandes: All people marry, all walk into that blessed land, where everything is supposed to be so wonderful – but I – between the blue dunes, on the heather-covered moors of Thyland, a long and sorry shadow is slinking lonely about, this is the last of the Mohicans. All his contemporaries are – married.
Letter 119, 1876, to Fraenkel: So [you are] married and a general practitioner – and me: dreizig Jahre und noch nichts für die Unsterblichkeit gehtan (times are getting worse, Schiller said zwanzig).
Letter 120, 1876, to Wilhelm Moeller: Fraenkel writes that he has married. All

marry, while I have to follow my own dark path.
Letter 147, 1877, to Edvard Brandes: I almost suspect you of believing that I am lying here and have fallen in love. Unfortunately not. Not at all. Oh God – no.
Letter 148, 1877, to Brandes: The deceased [Jacobsen here writing his own epitaph] did, despite his poor productivity, finish two-thirds of his existence; unfortunately existence finished him off before he had put the last third behind him.
Letter 220, 1879, to Brandes: Of course I am very lonely and never talk to anybody.

One letter in particular summarizes Jacobsen's situation. It introduces a concern of Jacobsen's that is also present in the poem. If this concern is not hidden in the letter, despite Jacobsen's personal beliefs, it is almost perfectly concealed in his "Arabesque."

The letter dates from April 28, 1880. Jacobsen is writing to his friend Edvard Brandes, brother to the celebrated literary critic George Brandes, but important in his own right for having spearheaded contemporary political and cultural debates in Denmark. Jacobsen writes from Thisted, a small provincial town in northern Jutland where he lives in relative isolation together with his mother.

> My last letter was probably so influenced by Thisted's lack of atmosphere that you did not sense a living person writing. It is not an unprofound remark by an old judge of human character or thousands that there are three–four sides of a human being, and now the same has happened to this sentence as to the elements: in the old days there were four, and now there are – sixty-three or more. Therefore it is not surprising that when a human being writes from one of his sixty-three remote sides he does not strike exactly the side that turns outside in the individual he addresses. I have therefore turned myself around. A little bit. – Have you ever thought about the last days of your future? Since you have neither lived in a provincial town nor had hangovers, I guess you would say, No.[568]

The issue Jacobsen here introduces is obvious. He doesn't need to know Nietzsche or Freud to figure out that a human being is not a unity. It has several 'sides,' and today these sides have even multiplied like the elements, which were once only four, but in the contemporary periodic table have multiplied to sixty-three. How then do we write, communicate, and understand each other, if understanding is supposed to be achieved only when there is conformity between these multiple 'sides' in the addresser

---

[568] This and all following quotes from Jacobsen's letter are to be found in Jacobsen, J.P.: "Breve," *Samlede Værker*, v. 6, p. 105–106.

and the addressee? How is sympathy achieved between communicating parties, between remitter and recipient? Because it has become difficult to realize this sympathy today, owing to the multiplication of 'sides,' Jacobsen tries to help Brandes' understanding of himself by turning 'a little bit.' Has Edvard ever thought about death? Can Jacobsen talk to Edvard about death? He is not entirely convinced, because Brandes has never lived a secluded provincial life. The Brandes brothers were cosmopolitans and perhaps too busy to think about death. Jacobsen, on the contrary . . .

Jacobsen posits the recipient of his letter as his contrary. It is on this level insignificant that the empirical receiver is Edvard Brandes, or significant only to the extent that Edvard is one of these 'contraries.' As the letter continues, it becomes clear that he dissolves into a much more general 'contrary.'

> If I were about to provide a title for the last three-four years of my life, which would form a very short chapter in my memoirs, I would choose either "Between the Battles" or, what I think would be more appropriate, "While they Struggled." – Because how have not all human beings lived while I have been lying with closed eyes looking around. Nevertheless! . . . I think I have won by sleeping. You will see that it goes with me as with the sluggards, I come out of the cave as young as I was when I entered. If not I have become even younger, and youth is what counts.

Jacobsen is reacting to what he thinks Edvard represents and at the same time is forgetting him for a while; his recipient is now everybody else – especially, we must presume, Danish middle class, all those busy with and absorbed in the concerns of ordinary life. While they struggle, Jacobsen does the opposite: he practices a unique passivity and indifference to life. By not living, by sleeping through his life, Jacobsen attains existential surplus value. As they get older, Jacobsen on the contrary grows even younger. It surprises even himself. At this point, he again remembers that Edvard is included in this imaginary group, these people living their busy and restless middle-class existence:

> All you people have allowed the world to touch you and play with you.

Is it too hazardous to translate 'world' with 'women' in this passage? If we do, he is saying that people have allowed women to touch them and play with them. This suggests that by sleeping, Jacobsen has become too young for women, while his adversaries have become too old. And it is, as he explicitly states, better to be young than old, and, by consequence, better to be too young than too old. He has gained not only youth, but also something

Edvard and his kind have lost. What this something is, is not easily explained: Jacobsen has gone untouched through the world and for his efforts has received a reward, a compensation of sorts; he has not only avoided a loss, he has even profited. He has not lost his 'gilding,' as everybody else has; moreover, he has also secured himself a surplus of gilding (if not gold):

> The gild has started to peel of some of you. But me [alternatively: Me, on the contrary] – speech is poor silver and silence is gold and all the gold I have muted in four long years will fall gildingly on my forgotten gestalt when I step forward again. If I had done this out of calculation it would have been merely talented, but I have done it out of sloth, and this is ingenious and genius is what one must be.

In Jacobsen's economy, silence is an investment one can finally cash in as gold; Jacobsen has an *economics of silence*. People living their inauthentic average babbling lives become shabby and bleak, while Jacobsen continues to shine. They talk their gold away, but Jacobsen's silence is an investment that after four years rains profitably down on him in the form of gold. Withholding and withdrawing himself from society has been a deposit of life and speech that finally earns him a return denied Edvard and his kind.[569] The final sentence reveals what the actual return is on this investment other than 'gilding': *genius*. Silence has now been worthwhile; *they* lose their youth, their gilding, and finally, most importantly, their *genius*. But not Jacobsen.

In the letter, this thought is not an undercurrent that must be disclosed; it has already surfaced as a subject's retaliation against the living others and as such seems to be plain enough: a subject invests; it is painful; the subject expects compensation; the compensation is revenge on those who never invested; they die, I stay immortal. The thought is, however, somewhat imprudent, and Jacobsen therefore tells us that it is 'hidden.' He holds a jewel up before our eyes and proclaims confidently, "You can't see it!" His letter is intended to be an enigma with which later readers may occupy themselves.

> – I shall not disturb the impression of the above written by the least hint on why it was written . . . this letter shall remain an enigma for Nic. Bøgh and O. Borchsenius, when they or their children one day publish my letters. Sat Eduar-

---

[569] Before Heidegger in an altogether different vocabulary expressed the notion of an existence that gains authenticity by recognizing its "being-toward-death" while avoiding "falling" into the everyday averageness of "the they" (*das Man*), Jacobsen gave voice to an identical thought.

do. / But you could try to tell me how you are, even though you may not succeed in doing it as distinctly as I have succeeded in telling you how lonely and world-forgotten I feel when exactly *this* turns up in me that is hidden in this letter.

Jacobsen simultaneously reveals truth and believes he disguises it. My truth is hidden, he says, while displaying it as an economy of which he is not fully conscious. He does not fully understand the rationale for this savings plan that never pays out a dividend, that cannot pay out a disbursement because the saved life is reimbursed only in the finality of death. If Jacobsen states "something turns up in me that is hidden in this letter," I would reformulate, "something turns up in this letter that is hidden from Jacobsen."

Supposedly, Jacobsen's publishers (Bøgh and Borchsenius) do not understand this truth, and he is not inclined to give them a hint of what he has left for them to see. They, or later scholars reading this letter, may even be inclined to believe him and start looking for something hidden, something that was never there. He secures their attention for himself after his death by making them look for something he held back. He *calculates a reader response*. In the last passage, silence is still gold. Jacobsen exercises yet again his economics of silence. Now he invests silence in future immortality: after death, golden genius shall rain down on him as a late compensation.

There is revenge in holding back life, talk, truth. Other people squander their lives; Jacobsen saves his and will continue to shine – perhaps not in this life, which is in any case unimportant, but after. On the other hand, the solitude obviously hurts. His pain is the other side of a coin that he tosses in this letter: now turning up the satisfaction of expected immortality, now the pain of actual solitude.

3. Reading the Poem

3.1. First Stanza: Repetition and Rebellion

Let us turn our attention to the poem: "Arabesque to a Drawing by Michelangelo (Profile of a Woman with Downcast Eyes in the Uffizi)," printed in its entirety with a parallel English translation by undersigned as a supplement to this appendix.

From the beginning, a question is being asked – or rather, two, for the first question is repeated. "*Did the wave reach land? / Did it reach land and drift slowly.*" This repetition makes the question more urgent and transforms it into an enigma. The intensification of pathos transports us, as readers, beyond the self-evident. Futhermore, when Jacobsen lets the wave break on the shore twice, the rhythm of the poem repeats the rhythm of waves, which break on the shore and roll back under new waves that repeat the movement. Form imitates content, as we say. Jacobsen continues: "*Rattling with the pearls of gravel / Back into the world of waves?*" The whole sequence was a question: do waves perpetually and repeatedly dash against the shore, or could they behave differently? There is apparently an alternative behavior for waves; apparently, they could transgress this rhythm. One word in particular changes the purely empirical connotation of the wave: the word "rattling" (*rallende*), connoting 'death rattle.' *Rallende* (death-rattling) is placed where it would have been more obvious to write *rullende* (rolling), and Jacobsen's publisher believed that the poet had made a spelling mistake by replacing the obvious "u" with a less obvious "a" (*rallende* ~ *rullende*). It seems to make more sense for a wave to roll back with gravel than for it to death-rattle back. However, Jacobsen answers his publisher in a letter in which he explicitly emphasizes his choice: "There is no spelling mistake in the 'Arabesque': the third line says *rallende*."[570] This substitution of a single letter is an inspired choice of the poet, because it changes everything.

Rallende connotes death and the death struggle. The wave image is now dysphoric, and the dysphoria consists (we must assume, since we have no other information) in the compulsive repetition of waves dashing upon the shore perpetually. It is the repetition-compulsion of this rhythm that connotes death and pain. Since now these first four lines are formed as a question, the poet-subject asks himself whether waves always have to follow this rhythm. Are waves fated to repeat this rolling/rattling back and forth compulsively, or could they transgress the rhythm? Is rebellion possible, or is repetition the given condition? "*No! It reared as a steed, / Raising high its wet chest.*" Rebellion is possible! The poem replaces "wave" with "steed," mediating the replacement by means of (1) the glistering foam, both the foam of the wave and the froth of the steed, and (2) the wet chest, indicating the wetness both of the wave and of the steed's chest.

As we shall see shortly, the rebellion of the wave or steed against the predictability of waves announces a sexual theme. For now, when the wave rears like a steed, it transgresses its own peak of culmination. Instead of dashing upon the shore, breaking in order to roll back into the sea beneath a wave that is bound to repeat the same movement, it overcomes the law of gravity in a joyful flight. The transgression of compulsive repetition and the

---

[570] Jacobsen, J.P.: "Digte," *Samlede Værker*, vol. 4, letter to Vilhelm Møller; illustration no. 158.

eruption into the air indicate desire and ecstasy. We are situated in a visual universe wherein the poet-subject's imaginative glance as (or within) a wave flies through the sky in rebellion against compulsive repetition. This transgression was provoked by the dysphoric *rallen*, that is, by a single well-placed 'a' indicating the death threat of compulsive repetition.

These lines express the rebellion of life against death, but death is not understood as a biological-empirical end of life. Here death is repetition – or rather, the repetitious play of death in life, the condition of being subjected to a predictable automatism. The world of death is here the anonymous world of the sea, and the dashing of the waves against the shore represents partial but unsuccessful attempts to escape the attraction of the dark water, the pull of the massive sea. The steed rears against this sea of predictability, in a desire for life and pleasure, a desire to achieve a state where rule-governed life is defeated, transfigured into a sprinkle of droplets reflecting the white sunlight. "*The foam sparkled through its mane / Snow-white as the back of a swan. / Sparkle-drops and rainbow-fog / Trembled up through the air: / Skin it cast off, / Skin it changed, / Flew on broad swan wings / Through the white light of the sun.*" The metonymical displacements in the first stanza are from wave to steed to swan according to the following associative pattern: wave (foam, white, wetness) → steed (froth, white, wetness) → swan (white).

Whiteness allows an association with the swan – one reason for introducing it into the poem. Yet another, more compelling reason impels the choice. Jacobsen uses a sketch by Michelangelo as a source of inspiration (in the Casa Buonarroti collections of Michelangelo's drawings, it is known as *Study for the Head of Leda* (circa 1530); Jacobsen, however, calls it 'Profile of a Woman with Downcast Eyes'). The sketch represented Michelangelo's preliminary study for his never-finished painting *Leda and the Swan*, a painting in which he intended to depict the mythological scene where Zeus, in the form of a swan, seduces Leda and impregnates her. The transformation of the wave into a seductive swan substantiates the assertion that a sexual theme is latent in the text. The swan-wave's trajectory through the white sunlight indicates the start of a sexual campaign. It is the disguised Zeus who for a brief moment speaks in the poem.

3.2. Second Stanza: Implosion and Castration

As soon as 'life' is introduced as an alternative to 'death' – that is, repetition – it is rejected again. Zeus hardly gets his sexual campaign started before he is stopped. "*I know your flight, you flying wave.*" With the silent scratching of his pen, Jacobsen may shout and scream about emancipation as much as he likes, but nothing happens, and he knows it. This is his most profound and most tragic knowledge. Every attempt at self-emancipation is doomed to fail. It is the first and only time an 'I' appears in the poem ("I know your . . ."). This highly efficient 'I' immediately stops the lawless attempt to escape simply by announcing its knowledge of the predictable outcome of the project. This 'I' is the poet-subject, speaking woefully – with the voice of a parent to a child – to the wave, the desire, resulting in its instant collapse after having raced through the air. This is the poet speaking as his mother to himself. With the arrival of this voice, the subject realizes that emancipation is futile, that the indicated omnipotence is illusory. And then follows the reason for its futility: "*But the golden day will sink, / Will, clothed in the dark frock of night, / Lie down, tired, to rest, / And the dew will gleam in his breath, / The flowers close around his bed / Before you reach your goal.*" There is metonymic proximity between day and wave; now, when the day is ending, the wave collapses too. With the arrival of night, it throws off the powerful sexual symbols by which it was represented (the steed and the swan) as it disintegrates and continues to live on only as creeping dew, as voyeur. Not only does it surrender its symbolic guises, it dissolves and evaporates. The reason for this transformation, this symbolic castration, is the arrival of the night, a logic that is at first incomprehensible and impenetrable. But as we will learn shortly, 'night' also connotes 'woman,' and the wave is consequently vanquished by the same female imagery toward which it initially strives in its attempt at emancipation: " – *And when you reach the golden grating / And sweep silently on wide wings.*" For the first time in the poem, we are introduced to a human world. From a wave that revolted and raised its chest in the glistering sun – still only wave and nature – the wave is closing in on the social world, but now in secretive voyeurism, sweeping silently across the ground in order to avoid detection. Once an omnipotent auto-affective and auto-erotic wave, the wave is now losing its power with the arrival of society. The rebellion is crushed. Through the nightly metamorphosis it is transformed into dew; it becomes a guilt-ridden, shy, and ashamed wave. "*Across the broad arcades of the garden / Across the waves of lavender and myrtle / Across the dark crown of magnolia, / Followed by its light, quietly blinking, / Followed by its staring flower-eyes.*" Nobody is more intensely looked at than the voyeur. The evaporated wave is now gliding through the flowerbeds, while the flowers, with their "quietly blinking, . . . staring flower-eyes," follow its movements intensely and attentively. This gaze is more than simply a metaphor for the corollas of the flowers. When the wave is surrounded by a gaze in the form of the silent and attentive flowers, it is placed under the gaze of the other. The wave now sees itself being seen, especially in its shame.

 The eye with which the wave sees, or rather sees blindly, does not understand, it does not differentiate. It sees all and nothing because it only senses. It does not see horizons or structured space; it sees only foreground as it zooms in on the foreground of flowers. Here the poem is more dreamlike than ever, staging a play between a sensing eye of desire and the staring gaze of a prohibiting other. "*Downward secretly whispering iris, / Carried and lulled by mild-weeping dreams / By the scent of geranium / By the heavy-breathing scent of roses and jasmines.*" Flowers are often depicted in the poetic universe of Jacobsen; they always indicate a mood of tranquility and serenity, a sense of nirvana. Their exotic names are recited joyously: lavender, myrtle, magnolia, iris, geranium, roses, jasmines. They seem to belong to another world, one with a more beautiful language and a more sublime poetry. It is also a world of innocence, sublimation, quiet, auto-affection, and nirvana. In this world, language has lost its communicative aspect; the speech of flowers, like sublime poetry, has no practical purpose. It is hardly more than a remote noise, a distant murmur: "secretly whispering iris." The poet is at home in this gentle and mild world where truth is heard but never understood. "Secretly whispering iris," "mild-weeping dreams," and "heavy-breathing scent" all indicate the finely balanced melancholia of the secluded poet.

Flowers seem to suggest a primary narcissism in which the individual is nonetheless still unified with the world and no split has yet divided subject and object. As symbol of innocence and auto-affection, the universe of flowers also represents an idyll preceding the introduction of language. But the idyll is fragile, and it splinters with the introduction of woman.[571] Before the woman steps onto the stage, the universe is without tension; serenity and stillness rule. This impression is amplified in the next lines. After the calming scent of flowers follows naturally the calm of the cypresses: "*Carried toward the white villa / With the moonlit windowpanes, / With its guard of tall, dark, / Tall, calm cypresses.*" This attempt to express silence fascinates Jacobsen. It is paradoxical because evidently a poetical representation of a language-free universe is possible only in language. Language becomes the necessary, but vexatious, tool for representing stillness – a tool that Jacobsen consequently does his best to mute. The paradoxical and impossible project is to neutralize writing.[572]

---

[571] This happens not only in this poem, but in several of Jacobsen's writings, most significantly in the introductory pages of Jacobsen's famous novel *Fru Marie Grubbe*. Here we are again presented to an auto-affective universe free of tension as we are introduced to the main character of the novel, Marie Grubbe. In the opening pages, she is still an innocent child playing in the backyard among wildflowers and other plants. At first this universe is silent, motionless, regular and unbroken. But when the child manifests the first signs of thinking, a transformation starts. As she seeks a small dark enclosure in the garden, the harmony shatters, and we are introduced to a dangerous sexual fantasy of a sadomasochistic nature. From this point onward, the child abandons innocent childhood. She is being born as a woman. Beneath her "downcast eyes," a woman appears, disturbing and disquieting, as an enigmatic, menacing, and fundamentally sensuous creature.

[572] How does one silence language by language? If the project were not impossible, Jacobsen in the *Gurre Songs* is as successful as one could get. Listen to these lines (and one may do well to listen to how Schönberg brilliantly captures the mood in *Gurre-Lieder*): "*Now the blue dusk mutes / Every sound from sea and land, / The flying clouds are resting / At the horizon of the sky, / The forest's airy dwelling, / Is gathered in soundless weight. / And the limpid waves of the sea / Have lulled themselves to rest. / In the west, the sun throws off / Her dazzling purple robes, / She draws the wave over her / While dreaming of the glory of the day / Not even the smallest bush stirs / Distracting my senses. / Not even the faintest tone is clanging / Lulling my soul in dance, / No, every power has sunk / Into the current of its own dreams, / And I am*

Let us return to the wave cautiously approaching the white villa guarded by tall, calm cypresses. The sight of the cypresses causes the wave to evaporate, for it is now being burned up from within (besides being conventional symbols of death, cypresses are specifically, in Jacobsen's poetry, guardians of death). *"Then you dissolve in fearful forebodings, / Burned up by your trembling longing, / Gliding ahead as a breeze from the sea, / And you die between the leaves of the grapevine, / The whispering leaves of the grapevine, / On the marble threshold of the balcony, / While the cold silk of the balcony curtain / Slowly sways in heavy folds."* The white villa – with the moonlit windows, the marble threshold, the cold silk of the balcony curtain – is a tomb guarded by cypresses. The wave cannot enter this tomb, and on its threshold the wave burns up because of something within itself. The image seems impossible: water is burned up because of something in the water. However, the image of something destroying itself from within is repeated several times in the poem: a drive is blocked and self-destructively turned inward. It is therefore not surprising if we now encounter, rising from the burned-out wave, what it consistently represented: longing, need, desire, and hope.

The wave has materialized and dematerialized in four stages: (1) first, rising from the wet element of water; (2) then existing vaporized as fog in the sunlight; (3) then evaporating as dew; and finally (4), being burned up in longing. Finally, the wave-glance is creeping along the ground, closing in on the danger with voyeuristic curiosity. Now, in the last lines of the stanza, we are confronted with an image of castration; an image that seems a logical consequence of the progressive evaporation and gradual disintegration of the wave: *"And the golden clusters of grapes / From the anguishedly wrought branches / Are felled into the grass of the garden."* This ends the stanza. The dematerialized wave has arrived at the villa or tomb, and we would expect the following stanza to continue from here. But instead of this natural progression, the third stanza appears as an interlude, a description of a Dionysic orgy. This interlude at first glance seems unmotivated. Not until the fourth stanza do we return to the wave facing the villa.

It is possible to understand the rationale for this interlude only if we read the fall of the grapes ("from the anguishedly wrought branches") as a symbolic castration – from here the writer goes berserk; latent anguish surfaces, and the description of a Dionysian orgy follows. Thus, whereas there is no

---

gently and silently / Thrown back upon myself. / . . . / Everything: an expression of what God dreamt" (Jacobsen, J. P.: "Digte," *Samlede Værker*, 4:88). This is how immaterial the universe is, merely God's dream, a dream even in past tense.

obvious narrative connection between second and third stanzas, there is a latent connection, a certain correspondence between the symbolic "castration" and the ensuing description of uncontrolled and death-threatening passion. First the grapes are cut from their branches, then follows the shock.

3.3. Third Stanza: The Blind Eye of Desire

In the third stanza, the poet-subject addresses the "burning night" – or "glowing night" – no fewer than five times. In the following, the "burning night" will be still better determined: *"Burning night! / Slowly you burn across the earth, / The strangely changing smoke of dreams / Flickers and swirls about in your path / Burning night!"* Usually night indicates darkness, but here night burns or glows. This night does the opposite of what nights usually do: it emits intense light and heat. So what is burning in this night? As one might expect, this burning is not related to fire; it is need, longing, or desire that is on fire in this night. In the previous stanza, the wave was *"burned up by . . . trembling longing,"* and in the next, it is again in the self that this burning flares: *"Why these fires of suffering and pain?"*

The night symbolizes something unknown – or, paradoxically, known only through its symbols. It stages a thought presentable only through metaphors: a thought about flaming desire that sucks out, hollows out, or burns out. As we shall see, in his attempt to qualify and explain this "burning night," the poet-subject exhibits its meaning on the textual surface, but unconsciously (at least, without noticing the textual surface). The poet stumbles in language, and in his fall, he grasps for the nearest metaphors; but he does not see what he holds in his hands. It is for us to take a closer look at these metaphors: " – *Wills are wax in your soft hand / And fidelity only a rush for a puff of your breath, / And what is wisdom leaned against your bosom? / And what is innocence charmed by your glance."* Against the burning night different human qualities must surrender, such as will, fidelity, wisdom, and innocence – qualities one would typically characterize as super-egoistical. These noble qualities surrender to the "soft hand," the "breath," the "bosom," or the "glance" of the night. So we are talking about a woman, or at least about fragments of a woman, insofar as the poet focuses on the body parts a child experiences when it is breast-fed: hand, mouth, bosom, and eyes. The burning night is a woman – specifically, a mother. When the "glance" of this night or mother is further qualified and explained, it becomes evident that the night is not a mother in a positive sense, but a mother threatening the child with seduction and incest. Thus, she sees with a glance *"that nothing sees, but wildly draws / The red stream of the vein to a stormy flood / As the moon draws the cold waters of the sea?"* The "red stream of the vein," the blood, is brought to a boil by this mysterious glance "that nothing sees, but wildly draws" (alternative translation: "wildly sucks") the blood like a tide – as the gravitational pull of the moon affects the sea. The glance is therefore a powerful cosmic force; like the moon, it is a blind eye, a "pale membrane," in the night. This glance does not see; it is not a glance that gives the child existence. On the contrary, this glance gives nothing; it takes or "draws" destructively. It is through this blind eye that the blood of the subject is whipped into a "stormy flood." The eye is blind, dead, and as such, it stirs a dangerous and violent passion in the poet-subject. We encounter here an enigmatic and uncanny relationship: woman ~ glance ~ blindness ~ desire. This chain of associations is explicitly indicated in the next two lines: " – *Burning night! / Huge, blind maenad!*" Here the night is explicitly addressed as a woman, and explicitly as a sensuous woman – a maenad – and, finally, explicitly as blind. So the interpretation of the foregoing lines must have been correct. Because the night is a huge blind maenad, and because maenads are sensuous women,[573] the night must consequently be a huge sensuous woman.

The maenad is all-embracing as the night; the night as mother is thus represented as a huge, excited matriarch embracing her children. This immense, passionate organism clearly threatens the 'child' with death, and the introduction of the figure is succeeded by intense anxiety. The dysphoria of the figure is so intense that the poet has difficulty giving his repulsion sufficiently strong expression. We are introduced to a tableau of lawless desire and to the consequences of this lawlessness: *"Forth through the darkness blink and fizzle / Strange waves of strange sounds: / The clang of goblets, / The quick, singing clang of steel, / The dripping of blood and the rattle of bleeding / And throaty mad cries mixed / With hoarse screams of scarlet-*

---

[573] Greek mythology tells us that maenads were female followers of the god of orgiastic religion, Dionysus, under whose influence they were driven to drunkenness and ecstasy. The well-read Jacobsen must have known this myth, and he must also have been familiar with Euripides' tragedy *Bacchae*, where a king denounces the divine status of Dionysus. In revenge, Dionysus transforms the king's female relatives into maenads. In their ecstasy they perceive their patron as a lion, mutilate and dismember him, then triumphantly bring home his head on a stake. According to legend, maenads are dangerous – castrating and mutilating – women. Jacobsen is also likely to have known Nietzsche's *Die Geburt der Tragödie* and the descriptions of Dionysian orgies at the beginning of this work. Indeed, the two female figures described in Jacobsen's poem could be seen as modeled over Nietzsche's distinction between Dionysus and Apollo.

red desire . . . " Chaos implies the cassation of language In the universe of night and maenads, we hear only the "rattle of bleeding," "mad cries," or "hoarse screams." Rattling, crying, and screaming characterize the inarticulate language expressed in the universe of Dionysus. The poet is pursuing the strongest possible expression for chaos and death; he tries to produce a fitting expression for the threat of castration, but no expression covers the experience. Consequently, the search for an expression to represent the dysphoria ends in silence: just after the "hoarse screams of scarlet-red desire," we read: " . . ." – an ellipsis. The sentence cannot be completed; instead, it is being opened up in order to refer to an instance outside the text, an instance that renders the author speechless, strikes him with silence and dumb horror. The strongest expression he has at his disposal is "dot, dot, dot." As usual, silence speaks louder than words.

The language of the night and the maenads is a language without the characteristics of language, without distinct and differentiating features. Not only do maenads threaten the subject with castration, they also threaten the writing of the poet-subject. Writing, as the highest representation of compulsive repetition (repetition itself being a death-in-life), is in danger of being overturned. Therefore, exposed to this new danger, the poet-subject ventures an objection, a reprimand of sorts: " *– But the sigh, burning night? / The sigh, that swells and dies, / Dies only to be born again, / The sigh, you burning night?*" The poet-subject asks the question cautiously, as if there were something the night had forgotten. The poet objects to the frivolity of the night for neglecting "the sigh." The sigh gives life instead of taking it; it "dies only to be born again" – that is, it never dies. It goes on living in its rhythm of inhalations and exhalations, a rhythm that imitates the dashing of waves against the seashore. Now the wave rhythm is repeated, but this time not as something one must escape from – rather, as an alternative the poet rushes toward, although this alternative indicates acquiescence, resignation, and sorrow. As such, there is a fundamental contradiction in the poem that the critic must of course expose, rather than excuse or mend. The movement of the wave, the repetition compulsion, is, on the one hand, something the poet tries to emancipate himself from because it threatens with death, with lifeless life. On the other hand, it is also what the poet must choose in order to protect himself from lawless desire (which initially he sets out to explore, as steed, as swan). Repetition initially implies death, but then it implies life, just as rebellion initially implies life, but then implies death. An awkward proposition emerges from the poem: both repetition and rebellion represent both life and death. At this point in the poem, rebellious life constitutes the greatest danger, and the flight into the non-life of repetition, with its promise of immortality, offers the greatest comfort. The termination of writing by the ellipsis after the scarlet-red screams represents an intolerable expenditure, a destruction of the economy of writing. When the poet-subject sees himself thrown into the oblivion of drunkenness and desire, a parsimonious economy is toppled, an economy wherein life is calculated and under control – the same tight economy Jacobsen described in the letter to Edvard Brandes with which I introduced the analysis.

Briefly, it is all about saving in order to become genius. It is all about economy. Genius implies dying in life in order to live after death. Given a choice between promised immortality and the fantasy of a life in the present, genius chooses immortality. Of the two choices, emancipation from repetition-automatism ('life') and acceptance of repetition-automatism ('death'), the latter is victorious because repetition gives hope, it defers and promises, while the loss of language, screams, and ellipses threaten this economy. In the latter case, the poet-subject sees himself sinking down into the incomprehensible abyss where demons and maenads have free play. Against this indescribable horror, genius chooses death in life, that is, the sigh, the resigned pain.

3.4. Fourth Stanza: Poetry and Death

The fourth stanza introduces a woman whose qualities are entirely different from those of the maenad. The maenad represented frenzy and raving, but the new tall, dark woman is calm and serene. If in the previous sequence we encountered a chaotic and claustrophobic universe, we now return to a universe characterized by quiet and tranquility. The tall, dark woman appears to be an aesthetic abstraction, a symbol of art, and is therefore no longer menacing. (We must assume that the inspirational correlate to this woman figure is Michelangelo's study for Leda.)

The previous stanza was interpolated parenthetically into the poem. It was a journey into the disturbing signification of night, partly produced by the symbolic castration ending the second stanza, but interposed also to allow the poem to present frivolity and sexuality as an alternative to be explored and, finally, rejected. Logically, the fourth stanza continues from where the second stanza left off. The wave was approaching the house, and now, as it reaches the marble stairs beneath the balcony, a woman steps forward from behind the curtains. "*Look, the silk folds of the curtain part / And a woman tall and wonderful / Outlined dark against the dark air.*" Behind a veil a woman is revealed. Just as previously the cypresses, she stands out dark against the dark air. Both figures are phallic, both are guarding something, and both are associated with death. The cypresses guard the villa as a tomb; the tall woman guards her knowledge of the truth of death – a precious knowledge, for it might explain the meaning of life. These two phallic figures are signifiers of the truth of death and, in consequence, of the truth of being. We notice that throughout the poem, the movement of the wave-glance is best described as a zooming in. First the wave zooms in on the villa, the tomb, in order to explore the truth of its interior. From the core of this tomb, a woman steps forward, and consequently the glance of the wave zooms in on her in order to probe her innermost thoughts. First, the woman is a signified stepping forward from the inner recesses of the tomb, but soon she herself becomes a signifier for her thoughts.

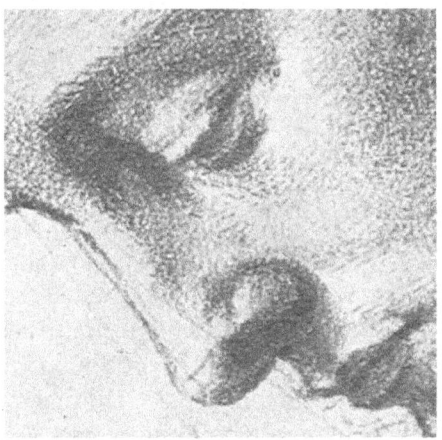

The woman seems to have an inexpressible knowledge of death, and it is this knowledge that fills her with sorrow: " – *Sacred sorrow in your eyes, / Sorrow, that nothing can help, / Hopeless sorrow, / Burning, doubtful sorrow.*" Her knowledge manifests itself as sorrow, a sorrow over existence as such. It is a sorrow the poet-subject knows as well as the woman – onto whom this "sacred," "hopeless," "burning, doubtful sorrow" is projected. Her sorrow concerns the relationship between existence and time: " – *Nights and days are humming over earth, / Seasons change like colors on a cheek, / Generation upon generation in long, dark waves / Roll over earth, / Roll and disappear, / While slowly time dies.*" So the reason for the sorrow is time. A cycle of nights and days rolls over earth, an eternal repetition of seasons and generations that arise only to vanish, "while slowly time dies" – logically speaking, a contradiction, because this cycle is everlasting and eternal, implying that we are talking about anything but the death of time. Since time never interrupts its counting, it never dies. Beings die in time, because time never dies. Life dies in time, because time continues its counting. However, what Jacobsen means to say – although he writes the opposite – is that time counts toward the death of beings. Life is granted a certain amount of time that will be spent, and after that expenditure comes death. It is time that makes death inescapable; thus the sorrow. (Although Jacobsen means that beings die, he writes that time dies – a slip of the pen and perhaps the fulfillment of a wish, for if time actually died he would secure eternal life – the underlying theme of the poem.)

Death implies not merely the end of the individual, but also the continuation of the lives of those he leaves behind. The individual does not merely die in the present; he also dies in the memories of succeeding generations. This adds insult to injury: generations continue while we are forgotten. Thus the desire of the poet-subject is to stop time. Jacobsen continues to distort logic by posing questions to which there are no answers: *"Why life? / Why death? / Why live when we yet must die? / Why struggle when we know that the sword / Will some time be wrested from our hand?"* These clichéd questions regarding the enigmas of life and death also constitute the most trivial lines in the poem. Why live when yet we shall die? If life ends, why then live? If we are going to live unto death why then live (. . . until death!)? Life is an enigma because it ends. Would it be possible to stop this relentless counting toward death? Could somebody give life beyond life by explaining death? The one who is supposed to know is the woman. However, she remains silent, remote and distant, notwithstanding the imploring poet-subject: *"Why these fires of suffering and pain: / A thousand hours of life in slow agony, / Slowly running out in death's agony? / Is that your thought, tall woman?"* Life is "running out in death's agony"! This is the most obvious translation of the Danish "livets . . . løben ud i Dødens Liden"; "liden" would usually be translated as "suffering" or "agony." However, it can also be understood as archaic Danish for something that is running toward an end. The phrase "time is running out" would approximately translate the archaic Danish "tiden lider hen."

If we choose the latter translation, the lines give the following meaning: a thousand hours of life are ending and are now running out in the running of death. Life is running, but death is running too? If life is running toward death, where does death run? As long as death is running too, we must assume that it still exists in life, that it is still running toward something unnamable and indeterminable. All of a sudden, death is not an end, because there is life in death. Just as it would be convenient if time died, so it would be convenient if there were no finality in death. In both cases (the "death of time" and the "running of death"), we are – on the unconscious level of the textual surface – promised eternal life.

Could the poet-subject just know about death, he could also master it. This is impossible, as he knows perfectly well even when he ignores this knowledge – for example, when he neutralizes it by means of the imaginary tale of how mastery might be achieved; the half-joke, half-fantasy from the letter above about becoming younger and younger . . . while living a passive life . . . without expenditure . . . lying asleep . . . looking around under a shower of gold . . . while people waste their lives. . . (etc.). Or is this certain? Do they waste their lives? Does he waste his? The discourse is insecure, because if this imaginary tale is false, he is suspending his life for no purpose. In that case, a passive life saves nothing and gives no return.

Consequently, the poet-subject asks the woman for an explanation. It is to her he directs his questioning, as if these questions were also her questions: "Is that your thought?" The question is whether she silently asks the same question as the poet-subject, and if so, whether she is also able to give answers. We do not know whether the woman has solved the riddle, but it is possible. When the poet-subject in his auto-affective economy asks himself, in the figure of a woman, for an answer, he is looking for the smallest sign of recognition from the woman figure onto whom he projects himself – just a nod. But the woman figure is merely a front. In the final analysis, the poet has only himself. He addresses his questions and inquiries auto-affectively to himself and within the soliloquizing space in himself, only to hear in the answer the reverberating echo of his questions.

3.5. Fifth Stanza: A Pen through the Heart of Night

The culmination of the poem, the final and most enigmatic lines, are now open to interpretation: *"Silently and calm she stands on the balcony, / Has no words, no sighs, no laments, / Outlined dark against the dark air / Like a sword through the heart of night."* The woman "outlined dark against the dark air / Like a sword through the heart of night" represents the rescue of the poet. With her help, the threats of the night are defeated. When the woman "like a sword" penetrates the heart of night, she effectively kills the living, pulsing, throbbing heart of the maenad.

Destruction of desire is represented by three identical phallic figures: the cypresses, the sword, and the woman (we might mention the pen). The poem halts at these phallic figures; to these images there is nothing more to add. Desire and the maenad represented extreme dangers in the poem, but in the final lines these dangers are defeated. The poet's worries and inquiries have been projected into the mind of the dark woman, and poet and woman are unified in their pursuit of an identical project. The woman no longer represents the (dangerous) other or difference; she is elevated into the same. In a sense, she no longer represents women, since she has been transformed and sublimated into the very principle of poetry itself. Thus, in the final lines, the auto-affective poet writes to himself – taking on the symbolic guise of a poet-woman – that with his pen he has killed the night, the maenad-woman. The woman-as-poet is death to the woman-as-desire.

4. Fundamental Ignorance

After this line-by-line reading, we might take a step back and try to determine the conflicts Jacobsen's poem is attempting to resolve.

The image of the woman, who, "like a sword through the heart of night," penetrates dangerous darkness, corresponds to the desire that the so-called phallus of poetry may defeat the so-called phallus of sexuality. As such, a persistent inner conflict is addressed, and the poet-subject has conjured up a satisfying poetic image resolving a tumultuous desire. The consequent "feeling" in the heroine, with whom the poet identifies, is one of calm and peacefulness: at last, "no words, no sighs." At last the voices have been brought to rest – at least for this brief and provisional moment (we can be sure that Jacobsen the next day is ready to repeat, ready to start a new poem, a new short story, or a new confessional letter).

We are allowed to understand this brief and transient moment of silence as the ultimate object of desire in a refashioned Nietzschean notion of the subject; the poem expresses a desire not so much for something as for nothing. Ultimately, it expresses a desire to alleviate the subject of a conflict within its fractious perspectival self; we may therefore call the desire conflict-resolving desire.

The image of the wave moving toward a desired but unapproachable woman figure could have been seen as representing desire of a sexual nature (e.g., according to certain psychoanalytical readings), but according to a Nietzschean model of the subject, such readings would now seem much too simple, too schematic, and too dogmatic. They would falsely suggest a reification of the desire lingering in the poem, because they would conceive desire as desire of something, while I suggest that conflict-resolving desire is desire of nothing; that is, desire of non-desire. (In a Nietzschean model of the subject, sexuality might be an issue, but it would be a relatively subordinate one, depending on how the historical subject interprets the importance of sexuality. If sexuality is not seen or understood as satisfying the subject's will to power, it remains divested of importance.)

Despite the final image with which the poet seems to resolve his inner mental conflict, we must still emphasize that the resolution is unsuccessful. It is accurate to say that the poem as a whole expresses a doubt rather than a dogma. It questions, rather than knows, what it wants (or what it fears). For example, the poem does not positively know that it wants sexuality, but it explores the possibility in order to reject it. This, on the other hand, does not necessarily imply that the poem positively knows that it does not want sexuality; it may simply imply that it wants it to be not wanted. It would be desirable if there were no desire: this is the desire. The poem explores whether or not death – as repetition in the form of repetitious "waves," "sighs," "resigned solitude," "writing," and so on – might be a good alternative to sexuality; and in its final image, it temporarily succeeds in arguing that death in that specific sense does defeat sexuality.

To emphasize again: the poem fundamentally does not know, but it suggests – in the modality of a very doubtful "perhaps" – that death as repetition, death for the sake of poetry, might be an absolute good, because if death can be seen as the true object of desire, then the poet is doing fine, then he has outperformed his more profane contemporaries. Hence, the poem wants it to be wanted. If the poem has a desire or a will to power, it is that it ought to be true that the tall, dark woman kills the maenad, that poetry defeats life. It wants death to be wanted and sexuality or life to be not wanted. It wants a want, and searches for an answer to the question, Is a life without expenditure spent more authentically than a life squandered? Can death be wanted and life not wanted? The poem desires to know this from the woman and stages her to confirm this suggestion.

Because in the last analysis the poet can address the woman only as a front for himself, he desires to reveal this secret from himself to himself, a secret he a priori does not have. He is playing that inconclusive one-player chess game. The poet nonetheless desires to win this futile game. He attempts the impossible: to calculate a definitive move that is not already anticipated by his other self. He requires answers, although the poem is honest enough to show that his questions remain unanswered. There can be no answer, because in this game the two players are held captive by the same ego.

Let me suggest this simplified formulaic expression for the fragmented self, playing within itself its futile game of chess: Jens Peter (&) Jacobsen, or, better, JP (&) J. If the underlying "wish" of this poem consists in a simple insistence on knowledge, on an answer to a fundamental ignorance, then the writing process constitutionally makes it impossible to satisfy this will to truth. A reflective subject can never meaningfully respond to its own doubts. Does he want death to be wanted and woman to be not wanted?

4. Fundamental Ignorance

Whether the answer is yes or no, it rings hollow in the inner forum of the self. The subject wants to hear absolute, capitalized Yeses or Nos that could drown its self-reflective discourse – some answer that could effectively stop these debating inner voices. And for a brief instant, the mere image of the swordlike, tall, dark woman seems to satisfy his will. Beyond this briefest of instances, however, we can be sure that the debate between JP (&) J continues:

JP: Is poetic genius better than average mediocrity?
J: Yes, of course it is, of course!
JP: But is this absolutely true . . . ?
J: No, other people enjoy life, love, and comfort!
JP: But I become immortal, and this is better!
J: Yes, of course it is, of course!
JP: But is this absolutely true . . . ?
J: Yes . . ? No . . ? I don't know . . ?

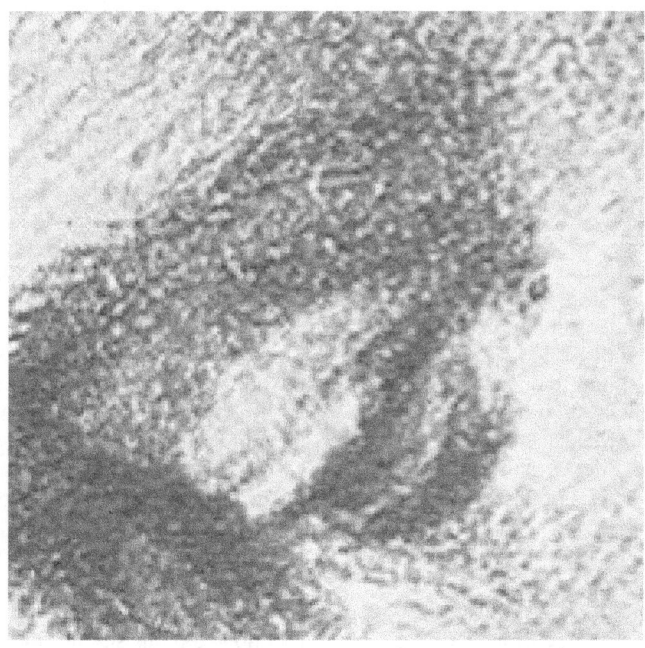

5. Jacobsen's Poem

"Arabesk til en Haandtegning af Michel Angelo (Kvindeprofil med Sænkede blikke i Ufficierne)"	"Arabesque to a Drawing by Michel angelo (Profile of a Woman with Downcast Eyes in the Uffizi)"
Stanza 1	*1st Stanza*
Tog Bølgen Land? Tog den Land og sived langsomt Rallende med Grusets Perler Atter ud i Bølgers Verden? Nej! Den stejled' som en Ganger, Løfted' højt sin vaade Bringe; Gjennem Manken gnistred' Skummet Snehvidt som en Svanes Ryg. Straalestøv og Regnbu'taage Sittred op igjennem Luften: Ham den kasted', Ham den skifted', Fløj paa brede svanevinger Gjennem Solens hvide Lys.	Did the wave reach land? Did it reach land and drift slowly Rattling with the pearls of gravel Back into the world of waves? No! It reared as a steed, Raising high its wet chest; The foam sparkled through its mane Snow-white as the back of a swan. Sparkle-drops and rainbow-fog Trembled up through the air: Skin it cast off, Skin it changed, Flew on broad swan-wings Through the white light of the sun
Stanza 2	*2nd Stanza*
Jeg kjender din Flugt du flyvende Bølge; Men den gyldne Dag vil segne, Vil, svøbt i Nattens dunkle Kappe, Lægge sig træt til Hvile. Og Duggen vil glimte i hans Aande, Blomsterne lukke sig om hans Leje Før du naar dit Maal. Og har du naa't det gyldne Gitter Og stryger tyst paa spredte Vinger Henover Havens brede Gange, Henover Lavrers og Myrthers Vover, Over Magnoliens dunkle Krone, Fulgt af dens lyse, roligt-blinkende, Fulgt af dens stirrende Blomsterøjne, Nedover hemmeligt-hvidskende Iris, Baaret og dysset i graadmilde Drømme Af Geraniernes Duft Af Tuberosers og Jasminers tungtaandende Duft, Baaret mod den hvide Villa	I know your flight, you flying wave; But the golden day will sink, Will, clothed in the dark frock of night, Lie down, tired, to rest. And the dew will gleam in his breath, The flowers close around his bed Before you reach your goal. – And when you reach the golden grating And sweep silently on wide wings Across the broad arcades of the garden Across the waves of lavender and myrtle Across the dark crown of magnolia, Followed by its light, quietly blinking, Followed by its staring flower-eyes, Downward secretly whispering iris, Carried and lulled by mild-weeping dreams By the scent of geranium By the heavy-breathing scent of roses and jasmines, carried toward the white villa

Med de maanelyste Ruder,	With the moonlit windowpanes,
Med dens Vagt af høje, dunkle,	With its guard of tall, dark,
Høje, rolige Cypresser,	Tall, calm cypresses,
da forgaar du i Anelsers Angst,	Then you dissolve in fearful forebodings,
Brændes op af din skjælvende Længsel,	Burned up by your trembling longing,
Glider frem som en Luftning fra Havet,	Gliding ahead like a breeze from the Sea,
Og du døer mellem Vinrankens Løv,	And you die between the leaves of the grapevine,
Vinrankens susende Løv,	The whispering leaves of the grapevine,
Paa Balkonens Marmortærskel,	On the marble threshold of the balcony,
Mens Balkongardinets kolde Silke	While the cold silk of the balcony curtain
Langsomt vugger sig I tunge Folder	Slowly sways in heavy folds
Og de gyldne Drueklaser	And the golden clusters of grapes
Fra de angstfuldt-vredne Ranker	From the anguishedly wrought branches
Fældes ned i Havens Græs.	Are felled into the grass of the garden.
Stanza 3	*3rd Stanza*
Glødende Nat!	Burning night!
Langsomt brænder du henover Jorden,	Slowly you burn across the earth,
Drømmenes sælsomt skiftende Røg	The strangely changing smoke of dreams
Flakker og hvirvles afsted i dit Spor	Flickers and swirls about in your path
Glødende Nat!	Burning night!
– Viljer er Voks i din Bløde Haand	– Wills are wax in your soft hand
Og Troskab Siv kun for din Aandes Pust,	And fidelity only a rush for a puff of your breath,
Og hvad er Klogskab lænet mod din Barm?	And what is wisdom leaned against your bosom?
Og hvad er Uskyld daaret af dit Blik,	And what is innocence charmed by your glance,
Der Intet seer, men suger vildt	That nothing sees, but wildly draws
Til stormflod Aarens røde Strøm	The red stream of the vein to a stormy flood
Som Maanen suger Havets kolde Vande?	As the moon draws the cold waters of the sea?
– Glødende Nat!	– Burning night!
Vældige, blinde Mænade!	Huge, blind maenad!
Frem igjennem Mulmet blinker og skummer	Forth through the darkness blink and fizzle
Sælsomme Bølger af sælsom Lyd:	Strange waves of strange sounds:
Bægeres Klang,	The clang of goblets,
Staalets hurtige, syngende Klang,	The quick, singing clang of steel,
Blodets Dryppen og Blødendes Rallen	The dripping of blood and the rattle of the bleeding
Og tykmælt vanvids Brølen blandet	And throaty mad cries mixed
Med purpurrøde Attraaes hæse Skrig . . .	With hoarse screams of scarlet-red desire . .
– Men Sukket, Glødende nat?	– But the sigh, burning night?
Sukket, der svulmer og døer,	The sigh, that swells and dies,
Døer for at fødes paany,	Dies only to be born again,

Sukket, du Glødende Nat?	The sigh, you burning night?
Stanza 4	*4th Stanza*
Se Gardinets Silkevover skilles Og en Kvinde høj og herlig Tegner mørk sig mod den mørke Luft. – Hellige Sorg i dit Blik, Sorg, der ej kan Hjælpes, Haabløs Sorg, Brændende, tvivlende Sorg. – Nætter og Dage summe over Jorden, Aarstider skrifte som Farver paa Kind, Slægter paa Slægt i lange, mørke Bølger	Look, the silk folds of the curtain part And a woman tall and wonderful Outlined dark against the dark air. – Sacred sorrow in your eyes, Sorrow, that nothing can help, Hopeless sorrow, Burning, doubtful sorrow. – Nights and days are humming over earth, Seasons change like colors on a cheek, Generation upon generation in long, dark waves
Rulle over Jord, Rulle og Forgaa, Medens Langsomt Tiden Døer. Hvorfor Livet? Hvorfor Døden? Hvorfor leve naar vi dog skal dø? Hvorfor Kæmpe naar vi veed at Sværdet Dog skal vristes af vor Haand en Gang? Hvortil disse Baal af Kval og Smerte: Tusind Timers Liv i langsom Liden, langsom Løben ud i Dødens Liden? Er det din Tanke, høje Kvinde?	Roll over earth, Roll and disappear, While slowly time dies. Why life? Why death? Why live when we yet must die? Why struggle when we know that the sword Will some time be wrested from our hand? Why these fires of suffering and pain: A thousand hours of life in slow agony, Slowly running out in death's agony? Is that your thought, tall woman?
Stanza 5	*5th Stanza*
Tavs og rolig staaer hun paa Balkonen, Har ej Ord, ej Suk, ej Klage, Tegner mørk sig mod den mørke Luft Som et Sværd igjennem Nattens Hjerte	Silently and calm she stands on the balcony, Has no words, no sighs, no laments, Outlined dark against the dark air Like a sword through the heart of night.

LIST OF LITERATURE

INDEX

LIST OF LITERATURE

Abbreviations:

KSA:	Nietzsche: Sämtliche Werke Kritische Studienausgabe. Edited by G. Colli & M. Montinari. Berlin/New York (Walter de Gruyter), 1967-77.
KSB:	Nietzsche: Sämtliche Briefe Kritische Studienausgabe. Edited by G. Colli & M. Montinari. Berlin/New York (Walter de Gruyter), 1986.
SW:	Schopenhauer: Sämtliche Werke Bd. 1-5. Edited by W. von Löhneysen. Frankfurt am Main (Suhrkamp Verlag), 1960.
WA:	Kant: Werkausgabe Bd. 1-12. Edited by W. Weischedel. Frankfurt am Main (Suhrkamp Verlag), 1968.
GW:	Freud: Gesammelte Werke: Chronologisch Geordnet (Frankfurt a/M: Fischer Taschenbuch Verlag, 1999).
KrV:	Kant: Kritik der reinen Vernunft, WA 3 & 4.
SzG:	Schopenhauer: Über die vierfache Wurzel des Satzes vom zureichenden Grunde, SW 3.
W1:	Schopenhauer: Die Welt als Wille und Vorstellung Bd. 1. SW 1.
W2:	Schopenhauer: Die Welt als Wille und Vorstellung Bd. 2. SW 2.
A:	Nietzsche: Antichrist, KSA 6.
EH:	Nietzsche: Ecce Homo, KSA 6.
FW:	Nietzsche: Die fröhliche Wissenschaft, KSA 3.
G:	Nietzsche: Götzendämmerung, KSA 6.
GM:	Nietzsche: Zur Genealogie der Moral, KSA 5.
GT	Nietzsche: Die Geburt der Tragödie, KSA 1.
HL:	Nietzsche:Von Nutzen und Nachteil der Historie für das Leben (UB II), KSA 1.
JGB:	Nietzsche: Jenseits von Gut und Böse, KSA 5.
M	Nietzsche: Morgenröte, KSA 3.
MA:	Nietzsche: Menschliches, Allzumenschliches, KSA 2
Nachlaß:	Nietzsche: Nachgelassende Fragmente, KSA 7-14.
SE:	Nietzsche: Schopenhauer als Erzieher (UB III), KSA 1.
UB:	Nietzsche: Unzeitgemässige Betrachtungen, KSA 1.

WL:	Nietzsche: Über Wahrheit und Lüge in aussermoralischen Sinne, KSA 1.
WM:	Nietzsche: Der Wille zur Macht. Stuttgart (Kröner Verlag), 1996.
Z:	Nietzsche: Also Sprach Zarathustra, KSA

Works by Nietzsche:

German Editions:

Sämtliche Werke Kritische Studienausgabe. Edited by G. Colli & M. Montinari. Berlin/New York (Walter de Gruyter), 1967-77.
Sämtliche Briefe Kritische Studienausgabe. Edited by G. Colli & M. Montinari. Berlin/New York (Walter de Gruyter), 1986.
"Zu Schopenhauer. Philosophische Notizen" in Spierling (ed.): Materialien (loc. cit.).
Also Sprach Zarathustra, KSA 5
Antichrist, KSA 6.
Der Wille zur Macht. Stuttgart (Kröner Verlag), 1996.
Die fröhliche Wissenschaft, KSA 3.
Die Geburt der Tragödie, KSA 1.
Ecce Homo, KSA 6.
Götzendämmerung, KSA 6.
Jenseits von Gut und Böse, KSA 5.
Menschliches, Allzumenschliches, KSA 2
Morgenröte, KSA 3.
Nachgelassende Fragmente, KSA 7-14.
Schopenhauer als Erzieher (UB III), KSA 1.
Über Wahrheit und Lüge in aussermoralischen Sinne, KSA 1.
Unzeitgemässige Betrachtungen, KSA 1.
Von Nutzen und Nachteil der Historie für das Leben (UB II), KSA 1.
Zur Genealogie der Moral, KSA 5.

English Editions:

Beyond Good and Evil. Translated by J. Norman. Cambridge. (Cambridge University Press), 2002.
Beyond Good and Evil. Translated by R. J. Hollingdale. London (Penguin Books), 1973.

Daybreak. Translated by R. J. Hollingdale. Cambridge (Cambridge University Press), 2002.
Ecce Homo. Translated by W. Kaufmann. New York (Vintage Books), 1969.
Human, All Too Human. Translated by R. J. Hollingdale,. Cambridge (Cambridge University Press), 1986.
On the Genealogy of Morals. Translated by D. Smith. Oxford (Oxford University Press), 1996.
On the Genealogy of Morals. Translated by W. Kaufmann. New York (Vintage Books), 1969.
On the Truth and Lie in an Extra-Moral Sense, in *Philosophy and Truth* (loc. cit.)
On Truth and Lying in a Non-Moral Sense, in *The Birth of Tragedy and other Writings* (loc. cit.).
Philosophy and Truth: Selections from Nietzsche's Notebooks of the Early 1820's. Edited & translated by D. Breazeale. Amherst (Humanities Books), 1999.
The Birth of Tragedy and Other Writings. Translated by R. Speirs. Cambridge: (Cambridge University Press), 1999.
The Birth of Tragedy. Translated by D. Lange. Oxford (Oxford Univeristy Press), 2000.
The Birth of Tragedy. Translated by W. Kaufmann. New York (Vintage Books), 1967.
The Gay Science. Edited by B. Williams. Translated by J. Nauckhoff. Cambridge (Cambridge University Press), 2001.
The Gay Science. Translated by W. Kaufmann. New York (Vintage Books. Random House), 1974.
The Twilight of the Idols. Translated by Duncan Large. Oxford (Oxford World Classics), 1998.
The Twilight of the Idols. Translated by R. J. Hollingdale. London (Penguin Books), 1968.
The Will to Power. Edited by W. Kaufmann. Translated by Kaufmann & R. J. Hollingdale. New York (Vintage Books), 1968.
Thus Spoke Zarathustra. Translated by R. J. Hollingdale. London (Penguin Books), 1961[69].
Untimely Meditations. Translated by R. J. Hollingdale. Cambridge (Cambridge University Press), 1983.

Literature:

Abel, Günter: "Bewußtsein – Sprache – Natur. Nietzsches Philosophie des Geistes," in Nietzsche-Studien, Band 30, 2001. Berlin/New York (Walter de Gruyter), 2001, pp. 1-43.
Abel, Günter: "Logic und Ästhetik," in *Nietzsche Studien* 16. Berlin, New York (Walter de Gruyter), 1987.
Abel, Günter: "Was ist Interpretationsphilosophie," in Simon (ed.): *Zeichen und Interpretation* (loc. cit.)
Abel, Günter: Interpretationswelten: Gegenwartsphilosophie jenseits von Essentialismus und Relativismus. Frankfurt (Suhrkamp), 1995.
Abel, Günter: Nietzsche: Die Dynamik des Willen zur Macht und die Ewige Wiederkehr. Berlin/New York (Walter de Gruyter), 1998.
Abraham, N. & Torok, M.: The Shell and the Kernel. Edited and translated by Nicolas Rand. Chicago (The University Press of Chicago,) 1994.
Abraham, Nicolas: Rhythms: On the Work, Translation, and Psychoanalysis. Edited by N. Rand & M. Torok. Translated by B. Thigpen & N. Rand. Stanford (Stanford University Press), 1995.
Adorno, Theodor W.: Studien zum autoritären Charakter. Frankfurt a/M (Suhrkamp Verlag), 1995.
Allison, David B. (ed.): The New Nietzsche. New York (A Delta Book), 1977.
Allison, David B.: Reading the New Nietzsche. Lanham (Rowman and Littlefield), 2001.
Allison, Henry: Kant's Transcendental Idealism. Yale (Yale University Press), 2004 (rev. ed.)
Aristotle: Ethica Nicomachea, in *The Basic Works of Aristotle*, edited by R. McKeon. New York (Random House), 1941.
Aristotle: Metaphysics, in *The Basic Works of Aristotle*, edited by R. McKeon. New York (Random House), 1941.
Assoun, Paul-Laurent: Freud and Nietzsche. Translated by R. L. Collier. London (The Athlone Press), 2000.
Austin, J. L.: How to Do Things with Words. Cambridge, Mass. (Harvard University Press), 1975.
Babich, Babette E. (ed.): Nietzsche, Epistemology, and Philosophy of Science. Dordrecht (Kluwer Academic Publishers), 1999.
Babich, Babette E.: "The Minotaur and the Dolphin," in *New Nietzsche Studies*, vol. 4:3/4, 2000-2001.

Babich, Babette E.: Nietzsche's Philosophy of Science. New York (State University of New York Press), 1994.
Babich, Babette E.: "Nietzsche's Imperative as a Friend's Encomium. On Becoming the One Your Are, Ethics, and Blessing," in: Nietzsche-Studien 32, Berlin, New York (Walter de Gruyter), 2003.
Barthes, Roland. *S/Z*. Trans. R. Miller. New York (Hill and Wang), 1974.
Bataille, Georges: On Nietzsche. Translated by B. Boone. St. Paul (Paragon), 1992.
Baumanns, Peter: Kants Philosophie der Erkenntnis. Würzburg (Könighausen & Neumann), 1997.
Beckett, Samuel: Three Novels: Molloy, Malone Dies, The Unnamable . New York (Grove Press), 1958.
Beckett, Samuel: Waiting for Godot. London (Faber and Faber), 1956.
Bentham, Jeremy: The Principles of Morals and Legislation. Amherst (Prometheus Books), 1988.
Benveniste, Emile: Problemes de linguistique générale. Paris (Éditions Gallimand), 1966.
Benveniste, Emile: Problems in General Linguistics. Translated by M. E. Meek. Miami (University of Miami Press), 1971.
Berkeley, George: Principles of Human Knowledge in *Principles of Human Knowledge.* (loc. cit.)
Berkeley, George: Principles of Human Knowledge. Oxford (Oxford University Press), 1996/99.
Berkeley, George: Three Dialogues between Hylas and Philonous in *Principles of Human Knowledge*, (loc. cit.)
Berkowitz, Peter: Nietzsche: The Ethics of an Immoralist. Cambridge, Mass. (Harvard University Press), 1995.
Bernet, R., Kern I., & Marbach E.: An Introduction to Husserlian Phenomenology. Evanston (Northwestern University Press), 1993.
Bittner, Rüdiger: "Ressentiment," in Schacht: *Nietzsche, Genealogy, Morality* (loc. cit.).
Blondel, Eric: "The Question of Genealogy," in Schacht: *Nietzsche, Genealogy, Morality* (loc. cit.).
Böhme, Germot & Helmut: Das Andere der Vernunft: Zur Entwicklung von Rationalitätsstrukturen am Beispiel Kants. Frankfurt (Suhrkamp), 1983
Böhme, Germot: Philosophieren mit Kant: Zur Rekonstruktion der Kantischen Erkenntnis- und Wissenschaftheorie. Frankfurt (Suhrkamp), 1986.

Boothby, Richard: Death and Desire: Psychoanalytic Theory in Lacan's Return to Freud. London/New York (Routledge), 1991.
Borch-Jacobsen, Mikkel: Lacan: The Absolute Master. Translated by D. Brick. Stanford (Stanford University Press), 1991.
Borch-Jacobsen, Mikkel: The Freudian Subject. Translated by C. Porter. Stanford (Stanford University Press), 1988.
Bornedal, Peter: On the Beginnings of Theory. Lanham/New York (University Press of America), 2006.
Bornedal, Peter: Skrift og Skribent: Undersøgerlser i Grammatologien. Copenhagen (MTP, The University of Copenhagen Press), 1985.
Bornedal, Peter: Speech and System. Copenhagen (MTP, The University of Copenhagen Press), 1997.
Bornedal, Peter: The Interpretations of Art. Lanham & New York (University Press of America), 1996.
Breazeale, Daniel (ed.): Philosophy and Truth: Selections from Nietzsche's Notebooks of the Early 1870's. Amherst (Humanity Books), 1999.
Breazeale, Daniel: "Introduction," in Breazeale (ed.): Philosophy and Truth.
Brentano, Franz: Psychology from an Empirical Standpoint. London (Routledge), 1995.
Brobjer, Thomas: "Nietzsche's Reading and Knowledge of Natural Science: An Overview" in Moore/Brobjer: *Nietzsche and Science*, (loc. cit.)
Brown, Bill (ed.): *Things*. Critical Inquiry vol. 28, no. 1. Chicago (The University of Chicago Press), 2001.
Brown, Bill: "Thing Theory" in Brown (ed.): *Things*, (loc. cit.)
Brusotti, Marco: "Wille zum Nichts, Ressentiment, Hypnose. 'Aktiv' und 'Reaktiv' in Nietzsche's *Genealogie der Moral*," in Nietzsche-Studien, Band 30, 2001. Berlin/New York: Walter de Gruyter, 2001), pp. 107-132.
Canetti, Elias: Crowds and Power. New York (Farrar, Strauss, & Giroux), 1984.
Carr, David: The Paradox of Subjectivity: The Self in the Transcendental Tradition. Oxford (Oxford University Press), 1999.
Cassirer, Ernst: Kant's Life and Thought. Translation J. Haden. New Haven & London (Yale University Press), 1981.
Cassirer, Ernst: The Philosophy of Symbolic Forms v. 1: Language. Translated by R. Manheim. New Haven (Yale University Press), 1955.

Chapelle, Daniel: Nietzsche and Psychoanalysis. New York (State University of New York Press), 1993.
Clark, Maudemarie: "Nietzsche's Immoralism and the Concept of Morality," in Schacht: *Nietzsche, Genealogy, Morality* (loc. cit.).
Clark, Maudemarie: Nietzsche on Truth and Philosophy. Cambridge (Cambridge University Press), 1991.
Conway, Daniel W. (ed.): Nietzsche: Critical Assessments, v. II: The World as Will to Power and Nothing Else. London, New York (Routledge), 1998.
Conway, Daniel W.: "Beyond Truth and Appearance," in Babech: *Nietzsche, Epistemology, and Philosophy of Science* (loc. cit.).
Conway, Daniel W.: "Genealogy and Critical Method," in Schacht: *Nietzsche, Genealogy, Morality* (loc. cit.).
Conway, Daniel W.: Nietzsche's Dangerous Game. Cambridge (Cambridge University Press), 2002.
Copleston, Frederick: A History of Philosophy, v. VII: From the Post-Kantian Idealists to Marx, Kierkegaard, and Nietzsche. New York/London (Image Books, Doubleday), 1994.
Couzens Hoy, Daniel: "Nietzsche, Hume, and the Genealogical Method," in Schacht: *Nietzsche, Genealogy, Morality* (loc. cit.).
Cowan, Michael: "'Nichts ist so sehr Zeitgemäss als Willensschwäche.' Nietzsche and the psychology of the Will." Nietzsche Studien no. 34. Berlin/New York (Walter de Gruyter), 2005.
Crawford, Claudia: The Beginnings of Nietzsche's Theory of Language. Berlin/New York (Walter de Gruyter), 1988.
Culler, Jonathan: On Deconstruction: Theory and Criticism after Structuralism. Ithaca (Cornell University Press), 1982.
Damasio, Antonio R.: Descartes' Error: Emotion, Reason, and the Human Brain. New York (Quill Harber Collins), 2000.
Damasio, Antonio R.: Looking for Spinoza: Joy, Sorrow, and the Feeling Brain. New York (Harcourt, Inc.), 2003.
Danto, Arthur C.: "Some Remarks of *The Genealogy of Morals,*" in Schacht: *Nietzsche, Genealogy, Morality* (loc. cit.).
Danto, Arthur: Nietzsche as Philosopher. New York (Columbia University Press), 1980.
Davidson, Donald: "Deception and Division" in Elster (ed.): *The Multiple Self* (loc. cit.).
De Man, Paul: "Anthropomorphism and the Trope in the Lyric" in *The Rhetoric of Romanticism*. New York (Columbia University Press) 1984;

De Man, Paul: Allegories of Reading. New Haven/London (Yale University Press), 1979.
De Man, Paul: The Rhetoric of Romanticism. New York (Columbia University Press), 1984.
Deleuze, G. & Guattari, F.: What is Philosophy? Translated by H. Tomlinson & G. Burchell. New York (Columbia University Press), 1994.
Deleuze, Gilles: "Nomad Thought" in Allison (ed.): *The New Nietzsche* (loc. cit.)
Deleuze, Gilles: Difference and Repetition. Translated by P. Patton. New York: (Columbia University Press), 1994.
Deleuze, Gilles: Nietzsche and Philosophy. Translated by H. Tomlinson. New York: (Columbia University Press), 1983.
Dennett, Daniel C.: Consciousness Explained. Boston/London/New York (Little, Brown, and Company), 1991.
Dennett, Daniel C.: Darwin's Dangerous Idea: Evolution and the Meaning of Life. New York (Touchstone), 1995.
Derrida, Jacques: "Freud and the Scene of Writing" in *Writing and Difference*. Translated by A. Bass. Chicago (The University of Chicago Press), 1978.
Derrida, Jacques: "Otobiographies" in *The Ear of the Other* (loc. cit.)
Derrida, Jacques: "Plato's Pharmakon" in: *Dissemination*. Translated by B. Johnson. Chicago (The University of Chicago Press), 1981.
Derrida, Jacques: "To Speculate: On Freud" in *The Post Card*. Translated by A. Bass. Chicago (The University of Chicago Press), 1987.
Derrida, Jacques: Dissemination. Translated by B. Johnson. Chicago (The University of Chicago Press), 1981.
Derrida, Jacques: Of Grammatology. Translated by G. Spivak. Baltimore (Johns Hopkins University Press), 1974.
Derrida, Jacques: Spurs: Nietzsche's Styles/Éperons: Les Sytles de Nietzsche. Translated by B. Harlow. . Chicago (The University of Chicago Press), 1979.
Derrida, Jacques: The Ear of the Other. Translated by P. Kamuf. Lincoln (The University of Nebraska Press), 1988.
Derrida, Jacques: The Postcard: From Socrates to Freud and Beyond. Translated by A. Bass. Chicago (The University of Chicago Press), 1993.
Derrida, Jacques: Writing and Difference. Translated by A. Bass. Chicago (The University of Chicago Press), 1978.
Descartes, Rene: Meditations on First Philosophy, in *The Philosophical Writings of Descartes*, vol. II (loc. cit.)

Descartes, Rene: Objections and Replies, in *The Philosophical Writings of Descartes*, vol. II (loc. cit.)
Descartes, Rene: The Philosophical Writings of Descartes, vol. I & II. Translated by J. Cottingham et al,. Cambridge: (Cambridge University Press), 1984.
Dier, Oliver: "Die Verwandlung der Wiederkunft," in Nietzsche-Studien, Band 30, 2001. Berlin/New York (Walter de Gruyter), 2001, pp. 133-174.
Djurić, Mihailo: Nietzsche und die Metaphysik. Berlin/New York (Walter de Gruyter), 1985.
Dor, Joel: Introduction to the Reading of Lacan. Northvale (Jason Aronson Inc.), 1997.
Dosse, Francois: History of Structuralism, vol. I & II. Translated by D. Glassman. Minneapolis (University of Minnesota Press), 1997.
Duclot & Todorov: Encyclopedic Dictionary of the Sciences of Language. Translated by C. Porter. Baltimore (The Johns Hopkins University Press) 1979.
Dühring, Eugen Karl: Der Wert des Lebens. (Eliborn Classics) 2006.
Elster, Jon (ed.): The Multiple Self. Cambridge (Cambridge University Press), 1986.
Elster, Jon: "Introduction," in Elster (ed.): *The Multiple Self* (loc. cit.).
Emden, Christian: "Metaphor, Perception and Consciousness: Nietzsche on Rhetoric and Neurophysiology," in Moore/Brobjer: *Nietzsche and Science*, loc. cit.
Emden, Christian: Nietzsche on Language, Consciousness, and the Body. Urbana and Chicago (Illinois University Press) 2005.
Fechner, Gustav: Elements of Psychophysics. New York, Chicago (Holt, Reinhart and Winston), 1966.
Feldstein R., Fink B., & Jaanus M. (eds.): Reading Seminar XI: Lacan's Four Fundamental Concepts of Psychoanalysis. Albany (SUNY Press), 1995.
Felman, Shoshana (ed.): Literature and Psychoanalysis. Baltimore (The Johns Hopkins University Press), 1982.
Feuerbach, Ludwig: The Essence of Christianity. Translated by G. Eliot. Amherst, New York (Prometheus Books), 1989.
Figal, Günter: Nietzsche: Eine philosophische Einführung. Stuttgart (Reclam), 2001.
Fink, Bruce: "The Real Cause of Repetition" in *Reading Seminar XI* (loc. cit.)
Fink, Eugen: Nietzsche's Philosophy. Translated by G. Richter. London, New York (Continuum), 2003.

Fink, Eugen: Nietzsches Philosophie. Stuttgart, Berlin (Verlag Kohlhammer), 1960.
Fischer, Kuno: "Schopenhauers Leben, Werke und Lehre" in Spierling (ed.): Materialien.
Fischer, Kuno: A Commentary on Kant's Critick of the Pure Reason. London (Longmans, Green, & Co.) 1866.
Fish, Stanley: Doing what Comes Naturally: Change, Rhetoric, and the Practice of Theory in Litrerary and Legal Studies. Durham, London (Duke University Press), 1989.
Fish, Stanley: Is There a Text in this Class?. Cambridge, Mass. (Harvard University Press), 1980.
Foot, Philippa: "Nietzsche's Immoralism," in Schacht: *Nietzsche, Genealogy, Morality*. (loc. cit.)
Foucault, Michel: Discipline and Punish: The Birth of the Prison. Translated by A. Sheridan. New York (Vintage Books), 1995.
Foucault, Michel: Madness and Civilization: A History of Madness in the Age of Reason. Translated by R. Howard. New York (Vintage Books), 1988.
Foucault, Michel: The Archaeology of Knowledge & The Discourse on Language. Translation, Sheridan Smith. New York (Pantheon Books) 1971.
Foucault, Michel: The Birth of the Clinic: An Archeology of Medical Perception. Translated by Sheridan Smith. New York (Vintage Books), 1994.
Foucault, Michel: The History of Sexuality: An Introduction. Translated by R. Hurley. New York (Vintage Books), 1978
Foucault, Michel: The Order of Things: An Archeology of the Human Sciences. New York (Vintage Books), 1994.
Frank, Manfred (ed.): Selbstbewußtseinstheorien von Fichte bis Sartre. Frankfurt a/M (Suhrkamp) 1991.
Frauenstädt, Julius: "Briefe über die Schopenhauersche Philosophie" in Spierling (ed.): *Materialien*.
Freud, Sigmund: Gesammelte Werke: Chronologisch Geordnet. Frankfurt a/M: Fischer Taschenbuch Verlag, 1999.
Freud, Sigmund: The Standard Edition of the Complete Psychological Works of Sigmund Freud, vol. 1-24. Edited by J. Strachey. London: The Hogarth Press and the Institute of Psychoanalysis, 1966.
Freud, Sigmund: "A Metapsychological Supplement to the Theory of Dreams" [1917], in SE 14.
Freud, Sigmund: "A Note upon the 'Mystic Writing Pad'," SE 19.

Freud, Sigmund: "An Outline of Psychoanalysis" [1940], in SE 23.
Freud, Sigmund: "Beyond the Pleasure Principle" [1920], in SE 18.
Freud, Sigmund: "Civilization and its Discontents" [1930] , in SE 12.
Freud, Sigmund: "Extracts from the Fliess Papers" [1896], SE 1.
Freud, Sigmund: "History of the Psychoanalytic Movement" [1914], in SE vol. 14.
Freud, Sigmund: "Instincts and their Vicissitudes" [1915] , in SE vol. 14.
Freud, Sigmund: "Negation" [1925] , in SE 19.
Freud, Sigmund: "Repression" [1915], in SE 14.
Freud, Sigmund: "The Economic Problem of Masochism" [1924] , in SE 19.
Freud, Sigmund: "The Ego and the Id" [1923] , in SE 19.
Freud, Sigmund: "The Unconscious" [1915], in SE 14.
Freud, Sigmund: "Two Principles of Mental Functioning, [1911], in SE 12.
Freud, Sigmund: A Moment of Transition: Two Neuroscientific Articles by Sigmund Freud. Edited and translated by M. Solms & M. Saling. London (Karnac Books), 1990.
Freud, Sigmund: Art and Literature. Penguin Freud Library vol. 14. London (Penguin Books), 1986.
Freud, Sigmund & Breuer, Joseph: Studies on Hysteria. SE. 2.
Freud, Sigmund: Introductory Lectures in Psychoanalysis, SE 3.
Freud, Sigmund: On Metapsychology. The Penguin Freud Library, vol. 11. London (Penguin Books), 1991.
Freud, Sigmund: Pre-Psychoanalytic Publications and Unpublished Drafts, SE 1
Freud, Sigmund: Project for a Scientific Psychology, SE 1.
Freud, Sigmund: The Interpretation of Dreams, SE 4 & 5.
Freud, Sigmund: Zur Auffassung der Aphasien. Leibniz und Wien (Franz Deutiche) 1891.
Gasser, Reinhard: Nietzsche und Freud. Berlin, New York (Walter de Gruyter), 1997.
Gaultier, Jules de: From Kant to Nietzsche. New York (Philosophical Library), 1961.
Gay, Peter: Freud: A Life for Our Time. New York (W. W. Norton & Company), 1988.
Gehlen, Arnold: "Die Resultate Schopenhauers" in Spierling (ed.): Materialien.
Gerber, Gustav: Die Sprache als Kunst, bd. I & II. Berlin (R. Gaertners Verlagsbuchhandlung), 1885.

Gerhardt, Volker: Vom Willen zur Macht: Anthropologie und Metaphysic der Macht am exemplarischen Fall Friedrich Nietzsches. Berlin, New York (Walter de Gruyter), 1996.
Goethe, Johann Wolfgang von: Faust vol. I & II. Translated by D. Luke. Oxford (Oxford University Press), 1994.
Golomb J. & Wistrich, R. S. (eds.): Nietzsche, Godfather of Fascism?: On the Uses and Abuses of a Philosophy. Princeton (Princeton University Press), 2002.
Granier, Jean: "Nietzsche's Conception of Chaos" in: Allison: *The New Nietzsche* (loc. cit.)
Granier, Jean: "Perspectivism and Interpretation" in: Allison: *The New Nietzsche* (loc. cit.)
Granier, Jean: Le problème de la Vérité dans la philosophie de Nietzsche. Paris (Éditions du Seuil), 1966.
Green, Michael Steven: Nietzsche and the Transcendental Tradition. Urbana & Chicago (University of Illinois Press), 2002.
Grimm, Herman Ruediger: Nietzsche's Theory of Knowledge. Berlin/New York (Walter de Gruyter), 1977.
Guyer, Paul: Kant and the Claims of Knowledge. Cambridge (Cambridge University Press), 1987.
Guyer, Paul: Kant. London, New York (Routledge), 2006.
Haar, Michel: Nietzsche and Metaphysics. New York (State University of New York Press), 1996.
Habermas, Jürgen: "On Nietzsche's Theory of Knowledge" in: Babich (ed.): *Nietzsche, Epistemology, and Philosophy of Science*, (loc. cit.).
Habermas, Jürgen: On the Theory of Communicative Action vol. I. Translated by T. McCarthy. Boston (Beacon Press), 1984;
Habermas, Jürgen: The Philosophical Discourse of Modernity. Translated by F. G. Lawrence. Cambridge, Mass. (The MIT Press), 1996.
Hales, S. D. & Welshon, R.: Nietzsche's Perspectivism. Urbana and Chicago (University of Illinois Press), 2000.
Harris, Roy: Reading Saussure. La Salle (Open Court), 1987.
Hartmann, Eduard von: Philosophie des Unbewussten bd. 1 & 2. Berlin (Carl Dunker's Verlag), 1870.
Hartmann, Eduard von: The Philosophy of the Unconscious. Translation by W. C. Coupland. London (Routledge), 2000.
Hatab, Lawrence J.: Nietzsche's Life Sentence: Coming to Terms with Eternal Recurrence. New York (Routledge), 2005.
Havas, Randal: Nietzsche's Genealogy: Nihilism and the Will to Knowledge. Ithaca/London (Cornell University Press), 1995.

Hawkes, Terence: Structuralism and Semiotics. Berkeley (University of California Press), 1977.
Heidegger, Martin: An Introduction to Metaphysics. Translated by R. Manheim. New Haven/London (Yale University Press), 1987.
Heidegger, Martin: Basic Writings. Edited & translated by D. F. Krell. San Francisco (HarperSanFrancisco), 1993.
Heidegger, Martin: Being and Time. Translated by J. Stambaugh. New York (State University of New York Press), 1996.
Heidegger, Martin: Identity and Difference. Translated by J. Stambaugh. New York (Harper Touchbooks), 1969.
Heidegger, Martin: Nietzsche, vols. I-IV. Edited & translated by D. F. Krell. San Francisco (Harper and Row), 1991.
Helmholtz, Hermann von: Science and Culture: Popular and Philosophical Lectures. Edited by D. Cahan. Chicago (The University of Chicago Press), 1995.
Helmholtz, Hermann von: Scientific Subjects. London (Longmans, Green, & co.), 1893.
Henrick, Dieter: The Unity of Reason. Translation R. L. Velkley. Cambridge (Harvard University Press), 1994.
Herbart, J. F.: Psychologie als Wissenschaft: Neu Gegründet auf Erfahrung, Metaphysik, und Mathematik. Amsterdam (E. J. Bonset) 1968.
Hill, Kevin R.: Nietzsche's Critiques: The Kantian Foundation for his Thought. Oxford (Clarendon Press), 2003.
Himmelmann, Beatrix (ed.): Kant und Nietzsche im Widerstreit. Berlin, New York (Walter de Gruyter), 2005.
Hjelmslev, Louis: Prolegomena to a Theory of Language. Translation, F. J. Whitfield. Madison (The University of Wisconsin Press), 1963.
Höffe, Otfried: Immanuel Kant. Translated by M. Farrier. New York (SUNY Press), 1994.
Hofmann, Johann Nepomuk: Wahrheit, Perspektive, Interpretation: Nietzsche und die philosophische Hermeneutik. Berlin, New York (Walter de Gruyter), 1994.
Holdcroft, David: Saussure: Signs, System, and Arbitrariness. Cambridge (Cambridge University Press), 1991.
Holder, Alex: "Einleitung" in Freud: *Das Ich und das Es: Metaphychologische Schriften* (loc. cit.)
Hollingdale, F. J.: Nietzsche: The Man and His Philosophy. Cambridge (Cambridge University Press), 1999.

Honneth, Andreas: Das Paradox des Augenblicks: "Zarathustras Vorrede" un Nietzsches Theorem der "ewigen Wiederkunft des Gleichen". Würzburg (Königshausen & Neumann), 2004.
Houlgate, Stephen: "Kant, Nietzsche, and the Thing-in-itself". Nietzsche Studien 22; Berlin, New York (Walter de Gruyter), 1993.
Hume, David: A Treatise of Human Nature. London (Penguin Classics), 1969.
Hume, David: An Enquiry Concerning Human Understanding. Indianapolis (Hackett Publishing Company), 1977.
Husserl, Edmund: Cartesianische Meditationen. Hamburg (Felix Meiner), 1995.
Husserl, Edmund: Erfahrung und Urteil. Hamburg (Felix Meiner), 1999.
Husserl, Edmund: Experience and Judgment: Investigations in a Genealogy of Logic. Edited by L. Landgrebe; translated by J. S. Churchill & K. Ameriks. Evanston (Northwestern University Press), 1973.
Husserl, Edmund: Grundprobleme der Phänomenologie 1910/11. Hamburg (Felix Meiner Verlag), 1977/92.
Husserl, Edmund: On the Phenomenology of the Consciousness of Internal Time. Translated by J. B. Brough. Dordrecht (Kluwer Academic Publishers), 1991.
Husserl, Edmund: Raum und Ding. Hamburg (Felix Meiner), 1985.
Husserl, Edmund: Texte zur Phänomenologie des Inneren Zeitbewußtseins (1895-1917). Hamburg (Felix Meiner), 1985.
Husserl, Edmund: The Crisis of European Sciences and Transcendental Phenomenology. Translated by D. Carr. Evanston (Northwestern University Press), 1970.
Husserl, Edmund: Thing and Space: Lectures of 1907. Translated by R. Rojcewicz. Dordrecht (Kluwer Academic Publishers), 1997.
Jacobsen, J. P. Samlede Værker. Vol. 1–6. København: Rosenkilde og Bagger, 1973.
Jakobson, Roman: On Language. Edited by Waugh & Burston. Cambridge, Mass.: Harvard University Press, 1990.
James, William: The Principles of Psychology, vol. I-II. New York: Henry Holt and Company, 1890.
Janaway, Christopher (ed.): The Cambridge Companion to Schopenhauer. Cambridge (Cambridge University Press), 1999.
Janaway, Christopher: Beyond Selflessness: Reading Nietzsche's *Genealogy*. Oxford (Oxford University Press), 2007.
Janaway, Christopher: Schopenhauer. Oxford (Oxford University Press), 1994.

Janaway, Christopher: Self and World in Schopenhauer's Philosophy. Oxford (Clarendon Press), 1989.
Jaspers, Karl: Nietzsche: An Introduction to the Understanding of his Philosophical Activity. Translated by C. F. Wallraff & F. J. Schmitz. Baltimore (The Johns Hopkins University Press), 1997.
Jordan, L.: "Nietzsche: Dekonstruktionist oder Konstruktivist?" in Nietzsche Studien 23. Berlin, New York (Walter de Gruyter), 1994.
Kafka, Franz: The Complete Stories. Translated by W. and E. Muir. New York (Schocken Books), 1971.
Kant, Immanuel: Werkausgabe 1-12. Ed.: W. Weischedel. Frankfurt am Main (Suhrkamp Verlag), 1968.
Kant, Immanuel: "De Mundi Sensibilis," in WA 5.
Kant, Immanuel: Critique of Pure Reason. Translated by W. S. Pluhar. Indianapolis (Hackett Publishing Company), 1996.
Kant, Immanuel: Critique of Pure Reason. Translated by Norman Kemp Smith. Houndmills (Palgrave Macmillian), 1918, 2003).
Kant, Immanuel: Grounding of a Metaphysics of Morals. Translated by J. W. Ellington. New York (Hackett Publishing Company), 1993.
Kant, Immanuel: Kritik der reinen Vernunft I, in WA 3.
Kant, Immanuel: Kritik der reinen Vernunft II, in WA 4.
Kant, Immanuel: Logik, in WA 6.
Kant, Immanuel: Prolegomena to Any Future Metaphysics. Translated by P. Carus. Indianapolis (Hackett Publishing Company), 1977.
Kant, Immanuel: Prolegomena zu einer jeden Künftigen Metaphysik, in WA 5.
Kaufmann, Walter: Discovering the Mind, vol. II: Nietzsche, Heidegger, Buber. New Brunswick/London (Transaction Publishers), 1992.
Kaufmann, Walter: Nietzsche: Philosopher, Psychologist, Antichrist. Princeton (Princeton University Press), 1974.
Kaulbach, Friedrich: Immanuel Kant. Berlin, New York (Walter de Gruyter), 1982.
Keller, Pierre: Kant and the Demands of Self-Consciousness. Cambridge (Cambridge University Press), 1998.
Kemp Smith, Norman: A Commentary to Kant's "Critique of Pure Reason". New York (The Humanities Press), 1950.
Kierkegaard, Søren: Either/Or. Translation, H. V. Hong and E. H. Hong. Princeton (Princeton University Press) 1987.

Kierkegaard, Søren: Repetition. Translated by H. V. & E. H. Hong. Princeton (Princeton University Press), 1983.
Kitcher, Patricia: Kant's Transcendental Psychology. Oxford (Oxford University Press), 1993.
Klein, Wayne: Nietzsche and the Promise of Philosophy. New York (State University of New York Press), 1997.
Klossowski, Pierre: Nietzsche and the Vicious Circle. Translated by D. W. Smith. Chicago (The University of Chicago Press), 1997.
Kofman, Sarah: Nietzsche and Metaphor. Translated by Duncan Large. Stanford (Stanford University Press), 1993.
Lacan, Jacques: Ecrits: A Selection. Translated by A. Sheridan. New York, London (Norton & Company), 1977.
Lacan, Jacques: The Four Fundamental Concepts of Psychoanalysis. Edited by J-A. Miller; translated by A. Sheridan. New York, London (Norton & Company), 1981.
Lacan, Jacques: The Language of the Self. Edited by A. Wilden. Baltimore (The Johns Hopkins University Press), 1981.
Lambert, Laurence: Nietzsche's Task: An Interpretation of 'Beyond Good and Evil'. New Haven/London (Yale University Press), 2002.
Lange, Frederick Albert: The History of Materialism. Translated by C. K. Ogden. New York (Routledge), 1865/2000.
Lange, Friedrich Albert: Geschichte des Materialismus und Kritik seiner Bedeutung in der Gegenwart bd. 1 & 2. Iserlohn (Verlag con J. Daedeker), 1873.
Langton, Rae: Kantian Humility: Our Ignorance of Things in Themselves. Oxford (Clarendon Press)l 1998.
Laplanche, J. & Pontalis, J-B.: The Language of Psychoanalysis. Translated by D. Nicholson-Smith. New York (W. W. Norton & Company), 1973.
Laplanche, Jean. Life and Death in Psychoanalysis. Trans. J. Mehlman. Baltimore (Johns Hopkins University Press), 1985.
Le Bon, Gustave: The Crowd: A Study of the Popular Mind. New York (Dover Publications), 2002.
LeDoux, Joseph: Synaptic Self: How our Brains Become Who We Are. New York (Viking), 2002.
Leibniz, G. W.: New Essays on Human Understanding. Translated & edited by P. Remnant & J. Bennett. Cambridge (Cambridge University Press), 1982.
Leibniz, G. W.: Philosophical Texts. Translated & edited by R. S. Woolhouse & R. Francks. Oxford (Oxford University Press), 1998.

Leiter, Brian: "Perspectivism in Nietzsche's *Genealogy of Morals*," in Schacht: *Nietzsche, Genealogy, Morality* (loc. cit.).
Leiter, Brian: Nietzsche on Morality. London/New York: Routledge Philosophical Guidebook), 2002.
Lomax, Harvey J.: The Paradox of Philosophical Education: Nietzsche's New Nobility and the Eternal Recurrence in *Beyond Good and Evil*. London, New York (Lexington), 2003.
Longuenesse, Béatrice: Kant and the Capacity to Judge: Sensibility and Discursivity in the Transcendental Analytic of the *Critique of Pure Reason*. Princeton (Princeton University Press), 1998.
Longuenesse, Beatrice: Kant on the Human Standpoint. Cambridge (Cambridge University Press), 2005.
Lotze, Hermann: Metaphysic in three Books; Ontology, Cosmology, and Psychology. Translation B. Bosanquet. Oxford (Clarendon Press), 1887.
Lotze, Hermann: Outlines of Metaphysic. Translated by G. T. Ladd. Boston (Ginn & Company), 1893.
Löwith, Karl: From Hegel to Nietzsche: The Revolution in Nineteenth-Century Thought. New York (Columbia University Press), 1964.
Löwith, Karl: Nietzsche's Philosophe der Ewigen Wiederkehr des Gleichen. Hamburg (Felix Meiner Verlag), 1978.
Löwith, Karl: Nietzsche's Philosophy of the Eternal Recurrence of the Same. Translated by J. H. Lomax. Berkeley (University of California Press), 1997.
Mach, Ernst: Erkenntnis und Irrtum. Leipzig (Verlag von Johann Ambrosius Barth), 1905.
Mach, Ernst: The Analysis of the Sensations and the Relation of the Physical to the Psychical. Translated by C. M. Williams New York (Dover Publications), 1959.
Macmillan, Malcolm: Freud Evaluated: The Completed Arc. Cambridge, Mass.: The MIT Press), 1997.
Magee, Brian: The Philosophy of Schopenhauer. Oxford (Clarendon Press), 1983.
Magnus, Bernd: "Nietzsche and Postmodern Criticism," in *Nietzsche Studien* 18. Berlin, New York (Walter de Gruyter), 1989.
Magnus, Bernd: Nietzsche's Existential Imperative. Bloomington (Indiana University Press), 1978.
Mann, Thomas: Death in Venice and seven other Stories. New York (Vintage International), 1989.

Mann, Thomas: Doctor Faustus. Translated by J. E. Woods. New York (Vintage Books), 1997.
Mann, Thomas: The Magic Mountain. Translated by J. E. Woods. New York: Vintage Books), 1995.
Marx, Karl: The Marx-Engels Reader. Edited by R. C. Tucker. New York (W. W. Norton), 1978.
McQuillan, Martin: Paul de Man. London, New York (Routledge), 2001.
Meijers, A. und Stengelin, M.: "Kondordanz zu . . . Gustav Gerbers *Die Sprache als Kunst* . . . und Nietzsches *Über Wahrheit und Lüge*," in Nietzsche Studien 17. Berlin, New York (Walter de Gruyter), 1888.
Meijers, Anthonie: "Gustav Gerber und Friedrich Nietzsche. Zum historischen Hintergrund der sprachphilosophichen Auffassungen des frühen Nietzsche," in *Nietzsche Studien* 17. Berlin, New York (Walter de Gruyter), 1888.
Meissner, M. M.: Freud and Psychoanalysis. Notre Dame (University of Notre Dame Press), 2000)
Mill, John Stuart: Autobiography. London (Penguin Books), 1989.
Mill, John Stuart: On Liberty and Other Essays, edited by J. Gray. Oxford (Oxford University Press), 1991.
Montinari, Mazzino: Friedrich Nietzsche: Eine Einführung. Berlin, New York (Walter de Gruyter), 1991.
Montinari, Mazzino: Nietzsche Lesen. Berlin (Walter de Gruyter), 1984.
Moore, G, & Brobjer T. (eds.): Nietzsche and Science. London (Ashgate), 2004.
Moore, Gregory: "Introduction"; in Moore/Brobjer: Nietzsche and Science, loc. cit. .
Moore, Gregory: Nietzsche, Biology and Metaphor. Cambridge (Cambridge University Press), 2002.
Moran, Dermot: Introduction to Phenomenology. London/New York (Routledge), 2000.
Morick, Harold (ed.): Challenges to Empiricism. Indianapolis (Hackett Publishing Company), 1980)
Müller-Lauter, Wolfgang: "On Judging in a World of Becoming"; in: Babich (ed.): *Nietzsche, Epistemology, and Philosophy of Science*, (loc. cit.)
Müller-Lauter, Wolfgang: Heidegger und Nietzsche: Nietzsche-Interpretationen III. Berlin, New York (Walter de Gruyter), 2000.
Müller-Lauter, Wolfgang: Nietzsche: His Philosophy of Contradictions and the Contradictions of His Philosophy. Translated by D. J.

Parent. Urbana and Chicago (University of Illinois Press), 1999.

Müller-Lauter, Wolfgang: Über Freiheit und Chaos: Nietzsche-Interpretationen II. Berlin, New York (Walter de Gruyter), 1999.

Müller-Lauter, Wolfgang: Über Werden und Wille zur Macht: Nietzsche Interpretationen I. Berlin/New York (Walter de Gruyter), 1999.

Musil, Robert: The Man Without Qualities. Translated by S. Wilkins & B. Pike. London (Picador), 1997.

Nehamas, Alexander: "The Eternal Recurrence" in Conway (ed.) *Nietzsche*, loc. cit.

Nehamas, Alexander: "The Genealogy of Genealogy," in Schacht: *Nietzsche, Genealogy, Morality* (loc. cit.).

Nehamas, Alexander: Nietzsche: Life as Literature. Cambridge, Mass. (Harvard University Press), 1985.

Norris, Christopher: Paul de Man: Deconstruction and the Critique of Aesthetic Ideology. London, New York (Routledge), 1988

Norris, Christopher: What's Wrong with Postmodernism: Critical Theory and the Ends of Philosophy. Baltimore (Johns Hopkins University Press), 1990.

Nussbaum, Martha C.: "Pity and Mercy: Nietzsche's Stoicism," in Schacht: *Nietzsche, Genealogy, Morality* (loc. cit.).

Olivier, Abraham: "Nietzsche and Neurology," in *Nietzsche-Studien,* Band 32, 2003. Berlin, New York (Walter de Gruyter), 2003), pp. 124-141.

Parkes, Graham: Composing the Soul: Reaches of Nietzsche's Psychology. Chicago (The University of Chicago Press), 1994.

Patai, D. & Corral, W. H. (eds.): Theory's Empire: An Anthology of Dissent. New York (Columbia University Press), 2005.

Patton, H. J.: Kant's Metaphysic of Experience, vol. I & II. New York (The Macmillan Company) 1936.

Penrose, Roger: The Emperor's New Mind: Concerning Computers, Minds, and the Laws of Physics. New York (Vintage), 1990.

Perelman, Ch. & Olbrechts-Tyteca, L.: The New Rhetoric: A Treatise of Argumentation. Translated by J. Wilkinson & P. Weaver. Notre Dame (The University of Notre Dame Press), 1969.

Plato: The Republic of Plato. Translated by F. M. Cornford. Oxford (Oxford University Press), 1945.

Poellner, Peter: "Causation and Force in Nietzsche" in Babech (ed.): *Nietzsche, Epistemology, and Philosophy of Science*, (loc. cit.).

Poellner, Peter: Nietzsche and Metaphysics. Oxford (Oxford University Press), 1995.
Pothast, Ulrich: Die eigentlich metaphysische Tätigkeit: Über Schopenhauers Ästhetic und ihre Anwendung durch Samuel Beckett. Frankfurt (Suhrkamp), 1982.
Powell, Thomas: Kant's Theory of Self-Consciousness. Oxford (Clarendon Press), 1990.
Prigogine, Ilya: The End of Certainty: Time, Chaos, and the New Laws of Nature. New York, London (The Free Press), 1996.
Raffnsøe, Sverre: Nietzsches *Genealogie der Moral*. Paderborn (Wilhelm Fink Verlag), 2007.
Ragland-Sullivan: Jacques Lacan and the Philosophy of Psychoanalysis. Urbana/Chicago (University of Illinois Press), 1987.
Richardson, John: Nietzsche's System. Oxford (Oxford University Press), 1996.
Richardson, John: Nietzsche's New Darwinism. Oxford (Oxford University Press), 2004
Ricoeur, Paul: Freud and Philosophy: An Essay on Interpretation. Translated by D. Savage. New Haven (Yale University Press), 1970.
Ricoeur, Paul: Oneself as Another. Translated by K. Blamey. Chicago (Chicago University Press), 1992.
Rittelmeyer, Friedrich: Friedrich Nietzsche und das Erkenntnisproblem. Elibron Classics.2005.
Rorty, Richard: Consequences of Pragmatism. Minneapolis (University of Minnesota Press), 1982.
Rorty, Richard: Contingency, Irony, and Solidarity. Cambridge (Cambridge University Press), 1989)
Russell, Bertrand: A History of Western Philosophy. New York, London (Simon & Schuster), 1972.
Salaquarda, Jörg: "Nietzsche und Lange," in *Nietzsche Studien* 7. Berlin, New York (Walter de Gruyter), 1978.
Saussure, Ferdinand de: Cours de Linguistique Générale. Edited by C. Bally & A Sechehaye. Paris (Payot), 1975.
Saussure, Ferdinand de: Course in General Linguistics. Translated by Wade Baskin. New York (McGraw Hill), 1966.
Schacht, Richard (ed.): Nietzsche, Genealogy, Morality: Essays on Nietzsche's 'On the Genealogy of Morals'. Berkeley (University of California Press), 1994.
Schacht, Richard: "Introduction," in Schacht: *Nietzsche, Genealogy, Morality* (loc. cit.).

Schacht, Richard: "Of Morals and *Menschen,*" in Schacht: *Nietzsche, Genealogy, Morality* (loc. cit.).
Schacht, Richard: Nietzsche. London, New York (Routledge), 1983.
Scheier, Claus-Arthur: "The Rationale of Nietzsche's *Genealogy of Morals,*" in Schacht: *Nietzsche, Genealogy, Morality* (loc. cit.).
Schelling, Thomas: "The Mind as a Consuming Organ". in Elster (ed.): *The Multiple Self* (loc. cit.).
Schlimgen, Erwin: Nietzsches Theorie des Bewußtseins. Berlin/New York (Walter de Gruyter), 1998.
Schmidt, Alfred: "Schopenhauer und der Materialismus" in Spierling (ed.): Materialien.
Schopenhauer, Arthur: Sämtliche Werke Bd. 1-5. Ed.: W. von Löhneysen. Frankfurt am Main (Suhrkamp Verlag), 1960.
Schopenhauer, Arthur: "Vom Verhältnis zwischen Subjekt und Objekt" in Spierling (ed.): Materialien.
Schopenhauer, Arthur: Die Welt als Wille und Vorstellung I, in SW 1.
Schopenhauer, Arthur: Die Welt als Wille und Vorstellung II, in SW 2.
Schopenhauer, Arthur: On the Fourfold Root of the Principle of Sufficient Reason. Translation E. F. J. Payne. La Salle (Open Court), 1974.
Schopenhauer, Arthur: Parerga und Paralipomena II, in SW 5.
Schopenhauer, Arthur: The World as Will and Representation, vol. I & II. Translated by E. F. J. Payne. New York (Dover Publications), 1969.
Schopenhauer, Arthur: Über das Sehn und die Farben, in SW 3.
Schopenhauer, Arthur: Über die vierfache Wurzel des Satzes vom zureichenden Grunde, in SW 3.
Schrift, Alan D.: Nietzsche and the Question of Interpretation: Between Hermeneutics and Deconstruction. New York/London (Routledge), 1990.
Schwenger, Peter: "Words and the Murder of the Thing"; in Brown (ed.): *Things* (loc. cit.)
Sedgwick, Peter R. (ed.): Nietzsche: A Critical Reader. Oxford (Blackwell), 1995.
Shakespeare, William: Hamlet. Edited by G. R. Hibbard. Oxford (Oxford University Press), 1994.
Shakespeare, William: The Merry Wives of Windsor. Edited by G. R. Hibbard. Oxford (Oxford University Press), 1994.
Sherover, Charles M. (ed.): The Human Experience of Time. Evanston (Northwestern University Press), 2001.

Simmel, George: Schopenhauer und Nietzsche. In Gesamtausgabe Bd. 10. Frankfurt am Main (Suhrkamp Verlag), 1907/2000.
Simon, Josef (ed.): Zeichen und Interpretation. Frankfurt am Main (Suhrkamp Verlag), 1994.
Simon, Josef: "Grammatik und Wahrheit," in *Nietzsche Studien* 1. Berlin, New York (Walter de Gruyter), 1972.
Simon, Josef: "Die Krise des Wahrheitsbegriffs als Krise der Metaphysik," in *Nietzsche Studien* 18. Berlin, New York (Walter de Gruyter), 1989.
Simon, Josef: "Zeichenkunst und Interpretationskunst," in Stegmaier (ed.): *Zeichen-Kunst* (loc. cit.).
Simon, Josef: "Zeichenphilosophie und Transcendentalphilosophie," in Simon (ed.) *Zeichen und Interpretation*.
Sleinis, E. E.: Nietzsche's Revaluation of Values: A Study in Strategies. Urbana/Chicago (The University of Illinois Press), 1994.
Sloterdijk, Peter: Thinker on Stage: Nietzsche's Materialism. Translation by J. O. Daniel. Minneapolis (University of Minnesota Press), 1989.
Small, Robin: Nietzsche in Context. Aldershot (Ashgate), 2001.
Soll, Ivan: "Nietzsche on Cruelty, Asceticism, and the Failure of Hedonism," in Schacht: *Nietzsche, Genealogy, Morality* (loc. cit.).
Soll, Ivan: "Reflections on Recurrence: A Reexamination of Nietzsche's Doctrine, Die Ewige Widerkehr des Gleichen," in Conway (ed.) *Nietzsche* (loc. cit.)
Solms, Mark & Turnbull, Oliver: The Brain and the Inner World: An Introduction to the Neuroscience of Subjective Experience. New York (Other Press), 2002.
Solms, Mark: "Freud Returns" in *Scientific American* vol. 290, Number 5. May 2004.
Solomon, Robert (ed.): Nietzsche: A collection of Critical Essays. Notre Dame (University of Notre Dame Press), 1980.
Solomon, Robert: "One Hundred Years of Ressentiment: Nietzsche's *Genealogy of Morals,*" in Schacht: *Nietzsche, Genealogy, Morality* (loc. cit.)
Spiekerman, Klaus: "Nietzsche and Critical Theory"; in: Babich (ed.): *Nietzsche, Epistemology, and Philosophy of Science*, (loc. cit.).
Spiekermann, Klaus: Naturwissenschaft als subjektlose Macht: Nietzsches Kritik physikalischer Grundkonzepte. Berlin, New York (Walter de Gruyter), 1992.

Spierling, Volker (ed.): Materialien zu Schopenhauers 'Die Welt als Wille und Vorstellung'. Frankfurt am Main (Suhrkamp), 1984.
Spierling, Volker: "Die Drehwende der Moderne. Schopenhauer zwischen Skeptizismus und Dogmatismus," in Spierling (ed.): *Materialien.*
Spierling, Volker: Arthur Schopenhauer. Zur Einführung. Hamburg (Junius), 2002.
Spierling, Volker: Schopenhauer ABC. Leipzig (Reclam), 2003.
Spir, Afrikan: Forschung nach der Gewissheit in der Erkenntniss der Wirklichkeit. Leibniz (Förster & Findel), 1869.
Stack, George: Lange and Nietzsche. Berlin, New York (Walter de Gruyter), 1983.
Stambaugh, Joan: "Thoughts on the Innocence of Becoming," in Conway (ed.) *Nietzsche* (loc. cit.)
Stambaugh, Joan: The Other Nietzsche. Albany (State University of New York Press), 1994.
Stambaugh, Joan: The Problem of Time in Nietzsche. Translated by J. F. Humphrey. Lewisburg: (Backwell University Press), 1987.
Staten, Henry: Nietzsche's Voice. Ithaca (Cornell University Press), 1990.
Stegmaier, Werner (ed.): Kultur der Zeichen. Frankfurt am Main (Suhrkamp Verlag), 1999.
Stegmaier, Werner (ed.): Zeichen-Kunst. Frankfurt am Main (Suhrkamp Verlag), 1999.
Stegmaier, Werner: "Darwin, Darwinismus, Nietzsche. Zum Problem der Evolution," in *Nietzsche Studien* 16. Berlin, New York (Walter de Gruyter), 1987.
Stegmaier, Werner: "Einleitung," in Stegmaier (ed.): *Kultur der Zeichen.*
Stegmaier, Werner: "Nietzsches Neubestimmung der Wahrheit" in *Nietzsche Studien* 14. Berlin, New York (Walter de Gruyter), 1988.
Stegmaier, Werner: "Weltabkürzungskunst. Orientierung durch Zeichen," in Josef Simon (ed.): *Zeichen und Interpretation* (loc. cit.)
Stegmaier, Werner: Interpretationen: Hauptwerke der Philosophie von Kant bis Nietzsche. Stuttgart (Philipp Reclam) 1997.
Stegmaier, Werner: Nietzsches 'Genealogie der Moral'. Darmstadt (Wissenschaftlische Buchgesellschaft), 1994.
Stegmaier, Werner: Philosophie der Orientierung. Berlin, New York (Walter de Gruyter), 2008.
Strachey, James: "Editor's Introduction" to *Project for a Scientific Psychology*, SE 1.

Strawson, P. F.: The Bounds of Sense: An Essay on Kant's *Critique of Pure Reason*. London, New York (Routledge), 1966.
Strong, Tracy B.: Friedrich Nietzsche and the Politics of Transfiguration. Urbana/Chicago (University of Illinois Press), 2000.
Tallis, Reymond: Not Saussure. New York (St. Martin's Press), 1995.
Tetens, Holm: Kants "Kritik der reinen Vernunft": Ein Systematischer Kommentar. Stuttgart (Reclam), 2006.
Tetens, Holm: Geist, Gehirn, Maschine: Philosophische Versuche über ihren Zusammenhang. Stuttgart (Philipp Reclam), 1994.
Vaihinger, Hans: Nietzsche als Philosoph. Porta Westfalica (Gerhard Bleick), 2002.
Vattimo, Gianni: Nietzsche: An Introduction. Translated by N. Martin. Stanford (Stanford University Press), 2001.
Volkelt, Johannes: "Arthur Schopenhauers Persönlichkeit, seine Lehre, sein Glaube" in Spierling (ed.): *Materialien*.
Vollmer, Gerhard: Biophilosophie: Stuttgart (Philipp Reclam), 1995
Wandel, Fritz: Bewusstsein und Wille: Dialektik als Movens für Nietzsche. Bonn (Bouvier Verlag), 1972.
Watkins, Eric: Kant and the Metaphysics of Causality. Cambridge (Cambridge University Press), 2005.
Watson, James: The Double Helix: A Personal Account of the Discovery of the Structure of the DNA. Touchstone (New York) 1968/2001.
Wheeler, Samuel C.: Deconstruction as Analytic Philosophy. Stanford: Stanford University Press), 2000.
White, Alan: Within Nietzsche's Labyrinth. New York/London (Routledge), 1999.
White, Richard: "The Return of the Master: An Interpretation of Nietzsche's *Genealogy of Morals*," in Schacht: *Nietzsche, Genealogy, Morality* (loc. cit.).
Wilcox, John T.: Truth and Value in Nietzsche: A Study of His Metaethics and Epistemology. Lanham (University Press of America), 1982.
Wilden, Anthony: "The Function of Language in Psychoanalysis," in *The Language of the Self*. Baltimore (The Johns Hopkins University Press), 1981.
Wilson, Fred: "Mill on Psychology," in *The Cambridge Companion to Mill*, edited by J. Skorupsky. Cambridge (Cambridge University Press), 1998.
Wittgenstein, Ludwig: On Certainty. New York (Harper Torchbooks), 1969.

Wittgenstein, Ludwig: Philosophische Untersuchungen/Philosophical Investigations. Oxford (Blackwell), 1997. Re-issued 2nd edition.
Wollheim, Richard: Freud. London (Fontana/Collins), 1971.
Wood, David: The Deconstruction of Time. Evanston (Northwestern University Press), 2001.
Wundt, Wilhelm: Grundriss der Psychologie. Leipzig (VDM Verlag), 1896.
Zöllner, Johann: Transcendental Physics. (Kessinger reprint edition) 1881.

INDEX

Subject Index

A priori judgments, 304, 309-10
Abbreviation, 17, 74, 115, 154-55, 160, 208, 211, 456
Absolute flow of time, 485
Absolute other, 15
Absolute time, 502
Active forgetfulness, 372
Active, 58, 92, 133, 160, 221-222, 225-227, 297, 366, 369-374, 380-387, 393, 395, 470, 516
Activity, 2, 31, 62, 76, 83, 88-91, 123-125, 135, 140, 149-150, 154, 158-162, 172-173, 203, 219, 231, 235, 243, 248-250, 259, 265, 272, 293-295, 303, 310, 313, 318, 332, 345, 363, 374, 376, 386, 418, 420-423, 429, 435-37, 453, 472, 487, 491, 516, 520, 524-526, 536, 542-543
Actor, 149-151, 198, 221, 293-295, 313, 400, 402, 516
Actor-action, 150, 294
Ad hoc amendment, 331
Aesthetic attitude, 27, 117, 445, 491, 492, 493
Aesthetic pleasure, 27
Aestheticism, 124
After-the-fact, 58, 212-13, 243, 302, 347-48, 518
Aggressive confused subject, 331, 416, 431
Amor Fati, 468-470, 475, 477
Analysis of Sensations, 45, 246, 253, 508
Analytic Philosophy, 8, 33, 53, 104, 106-07, 110, 116, 127, 134, 199, 407, 584, 591
Analytic, 13, 53, 303-05, 372
Anarchism, 24, 386-387, 521
Anglo-Saxon philosophers, 12
An-sich, 278, 456, 504
Antennas, 9, 263, 266, 318
Anthropomorphism, 16, 52, 63, 69, 95, 100, 121, 198, 314, 514-16
Anti-cathexis, 335
Anticipatory, 399, 498, 500

Anti-narcissism, 468-470
Anti-Semitism, 361-362
Appearance for-us, 16
Appearances, 5, 8, 15, 39, 41, 45-49, 53-54, 93, 100, 106, 117, 124, 131-33, 138, 146, 175, 178-180, 183, 192, 293-295, 311, 349, 364, 482-483, 574
Arbitrariness, 61, 135, 210
Arbitrary sensible sign, 244
Aristocratic cells, 269, 325
Aristotelian, 69, 306, 328, 349, 370
Ascetic ideal, 407-414, 417-418
Ascetic priest, 407-409, 413-414, 417-418, 430
Assertive configuration, 358-360, 376, 380, 384-387, 396, 398, 424, 429
Assertively configured subject, 394
Authoritarian voices, 20
Auto-affection, 329, 470, 551-52, 529
Becoming being, 478
Becoming What One Is, 476
Becoming, 15-16, 48, 76, 100, 112-16, 118, 120, 125, 128-37, 142-150, 201, 207, 209, 220, 232, 251-252, 261-62, 273, 278-88, 299, 313-14, 319, 326, 328, 342, 366, 381-82, 408, 439, 444, 446, 457-61, 464-70, 472, 474, 477-82, 485-89, 492, 495-98, 503-04, 518, 522, 530, 560
Beholding the sublime, 479
Being guilty, 55, 391, 393
Being-there, 482
Big Bang, 66, 70-71, 252, 301-02, 441
Biological subject, 312
Biological-linguistic subject, 231, 282
British Empiricists, 452, 454
Calculating a reader response, 547
Cartesian, 18, 128, 153, 156-65, 169-76, 179, 182, 349, 508
Castration threat, 533
Castration, 550
Categorical imperative, 26, 216, 219, 389-91, 476, 506
Categorical imperator, 219, 391
Categories, 38, 42, 57-59, 70, 195, 284-86, 293-97, 303-13, 524

Cathect, 21-24, 255, 264-72, 289, 318, 322, 333-37, 376-77, 399, 424, 463, 466
Cathexis, 264-68, 270-72, 277, 287, 320, 333-34, 375
Causality, 38-43, 57, 70, 106, 122, 147, 213, 243, 278, 292-97, 300, 308-10, 342, 345-46, 451, 453, 459, 462, 514, 515, 591.
Cause and effect, 301
Cause/Causes, 37, 42, 56, 61, 72-73, 79, 89, 122, 148-60, 167-73, 184, 194-95, 197-201, 208-13, 219, 243-44, 292-317, 337, 342-47, 351-56, 361, 364, 370, 382, 390, 416, 424, 433-34, 448, 453-60, 495-99, 513-21, 538-39, 553
Cause-effect, 42, 122, 148-52, 156-58, 170-71, 184, 197, 199-201, 208-09, 294, 296, 300-05, 308, 312-13, 342, 351, 355, 382, 513-14
Celebration of cruelty, 395
Chaos Theory, 6
Chaos, 5, 6, 15-16, 21-22, 91, 112, 121-23, 128, 134, 138-43, 202, 233, 242, 249, 251, 270, 273, 276, 278, 283-84, 287-89, 291, 296, 314, 322-23, 326-29, 332, 372, 378, 386-88, 466, 473, 481, 490, 537, 556
Chaosmos, 288
Characterize/characterization, 53, 169, 177, 186, 208, 262, 316, 319, 324, 370, 380, 389, 427, 454-55, 528-529, 535-38, 554, 556-57
Christian, 9, 24, 31, 35-36, 60, 64, 105, 156, 235-36, 251, 282, 335, 361, 364, 390, 402-03, 409, 576
Christianity, 24, 132, 213-14, 227, 361, 365, 390, 410-11, 417, 424, 428, 432, 576
Chronological order, 453
Chronological reversal, 58, 300-302, 345, 355, 453, 499
Chronologische Umdrehung, 345, 453-54, 478, 499
Circular confusion, 373, 376, 395, 427
Civilization, 396-97, 517, 578
Clever animal, 29, 37-38, 95
Clusters of signification, 20
Cogito, 163-67, 171-76, 197, 310, 508-09
Cognition, 7, 10-12, 20, 32-33, 38, 160, 178, 185, 218, 235-39, 355

Cognitive apparatuses, 347, 351
Cognitive Science, 344
Commander, 19, 24, 162, 207-09, 220-21, 336, 377, 394, 424
Communication, 18-20, 52, 69-70, 139, 156, 171, 189-92, 217-24, 350, 387, 460
Communicative action, 52-53, 92-93, 124, 191, 323, 387
Concept/conceptualization, 3-4, 7-8, 11-14, 25, 33-35, 39, 42, 47-54, 59-60, 63, 73-88, 92-95, 100-01, 117, 141-42, 147, 158, 172-74, 177-78, 185, 190, 195-208, 213-14, 219-21, 235, 237, 274, 284-87, 292, 297, 299, 302-05, 309, 314, 319-22, 338, 354-55, 392-93, 408-10, 415, 425, 428, 444, 455, 467, 471-73, 482, 491, 511, 542
Concept-formation, 75-76
Concept-structures, 8
Confused-aggression, 415
Confused-aggressive subject, 23, 334, 415
Conscious subject, 490, 505
Consciousness, 23, 27, 43, 67, 95, 109, 112-16, 136-37, 140, 144, 148, 153, 160-62, 176-78, 184-85, 191-98, 203, 206, 211-13, 232-37, 246-48, 252-53, 258-62, 265-67, 270, 277-79, 282, 289-90, 302-03, 306, 314-18, 322, 326, 332, 343-50, 355, 380-85, 396, 419-22, 429, 439, 446, 453-60, 467, 484-504, 510, 525, 534-35, 537
Conservation of energy, 249, 251
Constative, 2, 493
Contact-barrier, 254-58, 263
Contradiction, 13, 55, 105-08, 111, 197, 216, 227, 232, 287, 327, 330-33, 376, 389, 401, 411, 431, 466, 470, 476, 521, 527, 556, 558
Conventionally determined signified, 324
Correspondence theory of truth, 12, 14, 54, 92
Cosmos, 118-20, 288, 441, 501
Counter-ideals, 409, 412
Creditor, 392-93
Creditor-debtor, 393
Criticism of morality, 325
Critique of ideology, 21, 157-58, 228, 325
Cruelty, 223, 233, 379, 391-96, 401-06, 423, 428
Darwinism, 351, 587

Dead metaphor, 65, 71
Death-drive, 259, 334, 398, 406, 426, 495
Debt/deptor, 229, 383, 391-93
Debtor-creditor relationship, 392
De-cathected, 264, 371, 376-77, 424, 466
Deconstruction, 1-3, 7-8, 132, 158, 235, 342-44, 454, 496, 574, 586-88, 591-92
Deconstructionist, 1-3, 52, 343-44
Deconstructive method, 342
Deed, 43, 122, 150, 161, 172, 184, 200-04, 294-95, 303, 313, 365, 375-77, 416, 453, 465, 470
Defense-mechanism, 432, 434
Defensive layer, 258, 288
Defensive retaliation, 422, 430, 433-34
Delayed perception, 452
Demasculinized, 369
Der Wille zur Wahrheit, 109
Derridian, 3, 382
Dialogical structure, 19
Dionysian, 436-37, 484, 553, 555
Dionysus and Apollo, 555
Disintegration, 337-88, 421, 536-37, 550, 553
Dividuum/Dividuality, 19, 157, 191-92, 214-22, 424
Doer, 122, 150, 161, 172, 184, 200-01, 204, 294-96, 300, 313, 365, 465, 514-16
Double mirroring, 458
Double nihilism, 410-11
Double-deed, 295
Economics of silence, 546-47
Ecstatic, 493
Ego-cluster, 18-20, 239, 264, 267-70, 280-81, 291, 314, 318, 322, 325-27, 339, 370
Ego-configuration, 370
Ego-consciousness, 19, 196
Emotional word, 314
Empirical subject, 176, 186, 200, 203
Empiricist, 453
Empty perception, 253, 278, 457, 488, 495, 506
Entity/identity, 283, 313
Environment, 121, 350-55, 463, 479
Envy, 159, 335, 339, 367, 375, 388, 390, 414-15, 421, 485
Epistemological attitude, 445, 492
Epochè, 8, 10
Eros, 398, 405

Es gibt, 146-48, 204, 233, 374, 414, 425, 466, 469
Essential human in-essentiality, 363
Eternal Recurrence, 25-28, 74-75, 260, 435-47, 453, 464, 474, 479-83, 492-93, 503-04, 579, 584-86
Eternal-recurrence-subject, 28, 504, 506
Euphemistic re-labeling, 401
European man, 24, 390
Evolutionary process, 50, 119, 311-13, 353
Ewig Weibliche, 370
Ewigen Wiederkunft, 6
Excess of feeling, 422-26, 431
Existential subject, 18, 200
Existentialism, 487, 495, 506
Exploiting suffering, 407, 413
External reality, 60, 261, 288-89, 322, 499
Extra-real, 132
Facilitating passages, 144, 255-58, 264
Facilitation, 255-56, 264-65, 318, 481
Faculty, 114, 308-10, 383-87
Falsification, 22, 90, 104-08, 111, 115, 119, 122, 126, 133-34, 147-50, 160, 276, 287, 293, 327, 353, 368, 418
Falsification-thesis, 104-08, 111
Falsify/Falsifying, 16-17, 22, 104-08, 111-16, 119-21, 128-29, 131, 144-46, 149, 195, 258, 276-77, 284-88, 298, 327, 347, 494
Familiar, 19, 22, 41, 44, 62, 100, 138-40, 148, 159, 164, 200, 203, 210, 214, 217, 245, 297-99, 328, 330, 345-46, 354-55, 436, 451, 454-55, 500, 541, 555
Familiarization/Familiarize, 100, 450-52, 455
Familiarizing the Strange, 450-52
Fanaticization of the depressed individual, 424
Fanaticization, 423-24, 427
Fantasizing unity, 536
Fascism, 337, 361, 427-28, 579
Fatalism, 363, 475
Feeling of guilt, 391, 424
Feminine woman, 367-69, 533
Femininity, 366-69, 388
Feminism, 24
Fiction, 67, 117, 125-26, 134-35, 146-47, 156-57, 189, 194-95, 199-01, 227, 233, 287, 357-60, 382, 410, 463, 516, 528

Fictional/Fictionalism, 18, 32, 67, 90, 124-25, 147, 151, 154, 157, 186, 194, 198, 486
Filter, 134, 288
Filtration-apparatus, 17, 112, 248, 509
Fluctuation of meaning, 322, 338, 385, 407
Fluidity of meaning, 321
Forces, 13, 38, 48, 55, 60, 76, 99, 118-21, 141, 145, 152, 201-04, 225, 232-33, 251-52, 269-70, 283, 294-96, 299, 327, 329, 360, 366, 374, 378, 380, 395-96, 410, 417-18, 426, 463-71, 515
Forgetfulness, 82, 102, 366, 371-373, 380-89, 415, 420, 437, 484, 487
Formal conscience, 220-21, 377-78, 391, 396, 424
Fort-da game, 533
For-us, 17, 22, 41, 48, 56, 60, 77, 98, 245, 274, 313, 353
Fragmentation, 157, 197, 536
Fragmented self, 470, 540, 562
Fragmented subject, 4, 17, 20, 196, 203, 227-28, 238, 239, 335, 370
Frenetic defense, 23, 332-37
Fundamental Ignorance, 540, 561
Gaze, the, 27-28, 61, 68, 152, 288, 387, 485, 489-90, 509, 551
Genealogy, 9, 450
German nationalism/German nationalist, 361-62
Germans/Germany, 10, 333, 337, 361
Gesammtbewußtsein, 252
Gesamtzustand, 317
Gliding over existence, 491
God, 24, 70, 121, 128, 164, 166, 169-70, 214, 219, 252, 301, 304-05, 311, 338, 354, 365, 390-91, 394, 399, 402, 409, 416, 424, 440, 520, 533, 544, 553
Good and bad, 21, 290-91, 506
Good and evil, 374, 400-03, 490
Good will, 119, 364, 401
Grammatical subject, 18, 157, 173, 200
Grammatology, 7-8, 541, 575
Guilt/Guilty, 10, 389-99, 402, 416, 423-25, 551
Hallucination/Hallucinatory, 21, 260-67, 270-71, 277-79, 289-91, 329, 534-35
Happiness, 333, 517
Hate-objects, 24, 333-34, 337, 425

Hatred, 21-24, 153, 203, 228, 289, 333, 336-37, 377, 402, 414
Hedonistic, 524
Herd, 20, 219-20, 236-28, 358-60, 390, 415, 418, 421-23, 451, 518, 519
Hermeneutic, 4
Hetero-biography, 540
Honesty, 52, 78, 79
Horizontal superficiality, 362
Hostile object, 290, 316-17, 334, 500, 538
Human ground, 17, 113-16, 128-29, 134, 140-45, 147, 298, 351, 353
Human in-essentiality, 362
Human language, 68, 353
Human optics, 12, 16, 114, 353, 494
Human perspective, 71, 114, 121
Humanize/Humanization, 98, 100, 122, 149-51, 292-301, 313, 450-52
Hyper-cathect, 23-24, 334-37, 371-76, 388, 399
Hyper-reality, 116, 132-34, 138, 143-52, 278, 295. 492, 495
Hyper-surface, 27
I think, 18, 52, 150, 152-58, 159, 160-73, 177-87, 204, 227, 232, 509, 545
Idea as Ideal, 411
Idea, 5, 10, 24, 26, 28, 32-33, 37, 48, 52, 58-61, 80-82, 86, 89, 93, 95, 103, 105, 115, 123, 141, 149-51, 159, 162, 164, 172-75, 192, 197, 202-04, 212, 215-19, 222, 228-33, 236, 248, 254-56, 260, 267, 271, 281, 289, 293-98, 318, 322, 326, 330, 335-36, 346-47, 352, 355, 359, 375, 382, 410-11, 414, 418, 437, 439-41, 446, 453, 463-66, 474, 480-81, 484, 501-05, 508, 511, 516-17, 523, 529, 532
Ideal as such, 409-12
Ideal, 193, 409-14, 510, 526
Idealism, 8, 12, 39, 56, 98, 123, 126-28, 179, 291, 342-55, 361, 462, 571
Idealization, 367-70, 514
Idealization of the woman, 533
Ideational representation, 528
Identical cases, 117, 282, 451
Ideological exploitation, 427
Ideological subject, 24, 157-58, 239-40, 337
Ideologically emancipated subject, 24, 228, 325, 429

Ideologically infected subject, 24, 215, 228, 325
Ideologue, 24-25, 157-58, 225, 228-30, 240, 325-38, 414-16, 425-27
Ideology, 5, 23-25, 157, 214, 225-30, 239-40, 325, 336-37, 403, 410, 417, 427-32, 484, 535, 586
Illusion, 12-16, 32, 50-55, 77, 92-95, 100, 103, 108, 124, 147, 182, 226, 310, 429, 439, 489, 514, 531
Image, 1, 3, 10, 14-16, 34, 42, 55, 58-62, 70, 74, 77, 79-82, 87, 94-96, 122, 137, 141, 147, 182-83, 196, 198-99, 241-45, 255-65, 271-76, 282-87, 299-301, 314-20, 333, 341, 351-52, 371, 393-95, 410-11, 430, 445-49, 458-62, 470-71, 474, 487, 497, 528-32, 537, 542, 548, 553, 561-63
Imaginary Repair, 336
I-me distinction, 19
Immorality, 364, 402
Impressions, 17, 41-43, 56-59, 77, 112-16, 120, 131, 136-48, 162, 174-76, 232, 234, 242-48, 253, 257-59, 262, 273-74, 278, 283-84, 297, 305, 315-16, 319, 322, 345-49, 377, 381-82, 399, 453-62, 496-509, 513, 517
Incorporation, 286, 436, 487, 505, 536-37
In-decidability, 1, 7
Indication of reality, 267-68, 271-72, 289
Indifference to difference, 471
Individuum, 157, 191-92, 214-16, 394
Infinite receptivity, 253
Infinite retention, 253
Inhibited wish-fulfillment, 267
In-itself, 11-18, 28, 32, 36, 40-73, 93-94, 98-99, 104-06, 110, 117-32, 140, 145-46, 173, 184-86, 200, 205, 221, 241, 243, 253, 292, 299, 301, 311, 316, 320, 329, 349-53, 360, 364, 387, 459, 462, 493, 501, 511, 534, 536, 581
Inner experience, 22, 276, 327, 345, 349, 354-55, 453, 462, 499
Inner experience, 345, 455
Inner flow of time, 496-97, 501, 502
Inner interpretation-machine, 468
Inner life, 17, 19-20, 176, 191-92, 214, 218-19, 314, 322-23, 327, 355-56
Inner perspectivism, 22, 326
Inner processes, 315

Inner sense, 319, 354, 482, 483
Inner world, 22, 195, 213, 223, 232, 265, 277, 280-81, 316, 327, 329, 345-47, 354-56, 396, 453
Inner-mental, 21-22, 26, 28, 154, 158, 162, 175-76, 178, 182-83, 212, 232, 239, 258, 280, 289, 302, 322, 328-30, 352, 370, 400, 425, 445, 478, 501
Insincere promise, 476
Institution of Guilt, 389
Intention, 6, 15, 30-32, 67-68, 80, 84, 122, 149, 151, 171, 179, 184, 200, 204-05, 214, 216, 226, 293-303, 365, 370, 377, 434, 476, 490, 500, 526
Intentional harmlessness, 365
Intentional object, 9
Internal reality, 261, 289, 322
Internalization of guilt, 393
Internalization, 10, 19, 192, 221-223, 396-99, 504-05, 521
Internalizing the eternalized external, 491
Interpretability, 35, 87-91, 95
Interpretation, 3, 11-13, 24-27, 31, 35, 41-44, 48-49, 54, 57-61, 74, 79, 83, 86-91, 99, 100, 105, 110, 123-27, 131, 134-35, 147, 154, 160-61, 196-98, 202, 205-06, 232, 243, 251, 262, 269, 280, 290, 297, 300-01, 305, 310-12, 320-25, 328, 335-36, 339-45, 352-55, 362, 367, 371, 382, 388, 404, 409-10, 416, 418, 423-24, 429, 438, 440-55, 461-64, 468-69, 472, 474-79, 487, 495, 500-01, 511, 518, 524, 535, 555, 560
Interpretation-machine, 468, 469
Interpretation-process, 27, 443-45, 450, 462, 474, 479, 501
Interpretative community, 91
Interpretive pressure, 298
Interpretive processes, 22, 290, 438
Intrinsic Irrationality, 330
It thinks, 160-61, 172, 486
I-you, 19
Jew, 362
Joy, 28, 119, 133, 210, 223, 363, 390, 394, 396, 405-06, 436-82, 492-93, 519, 529
Judea/Judaic, 365, 379
Judgment, 52-55, 62, 72-74, 149, 159, 177-82, 205, 218-22, 261, 282, 284, 292-96, 303, 305-13, 319, 346, 390, 453, 455, 536

Kantian, 11-13, 30, 33, 36, 41-49, 56-57, 60, 67, 70, 72, 76, 93, 99, 104, 107, 133, 153, 158, 178, 186-87, 193-94, 211, 214, 241-43, 246, 278, 298, 303, 307-08, 311, 390, 442, 456, 480, 492, 574, 580, 583
Kantianism, 29-44, 56, 98, 241, 245
Kinetic and potential energy, 249
Kinetic energy, 250-51
Knowledge, 30, 36, 73, 94, 103, 147, 151, 231, 282-84, 296, 307, 347, 356, 435, 450-51, 510, 572-73, 577, 579
Knowledge, 5, 7, 10, 15, 18, 23, 26-41, 44, 49, 52-53, 67-86, 93, 95-96, 100-13, 117, 120-27, 132-35, 146, 154, 159-60, 168, 173-74, 177, 179, 184, 194, 203, 209, 236, 241, 247, 269, 280, 284-92, 298, 300-12, 322, 328, 332, 336, 343-46, 354, 357, 388, 401, 437-38, 444, 451, 461, 465, 467, 480, 488, 501, 505, 536, 542, 550, 558-562
Knowledge-formation, 305
Knowledge-production, 33, 34
Ku Klux Klan, 337
Lacanians, 529
Lack of truth, 368, 370
Language, 2-3, 7, 9, 12-26, 31-33, 49-51, 55-75, 80-81, 84, 87-88, 95, 102-03, 108, 113, 116, 118, 123-26, 133-53, 157-61, 166, 168, 172-73, 189-92, 200-04, 209, 211, 226-27, 237-39, 261, 268, 270, 274-76, 280-81, 290-96, 299, 302-03, 306, 313, 318-28, 334-38, 343, 345, 348-55, 437, 450, 455-56, 460-61, 463, 466, 471-72, 478-79, 484-89, 495, 501, 513, 533, 538, 541-42, 551-57
Language-dependent, 349, 350
Language-independent reality, 15, 68, 116, 142, 348-50, 488, 501
Language-metaphysics, 200, 353
Language-system, 19, 350
Law, 122, 385-89, 408, 426-27, 432
Life-affirmation, 418
Linguistic processes, 22, 290
Linguistic representation, 316, 538
Linguistic sign, 34, 61-62, 82, 88, 142-43, 244, 327
Linguistication/Linguisticize, 15, 34, 314, 329-31, 416

Linguistics, 4, 7, 53, 61, 116, 118, 138, 140, 141, 148, 187-92, 274-75, 281, 321-23, 572, 587
Literal and metaphorical language, 14, 67
Literary Criticism, 540
Living metaphor, 65, 71
Living-the-world-as-hyperreality, 485, 489
Logic, 53, 58, 74, 84, 94, 135, 255, 284-85, 313, 336, 528, 571, 581
Logical Subject, 186
Logical super-self, 22, 327
Logical thinking, 135, 287
Logicization/Logicize, 139-40, 331, 353
Loop, 448-54, 461, 463, 478, 492
Loss of life, 337
Loss of truth, 337
Love of one's self, 469, 471
Love of oneself, 469
Love-objects, 24, 333-34, 337
Machine, 199, 352, 464, 468-70, 478
Making life tolerable, 417
Manifold, 100, 130, 133, 146, 184-87, 258, 305-06, 347, 356, 408, 512, 515
Manipulatable subject, 427
Masochist, 403
Master, 2, 7-11, 21-25, 75, 107, 154, 157, 175, 185, 204, 222-25, 228, 284, 291, 296, 325-35, 358-60, 366-69, 372-74, 379, 383-88, 400, 404, 408, 410, 417-18, 495, 511, 518, 522-33, 530, 560
Master-distinction, 21, 204, 511
Mastering by interpreting, 452
Mastery of the will, 527
Materialism, 40-41, 45, 48, 56, 62, 241-45, 291, 295, 299, 583, 589
Materialist, 58, 243
Maxim, 167, 211, 216, 305, 321, 389, 412, 464-67, 472, 476
McCarthyism, 337
Meaning-addition, 322
Means of representation, 10, 197
Mechanical activity, 420
Memory system, 253, 259, 279
Memory traces, 253-54, 259, 268-69, 322, 387, 466
Memory, 20, 21, 27, 63, 71, 113, 116-18, 135-39, 144, 176, 235, 239, 253-60, 264, 268-74, 277-79, 282-83, 289-291, 314-16, 319, 322, 345, 355, 381-91,

445, 457-62, 466, 486-87, 495, 497, 501, 510, 513, 534, 538
Menschliche Optik, 113
Mental apparatus, 115, 138, 144, 253-55, 257, 261-63, 268, 275, 289, 314
Mephistopheles, 402, 519
Metaphor, 1, 3, 11-14, 30-35, 50-52, 58-73, 77, 87, 90, 137, 143, 222-24, 264, 301-03, 331, 337, 348, 351, 445, 450, 458, 460, 473, 523, 526, 551
Metaphorical language, 66-68, 445
Metaphoricity, 14, 31, 64, 71, 377
Metaphysics of seriousness, 2
Metonymy, 63, 71-73, 314
Mimetic, 373
Mind, 2-11, 17, 23, 26, 36, 38, 43, 46, 48, 60, 70, 74, 82, 85, 108-09, 112, 115-16, 154, 160-64, 168-70, 173, 175, 181-83, 187, 197-99, 205, 209-10, 213, 220, 229, 232, 236, 238, 243, 245, 248-53, 257, 265, 274, 282, 285, 290, 297, 304, 308-16, 320, 329, 336, 339, 340-49, 355-56, 396, 400-04, 411, 428, 434, 437, 444-45, 452, 454-57, 464, 476, 480-82, 488, 505, 509-13, 519, 524, 535-38, 560
Mirror of consciousness, 459, 485
Mirror, 45, 70, 74, 98, 123, 128, 183, 196, 203, 258, 274, 279-80, 289, 373-75, 424, 427, 458-62, 485, 489, 494
Mirror-image, 183, 196
Mnemic images, 260-65, 271-73, 289, 319-20
Moral discourse, 19-20, 24, 228
Moral imperative, 10, 330
Moral subject, 20, 24-25, 157, 214-15, 218-20, 223, 228, 325
Moral, 10, 19-20, 24-25, 51-52, 105-06, 121, 124, 157, 205, 214-28, 252, 309, 325-26, 330, 361-64, 373, 390-94, 403, 410, 422, 476, 513, 521, 526
Motor-image, 275, 315
Multiple identities, 370
Multiple-Self, 174
Multiplicity of forces, 233
Muting of sensibility, 419-20
My-world, 280, 496, 500
Narcissism of Human Knowledge, 29, 92
Narcissism, 95-98, 121, 371, 429, 470, 552
Natural selection, 347

Negation, 28, 47, 53, 402-03, 412, 418, 425, 505-06, 542
Neo-Kantian, 36, 40, 46, 48, 58, 241
Neo-Pragmatist, 35, 88
Nervenreiz → Bild → Laut, 351
Nerve-stimulus/-stimuli, 14, 34, 41, 55-56, 61, 77, 245, 352
Neuro-Epistemology, 231
Neurological network, 255, 264, 269, 320-22
Neuron system, 253, 278-79
Neuroscience, 112, 120, 155, 237, 263, 444, 536
New Criticism, 7
Nietzsche's 'Negative Ontologie des Dinges', 145
Nietzsche's Chiasma, 383
Nietzsche's epistemology, 6, 10, 124, 296, 499
Nietzsche's ontology, 15, 16, 110
Nietzschean chessboard, 332
Nietzschean Realism, 342, 353
Nietzschean *Traum(um)deutung*, 340
Nihilism/Nihilist, 92, , 410, 431, 579
Nirvana, 270, 495, 551
Noble, 25, 121, 124, 218, 223, 326, 358-66, 372-78, 384, 403, 416, 429, 431, 532, 554
Nodal point, 2, 9, 157, 182, 274, 279-80, 341
Noumenal Subject, 186
Noun-verb, 148-50
Nucleus, 66, 126, 255, 263, 265
Omega, 253, 259-65, 279-80, 288
Omega-interpreter-neuron, 262, 263
Omega-interpreter-system, 261-66, 280, 288-89
Opposing counter-ideals, 412
Optical image, 245
Original aggression, 24, 240, 337, 406
Original cruelty, 389, 401, 404
Original lack, 339, 363
Other, the, 215, 221-26, 323, 369, 376, 422, 451-52, 473, 540, 575
Outer world, 42-43, 234, 302, 319, 345-52, 356, 376, 450, 453, 457, 458, 462
Pain and pleasure, 517
Pain, 153, 217, 264-65, 273, 316-17, 345, 352, 383, 390-95, 404-06, 414-20, 423-26, 434, 438, 453, 485, 499, 509-10,

517-20, 523-26, 534-38, 547-48, 554, 557-59, 564
Pain-sensation as fantasy, 534
Paralogisms of Pure Reason, 18, 176, 310
Paralogistic confusion, 185, 186, 200
Pathos, 37, 262
Perception, 5, 7, 10-17, 21, 27, 32-33, 39-43, 56-62, 70, 74-77, 81, 92-94, 106-08, 112-23, 127-30, 134, 136-41, 144-48, 151-53, 174-75, 188, 194, 196, 200, 212, 216, 219, 238, 241-45, 248, 253-71, 276-77, 286, 289-91, 297, 306-07, 314, 346-56, 382, 407, 433, 438, 445, 450-62, 478-83, 488-96, 499-506, 517, 534
Perceptive images, 34, 42, 76, 88, 271, 353
Performative self-contradiction, 403
Performative, 168, 188, 275, 433, 493
Perspectival 'method', 22, 330
Perspectival conflict-resolution, 331-32
Perspective, 16, 21-22, 31, 47, 66, 71, 87-89, 104-05, 114, 118-22, 127-28, 238, 252, 273, 285, 321, 330-31, 390, 444, 453, 475, 488, 511, 513
Perspectivism, 105, 326, 390 510, 513, 579, 584
Perverse aggression, 393
Perverse guilt, 393
Petty pleasure, 420-23, 429
Phallo-logo-phono-centric, 2
Phallus, 367, 371-73, 388, 561
Phantasmatic, 272, 326, 444, 543
Phenomenalism, 345, 453
Phenomenology, 4, 7-8, 190, 355, 502
Phenomenon, 35, 41-42, 49, 66, 78-79, 92, 157, 178, 228, 245, 273, 296, 310, 343, 356, 474, 493, 502, 515-17, 526, 534
Phi, 253-56, 259-63, 278-280, 381
Philosophy of Mind, 342
Phi-receptor-neuron, 254, 256, 263
Pleasure as 'rhythm', 523
Pleasure of resistance of pleasure, 518
Pleasure-pains, 535
Pleasure-principle, 260, 265-67, 334, 517, 520-22, 526-27
Pleasure-theory, 523
Post-modernism/Post-modernist, 1, 2, 3, 6-7, 13-15, 106, 116, 123, 186, 236-37, 418
Power-Configurations, 325

Power-desire, 330
Power-quantities, 516
Power-struggle, 197, 317, 468, 520
Pragmatic communication, 191, 218, 219
Pragmatic, 4, 19, 46, 86, 116, 124, 127, 170, 173, 187, 191-92, 204, 218-19, 287, 326, 347, 401, 521
Pragmatism, 91, 287, 344, 587
Pre-cathected, 271
Pre-conscious, 279, 283, 326
Predicate, 53, 72-73, 148-150, 157, 160, 171-73, 179-80, 187, 199-200, 208, 292, 294-95, 303-07, 313
Pre-linguistic, 22, 59, 145, 207, 290
Presence of the present, 75, 117, 380, 381, 487
Presence, 10-12, 27-28, 75, 116, 126, 140, 148, 204, 259, 271-72, 278-79, 301-02, 351, 380-82, 411, 459-60, 478-79, 484-87, 490, 494-503
Present-being, 478
Priest, 9, 14, 20, 24-25, 157, 220-21, 225, 228-30, 325, 338, 394, 399, 407-10, 413-31
Primary aggression, 393, 395-96, 406, 426-27
Primary aggression, 403
Primary elaboration, 463
Primary process, 266
Principium individuationis, 438
Principle of contradiction, 304
Private language, 281, 461
Privately determined signified, 324
Production of emotions, 428
Projection-theory, 56, 289, 346, 352
Promises, 25, 26, 51, 218, 333, 339, 380, 383, 384, 385, 386, 388, 389, 391, 476, 532, 557
Protentional horizon, 498, 499, 395
Proto-masochism/-masochistic, 394-95, 405
Proto-sadism/-sadistic, 394, 395, 405
Psi, 253-59, 262-63, 268, 278-80, 289, 381
Psi-memory-neuron, 254, 256, 263
Psychoanalysis, 7, 161, 215, 221, 235, 330, 334, 367, 399, 406-07, 434, 528, 573, 578
Psychoanalyst, 117, 225, 434
Psychophysical, 249
Pure will to goodness, 402

Q-quantity, 255
Qualities, 43, 72, 78, 98, 113, 120, 127, 151, 182, 191, 261-62, 286, 312, 315, 326, 384, 432, 457, 524, 554, 557
Quantities, 72, 78, 113, 120, 255-56, 261-63, 270, 466, 516
Qη-energy, 256, 266, 318
Qη-quantity, 255, 259
Rational *super-subject*, 308
Rationalism, 98, 227
Reactive, 225-26, 373-74, 378, 383, 386-87, 395, 410
Realism, 97, 344, 351
Reality, 15, 112, 116, 127, 147, 166, 200, 259, 288, 462, 488
Reality-defense, 17, 115, 130, 135
Re-cathected, 377, 424
Re-constructive thinking, 3
Reconstructive thinking, 8
Recurrence, 11, 26-28, 140, 251-52, 418, 437-51, 462-63, 475-84, 490-95, 502-06, 515, 530
Re-direction of ressentiment, 415, 425
Reducing the other to the same, 452
Reflective communication, 192, 218-19
Refusal to be different, 469, 471
Relations-Welt, 118, 511, 516
Repetition, 435-36, 443-45, 474, 478, 547, 556, 575-76, 583
Repetitive Interpretation-Processes, 445, 492
Re-presentation, 279, 497
Repressed self-deception, 369
Res cogitans, 161, 166, 169, 172
Resistance, 98, 208, 252-55, 258, 279, 515, 518-19, 523-27, 532
Ressentiment, 375, 379, 386, 405, 408, 414-16, 425-31, 572-73, 589
Retention, 497-500
Retentional horizon, 75, 485, 497-499, 503
Retinal Image, 241
Return as self-repetition, 445
Revenge, 333, 340, 383, 386-88, 416, 419, 423, 426, 546-47, 555
Reversal of time, 302-03, 344, 458
Reversed chronology, 355
Rhetoric, 3, 7, 15, 30-33, 64, 68, 337-38, 369, 428, 431, 494
Rhythm, 335, 462, 522-23, 527-28, 530, 548, 556

Romanticism, 31, 376, 574-75
Rome, 379
Sadist, 403, 406
Schemata/Schematization, 135-38, 284, 301, 344, 450, 455, 482, 501, 515
Secondary aggression, 426-27
Secondary elaboration, 463
Secondary process, 266-68
Self-aggression, 392-93, 396, 415, 424-27
Self-conscious subject, 162, 169
Self-contradiction, 12-13, 55, 103-04, 107, 191, 311, 330-32, 403, 411, 414, 418, 433, 518
Self-interpretation, 23, 332, 468, 469
Self-other opposition, 18, 19, 218, 220
Self-presence, 17, 27, 46, 94, 117, 174, 209, 279, 301, 349, 443-45, 478, 484
Self-reflective discourse, 19, 563
Self-reflective, 19, 191-92, 563
Self-repetition of self-presence, 438, 478-79, 492
Self-repetition, 445
Self-self opposition, 19, 220
Self-*un*conscious, 437, 502-06
Semantic cluster, 9, 318, 330, 334, 401
Semantic ego-cluster, 280, 314, 370
Semantic networks, 315
Sensation and perception, 450
Sensation, 20, 32, 43, 45, 56-58, 61, 110, 113, 116, 122-23, 128-34, 138, 143, 205, 208-212, 235-50, 259-60, 264, 283-86, 289, 302-03, 312, 316, 342, 454-56, 500, 509-12, 515, 523, 534, 537-39
Sensational manifold, 347
Sense of guilt, 392-97, 424
Sense of identity, 188-90, 196, 227, 313
Sense of power, 207, 421, 432
Sense-apparatus, 56, 113, 129, 132, 261, 460, 496
Sense-impression, 56, 59, 80, 245, 343
Sense-perception, 40
Sensible sign, 61, 244
Sensory system, 288
Servile configuration, 358-360, 376-79, 383-84, 394-96, 398-99, 424
Servile subject, 429
Sexualization, 493
Signified, 80-82, 141-43, 274-75, 281, 318-23, 558

Signifier, 13, 80-82, 141-43, 274-75, 281, 317-23, 330, 335, 386, 527, 538, 558
Signifier-signified, 322-23
Sign-mediated, 15, 350
Sign-system, 455, 460
Simplification, 17, 22, 90, 94, 112-15, 122-24, 133-38, 144, 160, 196, 198, 202, 238, 248, 258, 280, 313-15, 327, 336, 347, 353, 400, 454-56, 460, 514-15
Simplification-apparatus, 17, 112, 134-38, 202, 460
Simplification-process, 248
Simplify, 5, 16, 22, 34-36, 66, 84-87, 94, 108, 115-19, 129-36, 144, 180, 195, 211, 258, 276-77, 284-87, 290, 314, 327-28, 347, 400, 456, 515, 536, 562
Slave, 9, 11, 20, 24, 28, 157, 161, 219, 222, 228, 296, 325, 335, 358-60, 365-79, 383-84, 386-89, 415-16, 422, 428-34, 525, 528
Smallest possible loop, 478
Socialism, 24
Soliloquizing self, 332
Soliloquy, 19, 191-92, 217-20, 531, 543
Solipsism, 343
Sovereign, 51, 213, 358, 383-88
Space and time, 40, 59, 76, 114, 119, 181, 305, 491
Spatial-temporal world, 19
Special Theory, 157, 192, 213, 218
Speech-act, 166, 275, 311
Speed of light, 229-30, 349, 502
Split subject, 17-18, 155-57, 192-94, 200-01, 204, 213-16, 226, 424
Split-off formation, 401-02
Stalinism, 337, 428
Stimulus/stimuli, 14, 20, 32, 41-48, 55-62, 77-79. 87, 235-41, 245-70, 278, 288, 314, 352, 375, 401, 494, 518-22, 536, 538
Structural Linguistics, 274
Structuralism, 4, 7, 287, 342, 352, 454, 574, 576, 580
Subject and predicate, 55, 149, 293-95, 304, 306
Subject of discourse, 18, 188
Subject of enunciation, 18, 187-88
Subjective deficiency, 433
Subjective emptiness, 25, 336
Subjective fragmentation, 239

Subjectivity, 2, 18, 28, 123, 157, 161, 185, 189-90, 198, 202, 210, 219-20, 227-28, 234, 237, 246, 282, 293, 308, 325, 328-30, 359, 370, 377-79, 424, 438, 459-61, 492, 506
Subject-predicate logic, 18, 148-52, 156-57, 161, 171-73, 199-202, 208, 293-96, 313
Subject-structure, 162, 239
Substance-accidence scheme, 18
Substance-attribute, 148
Suffering, the, 1, 9, 95, 108, 113, 216, 333, 365, 390-93, 403-05, 413-25, 430, 433-34, 519, 554, 559, 564
Sufficient reason, 56, 242-44, 440
Super-ego, 20, 215, 308, 340, 378, 391-93, 396-98, 425-29, 519
Superficial surface-desires, 469
Superficial/Superficiality, 15, 23, 38, 71, 78, 85, 100, 115, 124, 133, 188, 202, 218, 223, 285, 300-01, 310, 336, 344, 354, 361-66, 379-80, 384, 389, 426, 469, 476, 482, 489-92, 518-19, 524
Super-personality, 388
Super-superficial, 488
Surface, 5, 7, 12, 15-17, 21-23, 27-31, 39, 43-44, 54, 62-63, 69-78, 100, 130-31, 148-49, 173, 187, 204-05, 227, 245, 257, 277-78, 301-02, 310, 314-17, 322, 327, 336, 349, 355, 362-64, 370, 381, 420, 465-69, 471, 474, 489-94, 511, 554, 559
Surface-desire, 469
Synapses, 263, 266, 318, 322
Synthesis/Synthetic, 54-55, 71-73, 177, 182-84, 208, 292, 303-11, 327, 439, 442
Synthetic statement, 54
System of differences, 323
System-specific meaning, 14, 33-34, 68
Tabula rasa, 380-81, 385
Temporalization, 501
Temporally constructed world of being, 496, 500
Temptation-to-hallucinate, 265
Terra incognita, 226, 318, 535
Thanatos, 398, 405
The I, 18-20, 173, 177, 185, 194-200, 227, 472, 484
The me, 20, 473
Theory of irrationality 335

Theory, 23, 30, 35-37, 43, 54, 58, 73, 80, 103, 124-26, 141, 151, 157, 193-94, 200-04, 218, 226-29, 231, 244, 267, 274, 282, 287, 296, 326, 342-44, 351, 356, 454, 510, 517, 522, 573-80, 586-89
The-world, 288, 441-42, 485, 489, 496, 500
Thing itself, 64, 78, 199, 274
Thing-as-represented, 274
Thing-for-us, 41
Thing-images, 314
Thing-in-and-for-itself, 48
Thing-in-itself, 13, 41, 45-48, 60, 63, 99, 105-06, 110, 131, 243, 311
Thing-in-itself-for-us, 48
Thing-presentation, 274-76, 279-81, 317, 538
Thinking thing, 154, 166-69, 172, 177, 185
Threshold, 144, 234, 245-48, 251, 258, 418, 553, 564
Time-consciousness, 496
Time-delay, 342, 352
Time-dilation, 502
Time-reversal, 259, 300-03, 310, 352, 355, 452-53
Toleration of life, 417
Too much reality, 17, 68, 115, 130, 146, 258, 288, 456
Transcendental categories, 292, 347
Transcendental Ego, 311, 313
Translation, 20-22, 34, 37, 56, 60-61, 70, 110, 114, 140-141, 172, 202, 214, 224-25, 262, 276, 304, 327, 345, 455, 472, 547, 555, 559
True and false, 21, 267, 290-91, 506
Truth as illusion, 12-13, 32, 55, 63, 92-94, 103
Truth, 2, 4, 11-13, 20-23, 29, 32, 35-40, 44-56, 62-66, 73, 76, 92-111, 117, 125-26, 134, 146-48, 152, 164, 167, 170, 174, 190-94, 198-201, 210, 224, 229, 240, 267, 283-88, 293-94, 298-300, 310-13, 332-37, 346, 362, 366-73, 387-90, 436, 454, 459, 473-75, 489, 510, 521, 542, 547, 551, 558, 570, 573, 574, 591
Truth-candidates, 50, 93
Truth-drive, 50, 77
Truthfulness, 13, 32, 50-54, 63, 92, 94
Turkish fatalism, 474-75

Übermensch, 6, 236, 429-31, 448
Umwerthung aller Werthe, 5, 109
Unconscious subject, 234
Unified subject, 217, 325, 508
Uninhibited wish-fulfillment, 267
Untruth, 47, 63, 133
Urform, 82
Ur-ground, 16-17, 113-29, 134, 145-47, 298-99, 350-53
Utilitarianism, 524, 534
Utterance-subject, 168, 187-90, 196
Values, 6, 14, 120, 214, 219, 226, 247-48, 252, 364, 377, 379, 382, 400-02, 416, 524, 526
Vermögen, 233, 308-10
Vertical superficiality, 362
Vorstellung, 35, 38-41, 59, 82, 94, 197, 453, 537-38
Vorstellungsrepräsentanz, 528, 531, 534-35, 537
Wagnerian, 361, 437
Will to Power as Knowledge, 54, 100, 117
Will to truth, 23, 332, 562
Will/Willing, 22-23, 54, 99-100, 108-111, 117, 147, 167, 171, 200-08, 206-09, 212-13, 217, 233, 264, 269-70, 284, 297, 333, 372, 387-88, 404, 407, 410-11, 443-45, 454, 466, 514, 525-28, 550, 559, 564, 570, 574, 579, 588
Will-punctures, 204, 233, 466
Wills-to-power, 22, 204, 233, 269-70, 326
Will-to-nothing, 411
Will-to-power, 20-23, 99-100, 112, 119, 124, 167-69, 197, 201-04, 210-11, 217, 262-64, 267-70, 284, 288, 291, 296, 326, 329-35, 341, 359, 372-76, 385-90, 421, 443-45, 451, 468-69, 473, 519-22, 525-30, 561, 562
Will-to-power-complexes, 22
Will-to-power-processes, 211, 329-30, 444, 468
Wishfulfillment, 340-41
Woman/Women, 230, 331, 363-64, 366-69, 371, 419, 431-34, 468-69, 487, 532-33, 542-45, 555, 561
Word, 1, 9, 14-15, 33-34, 40, 45, 51, 55-64, 71, 79-87, 97-99, 108, 120-21, 138, 143, 148, 150, 169, 172, 177, 203-08, 213, 239, 259-61, 273-81, 292, 301,

309, 314-24, 354, 383-88, 400, 413, 446, 455, 486, 489, 527, 538, 548
Word-presentation, 261, 273-79, 281, 314, 317, 538
World of appearances, 39, 93, 311, 482
World-of-relations, 512
Yes-Saying/-affirmation, 416, 418, 504-06
Zarathustra, 224, 362, 371, 438, 445-49, 471-73, 479-83, 487, 493-94, 569-70
Zeit-Umkehrung, 303, 453-54, 478
Zero-tension resolution of conflict, 495
Zero-tension rest-position, 445

Name and Title Index

A History of Western Philosophy, 371, 587
Abel, Günter, 10, 22, 26, 100-01, 112, 127, 156, 162, 171, 201, 205, 237, 282, 290, 317, 442-444, 455, 462-63, 469, 500, 520, 526, 571
Achilles, 430
Adorno, Theodor W., 378, 432, 571
Allen, Woody, 320
Allison, David B, 362, 571
Also sprach Zarathustra, 471, 481
An Enquiry Concerning Human Understanding, 292, 452, 581
Analysis of Sensations, The, 45, 508
Antichrist, 106, 404, 431-432, 568-569, 582
Arabesque to a Drawing by Michelangelo, 540, 542, 547
Aristotle, 3, 14, 33, 59, 68, 89, 370, 521, 571
Assoun, Paul-Laurent, 215, 235-36, 400, 571
Augustine, 498, 520
Austin, 188, 275, 571
Babich, Babette, 116, 151, 236, 296, 464, 470, 571-572, 579, 585, 589
Bacon, Francis, 12, 108, 245, 299, 328, 451
Bang, Herman, 541
Baumgarten, Alexander, 491
Beckett, Samuel, 153, 207, 379, 572, 587
Bentham, Jemery, 524, 572
Benveniste, Emile, 18-19, 164, 187-92, 200, 572
Berkeley, George, 98, 123, 128, 267, 343-47, 352, 453, 464, 501, 572, 580, 584, 587
Berkowitz, Peter, 404
Beyond the Pleasure Principle, 238, 267, 533, 578
Birth of the Clinic, The, 356, 577
Book of Genesis, 445
Bohr, Niels, 108
Bornedal, Peter, 68, 442, 573
Boscovich, Roger, 195, 201
Brandes, Edvard, 545
Brandes, George, 508, 530, 541, 543-45, 557
Breazeale, Daniel, 37, 56, 104, 570, 573
Breuer, Josef, 139, 279, 368, 578
Brobjer, Torben 6, 36, 235-37, 573, 576, 585
Brusotti, Marco, 374-75, 573
Canetti, Elias, 417
Churchland, Patricia,11
City of God, 520
Clark, Maudemarie, 11, 14, 35-37, 49, 54-55, 104-12, 116-17, 574
Colli & Montinari, 111
Comte, Auguste, 99
Conway, Daniel, 430-31, 530, 574, 586, 589-90
Crawford, Claudia, 11, 30, 35, 37, 58, 80, 299, 574
Critique of Judgment, The, 481
Critique of Pure Reason, 37, 107, 304, 483, 582, 584, 591
Culler, Jonathan, 7, 342, 454, 574
Czermak, 242
Damasio, Antonio, 112, 154, 239, 574
Danto, Arthur, 14, 54, 574
Das Unbehagen in der Kultur, 399, 405, , 517, 519, 526
Dawkins, Richard, 338
De Bois-Reymond, 298, 299
De Man, Paul 7, 11, 31, 342-44, 454, 585-86
Death in Venice, 435, 584
Deleuze, Gilles, 4, 26, 162, 374, 378, 383-87, 395, 410, 438, 442, 476, 575
Dennett, Daaniel, 11, 112, 162, 178, 239, 269, 338, 353, 575
Der Wille zur Macht, 5, 109, 117, 119, 231, 465, 569
Derrida, Jacques, 2, 7, 31, 103, 130, 157, 224-25, 313, 382, 399, 484, 527, 532, 540-41, 575
Descartes, Rene, 18, 99, 154-55, 161-85, 190-97, 237-39, 299, 310, 574-76
Diary of a Seducer, The, 335
Die fröhliche Wissenschaft, 110, 131, 133, 137, 203, 220, 346, 438, 456, 459, 490, 517, 568, 569
Die Geburt der Tragödie, 437, 484, 555, 568, 569
Die Welt als Wille und Vorstellung, 29-30, 39, 47, 304-05, 492, 568, 588, 590
Dier, Oliver, 483, 503, 576

Discipline and Punish, 402, 577
Djurić, Mihailo, 473
Duclot, O., 188, 576
Ecce Homo, 224, 408, 463-71, 481, 568, 569-70
Ego and the Id, The, 238, 578
Einstein, Albert, 118, 157, 230, 502
Either/Or, 335, 339, 475, 582
Elias, Norbert, 417
Emden, Christopher, 6, 11, 31, 35-36, 60, 64, 156, 235-36, 282, 576
Eperons/Spurs, 541
Epic of Gilgamesh, The,412, 413
Essays Concerning Human Understanding, 62
Faust, 402, 430, 519, 520, 579
Fear and Trembling, 436
Fechner, Gustav, 234-36, 246-58, 576
Feuerbach, Ludwig, 99, 213-14, 444, 576
Feyerabend, 108
Figal, Günter, 75, 156, 204, 207, 215, 576
Fink, Eugen, 4, 112, 124, 146-48, 410-11, 417, 446, 473, 576-77, 587
Fischer, Kuno, 178, 181, 568, 577
Fish, Stanley, 35, 88-91, 577
Fliess, 238, 253, 277, 578
Forførerens Dagbog, 335
Foucault, Michel, 7, 108, 287, 356, 402, 417, 541, 577
Fourfold Root of the Principle of Sufficient Reason, The,56
Freud, Sigmund, 3, 113, 120, 137-39, 144-62, 172, 199, 215, 221-23, 228, 234-39, 247, 253-82, 287-88, 302, 314-19, 322, 329-35, 340-41, 367-68, 372, 377-78, 381-82, 386, 391, 393, 396-99, 405-07, 421, 426, 429, 437, 463, 474, 488, 494-95, 506, 517, 519, 522-28, 533, 537-40, 544, 568, 571-80, 584-89, 592
Friedrich, Casper David, 480
Fritsch, Theodor 362
Fru Marie Gruppe, 552
Zur Genealogie der Moral, 34, 86, 115, 135, 211, 321, 325, 329, 376, 417, 456, 573, 587, 590
Genealogy of Morals, The, 106, 150, 400, 574
Gerber, Gustav 30, 36, 58, 61-62, 69, 79, 585
Gersdorff, Carl von, 242

Geschichte des Materialismus, 30, 41, 298, 583
Gilgamesh, 412-13
Goethe, Johann Wolfgang, 363, 402, 430, 519, 579
Golomb, J, 362
Götzendämmerung, 203, 346, 568, 569
Gouldner, Alvin, 25
Green, Martin Steven, 104, 181, 193, 577, 579, 580
Greene, Brian, 503
Grimm, Herman-Rudiger, 4, 103, 112, 125, 282, 579
Groddeck, George, 161
Group Psychology and the Analysis of the Ego, 393, 421
Gurre Songs, 552
Gurre-Lieder, 541, 552
Guyer, Paul, 181, 579
Habermas, Jurgen, 86, 108, 124, 191, 218, 311, 387, 439, 579
Hales & Welshon, 326
Hamlet, 87, 588
Hartmann, Eduard von, 30, 36-37, 55, 234-36, 295, 579
Hatab, Lawrence, 26, 442, 579
Hawking, Stephen, 70
Haydn, Joseph, 435-40
Hegel, G. F. W., 99, 199, 439, 525, 541, 584
Heidegger, Martin, 4, 26-27, 46, 54, 100, 103, 112, 138, 147, 197, 236, 372, 387, 442-44, 546, 580-82, 585
Helmholtz, Hermann von, 29-30, 36-37, 39, 42-44, 55, 58, 60, 234-36, 241, 244, 249, 580
Henrich, Dieter, 186
Heraclitus, 381, 443, 496, 504
Herbart, J. F., 236, 580
Herder, 318-19
Hill, Kevin, 178
Hjelmslev, Louis, 140-43, 148, 580
Hölderlin, 153, 227
Hollingdale, F. J., 110-11, 532, 569-70, 580
Houlgate, Stephen, 48, 581
Hume, David, 99, 122, 149, 152-55, 174-78, 187-88, 214, 232, 237, 278, 292-97, 304, 307-08, 345-47, 355, 441, 452, 574, 581

Husserl, Edmund, 3, 7, 118, 199, 485, 497, 498, 500-03, 581
Interpretation of Dreams, The, 238, 277-79, 340-341, 578
Irigaray, Luce, 229, 230
Jacobsen, Jens Peter, 540-64, 573, 581
James, William, 4
Jameson, Frederic, 343
Janaway, Christopher, 39, 244, 417, 581, 582
Janz, Curt Paul, 480-81
Jenseits von Gut und Böse, 110, 131, 133, 220, 309, 360, 568, 569
Johnson, Samuel, 267
Kafka, Franz, 78, 378, 390, 471, 582
Kamuf, Peggy, 215, 575
Kant, Immanuel, 3, 6, 18, 26, 30, 36-56, 72, 74, 94, 98, 104, 106-07, 110, 116, 123, 131-32, 138, 140, 154-6, 162-64, 171-89, 193, 199-205, 209-16, 219, 227, 241-243, 274, 292-97, 304-13, 345-46, 353, 364, 389-90, 428, 451, 476, 479, 481-92, 504-06, 511, 521, 568-73, 577-87, 590-91
Kaufmann, Walter, 111, 236, 404, 423, 425, 570, 582
Kaulbach, Friedrich, 177, 582
Kierkegaard, Soeren, 335, 339, 436-37, 475, 574, 582, 583
Klein, Wayne, 11, 31, 104, 342, 454, 583
Klossowski, Pierre, 27, 444, 480
Kofman, Sara, 11, 31 583
Krell, D. F., 54, 100, 198, 387, 442, 580
Kritik der reinen Vernunft, 30, 176, 180, 568, 582, 591
Kritik der Urteilskraft, 492
Kuhn, Thomas, 108, 287
Köselitz, Heinrich, 480
Lacan, Jacques, 7, 183, 198, 275, 278, 573, 576, 583, 587
Lange, Friedrich A., 6, 30, 36, 39-41, 44-45, 48, 55-58, 62, 93, 195, 201, 234, 241, 245, 295, 298-99, 345, 570, 583, 587, 590
Laplanche, Jean, 254, 256
Large, Duncan, 31, 570, 583
LeDoux, Joseph, 239, 583
Leibniz, G. W., 43, 99, 136-37, 144, 146, 258-59, 440, 456-58, 578, 583, 590
Leiter, Brian, 109, 584

Levi-Strauss, Claude-Levi, 7
Licthenberg, Georg Christoph, 509
Locke, John, 3, 62, 289, 344-47, 427, 452, 457
Lomax, J. H., 464, 584
Löwith, Karl, 438, 464, 472, 584
Mach, Ernst, 45, 249, 508-16, 584
Madness and Civilization, 356, 577
Magee, Brian, 39, 584
Magnus, Bernd, 26, 438, 442, 476, 584
Mann, Thomas, 435
Marx, Karl, 25, 64, 338, 414, 436, 439, 574, 585
Masse und Macht, 417
Meijers, A., 30, 58, 61-62, 69, 79, 585
Menschliches, Allzumenschliches, 110, 214, 364, 474
Merchant of Venice, The, 392
Mill, John Stuart, 362, 369, 521, 524, 534, 585, 591
Miller, Hillis J., 31
Moore, Gregory, 6, 11, 36, 235-37, 241, 351, 477, 573, 576, 585
Morgenröte, 97, 110, 131-32, 216, 358, 398, 489, 568, 569
Müller, Johannes, 42, 241, 245
Müller-Lauter, W., 10, 22, 26, 99, 110, 112, 151, 201, 204, 237, 282, 296, 351, 442, 504-05, 585-86
Napoleon Bonaparte, 210, 362-63, 372, 530
Nehamas, Alexander, 4, 14, 49, 104, 127, 156, 196, 215, 417, 464-65, 470, 586
New Essays on Human Understanding, 136-37, 258, 456, 583
New Rhetoric, The, 64, 586
Nietzsche, Friedrich, 30, 58, 69, 79, 359, 480, 481, 585, 587, 591
Olbrechts-Tyteca, 64, 586
Olivier, Abraham, 237, 500
Parmenides, 443
Payne, F. J., 37, 588
Penrose, Roger, 11
Perelman, Ch., 14, 33, 64, 69, 586
Philosophie des Unbewußten, 295
Pinker, Steven, 239, 264
Piranesi, 378
Plato, 86, 116, 132, 427, 473, 521, 527, 575, 586
Poellner, Peter, 127

Poincaré, Henri, 108
Popper, Karl, 108, 287
Port Royal, 33
Principles of Psychology, The, 4, 581
Project for a Scientific Psychology, 113, 144, 236-38, 253, 278, 287, 381, 494, 538, 578, 590
Prolegomena to any Future Metaphysics, 45
Prolegomena zur einen jeden künftigen Metaphysik, 30, 45, 72, 141, 346, 504, 580, 582
Quine, W. O., 83
Raffensoe, Sverre, 417
Rees, Martin, 440
Richardson, John, 351, 587
Ricoeur, Paul, 188, 256, 587
Rohde, Erwin, 43
Rorty, Richard, 4, 97, 108, 587
Rousseau, Jean-Jacques, 31, 541
Russell, Bertrand, 316-17, 371, 587
Said, Edward, 541
Salaquarda, Jörg, 30, 41, 44, 587
Saussure, Ferdinand de, 7, 19, 80, 82, 140-43, 148, 244, 274-75, 318, 321, 350, 579-80, 587, 591
Schacht, Richard, 11
Schlimgen, Erwin, 10, 60, 155, 173, 184, 195-97, 205, 237, 282, 296, 327, 336, 343-44, 348-50, 453, 467, 588
Schönberg, Arnold, 541
Schopenhauer, Arthur, 6, 29-31, 36-49, 55-63, 70-86, 93-94, 98-104, 123, 205, 216, 234, 236, 241-44, 304-05, 335, 338, 345-39, 453, 479, 482, 492, 521, 568-69, 581-90
Searle, John, 188, 275, 311
Shakespeare, 87, 91, 375, 392, 588
Simmel, George, 26, 442
Simon, Josef, 10, 46, 116, 151, 202, 313, 456, 463, 477, 571, 587-90
Skowron, Michael, 448
Smith, Norman Kemp, 37, 582
Soll, Ivan, 26
Solms, Mark, 11, 112, 239, 264, 578, 589
Spiekemann, Klaus, 296
Spierling, Volker, 39, 590
Spinoza, B., 99, 112, 201, 239, 574
Spir, African, 193-94, 201-03, 590
Stack, George, 30, 201, 298, 590

Stambaugh, Joan, 27, 444, 448-49, 475, 487, 495, 580, 590
Staten, Henry, 4, 156-57, 196, 215, 403, 408, 428, 431, 470, 519, 540-41, 590
Stegmaier, Werner, 10, 22, 34, 46, 86, 115, 135, 151, 177, 211, 308, 321-23, 328, 351, 376, 383, 411, 417, 422, 452, 456, 461, 589, 590
Stingelin, M., 30, 61-62
Strachey, James, 256
Studies on Hysteria, 238, 368, 578
Summer, Andreas Urs, 6
Tegmark, Max 440
Tetens, Holm, 11, 180-81, 353, 591
Todorov, T., 188, 576
Traumdeuting, 340
Über den Ursprung der Sprache, 319
Über die vierfache Wurzel des Satzes vom zureichenden Grunde, 30, 47, 241, 568, 588
Über Wahrheit und Lüge im ausser-moralischen sinne, 11, 29-30, 300, 314, 569, 585
Unzeitgemässe Betrachtungen, 381, 484, 487
Vaihinger, Hans, 351, 591
Waiting for Godot, 379, 572
Watson, James, 126, 591
Weber, 246, 247
Wistrich, R. S, 362
Wohlheim, Richard, 254, 256
Wundt, Wilhelm, 236, 592
Yale School, 7
Zöllner, Johann, 30, 36. 43, 592
Zur Genealogie der Moral, 51, 220, 361, 363, 394, 409, 568, 569

www.ingramcontent.com/pod-product-compliance
Lightning Source LLC
Chambersburg PA
CBHW060328240426
43665CB00048B/2818